MUSIC
AN APPRECIATION

BY THE AUTHOR

The Norton Scores: An Anthology for Listening
Music: An Appreciation—Brief Edition

MUSIC

AN APPRECIATION

V

EDITION

Roger Kamien

Queens College
of the City University of New York
Zubin Mehta Chair in Musicology,
The Hebrew University of Jerusalem

McGraw-Hill, Inc.
New York St. Louis San Francisco Auckland Bogotá
Caracas Lisbon London Madrid Mexico Milan
Montreal New Delhi Paris San Juan Singapore
Sydney Tokyo Toronto

MUSIC: AN APPRECIATION

Acknowledgments appear on pages 695–697, and on this page by reference.

3 4 5 6 7 8 9 0   HAL HAL   9 0 9 8 7 6 5 4 3 2

ISBN 0–07–033677–6

This book was set in Palatino by York Graphic Services, Inc.
The editors were Cynthia Ward and Susan Gamer;
the designer was Joan E. O'Connor;
the production supervisor was Kathryn Porzio.
The photo editor was Elsa Peterson.
Arcata Graphics/Halliday was printer and binder.

Front cover photograph: Comstock
Back cover photograph: Four by Five

Library of Congress Cataloging-in-Publication Data

Kamien, Roger.
    Music, an appreciation / Roger Kamien.—5th ed.
        p.   cm.
    Includes bibliographical references and index.
    ISBN 0–07–033677–6
    1. Music appreciation.   I. Title.
MT6.K22M9   1992
780—dc20   91-46823

ABOUT THE AUTHOR

Roger Kamien was born in Paris in 1934 and was brought to the United States at the age of six months. He received his B.A. in music from Columbia College in New York, and his M.A. and Ph.D. in musicology from Princeton University. During 1957–1959, he returned to Paris as a Fulbright scholar, for research on eighteenth-century music.

Professor Kamien taught music history, theory, and literature for two years at Hunter College and then for twenty years at Queens College of the City University of New York, where he was coordinator of the music appreciation courses. During this time he was also active as a pianist, appearing both in the United States and in Europe. In 1983, he was appointed to the Zubin Mehta Chair of Musicology at the Hebrew University of Jerusalem.

In addition to *Music: An Appreciation*, Dr. Kamien is the editor of *The Norton Scores* and one of the coauthors of *A New Approach to Keyboard Harmony*. He has also written articles and reviews for journals including *Music Forum*, *Musical Quarterly*, *Journal of Music Theory*, and *Journal of the American Musicological Society*.

In recent years, he has formed a two-piano team with his wife, Anita Kamien—who has also contributed in many ways to *Music: An Appreciation*. The Kamiens have three children.

For Anita, David, Joshua, and Adina

CONTENTS

LISTENING OUTLINES LISTED BY COMPOSER

PREFACE

W hy another music appreciation text? Over thirty years' experience with music appreciation courses and college students has shown me the need for an accurate, clear, and engaging book that takes students' interests and knowledge into account. My goal has been to write a book that is useful both for study and in the classroom. This text provides an approach to perceptive listening and an introduction to musical elements, forms, and stylistic periods. Its discussions of composers' lives, individual styles, and representative works aim not merely to impart facts but to stimulate curiosity and enthusiasm. The book was written to heighten the readers' love of music as well as to develop their listening skills. The features outlined below have proved attractive to students and teachers alike.

ORGANIZATION

In addition to a comprehensive discussion of the musical style and sociological aspects of each historical period, the lives, individual styles, and representative works of many composers are examined in detail. Through repeated exposures to a variety of musical compositions, students are encouraged to listen for basic forms (such as A B A and theme and variations) as well as for elements of music (dynamics, tone color, rhythm, texture).

Part I of the book examines the elements of music both in general terms and with reference to illustrative pieces that are attractive, brief, and representative of a variety of periods. Notation is used sparingly in this part—usually in connection with familiar tunes like *Home on the Range* that allow students first to analyze music they are likely to have known since childhood. Parts II through VII deal with specific periods of music history from the Middle Ages to the present. Each part opens with a discussion of the stylistic characteristics of the period, its cultural trends, and the role of music and musicians in society. Jazz, American musical theater, and rock are considered in Parts VIII, IX, and X. Nonwestern music is surveyed in Part XI. Five appendixes provide a glossary (which includes a locator for music examples), a brief discussion of tone color and the harmonic series, a list of key signatures, a chronology, and a list of readings.

KEY FEATURES

Listening Outlines

A distinctive feature of this text is the use of "listening outlines" to enrich the discussion of many pieces. The listening outlines are meant to be followed while the compositions are heard. Each outline focuses attention on musical events as they unfold. The outlines can be followed easily and therefore are useful for outside listening assignments as well as for classroom work. However, since the text offers a general discussion of each composition represented, the listening outlines may be omitted.

Opera Texts

The study of opera is aided in this book by extended excerpts from librettos, making it unnecessary for teachers to supply them. Opera texts appear with brief marginal notes that indicate the relationship between words and music and help readers follow the drama.

Flexibility

Music: An Appreciation takes a chronological approach but can be adapted easily to individual teaching methods. Each stylistic period is subdivided into short, relatively independent sections that can be studied in any order; some could even be omitted.

While music examples are offered throughout the book, discussions of the compositions require no knowledge of music notation. The examples provide visual aids for those who want them; students may prefer simply to read the text and skip the details of notation.

Readability

The biographical sketches and the descriptions of composers' individual styles attempt to give the flavor of each composer's personality and music. Anecdotes and quotations from composers enliven the discussions.

Clarity of expression has been a chief goal. This is a book that students can feel comfortable with. They will recognize that it was written for them by a musician who loves music and who wants to convey its essentials without creating confusion or boredom. Musical terms are defined simply and appear in **bold italic** type. Basic terms are listed at the end of each section, and terms and definitions appear in the Glossary and Example Locator (Appendix 1).

NEW FEATURES IN THE FIFTH EDITION

Music: An Appreciation, Fifth Edition, expands the range of music discussed by broadening the coverage of choral music, music by women composers, twentieth-century French music, and the American musical theater. This new edition increases the number of listening outlines to forty-eight, and it provides new representative pieces that are attractive to students and effective for teaching. Timings and CD track numbers keyed to our recording sets have been added to listening outlines, vocal texts, and discussions of pieces. An innovative Glossary and Example Locator has been added as Appendix 1. This allows readers to combine a review of musical terms with easy reference to clear musical examples of these terms (elements, forms, genres, and compositional techniques) in the works included on our recording sets.

The discussion of musical elements (Part I) now includes Gershwin's *I Got Rhythm* to illustrate syncopation and Arlen's *Over the Rainbow* as an example of melody.

In Part II, on the Middle Ages, there is a new example of secular music: *Estampie.* Part IV, on the baroque period, now has a listening outline for Bach's Organ Fugue in G Minor *(Little Fugue).* Part V, on the classical period, now discusses Mozart's Piano Concerto No. 23 in A Major, K. 488 (with a listening outline), and Mozart's Requiem in D Minor. Part VI, on the romantic period, includes a new section on Clara Schumann, with her Romance in G Minor for Violin and Piano, Op. 22, No. 2, as a representative work (with a listening outline). Part VI also has new discussions of Schubert's song *Die Forelle (The Trout)* (which complements the analysis of the Fourth Movement of Schubert's Piano Quintet in A Major, *The Trout*); Robert Schumann's song *Im wunderschönen Monai Mai (In the Lovely Month of May), from Dichterliebe (Poet's Love);* Liszt's *Transcendental Étude* in F Minor for Piano (with a listening outline); Brahms's *German Requiem;* and the love scene from Act I of Wagner's *Die Walküre.*

Part VII, on the twentieth century, has a new section on Maurice Ravel, with *Bolero* as a representative work (with a listening outline). Other additions to Part VII are Debussy's *Voiles (Sails)* from Preludes for Piano (with a listening outline) and a new listening outline for the Theme and Variations on *Simple Gifts* from Copland's *Appalachian Spring.* The section on music since 1950 now includes discussions of John Adams's minimalist opera

Nixon in China; and Ellen Taaffe Zwilich's *Concerto Grosso 1985,* an example of "quotation music," with a listening outline.

New to this edition is Part IX, The American Musical, which includes a section on Leonard Bernstein and the *Tonight* ensemble from *West Side Story* (with a listening outline).

The entire book has been carefully revised to reflect recent musical scholarship, and Part X on rock and the discussion of electronic instruments have been updated. The fifth edition also includes many new color and black-and-white photos.

SUPPLEMENTARY MATERIALS

Recordings

This fifth edition is accompanied by a new, expanded listening program produced by PolyGram: a Basic Set of eight recordings and a Supplementary Set of four recordings, each available as compact disks, cassettes, and LPs. The CD sets are "internally tracked" so that the student or instructor can locate specific themes or sections within a composition at the push of a button. The cassettes have an announcement of composer and title before each composition. The recordings have all been chosen from the finest performances by leading artists and ensembles.

The Basic Set provides the "core" compositions or movements studied in introductory music courses—those most likely to be discussed in class or assigned for outside listening. It contains almost all the pieces discussed in Part I (Elements); representative works from all the historical periods; and examples of jazz, the American musical, and nonwestern music. The Supplementary Set offers additional listening examples—new compositions as well as additional movements of works represented by a single movement on the Basic Set. Together, these sets include all but one of the works described by the listening outlines.

Note that a listing of the recordings is provided at the end of the book (see page 687).

Study Guide and Student Workbook

The Study Guide/Workbook, developed by Professor Raoul Camus to interact with the text, provides students with exercises, reviews, self-tests, and other materials.

Instructor's Manual and Test Bank

The Instructor's Manual/Test Bank, also by Professor Camus, follows the organization of the text and provides objectives, suggested classroom activities, listening experiences, questions, discussion topics, student essays, and exams. The test file contains multiple-choice and true-false questions.

Computerized Test Generator

The Test Generator, for IBM, MacIntosh, and Apple computers, contains all the questions found in the test bank within the Instructor's Manual.

ACKNOWLEDGMENTS

My deep thanks go to many colleagues around the country whose valuable suggestions were incorporated into this edition: Joe David Bonner, Andrew D. Brown, Al Carnine, Ann Carruthers, John W. Clark, Don L. Collins, Jeff R. Cox, Ann Davenport, Lori Dewitt, Kathy Dougherty, Randall Ellis, John Fairfield, Larry Fritts, Charlotte Giles, James Henry, Howard Irving, Duke Jackson, Richard E. Jorgenson, James A. Keene, Paul Kirk, Ramon Kyser, Leslie A. Lambert, James McCray, Matthew A. McCready, Oho E. Mielenz, Gabriel Pegis, Susan Y. Porter, Cathy J. Risse, Rebecca Rollins, Ingrid Rosenhein, Richard C. Sang, Lisa Lee Sawyer, Susan Schoenfeld, Michael Tacchia, Donald R. Trentham, and Robert E. Williams.

Many musicians, teachers, and students very kindly read sections of previous editions in draft and have earned my deep gratitude: James Anthony, Geoffrey Block, Art Brownlow, Raoul F. Camus, Roger Collins, Raymond Comstock, David Debolt, JoAnn Domb, David Dworkin, G. Daniel Fairchild, Arthur Follows, Peter Gano, I. Calvin Greer, Janet Griffith, Deborah Hayes, Calvin R. Huber, Geo Humphrey, Frederic Johnson, Larry Keig, Katherine Kemler, David Z. Kushner, Margaret B. McArthur, S. Margaret William McCarthy, John Meyer, Robert W. Montgomery, Karl E. Moyer, Raymond Nilsson, Trygve Peterson, Jerry Rife, Thomas L. Riis, H. M. Savige, Mary Alice Spencer, Arthur Spiro, Gary Sudano, Robert Van Voorhis, George Weimer, and Jerry A. Young. All contributed valuable suggestions.

Colleagues in the Aaron Copland School of Music, Queens College, were extraordinarily generous and helpful. I am particularly indebted to Anthony Nwabuoku, Henry Burnett, and Hubert S. Howe, Jr., for their help with the sections on sub-Saharan Africa, Japan, and electronic instruments. Alan Buechner, Charles Burkhart, Lawrence Eisman, Raymond Erickson, Hubert Howe, Joel Mandelbaum, Arbie Orenstein, Carl Schachter, David Walker, Robert White, and Helen Wright all read portions of the text. I am especially grateful for the help of the following experts: David Loeb (Japanese music), Teddy Rosenthal (jazz), Elise Barnett (Indian music), Alvin Fosner (jazz), Raymond F. Kennedy (rock and nonwestern music) and James Kurtz (opera and the American musical). Susan Hellauer provided editorial help, and Grazia Lopez and Dr. Bathja Bayer assisted with translations.

For background in the American musical, I drew on two excellent theater texts published by McGraw-Hill: *The Theater Experience,* Fifth Edition, by Edwin Wilson; and *Theater: The Lively Art,* by Edwin Wilson and Alvin Goldfarb.

I am grateful for the expert assistance of my editors at McGraw-Hill, Cynthia Ward and Susan Gamer; the designer, Joan O'Connor; and the photo editor, Elsa Peterson. Special thanks are due to Patricia Rodney, who put the manuscript together.

I also wish to thank Professor Raoul Camus for the fine *Instructor's Manual* and the *Study Guide and Student Workbook* that accompany this text.

My wife, Anita Kamien, has contributed to every aspect of this book. She clarified ideas, helped choose representative pieces, and worked tirelessly to improve the listening outlines. Her advice and encouragement were essential to the completion of *Music: An Appreciation.*

Roger Kamien

ELEMENTS

Street musicians. Informal music making is a source of pleasure for both players and listeners.

The audience at a concert of the United States Marines Band. Whether in a public park or a concert hall, live performances have a special electricity.

(Paul Conklin/Uniphoto)

Concert by the Grateful Dead. The exchange between singer and audience contains a bit of magic, something direct and spellbinding.

I

ELEMENTS I

All the musical elements come together when people play or sing.

1 SOUND: PITCH, DYNAMICS, AND TONE COLOR

Sounds bombard our ears every day—the squeaks and honks of traffic noises, a child's laugh, the bark of a dog, the patter of rain. Through them we learn what's going on; we need them to communicate. By listening to the speech, cries, and laughter of others, we learn what they think and how they feel. But silence, an absence of sound, also communicates. When we hear no sound in the street, we assume no cars are passing. When someone doesn't answer a question or breaks off in the middle of a sentence, we quickly notice, and we draw conclusions from the silence.

Sounds may be perceived as pleasant or unpleasant. Fortunately we can direct our attention to specific sounds, shutting out those that don't interest us. At a party, we can choose to ignore the people near us and focus instead on a conversation across the room. We shut out most sounds, paying attention only to those of interest. The composer John Cage (b. 1912) may have meant to show this with his "composition" entitled *4'33"*, in which a musician sits at a piano for 4 minutes and 33 seconds—and does nothing. The silence forces the people in the audience to direct attention to whatever noises, or sounds, they themselves are making. In a sense, the audience "composes" this piece. To get the effect, listen to the sounds that fill the silence around you right now.

What are these sounds that we hear? What *is* "sound"? What causes it, and how do we hear it?

Sound begins with the vibration of an object, such as a table that is pounded or a string that is plucked. The vibrations are transmitted to our ears by a *medium*, which is usually air. As a result of the vibrations, our eardrums start vibrating too, and *impulses*, or signals, are transmitted to our brains. There the impulses are selected, organized, and interpreted.

Music is part of this world of sound, an art based on the organization of sounds in time. We distinguish music from other sounds by recognizing the four main properties of musical sounds: *pitch, dynamics* (loudness or softness), *tone color*, and *duration*. We'll look now at the first three of these properties of musical sound. Duration—the length of time a musical sound lasts—is discussed in Section 3, "Rhythm."

PITCH: HIGHNESS OR LOWNESS OF SOUND

Pitch is the relative highness or lowness that we hear in a sound. No doubt you've noticed that most men speak and sing in a lower range of pitches than women or children do. And when you sing the beginning of *The Star-Spangled Banner*, the pitch on *see* is higher than the one on *say:*

Without differences of pitch, speech would be boring, and—worse—there would be no music as we know it.

The pitch of a sound is decided by the frequency of its vibrations. The faster the vibrations, the higher the pitch; the slower the vibrations, the lower the pitch. Vibration frequency is measured in cycles per second. On a piano the highest-frequency tone is 4,186 cycles per second, and the lowest is about 27 cycles per second.

In general, the smaller the vibrating object, the faster its vibrations and the higher its pitch. All other things being equal, plucking a short string produces a higher pitch than plucking a long string. The relatively short strings of a violin produce higher pitches than do the longer strings of a double bass ("bass fiddle").

In music, a sound that has a definite pitch is called a *tone.* It has a specific frequency, such as 440 cycles per second. The vibrations of a tone are regular and reach the ear at equal time intervals. On the other hand, noiselike sounds (the squeaking of brakes or a clash of cymbals) have an indefinite pitch and are produced by irregular vibrations.

Two tones will sound different when they have different pitches. The "distance" in pitch between any two tones is called an *interval.* When tones are separated by the interval called an *octave,* they sound very much alike. Sing the opening of *The Star-Spangled Banner* again. Notice that the tone you produce on *see* sounds like your tone on *say,* even though it's higher. (Sing the *say* and *see* tones several times.) An octave lies between them. The vibration frequency of the *say* tone is exactly half that of the *see* tone. If the *say* tone were 440 cycles per second, the *see* tone—an octave higher—would be 880 cycles per second. A tone an octave lower than the *say* tone would be half of 440, or 220 cycles per second. When sounded at the same time, two tones an octave apart blend so well that they almost seem to merge into one tone.

The interval of an octave is important in music. It is the interval between the first and last tones of the familiar scale. Sing this scale slowly:

Seven different tones are produced by the white keys of the piano.

You will notice that you fill the octave with seven different pitches before arriving at the high *do*, which "duplicates" the low *do* you start on. You do not slide up as a siren does; you fill the octave with a specific number of pitches. If you start from the higher *do* and continue the scale upward, each of your original seven tones will be "duplicated" an octave higher. This group of seven tones was the basis of music in western civilization for centuries. The seven tones are produced by the white keys of the piano keyboard, as shown in the illustration at the left.

As time passed, five pitches were added to the original seven. They are produced by the black keys of the keyboard. All twelve tones, like the original seven, are "duplicated" in higher and lower octaves. Every tone has "close relatives" 1, 2, 3, or more octaves away. (In nonwestern music, the octave may be divided into a different number of tones, say, seventeen or twenty-two.)

The distance between the lowest and highest tones that a voice or instrument can produce is called its **pitch range,** or simply its *range*. The range of the average untrained voice is between 1 and 2 octaves; a piano's range is over 7 octaves. When men and women sing the same melody, they usually sing it an octave apart.

The organization of pitch is a composer's first resource. In Sections 5 and 6, where melody and harmony are explored, we will look at how pitch is organized. For now, we'll simply observe that composers can create a special mood in their music by using very low or very high pitches. For example, low pitches can intensify the sadness of a funeral march; high pitches can make a dance sound lighter. And a steady rise in pitch often increases musical tension.

Though most music we know is based on definite rather than indefinite pitches, noiselike sounds—such as those made by a bass drum or by cymbals—figure strongly in the rhythmic aspect of music. In parts of Africa, the indefinite pitches of drums are very important. And with recent developments in electronic music, indefinite pitches have come to play a vital role in western music as well.

DYNAMICS

Degrees of loudness or softness in music are called **dynamics.** Loudness is related to the amplitude of the vibration that produces the sound. The harder a guitar string is plucked (the farther it moves from the fingerboard), the louder its sound. When instruments are played more loudly or more softly, or when there is a change in how many instruments are heard, a dynamic change results; such a change may be made either suddenly or gradually. A gradual increase in loudness often creates excitement, particularly when the pitch rises too. On the other hand, a gradual decrease in loudness can convey a sense of calm.

A performer can emphasize a tone by playing it more loudly than the tones around it. We call an emphasis of this kind a **dynamic accent.** Skillful, subtle changes of dynamics add spirit and mood to performances. Sometimes these changes are written in the music; often they are not but are inspired by the performer's feelings about it.

Improvements in making musical instruments during the last 150 years have vastly increased our range of dynamics. In fact, today's electronic equipment has expanded it to the point where loudness can cause pain. Probably no culture has used so wide a dynamic range as ours does today.

When notating music for others to read, composers traditionally have used Italian words and abbreviations to indicate dynamics. The usual terms (shown in **bold italic** here), their abbreviations (in *italic*), and their meanings (roman type) are as follows:

pianissimo	*pp*	very soft
piano	*p*	soft
mezzo piano	*mp*	moderately soft
mezzo forte	*mf*	moderately loud
forte	*f*	loud
fortissimo	*ff*	very loud

For extremely soft and loud dynamic levels, a composer sometimes will use *ppp* or *pppp* and *fff* or *ffff*.

To show gradual changes in dynamics, the following words and symbols are used:

	decrescendo (*decresc.*)	
	or	gradually softer
	diminuendo (dim.)	
	crescendo (*cresc.*)	gradually louder

Like many elements of music, a dynamic indication is not absolutely precise. A tone has a dynamic level—is soft or loud—in relation to other tones around it. A single violin's loudest sound is tiny compared with an entire orchestra's, and even further from an amplified rock group's. But it can be considered fortissimo (very loud) within its own context.

TONE COLOR

We can tell a trumpet from a flute even when each of them plays the same tone at the same dynamic level. The quality of sound that distinguishes them is called **tone color,** or **timbre** (pronounced *tam'-ber*). Tone color is described by words like *bright, dark, brilliant, mellow,* and *rich.**

*An explanation of the physical basis of tone color appears in Appendix 2.

Like changes in dynamics, changes in tone color create variety and contrast. When the same melody is played by one instrument and then by another, it takes on different expressive effects because of each instrument's tone color. On the other hand, a contrast in tone color may be used to highlight a new melody: after violins play a melody, an oboe may present a contrasting one.

Tone colors also build a sense of continuity; it is easier to recognize the return of a melody when the same instruments play it each time. Specific instruments can reinforce a melody's emotional impact: the brilliant sound of a trumpet is suited to heroic or military tunes; the soothing tone color of a flute fits the mood of a calm melody. In fact, composers often invent a melody with a particular instrument's tone color in mind.

A practically unlimited variety of tone colors is available to composers. Combining different instruments—violin, clarinet, and trombone, for example—results in new colors that the instruments cannot produce by themselves. And tone color can be changed by varying the number of instruments or voices that perform a melody. Finally, electronic techniques developed in recent years allow composers to invent colors completely unlike those of traditional instruments.

LISTENING OUTLINES AND THE PROPERTIES OF SOUND

Reading about pitch, dynamics, and tone color without hearing music is too abstract. To understand and recognize the properties of sound, we must *listen for them.* In this book, listening outlines will help focus your attention on musical events as they unfold. These outlines must be read *as you listen to the music;* otherwise, their value to you is limited.

Each item in a listening outline describes some musical sound. It may point out dynamics, instruments used, pitch level, or mood. (Remember that indications of mood in music are subjective. What one person calls "triumphant" another may call "determined.")

Before you listen to a piece of music, it will help you to glance over the entire listening outline. Then, while hearing one item, look ahead to learn what's next. For example, in the listening outline for the Prelude to Act III of Richard Wagner's opera *Lohengrin,* the first item (1a) is "Full orchestra, very loud *(ff),* main melody in violins, cymbal crashes." While listening to the music described by item 1a, glance at item 1b: "Brass melody, pulsating accompaniment in strings."

Sometimes, not all the instruments playing are listed; instead, only those that are prominent at a given moment are shown. For example, item 2 in the *Lohengrin* listening outline reads "Soft *(p),* contrasting oboe melody. Melody repeated by flute. Clarinet and violins continue." Although other instruments can be heard, this description focuses attention on the instruments that play the melody.

Each listening outline is preceded by a description of the music's main features. Instrumentation, recording notes (where important), and duration of the selection in our recording are also given. Timings and compact disk track numbers appear to the left of items in the listening outline.

LOHENGRIN, PRELUDE TO ACT III, BY RICHARD WAGNER

Wagner makes wide and brilliant use of dynamic contrasts in the Prelude to Act III of *Lohengrin* to set the scene for the wedding of the opera's hero and heroine. The prelude opens with a feeling of exultation—great energy is conveyed by the massive sound of the full orchestra. Later, the music suddenly becomes calm and gentle as we hear fewer instruments, playing softly. This is followed by another sudden contrast when Wagner again employs the full orchestra.

Side 1, band 1
CD 1 [1]

Listening Outline   To be read while music is heard

LOHENGRIN, PRELUDE TO ACT III (1848),
BY RICHARD WAGNER (1813–1883)

3 flutes, 3 oboes, 3 clarinets, 3 bassoons, 4 French horns, 3 trumpets, 3 trombones, bass tuba, timpani, triangle, cymbals, tambourine, 1st violins, 2d violins, violas, cellos, double basses

(Duration, 3:00)

[1] 0:00	1.	*a.* Full orchestra, very loud *(ff),* main melody in violins, cymbal crashes.
[2] 0:22		*b.* Brass melody, pulsating accompaniment in strings.
1:06		*c.* Full orchestra, main melody in violins, cymbal crashes.
[3] 1:16	2.	Soft *(p),* contrasting oboe melody. Melody repeated by flute. Clarinet and violins continue.
[4] 2:13	3.	*a.* Full orchestra, very loud *(ff),* main melody in violins, cymbal crashes.
2:24		*b.* Brass melody, pulsating accompaniment in strings.
2:47		*c.* Cymbals. Becomes softer (decrescendo).

PRELUDE IN C MINOR FOR PIANO, OP. 28, NO. 20, BY FRÉDÉRIC CHOPIN

In Chopin's Prelude in C Minor, Op. 28, No. 20, dynamic change is produced by a single instrument, the piano. A decrease in volume from very loud *(ff)* to soft *(p),* and then to very soft *(pp),* contributes to a feeling of emotional progression within this miniature lasting only 1½ minutes; it's as though a majestic funeral march becomes increasingly personal.

Side 1, band 2
CD 1 [5]

Listening Outline To be read while music is heard

PRELUDE IN C MINOR FOR PIANO, OP.* 28, NO. 20 (1839),
BY FRÉDÉRIC CHOPIN (1810–1849)

(Duration, 1:32)

5	0:00	1. Heavy chords, very loud *(ff)*.
6	0:25	2. New section, soft *(p)*.
7	0:54	3. Very soft *(pp)* repeat of preceding section. Loud chord at end.

FIREBIRD SUITE, FINALE (1919 VERSION), BY IGOR STRAVINSKY

Side 1, band 3
CD 1 8

In the Finale of the *Firebird* Suite, Stravinsky repeats one melody over and over, creating variety and contrast through changes in dynamics, tone color, and rhythm. The *suite* is a set of dances from *The Firebird* (1910), a ballet in which the hero marries a beautiful princess during the music of the Finale.

The Finale begins softly but becomes increasingly grand as the music gradually gets louder (crescendo), more instruments play, and the melody is repeated at higher pitches. After this slow buildup to a climax, there's a sudden quiet as all instruments but the strings stop playing. A quick crescendo then leads to a brilliant concluding section.

Listening Outline To be read while music is heard

FIREBIRD SUITE, FINALE (1919 VERSION†),
BY IGOR STRAVINSKY (1882–1971)

Piccolo, 2 flutes, 2 oboes, 2 clarinets, 2 bassoons, 4 French horns, 2 trumpets, 3 trombones, tuba, timpani, bass drum, triangle, cymbals, harp, 1st violins, 2d violins, violas, cellos, double basses

(Duration, 2:49)

8	0:00	1. *a.* Melody in French horn, soft *(p)*, quivering string accompaniment.
	0:25	*b.* Violins, soft, melody an octave higher. Flutes join.
	0:37	*c.* Gets louder (crescendo) as more instruments enter.

*The abbreviation *op.* stands for *opus*, Latin for *work*. An opus number is a way of identifying a piece or set of pieces. Usually, within a composer's output, the higher a composition's opus number, the later it was written.
†Stravinsky composed three different versions of the *Firebird* Suite.

0:54	d. Violins and woodwinds, loud, melody at an even higher octave, crescendo to
1:06	e. Full orchestra, melody extremely loud *(fff)*.
1:20	f. Suddenly very soft *(pp)*, strings, quick crescendo to
[9] 1:27	2. a. Brasses, very loud *(ff)*, melody in quick detached notes, timpani (kettledrums). Melody slows down, full orchestra, *fff*, timpani.
2:27	b. Cymbals, sustained brass chords, extremely loud *(fff)*. Dynamic swell at end.

HOTTER THAN THAT,
BY LOUIS ARMSTRONG AND HIS HOT FIVE

A succession of different tone colors contributes to the variety within *Hotter Than That,* for jazz band. After an introduction played by the full band, we hear solos by the trumpet, clarinet, voice, guitar, and trombone. Louis Armstrong performs as both trumpeter and vocalist. His singing is like his trumpet playing in sound and style. Instead of lyrics he sings nonsense syllables like *dat-a bat-a dip-da.* In one section, the guitarist, Lonnie Johnson, imitates the melodic phrases sung by Armstrong, whose voice takes on a guitarlike twang.

Side 1, band 4
CD 1 [10]

Unlike the preceding compositions by Wagner, Chopin, and Stravinsky, this music was improvised by the performers. Their point of departure was the tune *Hotter Than That*, by Lillian Hardin Armstrong, the band's pianist.

Within item 2 of the listening outline, the trumpet is momentarily heard alone, without its accompaniment of piano and guitar. This unaccompanied solo should not be mistaken for the entrance of the clarinet (item 3), which sounds like a high-pitched whine.

Listening Outline To be read while music is heard

HOTTER THAN THAT (1927),
BY LOUIS ARMSTRONG (1900–1971) AND HIS HOT FIVE

Voice, clarinet, trumpet, trombone, piano, banjo, guitar

(Duration, 2:59)

[10] 0:00	1. All instruments, trumpet predominates.
0:09	2. Trumpet accompanied by piano and guitar. Trumpet briefly alone, piano and guitar rejoin.
[11] 0:43	3. Clarinet, high-pitched whine, piano and guitar accompany.
[12] 1:19	4. Voice, guitar accompaniment.
[13] 1:54	5. Twangy voice imitated by guitar. Piano leads into
[14] 2:17	6. a. Muted trombone accompanied by piano and guitar.
[15] 2:33	b. Trumpet, all instruments join. Guitar, trumpet, guitar at end.

9

BASIC TERMS

sound (page 2)
pitch (2)
tone (3)
interval (3)
octave (3)
pitch range (4)
dynamic accent (5)
tone color (timbre) (5)

dynamics (4–5):
  pianissimo
  piano
  mezzo piano
  mezzo forte
  forte
  fortissimo
  decrescendo (diminuendo)
  crescendo

[2] ELEMENTS PERFORMING MEDIA: VOICES AND INSTRUMENTS

VOICES

Throughout history, singing has been the most widespread and familiar way of making music. Ancient Greek drama included chanting choruses, and the Bible records that Moses, Miriam, and the Israelites sang to glorify the Lord. Singers seem always to have had a magnetic appeal, and even today adoring audiences imitate the looks and lifestyles of their favorites.

The exchange between singer and audience contains a bit of magic, something direct and spellbinding. Probably because the singer becomes an instrument, we identify with him or her especially—a human body like our own expressing emotions through sounds and words.

The voice's unique ability to fuse a word with a musical tone is the reason that poetry and singing have been inseparable in many cultures. Singing can make words easier to remember and heighten their emotional effect.

For many reasons, it is difficult to sing well. In singing we use wider ranges of pitch and volume than in speaking. And we hold vowel sounds longer. Singing demands a greater supply and control of breath. Air from the lungs is controlled by the lower abdominal muscles and the diaphragm. The air makes the vocal cords vibrate, and the singer's lungs, throat, mouth, and nose come into play to produce the desired sound. The pitch of the tone varies with the tension of the vocal cords; the tighter they are, the higher the pitch.

Throughout history, singing has been the most widespread way of making music. These vocal soloists, choristers, and instrumentalists are from the New England Conservatory of Music.

The range of a singer's *voice* depends both on training and on physical makeup. Professional singers can command 2 octaves or even more, whereas an untrained voice is usually limited to about 1½ octaves. Men's vocal cords are longer and larger than women's, and this difference produces a lower range of pitches. The classification of voice ranges for women and men follows, arranged from highest to lowest. (The four basic ranges are soprano, alto, tenor, and bass.)

Women	Men
soprano	*tenor*
mezzo-soprano	*baritone*
alto (or contralto)	*bass*

Because of differences in taste, methods of singing vary widely from culture to culture. Asian singing, for example, is more nasal than that of the west. While classical singers in our culture stand erect, singers in west

11

Africa stand bending forward; and in India they sit on the floor. In fact, there are differences in performing styles in the west alone: classical, popular, jazz, folk, and rock music are all sung differently. Classical singers, for example, normally don't rely on microphones, but rock gets its point across partly by amplification.

Until the late 1600s, most music of western culture was vocal. But by the end of the seventeenth century, instrumental music rivaled vocal music in importance. Since then, composers have continued to write vocal works—both solo and choral—with and without instrumental accompaniment. There are compositions for male chorus, female chorus, and mixed chorus, which usually combines sopranos, altos, tenors, and basses. Accompaniments to vocal works range from single instruments like guitar or piano to entire orchestras.

MUSICAL INSTRUMENTS

People around the world use musical instruments that vary greatly in construction and tone color. An instrument may be defined as any mechanism—other than the voice—that produces musical sounds. Western musicians usually classify instruments in six broad categories: *string* (such as guitar and violin); *woodwind* (flute, clarinet); *brass* (trumpet, trombone); *percussion* (bass drum, cymbals); *keyboard* (organ, piano); and *electronic* (synthesizer).*

An instrument is often made in different sizes that produce different ranges. For instance, the saxophone family includes soprano, alto, tenor, baritone, and bass saxophones.

An instrument's tone color may vary with the *register* (part of the total range) in which it is played. A clarinet sounds dark and rich in its low register, but its high register is brilliant and piercing.

Instrumental performers try to match the beautiful, flexible tone of a singer's voice. Yet most instruments have a wider range of pitches than the voice does. While a trained singer's range is about 2 octaves, many instruments command 3 or 4 octaves, and some have 6 or 7. And instruments usually produce tones more rapidly than the voice. When writing music for a specific instrument, composers have to consider its range of pitches and dynamics and how fast it can produce tones.

---

*The scientific classification of instruments, based on the way sound is made, has five categories: *chordophones* (a stretched string is the sound generator—our "string" category); *aerophones* (a column of air is the sound generator—our "woodwind" and "brass" categories); *idiophones* (instruments whose own material is the sound generator, such as cymbals, gongs, and bells—part of our "percussion" category); *membranophones* (instruments with a stretched skin or other membrane for the sound generator, such as drums—part of our "percussion" category); and *electrophones* (instruments generating their sounds by means of electricity—our "electronic" category).

Instruments provide entertainment and accompany singing, dancing, religious rites, and drama. But they have served other functions, too. In some cultures, instruments are thought to have magic powers. Bells are worn to guard against harm, and rattles are witch doctors' tools. In parts of Africa, drums are so sacred that religious rites are not performed without them, and special ceremonies and sacrifices are sometimes enacted when the drums are being made.

Instruments have been used for communication as well. Detailed messages have been sent by drumbeats; hunters have blown horns for signals; and musicians have announced the time by sounding brass instruments from towers. Trumpets have been used for military signals and to bolster soldiers' courage in battle. For centuries, trumpets and kettledrums announced kings and queens.

Musical instruments have even been status symbols. During the nineteenth and early twentieth centuries, the piano was a fixture in any home that aspired to be middle-class. "Proper" young ladies were expected to learn the piano as one of many "accomplishments." Such ideas lost their currency when women began to move more freely in the world (around the time of World War I), and when the radio and phonograph began to replace the piano as a source of home entertainment. Still, even today there are status implications in the type of audio equipment someone owns. Though a stereo is not a musical instrument, a connection can be made between the parlor piano of 1900 and today's elaborate "home entertainment centers."

Instruments' popularity rises and falls with changing musical tastes and requirements. Today only a fraction of all known instruments are used. However, interest in music of earlier times has led to the resurrection of long-forgotten instruments like the harpsichord, an ancestor of the piano, and the recorder, a relative of the flute. Modern replicas of ancient instruments are being built and played. In fact, modern musicians are flexible and far-ranging in their choice of instruments. Rock composers have used nonwestern instruments such as the Indian sitar (a plucked string instrument). Jazz musicians are turning to classical instruments like the flute, while classical composers are using instruments associated with jazz, such as the vibraphone.

Compositions may be written for solo instruments, for small groups, and for orchestras with over 100 musicians. Whatever the group, it may include instruments from only one category (say, strings) or from several. Modern symphony orchestras contain string, woodwind, brass, and percussion instruments. (The illustration on the following page shows a typical seating plan for a large orchestra.) Keyboard instruments also find their way into the modern orchestra as needed. Bands consist mainly of brass, woodwind, and percussion instruments.

Instruments commonly used for western music are described in this chapter, by categories. Nonwestern instruments are discussed in Part XI.

Above: The New York Philharmonic orchestra.

Below: Typical seating plan for a large orchestra (about 100 instrumentalists), showing the distribution of instruments.

Woodwinds	Brass	Strings	Percussion
3 flutes, 1 piccolo	4 trumpets	18 first violins	4 timpani (1 player),
3 oboes, 1 English horn	6 French horns	16 second violins	bass drum, snare
3 clarinets, 1 bass clarinet	4 trombones	12 violas	drum, cymbals,
3 bassoons, 1 contrabassoon	1 tuba	10 cellos	triangle, xylophone,
		8 double basses	celesta, glockenspiel,
1 piano			etc. (2 to 4 players)
2 harps			

Bands marching in the Steuben Day parade in New York City.

String Instruments

The *violin, viola, cello* (violoncello), and ***double bass*** ("bass fiddle," sometimes called simply a *bass*) form the symphony orchestra's string section.
They vary in tone color as well as in size and range: the violin is the smallest and has the highest range; the double bass is the largest and has the
lowest range. For symphonic music the strings are usually played with a
bow, a slightly curved stick strung tightly with horsehair (see the illustration on the following page). Symphonic strings are also plucked with the
finger.

Of all the instrument groups, the strings have the greatest versatility and
expressive range. They produce many tone colors and have wide ranges of
pitch and dynamics. String players can produce tones that are brilliant and
rapid or slow and throbbing; they can control tone as subtly as a singer.
Orchestral works tend to rely more on the strings than on any other group.
Even with their differing tone colors, the four string instruments blend
beautifully. Here it will be helpful to consider the strings' construction and
tone production; the violin can represent the entire family.

The hollow wooden body of the violin supports four strings made of gut
or wire. The strings stretch, under tension, from a *tailpiece* on one end over
a wooden *bridge* to the other end, where they are fastened around wooden
pegs. The bridge holds the strings away from the *fingerboard* so that they
can vibrate freely; the bridge also transmits the strings' vibrations to the
body, which amplifies and colors the tone. Each string is tuned to a different pitch by tightening or loosening the pegs. (The greater the tension, the
higher the pitch.)

The musician makes a string vibrate by drawing the bow across it with
the right hand. The speed and pressure of the bow stroke control the dynamics and tone color of the sound produced. Pitch is controlled by the

15

Violin and bow.

musician's left hand. By pressing a string against the fingerboard, the player varies the length of its vibrating portion and so changes its pitch. This is called *stopping* a string (because the vibrations are stopped at a certain point along the string's length). Thus a range of pitches can be drawn from each of the four strings.

Basically the viola, cello, and double bass are made in the same manner and produce sound by similar means. How the string instruments are played—what string performance techniques are used—determines which of many musical effects they will produce. The most frequently used techniques are listed here:

Pizzicato (plucked string): The musician plucks the string, usually with a finger of the right hand. In jazz, the double bass is played mainly as a plucked instrument, rather than being bowed.

Double stop (two notes at once): By drawing the bow across two strings, a string player can sound two notes at once. And by rotating the bow rapidly across three strings *(triple stop)* or four strings *(quadruple stop)*, three or four notes can be sounded almost—but not quite—together.

Vibrato: The string player can produce a throbbing, expressive tone by rocking the left hand while pressing the string down. This causes small pitch fluctuations which make the tone warmer.

Mute: The musician can veil or muffle the tone by fitting a clamp (mute) onto the bridge.

Tremolo: The musician rapidly repeats tones by quick up-and-down strokes of the bow. This can create a sense of tension, when loud, or a shimmering sound, when soft.

Harmonics: Very high-pitched tones, like a whistle's, are produced when the string player lightly touches certain points on a string. (See Appendix 2.)

Though the violin, viola, cello, and double bass are similar, they, like members of any family, have their differences. The photographs in this section show why each adds something distinctive to the orchestra's total sound.

Some string instruments are not played with a bow but are plucked instead, with the fingers or with a *plectrum* (plural, *plectra)*. The most important of these are the *harp* and the *guitar.* The harp is the only plucked string instrument that has gained wide acceptance in the symphony orchestra.

STRINGS

(Michael Putland/Retna Ltd.)

The violin (above) is often used as a solo instrument. In the orchestra, the violins are divided into first and second violins, with the first violins frequently playing the main melody. One of the world's best-known violinists is Itzhak Perlman.

(Steve J. Sherman)

Although eighteenth-century composers generally used the cello (above) in its bass and baritone registers, later composers exploited its upper registers as well. The cellist shown here is Yo-Yo Ma.

(Innervisions)

The body of the viola (left) is about 2 inches longer than that of the violin, and thus the viola's range is somewhat lower. Its tone color is darker, thicker, and a little less brilliant than the violin's.

The double bass (or bass, above left) has a very heavy tone and is less agile than other string instruments. It is often heard with the cello, but an octave lower.

The harp (above, right)—with forty-seven strings stretched on a triangular frame—has a wide range of 6 octaves. The harpist plucks the strings with the fingers of both hands. Shown here is the harpist Maria Casale.

The guitar (right) has six strings, which are plucked with the fingers of the right hand. Frets on the fingerboard mark the places where the strings are stopped (pressed) with the fingers of the left hand. The guitarist shown here is Carlos Montoya.

Woodwind Instruments

The woodwind instruments are so named because they produce vibrations of air within a tube that traditionally was made of wood. During the twentieth century, however, piccolos and flutes came to be made of metal. All the woodwinds have little holes along their length that are opened and closed by the fingers or by pads controlled by a key mechanism. By opening and closing these holes, the woodwind player changes the length of the vibrating air column and so varies the pitch.

The woodwind instruments of the symphony orchestra are as follows, arranged from highest (piccolo) to lowest (contrabassoon) in range. (The pairing indicates closely related instruments; the more important one of each pair is followed by an asterisk.)

$\begin{cases} piccolo \\ flute* \end{cases}$
$\begin{cases} oboe* \\ English\ horn \end{cases}$
$\begin{cases} clarinet* \\ bass\ clarinet \end{cases}$
$\begin{cases} bassoon* \\ contrabassoon \end{cases}$

Woodwind instruments are great individualists and are much less alike in tone color than the various strings. The flute, with its silvery tone, differs more from the nasal-sounding oboe than the violin does from the viola. The woodwinds' unique tone colors result largely from the different ways in which vibrations are produced. Flute and piccolo players blow across the edge of a mouth hole much as one makes sounds by blowing across the top of an empty bottle. (Players of the *recorder,* a relative of the flute, blow through a "whistle" mouthpiece.) The rest of the woodwind instruments rely on a vibrating reed. A *reed* is a very thin piece of cane, about 2½ inches long, that is set into vibration by a stream of air. There are single- and double-reed woodwinds. In *single-reed woodwinds* the reed is fastened over a hole in the mouthpiece and vibrates when the player blows into his or her instrument. The clarinet and bass clarinet are single-reed woodwinds. The *saxophone,* too, an instrument used mainly in bands, has a single reed.

In *double-reed woodwinds* two narrow pieces of cane are held between the musician's lips. The oboe, English horn, bassoon, and contrabassoon are double-reed woodwinds.

Heard by itself, a reed produces only a squawklike sound. Although the tone color of reed woodwinds is mainly determined by the bore of the instrument's tube, the reed does affect the tone color somewhat. Professional woodwind players spend much time soaking and shaping their supply of reeds to ensure the best possible tone.

WOODWINDS

The piccolo (top, left)—whose name is short for *flauto piccolo,* or *small flute*—is half the size of the flute and plays an octave higher. The piccolo's high register is shrill and whistlelike.

The flute (top, right) has a high range and is extremely agile, capable of producing rapid successions of tones. Its tone is full and velvety in the low register and bright and sparkling at the top. Shown here is the well-known flutist James Galway.

The oboe (above) has a nasal, intense, expressive tone. Because the oboe's pitch is difficult to adjust, the entire orchestra is tuned to its A. The oboist here is Heinz Holliger.

The recorder (left), like the flute and piccolo, has no reed. The recorder's tone resembles a flute's but is softer and gentler. Its five main sizes are sopranino, soprano, alto, tenor, and bass.

The English horn (top, left) is neither English nor a horn, but simply a low, or alto, oboe.

The clarinet (top, right) can produce tones very rapidly and has a wide range of dynamics and tone color. The clarinetist shown here is Richard Stoltzman.

The tone of the bassoon (bottom, left) is deeply nasal.

The bass clarinet (bottom, right) is larger than the clarinet and has a much lower range.

21

The contrabassoon (above) can produce the lowest pitch in the orchestra.

The saxophone (right) has a single-reed mouthpiece like a clarinet's, but its tube is made of brass. Its tone is rich, husky, and speechlike. Shown here is the jazz saxophonist Sonny Rollins.

Tone colors also differ greatly among the various registers of each woodwind instrument. In general, low registers tend to be breathy and thick, and top registers are more penetrating. Unlike the strings, which can double-stop, the woodwinds can produce only a single note at a time. In symphonic music they are frequently given melodic solos. Woodwind instruments are well suited for outdoors (shepherds have played simple woodwinds for thousands of years). Therefore they are often featured in music that evokes a rustic mood.

Brass Instruments

From high register to low, the main instruments of the symphony orchestra's brass section are the *trumpet, French horn* (sometimes called simply a *horn*), *trombone,* and *tuba.* Trumpets and trombones are often used in jazz and rock groups.

The vibrations of brass instruments come from the musician's lips as he or she blows into a cup- or funnel-shaped *mouthpiece.* The vibrations are amplified and colored in a tube that is coiled (to make it easy to carry and play). The tube is flared at the end to form a *bell.* Modern brass instruments are actually made of brass, but their earlier counterparts were made of hollow animal horns, elephant tusks, wood, and even glass.

Some brass instruments, such as the cornet, baritone horn, euphonium, and bass, are used mainly in concert and marching bands. The *cornet* is similar in shape to the trumpet, but its tone is more mellow. The *baritone horn* looks like a tuba and has the same range as the trombone. The *euphonium* is the tenor instrument of the tuba family. The *bass* corresponds to the tuba.

The pitch of brass instruments is regulated both by varying the lip tension and by using *slides* and *valves* to change the length of the tube through which the air vibrates. The trombone uses a slide, a U-shaped tube that fits into two parallel straight tubes. By pulling the slide in or pushing it out, the player changes the length of tubing and makes it possible to play different pitches. The trumpet, French horn, and tuba use three or four valves to divert air through various lengths of tubing. The longer the length of tubing through which air is diverted, the lower the possible pitch. Valves came into common use around 1850. Before then, French horn and trumpet players would insert additional curves of tubing (called *crooks*) into their instruments to change the range of available pitches. When valves came into use, these instruments could produce many more tones and became much more flexible. Brass players can also alter the tone of their instruments by inserting a *mute* into the bell. A mute for a brass instrument is a hollow, funnel-shaped piece of wood or plastic.

Brasses are powerful instruments; when played loudly they can almost drown out the rest of the orchestra. Brasses are used at climaxes and for bold and heroic statements. They cannot play as rapidly as most of the string or woodwind instruments and serve less often as soloists. We often think of the brasses in connection with military marches or outdoor ceremonies. For many centuries they were simple instruments capable of producing only a few pitches and were used mainly for military signals, religious rites, or hunting calls.

BRASS

The trumpet (left, top) sounds brilliant, brassy, and penetrating. The trumpeter shown here is Wynton Marsalis.

The French horn (above) has a tone that is less brassy, more mellow, and more rounded than the trumpet's.

The trombone (left, middle) has a tone that combines the trumpet's brilliance with the French horn's mellowness.

The thick, heavy tone of the tuba (left, bottom) is used to add weight to the lowest orchestral register.

Percussion Instruments

Most percussion instruments of the orchestra are struck by hand, with sticks, or with hammers. Some are shaken or rubbed. Percussion instruments are subdivided into instruments of definite and indefinite pitch, depending on whether they produce a tone or a noiselike sound.

Definite Pitch		Indefinite Pitch	
timpani	*xylophone*	*snare drum*	*triangle*
(kettledrums)	*celesta*	*(side drum)*	*cymbals*
glockenspiel	*chimes*	*bass drum*	*gong*
		tambourine	*(tam-tam)*

The vibrations of percussion instruments are set up by stretched membranes, like the calfskin of the kettledrum, or by plates or bars made of metal, wood, or other sonorous materials. Extremely loud sounds may be drawn from percussion instruments like the bass drum or cymbals; however, percussion sounds die away more quickly than those of other instruments. In a symphony orchestra, one percussionist may play several different instruments during a composition.

PERCUSSION

The timpani (kettledrums, below) are the only orchestral drums of definite pitch. A calfskin head is stretched over a copper, hemispherical shell. The pitch of the timpani is changed by varying the tension of the head. Screws around the shell's rim are tightened or loosened by hand or by a foot pedal. One percussionist generally plays two to four timpani, each tuned to a different pitch.

(Innervisions)

The metal bars of the glockenspiel (orchestral bells; left, top) are struck with two hammers to produce a tone that is bright and silvery.

The xylophone (left, middle) consists of a set of wooden bars which are struck with two hard hammers to produce a dry, wooden tone.

The celesta (left, bottom) looks like a small upright piano, but its sounding mechanism is like a glockenspiel's. Metal bars are struck by hammers that are controlled by a keyboard. The celesta's tone is tinkling and graceful.

Chimes (above) are a set of metal tubes hung from a frame. They are struck with a hammer and sound like church bells.

The bass drum (left, top)—the largest of the orchestral drums—is almost 3 feet in diameter.

The dry rattling sound of the snare drum or side drum (left, middle) is produced by the vibration of snares—strings which are tightly stretched against the bottom head. The snare drum is often used in marches.

The tambourine (left, bottom) is often used to create Spanish or Gypsy effects. The player shakes it or strikes its head with the knuckles.

The triangle (top, right) is struck with a metal beater and makes a tinkling, bell-like sound.

When struck by a bass drum's stick with a soft head, the gong or tam-tam (above) produces long-lasting sounds that can seem solemn, mysterious, or frightening.

(Clemens Kalischer)

Cymbals (left) are round brass plates. They are usually struck together with a sliding motion, and their sound penetrates like a sharp crash.

Percussion instruments have long been used to emphasize rhythm and to heighten climaxes. But until about 1900, they played a far less important role in western music than strings, woodwinds, or brasses. Composers of our century have been more willing to exploit the special colors of the percussion group and have occasionally written entire pieces to show it off, such as *Ionisation* (1931) by Edgard Varèse. Jazz and rock musicians have, of course, made good use of percussion instruments. Yet, for all these recent explorations, western musicians barely approach the incredibly varied use of percussion found in Africa and Asia, where subtle changes of rhythm, tone color, and dynamics are used with great imagination.

Keyboard Instruments

The piano, harpsichord, organ, and accordion are the best-known keyboard instruments. A keyboard permits the performer to play several tones at the same time with ease and rapidity. This capacity justifies grouping instruments that are otherwise quite different: the piano and harpsichord produce sounds through vibrating strings; the organ uses vibrating air columns. The piano and, to a lesser extent, the organ are sometimes used in modern symphony orchestras for coloristic effects. All keyboard instruments are played solo, as well.

During the last two centuries, more great music has been written for the *piano* than for any other solo instrument. The piano is exceptionally versatile. A pianist can play many notes at once, including both a melody and its accompaniment. The piano commands a wide range of pitches. Its eighty-eight keys span more than 7 octaves. The dynamic range is broad, from a

KEYBOARD INSTRUMENTS

The piano (above) is exceptionally versatile. Shown here is the pianist Mitsuko Uchida.

The harpsichord (below) has plucked strings controlled from one or two keyboards.

(Lawrence Migdale/Photo Researchers)

A pipe organ (above) has many sets of pipes, controlled from several keyboards.

faint whisper to a powerful fortissimo. Because of its dynamic flexibility, the Italians named it the *pianoforte* (meaning *soft-loud*).

When a pianist's finger strikes a key, a felt-covered hammer swings up against a string. The greater the force on the key, the more powerful the hammer's blow on the string, and the louder the tone produced. When the pianist releases the key, a felt *damper* comes down on the string to stop the vibrations and end the tone. The steel strings are held under tension by an iron frame. Below the strings is a wooden sounding board, which amplifies and colors the strings' vibrations.

There are usually three pedals on a piano. Most important is the *damper pedal*, on the right, which allows a pianist to sustain tones even after the keys are released. The *una corda* pedal, on the left, commonly known as the *soft pedal*, veils the sound. The *sostenuto* pedal, in the middle, is rarely used (and in fact is often missing from upright pianos); it allows the pianist to sustain some tones without sustaining others.

The piano was invented around 1700, came into fairly wide use in the 1780s, and was mechanically perfected by the 1850s. Today it is among the most popular instruments and is used for solos, for accompaniments, and in combination with one other instrument or many other instruments.

The **harpsichord** has strings that are plucked by a set of *plectra* (little wedges of plastic, leather, or quill). These are controlled by one or two keyboards. The harpsichord was the main keyboard stringed instrument from about 1500 to 1775, when it was gradually replaced by the piano. Although largely forgotten during the nineteenth century, the harpsichord has been revived during the twentieth century for the performance of music composed before 1750. It has also been put to new use in works by twentieth-century composers.

Pipe organs have many sets of pipes controlled from several keyboards, including a pedal keyboard played by the organist's feet. The keys control valves from which air is blown across or through openings in the pipes. Various sets of pipes are brought into play by pulling knobs called *stops*. Each set of pipes has a particular tone color which the organist uses alone or with others. The larger the organ, the more tone colors available. Organists, unlike pianists, cannot make subtle changes of dynamics by varying finger pressure. Instead, dynamic change is produced by adding to or reducing the number of pipes being played, by moving from one keyboard to another, or by opening and closing the shutters (much like Venetian blinds) which surround some groups of pipes. The organ has a greater range of pitch, volume, and tone color than any other traditional instrument. Its tones last for as long as a finger or a foot is held on a key or pedal.

The greatest period of organ music and organ building was from 1600 to 1750, when the organ was known as the "king of instruments." Although mostly connected with religious services, today the organ is found in many auditoriums and is used in concerts.

The *accordion* has free steel reeds that are controlled by a treble keyboard with piano keys—played by the right hand—and a bass keyboard with buttons—played by the left hand. The reeds are caused to vibrate by air pressure from a bellows.

Electronic Instruments

Electronic instruments produce or amplify sound through electronic means; they were invented as early as 1904 but have had a significant impact on music only since 1950. Today, electronic and computer technologies are developing rapidly, changing continually, and increasingly blending together. Electronic instruments for performing and composing music include amplified instruments, such as the electric piano, organ, and guitar; tape studios; synthesizers; computers; and various "hybrid" technologies.

The *tape studio* was the main tool of composers of electronic music during the 1950s. (In Part VII, we'll study Edgard Varèse's *Poème électronique*, which was created in a tape studio.) The raw material in tape studios consisted of recorded sounds of definite and indefinite pitch which might be electronic or from "real life"—flutes, bird calls, etc. The composer manipulated these in various ways: by speeding them up or slowing them down, altering their pitch and duration, giving them echos, filtering them to

(Patricia Sener)

Today's electronic music studios integrate a wide variety of equipment, including tape recorders, synthesizers, computers, and devices for mixing and filtering sound.

change tone color, mixing them, and editing the tape (as by cutting and splicing) to play them in any desired order. Rhythm could be fully controlled, because the duration of a sound depended only on the length of a tape segment. However, tape splicing and rerecording was a difficult, inaccurate, and time-consuming process, and many composers of the 1960s turned to synthesizers, which appeared around 1955.

Synthesizers are systems of electronic components which generate, modify, and control sound. They can generate a huge variety of musical sounds and noises, and the composer has complete control over pitch, tone color, loudness, and duration. Most synthesizers can be "played" by means of a keyboard—an addition to the mechanisms of the tape studio.

Synthesizers vary in size and capacity. For example, Milton Babbitt created his *Composition for Synthesizer* (which we'll study in Part VII) on an enormous (and unique) vacuum-tube synthesizer occupying an entire wall of the Columbia-Princeton Electronic Music Center in New York City. During the 1960s and 1970s, smaller, less expensive transistorized synthesizers such as the Moog and Buchla were developed; these were installed in electronic music studios at universities and advertising agencies, played in live rock concerts and concerts of electronic music, and used to create film and television scores. Highly sophisticated synthesizers using computer capabilities have now been developed, and several different technologies are in use.

Analog synthesis—the earliest of the synthesizer technologies, which predominated until about 1980—uses a mixture of complex sounds that are shaped by filtering. Like all analog technology, it is based on representing data in terms of measurable physical quantities, in this case sound waves.

Digital frequency modulation (FM) synthesis, invented by John Chowning, was patented by Yamaha and has been associated with Yamaha instruments. Like all digital technology, it is based on representing physical quantities—here, points on sound waves—as numbers.

Effects devices, which include reverberators, echo devices, and stereo splitters, are often integrated into synthesizers and the synthesis process. They are used in almost all recorded music (especially popular music) and in some live music.

Sampling is considered a synthesizer technology, since it involves placing brief digital recordings of live sounds under the control of a synthesizer keyboard; but although the sounds can be modified during playback, no actual synthesis is present. Sampling can be seen as an advanced form of composing by tape splicing: it allows the composer to record short segments of sounds (these are the "samples") digitally and then manipulate them. Sampling has been integrated into relatively inexpensive computer-linked keyboards and is one of the most important aspects of today's electronic music making.

A significant development in synthesizing technology is known as *musical instrument digital interface (MIDI)*: this is a standard adopted by manufacturers for interfacing synthesizer equipment. MIDI has allowed the device actually played on to be separated from tone generation; thus there are now keyboards that look, feel, and play like a piano; wind controllers played like a woodwind instrument; and string controllers played like a violin or cello. Also, control signals can be fed to and from a MIDI instrument into and out of a personal computer, and users can store and edit music and convert to and from musical notation.

Historically, **computers** were the third means of producing sounds on audiotape; they were developed for this purpose after the tape studio and synthesizers. Since the vibrating waves which produce any sound can be represented by a series of numbers, a computer can be programmed to accept musical specifications fed into it by a composer; it then changes these specifications into numbers that represent the final sounds. Later, the numbers are passed through a converter so that the music may be heard or recorded.

The 1970s and 1980s saw the development of small computers with which composers could instantly hear the music they programmed; since then, computers have become even more sophisticated. Computers are used for music synthesis (mainly to produce sounds not otherwise obtainable), to help composers write scores (following rules selected by the composer), to store samples of audio signals, to control synthesizing mechanisms, and so on.

Obviously, it is not entirely possible (or particularly useful) to consider modern electronic music devices and processes separately: the distinction between synthesizer technology and computer technology is not clear-cut. To increase the variety of sound and the composer's control over it, today's electronic music studios contain and integrate a wide variety of equipment, including tape recorders, synthesizers, computers, and devices for mixing and filtering sound.

All this equipment enables the composer to exploit the entire spectrum of sound as never before. But the quality of the music produced is still dependent upon the imagination and organizing power of the human mind.

THE YOUNG PERSON'S GUIDE TO THE ORCHESTRA, OP. 34 (1946), BY BENJAMIN BRITTEN (1913–1976)

Supplementary sets:
Side 1, band 1
CD 1 [1]

Benjamin Britten, an English composer, wrote the attractive *Young Person's Guide to the Orchestra* in 1946 as an introduction to the instruments of the orchestra. He used a theme by Henry Purcell, a great English composer of the seventeenth century. (A *theme* is a melody used as the basis for a musical composition.)

The majestic theme is first presented as follows:

Theme

[1] 0:00   *a.* Full orchestra
[2] 0:23   *b.* Woodwind section
[3] 0:45   *c.* Brass section
[4] 1:04   *d.* String section
[5] 1:21   *e.* Percussion section
[6] 1:37   *f.* Full orchestra

Thirteen variatons, or varied repetitions of the theme, are then heard. Each highlights a different instrument. Together, they vary in dynamics, speed, and tone color, as well as mood. The variations follow each other without pause and range from about 30 seconds to 1 minute in length. (Variation 13, however, which features many percussion instruments, lasts almost 2 minutes.)

Within each of the instrumental groups, instruments are generally presented from highest to lowest in range, as follows:

Woodwinds

[7] 1:56   *Variation 1:*   Flutes and piccolo
[8] 2:28   *Variation 2:*   Oboes
[9] 3:32   *Variation 3:*   Clarinets
[10] 4:08 *Variation 4:*   Bassoons

Strings
Variation 5:	Violins	11	5:01
Variation 6:	Violas	12	5:37
Variation 7:	Cellos	13	6:36
Variation 8:	Double basses	14	7:53
Variation 9:	Harp	15	8:52

Brasses
Variation 10:	French horns	16	9:40
Variation 11:	Trumpets	17	10:24
Variation 12:	Trombones and tuba	18	10:58

Percussion

Variation 13:

a.	Timpani (kettledrums); bass drum and cymbals.	19	11:56
b.	Tambourine and triangle; snare drum (side drum) and Chinese block (a hollow wooden block that is struck with a drumstick)	20	12:23
c.	Xylophone	21	12:44
d.	Castanets and gong	22	12:54
e.	Whip (two hinged pieces of wood that are slapped against each other)	23	13:04
f.	Entire percussion section; xylophone and triangle	24	13:12

25 13:43

Variation 13 is followed immediately by a lively new tune played by an unaccompanied piccolo. Then, other instruments enter, each playing the same tune. After woodwind, string, brass, and percussion instruments have had their turn, the brasses bring back the main theme and provide an exciting conclusion.

THE STARS AND STRIPES FOREVER, BY JOHN PHILIP SOUSA

One of the most popular of all band marches, *The Stars and Stripes Forever* (1897), was written by John Philip Sousa (1854–1932), the American composer and conductor nicknamed the "march king." *The Stars and Stripes Forever* displays the power and vitality of band music. The march begins with a short introduction that is followed by two different melodies that are predominantly loud. We then hear the flowing main melody, which is played softly. After a transitional passage, there is a return of the main melody, this time combined with a new piccolo tune. *The Stars and Stripes Forever* builds to a climactic concluding section in which the main melody—now played loudly—and the piccolo tune are accompanied by a new trombone melody.

Side 1, band 5
CD 1 16

35

Listening Outline To be read while music is heard

THE STARS AND STRIPES FOREVER (1897),
BY JOHN PHILIP SOUSA (1854–1932)

Piccolo, 2 flutes, 2 oboes, 1st clarinets, 2d clarinets, 3d clarinets, alto clarinet, bass clarinet, 2 bassoons, 2 alto saxophones, tenor saxophone, baritone saxophone, bass saxophone, 3 cornets, 2 trumpets, 4 French horns, baritone horn, euphonium, 3 trombones, 2 basses, double bass, timpani, bass drum, snare drum, cymbals

(Duration, 3:22)

<table>
<tr><td>16</td><td>0:00</td><td>1. a. Band, ff, introduces</td></tr>
<tr><td></td><td>0:04</td><td>b. First melody, ff, in quick detached notes, cymbal crashes, soft, suddenly loud, soft. First melody repeated.</td></tr>
<tr><td>17</td><td>0:32</td><td>2. Brasses, ff, second melody in longer notes, cymbal crashes. Second melody repeated.</td></tr>
<tr><td>18</td><td>1:02</td><td>3. Soft and flowing main melody, saxophones, clarinets.</td></tr>
<tr><td></td><td>1:32</td><td>4. Brasses, ff, low tones alternating with high tones, rise to climax, cymbal crashes, snare drum. Becomes softer (decrescendo).</td></tr>
<tr><td>19</td><td>1:55</td><td>5. High piccolo tune combined with soft main melody.</td></tr>
<tr><td></td><td>2:24</td><td>6. Brasses, ff, low tones alternating with high tones, rise to climax, cymbal crashes, snare drum.</td></tr>
<tr><td></td><td>2:48</td><td>7. High piccolo tune and loud main melody accompanied by new trombone melody. Full band, fff, at end.</td></tr>
</table>

BASIC TERMS

Voices

soprano (page 11)	tenor (11)
mezzo-soprano (11)	baritone (11)
alto (11)	bass (11)

Musical Instruments
register (12)

String Instruments

violin (15)	vibrato (16)
viola (15)	mute (16)
cello (15)	tremolo (16)
double bass (15)	harmonics (16)
bow (15)	plectrum (17)
pizzicato (16)	harp (17)
stop (double, triple, quadruple) (16)	guitar (17)

36

Woodwind Instruments
piccolo (19)
flute (19)
oboe (19)
English horn (19)
clarinet (19)
bass clarinet (19)
bassoon (19)
contrabassoon (19)
recorder (19)
reed (19)
single-reed woodwinds (19)
saxophone (19)
double-reed woodwinds (19)

Brass Instruments
trumpet (23)
French horn (23)
trombone (23)
tuba (23)
cornet (23)
baritone horn (23)
euphonium (23)
bass (23)
mute (23)

Keyboard Instruments
piano (28)
harpsichord (30)
pipe organ (31)
accordion (31)

Percussion Instruments
timpani (kettledrums) (25)
glockenspiel (25)
xylophone (25)
celesta (25)
chimes (25)
snare drum (side drum) (25)
bass drum (25)
tambourine (25)
triangle (25)
cymbals (25)
gong (tam-tam) (25)

Electronic Instruments (31)
tape studio (31)
synthesizer (32)
computer (33)

RHYTHM

Rhythm is basic to life. We see it in the cycle of night and day, the four seasons, the rise and fall of tides. More personally, we feel rhythm as we breathe. We find it in our heartbeats and our walking.

The essence of rhythm is a recurring pattern of tension and release, of expectation and fulfillment. This rhythmic alteration seems to pervade the flow of time. Time, as we live it, has fantastic diversity; each hour has sixty minutes, but how different one hour may seem from another!

Rhythm forms the lifeblood of music, too. In its widest sense, *rhythm* is the ordered flow of music through time. Musical time is like lived time in its endless variety. It also seems to pass at varying speeds and intensities. Yet there is an essential difference between music and life. A composer can control the passage of time in music. In life, such order eludes us. We delight in surrendering to a musical time world that is ordered yet somehow related to our feelings and moods. We also enjoy letting the rhythm of music stimulate movement in our bodies, as when we dance.

Just as rhythm pervades our lives, so we find it everywhere in music—in pitch, tone color, and volume. How these elements change in time, and their rate of change, have to do with rhythm. The many interrelated aspects of rhythm will be considered one at a time.

37

(Martha Swope)

Dancing is closely linked to the rhythms of music. The ballet dancer Mikhail Baryshnikov is shown here in a performance of Tchaikovsky's *Nutcracker*.

BEAT

When you clap your hands or tap your foot to music, you are responding to its beat. The *beat* is a regular, recurrent pulsation that divides the music into equal units of time. Beats can be represented by marks on a time line (see the illustration below). In music, such beats occur as often as every ¼ second or as seldom as every 1½ seconds. Sometimes the beat is powerful and easy to feel, as in marches or rock music. Or it may be barely noticeable, suggesting feelings like floating or aimlessness.

The pulse of music is communicated in different ways. Sometimes the beat is explicitly pounded out—by a bass drum in a marching band, for instance. At other times the beat is sensed rather than actually heard.

Beats can be shown as a succession of marks on a time line.

Beats

Time

Sing the beginning of *America* up to the words *Land where my fathers died:*

My	coun- try,	'tis	of thee,	Sweet land of	lib-	er- ty,

My coun- try, 'tis of thee, Sweet land of lib- er- ty,
| | | | | | | | | | | |

Of thee I sing. Land (etc.)
| | | | | | |

Each of the marks represents a beat. Did you notice that you held *sing* for 3 beats automatically? You *sensed* the beat because you were aware of it and expected it to continue.

Beats form the background against which the composer places notes of varying lengths. Beats are basic units of time by which all notes are measured. Notes last either a fraction of a beat, an entire beat, or more than a beat. In the excerpt from *America,* for example, each of the three syllables in the words *My coun-try* lasts 1 beat; *'tis* lasts 1½ beats; and *of* lasts only ½ beat. It was already noted that *sing* is held for 3 beats. Thus in this portion of the song we have notes ranging in length from ½ beat to 3 beats.

When we talk about the combination of different note lengths in *America,* we are considering its rhythm. Earlier, rhythm was broadly defined as the ordered flow of music through time. More specifically, **rhythm** can be defined as the particular arrangement of note lengths in a piece of music. The rhythm of a melody is an essential feature of its personality. Indeed, we might recognize *America* merely by clapping out its rhythm without actually singing the tones. *America's beat* is an even, regular pulsation. But its *rhythm* flows freely, sometimes matching the beat, sometimes not.

METER

When we sing *America,* some beats feel stronger or more stressed than others. The stress comes regularly on the first of every 3 beats:

My	coun-	try,	'tis		of thee,
beat	beat	beat	**beat**	beat	beat

Therefore we count the beats of *America* as **1–2–3, 1–2–3:**

My	coun- try,	'tis		of thee,
1	2 3	**1**	2	3

Sweet land	of	lib-		er- ty,
1 2	3	**1**	2	3

Of	thee I	sing.		
1	2 3	**1**	2	3

In music we find a repeated pattern of a strong beat plus one or more weaker beats. The organization of beats into regular groups is called *meter.* Such a group containing a fixed number of beats is called a *measure.* There are several types of meter, which are based on the number of beats in a measure.

When a measure has 2 beats, it is in *duple meter;* we count 1–2, 1–2, etc.:

	Ma- ry	had	a	lit- tle	lamb,	lit- tle	lamb,	lit- tle	lamb,	
	1	2		**1**	2	**1**	2	**1**	2	

The vertical lines mark the beginning or end of the measure. The first, or stressed, beat of the measure is known as the *downbeat.*

A pattern of 3 beats to the measure is known as *triple meter.* As we have seen in *America,* we count 1–2–3, 1–2–3, etc. All waltzes are in triple meter.

Another basic metrical pattern is *quadruple meter,* which contains 4 beats to the measure. As usual, the downbeat is strongest; but there is another stress on the third beat, which is stronger than the second and fourth beats and weaker than the first: **1**–2–3–4, **1**–2–3–4. In the following example of quadruple meter the first word is on the *upbeat,* an unaccented pulse preceding the downbeat:

Mine	eyes	have	seen the	glo- ry	of the	com- ing	of	the	Lord;	He	is	
1		2	3	4	**1**		2		3	4		

Marches, jazz, and rock music are usually in quadruple meter. Both duple and quadruple meter reflect the left-right, left-right pattern of walking or marching.

Sextuple meter contains six rather quick beats to the measure. The downbeat is strongest, and the fourth beat also receives a stress: 1–2–3–4–5–6. For example:

Oh,	give	me	a	home	where the buf-	fa- lo	roam,	where the	
1	2	3	4	5	6	**1** 2 3	4 5 6		

Note that the measure is subdivided into two groups of 3 beats each: 1–2–3/4–5–6. Thus sextuple meter is a combination of duple and triple meter. Melodies in sextuple meter often create a feeling of smooth flow, as in *Silent Night.*

Quintuple meter, with 5 beats to the measure, and *septuple meter,* with 7 beats to the measure, occur frequently in twentieth-century music and are found occasionally in earlier music. Each of these meters combines duple and triple meter. In quintuple meter, for example, the measure is subdivided into groups of 2 and 3 beats: 1–2–3/4–5 or 1–2/3–4–5.

ACCENT AND SYNCOPATION

An important aspect of rhythm is the way individual notes are stressed—how they get "special emphasis." A note is emphasized most obviously by being played louder than the notes around it, that is, by receiving a dynamic *accent.* A note is sometimes especially accented when it is held longer or is higher in pitch than those notes near it. In *The Star-Spangled Banner, see* is naturally accented by its being longer and higher in pitch than *Oh, say can you.* In speech as well, we stress individual words through loudness, length, and pitch.

When an accented note comes where we normally would *not* expect one, the effect is known as *syncopation.* There is a syncopation when an "offbeat" note is accented, when the stress comes *between* two beats. In the following example, syncopation occurs on the accented *my,* which comes between beats 1 and 2:

Give	**my**	re-	gards	to		Broad-		way		
1	2	3	4		| 1	2	3	4		|

A syncopation also occurs when a weak beat is accented, as in 1–**2**–3–4 or 1–2–3–**4.** Such contradictions of the meter surprise the listener and create rhythmic excitement. Syncopation is a characteristic feature of jazz.

TEMPO

We've seen that the speed of the beat may be fast or slow. The speed of the beat is known as *tempo,* the basic pace of the music. A fast tempo is associated with a feeling of energy, drive, and excitement. A slow tempo often contributes to a solemn, lyrical, or calm mood. Such associations are rooted in the way we feel and act. When we're excited, our hearts beat more rapidly than when we're calm; we tend to move and speak more quickly.

A *tempo indication* is usually given at the beginning of a piece. As in the case of dynamics, the terms that show tempo are in Italian (they are set here in *bold italic* type):

largo	very slow, broad
grave	very slow, solemn
adagio	slow
andante	moderately slow, a walking pace
moderato	moderate
allegretto	moderately fast
allegro	fast
vivace	lively
presto	very fast
prestissimo	as fast as possible

Qualifying words are sometimes added to tempo indications to make them more specific. The two most commonly used are *molto (much)* and *non troppo (not too much)*. We thus get phrases like *allegro molto (very fast)* and *allegro non troppo (not too fast)*.

As with dynamics, all these terms indicate only approximate tempos; they are relative. A piece marked *andante*, for example, might be played faster by one musician than by another. With the markings as a guide, each performer chooses the tempo that seems appropriate for a piece. But there is no one "right" tempo. A piece can sound equally convincing at slightly different speeds.

The same tempo is not always used throughout a piece. A gradual quickening of tempo may be indicated by writing *accelerando (becoming faster)*, and a gradual slowing-down of tempo by *ritardando (becoming slower)*. An accelerando, especially when combined with a rise in pitch and volume, increases excitement, and a ritardando is associated with less tension and a feeling of conclusion.

Since about 1816, composers have been able to indicate their preferred tempos by means of a **metronome,** an apparatus which produces ticking sounds or flashes of light at any desired musical speed. The metronome setting indicates the exact number of beats per minute. For example, andante might be represented by the metronome number 60 and allegro by the number 116.

I GOT RHYTHM (1930),
BY GEORGE GERSHWIN (1898–1937)

Side 1, band 6
CD 1 [20]

Pervasive syncopations give a jazzy feeling to Gershwin's song *I Got Rhythm*, which was written for the musical comedy *Girl Crazy*. The song is in duple meter, with two quick beats to the measure.

In the opening rhythmic pattern to the words *I got rhy-thm*, a syncopation occurs when the accented tone *I* comes on the "offbeat," *between* beats 1 and 2. In our recording, beat 1 preceding the word *I* is marked by a brief silence and is sensed rather than heard.

	I		got	rhy-	thm		I		got	mu-	sic	
1		2		|1	2	|1		2		|1	2	|

The next emphasized tone *rhy-(thm)* falls *on* the first beat and therefore is *not* syncopated.

This opening rhythmic pattern is repeated for *I got music* and for later parts of the melody.

	Old		Man	Troub-	le		You		won't	find	him	
1		2		|1	2	|1		2		|1	2	|

The recurrence of the rhythmic pattern on different pitches helps give *I Got Rhythm* its wonderful sense of unity and drive.

UNSQUARE DANCE (1961), BY DAVE BRUBECK (b. 1920)

Side 1, band 7
CD 1 [21]

Brubeck's *Unsquare Dance* is in septuple meter, with 7 quick beats to the measure. The composer writes that this unusual meter makes *Unsquare Dance* "a challenge to the foot-tappers, finger-snappers, and hand-clappers. Deceitfully simple, it refuses to be squared." The piece is performed by a small jazz group consisting of piano, double bass, and percussion. It begins with only a pattern of beats and then becomes more active rhythmically and melodically. The meter is established by pizzicato bass tones on beats 1, 3, and 5, and by hand claps on beats 2, 4, 6, and 7:

```
        Clap        Clap        Clap  Clap
  1      2     3     4     5     6     7
 Bass         Bass        Bass
```

(This septuple meter combines duple and triple meter. Each measure is subdivided into groups of 2 and 3 beats: 1–2, 3–4, 5–6–7.) Exciting syncopations occur when weak beats 2 and 4 are accented by hand claps.

After the opening 6 measures, the piano enters with an introductory musical idea that begins on the upbeat and emphasizes the first beat of each measure. Soon the piano part becomes more tuneful and rhythmically intricate. After the piano solo, the bass and hand claps are joined by percussive sounds in a rhythm that is faster than the beat. The final piano solo rounds off *Unsquare Dance* on a comic note.

BASIC TERMS

rhythm (page 37)
beat (38)
meter (40):
   duple meter
   triple meter
   quadruple meter
   quintuple meter
   sextuple meter
   septuple meter

measure (40)
downbeat (40)
upbeat (40)
accent (41)
syncopation (41)
tempo (41)
tempo indication (41):
   largo
   grave

adagio
andante
moderato
allegretto
allegro
vivace
presto
prestissimo
metronome (42)

[4] MUSIC NOTATION

We use written words to express our thoughts and communicate with others when we can't be with them. In music, ideas are also written down, or *notated,* so that performers can play pieces unknown to them.

Notation is a system of writing music so that specific pitches and rhythms can be communicated. It is explained here—very briefly— primarily to help you recognize rising and falling melodic lines and long and short notes so that you can follow the music examples in this book. (You will find it helpful to review the material on pitch and rhythm in Sections 1 and 3.)

NOTATING PITCH

With music notation, we can indicate exact pitches by the upward or downward placement of symbols—called *notes*—on a *staff.* A **note** is an oval. (Its duration is indicated by whether it is black or white or has a *stem* and *flags,* as will be explained later, under "Notating Rhythm.") A **staff** (plural, *staves*) is a set of five horizontal lines. Notes are positioned either on the lines of the staff or between them, in the spaces; the higher a note is placed on the staff, the higher its pitch:

If a pitch falls above or below the range indicated by the staff, short, horizontal *ledger lines* are used:

Seven of the twelve pitches (tones) that fill the octave in western music are named after the first seven letters of the alphabet: A, B, C, D, E, F, G. This sequence is repeated over and over to represent the "same" tones in higher and lower octaves, and it corresponds to the white keys of the piano. The other five tones of the octave correspond to the black keys of the piano and are indicated by one of the same seven letters plus a *sharp sign* (♯) or a *flat sign* (♭) (see the illustration on the opposite page). Thus the pitch between C and D may be called C sharp (C♯; higher than C) or D flat (D♭; lower than D). A *natural sign* (♮) is used to cancel a previous sharp or flat sign.

The twelve pitches of the octave and their position on the piano keyboard.

A *clef* is placed at the beginning of the staff to show the pitch of each line and space. The two most common clefs are the **treble clef,** used for relatively high ranges (such as those played by a pianist's right hand), and the **bass clef,** used for relatively low ranges (played by the pianist's left hand):

Treble clef

Bass clef

Keyboard music calls for a wide range of pitches to be played by both hands; for such music, the **grand staff**—a combination of the treble and bass staves—is used. The illustration below shows how the notes on the grand staff are related to the piano keyboard. Note that the C nearest to the middle of the keyboard is called **middle C.**

Notes on the grand staff and their positions on the piano keyboard.

Middle C

NOTATING RYHTHM

Music notation does not indicate the exact duration of tones; instead, it shows how long one tone lasts in relation to others in the same piece. A single note on the staff lasts longer or shorter depending on how it looks—on whether it is white or black and has a *stem* or *flags.*

Following is a chart that shows the relationships of the duration symbols:

1 whole note

= 2 half notes:

= 4 quarter notes:

= 8 eighth notes:

= 16 sixteenth notes:

One whole note lasts as long as 2 half notes or 4 quarter notes, and so on. As shown, the flags of several eighth notes or sixteenth notes in succession are usually joined by a horizontal **beam.**

To lengthen the duration of a tone (and add rhythmic variety), we can make it a *dotted note;* adding a dot (·) to the right of a note increases its duration by half. Thus, 1 quarter note ordinarily equals 2 eighth notes, but 1 dotted quarter note equals 3 eighth notes:

but

Frequently, a dotted note is followed by one that is much shorter; this long-short pattern, called *dotted rhythm,* strongly emphasizes the beat (and is therefore often used in marches).

A *tie* (⌢) is another way to lengthen the duration of a note. When two notes in a row are the same pitch and are connected by a tie, the first note is lengthened by the duration of the second. In the following example, the note on *dell* lasts as long as 1 dotted quarter note plus 1 quarter note; the two tied notes become one continuous sound:

The farm - er   in   the dell,   The farm - er   in   the dell,

We can also add rhythmic variety by shortening the duration of a note. One method is the *triplet,* three notes of equal duration notated as a group within a curved line and the number 3. Such a group lasts only as long as if it were two notes of equal value:

NOTATING SILENCE (RESTS)

Duration of silence is notated by using a symbol called a *rest.* Rests are pauses; their durations correspond to those of notes:

| whole rest | half rest | quarter rest | eighth rest | sixteenth rest |

NOTATING METER

A *time signature* (or *meter signature*) shows the meter of a piece. It appears at the beginning of the staff at the start of a piece (and again later if the meter changes) and consists of two numbers, one on top of the other. The upper number tells how many beats fall in a measure; the lower number tells what kind of note gets the beat (2 = a half note, for instance, and 4 = a quarter note). Thus a $\frac{2}{4}$ time signature shows that there are 2 beats to the measure (duple meter) and a quarter note gets 1 beat. Duple meter may also be shown as $\frac{2}{2}$ (or by its symbol, ¢); quadruple meter is usually $\frac{4}{4}$ (or c). The most common triple meter is $\frac{3}{4}$.

BASIC TERMS

Notation of Pitch

notation (page 44)
note (44)
staff (44)
ledger lines (44)
sharp sign (♯) (44)

flat sign (♭) (44)
natural sign (♮) (44)
clef (treble and bass) (45)
grand staff (45)
middle C (45)

Notation of Rhythm

stem (46)
flag (46)
beam (46)
dotted note (46)
dotted rhythm (46)

tie (46)
triplet (47)
rest (47)
time signature (meter signature) (47)

A page from the orchestral score of Tchaikovsky's *Romeo and Juliet*.

THE SCORE

An orchestral *score* shows the music for each instrumental or vocal category in a performing group; often, a score will show more than twenty different staves of notation (see the illustration above).

MELODY

For many of us, music means melody. We've sung in schools, cars, camps, and the shower. After hearing a piece of music, we usually remember its melody best. Familiar melodies have the power to recall past emotions and experiences. Words and instruments aren't required; we don't need singers and large orchestras—just a few notes.

Melody is easier to recognize than to define. Yet it must have something special; melody is common to the music of all times and all peoples. Probably the elusive "something" that evokes so much feeling will never be trapped in a dictionary definition. We do know that a *melody* is a series of single tones that add up to a recognizable whole. A melody begins, moves, and ends; it has direction, shape, and continuity. The up-and-down movement of its pitches conveys tension and release, expectation and arrival. This is the melodic curve, or line.

A melody moves by small intervals called *steps* or by larger ones called *leaps.* A step is the interval between two adjacent tones in the *do-re-mi* scale (from *do* to *re, re* to *mi,* etc.). Any interval larger than a step is known as a leap (*do* to *mi,* for example). Besides moving up or down by step or leap, a melody may simply repeat the same note. A melody's range, or the distance between its lowest and highest tones, may be wide or narrow. *Mary Had a Little Lamb* moves mostly by step within a narrow range; *Rock-a-Bye Baby* has a wider range and lots of leaps as well as steps. Melodies written for instruments tend to have a wider range than those for voices, and they often contain wide leaps and rapid notes that would be difficult to sing.

The specific order of the long and short notes in a melody is important. A well-known melody can be almost unrecognizable if it is not sung in proper rhythm. Note durations, as well as pitches, contribute to the distinctive character of a melody. For example, the smooth, even rhythm of *Twinkle, Twinkle, Little Star* is calm but the snappy, dotted (long-short) rhythm of *The Battle Hymn of the Republic* is exciting. Try reversing these rhythms: the first melody will lose its calmness, and the second will lack excitement.

How the tones of a melody are performed can vary its effect, too. Sometimes they are sung or played in a smooth, connected style called *legato.* Or they may be performed in a short, detached manner called *staccato.*

Many melodies are made up of shorter parts called ***phrases.*** These short units may have similar pitch and rhythm patterns that help unify the melody. On the other hand, contrasting phrases can furnish variety. Phrases often appear in balanced pairs; a first phrase of rising pitches may be followed by a second phrase of falling pitches. The second phrase may partly repeat the first one but have a more conclusive ending, a point of arrival. Such a resting place at the end of a phrase is called a ***cadence.***

As you get further into the music explored in this book, you'll find a wealth of melodies: vocal or instrumental, long or short, simple or complex. To help sort them, let's see how some basic melodic principles apply to four familiar tunes. These are short melodies, easy to sing and easy to remember.

Row, Row, Row Your Boat is first. Sing the tune only up to the word *stream.* Notice that on *stream* the melody comes to a point of arrival, a resting place. This ends the first phrase of the melody. But the melody seems incomplete, as though it had posed a question. Now sing the rest of the melody, the second phrase, beginning on *merrily.* It ends conclusively and seems to answer the question. Each phrase has a point of arrival, a cadence. The first phrase ends with an ***incomplete cadence,*** which sets up expectations; the second phrase ends with a ***complete cadence,*** which gives an answer, a sense of finality.

Each phrase of *Row, Row, Row Your Boat* is the same length, a formula typical of many melodies called *tunes.* The two phrases create a feeling of symmetry and balance. The first begins with repeated notes (C–C–C— *Row, row, row*) and then moves upward by step (D–E–F–G—*your boat, Gently down the stream*); the second moves downward by leap (C–G–E– C—*Merrily, merrily, merrily, merrily*) and finally by step (G–F–E–D–C— *Life is but a dream*). Often the highest tone of a melody will be the ***climax,*** or emotional focal point. In this song the climax comes on the first *merrily,* at the beginning of the second phrase. The leaps create a carefree quality in the quick notes on the repeated *merrily.*

The two contrasting phrases of the song can be symbolized by the letters a and b. In discussing music it's helpful to let letters represent various sections of a piece. Lowercase letters (a, b, etc.) are used for phrases and relatively short sections, while capital letters (A, B, etc.) are used for longer sections. When the phrases or sections of the music differ significantly, as in this song, we use different letters: a b. When one section exactly repeats another, the letter is repeated: a a. When a section is a varied repetition of a previous one, the previous letter is repeated but with a prime mark: a a'.

Now sing the entire nursery tune *Mary Had a Little Lamb:*

As in *Row, Row, Row Your Boat,* this melody has two balancing phrases, the first ending up in the air with an incomplete cadence, and the second ending conclusively with a complete cadence. However, the two songs also differ from each other. In *Mary Had a Little Lamb* the second phrase begins exactly like the first. The melody starts over again but proceeds to a different, more conclusive ending. This partial repetition serves to unify the melody. The phrases in *Mary Had a Little Lamb* may be symbolized as a a'. It will be shown that melodic repetition, both exact and varied, plays an important unifying role in all kinds of music.

Both repeated and contrasting phrases can be heard in the cowboy song *Home on the Range:*

A yearning quality is projected here through a longer and more complex form than that of the two other tunes. There are four phrases, and, as in *Mary Had a Little Lamb,* the second phrase is a repetition of the first but has a more conclusive ending. (Sing the first two phrases a few times, comparing the note on *play* with that on *day.*) The first two phrases may be outlined a a' (to show repetition with variation). Contrast is introduced in the third phrase of the melody, the climactic refrain *Home, home on the range.* This phrase begins in a new way—on the highest pitch of the melody—and may be labeled b. The concluding fourth phrase *(Where seldom is heard)* is a repetition of the beginning but with a final ending. Thus the song as a whole is outlined a a' b a'. The principle of *statement* (a a'), *departure* or *contrast* (b), and *return* (a') that governs *Home on the Range* is an essential one in the creation of form in music.

Our final example, *America,* differs from the other songs in that its phrases are not of equal length:

The second phrase (starting from *Land*) is longer than the first and creates a feeling of continuation rather than one of balance or symmetry. An interesting aspect of *America* is the way a repeated rhythmic pattern is used to unify the melody. The rhythmic pattern for *My country 'tis of thee* is repeated for *Sweet land of liberty, Land where my fathers died,* and *Land of the Pilgrims' pride.*

Notice that the melody for *Land of the Pilgrims' pride* is simply a repetition a little lower of the preceding *Land where my fathers died.* Such a repetition of a melodic pattern on a higher or lower pitch is called a **sequence.** This is an impelling device of varied repetition that gives a melody a strong sense of direction.

We've considered tunes that are complete in themselves. Frequently, a melody will serve as the starting point for a more extended piece of music and, in stretching out, will go through all kinds of changes. This kind of melody is called a **theme.**

The concepts and vocabulary introduced in this chapter can be used to study melodies of any style. Try using them to examine your favorite songs. You may pinpoint parts that you like and, consequently, enjoy the melodies a bit more because you know what makes them tick.

OVER THE RAINBOW (1938), BY HAROLD ARLEN (1905–1986)

A beautiful melody creates a feeling of wonderment in *Over the Rainbow*, from the movie *The Wizard of Oz* (1939), starring the young Judy Garland. Like many popular songs, *Over the Rainbow* contains a main melody (A) and a contrasting one (B). The song can be outlined as A A B A, followed by a closing part. The main melody (A: *Somewhere over the rainbow way up high . . .*) is presented and then repeated with different words (A: *Somewhere over the rainbow skies are blue . . .*). Then we hear the contrasting melody (B: *Someday I'll wish upon a star . . .*), and then a return of the main melody (A: *Somewhere over the rainbow bluebirds fly . . .*). The closing part of the song (*If happy little bluebirds fly . . .*) is a varied and abridged return of the contrasting melody.

The main melody (A) grows out of the opening upward leap of an octave that beautifully expresses the word *somewhere*.

Side 1, band 8
CD 1 [22]

Main melody (A)
[22] 0:00

Contrasting
melody (B)
[23] 0:45

Return of
main melody (A)
[24] 1:13

Melody A

a

> Some - where   o - ver the rain - bow   way   up   high,

a'

> There's   a   land that I heard of   once in a lull - a - by,

A large upward leap followed by a downward step appears three times, with changes of pitch, giving the melody a sense of unity and direction.

The second upward leap, which is slightly smaller than the first, is appropriate for the words *way up*. In all, the melody features upward leaps from low tones to higher tones that gradually descend.

Melody A is made up of two related phrases that can be symbolized as a *(Somewhere over the rainbow . . .)* and a' *(There's a land . . .)*. The second phrase (a') begins somewhat like the first; but it starts on a lower pitch, and its upward leap is smaller. Whereas the first phrase (a) ends up in the air with an incomplete cadence (on *high)*, the second phrase (a') ends definitively with a complete cadence (on *lullaby*). The feeling given by A of motion to a conclusion is heightened by a sequence: the melodic pattern for *land that I heard of* is repeated on a lower pitch for *once in a lulla(by)*.

Melody B is more speechlike in character.

Melody B

It moves in a narrower range, uses quicker rhythms, and repeats two-note patterns. Like the main tune, melody B contains two phrases: b *(Someday I'll wish . . .)* and b' *(Where troubles melt . . .)*. It rises to a climax on its next-to-last tone *(find)*. Together, melodies A and B produce a satisfying feeling of balance in this enchanting song.

BASIC TERMS

melody (page 49)	staccato (49)	complete cadence (50)
step (49)	phrase (50)	climax (50)
leap (49)	cadence (50)	sequence (52)
legato (49)	incomplete cadence (50)	theme (52)

HARMONY

When folksingers accompany themselves on a guitar, they add support, depth, and richness to the melody. We call this *harmonizing*. Most music in western culture is a blend of melody and harmony.

Harmony refers to the way chords are constructed and how they follow each other. A ***chord*** is a combination of three or more tones sounded at once. Essentially, a chord is a group of simultaneous tones, and a melody is a series of individual tones heard one after another. As a melody unfolds, it provides clues for harmonizing—some of the tones of the melody are usually included in the chords of the accompaniment. But a melody does not always dictate a specific series, or ***progression,*** of chords. A melody may be harmonized in several musically convincing ways. A musician such as a folksinger will experiment and choose the chords that best fit a melody's mood. Chord progressions will enrich a melody by adding emphasis, surprise, suspense, or finality. In today's popular music, a songwriter often composes the melody while an arranger supplies the accompanying chords. Composers of classical music create both the melody and the harmony, often at the same time.

There is a tendency to think that a melody is composed first and that the

(Larry Busacca/Retna Ltd.)

The singer Tracy Chapman blends melody and harmony by accompanying herself on the guitar.

55

chords are added later. Actually, it's often the other way around. For centuries, repeated chord progressions have given rise to improvised melodies. In jazz, for example, a pianist may play the same basic progression of chords over and over again while a trumpet player invents a continually changing melody to fit the piano's pattern. When several jazz musicians improvise different melodies at once, their music is held together by the organized chordal background—by the harmony.

As different as Bach, Beethoven, jazz, folk, and rock may seem, some of the same chord progressions can be heard in all. Although new chords and new progressions continually enter the language of music, the basic chordal vocabulary has remained fairly constant. We'll look now at a few principles of harmony that have proved so useful for so long.

CONSONANCE AND DISSONANCE

Some chords have been considered stable and restful, others unstable and tense. A tone combination that is stable is called a *consonance*. Consonances are points of arrival, rest, and resolution. (Whoever coined the phrase *living in harmony with others* had consonance in mind.) A tone combination that is unstable is called a ***dissonance.*** Its tension demands an onward motion to a stable chord. A dissonance has its ***resolution*** when it moves to a consonance. When this resolution is delayed or accomplished in unexpected ways, a feeling of drama, suspense, or surprise is created. In this way a composer plays with the listener's sense of expectation. Dissonant chords are active and move music forward. Traditionally they have been considered harsh and have colored music that expresses pain, grief, and conflict.

Now that consonance and dissonance have been defined, be aware that they can exist in various degrees. Some consonant chords are more stable than others, just as dissonant chords vary in their levels of tension. Dissonant chords have been used with increasing freedom over the centuries, so that a chord considered intolerably harsh in one period has often come to seem rather mild in a later one.

THE TRIAD

A great variety of chords have been used in music. Some chords consist of three different tones; others have four, five, or even more. Depending on their makeup, chords sound simple or complex, calm or tense, bright or dark.

The simplest, most basic chord is the ***triad*** (pronounced *try'-ad),* which consists of three tones. To indicate that a triad's three tones are played at one time, it is notated:

A triad is made up of alternate tones of the scale, such as the first *(do)*, third *(mi), and fifth (sol)* tones. The bottom tone is called the *root;* the others are a third and a fifth above the root. (From *do* to *mi* in the scale is an interval of a third; from *do* to *sol* is the interval of a fifth.)

A triad built on the first, or tonic, note of the scale *(do)* is called the **tonic chord** *(do-mi-sol);* it is the main chord of a piece, the most stable and conclusive. Traditionally, the tonic chord would usually begin a composition and almost always end it.

The triad built on the fifth note of the scale *(sol)* is next in importance to the tonic. It is called the **dominant chord** *(sol-ti-re).* The dominant chord is strongly pulled toward the tonic chord. This attraction has great importance in music. A dominant chord sets up tension that is resolved by the tonic chord. The progression from the dominant to the tonic gives a strong sense of conclusion, and that's why it is used so often at the end of a phrase, melody, or entire piece. In *America,* for example, the next-to-last syllable is harmonized by a dominant chord, and the last word is harmonized by the tonic chord:

A progression from the dominant chord to the tonic chord is called a **cadence.** The word *cadence* means both the resting point at the end of a melodic phrase (as was noted in Section 5) and a chord progression that gives a sense of conclusion.

BROKEN CHORDS (ARPEGGIOS)

A chord has just been described as a group of tones played together, as a block of sound. But the tones of a chord may be presented in other ways, too. When the individual tones of a chord are sounded one after another, it is called a **broken chord,** or **arpeggio.** Arpeggios may appear in the melody or in the accompaniment. *The Star-Spangled Banner* is a melody that begins with such a broken chord, or arpeggio. The notes of the tonic chord are heard one after another instead of together:

As you go on with your study of music in this book, the importance of harmony will become more and more apparent. You'll see that chord progressions can produce powerful emotional effects and be more than simply a background for melody. Sometimes a melody depends on the accompanying harmony for its expressiveness, as in Chopin's Prelude in E Minor, which will be examined shortly.

Harmony helps give music variety and movement. There's a relaxation of tension when a dissonant chord resolves to a consonant chord, a sense of conclusion when the dominant chord moves to the tonic. The effects of harmony are endless, varying with the style of a particular era and the desires of individual composers.

PRELUDE IN E MINOR FOR PIANO, OP. 28, NO. 4 (1839), BY FRÉDÉRIC CHOPIN

Side 1, band 9
CD 1 25

Chopin's harmony makes a vital contribution to the brooding quality of this miniature lasting less than 2 minutes. Without the pulsating chords of its accompaniment, the melody might seem aimless and monotonous. It hardly moves, alternating obsessively between a long note and a shorter one right above it. But the returning long note seems to change in color, because each time, there is a different dissonant chord below it. The dissonant chords underscore the melancholy of this prelude, which is meant to be played *espressivo (expressively)*.

Toward the end of the piece, a mildly dissonant chord is followed by a brief pause. This silence is filled with expectancy, as we wait for the dissonance to resolve. Finally the tension is released in the three solemn chords of the closing cadence.

BASIC TERMS

harmony (page 55)
chord (55)
progression (55)
consonance (56)
dissonance (56)
resolution (56)

triad (56)
tonic chord (57)
dominant chord (57)
cadence (57)
broken chord (arpeggio) (57)

KEY

Practically all familiar melodies are built around a central tone. The other tones of the melody gravitate toward this central one. Since the central tone is especially stable and restful, a melody usually ends on it. To feel the gravitational pull of a central tone, sing *America* and stop after the next-to-last word, *freedom;* then, after a few seconds, sing the ending tone of *ring.*

My coun-try, 'tis of thee, Sweet land of lib - er - ty,

Of thee I sing. Land where my fa - thers died,

Land of the Pil - grims' pride, From ev - 'ry

moun - tain-side, Let free - dom ring.

You probably felt uneasy until you supplied the last tone. This central tone is the **keynote,** or **tonic,** of the melody. When a piece is in the key of C, for example, C is the keynote, or tonic. The keynote can also be E, or A, or any of the twelve tones that fill the octave in western music.

Key involves not only a central tone, but a central scale and chord as well. A piece in the key of C has a basic scale, *do-re-mi-fa-sol-la-ti-do,* with C as its *do,* or tonic. And the basic chord of a piece in C is a tonic triad with C as its root, or bottom tone. As was noted in Section 6, the tonic triad is made up of *do-mi-sol,* or the first, third, and fifth tones of the basic scale. Just as familiar melodies generally end on the keynote, compositions traditionally end with the restful tonic chord. Key, then, refers to the presence of a central note, scale, and chord within a piece. All other tones of a composition are heard in relationship to the central ones. Another term for key is **tonality.**

After 1900, some composers abandoned the traditional system, but even today much of the music we hear is built around a central tone, chord, and scale.

THE MAJOR SCALE

So far, we've referred to the *do-re-mi-fa-sol-la-ti-do* scale as a main element of key, but have not actually defined what a scale is. A **scale** is made up of the basic pitches of a piece of music arranged in order from low to high or from high to low. Many different scales have been used in various eras and cultures. The basic scales of western music from the late 1600s to 1900 were the *major* and *minor.* These scales have continued to be widely used during our own century.

Let's first consider the **major scale,** the familiar *do-re-mi-fa-sol-la-ti-do.* Sing this scale and note that you produce seven different pitches and then arrive at the high *do*—the eighth tone—which is really a duplication of the first tone an octave higher. As was pointed out in Section 1, the octave is the distance or interval between the first and eighth tones of the major scale. The major scale has a specific pattern of intervals between its successive tones.

Two kinds of intervals are found in the major scale: *half steps* and *whole steps.* The **half step** is the smallest interval traditionally used in western music. The **whole step** is twice as large as the half step. The illustration below shows the pattern of whole and half steps that makes up the major scale. There is an especially strong pull from *ti* to *do,* because the interval is a small one, a half step. You'll feel this pull when you sing the scale and stop on *ti.*

Pattern of whole and half steps making up the major scale.

whole step	whole step	half step	whole step	whole step	whole step	half step
do	re	mi	fa	sol	la	ti do

STAFF

Major scale beginning on C.

The illustration above shows a major scale with C as the beginning tone.

The C major scale uses only the white keys of the piano. There are half steps between E and F, and between B and C; these pairs of tones are not separated by black keys. *America* as notated near the beginning of this section is based on the C major scale; it is in the key of C major.

We can construct similar major scales by starting on any one of the twelve tones that fill an octave. The same pattern of intervals can begin on any of these tones, and so there are twelve possible major scales. To understand this better, imagine the major scale as a ruler on which eight marks are spaced irregularly (as shown in the *do-re-mi* diagram on page 60). The pattern of marks stays the same no matter where the "ruler" is placed. Similarly, the pattern of whole and half steps that makes up a major scale sounds the same even when the scales start on different keynotes.

To us the important point is not the technicality of half and whole steps but the idea of a scale as a pattern of intervals. Also important is the idea of the keynote (or beginning, or tonic) of the major scale; it is the scale's central tone toward which all others seem to pull. The conclusive quality we hear in the keynote is not a result of any law of nature—it's rooted in cultural conditioning.

THE MINOR SCALE

Along with the major scale, the minor scale is fundamental to western music. *Joshua Fought the Battle of Jericho* is a tune based on a minor scale:

Josh-ua fought the bat-tle   of   Jer - i - cho, Jer - i - cho, Jer - i - cho;

Josh-ua fought the bat-tle   of   Jer - i - cho, and the walls came tum-bl-ing down.

The *minor scale*—like the major—consists of seven different tones and an eighth tone that duplicates the first an octave higher; but it differs from the major scale in its pattern of intervals. The minor scale's pattern can also begin on any of the twelve tones in an octave, and so there are twelve possible minor scales. As just notated, *Joshua Fought the Battle of Jericho* is based on a minor scale beginning on C; it is in the key of C minor. Here is a comparison between a major and a minor scale both starting on C:*

C major scale	whole step		whole step	half step	whole step		whole step		whole step	half step
	C	D		E	F	G		A		B	C

C minor scale	whole step	half step	whole step		whole step	half step	whole step		whole step	
	C	D	E♭		F		G	A♭		B♭	C

The crucial difference between major and minor is that in the minor scale there is only a half step between the second and third tones. A major scale has a whole step here. This small difference greatly changes the sound of a scale and the mood of music using that scale. Music based on minor scales tends to sound serious or melancholy. Almost all funeral marches, for ex-

*The minor scale shown in this example is the *natural minor*, one of three minor scales. The other two kinds are the *harmonic minor* and the *melodic minor* scales. The three types of minor scales have slight variations in their patterns of intervals, but all can begin on any tone of the octave, and all will produce a sound that contrasts with the major scale as described here.

ample, are in minor keys. Also, the tonic triad built from a minor scale is a minor chord, while one built from a major scale is a major chord. Minor chords sound darker than major ones. Composers use the differences between minor and major to create contrasts of mood. A serious or agitated melody in C minor may be followed by a brighter tune in C major. We learn to tell the difference between minor and major as we learn to distinguish one color from another, by repeated exposure.

THE KEY SIGNATURE

When a piece of music is based on a major scale, we say that it is in a ***major key;*** when it is based on a minor scale, it is said to be in a ***minor key.*** For instance, a piece based on a major scale with D as its keynote is in the key of D major. Similarly, if a composition is based on a minor scale with the keynote F, the composition is in the key of F minor. Each major and minor scale has a specific number of sharps or flats ranging from none to seven. To indicate the key of a piece of music, the composer uses a ***key signature,*** consisting of sharp or flat signs immediately following the clef sign at the beginning of the staff. To illustrate, here is the key signature for D major, which contains two sharps:

By using a key signature, a composer avoids the problem of having to write a sharp or a flat sign before every sharped or flatted note in a piece. (The seven sharps in the key of C sharp major and the seven flats in the key of C flat major would otherwise make notation very complicated!) Appendix 3 shows the key signatures for the different major and minor scales.

THE CHROMATIC SCALE

The twelve tones of the octave—*all* the white and black keys in one octave on the piano—form the ***chromatic scale.*** Unlike those of the major or minor scales, tones of the chromatic scale are all the same distance apart. As the illustration on the following page shows, each tone is a half step away from the next one.

The word *chromatic* comes from the Greek word *chroma, color.* Its derivation provides a clue to the chromatic scale's traditional function, which is to color or embellish the tones of the major and minor scales. The chromatic scale is not like the major and minor: it does not define a key. Its tones contribute a sense of motion and tension. Composers throughout history

The chromatic scale consists of all twelve tones of the octave—all the white keys and black keys in one octave on the piano.

have used it to evoke strong feelings of grief, loss, and sorrow. We'll see that in the twentieth century it has become independent of major and minor scales and is used as the basis for entire compositions.

MODULATION: CHANGE OF KEY

Most short melodies we know remain in a single key from beginning to end. However, in longer pieces of music, variety and contrast are created by using more than one key. A composition may begin in the key of C major, for example, and then proceed to G major. A shift from one key to another within the same piece is called a *modulation.* A modulation is like a temporary shift in the center of gravity. When the music starts out in the key of C major, C is the central tone, and the C major scale and chord predominate. With the modulation to G major, G temporarily becomes the central tone, and the G major scale and chord are now the main ones. Though modulations are sometimes subtle and difficult to spot, they produce subconscious effects that increase our enjoyment of the music.

TONIC KEY

No matter how often a piece changes key, there usually is one main key, called the *tonic* or *home key.* The tonic key is the central key around which the whole piece is organized. Traditionally, a piece would usually begin in the home key and practically always end in it. A composition in the key of C major, for example, would begin in the home key, modulate to several other keys—say, G major and A minor—and finally conclude in the home key of C major. The other keys are subordinate to the tonic.

Modulating away from the tonic key is like visiting: we may enjoy ourselves during the visit, but after a while we're glad to go home. In music, modulations set up tensions that are resolved by returning to the home key. For centuries, the idea of a central key was a basic principle of music. But after 1900, some composers wrote music that ignored the traditional system. The results of this revolutionary step are explored in Part VII, The Twentieth Century.

BASIC TERMS

keynote (tonic) (page 59)

key (tonality) (60)

scale (60)

major scale (60)

half step (60)

whole step (60)

minor scale (62)

major key (63)

minor key (63)

key signature (63)

chromatic scale (63)

modulation (64)

tonic key

  (home key) (65)

MUSICAL TEXTURE ⟦ ELEMENTS **8** ⟧

At a particular moment within a piece, we may hear one unaccompanied melody, several simultaneous melodies, or a melody with supporting chords. To describe these various possibilities, we use the term *musical texture;* it refers to how many different layers of sound are heard at once, to what kind of layers they are (melody or harmony), and to how they are related to each other.

Like fabric, musical texture is described as transparent, dense, thin, thick, heavy, or light. Composers can vary the textures within their music to create contrast and drama. We'll look now at the three basic musical textures—*monophonic, polyphonic,* and *homophonic.*

MONOPHONIC TEXTURE

The texture of a single melodic line without accompaniment is **monophonic,** meaning literally *one sound*. If you sing alone, you make monophonic music. Performance of a single melodic line at the same pitch by more than one instrument or voice is playing or singing in **unison** and results in a fuller, richer-sounding monophonic texture. Examples of unison singing, where men and women sing the same notes in different octaves, appear in the *Hallelujah* chorus by George Frideric Handel, analyzed on pages 194–195.

POLYPHONIC TEXTURE

Simultaneous performance of two or more melodic lines of relatively equal interest produces the texture called **polyphonic,** meaning *many-sounding.* In polyphony several melodic lines compete for attention. (When several jazz musicians improvise different melodies at once, they produce polyphony.) Polyphony adds a dimension that has been compared to perspective in painting: each line enriches and heightens the expression of the other.

This mutual enhancement points up a difference between music and speech. If many people are saying different things at one time, the result can be confusing. But when several different melodies are sung together, highly expressive sounds may be created. This technique of combining several melodic lines into a meaningful whole is called **counterpoint.** (The term *contrapuntal texture* is sometimes used in place of *polyphonic texture*).

To fully enjoy the simultaneous flow of several melodic lines, you may have to hear a piece of music a few times. Repeated hearings lead to a satisfying awareness of how the whole is woven from its parts. It's often helpful to listen first for the top line, then for the bottom, and then for the middle lines. Such selective listening increases our appreciation of contrasting rhythms and melodic shapes and gives us a chance to hear how different lines are emphasized at any given moment.

Polyphonic music often contains **imitation,** which occurs when a melodic idea is presented by one voice or instrument and then restated immediately by another voice or instrument. It's as though different lines of texture play follow the leader. Imitation is familiar to anyone who has sung *Row, Row, Row Your Boat:*

This familiar tune is a *round*, a song in which several people sing the same melody but each singer starts at a different time. By the time the first singer has reached *Merrily, merrily*, etc., the second singer is only at *Gently down the stream* and the third is just beginning *Row, row, row your boat*. At any one time, all the voices are singing different parts of the same tune.

A round like *Row, Row, Row Your Boat* is an example of strict imitation; the different voices play follow the leader with exactly the same melody. But imitation is usually freer—the imitating line begins like the first one but then goes off on its own. A delightful feeling of give-and-take results when a short melodic idea is quickly passed from one voice or instrument to another. This happens often in polyphonic texture.

HOMOPHONIC TEXTURE

When we hear one main melody accompanied by chords, the texture is *homophonic.* Attention is focused on the melody, which is supported and colored by sounds of subordinate interest. Homophonic texture is familiar to anyone who has heard a folksinger accompany himself or herself on a guitar. Though the accompaniment may be quite distinctive, it is there primarily to help carry the sound and meaning of the melody. *Row, Row, Row Your Boat*, when harmonized by chords, is an example of homophonic texture:

A hymn tune is another example of homophony. The hymn's melody is sung by the voice on top, while other voices have lower lines that harmonize, or blend, with the melody but are less individual. Generally, these lower voices sing notes that are different from the main tune but move in the same rhythm. All the voices moving together produce a progression of chords, one for each syllable of the hymn's text.

Accompaniments in homophonic music vary widely in character and importance. They range from subdued background chords to surging sounds that almost hide the main melody. An expressive quality in the melody can be strengthened by the rhythm or harmony that accompanies it. Sometimes a subordinate line may assert its individuality briefly and compete for the listener's attention. At such times the texture is probably best described as being between homophonic and polyphonic.

CHANGES OF TEXTURE

A composer can create variety and contrast by changing textures within a composition. He or she might begin with a melody and a simple accompaniment and later weave the melody into a polyphonic web. Or the composer might create drama by contrasting a single voice with massive chords sung by a chorus. A good example of textural variety is Georges Bizet's *Farandole*.

FARANDOLE FROM *L'ARLÉSIENNE* SUITE NO. 2, BY GEORGES BIZET

Side 1, band 10
CD 1 26

The *Farandole* comes from Bizet's music for the play *L'Arlésienne (The Woman of Arles)*, which is set in southern France. Two contrasting themes are heard in this exciting orchestral piece. The first, in minor, is a march theme adapted from a southern French folk song. The lively second theme, in major, has the character of the *farandole*, a southern French dance.

Many changes of texture contribute to the *Farandole*'s exciting mood. The piece contains two kinds of homophonic texture: in one, the accompaniment and melody have the same rhythm; in the other, the rhythm of the accompaniment differs from that of the melody. The *Farandole* opens with the march theme and its accompaniment in the same rhythm. But when the lively dance theme is first presented, its accompanying chords do not duplicate the rhythm of the melody; instead, they simply mark the beat.

The *Farandole* also includes two kinds of polyphony: with and without imitation. Soon after the opening, the march theme is presented by the violins and then is imitated by the violas. At the end of the piece, polyphony results when the march and dance themes—previously heard in alternation—are presented simultaneously. In this concluding section, both themes are in major.

The *Farandole* also contains monophonic texture, which sets off the homophony and polyphony. Monophony is heard when the march theme is played by the strings in unison.

Listening Outline To be read while music is heard

FARANDOLE FROM *L'ARLÉSIENNE* SUITE NO. 2 (1879),
BY GEORGES BIZET (1839–1875)*

Allegro deciso (forceful allegro), march tempo, quadruple meter ($\frac{4}{4}$), D minor

Piccolo, 2 flutes, 2 oboes, 2 clarinets, 2 bassoons, 4 French horns, 2 trumpets, 2 cornets, 3 trombones, timpani, tambourine, bass drum, cymbals, 1st violins, 2d violins, violas, cellos, double basses

(Duration, 3:08)

26 0:00   1. *a.* Full orchestra, *ff*, march theme; homophonic (accompaniment in same rhythm as melody), minor.

L'Arlésienne Suites No. 1 and No. 2 are sets of pieces from the theater music composed by Bizet. Suite No. 2 was arranged by Bizet's friend Ernest Guiraud after the composer's death.

[27] 0:16		*b.* Violins imitated by violas, march theme; polyphonic, minor.
[28] 0:33		2. *a.* High woodwinds, *ppp*, dance theme; faster tempo, homophonic (accompanying chords on beat), major; decorative rushes in violins, long crescendo to *ff* as dance theme is repeated.

ppp   *poco a poco crescendo* _____

1:13		*b.* Full orchestra, *fff*, dance theme.
[29] 1:23		3. *a.* Strings only, *ff*, march theme in faster tempo; monophonic, minor.
1:34		*b.* High woodwinds, *ppp*, dance theme; homophonic.
1:39		*c.* Strings only, *ff*, continue march theme; monophonic, then homophonic as lower strings accompany melody.
1:50		*d.* High woodwinds, *ppp*, dance theme; homophonic. Crescendo to
[30] 2:12		4. Full orchestra, *fff*, dance and march themes combined; polyphonic, major. Homophonic ending.

BASIC TERMS

musical texture (page 65) counterpoint (66)
monophonic texture (66) imitation (66)
unison (66) homophonic texture (67)
polyphonic texture (66)

ELEMENTS
9

MUSICAL FORM

The word *form* is associated with shape, structure, organization, and coherence. Form calls to mind the human body or the balanced arrangement of figures in a painting.

Form in music is the organization of musical ideas in time. Music exists only in time; there its sounds begin, vary, repeat, and end. In the flow of time, a composer creates something cohesive out of all the musical elements that were examined in the previous sections—pitch, tone color, dynamics, rhythm, melody, harmony, and texture. In a logically organized piece of music, one thought grows from another, and all the parts are interrelated. Our memories let us perceive the overall form by recalling the various parts and how they relate. As awareness and recall of these parts are developed through repeated listening, the form becomes clearer and takes on an emotional meaning of its own.

TECHNIQUES THAT CREATE MUSICAL FORM

Form has already been explored in connection with simple tunes like *Mary Had a Little Lamb* and *Home on the Range* (see Section 5). These tunes have phrases that are repeated—exactly or with variation—and phrases that are contrasted. Repetition, contrast, and variation are essential techniques in short tunes as well as in compositions lasting much longer. *Repetition* creates a sense of unity; *contrast* provides variety; and *variation,* in keeping some elements of a musical thought while changing others, gives a work both unity and variety at the same time.

Repetition

Musical repetition appeals to the pleasure we get in recognizing and remembering something. In a play, a scene or act is rarely repeated, but in music the repetition of melodies or extended sections is a technique widely used for binding a composition together. Through repetition a melody is engraved in the memory.

The passage of time in music, as in life, influences the way we react to events. When a musical idea returns during a piece, the effect produced is not duplication but balance and symmetry.

Contrast

Forward motion, conflict, and change of mood all come from contrast. Opposition—of loud and soft, strings and woodwinds, fast and slow, major and minor—propels and develops musical ideas. Sometimes a common element will exist between the opposing ideas to establish a sense of continuity. At other times the contrast will be complete. (The contrast between black and white is different from the contrast between black and gray.) The separate identities of contrasting ideas are heightened if they are placed near each other. A composer can emphasize the power and excitement of a musical idea by contrasting it with one that is calm and lyrical, much as a photographer can show the height of a building by including a human figure in the photograph.

Variation

In the variation of a musical idea, some of its features will be retained while others are changed. For example, the melody might be restated with a different accompaniment. Or the pitches of a melody might stay the same while its rhythmic pattern is changed. A whole composition can be created from a series of variations on a single musical idea.

TYPES OF MUSICAL FORM

When form was defined at the beginning of this section, it was explained that a composition is made up of ideas that are interrelated. We looked at the basic techniques for combining these ideas into a coherent whole; repetition, contrast, and variation are used constantly in music of different styles and times. In Section 5 you studied several such patterns. (Remember that lowercase letters represented phrases or relatively short sections, and capital letters represented longer sections.) *Home on the Range,* for example, was outlined as a a' b a'. Other songs could be outlined by the same pattern of letters. (Think of *Oh, Susanna* or *Deck the Halls with Boughs of Holly.*) These songs are said to have the same form, or to be of the same formal type. It's important to note, however, that two compositions having the same form may be different in every other respect.

Composers have used certain forms or patterns to organize their musical ideas. As listeners, we can respond more fully to music when we appreciate its form. We'll look now at two of the basic types of musical form.

Three-Part (Ternary) Form: A B A

During the last few centuries *three-part form (A B A)* has probably been used most frequently. This form can be represented as *statement* (A), *contrast* or *departure* (B), *return* (A). When the return of A is varied, the form is outlined A B A'. Wagner's Prelude to Act III of *Lohengrin,* analyzed in Section 1, is in A B A' form. In the prelude, the A and A' sections are very loud, played by full orchestra (items 1 and 3 in the outline); the B section (item 2 in the outline) is softer, played by fewer instruments. But contrast can be of *any* kind. The A section might be softer than the B, not louder, as in Wagner's prelude. Or the relative lengths of the three sections might vary; section B might be shorter or longer than A.

The way in which A returns after B also differs from piece to piece. Sometimes, as in the prelude by Wagner, A returns suddenly; it's unexpected. More often, the return of A is clearly signaled. The B section will come to a definite end with a cadence and pause. The listener is thus alerted for what happens next. Or a transition might smoothly link B with A and lead into the return.

The sections of a composition in A B A form can be subdivided. One possible subdivision might be:

$$
\begin{array}{ccc}
\text{A} & \text{B} & \text{A} \\
\text{a b a} & \text{c d c} & \text{a b a}
\end{array}
$$

In this case, each large A section is divided into three subsections, a b a, and the large B section is divided into c d c. Depending on the piece, a listener might mistake the subsection b within the first large A section for the arrival of B. But as the music progresses, the greater contrast one hears with B will make it clear that b is a subsection within section A.

DANCE OF THE REED PIPES FROM NUTCRACKER SUITE, BY PETER ILYICH TCHAIKOVSKY

Side 1, band 11
CD 1 [31]

The *Nutcracker* Suite is a set of dances from Tchaikovsky's fairy tale ballet, *The Nutcracker*. The *Dance of the Reed Pipes* is a particularly clear example of A B A' form. Section A features three flutes playing a staccato melody which conveys a light, airy feeling and is repeated several times. The B section contrasts in tone color, melody, and key—it features a trumpet melody accompanied by brasses and cymbals. This melody moves by step within a narrow range, in contrast to the opening flute melody, which has a wide range and lots of leaps as well as steps. The F sharp minor key of the middle section contrasts with the D major key of the opening section. The concluding A' section, in D major, is a shortened version of the opening A section.

Listening Outline To be read while music is heard

DANCE OF THE REED PIPES FROM *NUTCRACKER* SUITE (1892), BY PETER ILYICH TCHAIKOVSKY (1840–1893)

Three-part (ternary) form: A B A'

Moderato assai (very moderate), duple meter ($\frac{2}{4}$), D major

3 flutes, 2 oboes, English horn, 2 clarinets, bass clarinet, 2 bassoons, 4 French horns, 2 trumpets, 3 trombones, tuba, timpani, cymbals, 1st violins, 2d violins, violas, cellos, double basses

(Duration, 2:17)

A

[31] 0:00   1. *a.* Low pizzicato strings, *p*, introduce
0:04   *b.* 3 flutes, staccato melody in major, pizzicato strings accompany. Melody repeated.

c. English horn melody, legato, flutes accompany, staccato.

0:45 *d.* 3 flutes, staccato melody, pizzicato strings accompany. Melody repeated. Cadence.

B

[32] 1:13 2. *a.* Trumpet melody in minor, brasses and cymbals accompany.

A′ 1:26 *b.* Strings repeat trumpet melody. Flutes lead back to

[33] 1:46 3. 3 flutes, staccato melody in major, strings accompany. Melody repeated. Cadence.

Two-Part (Binary) Form: A B

A composition subdivided into two large sections is in *two-part form (A B).* Two-part form gives a sense of *statement* (A) and *counterstatement* (B). A composition in A B form might be represented by A A B or A B B or A A B B if either or both of its large sections are immediately repeated. For example, Chopin's Prelude No. 20 in C Minor, analyzed in Section 1, is in two-part form and is outlined A B B (items 1, 2, and 3 in the outline). Again, differences between A and B may be of any kind, and the two sections may be equal or unequal in length. Like the sections in three-part form, the large sections in two-part form may be divided into subsections. The B section almost always returns to the home key and gives a sense of finality.

BADINERIE FROM SUITE NO. 2 IN B MINOR, BY JOHANN SEBASTIAN BACH

Side 1, band 12
CD 1 [34]

The *Badinerie* (French for *jest* or *banter*) is the lighthearted finale of Bach's Suite No. 2 in B Minor for solo flute, string orchestra, and harpsichord. It is in two-part (binary) form and is outlined A A B B, because each part is repeated. Parts A and B differ in key and length but are similar in melody and rhythm. The first part begins in B minor and then modulates to F sharp minor, and the longer second part begins in F sharp minor and then modulates back to the tonic key of B minor. Section A opens with a descending phrase that reappears at the beginning of section B but at a lower pitch. Each section of this playful miniature is rounded off by a cadence.

Listening Outline To be read while music is heard

BADINERIE FROM SUITE NO. 2 IN B MINOR (LATE 1730S),
BY JOHANN SEBASTIAN BACH (1685–1750)

Two-part (binary) form: **A A B B**

Duple meter ($\frac{2}{4}$), B minor

Solo flute, string orchestra, harpsichord

(Duration, 1:26)

A

[34] 0:00
1. Flute, descending phrase in minor,

phrase repeated, running notes lead to cadence in minor. Section A repeated.

B

[35] 0:31
2. Descending phrase, lower in pitch than section A,

running notes, flute melody descends and leads to cadence in minor. Section
B repeated.

LISTENING FOR FORM

The musical patterns covered in this section fall into clearly defined units.
But music is continuous in its flow and sometimes can't be subdivided
quite so easily. Short pieces often fall into a more elusive category. And
some music seems to fit none of the frequently used patterns. Such music
is not without form; it has a unique form that the listener can discover
through repeated hearings.

Again, it's important to lean on memory when you listen to music. Spot-
ting musical ideas when they occur is fine, but it's only the beginning. The
goal is to put the related ideas together by recognizing and remembering
them and by finding their relationships. Through alert, repeated listening
their overall shape will be made clear, and your response to music will be
more satisfying.

75

ELEMENTS 10

PERFORMANCE

Without a performer, music would remain soundless on a page. Unlike books and paintings, music speaks to us through a re-creator, a musician who makes the printed music sound. A composition, even a familiar one, can be a fresh experience each time it's performed.

It's the job of the *performer* to bring life to the printed symbols laid out by a composer. Just how loud is a chord marked *f*? How fast is a section labeled *allegro*? No matter how many specific indications of rhythm, dynamics, or accent are on a page, much is left to the performer. Like that of an actor, his or her interpretation is full of subtle timings and inflections. Performers project to an audience a mixture of their own feelings and the composer's intentions. Critics sometimes say about a particularly convincing interpretation that a performer is "identified" with a work and its composer. That's how close their relationship can be.

Music created at the same time it's performed is called *improvisation.* Bach at the organ and Beethoven at the piano were brilliant improvisers; their musical ideas flowed instantly from brain to fingers. Improvisation today is a vital aspect of jazz and nonwestern music.

Before the nineteenth century, performers were expected to add certain *ornaments,* or embellishing notes, not indicated in the printed music. Such *embellishments* offered variety and a sense of the performer's individuality. The many musicians today who perform music of the seventeenth and eighteenth centuries have made a point of learning these devices from the past. With such knowledge they can play the music as the composer intended it to be played. Music composed before 1600 presents the challenge of deciding what instruments to use. Often these were not specified by early composers, and to make things more difficult, some of the original instruments are not readily available today.

Performance styles change from generation to generation. Some performers today believe in making a work sound as it did when composed; a keyboard artist will play Bach on the harpsichord rather than on the piano. The size of an orchestra or chorus will be reduced to what was available to a church in 1630, or to a castle in 1760. Other performers believe that they need to reinterpret a past work in a contemporary spirit because their audiences are used to a much wider range of dynamics and listen in larger concert halls. These musicians choose to use all our modern resources to make the composer's message come alive.

The virtuoso violinist Isaac Stern, an artist of extraordinary technical mastery.

THE PERFORMER

Outstanding performers of music, nearly always, have been people with special talents that were recognized in childhood—a beautiful voice, unusual manual dexterity, an excellent ear for pitch, or a keen memory. Like athletes, they have exceptional coordination, strength, and competitive drive. Most solo pianists and violinists play professionally before the age of ten. Singers and woodwind players wait longer for serious training, because their bodies need to mature.

Natural gifts are not enough. A developing performer studies for years with fine teachers, practices many hours a day, and cultivates musical taste and a sense of style. Out of all this may come a *virtuoso,* an artist of extraordinary technical mastery. The great solo performers are a breed apart. Above and beyond their natural gifts and training, they project a

77

personal magnetism that can draw cheers from an audience. These rare few are constantly renewed by the challenge of performance and can make their hundredth playing of a work as exciting as their first. The discomforts of constant travel and the drain on their energies are minor matters—they thrive on communication through music.

What happens to the many fine instrumentalists who are not among the "rare few"? They teach, or play in orchestras, or both. Until fairly recently, wages for orchestral musicians were notoriously low. After lengthy and expensive training, instrumentalists were making less than sanitation workers. Musicians therefore formed orchestral committees and improved their lives through collective bargaining. But even with higher pay and increased benefits, players must often engage in additional free-lance work. Many feel that they're subsidizing their art, but they're willing to do so. As a member of their audience, one does well to appreciate that performers today—however glamorous they may seem—do not have an easy life.

THE CONDUCTOR

A *conductor,* the leader of a group of musicians, represents responsibility and authority. The conductor's "instruments" are the orchestra, band, and chorus. He or she holds performers together and makes them translate a piece into a meaningful whole. Many, though not all, conductors hold a thin stick called a *baton* in one hand to beat time and indicate pulse and tempo. With the other hand they control the balance among the instruments or voices so that the most important musical ideas will be brought out. Conducting styles vary greatly among these powerful individuals, but usually a conductor will use the left hand to indicate expression and to cue musicians.

Most of the conductor's work is done in rehearsal, where technical problems and expressive possibilities are worked over to his or her satisfaction. When a hundred instruments or voices sound at once, the conductor must be able to detect mistakes and performers who are out of tune. Conductors read the orchestral score and "hear" it in their minds. (An example of such a score—from Tchaikovsky's *Romeo and Juliet*—is shown on page 48.) Often conductors memorize the score so that they will be free to hold the eyes of the musicians and thus control fine points of interpretation. In performance, different conductors seem flamboyant, reserved, graceful, or angular. But however they look, all conductors are trying to project an overall concept of a musical work.

The experience of most conductors includes mastery of at least one instrument and extended study of orchestration, music theory, and composition. Conductors are, as needed, diplomats, dictators, and teachers; their role traditionally has been thought of as the most glamorous in the music

Michael Tilson Thomas conducting the New World Orchestra.

profession. In the early nineteenth century, composers began to write increasingly complex music that demanded more and more musicians. This trend fostered the rise of the virtuoso conductor—one who can hold all the forces together and make interpretive sense of their sounds.

Before the nineteenth century, the time beat was given either by the first violinist or by the keyboard player, or both. From this early custom came a title still used today—*concertmaster*. In a modern symphony orchestra the **concertmaster** is the principal first violinist, who sits at the conductor's immediate left. Solo violin music that occurs in symphonic works is played by the concertmaster. He or she also serves as the conductor's assistant by seeing that the players' music contains special markings and checking the tuning of the orchestra before the conductor appears.

RECORDED AND LIVE PERFORMANCE

Recorded performance is a sensational innovation of our time. Our homes resound with medieval music, rock, Beethoven, and Indian ragas. The living room is a new kind of concert hall where we can hear and repeat what we want. Performances heard as recordings may never even have existed "live," played through from beginning to end. Instead, they are often made up of spliced tape from several performances. (It's understandable that performers who have smudged some notes would like them cleaned up by the splicing process. However, too much cleaning of a tape results in a loss of natural vitality, and the long interpretive line can be destroyed.)

Through *dubbing,* recordings have made available new listening experiences not possible in live performance. Beeps, clangs, whistles, never-ending gongs, and other effects can be added to music at a composer's electronic whim. Echo chambers and other equipment have given a new dimension to tone.

It's only in the last 200 years or so that concert-hall listening has developed. Before that, music was heard in a church or palace, on the street, or at home. Much music was intended for amateurs to enjoy around their fireplaces. In church, at dances, or on ceremonial occasions, the listener often was also a performer.

In a live performance, artists put themselves on the line; training and magnetism must overcome technical difficulties to involve the listeners' emotions. What is performed, how it sounds, how the artist feels about it that evening—all this exists for a fleeting moment and can never be repeated. An audience responds to the excitement of such a moment, and feelings are exchanged between stage and hall.

Despite the special electricity of a live performance, there are people who object to coughs and sneezes, the price of tickets, and the fact that seats in a concert hall don't recline. They prefer the living room, where they can choose in comfort from a staggering variety of music and performers on recordings. But in the living room, recorded music can become background sound. Carried to extremes, this can lessen the ability to concentrate. Total satisfaction from music requires that we focus attention as we would at a live performance.

Although recordings have wooed some people away from concert halls, it's also true that they have helped to build audiences for live performances. Enthusiasm for a recording has filled innumerable seats in concert halls. So even though it's an individual matter, most alert listeners will try to strike a happy balance between the voltages offered by the concert hall and by the wall socket.

JUDGING PERFORMANCE

If you have listened to two music lovers arguing after a concert about the merits of what they had just heard, you know how much heat can be generated. Our response to a musical composition or an artist is very subjective and is rooted in deep feeling. Even professional critics can differ strongly in their evaluations of a performance. One will be bowled over by how clearly an artist has revealed the structure of a piece, and another will find the performance cold and unrewarding. There is no one "truth" about what we hear and feel.

Is a concept, an overall idea, projected by the performer? Do some sections of a piece communicate something to you, but not others? Can you figure out why? Subtle effects of phrasing, dynamics, tone color, and tempo become more noticeable to someone who has listened to a number of performers. Listen to the same work played by three different musicians—say, pianists. At first, you may like the second pianist best, but by the third hearing you may decide that it was the first pianist who made the most of what the composer tried to say. All three pianists have played the same notes and yet made three different statements. This is what *molding an interpretation* means.

To a large extent, it's up to us as listeners to evaluate the performance of music. We can do that in the most sensitive way by being alert and open-minded. These qualities will enhance our ability to compare performances and judge music so that we can get full enjoyment from it.

BASIC TERMS

performer (page 76)
improvisation (76)
embellishments (76)
virtuoso (77)
conductor (78)
baton (78)
concertmaster (79)
dubbing (80)

MUSICAL STYLE

ELEMENTS

11

We use the word *style* in reference to everything from clothing to cooking, automobiles to paintings. In music, **style** refers to a characteristic way of using melody, rhythm, tone color, dynamics, harmony, texture, and form. The particular way these elements are combined can result in a total sound that's distinctive or unique.

When we hear an unfamiliar piece on the radio and identify it as jazz, Italian opera, or a symphony by Beethoven, we are responding to its style.

We speak of the musical style of an individual composer, a group of composers, a country, or a particular period in history. Compositions created in the same geographical area or around the same time are often similar in style. Yet composers using the same musical vocabulary can create a personal manner of expression, just as people dressed in a similar style can have an individual look.

Like most other things, musical styles change from one era in history to the next. These changes are continuous, and so any boundary line between one stylistic period and the next can be only an approximation. Though sudden turning points do occur in the history of music, even the most revolutionary new styles are usually foreshadowed in earlier compositions. And few changes of style sweep away the past entirely. Even after a new style has become established, elements of the previous style are usually preserved in the musical language.

The history of western art music can be divided into the following stylistic periods:

Middle Ages (450–1450)
Renaissance (1450–1600)
Baroque (1600–1750)
Classical (1750–1820)
Romantic (1820–1900)
Twentieth century to 1950
1950 to the present

The chapters that follow will describe the general features of each period and show how it differs from the preceding one. An awareness of the characteristics of a style helps you to know what to listen for in a composition written in a particular period. And by knowing the common practice of a period, you can better appreciate the innovative or unique features of a particular composition.

Music is not created in a vacuum. To fully understand the style of a composition, one has to be aware of its function in society. Is a piece meant to provide entertainment in an aristocrat's castle, a concert hall, or a middle-class home? Is it designed to accompany singing, dancing, religious rites, or drama? Musical style is shaped by political, economic, social, and intellectual developments as well. And often, similar features of style can be found in different arts of the same period.

The history of music is probably as old as the history of the human race itself. There is pictorial evidence of musical activity in Egypt as early as 3000 B.C. We know that music played an important role in the cultures of ancient Israel, Greece, and Rome. But hardly any notated music has survived from these ancient civilizations.

The first stylistic period to be considered in this book is the European Middle Ages, from which notated music *has* come down to us. Through the power of notation, music created over 1000 years ago can come alive today.

BASIC TERM

style (81)

THE MIDDLE AGES

Sacred music was dominant during the Middle Ages. This miniature from
a twelfth-century psalter shows King David playing the harp, and ten
other musicians.

1 MUSIC IN THE MIDDLE AGES (450–1450)

A thousand years of European history are spanned by the phrase *Middle Ages.* Beginning around 450 with the disintegration of the Roman Empire, this era witnessed the "dark ages," a time of migrations, upheavals, and wars. But the later Middle Ages (until about 1450) were a period of cultural growth: romanesque churches and monasteries (1000–1150) and gothic cathedrals (1150–1450) were constructed, towns grew, and universities were founded.

During the Middle Ages a very sharp division existed among three main social classes: nobility, peasantry, and clergy. Nobles were sheltered within fortified castles surrounded by moats. During wars, noblemen engaged in combat as knights in armor, while noblewomen managed estates, ran households, and looked after the sick. In peacetime, they amused themselves with hunting, feasting, and tournaments. Peasants—the vast majority of the population—lived miserably in one-room huts. Many were serfs, bound to the soil and subject to feudal overlords. All segments of society felt the powerful influence of the Roman Catholic church. In this age of faith, hell was very real, and heresy was the gravest crime. Monks in monasteries held a virtual monopoly on learning; most people—including the nobility—were illiterate.

Just as the cathedral dominated the medieval landscape and mind, so was it the center of musical life. Most important musicians were priests and worked for the church. An important occupation in thousands of monasteries was liturgical singing. Boys received music education in schools associated with churches and cathedrals. Women were not allowed to sing in church but did make music in convents. Nuns learned to sing, and some—like Hildegard of Bingen (1098–1179), abbess of Rupertsberg—wrote music for their choirs. With this preeminence of the church, it's no surprise that for centuries only sacred music was notated.

Most medieval music was vocal, though a wide variety of instruments served as accompaniment. Few music manuscripts of the time indicate specific instruments, but from paintings and literary descriptions we know that instruments were used. The church frowned upon instruments, because of their earlier role in pagan rites.

After about 1100, however, instruments were used increasingly in church. The organ was most prominent. At first, it was a primitive instrument; the keys were operated by heavy blows with the fists. It was so loud that it could be heard for miles around. Gradually it evolved into a flexible instrument that could play intricate polyphonic music. Throughout the period, the clergy complained about noisy instruments that distracted wor-

Architecture changed during the Middle Ages from the Romanesque style, seen in the eleventh-century nave above, to the gothic of the thirteenth-century Cathedral of Reims (left).

shipers. "Whence hath the church so many Organs and Musical Instruments?" complained a twelfth-century abbot. "To what purpose, I pray you, is that terrible blowing of Bellows, expressing rather the cracks of thunder than the sweetness of a Voyce? . . . In the meantime, the common people standing by, trembling and astonished, admire the sound of Organs, the noise of Cymballs and Musical Instruments." In the later Middle Ages, instruments were a source of constant struggle between composers, who wanted to create elaborate compositions, and church authorities, who wanted music only as a discreet accompaniment to the religious service.

During the Middle Ages, artists were concerned more with religious symbolism than with lifelike representation. Sculptures from the late-twelfth-century church of St. Trophime at Arles (in southern France) show Christ surrounded by symbols of the four evangelists.

MIDDLE AGES

2

GREGORIAN CHANT

For over 1000 years, the official music of the Roman Catholic church has been *Gregorian chant,* which consists of melody set to sacred Latin texts and sung without accompaniment. (The chant is monophonic in texture.) The melodies of Gregorian chant were meant to enhance parts of religious services. They set the atmosphere for specific prayers and ritual actions. For centuries, composers have based original compositions on chant melodies. (Since the Second Vatican Council of 1962–1965, most Roman Catholic services have been celebrated in the native language of each country, and so today Gregorian chant is not common.)

Gregorian chant conveys a calm, otherworldly quality; it represents the voice of the church, rather than of any single individual. Its rhythm is flexible, without meter, and has little sense of beat. The exact rhythm of chant melodies is uncertain, because precise time values were not notated. But its free-flowing rhythm gives Gregorian chant a floating, almost improvisational character. The melodies tend to move by step within a narrow range of pitches. Depending on the nature and importance of the text, they are simple or elaborate; some are little more than recitations on a single tone; others contain complex melodic curves.

Gregorian chant is named after Pope Gregory I (the Great), who reorganized the Catholic liturgy during his reign from 590 to 604. Although medieval legend credits Pope Gregory with the creation of Gregorian chant, we know that it evolved over many centuries. Some of its practices, such as the singing of psalms, came from the Jewish synagogue of the first centuries after Christ. Most of the several thousand melodies known today were created between A.D. 600 and 1300.

At first Gregorian melodies were passed along by oral tradition, but as the number of chants grew to the thousands, they were notated to ensure musical uniformity throughout the western church. (The illustration on page 90 shows an example of medieval chant notation). The earliest surviving chant manuscripts date from about the ninth century. The composers of Gregorian chant—like the sculptors who decorated early medieval churches—remain almost completely unknown.

THE CHURCH MODES

The "otherworldly" sound of Gregorian chant results partly from the unfamiliar scales used. These scales are called the *church modes* (or sometimes simply *modes)*. Like major and minor scales, church modes consist of seven different tones and an eighth tone that duplicates the first an octave higher. However, their patterns of whole and half steps are different. The church modes were the basic scales of western music during the Middle Ages and Renaissance and were used in secular as well as sacred music. Much western folk music follows the patterns of the church modes. For example, the sea chantey *What Shall We Do with the Drunken Sailor?* is in a mode called *Dorian*, and the Civil War song *When Johnny Comes Marching Home* is in the *Aeolian* mode.

Medieval chant notation for *Alleluia: Vidimus stellam.*

ALLELUIA: VIDIMUS STELLAM
(WE HAVE SEEN HIS STAR)

Side 1, band 13
CD 1 [36]

An elaborate and jubilant Gregorian chant is the Alleluia from the Mass for Epiphany. The word *alleluia* is a Latinized form of the Hebrew *hallelujah (praise ye the Lord)*. In this chant (shown here in medieval notation), many notes are sung to single syllables of text. The long series of tones on *ia* is an expression of wordless joy and religious ecstasy. The monophonic texture of the chant is varied by an alternation between a soloist and a choir singing in unison. The chant is in A B A form; the opening Alleluia melody is repeated after a middle section that is set to a Biblical verse.

[36] 0:00	Solo voice:	*Alleluia* phrase.		A
	Chorus:	Long series of tones on *ia*.		
[37] 0:23	Chorus:	*Vidimus stellam*	We have seen His star	B
		ejus in Oriente,	in the East	
		et venimus cum muneribus	and are come with gifts	
		adorare Dominum.	to worship the Lord.	
[38] 1:43	Chorus:	*Alleluia* phrase with long series of tones on *ia*.		A

BASIC TERMS

Gregorian chant (page 88)
church modes (89)

[**3**] SECULAR MUSIC IN THE MIDDLE AGES

Despite the domination of Gregorian chant throughout the Middle Ages, there was much music outside the church, too. The first large body of secular songs that survives in decipherable notation was composed during the twelfth and thirteenth centuries by French nobles called *troubadours* and *trouvères*. Among the best known of these poet-musicians were the troubadour Guillaume IX, duke of Aquitaine, from southern France, and the trouvère Chastelain de Couci, from northern France. During this age of chivalry, knights gained great reputations as musical poets, as they might have done earlier by fighting bravely. Many of the love songs they sang have been preserved because nobles had clerics write them down. These songs were usually performed by court minstrels, and most of them deal with love; but there are also songs about the Crusades, dance songs, and spinning songs. In southern France, there were women troubadours—such as Beatriz de Dia—who addressed their songs to men.

Some 1,650 troubadour and trouvère melodies have been preserved. The notation does not indicate rhythm, but it's likely that many had a regular meter with a clearly defined beat. They thus differ from the free, nonmetrical rhythm of Gregorian chant.

During the Middle Ages, wandering minstrels (or *jongleurs—juggler* comes from this French word) performed music and acrobatics in castles, taverns, and town squares. Without civil rights and on the lowest social level, with prostitutes and slaves, only a lucky few found steady work in the service of the nobility. But they were an important source of information in a time when there were no newspapers. They usually sang songs written by others and played instrumental dances on harps, fiddles (ancestors of the violin), and lutes (plucked string instruments).

ESTAMPIE (THIRTEENTH CENTURY)

Side 1, band 14
CD 1 [39]

The *estampie*, a medieval dance, is one of the earliest surviving forms of instrumental music. In the manuscript for this estampie, a single melodic line is notated and, as usual, no instrument is specified. In our recording, the melody is played on a *rebec* (a bowed string instrument) and a *pipe* (a tubular wind instrument). Since medieval minstrels probably improvised modest accompaniments to dance tunes, the performers have added a drone—two simultaneous, repeated notes at the interval of a fifth, played on a *psaltery* (a plucked or struck string instrument). The estampie is in triple meter and has a strong, fast beat.

Many secular songs in the Middle Ages dealt with love. The illustration at the left shows the German poet-composer Frauenlob (c. 1255–1318) with a group of musicians.

Dances in the Middle Ages were often accompanied by instrumental music, as shown below.

Les ier ot vaurs la louche gente

[4] THE DEVELOPMENT OF POLYPHONY: ORGANUM

For centuries, western music was basically monophonic, having a single melodic line. But sometime between 700 and 900, the first steps were taken in a revolution that eventually transformed western music. Monks in monastery choirs began to add a second melodic line to Gregorian chant. In the beginning, this second line was improvised, not written down; it duplicated the chant melody at a different pitch. The two lines were in parallel motion, note against note, at the interval of a fourth or a fifth. (The interval from *do* to *fa* is a fourth; from *do* to *sol* is a fifth.)

Sit glo - ri - a Do - mi - ni in se - cu - la

Medieval music that consists of Gregorian chant and one or more additional melodic lines is called **organum.** Between 900 and 1200, organum became truly polyphonic, and the melody added to the chant became more independent. Instead of moving strictly parallel to the chant, it developed a melodic curve of its own. Sometimes this line was in contrary motion to the chant, moving up as the original melody moved down. The second line became even more independent around 1100, when the chant and the added melody were no longer restricted to a note-against-note style. Now the two lines differed rhythmically as well as melodically. The chant, on the bottom, was sung in very long notes while the added melody, on top, moved in shorter notes.

Medieval listeners must have been startled to hear religious music in which the added melody was more attractive than the chant. In fact, at times the chant tones were so slow and dronelike that the original melody was hardly recognizable. Nonetheless, the chant represented the authority of the church. And respect for the church was so great that for centuries most polyphonic music was created by placing new melodic lines against known chants.

THE MIDDLE AGES

Interior of the Sainte-Chapelle in Paris (1243–1248). During the Middle Ages, religious teachings were imparted, and beliefs were strengthened, by the biblical scenes depicted in stained-glass windows.

Madonna and Child Enthroned, by an anonymous Byzantine artist (late thirteenth century). Like Gregorian chant, medieval painting often expressed an otherworldly feeling. It represented the voice of the church, rather than of any individuals.

THE RENAISSANCE

Saint Anne, the Virgin, and Child (1506–1510), by Leonardo da Vinci. The Renaissance was an age of curiosity and individualism, exemplified in the remarkable life of Leonardo da Vinci (1452–1519), who was an important painter, a sculptor, an architect, an engineer, and a scientist—and a fine musician as well. Renaissance painters emphasized balance and human beauty and used perspective to create an illusion of depth.

(Metropolitan Museum of Art, John Stewart Kennedy Fund, 1910)

Mars and Venus United by Love (1576), by Paolo Veronese. Classical mythology was an important source of inspiration for Renaissance art. Veronese, and other Venetian painters of his time, reveled in rich colors and textures.

A supreme monument of gothic architecture, the Cathedral of Notre Dame in Paris was the center of polyphonic music around 1200.

SCHOOL OF NOTRE DAME: MEASURED RHYTHM

After 1150, Paris—the intellectual and artistic capital of Europe—became the center of polyphonic music. The University of Paris attracted leading scholars, and the Cathedral of Notre Dame (begun in 1163) was the supreme monument of gothic architecture. Two successive choirmasters of Notre Dame, Leonin and Perotin, are the first notable composers known by name. They and their followers are referred to as the *school of Notre Dame.*

From about 1170 to 1200, the Notre Dame composers developed rhythmic innovations. Earlier polyphonic music was probably performed in the free, unmeasured rhythms of Gregorian chant. But the music of Leonin and Perotin used *measured rhythm,* with definite time values and a clearly defined meter. For the first time in music history, notation indicated precise rhythms as well as pitches. At first the new notation was limited to only certain rhythmic patterns, and the beat had to be subdivided into

95

threes, the symbol of the Trinity. Despite these limitations, much fine polyphonic music was composed during the late twelfth and thirteenth centuries.

Modern listeners sometimes find medieval polyphony hollow and thin, probably because it has relatively few triads, which in later periods became the basic consonant chords. The triad contains two intervals of a third; medieval music theorists considered this interval a dissonance. (An interval of a third separates *do* and *mi,* and *mi* and *sol*). But as the Middle Ages advanced, triads and thirds were used more often, and polyphonic music gradually became fuller and richer by our standards. As an example of Notre Dame polyphony, we'll listen to *Alleluia: Nativitas,* by Perotin.

ALLELUIA: NATIVITAS (THE BIRTH; 1200?), **BY PEROTIN**

Side 2, band 1
CD 1 40

Perotin (late twelfth to early thirteenth century) was the first known composer to write music with more than two voices. *Alleluia: Nativitas,* an organum in three voices, is based on a Gregorian alleluia melody—for the nativity of the Virgin Mary—that Perotin placed in the lowest voice part. In our recording, the lowest part (the chant) is played on an instrument, while the two upper parts are sung by vocal soloists who are reinforced by instruments.

Al - le - - - - lu - - - - - ya.

A chant that is used as the basis for polyphony is known as a *cantus firmus (fixed melody).* Above the cantus firmus, or preexisting melody, Perotin wrote two additional lines that move much more quickly. As many as sixty-six tones of the upper voices are sung against one long, sustained tone of the chant. But only three chant tones—the first, second, and last—are treated in this dronelike way. In the middle of the piece, the chant tones are speeded up so that only about three tones are sung above each chant tone. (This speeding up was a practical necessity, since a chant sung entirely in long notes seems endless, and church services were already long enough!)

The top voices of *Alleluia: Nativitas* have a clearly defined meter, which we would notate today as a fast § (1–2–3–4–5–6). They relentlessly repeat rhythmic patterns: long-short-long, long-short-long. The rhythmic contrast between bottom and top voices is typical of medieval polyphony. The narrow range of the three voices is also characteristic; they are never more than an octave apart. When sung together, the tones of the different parts produce chords that have a hollow ring. As the three voices of *Alleluia: Nativitas* resounded under the vaulted ceilings of Notre Dame, they must have seemed like a cathedral of tones.

BASIC TERMS

organum (page 94)
cantus firmus (96)

FOURTEENTH-CENTURY MUSIC: THE "NEW ART" IN FRANCE

MIDDLE AGES

5

In the fourteenth century, an age of disintegration, Europe suffered through the Hundred Years' War (1337–1453) and the black death—or bubonic plague (around 1350)—which destroyed one-fourth of Europe's population. By this time, both the feudal system and the authority of the church had been weakened. From 1378 to 1417, two rival popes claimed authority; and at one time there were three. Even devout Christians were confused. Literature of the time, such as Chaucer's *Canterbury Tales* (1387–1400) and Boccaccio's *Decameron* (after 1348), stressed graphic realism and earthly sensuality rather than virtue and heavenly reward.

Given this atmosphere, it's not surprising that secular music became more important than sacred music in the fourteenth century. Composers wrote polyphonic music that was *not* based upon Gregorian chants, including drinking songs and pieces in which bird calls, dog barks, and hunting shouts were imitated.

By the early fourteenth century, a new system of music notation had evolved, and a composer could specify almost any rhythmic pattern. Now beats could be subdivided into two as well as three. Syncopation—rarely used earlier—became an important rhythmic practice. Changes in musical style in the fourteenth century were so profound that music theorists referred to French and Italian music as the "new art" (*ars nova*, in Latin). As examples of fourteenth-century music, we'll study a love song and a mass by Guillaume de Machaut, the foremost French composer of the time.

GUILLAUME DE MACHAUT

Guillaume de Machaut (about 1300–1377), who was famous as both musician and poet, was born in the French province of Champagne. Though a priest (he studied theology and took holy orders), Machaut spent most of his life as a court official for various royal families. In 1323, he became secretary to John, king of Bohemia, whom he accompanied on trips and military campaigns throughout Europe. After the king died in battle, Machaut served the royal family of France. In his later years he lived mainly in Reims, where he served as an important church official.

When he was sixty, Machaut fell in love with Péronne d'Armentières, a beautiful young noblewoman of nineteen. For several years they exchanged poems and letters, but the difference in age eventually proved too great and their relationship ended in mutual disappointment. Machaut immortalized their love in his greatest narrative poem, *Voir dit (Tale of Truth)*.

Machaut traveled to many courts and presented beautifully decorated copies of his music to noble patrons. These copies make Machaut one of the first important composers whose works have survived. The decline of the church in the fourteenth century is reflected by Machaut's output, which consists mainly of love songs for one or two voices and instrumental accompaniment. We'll consider, first, one of his secular songs and then the *Notre Dame* Mass, the best-known composition of the fourteenth century.

JE SUIS AUSSI (I TOO AM; MID-FOURTEENTH CENTURY)

Supplementary sets:
Side 1, band 2
CD 1 26

Machaut wrote both the music and the poetry of *Je suis aussi,* a tender song about the power of love. Its ornate vocal melody is accompanied by two unspecified instrumental parts. In our recording, these parts are performed on a recorder (an early flute) and a *vielle* (the main bowed string instrument of the Middle Ages).

Je suis aussi exploits the new rhythmic possibilities of fourteenth-century music: there are many syncopations, and beats are subdivided into 2 rather than 3.

Je   suis -   -   -   -   aus -   -   si

Its rhythm is varied and flexible, in contrast to the repeated rhythms of Perotin's *Alleluia: Nativitas,* which was discussed in Section 4. The flowing melody moves mostly by step within a wide range and often contains several tones sung on a single syllable of text.

Je suis aussi is a **ballade,** a French poetic and musical form that was introduced by the troubadours. It may be outlined A A' B. The sweet melancholy of the music of *Je suis aussi* re-creates the vanished world of courtly love.

Je suis aussi com cilz qui est ravis,	I too am like one ravished,	A	26 0:00
Qui n'a vertu, sens ne entendement,	Who has no strength, sense, or understanding,		
Car je ne sui a nulle riens pensis,	For unceasingly I think of nothing else,	A'	27 0:51
Jour ne demi, temps, heure ne moment,	At any day, time, hour or moment,		
Fors seulement a m'amour	But of my love alone	B	28 1:53
Et sans partir en ce penser demour.	And I remain fixed in that thought.		
Soit contre moy, soit pour moy, tout oubli	For better or worse, I forget all		
Fors li qu'aim mieus cent mille fois que mi.	But the one I love a hundred thousand times more than myself.		

NOTRE DAME MASS (MID-FOURTEENTH CENTURY)

Machaut's *Notre Dame* Mass, one of the finest compositions known from the Middle Ages, is also of great historical importance: it is the first polyphonic treatment of the mass ordinary by a known composer.

The *mass ordinary* consists of texts that remain the same from day to day throughout most of the church year. The five sung prayers of the ordinary are the Kyrie, Gloria, Credo, Sanctus, and Agnus Dei. Since the fourteenth century, these five texts have often been set to polyphonic music and have inspired some of the greatest choral works. In each age, composers have responded to the mass in their own particular style. This centuries-old tradition of the mass gives invaluable insight into the long span of music and its changing styles.

The *Notre Dame* Mass is written for four voices, some of which were probably performed or doubled by instruments. How Machaut wanted his mass performed and which instruments were used to support the voices are unknown. We also do not know when or why the mass was composed. We'll examine the Agnus Dei of the mass as an example of fourteenth-century polyphony.

Agnus Dei

Side 2, band 2
CD 1 [41]

Machaut's music for the Agnus Dei—a prayer for mercy and peace—is solemn and elaborate. It is in triple meter. Complex rhythmic patterns contribute to its intensity. The two upper parts are rhythmically active and contain syncopation, a characteristic of fourteenth-century music. The two lower parts move in longer notes and play a supporting role. In our recording, one low part is played on an instrument, and the three other parts are sung by vocal soloists who are reinforced by instruments.

The Agnus Dei is based on a Gregorian chant, which Machaut furnished with new rhythmic patterns and placed in the tenor, one of the two lower parts. Since the chant, or cantus firmus, is rhythmically altered within a polyphonic web, it is more a musical framework than a tune to be recognized.

The harmonies of the Agnus Dei include stark dissonances, hollow-sounding chords, and full triads. The Agnus Dei sounds fuller than Perotin's *Alleluia: Nativitas*, which was studied as an example of earlier medieval polyphony. Here there are four parts instead of three, and the total range of pitch is wider.

Like the chant melody on which it is based, the Agnus Dei is in three sections. It may be outlined as follows:

Agnus Dei (I)	Agnus Dei (II)	Agnus Dei (III)
A	B	A

The same text appears in each section, except for a change from *miserere nobis (have mercy on us)* to *dona nobis pacem (grant us peace)* in the concluding Agnus Dei (III). A and B are similar in mood, rhythm, and texture and end with the same hollow-sounding chord. The division into three sections is thought to symbolize the Trinity. In Machaut's time, music was meant to appeal to the mind as much as to the ear.

[41] 0:00	*Agnus dei, qui tollis peccata mundi: miserere nobis.*	Lamb of God, who taketh away the sins of the world, have mercy on us.	A
[42] 0:59	*Agnus dei, qui tollis peccata mundi: miserere nobis.*	Lamb of God, who taketh away the sins of the world, have mercy on us.	B
[43] 2:21	*Agnus dei, qui tollis peccata mundi: dona nobis pacem.*	Lamb of God, who taketh away the sins of the world, grant us peace.	A

BASIC TERMS

ballade (page 99)   mass ordinary (99)

III

THE RENAISSANCE

III

During the Renaissance, music was an important leisure activity; every educated person was expected to play an instrument and read musical notation. *The Concert,* a sixteenth-century painting by the "Master of the Female Half-Lengths," shows a flutist, a lutenist, and a singer.

1 MUSIC IN THE RENAISSANCE (1450–1600)

The fifteenth and sixteenth centuries in Europe have come to be known as the Renaissance. People then spoke of a "rebirth," or "renaissance," of human creativity. It was a period of exploration and adventure—consider the voyages of Christopher Columbus (1492), Vasco da Gama (1498), and Ferdinand Magellan (1519–1522). The Renaissance was an age of curiosity and individualism, too, as can be seen in the remarkable life of Leonardo da Vinci (1452–1519), who was a painter, sculptor, architect, engineer, and scientist—and a fine musician as well.

During the Renaissance, the dominant intellectual movement, which was called *humanism*, focused on human life and its accomplishments. Humanists were not concerned with an afterlife in heaven or hell. Though devout Christians, they were captivated by the pagan cultures of ancient Greece and Rome. They became intoxicated with the beauty of ancient languages—Greek and Latin—and by the literature of antiquity. Humanism strongly influenced art throughout the Renaissance. Sculptors and painters once again depicted the nude human body, a favorite theme of antiquity, but a subject of shame and concealment during the Middle Ages. And they no longer treated the madonna as a childlike, unearthly creature; they showed her as a beautiful young woman.

The Catholic church was far less powerful during the Renaissance than it had been during the Middle Ages, for the unity of Christendom was exploded by the Protestant Reformation led by Martin Luther (1483–1546). No longer did the church monopolize learning. Aristocrats and the upper middle class now considered education a status symbol, and they hired scholars to teach their children. The invention of printing with movable type (around 1450) accelerated the spread of learning. Before 1450, books were rare and extremely expensive because they were copied entirely by hand. But by 1500, 15 to 20 million copies of 40,000 editions had been printed in Europe.

MUSIC AND RENAISSANCE SOCIETY

The Renaissance in music occurred between 1450 and 1600. (Some historians place the beginning of the Renaissance as early as 1400.) As with the other arts, musical horizons were expanded greatly. The invention of printing widened the circulation of music, too, and the number of composers and performers increased.

Renaissance sculptors and painters once again depicted the nude human body, which had been a subject of shame and concealment during the Middle Ages. *The Birth of Venus* (1480), by Botticelli (above).

David (1504), by Michelangelo (shown at left).   105

(National Gallery of Art, Washington, D.C.)

During the Renaissance, the madonna was depicted as a beautiful young woman.
The *Niccolini-Cowper Madonna* (1510), by Raphael.

In keeping with the Renaissance ideal of the "universal man," every educated person was expected to be trained in music. "I am not pleased with the courtier if he be not also a musician," Castiglione wrote in *The Book of the Courtier* (1528). Shakespeare's stage directions call for music over 300 times, and the plays are full of beautiful tributes to music:

> The man that hath no music in himself,
> Nor is not mov'd with concord of sweet sounds,
> Is fit for treasons, stratagems and spoils.
> *(The Merchant of Venice)*

As in the past, musicians worked in churches, courts, and towns. Church choirs grew in size. (The Papal Choir in Rome increased from ten singers in 1442 to twenty-four in 1483.) Although polyphonic church music in the Middle Ages was usually sung by several soloists, during the Renaissance it was performed by an entire (male) choir. The church remained an important patron of music, but musical activity gradually shifted to the courts. Kings, princes, and dukes competed for the finest composers. Court musicians ranged in number from ten to sixty and included singers as well as instrumentalists. Women functioned as virtuoso singers at several Italian courts during the late Renaissance. A court music director would compose secular pieces to entertain the nobility and sacred works for the court chapel. The nobility often brought along their musicians when traveling from one castle to another.

Renaissance town musicians played for civic processions, weddings, and religious services. In general, musicians enjoyed higher status and pay than ever before. Composers no longer were happy to remain unknown; like other artists, they sought credit for their work.

Many leading Renaissance composers came from the low countries (Flanders), an area which now includes parts of Holland, Belgium, and northern France. These Flemish composers were regarded highly and held important positions throughout Europe, but especially in Italy, which became the leading music center in the sixteenth century. Other countries with vibrant musical lives in the Renaissance were Germany, England, and Spain.

CHARACTERISTICS OF RENAISSANCE MUSIC

Words and Music

In the Renaissance, as in the Middle Ages, vocal music was more important than instrumental music. The humanistic interest in language influenced vocal music, creating a close relationship between words and music. Renaissance composers wrote music to enhance the meaning and emotion of the text. "When one of the words expresses weeping, pain, heartbreak, sighs, tears and other similar things, let the harmony be full of sadness," wrote Zarlino, a music theorist of the sixteenth century. By contrast, medieval composers had been relatively uninterested in expressing the emotions of a text.

Renaissance composers often used *word painting,* a musical representation of specific poetic images. For example, the words *descending from heaven* might be set to a descending melodic line, and *running* might be heard with a series of rapid notes. Yet, despite this emphasis on capturing the emotion and imagery of a text, Renaissance music may seem calm and restrained to us. While there *is* a wide range of emotion in Renaissance music, it is usually expressed in a moderate, balanced way, with *no* extreme contrasts of dynamics, tone color, and rhythm.

Texture

The texture of Renaissance music is chiefly polyphonic. A typical choral piece has four, five, or six voice parts of nearly equal melodic interest. Imitation among the voices is common: each presents the same melodic idea in turn, as in a round. Homophonic texture, with successions of chords, is also used, especially in light music, like dances. The texture may vary within a piece to provide contrast and bring out aspects of the text as it develops.

Renaissance music sounds more full than medieval music. The bass register is used for the first time, expanding the pitch range to more than 4 octaves. With this new emphasis on the bass line came richer harmony. Composers began to think in terms of chords as well as individual melodic lines. Now all the melodic lines were conceived at the same time. Earlier, during the Middle Ages, a complete melodic line was conceived and then another was added on top of it, with relatively little attention to the total harmonic effect. Renaissance music sounds mild and relaxed, because stable, consonant chords are favored; triads occur often, while dissonances are played down.

Renaissance choral music did not need instrumental accompaniment. For this reason, the period is sometimes called the "golden age" of unaccompanied—*a cappella*—choral music. Even so, instruments were often combined with voices. Instruments might duplicate the vocal lines to reinforce the sound, or they might take the part of a missing singer. But parts written exclusively for instruments are rarely found in Renaissance choral music.

Rhythm and Melody

In Renaissance music, rhythm is more a gentle flow than a sharply defined beat. This is because each melodic line has great rhythmic independence:

when one singer is at the beginning of his or her melodic phrase, the others may already be in the middle of theirs. This technique makes singing Renaissance music both a pleasure and a challenge, for each singer must maintain an individual rhythm. But pitch patterns in Renaissance melodies are easy to sing. The melody usually moves along a scale with few large leaps.

BASIC TERMS

word painting (page 108)
a capella (108)

SACRED MUSIC IN THE RENAISSANCE

The two main forms of sacred Renaissance music are the motet and the mass. They are alike in style, but a mass is a longer composition. The Renaissance *motet* is a polyphonic choral work set to a sacred Latin text other than the ordinary of the mass. The Renaissance *mass* is a polyphonic choral composition made up of five sections: Kyrie, Gloria, Credo, Sanctus, and Agnus Dei.

JOSQUIN DESPREZ AND THE RENAISSANCE MOTET

Josquin Desprez (about 1440–1521), a contemporary of Leonardo da Vinci and Christopher Columbus, was a master of Renaissance music. Like many Flemish composers, he had an international career. Josquin was born in the province of Hainaut—today part of Belgium—and spent much of his life in Italy, serving in dukes' private chapels and in the Papel Choir at Rome. In later years, he worked for Louis XII of France and held several church posts in his native land.

Josquin's compositions, which include masses, motets, and secular vocal pieces, strongly influenced other composers and were praised enthusiastically by music lovers. Martin Luther, for example, remarked: ''God has His Gospel preached also through the medium of music; this may be seen from the compositions of Josquin, all of whose works are cheerful, gentle, mild, and lovely; they flow and move along and are neither forced nor coerced and bound by rigid and stringent rules, but, on the contrary, are like the song of the finch.''

AVE MARIA . . . VIRGO SERENA
(HAIL, MARY . . . SERENE VIRGIN; 1502)

Side 2, band 3
CD 1 44

Josquin's four-voice motet *Ave Maria . . . virgo serena* is an outstanding Renaissance choral work. This Latin prayer to the Virgin is set to delicate and serene music. The opening uses polyphonic imitation, a technique typical of the period.

The short melodic phrase on *Ave Maria* is presented by the soprano voice and then imitated in turn by the alto, tenor, and bass. The next two words, *gratia plena (full of grace),* have a different melody, which also is passed from voice to voice. Notice that each voice enters while the preceding one is in the middle of its melody. This overlapping creates a feeling of continuous flow. Josquin adapted the melody for the opening phrases from a Gregorian chant, but the rest of the motet was not based on a chant melody.

Josquin skillfully varies the texture of this motet; two, three, or four voices are heard at one time. In addition to the imitation among individual voices, there is imitation between pairs of voices: duets between the high voices are imitated by the two lower parts. Sometimes the texture almost becomes homophonic, as at the words *Ave, vera virginitas*. Here, also, is a change from duple to triple meter, and the tempo momentarily becomes more animated. But soon the music returns to duple meter and a more peaceful mood. *Ave Maria* ends with slow chords that express Josquin's personal plea to the Virgin: *O Mother of God, remember me. Amen.*

Ava Maria *gratia plena* *dominus tecum,* *virgo serena.*	Hail Mary, full of grace, the Lord is with thee, serene Virgin.	Each soprano phrase imitated in turn by alto, tenor, and bass. Duple meter.	44 0:00
Ave, cuius conceptio,	Hail, whose conception,	High duet imitated by three lower voices.	0:49
solemni plena gaudio, *coelestia terrestria* *nova replet laetitia.*	full of great jubilation, fills Heaven and Earth with new joy.	All four voices. Increased rhythmic animation reflects "new joy."	
Ave, cuius nativitas *nostra fuit solemnitas,* *ut lucifer lux oriens* *verum solem praeveniens.*	Hail, whose birth brought us joy, as Lucifer, the morning star, went before the true sun.	High duet imitated by low duet. Soprano phrase imitated by alto, tenor, and bass.	1:32
Ave, pia humilitas, *sine viro fecunditas,* *cuius annuntiatio* *nostra fuit salvatio.*	Hail, pious humility, fruitful without a man, whose Annunciation brought us salvation.	High duet imitated by low duet. High duet. Low duet.	2:17
Ave, vera virginitas, *immaculata castitas,* *cuius purificatio* *nostra fuit purgatio.*	Hail, true virginity, immaculate chastity, whose purification brought our cleansing.	Triple meter.	45 2:50
Ave, praeclara omnibus *angelicis virtutibus,* *cuius assumptio* *nostra glorificatio.*	Hail, glorious one in all angelic virtues, whose Assumption was our glorification.	Duple meter, high duets imitated by lower voices. Brief pause.	46 3:16
O mater Dei, *memento mei. Amen.*	O Mother of God, remember me. Amen.	Sustained chords.	

PALESTRINA AND THE RENAISSANCE MASS

During the sixteenth century, Italian composers attained the excellence of such earlier Flemish musicians as Josquin Desprez. Among the most important Italian Renaissance composers was Giovanni Pierluigi da Palestrina (about 1525–1594), who devoted himself to music for the Catholic church. His career thus centered in Rome, where he held important church positions, including that of music director for St. Peter's.

A mass at the court of Philip the Good of Burgundy is shown in this miniature
(c. 1460) by a pupil of Jean le Tavernier.

Palestrina's music includes 104 masses and some 450 other sacred works; it is best understood against the background of the Counter-Reformation. During the early 1500s, the Catholic church was challenged and questioned by the Protestants and, as a result, sought to correct abuses and malpractices within its structure, as well as to counter the move toward Protestantism. This need to strengthen the church led to the founding of the Jesuit order (1540) and the convening of the Council of Trent (1545–1563), which considered questions of dogma and organization.

During its deliberations, the council discussed church music, which many felt had lost its purity. Years before, the scholar Desiderius Erasmus (about 1466–1536) had complained: "We have introduced an artificial and theatrical music into the church, a bawling and agitation of various voices, such as I believe had never been heard in the theaters of the Greeks and Romans. . . . Amorous and lascivious melodies are heard such as elsewhere accompany only the dances of courtesans and clowns." At the council sessions, church music was attacked because it used secular tunes, noisy instruments, and theatrical singing. Some complained that complex polyphony made it impossible to understand the sacred texts; they wanted only monophonic music—Gregorian chant—for the mass. The council finally decreed that church music should be composed not "to give empty pleasure to the ear," but to inspire religious contemplation.

The restraint and serenity of Palestrina's works reflect this emphasis on a more spiritual music. For centuries, church authorities have regarded his masses as models of church music because of their calmness and "otherworldly" quality. And even today the technical perfection of his style is a model for students of counterpoint.

POPE MARCELLUS MASS (1562–1563)

Palestrina's *Pope Marcellus* Mass, his most famous mass, was long thought to have convinced the Council of Trent that polyphonic masses should be kept in Catholic worship. While we now know that this work did *not* play that role, it does reflect the council's desire for a clear projection of the sacred text. It is dedicated to Pope Marcellus II, who reigned briefly in 1555 while Palestrina was a singer in the Papal Choir.

The *Pope Marcellus* Mass is written for an a cappella choir of six voice parts: soprano, alto, two tenors, and two basses. We'll focus on the first section of the mass, the Kyrie.

Kyrie

The Kyrie has a rich polyphonic texture. Its six voice parts constantly imitate each other, yet blend beautifully. This music sounds fuller than

Supplementary sets: Side 1, band 3 CD 1 29

Josquin's *Ave Maria,* in part because six voices are used rather than four. The elegantly curved melodies summon the spirit of Gregorian chant. They flow smoothly and can be sung easily. Upward leaps are balanced at once by downward steps, as in the opening melody:

Soprano

Ky - rie e - lei - - - - - son,

The Kyrie of the *Pope Marcellus* Mass is written in three sections:

29 0:00
30 1:35
31 3:29

1. *Kyrie eleison.*   Lord, have mercy upon us.
2. *Christe eleison.*   Christ, have mercy upon us.
3. *Kyrie eleison.*   Lord, have mercy upon us.

This text is short, and words are repeated with different melodic lines to express calm supplication. The rhythm flows continuously to the end of each section, when all voices come together on sustained chords. Each of the three sections begins in a thin texture with only some of the voices sounding, but as the other voices enter, the music becomes increasingly full and rich.

BASIC TERMS

motet (page 109)
mass (109)

RENAISSANCE
3

SECULAR MUSIC IN THE RENAISSANCE

VOCAL MUSIC

During the Renaissance, secular vocal music became increasingly popular. Throughout Europe, music was set to poems in various languages, including Italian, French, Spanish, German, Dutch, and English.

The development of music printing helped spread secular music, and thousands of song collections became available. Music was an important leisure activity; every educated person was expected to play an instrument and read notation. The Elizabethan composer Thomas Morley describes the embarrassment of being unable to participate in after-dinner music making: "But supper being ended, and Musicke bookes (according to the custome) being brought to the tables, the mistresse of the house presented me with a part, earnestly requesting me to sing. But when, after many excuses, I protested unfainedly that I could not: every one began to wonder. Yea, some whispered to others, demanding how I was brought up."

Renaissance secular music was written for groups of solo voices and for solo voice with the accompaniment of one or more instruments. Word painting—musical illustration of a text—was common. Composers delighted in imitating natural sounds such as bird calls and street cries. In a famous piece entitled *La Guerre (The War)*, the Frenchman Clément Janequin (about 1485–1560) vividly imitated battle noises, drumbeats, and fanfares. Secular music contained more rapid shifts of mood than sacred music did. As Morley advised one composer, "You must in your music be wavering like the wind, sometimes wanton, sometimes drooping, sometimes grave and staid; . . . and the more variety you show the better shall you please."

The Renaissance Madrigal

An important kind of secular vocal music during the Renaissance was the *madrigal,* a piece for several solo voices set to a short poem, usually about love. A madrigal, like a motet, combines homophonic and polyphonic textures. But it more often uses word painting and unusual harmonies.

The Renaissance madrigal began in Italy around 1520, along with a creative explosion in Italian poetry. Madrigals were published by the thousands in sixteenth-century Italy, where they were sung by cultivated aristocrats. Among the many Italian madrigalists were Luca Marenzio (1553–1599) and Carlo Gesualdo (about 1560–1613), the infamous prince of Venosa who had his wife and her lover murdered after finding them together in bed.

In 1588—the year of the defeat of the Spanish armada—a volume of translated Italian madrigals was published in London. This triggered a spurt of madrigal writing by English composers, and for about thirty years there was a steady flow of English madrigals and other secular vocal music. The time of Queen Elizabeth (1533–1603) and William Shakespeare (1564–1616) was as much a golden age in English music as it was in English literature. The impetus for both arts arose in Italy. But the English madrigal became lighter and more humorous than its Italian model, and its melody and harmony were simpler.

AS VESTA WAS DESCENDING (1601), BY THOMAS WEELKES

Side 2, band 4
CD 1 47

Among the finest English madrigalists was Thomas Weelkes (about 1575–1623), an organist and church composer. Weelkes's *As Vesta Was Descending* comes from *The Triumphes of Oriana* (1601), an anthology of English madrigals written to honor Queen Elizabeth, who was often called Oriana. The text of this six-voice madrigal pictures Vesta (the Roman goddess of the hearth) coming down a hill with her attendants, "Diana's darlings." (Diana was the Roman goddess of chastity, hunting, and the moon.) At the same time, the "maiden queen," Oriana (Elizabeth), is climbing the hill with her shepherd gallants. Vesta's attendants desert her and race down the hill to join Oriana.

As Vesta Was Descending has the light mood typical of English madrigals. Word painting is plentiful. For example, the word *descending* is sung to downward scales, and *ascending* to upward ones.

When Vesta's attendants run down the hill, "first *two* by *two*, then *three* by *three together*, leaving their goddess all *alone*," we hear first *two* voices, then *three* voices, then *six* voices, and finally a *solo* voice. In the extended concluding section, "*Long* live fair Oriana," a joyous phrase is imitated among the voices. And in the bass this phrase is sung in long notes, with the longest note on the word *long*.

47

As Vesta was from Latmos hill descending,	Descending scales.
she spied a maiden queen the same ascending,	Ascending scales.
attended on by all the shepherds swain,	
to whom Diana's darlings	
came running down amain.	Rapid descending figures.
First two by two,	Two voices.
then three by three together,	Three voices; all voices.

116

leaving their goddess all alone, hasted thither,
and mingling with the shepherds of her train
with mirthful tunes her presence entertain.
Then sang the shepherds and nymphs of Diana,
Long live fair Oriana!

Solo voice.

Brief joyful phrase
imitated among
voices; long notes
in bass.

The Renaissance Ballett (Fa-la)

A simpler type of secular vocal music than the madrigal was the *ballett* (or *fa-la*), a dancelike song for several solo voices. In contrast to much Renaissance music, the ballett was mostly homophonic in texture, with the melody in the highest voice. The same music is repeated for each stanza of the poem, and the syllables *fa-la* are used as refrain (hence the name). Like the madrigal, the Renaissance ballett originated in Italy. It was cultivated in England from around 1595 to the 1620s.

NOW IS THE MONTH OF MAYING (1595), BY THOMAS MORLEY

Among the most widely performed of all balletts is *Now Is the Month of Maying*, written by Thomas Morley (1557–1603), an English composer best known for his madrigals. The words of this five-voice ballett describe flirtation and courtship in the springtime, when young couples dance in the fields and play hide-and-seek games ("barley break"). Morley's carefree melody gracefully evokes the flirtatious mood of the poem. Each of the poem's three stanzas is set to the same music, which has a clear beat and the swing of an English folk dance. As in nearly all balletts, the music of each stanza consists of two repeated parts: aa bb. Parts a and b both end with a fa-la refrain. While most of the ballett is homophonic in texture, the fa-la section ending part b contains graceful polyphonic imitation among the voices.

Supplementary sets:
Side 1, band 4
CD 1 32

32

Now is the month of maying,
When merry lads are playing, fa la,
Each with his bonny lass
Upon the greeny grass. Fa la.

The spring, clad all in gladness,
Doth laugh at winter's sadness, fa la.
And to the bagpipe's sound
The nymphs tread out their ground. Fa la.

Fie then! why sit we musing,
Youth's sweet delight refusing? Fa la.
Say, dainty nymphs, and speak,
Shall we play barley break? Fa la.

INSTRUMENTAL MUSIC

Though still subordinate to vocal music, instrumental music did become more important during the Renaissance. Traditionally, instrumentalists accompanied voices or played music intended for singing. Even in the early 1500s instrumental music was largely adapted from vocal music. Instrumental groups performed polyphonic vocal pieces, which were often published with the indication *to be sung or played*. Soloists used the harpsichord, organ, or lute (a versatile plucked string instrument with a body shaped like half a pear) to play simple arrangements of vocal works.

During the sixteenth century, however, instrumental music became increasingly emancipated from vocal models. More music was written specifically for instruments. Renaissance composers began to exploit the particular capacities of the lute or organ when writing instrumental solos. They developed purely instrumental forms, such as theme and variations.

Much of this instrumental music was intended for dancing, a popular Renaissance entertainment. Every cultivated person was expected to be skilled in dance, which was taught by professional dancing masters. Court dances were often performed in pairs. A favorite pair was the stately *pavane*, in duple meter, and the lively *galliard*, in triple meter. Dance music was performed by instrumental groups or by soloists like harpsichordists and lutenists. A wealth of dance music published during the sixteenth century has come down to us.

(Alinari/Art Resource)

Much instrumental music of the Renaissance was intended for dancing. Three shawms and a slide trumpet accompany a dance in this detail from the Adimari wedding chest, Florence, c. 1450.

A wide variety of instruments were used during the Renaissance. Hans Burgkmair's woodcut of the emperor Maximilian with his musicians (1505–1516) shows (left) an organ and a cornett; (center) a harp; (on floor) a drum, a kettledrum, a trumsheit (string instrument), and a sackbut; (on table) a viola da gamba, an oblong keyboard instrument, a flute, recorders, a cornett, and a krummhorn.

Renaissance musicians distinguished between loud, outdoor instruments, like trumpets and shawms (a double-reed ancestor of the oboe), and soft, indoor instruments, like *lutes* and recorders (an early flute). The many instruments used in the Renaissance produced softer, less brilliant sounds than we hear from instruments today; most came in families of from three to eight instruments, ranging from soprano to bass. Recorders and *viols* (bowed string instruments) were among the most important Renaissance instruments. Often several members of the same instrumental family were played together, but Renaissance composers did not specify the instruments they wanted. A single work might be performed by recorders, viols, or several different instruments, depending on what was available. Today's standardized orchestra did not exist. Large courts might employ thirty instrumentalists of all types. And on state occasions such as a royal wedding, guests might be entertained by woodwinds, plucked and bowed strings, and keyboard instruments all playing together.

RICERCAR IN THE TWELFTH MODE (SIXTEENTH CENTURY), BY ANDREA GABRIELI

Side 2, band 5
CD 1 48

Andrea Gabrieli (about 1520–1586) was organist at St. Mark's Cathedral in Venice from 1564 until his death. He was an important composer of both sacred and secular vocal music, as well as instrumental music. Gabrieli's Ricercar in the Twelfth Mode was written for four unspecified instruments (soprano, alto, tenor, and bass). In our recording, the ricercar is performed by a group of recorders ranging from soprano to bass. (A *ricercar* is a polyphonic instrumental composition employing imitation. That this one is "in the twelfth mode" means that it is based on a scale corresponding to C major.)

Section A
48 0:00
Section B
49 0:22
Section C
50 0:47
Section A returns
51 1:35

This short, lively piece is composed of several contrasting sections; its form is A B CC A. Gabrieli unifies the ricercar by bringing back the opening material (A) after the two middle sections. Most of section C is in triple meter and contrasts with the duple meter of sections A and B. The work features imitation among the individual instruments and rapid echoes between the two lower and two upper parts. Though relatively simple, the piece is an early step toward the more elaborate instrumental music that developed in the baroque period.

LA BOURÉE (1612), BY MICHAEL PRAETORIUS

Side 2, band 6
CD 1 52

La Bourée comes from *Terpsichore,* a collection of over 300 French dance tunes arranged for instrumental ensemble by Michael Praetorius (1571–1621), a German composer and theorist. (Terpsichore was the Greek muse, or goddess, of the dance.) During the Renaissance, the bourrée (this is the usual spelling) was a folk dance, but later—from about 1650 to 1750—it became an important court dance and instrumental form.

La Bourée is a spritely dance in duple meter written for four instrumental parts (soprano, alto, tenor, and bass). In our recording, it is performed by a Renaissance band that includes loud shawms and soft recorders and krummhorns (a krummhorn is a double-reed instrument with a curved end). A triangle and tambourine also contribute to the festive sound. *La Bourée* consists of four sections, each in two-part (binary) form. The following outline will clarify the instrumentation and form:

1	recorders (soft)	a a b b		52 0:00
2	shawms (loud)	c c d d		53 0:39
3	krummhorns (soft)	e e d' d'	shawms (loud)	54 1:05
4	recorders (soft)	a b		55 1:31

The soprano recorder player adds embellishments to the melody when parts a and b are repeated, in accordance with the performance practice of the time.

Like most dance music of the late Renaissance, *La Bourée* has balanced phrases and a clear beat and meter. It is homophonic in texture, with the tuneful melody in the highest part, yet the three lower parts have a rhythmic vitality of their own. The distinctiveness of the accompaniment suggests that *La Bourée* was designed not only for dancing but for listening as well. And from the Renaissance to the present day, dance rhythms have inspired a great diversity of music meant for listening rather than dancing.

BASIC TERMS

madrigal (page 115)   lute (119)   ricercar (120)
ballett (fa-la) (117)   viol (119)

THE VENETIAN SCHOOL: FROM RENAISSANCE TO BAROQUE

RENAISSANCE

4

During the sixteenth century, Venice—an independent city-state on the northeastern coast of Italy—became a center of instrumental and vocal music. Venice is a seaport built on tiny islands separated by canals; it was a thriving commercial center for trade between Europe and the near east. Venice proclaimed its importance both by means of magnificent processions and through its architecture and painting. Venetian painters such as Titian, Tintoretto, and Veronese were inspired by the city's special light and used rich and brilliant colors.

The focal point for music in Venice was St. Mark's Cathedral. Colorful and wealthy, it employed up to twenty instrumentalists and thirty singers for grand ceremonies within the cathedral and in St. Mark's Square. The music directors and organists at St. Mark's, such as Adrian Willaert (about 1490–1562), Andrea Gabrieli (whose ricercar we studied in Section 3), and his nephew Giovanni Gabrieli, were among the finest composers of the Renaissance. They and their colleagues are called the *Venetian school.*

Gentile Bellini (c. 1429–1507), *Procession in St. Mark's Square.* The focal point for music in Venice was St. Mark's Cathedral.

Venetian composers were stimulated by an architectural feature of St. Mark's Cathedral—two widely separated choir lofts, each with an organ—and wrote much music for several choruses and groups of instruments. Unlike most Renaissance choral music, Venetian choral music of the late sixteenth century often contains parts that are written exclusively for instruments. This conscious use of instrumental color brings some works of the Venetian school close to the early baroque style. Another early baroque feature of some Venetian music is the tendency toward homophonic texture, rather than the polyphonic texture typical of Renaissance music.

GIOVANNI GABRIELI AND THE POLYCHORAL MOTET

Giovanni Gabrieli (about 1555–1612), a native of Venice, was the most important Venetian composer of the late Renaissance. He studied with his uncle Andrea Gabrieli and was an organist at St. Mark's from 1585 until his death. His compositions include organ and instrumental ensemble works and *polychoral motets* (motets for two or more choirs, often including groups of instruments). Gabrieli's *Sonata pian e forte* (1597) is famous as one of the earliest instrumental ensemble pieces in which dynamic indications and the desired instruments are specified by the composer. His polychoral motets for two to five choirs call for an unprecedentedly large number of performers and brilliantly exploit contrasts of register, sonority, and tone color.

PLAUDITE (CLAP YOUR HANDS; 1597)

Giovanni Gabrieli's spectacular polychoral motet *Plaudite* was intended for a joyful ceremony at St. Mark's Cathedral. Its Latin text calls for praise of God. The motet is written for a large vocal and instrumental ensemble of twelve voice parts divided into three "choirs," or performing groups, that contrast in register. There is one low choir, one choir in a middle register, and one high choir. The choice of instruments is left to the performers. In our recording, some of the voices are reinforced by brass instruments or by an organ.

Supplementary sets:
Side 1, band 5
CD 1 33

Gabrieli exploits the "stereophonic" possibilities of St. Mark's by rapidly tossing short phrases among the three separate choirs. Often the choirs combine to produce splendidly massive sonorities. Gabrieli unifies the motet by using the same music for each of four short *alleluia* sections. These sections are in triple meter and contrast with the prevailing duple meter of the motet. With its homophonic texture and its flamboyant use of contrasting sonorities, *Plaudite* is at the border between the Renaissance and early baroque styles.

Plaudite, Psallite, *Jubilate Deo* *omnis terra:*	Clap your hands, sing praises, sing joyfully to God, all the earth.	33 0:00
alleluia,	Alleluia.	0:12
benedicant Dominum *omnes gentes,* *collaudantes eum:*	Let all the nations bless the Lord, together praising Him.	
alleluia,	Alleluia.	0:51
quia fecit nobiscum Dominus *misericordiam suam:*	For the Lord hath acted in His mercy with us.	
alleluia,	Alleluia.	1:30
et captivam duxit captivitatem, *admirabilis et gloriosus* *in saecula:*	And led captivity captive. Admirable and glorious [He is] forever.	
alleluia.	Alleluia.	2:24

BASIC TERMS

Venetian school (page 121)
polychoral motet (122)

THE BAROQUE PERIOD

IV

During the late baroque period, instrumental music became as important as vocal music for the first time. Jan Vermeer, *A Lady and Gentleman at the Virginals* (1664). The instruments shown are a viola da gamba and a virginal, which is a type of small harpsichord.

BAROQUE MUSIC
(1600–1750)

1

Though the word *baroque* has at various times meant bizarre, flamboyant, and elaborately ornamented, modern historians use it simply to indicate a particular style in the arts. An oversimplified but useful characterization of baroque style is that it fills space—canvas, stone, or sound—with action and movement. Painters, sculptors, and architects became interested in forming a total illusion, like a stage setting. Artists such as Bernini, Rubens, and Rembrandt exploited their materials to expand the potentials of color, detail, ornament, and depth; they wanted to create totally structured worlds.

Such a style was very well suited to the wishes of the aristocracy, who also thought in terms of completely integrated structures. In France, for example, Louis XIV held court in the Palace of Versailles, a magnificent setting that fused baroque painting, sculpture, and architecture into a symbol of royal wealth and power.

Baroque artists exploited their materials to expand the potential of color, ornament, detail, and depth. Rembrandt, *Christ Preaching* (c. 1652).

(Metropolitan Museum of Art, The H. O. Havemeyer Collection, 1929)

126

(Michael J. Howell)

(Alinari-Anderson/Art Resource)

The palace of Versailles, in France (above), fused baroque architecture, sculpture, and painting into a symbol of royal wealth and power.

Left: Bernini's *David Slaying Goliath* (1623) fills space with action and movement. It is far more dynamic than Michelangelo's *David*, shown on page 105.

The baroque style was also shaped by the needs of churches, which used the emotional and theatrical qualities of art to make worship more attractive and appealing. The middle class, too, influenced the development of the baroque style. In Holland, for example, prosperous merchants and doctors commissioned realistic depictions of landscapes and scenes from everyday life.

It's also helpful to think of baroque style against the backdrop of scientific discoveries during the seventeenth-century. The work of Galileo (1564–1642) and Newton (1642–1727) represented a new approach to science based on the union of mathematics and experiment; they discovered mathematical laws governing bodies in motion. Such scientific advances led to new inventions and the gradual improvement of medicine, mining, navigation, and industry during the baroque era. Baroque art is a complex mixture of rationalism, sensuality, materialism, and spirituality.

In music, the baroque style flourished during the period from 1600 to 1750. The two giants of baroque composition were George Frideric Handel and Johann Sebastian Bach. Bach's death in 1750 marks the end of the period. Other baroque masters—Claudio Monteverdi, Henry Purcell, Arcangelo Corelli, Antonio Vivaldi—were largely forgotten until the twentieth century. But the appearance of long-playing records in the late 1940s spurred a "baroque revival" that made these long-forgotten musicians familiar to many music lovers.

The baroque period can be divided into three phases: early (1600–1640), middle (1640–1680), and late (1680–1750). Though the baroque music best known today comes from the latest phase, the earliest was one of the most revolutionary periods in music history. Monteverdi (1567–1643), for instance, strove to create unprecedented passion and dramatic contrast in his works. In Italy, especially, music was composed for texts conveying extreme emotion, and the text ruled the music. With this stress on drama and text, it is not surprising that Italian composers of the early baroque created opera—a drama sung to orchestral accompaniment. Their melodic lines imitated the rhythms and inflections of speech.

Early baroque composers favored homophonic texture over the polyphonic texture typical of Renaissance music. They felt that words could be projected more clearly by using just one main melody with a chordal accompaniment. But note that this new emphasis on homophonic texture characterizes only the *early* baroque; by the *late* baroque period, polyphonic texture returned to favor.

To depict the extreme emotions in their texts, early baroque composers used dissonances with a new freedom. Never before were unstable chords so prominent and emphatic. Contrasts of sound were stressed—one or more solo singers against a chorus, or voices against instruments. In Renaissance choral music, instruments—if used at all—duplicated a singer's melody. But in the early baroque, voices were accompanied by melodic lines designed for instruments.

During the middle phase of the baroque (1640–1680), the new musical style spread from Italy to practically every country in Europe. The medieval or church modes—scales that had governed music for centuries—gradually gave way to major and minor scales. By about 1680, major or minor scales were the tonal basis of most compositions. Another feature of the middle baroque phase was the new importance of instrumental music. Many compositions were written for specific instruments, the violin family being most popular.

We will focus mainly on the late baroque period (1680–1750), which yielded most of the baroque music heard today. Many aspects of harmony—including the emphasis of the dominant chord's attraction to the tonic—arose in this period. During the late baroque, instrumental music became as important as vocal music for the first time. Early baroque composers had emphasized homophonic texture; late baroque composers gloried in polyphony. Let's look more closely at some features of late baroque style. (From now on the word *baroque* will pertain to the late baroque phase.)

CHARACTERISTICS OF BAROQUE MUSIC

Unity of Mood

A baroque piece usually expresses one basic mood—what begins joyfully will remain joyful throughout. Emotional states like joy, grief, and agitation were represented. (At the time, these moods were called *affections*.) Composers molded a musical language to depict the affections; specific rhythms or melodic patterns were associated with specific moods. This common language gives a family resemblance to much late baroque music.

The prime exception to this baroque principle of unity of mood occurs in vocal music. Drastic changes of emotion in a text may inspire corresponding changes in the music. But even in such cases, one mood is maintained at some length before it yields to another.

Rhythm

Unity of mood in baroque music is conveyed, first of all, by continuity of rhythm. Rhythmic patterns heard at the beginning of a piece are repeated throughout it. This rhythmic continuity provides a compelling drive and energy—the forward motion is rarely interrupted. The beat is emphasized far more in baroque music than in most Renaissance music, for example.

Melody

Baroque melody also creates a feeling of continuity. An opening melody will be heard again and again in the course of a baroque piece. And even when a melody is presented in varied form, its character tends to remain constant. There is a continuous expanding, unfolding, and unwinding of melody. This sense of directed motion is frequently the result of a melodic sequence, that is, successive repetition of a musical idea at higher or lower pitch levels. Many baroque melodies sound elaborate and ornamental, and they are not easy to sing or remember. The baroque melody gives the impression of dynamic expansion rather than of balance and symmetry. A short opening phrase is often followed by a longer phrase with an unbroken flow of rapid notes.

Terraced Dynamics

Continuity Dynamics

Paralleling continuity of rhythm and melody in baroque music is a continuity of dynamic level: the volume tends to stay constant for a stretch of time. When the dynamics do shift, it's sudden, as though one had physically stepped from one level to another. This alternation between loud and soft is called **terraced dynamics.** *Gradual* changes through crescendo and decrescendo are *not* prominent features of baroque music. However, singers and instrumentalists no doubt made some subtle dynamic inflections for expressive purposes.

The main keyboard instruments of the baroque period were the organ and harpsichord, both well suited for continuity of dynamic level. An organist or harpsichordist could not obtain a crescendo or decrescendo by varying finger pressure, as pianists today can. A third keyboard instrument, the *clavichord,* could make gradual dynamic changes, but only within a narrow range—from about *ppp* to *mp.* Sound was produced on it by means of brass blades striking the strings. The clavichord was usually not used in large halls, since its tone was too weak. But for home use by amateurs it was ideal; its cost was low and its expressive sound satisfying. It had especially wide popularity in Germany.

Texture

We've noted that late baroque music is predominantly polyphonic in texture: two or more melodic lines compete for the listener's attention. Usually, the soprano and bass lines are the most important. Imitation between the various lines, or "voices," of the texture is very common. A melodic idea heard in one voice is likely to make an appearance in the other voices as well.

However, not all late baroque music was polyphonic. A piece might shift in texture, especially in vocal music, where changes of mood in the words demand musical contrast. Also, baroque composers differed in their treatment of musical texture. Bach inclined toward a consistently polyphonic texture, whereas Handel used much more contrast between polyphonic and homophonic sections.

Chords and the Basso Continuo (Figured Bass)

Chords became increasingly important during the baroque period. In earlier times, there was more concern with the beauty of individual melodic lines than with chords formed when the lines were heard together. In a sense, chords were mere by-products of the motion of melodic lines. But in the baroque period chords became significant in themselves. As composers wrote a melodic line, they thought of chords to mesh with it. Indeed, sometimes they composed a melody to fit a specific chord progression. This interest in chords gave new prominence to the bass part, which served as the foundation of the harmony. The whole musical structure rested on the bass part.

The new emphasis on chords and the bass part resulted in the most characteristic feature of all baroque music, an accompaniment called the *basso continuo,* or *figured bass.* This is made up of a bass part together with numbers (figures) which specify the chords to be played above it. The continuo—to use the common abbreviation for *basso continuo*—is usually played by at least two instruments: an organ or a harpsichord and a low melodic instrument like the cello or bassoon. With the left hand, the organist or harpsichordist plays the bass part, which is also performed by the cello or bassoon. With the right hand, the keyboard player improvises chords or even a melodic line, following the indications of the numbers. These numbers specify only a basic chord, not the exact way in which the chord should be played. Thus, the performer is given a great deal of freedom. (This shorthand system is similar in principle to the chord indications found on the modern song sheets from which jazz pianists improvise.)

The basso continuo offered the advantage of emphasizing the all-important bass part, besides providing a steady flow of chords. Practically, the use of numbers, rather than chords with all their notes written out, saved time for busy baroque composers. It also saved paper at a time when paper was expensive.

Words and Music

Like their Renaissance predecessors, baroque composers used music to depict the meaning of specific words. *Heaven* might be set to a high tone, and *hell* to a low one. Rising scales represented upward motion; descending scales depicted the reverse. Descending chromatic scales were associated with pain and grief. This descriptive musical language was quite standardized: a lament for a lost love might call forth the same descending chromatic scale used to depict suffering in the *Crucifixus* of the mass.

Baroque composers emphasized words by writing many rapid notes for a single syllable of text; this technique also displayed a singer's virtuosity. The individual words and phrases of a text are repeated over and over as the music continuously unfolds.

THE BAROQUE ORCHESTRA

During the baroque period, the orchestra evolved into a performing group based on instruments of the violin family. By modern standards, the baroque orchestra was small, consisting of from ten to thirty or forty players. Its instrumental makeup was flexible and could vary from piece to piece. At its nucleus were the basso continuo (harpsichord plus cello, double bass, or bassoon) and upper strings (first and second violins and violas). Use of woodwind, brass, and percussion instruments was variable. To the strings and continuo could be added recorders, flutes, oboes, trumpets, horns, trombones, or timpani. One piece might use only a single flute, while another would call for two oboes, three trumpets, and timpani. Trumpets and timpani joined the orchestra mainly when the music was festive. This flexibility contrasts with the standardized orchestra of later periods, composed of four sections: string, woodwind, brass, and percussion.

The baroque trumpet (like the early French horn) had no valves but was given rapid, complex melodic lines to play in a high register. Because the instrument was difficult to play and had a traditional association with royalty, the trumpeter was the aristocrat of the baroque orchestra. When prisoners of war were exchanged, trumpeters, if they had been captured, were treated like military officers.

Bach, Handel, Vivaldi, and others chose their orchestral instruments with care and obtained beautiful effects from specific tone colors. They loved to experiment with different combinations of instruments. However, in the baroque period tone color was distinctly subordinate to other musical elements—melody, rhythm, and harmony. Composers frequently rearranged their own or other composers' works for different instruments. A piece for string orchestra might become an organ solo, losing little in the process. Often, one instrument was treated like another. An oboe would play the same melody as the violins, or the flute and trumpet would imitate each other for extended sections of a piece.

BAROQUE FORMS

It has been noted that a piece of baroque music—particularly instrumental music—usually has unity of mood. Yet many baroque compositions include a set of pieces, or movements, that contrast. A *movement* is a piece that sounds fairly complete and independent but is part of a larger composition. Usually, each movement has its own themes, comes to a definite end, and is separated from the next movement by a brief pause. Thus, a baroque composition in three movements may contain contrasts between a fast and energetic opening, a slow and solemn middle, and a conclusion that is quick, light, and humorous.

All the form types described in Part I, Section 9—"Musical Form"—appear in baroque music. Three-part form (A B A), two-part form (A B), and continuous or undivided form are all common. We'll consider examples of these and other forms in the sections that follow.

Regardless of form, baroque music features contrasts between bodies of sound. Often there is a quite regular alternation between a small and a large group of instruments, or between instruments and voices with instrumental accompaniment. This exploration of contrasting sounds was pursued with great imagination and provides a key to the understanding and enjoyment of baroque music.

BASIC TERMS

terraced dynamics (page 130)   basso continuo (figured bass) (131)
clavichord (130)   movement (132)

MUSIC IN BAROQUE SOCIETY

BAROQUE

2

Before 1800, most music was written to order, to meet specific demands that came mainly from churches and aristocratic courts. (There were many such courts. Germany, for example, was divided into about 300 territories, each governed separately.) Opera houses and municipalities also required a constant supply of music. In every case, the demand was for *new* music; audiences did not want to listen to pieces in an "old-fashioned" style.

The ruling class was enormously rich and powerful. While most of the population barely managed to survive, European rulers surrounded themselves with luxury. Each ruler proclaimed greatness by means of splendid palaces and magnificent court entertainments. Indeed, entertainment was necessary; most courtiers did no real work and tried to avoid boredom as much as possible.

Music was a main source of diversion. One court might employ an orchestra, a chapel choir, and opera singers—the size of the musical staff depending on the court's wealth. Bach directed about eighteen players in the orchestra of a small German court in 1717; but a large court might have more than eighty performers, including the finest opera singers of the day. The music director supervised performances and composed much of the music required, including operas, church music, dinner music, and pieces for court concerts. This overworked musician also was responsible for the

During the baroque period, musicians often played with amateurs in music clubs or university music societies, getting together at private homes, coffeehouses, and taverns. The ensemble shown here includes three singers, three violins, six wind instruments, and a basso continuo made up of a harpsichord and a cello.

discipline of other musicians, and for the upkeep of the instruments and music library.

The music director's job had good and bad features. Pay and prestige were quite high, and anything the composer wrote would be performed. But no matter how great, the composer was still a high-class servant who could neither quit nor take a trip without the patron's permission. Like everyone in baroque society, musicians had to curry favor with the aristocracy.

It is in this light that we must understand dedications like the one which Bach addressed to a nobleman along with his *Brandenburg* Concertos: "Begging Your Highness most humbly not to judge their imperfection with the rigor of the fine and delicate taste which the whole world knows Your Highness has for musical pieces; but rather to infer from them in benign Consideration the profound respect and the most humble obedience which I try to show Your Highness." Yet sometimes musicians formed personal friendships with their patrons, as did Arcangelo Corelli, who thus gained a private apartment in a palace.

Some rulers were themselves good musicians. Frederick the Great, king of Prussia during the mid-eighteenth century, was a flutist and good composer, as well as a feared general. At his nightly court concerts, Frederick played his own works and some of the hundreds of pieces supplied by his flute teacher, Johann Quantz. (Quantz was "granted the privilege" of shouting "Bravo!" after a royal performance.)

Churches also needed music, and what music they had was often very grand. Along with an organ and a choir, many baroque churches had an orchestra to accompany the services. Indeed, church was where most ordinary citizens heard music. There were few public concerts, and the populace was rarely invited to the palace. The music director of a church, like the music director at a court, had to produce a steady flow of new music and was also responsible for the music training of choristers in the church school. Fine church music contributed to the prestige of cities, which often competed to attract the best musicians.

Church musicians earned lower pay and had less status than court musicians. Their meager income was supplemented by allotments of firewood and grain and by irregular fees for weddings and funerals. They suffered a financial pinch when "a healthy wind" blew and there were fewer funerals than usual, a situation Bach once complained about.

Large towns employed musicians to perform a variety of functions—to play in church, in processions, in concerts for visiting dignitaries, and for university graduations. These town musicians often played with amateurs in music clubs or university music societies, getting together at private homes, coffeehouses, and taverns.

Some baroque musicians earned money by writing operas for commercial opera houses; such houses were located mainly in Italy. In Venice, a city of 125,000 people, six opera companies performed simultaneously between 1680 and 1700. In London, Handel became music director of a commercial opera company in 1719. Backed by English nobles, this company was a corporation with shares listed on the London stock exchange. When the company went bankrupt in 1728, Handel formed his own company, for which he wrote operas and served as conductor, manager, and impresario. In filling these many roles, Handel became one of the first great "freelance" musicians.

How did one become a musician in the baroque period? Often the art was handed from father to son; many leading composers—such as Bach, Vivaldi, Purcell, Couperin, and Rameau—were sons of musicians. Or boys sometimes were apprenticed to a town musician and lived in his home. In return for instruction, the boys did odd jobs, such as copying music. Many baroque composers began their studies as choirboys, learning music in the choir school. In Italy, music schools were connected with orphanages. (*Conservatory* comes from the Italian for *orphans' home.*) There, orphans, foundlings, and poor children—boys and girls—were given thorough musical training, and some became the most sought-after opera singers and instrumentalists in Europe. Eminent composers such as Vivaldi were hired to teach and direct concerts in these schools. Vivaldi's all-female orchestra in Venice was considered one of the finest ensembles in Italy. During the baroque period, women were not permitted to be employed as music directors or as instrumentalists in court or opera orchestras. Nevertheless, a number of women—including Francesca Caccini, Barbara Strozzi, and Elisabeth-Claude Jacquet de la Guerre—succeeded in becoming respected composers.

To get a job, musicians usually had to pass a difficult examination, performing and submitting compositions. Sometimes there were nonmusical job requirements, too. An applicant might be expected to make a "voluntary contribution" to the town's treasury, or even to marry the daughter of a retiring musician. Bach and Handel turned down the same job because one of the conditions was marriage to the organist's daughter. Italian musicians held the best posts in most European courts and were frequently paid twice as much as local musicians.

Composers were an integral part of baroque society, working for courts, churches, towns, and commercial opera houses. And even though they wrote their music to fit specific needs, its quality is so high that much of it has become standard in today's concert repertory.

[BAROQUE 3] THE CONCERTO GROSSO AND RITORNELLO FORM

Large

We've seen that the contrast between loud and soft sounds—between large and small groups of performers—is a basic principle of baroque music. This principle governs the concerto grosso, an important form of orchestral music in the late baroque period. In the *concerto grosso*, a small group of soloists is pitted against a larger group of players called the *tutti* *(all)*. Usually, between two and four soloists play with anywhere from eight to twenty or more musicians for the tutti. The tutti consists mainly of string instruments, with a harpsichord as part of the basso continuo. A concerto grosso presents a contrast of texture between the tutti and the soloists, who assert their individuality and appeal for attention through brilliant and fanciful melodic lines. The soloists were the best and highest-paid members of the baroque orchestra, because their parts were more difficult than those of the other players. Concerti grossi were frequently performed by private orchestras in aristocratic palaces.

The concerto grosso consists of *several movements that contrast in tempo and character*. Most often there are three movements: (1) fast, (2) slow, (3) fast. The opening movement is usually vigorous and determined, clearly showing the contrast between tutti and soloists. The slow movement is quieter than the first, often lyrical and intimate. The last movement is lively and carefree, sometimes dancelike.

The first and last movements of concerti grossi are often in *ritornello form,* which is based on alternation between tutti and solo sections. In ritornello form the tutti opens with a theme called the *ritornello (refrain).* This theme, always played by the tutti, returns in different keys throughout the movement. But it usually returns in fragments, not complete. Only at the end of the movement does the entire ritornello return in the home key. Although the number of times a ritornello (tutti) returns varies from piece to piece, a typical concerto grosso movement might be outlined as follows:

1. *a.* Tutti *(f),* ritornello in home key
   b. Solo
2. *a.* Tutti *(f),* ritornello fragment
   b. Solo
3. *a.* Tutti *(f),* ritornello fragment
   b. Solo
4. Tutti *(f),* ritornello in home key

In contrast to the tutti's ritornello, the solo sections offer fresh melodic ideas, softer dynamics, rapid scales, and broken chords. Soloists may also expand short melodic ideas from the tutti. The opening movement of Bach's *Brandenburg* Concerto No. 5 is a fine example of ritornello form in the concerto grosso.

BRANDENBURG CONCERTO NO. 5 IN D MAJOR (1721), BY JOHANN SEBASTIAN BACH

With his set of six *Brandenburg* Concertos, Bach brought immortality to a German aristocrat, the margrave of Brandenburg. Bach met the margrave in 1718, when he was music director for another patron. The margrave loved music and asked Bach to send him some original compositions. About three years later, Bach sent him the *Brandenburg* Concertos with the flattering dedication quoted in Section 2, probably hoping for money or favors in return. (We don't know whether he got any.) These concertos had actually been composed for, and performed by, the orchestra of Bach's employer, the prince of Cöthen. Each of the concertos is written for a different and unusual combination of instruments.

The *Brandenburg* Concerto No. 5 uses a string orchestra and a group of soloists consisting of a flute, a violin, and a harpsichord. This was the first time that a harpsichord had been given the solo role in a concerto grosso. In 1719, the prince of Cöthen bought a new harpsichord; Bach probably wanted to show off this instrument (as well as his skill as a keyboard player), and so he gave it a solo spot. The tutti is written for violins, violas, cellos, and double bass. During the tutti sections the solo violinist plays along, as does the harpsichordist, who supplies the figured bass.

Here, we'll focus on the first movement of the *Brandenburg* Concerto No. 5; the second and third movements are discussed later (see pages 168–170).

First Movement: Allegro Fast #41

Side 3, band 1
CD 2 1

The allegro movement opens with the ritornello, which is an almost continuous flow of rapid notes. After the ritornello ends very definitely, the soloists present short melodic ideas, the flute and violin imitating each other playfully. The appearance of the soloists brings a lower dynamic level and the new tone color of the flute. After a while, the tutti returns loudly with a brief fragment of the ritornello, only to give way again to the soloists. This alternation between brief, loud ritornello fragments in the tutti and longer, softer solo sections continues throughout the movement.

The soloists' music tends to be brilliant, fanciful, and personal when compared with the more vigorous and straightforward tutti sections. Solo sections are also more polyphonic in texture than the tutti and stress imitation between the flute and violin. The soloists play new material of their own or varied fragments from the ritornello. These solo sections build tension and make the listener anticipate the tutti's return. Listen especially for the suspenseful solo section that begins with a new theme in minor and ends with the fluttery sound of trills in the flute and violin. (A *trill* is an ornament consisting of the rapid alternation of two tones that are a whole or half step apart.)

Only the harpsichord plays during the long final solo section. And it is spectacular! Bach builds a tense high point for the movement through irresistible rhythm and dazzling scale passages that require a virtuoso's skill. His audience must have marveled at this brilliant harpsichord solo within a concerto grosso. Audiences still do.

Listening Outline   To be read while music is heard

BRANDENBURG CONCERTO NO. 5 IN D MAJOR (1721),
BY JOHANN SEBASTIAN BACH

First Movement: Allegro

Ritornello form, duple meter ($\frac{2}{2}$), D major

Flute, violin, harpsichord (solo group); string orchestra, continuo (tutti)

(Duration, 9:44)

Tutti

☐1 0:00   1. *a.* Strings, *f,* ritornello.

Solo

☐2 0:20   *b.* Flute, violin, harpsichord, major key.

Tutti

0:45   2. *a.* Strings, *f,* ritornello fragment.

Solo

☐3 0:49   *b.* Flute, violin, harpsichord, varied ritornello fragment.

Tutti

1:10   3. *a.* Strings, *f,* ritornello fragment.

Solo

1:17   *b.* Violin, flute, harpsichord.

Tutti

1:36   4. *a.* Strings, *f,* ritornello fragment, minor.

Solo

1:42   *b.* Harpsichord, flute, violin.

Tutti

2:23   5. *a.* Strings, *f,* ritornello fragment, major.

Solo

2:30   *b.* Flute, harpsichord, violin, varied ritornello fragment, *pp.*

☐4 2:55   *c.* New theme in minor, *pp,* tossed between flute and violin; tension mounts.

Trills in flute and violin lead to

Tutti

4:08   6. *a.* Strings, *f,* ritornello fragment, major.

Solo

4:12   *b.* Violin, flute, harpsichord.   139

BASIC TERMS

concerto grosso (page 136)
tutti (136)
ritornello form (137)
ritornello (137)
trill (138)

[BAROQUE]

4 THE FUGUE

One cornerstone of baroque music is the fugue. A fugue can be written for a group of instruments or voices, or for a single instrument like an organ or harpsichord. The *fugue* is a polyphonic composition based on one main theme, called a *subject.* Throughout a fugue, different melodic lines, or "*voices,*" imitate the subject. The top melodic line—whether sung or played—is the soprano voice, and the bottom is the bass. A fugue's texture usually includes three, four, or five voices. Though the fugue's subject remains fairly constant throughout, it takes on new meanings when shifted to different keys or combined with different melodic and rhythmic ideas.

The form of a fugue is extremely flexible; in fact, the only constant feature of fugues is how they begin—the subject is almost always presented in a single, unaccompanied voice. By thus highlighting the subject, the composer tells us what to remember and listen for. In getting to know a fugue, try to follow its subject through the different levels of texture. After its first presentation, the subject is imitated in turn by all the remaining voices.

The opening of a fugue in four voices may be represented as follows:

Soprano	Subject _____	etc.
Alto	Subject _____	etc.
Tenor	Subject _____	etc.
Bass	Subject _____	etc.

In this case, the top voice announces the subject and then the lower voices imitate it. However, the subject may be announced by *any* voice—top, bottom, or middle—and the order in which the remaining voices imitate it is also completely flexible.

This may seem reminiscent of a round like *Row, Row, Row Your Boat,* but in a fugue the game of follow the leader (exact imitation of the subject) does not continue indefinitely. The dotted lines in the fugue diagram just given show that *after a voice has presented the subject, it is free to go its own way with different melodic material.* A fugue's opening differs from a round's in another way: in a round, each voice presents the melody on the same tones. If the melody begins with the tones C–D–E, each voice will begin with these tones, whether at a higher or lower register. But in the opening of a fugue, *the subject is presented in two different scales.* The first time, it is based on the notes of the *tonic scale.* But when the second voice presents the subject, it is in the *dominant scale*—five scale steps higher than the tonic—and it is then called the *answer.* A subject beginning with the notes C–D–E, for example, would be imitated by an answer five steps higher, on G–A–B. This alternation of subject and answer between the two scales creates variety.

In many fugues, the subject in one voice is constantly accompanied in another voice by a different melodic idea called a ***countersubject.*** A constant companion, the countersubject always appears with the subject, sometimes below it, sometimes above it.

After the opening of a fugue, when each voice has taken its turn at presenting the subject, a composer is free to decide how often the subject will be presented, in which voices, and in which keys. Between presentations of the subject, there are often transitional sections called ***episodes,*** which offer either new material or fragments of the subject or countersubject. Episodes do *not* present the subject in its entirety. They lend variety to the fugue and make reappearances of the subject sound fresh. Bach called one composer of fugues "pedantic" because he "had not shown enough fire to reanimate the theme by episodes."

Several musical procedures commonly appear in fugues. One is ***stretto,*** in which a subject is imitated before it is completed; one voice tries to catch the other. Another common procedure is *pedal point* (or *organ point*), in which a single tone, usually in the bass, is held while the other voices produce a series of changing harmonies against it. (The term is taken from organ music, where a sustained low tone is produced by the organist's foot on a key of the pedal keyboard.)

A fugue subject can be varied in four principal ways:

1. It can be turned upside down, a procedure known as *inversion.* If the subject moves *upward* by leap, the inversion will move *downward* the same distance; if the subject moves *downward* by step, the inversion will move *upward* by step. In inversion, each interval in the subject is reversed in direction.
2. The subject may be presented *retrograde,* that is, by beginning with the last note of the subject and proceeding backward to the first.
3. The subject may be presented in *augmentation,* in which the original time values are lengthened.
4. The subject may appear in *diminution,* with shortened time values.

Fugues usually convey a single mood and a sense of continuous flow. They may be written as independent works or as single movements within larger compositions. Very often an independent fugue is introduced by a short piece called a *prelude.*

Bach and Handel each wrote hundreds of fugues; their fugues represent the peak among works in the form. In the baroque period, as a friend of Bach's observed, "Skill in fugue was so indispensable in a composer that no one could have attained a musical post who had not worked out a given subject in all kinds of counterpoint and in a regular fugue." Fugal writing has continued into the nineteenth and twentieth centuries. It is not used as frequently today as in the baroque period; yet to this day, musicians study how to write fugues as part of their training.

ORGAN FUGUE IN G MINOR *(LITTLE FUGUE;* ABOUT 1709), BY JOHANN SEBASTIAN BACH

Side 2, band 10
CD 1 64

One of Bach's best-known organ pieces is the *Little Fugue* in G Minor, so called to differentiate it from another, longer fugue in G minor. The opening section of this fugue corresponds to the diagram on page 141. Each of the fugue's four voices takes its turn presenting the tuneful subject, which is announced in the top voice and then appears in progressively lower voices, until it reaches the bass, where it is played by the organist's feet on the pedal keyboard. Like many baroque melodies, the subject gathers momentum as it goes along, beginning with relatively long time values (quarter notes) and then proceeding to shorter ones (eighth and sixteenth notes).

Starting with its second appearance, the subject is accompanied by a counter-subject that moves in short time values.

After the opening section, the subject appears five more times, each time preceded by an episode. The first episode uses both new material and a melodic idea from the countersubject.

This episode contains downward sequences, which are melodic patterns repeated in the same voice but at lower pitches.

For harmonic contrast, Bach twice presents the subject in major keys rather than minor. The final statement of the subject—in minor—exploits the powerful bass tones of the pedal keyboard. Though the fugue is in minor, it ends with a major chord. This was a frequent practice in the baroque period; major chords were thought more conclusive than minor chords.

Listening Outline <small>To be read while music is heard</small>

ORGAN FUGUE IN G MINOR (*LITTLE FUGUE*; 1709?),
BY JOHANN SEBASTIAN BACH

Fugue, quadruple meter ($\frac{4}{4}$), G minor
Organ

(Duration, 4:13)

64	0:00	1. *a.*	Subject, soprano voice alone, minor key.
	0:18	*b.*	Subject in alto, countersubject in running notes in soprano.
	0:41	*c.*	Subject in tenor, countersubject above it.
	0:58	*d.*	Subject in bass (pedals), countersubject in tenor.
65	1:14	*e.*	Brief episode, downward sequence.
	1:24	2. *a.*	Subject begins in tenor, continues in soprano, accompanied by sustained tone in bass; subject leads to
	1:43	*b.*	Brief episode, running notes in a downward sequence.
66	1:52	3. *a.*	Subject in alto, major key; countersubject in soprano; subject leads to
	2:17	*b.*	Episode in major, upward leaps and running notes.
	2:29	*c.*	Subject in bass (pedals), major key, countersubject and long trill above it.
	2:45	*d.*	Longer episode, downward sequence; begins in major, ends in minor.
	3:03	4. *a.*	Subject in soprano, minor key, countersubject below it.
	3:19	*b.*	Most extended episode, running notes in a downward sequence; upward sequences lead to sustained high tones which usher in
	3:49	*c.*	Subject in bass (pedals), countersubject in soprano. Fugue ends with major chord.

BASIC TERMS

fugue (page 140)
subject (140)
answer (141)
countersubject (141)
episode (141)
stretto (141)
pedal point (organ point) (142)
inversion (142)
retrograde (142)
augmentation (142)
diminution (142)
prelude (142)

144

Baroque mainly tragic, MYTHALOGICAL

THE ELEMENTS OF OPERA

The baroque era witnessed the development of a major innovation in music—*opera,* or drama that is sung to orchestral accompaniment. This unique fusion of music, acting, poetry, dance, scenery, and costumes offers a theatrical experience of overwhelming excitement and emotion. Since its beginnings in Italy around 1600, opera has spread to many countries, and even today it remains a powerful form of musical theater. In Section 6, we'll look closely at opera in the baroque period; but first, a general discussion of opera is in order.

An opera's characters and plot are revealed through song, rather than the speech used in ordinary drama. Once we accept this convention, opera offers us great pleasure; its music both delights the ear and heightens the emotional effect of the words and story. Music makes even a complicated plot believable by depicting mood, character, and dramatic action. The flow of the music carries the plot forward. In opera, the music *is* the drama.

Opera demands performers who can sing and act simultaneously. On stage are star solo singers, secondary soloists, a chorus, and sometimes dancers—all in costume. Besides the chorus of professional singers, there may be "supers" (supernumeraries, or "extras"), who don't sing but who carry spears, fill out crowds, drink wine, or do other things that add to the opera's effect. Scenery, lighting, and stage machinery are intricate. They're called upon to create illusions of fires, floods, storms, and supernatural effects. In the orchestra pit are the instrumentalists and the conductor, whose awesome responsibility it is to hold everything together. A large opera's personnel—from conductor to stage director and assorted vocal coaches, rehearsal accompanists, technicians, and stagehands—may reach a startling total of several hundred people.

The capacity of this combined force to create spectacle and pageantry accounts for much of opera's appeal. Historically, opera has been associated with high social status. It originated in the courts of kings and princes (who could afford it) and long continued as a form of aristocratic entertainment. But as opera became more concerned with "real" people and less with royal figures, it attracted popular audiences. Today, radio and television broadcasts, videos, and recordings have changed opera's image as an exotic and expensive diversion for the very rich. Millions of people from every economic background know opera for what it is: a powerful and pleasurable emotional experience.

The creation of an opera results from the joint efforts of a composer and a dramatist. The *libretto,* or text, of the opera is usually written by the *librettist,* or dramatist, and then set to music by the composer. But composers often collaborate with dramatists to ensure that the texts meet their

145

Martti Talvela as Boris in a scene from the Metropolitan Opera production of *Boris Godunov* (1874), by Modest Mussorgsky.

musical needs. W. H. Auden has said that a good libretto "offers as many opportunities as possible for the characters to be swept off their feet by placing them in situations which are too tragic or too fantastic for words. No good opera plot can be sensible, for people do not sing when they are feeling sensible." And that is true—opera characters are people overwhelmed by love, lust, hatred, and revenge. They wear fantastic disguises and commit extraordinary acts of violence. Yet the music makes them human and real. It evokes the haughtiness of a countess or the simplicity of a peasant girl. It creates a dramatic entrance for an outraged father, depicts the tension behind sword thrusts in a duel, and portrays the bleakness of a winter dawn. A great opera composer is a master of musical timing and characterization and has a keen sense of the theater, knowing just when to have a character sing a simple phrase or a soaring melody, when to provide a stirring chorus or a graceful dance. Through the music, the composer paces the drama, controlling the speed of gestures, entrances, exits, and stage movements.

Some operas are serious, some comic, some both. Operas may contain spoken dialogue, but most are sung entirely. (Spoken dialogue is used mainly in comic opera, where stage action must be performed quickly for the most humorous effect.) Since it normally takes longer to sing than to speak words, the text of a 3-hour opera is shorter than that of a 3-hour play. The librettist allows time for the composer's musical elaboration.

The range of characters found in opera is broad and varied; gods, empresses, dukes, servants, priests, prostitutes, peasants, clowns, and cowboys all make appearances. Opera soloists must create all these characters and so need acting skill as well as vocal artistry. During rehearsals, the stage director coaches the singers to move well, gesture meaningfully, and identify with their characters.

The basic voice ranges (soprano, alto, tenor, bass) are divided more finely in opera. Some of the *voice categories of opera* are as follows:

Coloratura soprano	Very high range; can execute rapid scales and trills
Lyric soprano	Rather light voice; sings roles calling for grace and charm
Dramatic soprano	Full, powerful voice; is capable of passionate intensity
Lyric tenor	Relatively light, bright voice
Dramatic tenor	Powerful voice; is capable of heroic expression
Basso buffo	Takes comic roles; can sing very rapidly
Basso profundo	Very low range, powerful voice; takes roles calling for great dignity

[Handwritten annotations: "female" and "Rare" near Coloratura soprano; "Common" near Lyric soprano; "Carries well" near Dramatic soprano; bracket with "Test"]

Like plays, operas have from one to five acts subdivided into scenes. An act presents a variety of vocal and orchestral contrasts. For example, a tenor solo might be followed by a duet for soprano and bass, and then by a chorus or an orchestral interlude. A section may end definitely—and provide an opportunity for applause—or it may be linked with the next section to form a continuous flow of music within an act.

The main attraction for many opera fans is the *aria,* a song for solo voice with orchestral accompaniment. It's an outpouring of melody that expresses an emotional state. In an aria, *I love you* might be sung ten times to accommodate the expansion of the idea. Often the action stops while the character's feelings are revealed through music. An aria usually lasts several minutes. It is a complete piece with a definite beginning, high point, and end. If the performance of an aria is brilliant, the audience responds with an ovation at its conclusion. This breaks the dramatic flow but allows the audience to release its feelings through applause and shouts of *bravo!* or *brava!*

Opera composers often lead into an aria with a *recitative,* a vocal line that imitates the rhythms and pitch fluctuations of speech. In a recitative (from the Italian word for *recite*), words are sung quickly and clearly, often on repeated tones. In a recitative, there's usually only one note to each syllable—as opposed to an aria, where one syllable may be stretched over many notes. Recitative is used for monologues and dialogues that connect the more melodic sections of the opera. It carries the action forward and quickly presents routine information.

Besides arias, the soloists in an opera will sing compositions for two or more singers: duets (for two singers), trios (for three), quartets (for four), quintets (for five), and sextets (for six). When three or more singers are involved, the composition is called an *ensemble.* In a duet or ensemble, the performers either face the audience or move through action that develops the plot. Each character expresses his or her own feelings. Conflicting emotions like grief, happiness, and anger can be projected simultaneously when different melodies are combined. This special blend of feelings is the glory of opera and is possible only through music; it cannot be duplicated in spoken drama.

An opera chorus generates atmosphere and makes comments on the action. Its members might be courtiers, sailors, peasants, prisoners, ballroom guests, and so on. Their sound creates a kind of tonal background for the soloists.

Rising just over the edge of center stage, near the footlights, is the prompter's box. In this cramped space, invisible to the audience, is the *prompter,* who gives cues and reminds the singers of words or pitches if they momentarily forget. Occasional memory lapses are inevitable with so much activity on stage.

Dance in opera is generally incidental. It provides an ornamental interlude that contrasts with and relaxes the thrust of the plot. By and large, dance occurs as part of the opera's setting—in a ballroom, at a country fair, in a pagan court—while the soloists, downstage, advance the action of the plot and work out their destinies.

The nerve center of an opera in performance is the orchestra pit—a sunken area directly in front of the stage. An opera orchestra has the same instruments as a full symphony orchestra, but usually it has a smaller string section. Covered lights attached to the players' music stands leave the orchestra in a deep shadow that doesn't interfere with the audience's view of the stage. The orchestra not only supports the singers but depicts mood and atmosphere and comments on the stage action. During the performance, the conductor shapes the entire work. He or she sets tempos, cues in singers, and indicates subtle dynamic gradations.

Most operas open with a purely orchestral composition called an *overture,* or *prelude.* Since the eighteenth century, the music for an overture has been drawn from material heard later in the opera. The overture is thus a short musical statement that involves the audience in the overall dramatic mood. Orchestral introductions to acts in the opera other than the first are always called *preludes.* We've already discussed one of these, the Prelude to Act III of *Lohengrin,* where Wagner anticipates the wedding of the opera's hero and heroine. Because overtures and preludes, like arias, are complete compositions, they frequently appear on symphony orchestra programs.

Should opera be translated? This question has long aroused controversy, and the battle continues. Most of the best-loved operas are in Italian, German, or French. Champions of translations into English argue that an audience should be able to understand the plot as it develops. Why tell jokes in a comic opera if they can't be understood? On the other hand, a composer takes pains to make a special fusion of pitch and the original words. This results in a tonal color that seems absolutely right. But no matter how well a singer articulates, some words are bound to be lost, whatever the language. For example, a sung melody can stretch one vowel over many notes; it takes a while to get to the end of a word. If the melody is placed in a soprano's highest range, the listener is really aware only of the silvery vowel and not of the word as a whole. Some operas seem to work well in translation; others don't. Much depends on the style of the opera and on the sensitivity of the translator.

In many recent opera productions, a translation of the libretto is projected above the stage. This device—called *supertitles*—has also been a source of controversy. Its advocates consider that it provides the best of both worlds, since it allows an opera to be sung in the original language while the audience is enabled to understand the words. But its opponents feel that it detracts from the music and the action on stage.

Before you attend a live opera performance, in any language and with or without supertitles, it's a good idea to read the libretto or a synopsis of the plot. Even better, watch a video or listen to a recording while following the libretto. This way, you're freer at the performance to appreciate the quality of production and interpretation.

BASIC TERMS

opera (page 145)
libretto (145)
librettist (145)

voice categories
  of opera (147)
aria (147)
recitative (147)

ensemble (148)
prompter (148)
overture (prelude) (148)

OPERA IN THE BAROQUE ERA [BAROQUE **6**]

Opera was born in Italy. Its way was prepared by musical discussions among a small group of nobles, poets, and composers who began to meet regularly in Florence around 1575. This group was known as the *Camerata* (Italian for *fellowship* or *society*) and included the composer Vincenzo Galilei, father of the astronomer Galileo.

The Camerata wanted to create a new vocal style modeled on the music of ancient Greek tragedy. Since no actual dramatic music had come down to them from the Greeks, they based their theories on literary accounts that had survived. It was believed that the Greek dramas had been sung throughout in a style that was midway between melody and speech. The Camerata wanted the vocal line to follow the rhythms and pitch fluctuations of speech. Because it was modeled after speech, the new vocal style became known as *recitative (recited)*. It was sung by a soloist with only a simple chordal accompaniment. The new music was therefore homophonic in texture. Polyphony was rejected by the Camerata because different words sounding simultaneously would obscure the all-important text.

Euridice by Jacopo Peri is the earliest opera that has been preserved. It was composed for the wedding of King Henri IV of France and Marie de' Medici and was performed in Florence in 1600. Seven years later Monteverdi composed *Orfeo*—the first *great* opera—for the court of the Gonzaga family in Mantua. Both these operas are based on the Greek myth of Orpheus's descent into hades to bring back his beloved Eurydice.

Much baroque opera was composed for ceremonial occasions at court and was designed as a display of magnificence and splendor. The subject matter was drawn from Greek mythology and ancient history. Not only were aristocratic patrons of the baroque fascinated by the classical civilizations of Greece and Rome, but they identified with their heroes and divinities. Opera did indeed reflect the creative urge of composer and librettist, but it also was a way to flatter the aristocracy. The radiant appearance of Apollo (god of poetry, music, and the sun) might symbolize a prince's enlightened rule.

In Venice in 1637, the first public opera house opened; now anyone with the price of admission could attend an opera performance. Between 1637 and 1700 there were seventeen opera houses in Venice alone, as well as many in other Italian cities—ample evidence that opera was born in the right place at the right time. Hamburg, Leipzig, and London had public opera houses by the early 1700s, but, on the whole, public opera outside Italy took longer to develop.

Venetian opera became a great tourist attraction. An English traveler wrote in 1645 about the opera and its "variety of scenes painted and contrived with no less art of perspective, and machines for flying in the air, and other wonderful motions; taken together, it is one of the most magnificent and expensive diversions the wit of man can invent." The stage machinery of baroque opera bordered on the colossal; stage effects might include gods descending on clouds or riding across the sky in chariots, ships tossing, boulders splitting. And set design was an art in itself. Painters turned backdrops into cities with arches and avenues that stretched into the distant horizon.

Baroque opera marked the rise of virtuoso singers. Chief among these was the **castrato,** a male singer who had been castrated before puberty. A castrato combined the lung power of a man with the vocal range of a

(Museo Civico di Torino)

Much baroque opera was designed to display magnificent extravagance. Pietro Domenico Olivero's painting of the interior of the Royal Theater, Turin (1740), shows a performance of Francesco Feo's opera *Arsace*.

woman. His agility, breath control, and unique sound (which was not like a woman's) intrigued listeners. Castrati received the highest fees of any musicians. With their soprano or alto vocal ranges, they played male roles such as Caesar and Nero—baroque audiences evidently were more interested in vocal virtuosity than dramatic realism. Some baroque operas cannot be done today, because contemporary singers aren't able to manage the fiendishly difficult castrato parts. (The castration of boy singers was common in Italy from 1600 to 1800; this was usually done with the consent of impoverished parents who hoped their sons would become highly paid opera stars.)

During the late baroque, operas consisted largely of arias that were linked by recitatives. These recitatives were usually accompanied only by a basso continuo, in which case they are called *secco recitatives.* At emotional high points and moments of tension, however, they might be supported by the orchestra; they are then called *accompanied recitatives.*

All action stopped during the aria, when the singer faced the audience, expressed the feelings of the character, and displayed vocal virtuosity. The form of a typical late baroque aria is A B A. An aria in A B A form is called a *da capo aria:* after the B section, the term *da capo* is written; this means *from the beginning* and indicates a repetition of the opening A section. However, the repetition was usually not literal, because the singer was expected to embellish the returning melody with ornaments.

By combining virtuosity, nobility, and extravagance, baroque opera perfectly expressed the spirit of a grand age.

BASIC TERMS

Camerata (page 149)
castrato (plural, castrati) (150)
secco recitative (152)
accompanied recitative (152)
da capo aria (152)
da capo (152)

BAROQUE

7   CLAUDIO MONTEVERDI

Claudio Monteverdi (1567–1643), one of the most important composers of the early baroque era, was born in Cremona, Italy. He served at the court of Mantua for twenty-one years, first as a singer and violist, then as music director. For this court Monteverdi created the earliest operatic masterpiece, *Orfeo (Orpheus,* 1607). Though widely recognized as a leading composer in Mantua, Monteverdi received little pay or respect: "I have never suffered greater humiliation," he wrote, "than when I had to go and beg the treasurer to obtain what was due me."

Life improved for Monteverdi in 1613, when he was appointed music director at St. Mark's in Venice, the most important church position in Italy. He stayed at St. Mark's for thirty years, until his death in 1643. There he composed not only the required sacred music but also secular music for the aristocracy. He wrote operas for San Cassiano in Venice, the first public opera house in Europe. At the age of seventy-five, Monteverdi wrote his last opera, *L'incoronazione di Poppea (The Coronation of Poppea,* 1642).

Monteverdi is a monumental figure in the history of music. His works form a musical bridge between the sixteenth and seventeenth centuries and greatly influenced composers of the time. All his music—madrigals, church music, opera—is for voices, ordinarily supported by a basso continuo and other instruments.

Monteverdi wanted to create music of emotional intensity. He felt that earlier music had conveyed only moderate emotion, and he wanted to extend its range to include agitation, excitement, and passion. To achieve this intensity, he used dissonances with unprecedented freedom and daring. And to evoke the angry or warlike feelings in some of his texts, he introduced new orchestral effects, including pizzicato and tremolo.

[handwritten note: Plucked — quick up and down strokes of Bow]

Monteverdi was the first composer of operatic masterpieces. Only three of the twelve operas he wrote are preserved, but they truly blend music and drama. His vocal lines respond marvelously to the inflections of Italian while maintaining melodic flow.

ORFEO (ORPHEUS, 1607)

Fittingly enough, Monteverdi's first opera is about Orpheus, the supremely gifted musician of Greek myth. Orpheus, son of the god Apollo, is ecstatically happy after his marriage to Eurydice. But this joy is shattered when his bride is killed by a poisonous snake. Orpheus goes down to hades hoping to bring her back to life. Because of his beautiful music, he is granted this privilege—on the condition that he not look back at Eurydice while leading her out of hades. During a moment of anxiety, however, Orpheus does look back, and Eurydice vanishes. Nonetheless, there is a happy ending, of sorts. Apollo pities Orpheus and brings him up to heaven, where he can gaze eternally at Eurydice's radiance in the sun and stars.

Orfeo was composed in 1607 for the Mantuan court, and no expense was spared to make it a lavish production. There were star soloists, a chorus, dancers, and a large orchestra of about forty players. The aristocratic audience was wildly enthusiastic and recognized the historic significance of the performance.

Monteverdi creates variety in *Orfeo* by using many kinds of music—recitatives, arias, duets, choruses, and instrumental interludes. He uses the opera orchestra to establish atmosphere, character, and dramatic situation. With the simplest of musical means, Monteverdi makes his characters come alive. Through vocal line alone he quickly characterizes the hero's joy and despair. Monteverdi sets his text in a very flexible way, freely alternating recitatives with more melodious passages, depending on the meaning of the words.

We'll now consider one well known passage from this opera, Orpheus's recitative *Tu se' morta (You are dead)*.

Act II

Recitative: *Tu se' morta (You are dead)*

Side 2, band 7
CD 1 [56]

Monteverdi's mastery of the then-novel technique of recitative is shown in *Tu se' morta*, sung by Orpheus after he is told of Eurydice's death. Orpheus resolves to bring her back from hades, and he bids an anguished farewell to the earth, sky, and sun. His vocal line is accompanied only by a basso continuo played by a small portable organ and a bass lute. (In modern performances, other instruments are sometimes substituted.)

The texture is homophonic, as the accompaniment simply gives harmonic support to the voice. The vocal line is rhythmically free, with little sense of beat or meter, and its phrases are irregular in length. This flexible setting of text is meant to suggest the passionate speech of an actor declaiming his lines.

Monteverdi frequently uses word painting, the musical representation of poetic images that was favored by baroque composers. For example, words like *stelle* (stars) and *sole* (sun) are sung to climactic high tones, whereas *abissi* (abysses) and *morte* (death) are sung to somber, low tones. Three times during the recitative the melodic line rises to a climax and then descends. Through such simple means, Monteverdi makes Orpheus's passion come alive.

[56]

Tu se' morta, se' morta, mia vita,	You are dead, you are dead, my dearest,
ed io respiro; tu se' da me partita,	And I breathe; you have left me,
se' da me partita per mai più,	You have left me forevermore,
mai più non tornare, ed io rimango—	Never to return, and I remain—
no, no, che se i versi alcuna cosa ponno,	No, no, if my verses have any power,
n'andrò sicuro a' più profondi abissi,	I will go confidently to the deepest abysses,
e, intenerito il cor del re de l'ombre,	And, having melted the heart of the king of shadows,
meco trarotti a riverder le stelle,	Will bring you back to me to see the stars again,
o se ciò negherammi empio destino, rimarrò teco in compagnia di morte.	Or, if pitiless fate denies me this, I will remain with you in the company of death.
Addio terra, addio cielo, e sole, addio.	Farewell earth, farewell sky, and sun, farewell.

HENRY PURCELL

Henry Purcell (about 1659–1695), called the greatest of English composers, was born in London to a musician in the king's service. At about the age of ten, Purcell became a choirboy in the Chapel Royal, and by his late teens his extraordinary talents were winning him important musical positions. In 1677, at about eighteen, he became composer to the king's string orchestra; two years later he was appointed organist of Westminster Abbey; and in 1682, he became an organist of the Chapel Royal. During the last few years of his short life, Purcell was also active composing music for plays.

Acclaimed as *the* English composer of his day, Purcell, who died at 36, was buried beneath the organ in Westminster Abbey. He was the last native English composer of international rank until the twentieth century.

Purcell mastered all the musical forms of late seventeenth-century England. He wrote church music, secular choral music, music for small groups of instruments, songs, and music for the stage. His only true opera is *Dido and Aeneas* (1689), which many consider the finest ever written to an English text. His other dramatic works are spoken plays with musical numbers in the form of overtures, songs, choruses, and dances.

Few composers have equaled Purcell's handling of the English language. His vocal music is faithful to English inflection and brings out the meaning of the text. Purcell developed a melodious recitative that seems to grow out of the English language. His music is filled with lively rhythms and a fresh melodic style that captures the spirit of English folk songs. He treated the chorus with great variety and was able to obtain striking effects through both simple homophonic textures and complex polyphony. His music is spiced with dissonances that seemed harsh to the generation of musicians that followed him. Some of Purcell's finest songs use a variation form found in many baroque works—a ground bass.

GROUND BASS

Often, in baroque works, a musical idea in the bass is repeated over and over while the melodies above it constantly change. The repeated musical idea is called a **ground bass,** or **basso ostinato** (*obstinate* or *persistent bass*). The ground bass pattern may be as short as four notes or as long as eight measures. In this type of variation form, the constant repetition of the bass pattern gives unity, while the free flow of the melodic lines above it results in variety. Composers have used a ground bass in both vocal and instrumental music. We'll hear a ground bass in Purcell's opera *Dido and Aeneas*, as well as in Bach's Mass in B Minor (Section 12).

155

DIDO AND AENEAS (1689)

Dido and Aeneas, a masterpiece of baroque opera, was written for students at a girls' boarding school. The opera lasts only an hour, is scored only for strings and harpsichord continuo, and requires no elaborate stage machinery or virtuoso soloists. Most of its solo roles are for women. Purcell used many dances in this opera, because the director of the school was a dancing master who wanted to display the students' accomplishments. The chorus plays a prominent role, both participating in the action and commenting on it.

The libretto of *Dido and Aeneas*, by Nahum Tate, was inspired by the *Aeneid*, the epic poem by the Roman poet Virgil (70–19 B.C.). The opera's main characters are Dido, queen of Carthage; and Aeneas, king of the defeated Trojans. After the destruction of his native Troy, Aeneas has been ordered by the gods to seek a site for the building of a new city. He sets out on the search with twenty-one ships. After landing at Carthage, a north African seaport, Aeneas falls in love with Dido. A sorceress and two witches see this as an opportunity to plot Dido's downfall. (In Purcell's time, people really believed in witches: nineteen "witches" were hanged in Massachusetts in 1692, three years after *Dido*'s first performance.) A false messenger tells Aeneas that the gods command him to leave Carthage immediately and renew his search. Aeneas agrees but is desolate at the thought of deserting Dido.

In the last act, which takes place at the harbor, Aeneas's sailors sing and dance before leaving, and the witches look on in glee. An emotional scene follows between Aeneas and Dido, who enters with her friend Belinda. Dido calls Aeneas a hypocrite and refuses his offer to stay. After he sails, Dido sings a noble, deeply tragic lament and kills herself. The opera concludes with the mourning of the chorus.

Act III:
Dido's Lament

Side 2, band 8
CD 1 [57]

A melodic recitative accompanied only by the basso continuo sets the sorrowful mood for *Dido's Lament*, the climax of the opera. This aria is built upon a chromatically descending ground bass that is stated eleven times. (Such chromatic ground basses were commonly used to show grief in the baroque period.) As shown in the music example on the opposite page, Dido's melody moves freely above this repeated bass line, creating touching dissonances with it.

Dido's repeated *Remember me* reaches the highest note of the aria and haunts the listener. The emotional tension is sustained in the orchestral conclusion, where a chromatically descending violin melody movingly expresses the tragedy of Dido's fate.

Thy hand, Belinda, darkness shades me,

On thy bosom let me rest;

More I would but Death invades me;

Death is now a welcome guest.

Recitative, descending melody, basso continuo accompanies.

57 0:00

When I am laid, am laid in earth, may my wrongs create

No trouble, no trouble in thy breast.

Remember me! But ah! forget my fate.

Dido's Lament (aria), low strings introduce chromatically descending ground bass.

58 0:56

Upper strings join accompaniment.

Orchestral conclusion, violin melody descends chromatically.

BASIC TERM

ground bass (basso ostinato) (page 155)

9 THE BAROQUE SONATA

Instrumental music gained importance dramatically and rapidly during the baroque period. One of the main developments in instrumental music was the *sonata,* a composition in several movements for one to eight instruments. (In later periods, the term *sonata* took on a more restricted meaning.)

Composers often wrote **trio sonatas,** so called because they had three melodic lines: two high ones and a basso continuo. Yet the word *trio* is misleading, because the "trio" sonata actually involves *four* instrumentalists. There are two high instruments (commonly, violins, flutes, or oboes) and two instruments for the basso continuo—a keyboard instrument (organ or harpsichord) and a low instrument (cello or bassoon).

The sonata originated in Italy but spread to Germany, England, and France during the seventeenth century. Sonatas were played in palaces, in homes, and even in churches—before, during, or after the service. Sometimes composers differentiated between the *sonata da chiesa (church sonata),* which had a dignified character and was suitable for sacred performance, and the *sonata da camera (chamber sonata),* which was more dancelike and was intended for court performance.

BASIC TERMS

sonata (page 158)
trio sonata (158)

10 ARCANGELO CORELLI

The most prominent Italian violinist and composer of string music around 1700 was Arcangelo Corelli (1653–1713). Corelli studied in Bologna but spent most of his adult life in Rome. He was friend and music director to Cardinal Ottoboni, in whose palace he lived. There he mingled with the intellectual and aristocratic elite of Rome.

As a teacher, Corelli instructed some of the most eminent musicians of his time and laid the foundations of modern violin technique. He was one of the first to write double stops and chords for the violin. He was unique among Italian composers of the period in that he wrote only instrumental music: sixty sonatas and twelve concertos, all for strings.

THE BAROQUE PERIOD

Rape of the Sabine Women (1636–1637), by Nicolas Poussin. The French painter Poussin combined dynamic motion with logic and balance.

Adoration of the Magi (1634), by Peter Paul Rubens. Baroque artists became interested in forming a total illusion, like a stage setting. Both baroque painting and baroque opera were often created for the nobility and designed to display magnificent extravagance.

Worship of the Holy Name of Jesus (1670–1683), by Giovanni Battista Gaulli. Baroque painters emphasized grandeur, movement, and drama. This painting of angels, saints, and sinners is a ceiling fresco in the Jesuit church Il Gesù, in Rome. It breaks through its frame and creates the illusion that the spectator is gazing into heaven.

Though little is known about Corelli's personality, he is generally described as gentle and calm. But when he played, he seemed transformed. According to a contemporary report, "Whilst he was playing on the violin it was usual for his countenance to be distorted, his eyes to become as red as fire, and his eyeballs to roll as in an agony."

TRIO SONATA IN E MINOR, OP. 3, NO. 7 (1689)

Corelli's Trio Sonata in E Minor, Op. 3, No. 7, is a fine example of the baroque trio sonata. The basso continuo is for organ and cello; the upper lines are taken by two violins that play in the same high register. The violins are the center of attention; they seem to be rivals, taking turns at the melodic ideas, intertwining, and sometimes rising above each other in pitch. Though the bass line is subordinate to the two upper voices, it is no mere accompaniment. It imitates melodic ideas presented by the violins.

The sonata consists of four short movements: (1) slow, (2) fast, (3) slow, (4) fast. All are in the same key, but they differ in meter, mood, and tempo. Each movement alone, however, has only a single mood, as is typical in baroque instrumental music.

A solemn, dignified slow movement in quadruple meter opens the sonata. The main motive is presented by the first violin and immediately imitated in turn by the other instruments before it has been completed. It's as though one instrument tries to catch the others.

Stretto

Supplementary sets:
Side 2, band 1
CD 1 [34]

The second movement, a vigorous allegro, is fuguelike and written in duple meter. Fugal second movements were characteristic of baroque trio sonatas.

Supplementary sets:
Side 2, band 2
CD 1 [35]

The third movement is songlike and soulful, an adagio in triple meter. The two violins play in a high register until the concluding measures of the movement, when they sustain a single low tone while the cello plays a slow descending scale.

Slow

Supplementary sets:
Side 2, band 3
CD 1 [36]

Supplementary sets:
Side 2, band 4
CD 1 37

The lightest movement of the sonata is the concluding allegro, a dance-like piece in triple meter. This movement is in two-part form, and each part is repeated: A A B B. Section B is almost twice as long as section A. At the end of section B, Corelli uses his only dynamic change in the sonata: the concluding phrase is repeated softly, like an echo.

[BAROQUE **11**] ANTONIO VIVALDI

Antonio Vivaldi (1678–1741), a towering figure of the late Italian baroque, was born in Venice; he was the son of a violinist at St. Mark's Cathedral. Along with his musical training, he prepared for the priesthood. He took holy orders at the age of about twenty-five, but poor health caused him to leave the ministry after a year. Because of his religious background and his red hair, Vivaldi was known as the "red priest" *(il prete rosso)*.

For most of his life, Vivaldi was a violin teacher, composer, and conductor at the music school of the Pietà, an institution for orphaned or illegitimate girls in Venice. Every Sunday and holiday, about forty young women presented a concert of orchestral and vocal music in the chapel. They were placed in a gallery, "hid from any distinct view of those below by a lattice of ironwork." For this all-female group—considered one of the finest orchestras in Italy—Vivaldi composed many of his works. He also wrote for Venetian opera houses and sometimes took leave to visit foreign courts.

Vivaldi was famous and influential as a virtuoso violinist and composer. Bach arranged some of his concertos. Emperor Charles VI, a passionate music lover, was said to have talked longer to Vivaldi "alone in fifteen days, than he talked to his ministers in two years."

But Vivaldi's popularity waned shortly before his death in 1741, and he died in poverty. Although he was acclaimed during his lifetime, he was almost forgotten for 200 years after his death. The baroque revival of the 1950s established his reputation among modern music lovers.

Although Vivaldi composed operas and fine church music, he is best known for his 450 or so concerti grossi and solo concertos. A *solo concerto* is a piece for a *single* soloist and an orchestra. Vivaldi exploited the resources of the violin as well as other instruments. (There are Vivaldi concertos for solo flute, piccolo, cello, bassoon, and even mandolin.) His fast movements feature tuneful themes in vigorous rhythms, and his slow movements have impassioned, lyrical melodies that would be appropriate in an opera aria.

LA PRIMAVERA (SPRING), CONCERTO FOR VIOLIN AND STRING ORCHESTRA, OP. 8, NO. 1, FROM *THE FOUR SEASONS* (1725)

Vivaldi's most popular work is the concerto *La Primavera (Spring)* from *The Four Seasons*, a set of four solo concertos for violin, string orchestra, and basso continuo. Each of these concertos depicts sounds and events associated with one of the seasons, such as the bird songs heard in spring and the gentle breezes characteristic of summer. The descriptive effects in the music correspond to images and ideas found in the sonnets that preface each of the four concertos. To make his intentions absolutely clear, Vivaldi placed lines from the poems at the appropriate passages in the musical score and even added such descriptive labels as *sleeping goatherd* and *barking dog*. The *Spring, Summer, Autumn,* and *Winter* concertos are examples of baroque *program music*, or instrumental music associated with a story, poem, idea, or scene. They are forerunners of the more elaborate program music that developed during the romantic period.

The *Spring* Concerto was as popular in Vivaldi's time as it is in ours and was a special favorite of Louis XV, king of France. Once, when the violinist Guignon gave a concert at the court, the king asked for *Spring* as an encore. This posed a problem, since the king's orchestra was not present. Rising to the occasion, a group of nobles at the court volunteered to accompany the violin soloist. A Paris newspaper reported that "this beautiful piece of music was performed perfectly."

Like most of Vivaldi's concertos, *Spring* has three movements: (1) fast, (2) slow, (3) fast. Both the first and last movements are in ritornello form.

Typical of baroque Concertos

First Movement:
Allegro

Spring has come, and joyfully,
The birds greet it with happy song.
And the streams, fanned by gentle breezes,
Flow along with a sweet murmur.
Covering the sky with a black cloak,
Thunder and lightning come to announce the season.
When these have quieted down, the little birds
Return to their enchanting song.

The allegro, in E major, opens with an energetic orchestral ritornello depicting the arrival of spring. Each of the ritornello's two phrases is played loudly and then repeated softly, in the terraced dynamics typical of baroque music. After the ritornello, the movement alternates between ex-

Side 2, band 9
CD 1 59

not decrescendo crescendo

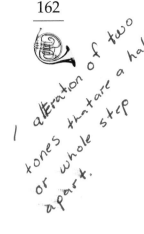

[handwritten margin note:] alteration of two tones that are a half or whole step apart.

tended solo sections containing musical tone painting and brief tutti sections presenting part of the ritornello theme. In the first solo section, bird songs are imitated by high trills and repeated notes played by the violin soloist and two violins from the orchestra. In the second descriptive episode, murmuring streams are suggested by soft running notes in the violins. The next solo section contains string tremolos and rapid scales representing thunder and lightning. Following the storm, the ritornello appears in minor instead of in major. All the pictorial passages in this movement provide contrasts of texture and dynamics between returns of the ritornello theme. The allegro's tunefulness, rhythmic vitality, and light, homophonic texture evoke the feeling of springtime.

[handwritten:] *MODULATION

[handwritten:] //rapidly repeats tones by quick up and down strokes of the bow.

Listening Outline   To be read while music is heard

LA PRIMAVERA (SPRING),
CONCERTO FOR VIOLIN AND STRING ORCHESTRA, OP. 8, NO. 1,
FROM *THE FOUR SEASONS* (1725), BY ANTONIO VIVALDI

First Movement: Allegro

Ritornello form, quadruple meter ($\frac{4}{4}$), E major

Solo violin, string orchestra, harpsichord (basso continuo)

(Duration, 3:15)

Spring
has come
59 0:00   1. *a.* Tutti, ritornello opening phrase, *f,* repeated p

closing phrase, *f,* repeated *p,* major key.

Song of
the birds
60 0:30   *b.* Solo violin joined by two violins from orchestra, high trills and repeated notes.

1:03 Murmuring streams	2. *a.* Tutti, ritornello closing phrase, *f.*
[61] 1:10	*b.* Violins, *p*, running notes, cellos, *p*, running notes below sustained tones in violins.
1:33 Thunder and lightning	3. *a.* Tutti, ritornello closing phrase, *f.*
[62] 1:40	*b.* String tremolos, *f*, upward rushing scales introduce high solo violin, brilliant virtuoso passages answered by low string tremolos.
2:06 Song of the birds	4. *a.* Tutti, ritornello closing phrase in minor key, *f.*
[63] 2:13	*b.* Solo violin joined by two violins from orchestra, high repeated notes and trills, minor key.
2:30	5. *a.* Tutti, ritornello opening phrase varied, *f*, ends in major key.
2:40	*b.* Solo violin, running notes accompanied by basso continuo.
2:54	6. Tutti, ritornello closing phrase, *f*, repeated *p*, major key.

Second Movement:

Largo e pianissimo sempre (very slow and very soft throughout)

And then, on a pleasant meadow covered with flowers,
Lulled by the soft murmuring of leaves and branches,
The goatherd sleeps, his faithful dog at his side.

The peaceful slow movement, in C sharp minor, is much quieter than the energetic opening movement. It uses only the solo violin and the orchestral violins and violas, omitting the cellos, basses, and harpsichord. A tender, expansive melody for the solo violin depicts the goatherd's slumber, while a soft, rocking figure in the violins suggests the rustling of leaves. The violas imitate the barking of the goatherd's "faithful dog" with a repeated-note figure in short-long rhythm. The tranquillity of this pastoral scene is evoked by the movement's unchanging texture, rhythm, and dynamic level.

Supplementary sets:
Side 2, band 5
CD 1 [38]

Third Movement:

Danza pastorale (Pastoral Dance)

To the festive sounds of country bagpipes,
Dance nymphs and shepherds in their beloved fields,
When spring appears in all its brilliance.

Like the first movement, the concluding *Danza pastorale (Pastoral Dance)*, in E major, alternates between tutti and solo sections. The playful ritornello theme, with its dotted rhythms, suggests nymphs and shepherds dancing

Supplementary sets:
Side 2, band 6
CD 1 [39]

in the fields. Sustained tones in the lower strings imitate the drone of country bagpipes. The sections for solo violin contain brilliant passages with many melodic sequences, which are typical of baroque style.

The following outline will clarify the movement's ritornello form:

39 0:00

0:27

0:49

1:18

1:48

2:11

2:43

3:07

1. *a.* Tutti, ritornello, lilting melody in major.
    b. Solo violin accompanied by basso continuo.
2. *a.* Tutti, varied ritornello in minor.
    b. Solo violin joined by violin from orchestra, major.
    c. Solo violin, staccato, accompanied by violins, faster rhythms.
3. *a.* Tutti, ritornello, major, varied in minor.
    b. Solo violin accompanied by sustained tone in cellos and basses, minor.
4. Tutti, ritornello in major.

BAROQUE 12 JOHANN SEBASTIAN BACH

The masterpieces of Johann Sebastian Bach (1685–1750) mark the high point of baroque music. Bach came from a long line of musicians: his father, grandfather, and great-grandfather were all church organists or town musicians in Germany. In fact, so many members of the family were musicians that the name *Bach* became synonymous with *town musician*. Annual family gatherings might assemble over a hundred Bachs to celebrate and make music. Johann Sebastian Bach passed on this musical heritage—he was father to twenty children, of whom nine survived him and four became well-known composers.

In Eisenach, his birthplace, Bach probably received his first musical training from his father, the town musician; and his cousin, the church organist. But when he was nine, both his parents died and Johann went to live with his oldest brother, the organist in a nearby town. At fifteen, Bach left his brother's crowded home and moved to yet another town, where he went to school and supported himself by singing in the church choir and playing the organ and violin. By this time his love of music was so great that he would walk up to thirty miles to hear a famous organist.

When he was eighteen, Bach became church organist in Arnstadt, a town not far from his birthplace. Here he came into conflict with church authorities, because they felt that his music was too complicated; they also questioned his meeting "a strange maiden" in the empty church to accompany her singing. Bach resolved both issues when he was twenty-three by finding a better position at Mühlhausen and by marrying the "strange maiden," his cousin Barbara. His reputation as an organist was growing steadily through his virtuoso performances, which included improvising elaborate fugues and, reportedly, playing with his feet (on the pedal keyboard) better than many performers could with their fingers.

After these two jobs as church organist, Bach obtained a more important post in 1708 as court organist in Weimar. He stayed there for nine years, becoming concertmaster of the court orchestra, but decided to leave when he was passed over for promotion. The duke of Weimar was so annoyed at Bach's obstinacy in requesting dismissal that he put him in jail for a month. (Such was the power of a minor German aristocrat!) But all his life Bach kept demanding his rights, never fearing controversy.

Bach's most lucrative and prestigious post was as court conductor for the prince of Cöthen. His salary equaled that of the marshal of the court, the second highest official. But more important, this was the first time in Bach's career that he was not involved with church or organ music. The prince belonged to the Reformed (Calvinistic) church, where only simple psalm singing was permitted in the service. For the six years from 1717 to 1723, Bach directed the prince's small orchestra of about eighteen players and composed music for it. The *Brandenburg* Concertos grew out of this productive period.

In 1720, Bach's wife died, leaving him with four young children. The next year, at thirty-six, he married a twenty-one-year-old singer at the court of Cöthen, and the second marriage was apparently as happy as the first.

Because he was an ardent amateur musician, the prince of Cöthen treated Bach as a friend. However, the prince's interest began to wane when he married a young princess who did not like music, and Bach decided to look for a new job.

He found one in 1723: the position of cantor (director of music) of St. Thomas Church in Leipzig, a position that involved responsibility for the four main municipal churches. Bach remained here for the last twenty-seven years of his life. Though one of the most important church posts in Germany, the position carried less prestige and paid less than the one with the prince of Cöthen. But Bach probably was interested because it was in Leipzig, a comparatively large city of 30,000, where his children could receive a good Lutheran education and go to the university. Then, too, Bach was a deeply religious man. At the beginning of each sacred composition he wrote the letters *J.J.*, for *Jesu Juva (Jesus help)*, and at the end he put *S.D.G.*, for *Soli Deo Gloria (to God alone the glory)*.

(Barenreiter Bild-Archiv)

Though recognized as the most eminent organist, harpsichordist, improviser, and master of fugue, Bach was by no means considered the greatest composer of his day; his music was largely forgotten and remained unpublished for years after his death.

At Leipzig, Bach rehearsed, conducted, and usually composed an extended composition for chorus, soloists, and orchestra for each Sunday and holiday of the church year. He was responsible for the musical education of some fifty-five students in the St. Thomas school. After some years in Leipzig he became director of the Leipzig Collegium Musicum, a student organization that gave concerts every Friday night at a coffeehouse. He was also an eminent teacher of organ and composition, gave organ recitals, and was often asked to judge the construction of organs. It's hard to imagine how he did all this while surrounded by children, relatives, and students—and living in the school building next to a classroom.

During the 1740s, Bach's eyesight deteriorated, yet he continued to compose, conduct, and teach. In 1750, the year of his death, Bach became completely blind.

Though recognized as the most eminent organist, harpsichordist, improviser, and master of fugue, Bach was by no means considered the greatest composer of his day. He was little known outside Germany, and even his Leipzig post was offered to him only after two other noted musicians had turned it down. By the time of Bach's maturity, the baroque style had begun to go out of fashion; people wanted light, uncomplicated music. Many thought his works too heavy, complex, and polyphonic.

Bach's music was largely forgotten and remained unpublished for years after his death. But a few composers of the generations following knew some of his compositions and were aware of his genius. In 1829, Felix Mendelssohn presented the *St. Matthew Passion,* and Bach's music has been the daily bread of every serious musician since then.

BACH'S MUSIC

Bach created masterpieces in every baroque form except opera. Throughout, he fused technical mastery and emotional depth. His instrumental music includes pieces for orchestra, for small groups, and for solo organ, harpsichord, clavichord, violin, and cello. The excellence and number of these works show how prominent instrumental music had become in the baroque period. Bach's vocal music—the bulk of his output—was written mostly for the Lutheran church and was often based on hymns familiar to the congregation.

In forming his personal style, Bach drew on the musical resources of three different lands. He avidly studied Italian concertos and French dance pieces, as well as the church music of his native Germany.

Bach's music is unique in its combination of polyphonic texture and rich harmony. Several melodic lines of equal importance often occur at once; and so many things might go on at the same time that the music will convey an awesome complexity and elaboration. Yet even with the great interest that the individual voices convey, it is the progression of chords that directs the musical motion. Bach used complex and dissonant harmonies more imaginatively than his contemporaries. His works show an astounding mastery of harmony and counterpoint, and they are used as models by music students today.

Baroque music leans toward unity of mood, and this is particularly true of Bach, who liked to elaborate a single melodic idea in a piece. Bach's melodies can be intricate, unpredictable, and highly embellished, but unity of mood is created by an insistent rhythmic drive. Whether slow or fast, Bach's works generate perpetual motion.

By Bach's time there was little difference in style between secular and sacred music. In fact, he often created sacred music simply by rearranging instrumental pieces or works originally written for secular texts. His church music also uses operatic forms like the aria and recitative.

Bach liked to illustrate religious or pictorial ideas through musical symbolism. In an organ piece based upon the hymn tune *Durch Adams Fall (Through Adam's Fall)*, Bach represents the serpent by twisting inner voices, and man's fall by downward leaps in the bass. And in one called *These Are the Holy Commandments*, Bach uses the theme exactly ten times.

Sometimes Bach composed music to demonstrate what he could do with a specific musical form. His *Art of the Fugue*, for example, is a collection which displays all the resources of fugue writing. He also explored with unprecedented thoroughness a system of tuning that was being developed at the time. This system made it possible for a composer to write in all twenty-four keys, not just in the simple ones. Bach used every major and minor key in his collection of forty-eight preludes and fugues, *The Well-Tempered Clavier* (which means, roughly, *The Well-Tuned Keyboard Instrument)*. The collection is in two volumes (1722, 1744), each with twenty-four preludes and fugues, one in each major and minor key. Today, the pieces are basic to the repertoire of keyboard players.

BRANDENBURG CONCERTO NO. 5 IN D MAJOR (1721)

Second Movement:
Affettuoso (affectionately, tenderly)

Side 3, band 2
CD 2 [6]

We have already examined the opening movement (allegro) of the Fifth *Brandenburg* Concerto in Section 3, "The Concerto Grosso and Ritornello Form." Here we'll study the two remaining movements of this concerto grosso for flute, violin, harpsichord, and orchestra.

The affettuoso is in marked contrast to the vigorous opening movement; it's slow, in a minor key, and much quieter. It uses only the three solo instruments and a cello, which duplicates the bass line (left hand) of the harpsichordist. The harpsichord has both an accompanying and a solo role in the movement. Sometimes, as at the beginning, it serves merely as a basso continuo accompaniment to a duet between the violin and flute. In these sections, there is no notated part for the right hand; the harpsichordist is expected to improvise chords as guided by Bach's figured bass. (In modern performing editions, the editor supplies these chords for the player.) In other sections, Bach gives the harpsichordist's right hand a melody of its own, and the instrument becomes a center of attention.

The affettuoso projects a single, rather serious mood throughout and is woven entirely from two brief motives that are constantly passed among the instruments. Bach creates melodic variety by turning his motives upside down. The following example shows the two motives, marked *a* and *b,* and their inversions:

Third Movement:

Allegro

The concluding allegro is dancelike in character. It is in A B A form; the A sections are in major, and the B section is in minor. The movement begins like a fugue, with a rollicking subject introduced by the solo violin and then imitated by the flute and harpsichord.

Side 3, band 3
CD 2 [7]
Section A
[7] 0:00

After a while, the instruments of the tutti—not heard since the opening movement—join in playing the subject.

The middle section, in minor, begins softly with a lyrical melody for the flute.

Section B
[8] 1:16

This melody starts like the main subject but contains long notes, which

Imitation

give it a songlike character. After the flute, the violin and harpsichord take turns playing this melody. The main subject also has a prominent role throughout the middle section and can be heard in a harpsichord solo. Bach achieves both unity and variety by combining within the middle section the main subject and the new lyrical melody related to it.

Return of section A
9   3:44

A loud tutti signals the conclusion of the middle section. Then the solo violin, imitated by the flute, announces the return of the opening section A. The major key and lively rhythms seem even more joyful after the minor key and reflective quality of the middle section.

MASS IN B MINOR (BEGUN 1733)

Over a period of years, Bach, a pious Lutheran, composed what is probably the most monumental setting of the Roman Catholic mass. In 1733, he wrote the first two sections (the Kyrie and Gloria) and sent them to a Catholic monarch with a request for the honorary title of court composer. Years later, he finished the mass by composing new music and by fitting the Latin text to some of his earlier Lutheran church pieces. Bach probably never heard the entire work performed. Since it is far too long to be used in the Catholic service, Bach's reasons for creating it are unknown. He may simply have wanted to show what he could do with this ancient and imposing form.

Bach's B Minor Mass contrasts strikingly with the Renaissance mass studied in Part III. It has specific orchestral accompaniments for the voices. And each major section of the mass—such as the Kyrie or Credo—is subdivided into arias, duets, and choruses. Thus this mass has more variety within each large section than a Renaissance mass has in its sections. Each part of Bach's B Minor Mass expresses the meaning and emotion of the text.

Let us explore two contrasting movements from the Credo: the *Crucifixus*, a profound expression of grief at Christ's crucifixion, and *Et resurrexit*, which expresses joy at Christ's resurrection.

Crucifixus

Crucifixus etiam pro nobis sub Pontio Pilato, passus et sepultus est.

And was crucified also for us under Pontius Pilate. He suffered and was buried.

Supplementary sets:
Side 2, band 7
CD 1   40

The *Crucifixus* is scored for four voice parts and a small orchestra of strings, two flutes, and continuo. (In our recording, the voice parts are sung by four soloists.) It is built upon a chromatically descending ground bass, or basso ostinato, the traditional symbol of grief in baroque music (you heard one in *Dido's Lament*, by Purcell).

Over the constantly repeating ground bass, the soprano, alto, tenor, and bass sing ever-changing melodic lines that produce dissonant harmonies. Minor key, slow tempo, and hushed dynamics—together with the generally downward-moving melodies—contribute to a feeling of infinite sorrow. One particularly sublime moment occurs at the very end of this movement, when there is an unexpected shift from minor to major and the sopranos descend chromatically to their lowest tone. At this point of deepest sorrow, the major key implies hope.

Et Resurrexit

Et resurrexit tertia die secundum scripturas. Et ascendit in coelum, sedet ad dexteram Dei Patris, et iterum venturus est cum gloria judicare vivos et mortuos, cujus regni non erit finis.

And the third day he rose again according to the scriptures. And ascended into Heaven. And sitteth at the right hand of God the Father. And he shall come again with glory to judge both the living and the dead; whose kingdom shall have no end.

The jubilant *Et resurrexit* fulfills the hope implied in the *Crucifixus*. Now Bach uses a chorus and full orchestra, including three trumpets, timpani, and two oboes. The movement is in major; a fast tempo and bright-sounding trumpets make it festive. Typically baroque is the rising melodic line on the words *Et resurrexit (and he rose).*

Supplementary sets:
Side 2, band 8
CD 1 41

Variety is achieved through repeated alternations between orchestral sections and those using voices and instruments.

[13] THE BAROQUE SUITE

Instrumental music has always been closely linked with dancing; in the past, much of it was written for use in palace ballrooms. During the Renaissance, dances often came in pairs—a dignified dance in quadruple meter was often followed by a lively one in triple meter. In the baroque period and later, music was written that—while meant for listening, not dancing—was related to specific dance types in tempo, meter, and rhythm.

Baroque composers wrote *suites,* which are sets of dance-inspired movements. Whether for solo instruments, small groups, or orchestra, a baroque suite is made up of movements that are all written in the same key but differ in tempo, meter, and character. The dancelike movements also have a variety of national origins: the moderately paced *allemande* (from Germany) might be followed by a fast *courante* and a moderate *gavotte* (from France), a slow and solemn *sarabande* (from Spain), and a fast *gigue* (jig, from England and Ireland). Suites were played in private homes, at court concerts, or as background music for dinner and outdoor festivities.

Dance pieces have a diverse past. Some began as folk dances, while others sprang from aristocratic ballrooms. Even the character of a dance might show dramatic evolution. The slow, solemn sarabande grew out of a sexually suggestive song and dance that a sixteenth-century moralist condemned as "so lascivious in its words, so ugly in its movements, that it is enough to inflame even very honest people." In the seventeenth century, however, the sarabande became respectable enough to be danced by a cardinal at the French court.

The movements of a suite are usually in two-part form with each section repeated; that is, in the form A A B B. The A section, which opens in the tonic key and modulates to the dominant, is balanced by the B section, which begins in the dominant and returns to the tonic key. Both sections use the same thematic material, and so they contrast relatively little except in key.

Suites frequently begin with a movement that is *not* dance-inspired. One common opening is the French overture, which is also the type of piece heard at the beginning of baroque oratorios and operas. Usually written in two parts, the *French overture* first presents a slow section with dotted rhythms that is full of dignity and grandeur. The second section is quick and lighter in mood, often beginning like a fugue. Sometimes part of the opening section will return at the end of the overture.

The suite was an important instrumental form in the baroque. Even compositions not called "suite" often have several dance-inspired movements.

172

Music influenced by dance tends to have balanced and symmetrical phrases of the same length, because formal dancing has a set of steps in one direction symmetrically balanced by a similar motion in the opposite direction.

Bach wrote four suites for orchestra. We don't know exactly when they were composed, but it seems likely that the Collegium Musicum performed them in a Leipzig coffeehouse.

SUITE NO. 3 IN D MAJOR (1729–1731), BY JOHANN SEBASTIAN BACH

2 oboes, 3 trumpets, timpani, strings, basso continuo
First Movement: Overture

The suite opens with a majestic French overture, which exploits the bright sounds of trumpets. After a slow opening section with dotted rhythms, we hear the energetic fast section. This begins like a fugue, with an upward-moving theme introduced by the first violins and then imitated by the other instruments.

The fast section is like a concerto grosso in its alternation of solid tutti passages with lightly scored ones highlighting the first violins. After the fast section, the slow tempo, dotted rhythms, and majestic mood of the opening return.

Second Movement: Air

The second movement, the air, contains one of Bach's best-loved melodies. It is scored for only strings and continuo and is serene and lyrical, in contrast to the majestic and bustling French overture. The title suggests that the movement is written in the style of an Italian aria. Like the opening movement, the air is not related to dance. In its A A B B form, the B section is twice as long as the A section. The air combines a steadily moving bass (which proceeds in upward and downward octave leaps) with a rhapsodic and rhythmically irregular melody in the violins.

Side 4, band 1
CD 2 [17]
Section A
[17] 0:00
Section B
[18] 1:32

Third Movement: Gavotte

All the movements that follow the overture and the air are inspired by dance, beginning with the gavotte, which is written in duple meter and in a moderate tempo and uses the full orchestra again. It may be outlined as follows: gavotte I (A A B B); gavotte II (C C D D); gavotte I (A B). Notice the contrast between the sections for full orchestra and those without trumpets and timpani.

Fourth Movement: Bourrée

Side 4, band 2
CD 2 [19]
Section A
[19] 0:00
Section B
[20] 0:17

The bourrée is an even livelier dance, also in duple meter. Its form is A A B B, and it is the shortest movement of the suite. Section A employs the full orchestra, including trumpets and timpani. Section B is three times as long as section A and alternates loud tutti passages with softer ones for strings and oboes.

Fifth Movement: Gigue

Side 4, band 3
CD 2 [21]
Section A
[21] 0:00
Section B
[22] 0:55

The suite concludes with a rollicking gigue in $\frac{6}{8}$ time, which is also in the form A A B B. Here, Bach's manner is simple and direct. Listen for the splendid effect when timpani and trumpets periodically join the rest of the orchestra.

BASIC TERMS

suite (page 172)
French overture (172)

[14] THE CHORALE AND CHURCH CANTATA

BAROQUE

In Leipzig in Bach's time, the Lutheran church service on Sunday was the social event of the week: it started at seven in the morning and lasted about 4 hours. The sermon alone could take an hour.

Music was a significant part of the Lutheran service. While most religious services today use no more than a chorus and organ, Bach's church had a small orchestra of between fourteen and twenty-one players to accompany the twelve or so men and boys of the choir. The service was filled with music; single compositions might last half an hour.

To further the direct communication that Lutheranism stressed between the believer and Christ, the rite was largely in the vernacular—German. Each service included several hymns, or chorales. The *chorale,* or hymn tune, was sung to a German religious text. Chorales were easy to sing and remember, having only one note to a syllable and moving in steady rhythm. They were tunes that had been composed in the sixteenth and seventeenth centuries or had been adapted from folk songs and Catholic hymns. The members of the congregation had sung these tunes since childhood, and each tune carried religious associations. Congregational

(Bettmann Archive)

Music was a significant part of the Lutheran church service in Germany during the baroque period. This engraving shows a performance of a cantata in Bach's time.

singing of chorales was an important way for people to participate directly in the service. These melodies were often harmonized for church choirs. The hymn melody was sung in the top part, and the tones of the supporting harmonies were sung in the three lower parts.

New church music was often based on traditional melodies written as far back as two centuries earlier. Before the congregation began to sing a hymn, the organist might play a *chorale prelude,* a short composition based on the hymn tune that reminded the congregation of the hymn's melody. By using traditional tunes in their works, composers could involve the congregation and enhance the religious associations.

THE CHURCH CANTATA

The principal means of musical expression in the Lutheran service, and one which employed chorales, was the church *cantata. Cantata* originally meant a piece that was *sung,* as distinct from a sonata, which was *played.* Many kinds of cantatas were being written in Bach's day, but we shall focus only on the cantata designed for the Lutheran service in Germany in the early 1700s. It was usually written for chorus, vocal soloists, organ, and a small orchestra. It had a German religious text, either newly written or drawn from the Bible or familiar hymns. In the Lutheran services, there were different Gospel and Epistle readings for each Sunday and holiday, and the cantata text was related to them. In a sense, the cantata was a sermon in music which reinforced the minister's sermon, also based on the Gospel and Epistle readings. The cantata of Bach's day might last 25 minutes and include several different movements—choruses, recitatives, arias, and duets. You'll see that in its use of aria, duet, and recitative, the cantata closely resembled the opera of the time and thus is typical of the baroque fusion of sacred and secular elements in art and music.

The cantor, or music director, had to provide church cantatas for every Sunday and holiday. Bach wrote about 295; about 195 are still in existence. In his first few years as cantor in Leipzig, he composed cantatas at the staggering rate of almost three a month. During the remaining twenty-five years of his tenure, he was inclined to reuse cantatas, and so his output dropped.

CANTATA NO. 140: *WACHET AUF, RUFT UNS DIE STIMME (AWAKE, A VOICE IS CALLING US;* 1731), BY JOHANN SEBASTIAN BACH

Wachet auf, ruft uns die Stimme (Cantata No. 140) is Bach's best-known cantata. To fully appreciate it, we perhaps should imagine ourselves as pious Lutherans of his time. It was composed for the twenty-seventh Sunday after Trinity Sunday, when the Gospel reading was the parable of the wise and foolish virgins (Mathew, 25). The Christian believers are represented by virgins, and Christ by the bridegroom:

> Then shall the kingdom of heaven be likened unto ten virgins, which took their lamps and went forth to meet the bridegroom. And five of them were wise, and five were foolish. . . . And at midnight there was a cry made, Behold the bridegroom cometh; go ye out to meet him. Then all those virgins arose, and trimmed their lamps. And the foolish said unto the wise, Give us of your oil; for our lamps are gone out. But the wise answered, saying, Not so; lest there not be enough for us and you: but go ye rather to them that sell, and buy for yourselves. While they were away the bridegroom arrived; and those who were ready went in with him to the wedding; and the door was shut. . . . Keep awake then; for you never know the day or the hour. . . .

Bach based his cantata on the chorale tune *Wachet auf,* because its text was inspired by the Gospel for this particular Sunday. The text and melody of the chorale had been written by Philipp Nicolai (1556–1608) in about 1597—over 130 years before Bach used it. This was a widely known chorale tune that had been used by other composers before Bach. The hymn has three stanzas, and all are sung to the same melody. Bach used the chorale melody and text in three of the seven movements in the cantata:

Movement	Use of Chorale	Content of Text
1. Chorus with orchestra.	Chorale, stanza 1	Virgins awakened by the watchmen announcing the coming of the bridegroom.
2. Recitative for solo tenor with continuo.		The bridegroom is coming.
3. Duet for soprano and bass with violino piccolo and continuo.		Dialogue between a longing soul (soprano) and Jesus (bass).
4. Tenors of chorus sing chorale in unison; strings and continuo.	Chorale, stanza 2	Zion (Christian believers) rejoices at the arrival of Lord Jesus, God's son.
5. Recitative for bass, accompanied by strings and continuo.		Jesus lovingly greets the bride.
6. Duet for soprano and bass with oboe and continuo.		Joyous union between Christ (bass) and Christian (soprano).
7. Chorus doubled by orchestra.	Chorale, stanza 3	Christians praise God and rejoice in union with him.

Last movement:
Side 3, band 6
CD 2 16

According to a Protestant theologian and music scholar, the chorale text interprets the relationship of the bridegroom and bride "as a picture of the union of God with his people, of Christ with the Church." The other texts of Cantata No. 140, for duets and recitatives, were written by an unknown author and depict "the relationship between Jesus and the pious individual soul." They are based on the Song of Songs (or Song of Solomon) in the Bible.

Before listening to all of Cantata No. 140, it's helpful to become acquainted with the chorale tune, which the last movement presents unadorned. The melody has the form A A B.

There are nine melodic phrases, of which the first three (which make up the A section) are repeated immediately. The last phrase of the A section (phrase 3) reappears at the end of the B section (phrase 9) and beautifully rounds off the chorale melody.

Now let's consider movements 1 and 4–7.

First Movement: Chorus and Orchestra

2 oboes, English horn, French horn, 1st violins, 2d violins, violas, basso continuo (organ, bassoon, cello)

In the chorale text of the first movement, watchmen on the towers of Jeru- Side 3, band 4 CD 2 [10] salem call on the wise virgins (Christians) to awake because the bridegroom (Christ) is coming. The movement opens with an orchestral ritornello that may have been intended to suggest a procession or march. As shown in the music example which follows, there are dotted rhythms (long-short, long-short), a rising figure with syncopation, and a series of rising scales.

At the ritornello's closing cadence the sopranos enter and sing the first phrase of the chorale in long notes. Soon the three lower voices engage in an imitative dialogue based on a new motive in shorter note values. Throughout, the orchestra continues to play still shorter notes.

179

Thus there are three layers of sound: the chorale phrases in long notes in the soprano; the imitative dialogue in shorter note values in the three lower voices; and the ever-busy orchestra playing motives from the ritornello in even shorter notes. The chorale tune (in the soprano) is presented not as a continuous whole but rather phrase by phrase, with breaks between. After each phrase, the voices pause while the orchestra continues to play interludes made up of either the whole ritornello or sections from it. Sometimes the motives in the three lower voices illustrate the text, as when they have rising scale figures at the word *hoch (high)* and exclamations at the repeated *wo (where)*.

Once during the movement, the three lower voices become emancipated from the soprano and jubilantly sing a melody in rapid notes on *Alleluja*. This, perhaps, is the most exciting moment in the movement.

[10] 0:00			Orchestral ritornello.
[11] 0:28	*Wachet auf, ruft uns die Stimme*	"Awake," the voice of watchmen	
			Brief orchestral interlude.
0:50	*der Wächter sehr hoch auf der Zinne*	calls us from high on the tower,	Rising scales in lower voices depict *hoch (high)*.
			Brief orchestral interlude.
	wach auf, du Stadt Jerusalem!	"Awake, you city of Jerusalem!"	
1:36			Orchestral ritornello.
2:01	*Mitternacht heisst diese Stunde;*	Midnight is this very hour;	
			Brief orchestral interlude.
	sie rufen uns mit hellem Munde:	they call to us with bright voices:	

		Brief orchestral interlude.	
wo seid ihr klugen Jungfrauen?	"Where are you, wise virgins?"		
		Long orchestral interlude.	3:07
Wohl auf, der Bräut'gam kömmt,	Take cheer, the Bridegroom comes,		
		Brief orchestral interlude.	
steht auf, die Lampen nehmt!	arise, take up your lamps!		
Alleluja!	Hallelujah!	Altos, jubilant melody in rapid notes. Imitation by tenors, then basses.	12 4:00
Alleluja!	Hallelujah!	Sopranos, chorale in long notes.	4:26
		Orchestral interlude.	
Macht euch bereit	Prepare yourselves		
		Orchestral interlude.	
zu der Hochzeit	for the wedding,		
		Brief orchestral interlude.	
ihr müsset ihm entgegen gehn.	you must go forth to meet him.		
		Orchestral ritornello.	5:36

Fourth Movement: Tenor Chorale
Violins and violas in unison, basso continuo

Side 3, band 5
CD 2 13

The chorale tune returns in the fourth movement, the most popular of the cantata. Bach liked this section so much that toward the end of his life he rearranged it as a chorale prelude for organ. With miraculous ease, he sets two contrasting melodies against each other. First we hear the unison strings supported by the continuo playing the ritornello, a warm, flowing melody that Bach may have intended as a dancelike procession of the maidens as they "all follow to the joyful hall and share in the Lord's supper." This melody is repeated and varied throughout while the tenors sing the chorale tune against it.

Zi - on hört die Wäch - ter sin - gen

das Herz tut ihr vor Freu - den sprin - gen,

The chorale tune moves in faster rhythmic values than it did in the opening movement, but here, too, it is broken into component phrases linked by the instrumental melody. It's helpful to listen several times to this movement, first focusing on the rapid rhythms of the graceful string melody, then on the sturdy, slower rhythms of the chorale tune, and finally on all lines at once.

13	0:00			String ritornello.
14	0:39	*Zion hört die Wächter singen,*	Zion hears the watchmen singing,	
		das Herz tut ihr vor Freuden springen,	for joy her very heart is springing,	
		sie wachet und steht eilend auf.	she wakes and rises hastily.	
				Ritornello.
	1:45	*Ihr Freund kommt von Himmel prächtig,*	From heaven comes her friend resplendent,	
		von Gnaden stark, von Wahrheit mächtig,	sturdy in grace, mighty in truth,	
		Ihr Licht wird hell, ihr Stern geht auf.	her light shines bright, her star ascends.	
				Ritornello.
15	2:36	*Nun komm, du werte Kron,*	Now come, you worthy crown,	
		Herr Jesu, Gottes Sohn.	Lord Jesus, God's own Son,	
	2:53	*Hosianna!*	Hosanna!	Ritornello in minor.
	3:15	*Wir folgen all' zum Freudensaal und halten mit das Abendmahl.*	We all follow to the joyful hall and share the Lord's Supper.	

182

Fifth Movement: Recitative for Bass (Jesus)
Strings, basso continuo

Sixth Movement: Duet for Bass (Jesus) and Soprano (Soul)
Oboe, basso continuo

An operatic atmosphere is suggested in movements 5 and 6, a recitative and duet. The fifth movement is an accompanied recitative in which the voice is supported by strings as well as continuo. The dancelike, joyful duet (sixth movement) depicts the happy union of Christ and the soul—but it could well suggest the bliss of any newlywed couple. A solo oboe first plays an opening ritornello and then intertwines with the voices almost throughout.

Supplementary sets:
Side 2, bands 9–10
CD 1 [42]–[43]

Perhaps to suggest their union, the soprano and bass imitate each other and often sing together harmoniously. The movement is in A B A form.

So geh herein zu mir, du mir erwählte Braut!	Come enter in with me, my chosen bride!	Recitative, accompanied by strings. [42]
Ich habe mich mit dir in Ewigkeit vertraut.	I have pledged my troth to you in eternity!	
Dich will ich auf mein Herz,	I will set you as a seal upon my heart,	
auf meinen Arm gleich wie ein Siegel setzen,	and as a seal upon my arm,	
und dein betrübtes Aug'ergötzen.	and restore delight to your sorrowful eye.	
Vergiss, o Seele,	Forget now, o soul	
nun die Angst, den Schmerz, den du erdulden müssen;	the anguish, the pain which you had to suffer;	
auf meiner Linken sollst du ruh'n,	on my left you shall rest,	
und mein Rechte soll dich küssen.	and my right shall kiss you.	
		Duet
		Section A; oboe ritornello. [43] 0:00
Mein Freund ist mein!	Soul: My friend is mine!	

183

Und ich bin dein!	Jesus: and I am thine!
Die Liebe soll nichts scheiden!	Both: Love shall separate nothing!

44 2:49

Oboe ritornello
Section B

Ich will mit dir in Himmels Rosen weiden,	Soul: I will feed with you among heaven's roses,
Du sollst mit mir in Himmels Rosen weiden,	Jesus: You shall feed with me among heaven's roses,
Da Freude die Fülle, da Wonne wird sein!	Both: There fullness of joy, there rapture shall be!

Section A
repeated;
oboe ritornello.

45 4:36

Mein Freund ist mein!	Soul: My friend is mine!
Und ich bin dein!	Jesus: and I am thine!
Die Liebe soll nichts scheiden!	Both: Love shall separate nothing!

Oboe ritornello.

When Bach was hired as cantor by the Leipzig town council, he specifically agreed to compose church music that would *not* "make an operatic impression." The fifth and sixth movements, which would be appropriate for a love scene in a baroque opera, show that Bach did not take his contract literally.

Seventh Movement: Chorale
Chorus doubled by orchestra

Side 3, band 6
CD 2 16

Bach rounds off Cantata No. 140 by bringing back the chorale once more. For the first time since the first movement, all voices and instruments take part. Here the chorale is set in a relatively simple, homophonic texture for four voices, with the instruments simply doubling them, not playing melodies of their own. Now the chorale is heard as a continuous melody, without interludes between its phrases. The rich sound, full harmonies, and regular rhythms express praise of God, faith in him, and joy in being in his kingdom. No doubt the congregation joined in the singing of the final chorale, which so firmly expressed their unity and belief.

16

Gloria sei dir gesungen	Gloria be sung to you
mit Menschen- und englischen Zungen,	with men's and angel's tongues,

mit Harfen und mit Zimbeln schon.	with harps and beautiful cymbals.
Von zwölf Perlen sind die Pforten	Of twelve pearls are the gates
an deiner Stadt; wir sind Konsorten	at your city; we are consorts
der Engel hoch um deinen Thron.	of the angels high about your throne.
Kein Aug' hat je gespürt,	No eye has ever sensed,
kein Ohr hat je gehört	no ear has ever heard
solche Freude.	such a delight.
Des sind wir froh,	Of this we rejoice,
io, io!	io, io,
ewig in dulci jubilo.	forever in sweet joy.

BASIC TERMS

chorale (page 174)
chorale prelude (176)
cantata (176)

THE ORATORIO

BAROQUE
15

Together with the opera and cantata, the oratorio stands as a major development in baroque vocal music. Like opera, the *oratorio* is a large-scale composition for chorus, vocal soloists, and orchestra; it is usually set to a narrative text. Oratorio differs from opera in that it has no acting, scenery, or costumes. Most oratorios are based on biblical stories, but usually they are not intended for religious services. Today they are performed in either concert halls or churches.

An oratorio contains a succession of choruses, arias, duets, recitatives, and orchestral interludes. The chorus is especially important and serves either to comment on or to participate in the drama. A narrator's recitatives usually relate the story and connect one piece with another. Oratorios are longer than cantatas (they sometimes last over 2 hours) and have more of a story line.

Oratorios first appeared in early seventeenth-century Italy as musical dramatizations of biblical stories and were performed in prayer halls called *oratorios*. During the baroque period, the oratorio spread to other countries and assumed many forms. *Messiah*, by George Frideric Handel, has for decades been the best-known and most-loved oratorio.

BAROQUE **16** GEORGE FRIDERIC HANDEL

George Frideric Handel (1685–1759), a master of Italian opera and English oratorio, was born in Halle, Germany, one month before J. S. Bach. Handel was not from a musical family; his father was a barber-surgeon who wanted his son to study law, not music. By the time Handel was nine, however, his musical talent was so outstanding that his father relented somewhat and permitted him to study with the local organist, who also was a composer. By the age of eleven, he was able not only to compose but also to give organ lessons. Perhaps to honor the wishes of his father, who had died when Handel was twelve, he entered Halle University at seventeen to study law. But a year later he left the university and set out for Hamburg.

Handel was drawn to the renowned opera house in Hamburg. There he became a violinist and harpsichordist in the orchestra, and when he was twenty, one of his operas was successfully produced.

Handel was a man of temperament and conviction. At the Hamburg opera one incident almost cost him his life. The company was performing an opera by one of Handel's friends, who insisted that he, not Handel, play the harpsichord. Handel refused to give up his post, and their argument led to a duel. A metal button on Handel's coat broke his opponent's sword. It was a button's great contribution to posterity.

Handel's good fortune continued. At twenty-one he went to Italy to establish his career and spent three highly productive years. There he wrote Italian operas that were acclaimed far and wide. He mingled with princes and famous musicians; even cardinals wrote librettos for him to set to music.

Returning to Germany in 1710, Handel took a well-paid position as music director for Elector Georg Ludwig of Hanover. After just a month, he asked for a leave to go to London, where his opera *Rinaldo* was being produced. *Rinaldo* was a triumph, and he returned to Hanover. A year later Handel again asked the elector for an English leave. It was granted on the condition that Handel stay only a reasonable length of time in London.

(Metropolitan Museum of Art, Bequest of Alexandrine Sinsheimer, 1959)

Handel's triple career as impresario, composer, and performer brought him success and fame but led to political infighting and two nervous breakdowns.

This turned out to be the next half-century (1712–1759). Handel's fame in England grew as rapidly as it had in Italy. He became England's most important composer and a favorite of Queen Anne, who gave him a subsidy of £200 a year. On Queen Anne's death, a complicated arrangement made the elector of Hanover, Georg Ludwig, King George I of England (1714). Evidently the king had not taken offense at Handel's absence; the composer's subsidy was increased to £400 annually, and he taught music to the king's granddaughters.

Italian opera in London was an exotic entertainment for the pleasure of the aristocracy. Middle-class audiences had little desire to see works with mythological plots they considered absurd. Therefore a few aristocrats provided the base of support for opera in London. They ran a commercial opera company called the Royal Academy of Music; in 1719, Handel became its music director. After nine seasons the company folded because of inadequate support. But in that period Handel had composed a number of brilliant operas for outstanding sopranos and castrati.

Handel's reputation continued to grow, and after the collapse of the Royal Academy, he decided to form a company to produce his works. (For years he had a triple career as impresario, composer, and performer.) Opera had become a political weapon. To spite him, a company called the Opera of the Nobility was formed. Its backers opposed the party in power, and Handel—a friend of the king and an establishment composer—became a scapegoat.

Both opera companies went bankrupt as a result of the competition, and Handel suffered a breakdown. He went to Germany to recuperate, and his condition moved the future king of Prussia to write, in 1737, "Handel's great days are over, his inspiration is exhausted, and his taste behind the fashion."

But the king of Prussia was mistaken. Handel recovered, returned to London, and—though heavily in debt—managed again to produce operas on his own. To these he added his oratorios, opening a glowing new chapter in music history.

For the English public, oratorios were a novelty. But the English people knew the Old Testament and liked hearing English on stage. Handel offered his oratorios during Lent, when operas were prohibited. Oratorios, unlike opera, required no expensive sets, stage machinery, or costumes, and were thus cheaper to produce. Even though Handel charged high prices, he attracted a new, middle-class audience.

In 1741, the year he composed *Messiah*, Handel stopped writing operas entirely. Oratorios poured from his pen. At first, some people were scandalized that biblical words were sung in a public theater. One newspaper received a letter asserting that "the People of England were arriv'd to such a Height of *Impiety* and *Prophaneness*, that the most sacred *Things* were suffer'd to be us'd as *publick Diversions*."

Despite the sniping, the oratorio seasons were acclaimed; they had the added attraction of Handel himself performing his organ concertos between acts. But too much success can bring trouble. Some aristocrats began to plot Handel's ruin. To them, the idea of a foreign-born musician's attaining power and prominence was too much. Concert posters were torn down, hired hoodlums robbed and assaulted concertgoers, and aristocrats made a point of giving private concerts and balls on oratorio evenings. Gradually, all this simmered down, but not before Handel had another breakdown. Again, he recovered rapidly and went on producing oratorios.

By 1753, Handel was still conducting and giving organ concerts, though he was almost blind. During his lifetime a statue of him was erected in a public park, and when he died in 1759, 3000 mourners attended his funeral in Westminster Abbey. He was wealthy, generous, cultivated—and stubborn. But above all, he was a master composer whose dramatic sense has rarely been equaled.

HANDEL'S MUSIC

Handel shares Bach's stature among composers of the late baroque. Although he wrote a great deal of instrumental music—suites, organ concertos, concerti grossi—the core of his huge output consists of English oratorios and Italian operas.

Handel's English oratorios are usually based on stories from the Old Testament and have titles like *Israel in Egypt, Saul, Joshua,* and *Judas Maccabaeus.* They are *not* church music, however; they were composed to entertain paying audiences in public theaters. Most have plots and characters, even though they are performed without acting, scenery, or costumes. As we'll see, *Messiah* is an exception, in that it deals with a New Testament subject and is without a plot.

The chorus is the focus of the Handelian oratorio. Sometimes the chorus participates in the narrative, representing the Israelites or their heathen enemies. But it also comments on the action, lamenting or exulting. Handel treats the combination of chorus and orchestra with flexibility and imagination. In his hands, a chorus can project delicacy, drama, or grandeur. Even Beethoven marveled at Handel's ability to "achieve great effects with simple means."

Handel never hesitated to reinforce an idea in his text by interrupting a polyphonic flow of music with a series of chords. Changes in texture are more frequent in his music than in Bach's. And he liked to present two different melodic ideas and then combine them polyphonically. Handel achieved sharp changes of mood by shifting between minor keys and major keys.

Handel's thirty-nine Italian operas, almost all written in London, are less well known today than the oratorios. But after two centuries of neglect, these operas are being revived successfully by modern opera companies. Handel's operas are nearly all serious. They are based on ancient Greek and Roman history or mythology. The heroes and heroines are royal figures like Julius Caesar and Cleopatra. Most noteworthy in Handel's opera are the arias, which are connected by long passages of recitative in which the plot develops. The arias show Handel's outstanding ability to evoke a mood or emotion. They were often written to display the virtuosity of singers, some of whom were castrati.

MESSIAH (1741)

Messiah lasts about 2½ hours and was composed in just twenty-four days. Handel wrote it before going to Ireland to attend performances of his own works that were being given to dedicate a concert hall. About five months after his arrival in Dublin (in 1742), Handel gave the first performance of *Messiah;* the occasion was a benefit for those lingering in debtors' prisons. The rehearsals attracted wide attention: one newspaper commented that *Messiah* was thought "by the greatest Judges to be the finest Composition of Musick that ever was heard." Normally, the concert hall held 600 people; but to increase the capacity, women were asked not to wear hoopskirts, and men were asked to leave their swords at home.

Although the premiere was a success, the first London performance (1743) was poorly received, mainly because of religious opposition to using a Christian text in a theater. It took *Messiah* almost a decade to find popularity in London. Not until it was performed yearly at a benefit for a London orphanage did it achieve its unique status. A contemporary wrote that *Messiah* "fed the hungry, clothed the naked, fostered the orphan."

Messiah is in three parts. Part I starts with the prophecy of the Messiah's coming and makes celestial announcements of Christ's birth and the redemption of humanity through his appearance. Part II has been aptly described by one Handel scholar as "the accomplishment of redemption by the sacrifice of Jesus, mankind's rejection of God's offer and mankind's utter defeat when trying to oppose the power of the Almighty." Part III expresses faith in the certainty of eternal life through Christ as redeemer.

Unlike most of Handel's oratorios, *Messiah* is meditative rather than dramatic; it lacks plot action and specific characters. *Messiah* is Handel's only English oratorio that uses the New Testament as well as the Old. Charles Jennings, a millionaire and amateur literary man, compiled the text by taking widely separated passages from the Bible—Isaiah, Psalms, and Job from the Old Testament; Luke, I Corinthians, and the Book of Revelations from the New.

Over the years, Handel rewrote some movements in *Messiah* for different performers and performances. In Handel's own time, it was performed with a smaller orchestra and chorus than we are used to. Handel's own chorus included twenty singers, all male, and his small orchestra had only strings and continuo, with trumpets and timpani used in some sections. Today we sometimes hear arranged versions; Mozart made one, and still later versions are often played by orchestras of one hundred and choruses of several hundred.

Messiah has over fifty movements, and Handel ensures variety by skillfully contrasting movements and grouping them. He achieves profound effects through simple alternations of major and minor. We will focus on the Sinfonia for Orchestra; *Comfort ye, my people; Ev'ry valley shall be exalted;* and *For unto us a Child is born* (all from Part I)—and on the *Hallelujah* Chorus, which ends Part II.

Sinfonia for Orchestra (French Overture)
Grave; Allegro moderato (moderate allegro)

Messiah opens with a French overture in minor. As is customary, a slow section featuring dotted rhythms is followed by a quite rapid section beginning like a fugue. A lively subject is passed from higher instruments to lower.

Side 4, band 4
CD 2 [23]
Grave
[23] 0:00
Allegro moderato
[24] 1:53

After this, the imitation mainly involves fragments of the subject. Near the end of the movement is a feature typical of Handel: an energetic orchestral motion is suddenly broken off by a brief pause that ushers in a closing cadence of slow chords. It's as though Handel had applied a brake to bring the music to a decisive end.

Comfort Ye, My People
Accompanied recitative for tenor and orchestra
Larghetto (slow, but less so than largo)

> Comfort ye, comfort ye my people, saith your God. Speak ye comfortably to Jerusalem, and cry unto her, that her warfare is accomplish'd, that her iniquity is pardon'd. The voice of him that crieth in the wilderness, Prepare ye the way of the Lord, make straight in the desert a highway for our God. (Isaiah 40:1–3)

Comfort ye, my people opens with an orchestral ritornello in major that seems "comforting" after the overture's minor key. The material of the ritornello returns repeatedly. The second movement is an *arioso*—the vocal line is something between a recitative and an aria, more lyrical than

Side 4, band 5
CD 2 [25]

191

26 2:39 one, less elaborate than the other. At the end, however, a heavenly voice is heard *(The voice of him that crieth in the wilderness),* and the vocal line becomes pure recitative.

The tenor's opening *Comfort ye* motive (long-short-long) is echoed by the strings, which repeat it reassuringly throughout.

Ev'ry Valley Shall Be Exalted
Aria for tenor
Andante

Ev'ry valley shall be exalted, and ev'ry mountain and hill made low, the crooked straight, and the rough places plain. (Isaiah 40:4)

Like many baroque arias, *Ev'ry valley shall be exalted* opens and closes with Side 4, band 6 CD 2 [27] an orchestral ritornello. This aria is striking in its vivid word painting, so characteristic of baroque music. On a single syllable of *exalted (raised up)*, forty-six rapid notes form a rising musical line.

Shall be_____ ex-alt - - - - - - - -
- - - - - - - ed,

Notice, too, the rising and falling direction of the phrase *and every mountain and hill made low:*

and ev-'ry moun-tain and hill____ made low;

The crooked straight is represented as follows:

the crook - ed straight,

In the line *and the rough places plain*, the word *plain (smooth* or *level)*, is expressed by sustained tones and a long, legato melodic line.

For unto Us a Child Is Born
Chorus

> For unto us a Child is born, unto us a Son is given, and the government shall be upon His shoulder, and His Name shall be called: Wonderful, Counsellor, the Mighty God, the Everlasting Father, the Prince of Peace! (Isaiah 9:6)

For unto us a Child is born is some of Handel's most joyful music. The texture is light, often with only one or two voices singing at a time. After the sopranos announce a motive, it is imitated by the tenors; then both voices—with different rhythms—are combined. Side 4, band 7 CD 2 [28]

29 0:58 The words *and the government shall be upon His shoulder* bring a new melodic idea in dotted rhythm:

30 1:15 Handel keeps the dynamics subdued until the striking chordal outburst on *Wonderful, Counsellor.* This change of texture and dynamics is a master's stroke.

With such a close fusion of words and music, it may be disconcerting to learn that most of the melodic ideas in this chorus came from Handel's Italian duet for the words *No, I will not trust you, blind love, cruel Beauty! You are too treacherous, too charming a deity!* (The musical idea for *Wonderful* is new.) But remember that in Handel's time there was little difference in style between sacred and secular music. Amorous joy and religious joy could therefore be conveyed in the same manner.

Hallelujah Chorus

Side 4, band 8
CD 2 31 The *Hallelujah* Chorus is one of the world's most famous choral pieces. In this vigorous chorus, Handel offers sweeping variety by sudden changes among monophonic, polyphonic, and homophonic textures. The monophonic texture is very full-sounding as all the voices and instruments perform in unison at the proclamation *for the Lord God Omnipotent reigneth.*

194

The texture becomes polyphonic when this majestic proclamation is set against joyful repeated exclamations of *Hallelujah* in quick rhythms. Polyphony gives way to homophony as the chorus sings *The kingdom of this world* to hymnlike music.

In the *Hallelujah* chorus, words and phrases are repeated over and over, as has been common practice in choral music for several centuries. (In the following text, braces connect lines sung at the same time.) Handel took his text from the Revelation of St. John, which celebrates God as the almighty and everlasting ruler.

	Orchestral introduction	31
Hallelujah!	Chorus joins, homophonic, quick exclamations	
for the lord God Omnipotent reigneth;	Monophonic, longer notes	32
Hallelujah!	Homophonic, quick exclamations	
for the Lord God Omnipotent reigneth;	Monophonic, longer notes	
Hallelujah!	Homophonic, quick exclamations	
{ for the Lord God Omnipotent reigneth; { Hallelujah!	Longer-note melody against quick exclamations, polyphonic	33
The kingdom of this world is become the Kingdom of our Lord and of His Christ:	Hymnlike in longer notes, homophonic	34
and He shall reign for ever and ever,	Bass melody, monophonic	35
	Other voices imitate, polyphonic	
{ King of Kings, and Lord of Lords. { for ever and ever, Hallelujah, Hallelujah!	Long repeated tones against quick exclamations; phrases repeated at higher pitches	36
and He shall reign for ever and ever,	Polyphonic, imitation	
{ King of Kings, and Lord of Lords, { for ever and ever, Hallelujah, Hallelujah!	Long repeated tones against quick exclamations	
and He shall reign for ever and ever,	Polyphonic	
King of Kings, and Lord of Lords.	Homophonic	
and He shall reign for ever and ever,	Polyphonic	
{ King of Kings, and Lord of Lords, { for ever and ever, for ever and ever,	Quick exclamations	
Hallelujah, Hallelujah, Hallelujah, Hallelujah!		
	Pause	
Hallelujah!	Sustained chords, homophonic	

BASIC TERM
arioso (191)

THE CLASSICAL PERIOD

V

Louis Carrogis de Carmontelle, *Misses Royer, Daughters of the Musician, Composer of "Zaide"* (1760).

[CLASSICAL **1**] THE CLASSICAL STYLE (1750–1820)

In looking at the baroque era, we found that the scientific methods and discoveries of geniuses like Galileo and Newton vastly changed people's view of the world. By the middle of the eighteenth century, faith in the power of reason was so great that it began to undermine the authority of the social and religious establishment. Philosophers and writers— especially Voltaire (1694–1778) and Denis Diderot (1713–1784)—saw their time as a great turning point in history and referred to it as the "age of enlightenment." They believed in progress, holding that reason, not custom or tradition, was the best guide for human conduct. Their attacks on the privileges of the aristocracy and clergy reflected the outlook of the middle class, which was struggling for its rights. This new climate of opinion prepared the way for the American and French revolutions at the end of the eighteenth century.

Revolutions in thought and action were paralleled by shifts of style in the visual arts. During the early eighteenth century, the heavy, monumental baroque style gave way to the more intimate rococo style, with its light colors, curved lines, and graceful ornaments. The painters Antoine Watteau (1684–1721) and Jean Honoré Fragonard (1732–1806) depicted an enchanted world peopled by elegant men and women in constant pursuit of pleasure. But by the later eighteenth century there was yet another change in taste, and rococo art was thought frivolous, excessively ornamented, and lacking in ethical content. The rococo style was superseded by the *neoclassical* style, which attempted to recapture the "noble simplicity and calm grandeur" of ancient Greek and Roman art. Neoclassical artists emphasized firm lines, clear structures, and moralistic subject matter. The painter Jacques Louis David (1748–1825), who took part in the French Revolution, sought to inspire heroism and patriotism through his scenes of ancient Rome.

The artistic response to the decline of traditional power is evidenced further by the English painter William Hogarth (1697–1764), whose socially conscious paintings satirized the manners and morals of the British aristocracy and middle class, and by the Spanish painter Francisco Goya (1746– 1828), whose highly personal vision lashed out against hypocrisy, oppression, and inhumanity.

In music history, the transition from the baroque style to the full flowering of the classical is called the *preclassical* period; it extends from roughly 1730 to 1770. The shift in musical taste parallels the similar, earlier trend in the visual arts. It was developing even as Bach and Handel were creating

The rococo painter Jean Honoré Fragonard showed the game of love in
The Pursuit, c. 1771.

In *The Oath of the Horatii* (1784), the neoclassical painter Jacques-Louis David depicted Romans swearing loyalty to their cause.

baroque masterpieces. Among the important pioneers in this new style were Bach's sons, Carl Philipp Emanuel (1714–1788) and Johann Christian (1735–1782). Around the middle of the eighteenth century, composers concentrated on simplicity and clarity, discarding much that had enriched late baroque music. Polyphonic texture was neglected in favor of tuneful melody and simple harmony. Carl Philipp Emanuel Bach described music with strict polyphonic imitation as "dry and despicable pieces of pedantry." Mid-eighteenth-century composers entertained their listeners with music offering contrasts of mood and theme. The term *style galant (gallant style)* was applied to this light, graceful music.

The term *classical* is confusing because it has so many different meanings. It may refer to an aspect of Greek or Roman antiquity, or it may be used for any supreme accomplishment of lasting appeal (as in the expres-

Monticello, Thomas Jefferson's home, shows the influence of ancient Greek and Roman architecture.

sion *movie classic*). Many people take *classical music* to mean anything that is *not* rock, jazz, folk, or popular music.

Music historians have borrowed the term *classical* from the field of art history, where it is more appropriate. The painting, sculpture, and architecture of the late eighteenth and early nineteenth centuries were often influenced by Greek and Roman models. But the music of this period shows little direct relationship to antiquity. The significant parallel between "classical" music and "neoclassical" art is a common stress on balance and clarity of structure. These traits can be found in the fully developed classical style in music, which we will focus on. The style flourished from about 1770 to 1820, and its master composers were Joseph Haydn (1732–1809), Wolfgang Amadeus Mozart (1756–1791), and Ludwig van Beethoven (1770–1827). First, we'll study the characteristics of their work.

CHARACTERISTICS OF THE CLASSICAL STYLE

Contrast of Mood

Great variety and contrast of mood received new emphasis in classical music. While a late baroque piece may convey a single emotion, a classical composition will fluctuate in mood. Dramatic, turbulent music might lead into a carefree dance tune. Not only are there contrasting themes within a movement, but there also may be striking contrasts within a single theme.

Mood in classical music may change gradually or suddenly, expressing conflicting surges of elation and depression. But such conflict and contrast are under the firm control of the classical composer. Masters like Haydn, Mozart, and Beethoven were able to impart unity and logic to music of wide emotional range.

Rhythm

Flexibility of rhythm adds variety to classical music. A classical composition has a wealth of rhythmic patterns, whereas a baroque piece contains a few patterns that are reiterated throughout. Baroque works convey a sense of continuity and perpetual motion, so that after the first few bars one can predict pretty well the rhythmic character of an entire movement. But the classical style also includes unexpected pauses, syncopations, and frequent changes from long notes to shorter ones. And the change from one pattern of note lengths to another may be either sudden or gradual.

Texture

In contrast to the polyphonic texture of late baroque music, classical music is basically homophonic. However, texture is treated as flexibly as rhythm. Pieces shift smoothly or suddenly from one texture to another. A work may begin homophonically with a melody and simple accompaniment but then change to a more complex polyphonic texture that features two simultaneous melodies or melodic fragments imitated among the various instruments.

Melody

Classical melodies are among the most tuneful and easy to remember. The themes of even highly sophisticated compositions may have a folk or popular flavor. Occasionally, composers simply borrowed popular tunes. (Mozart did, in his variations on the French song *Ah, vous dirai-je, maman,* which we know as *Twinkle, Twinkle, Little Star.*) More often, they wrote original themes with a popular character.

Classical melodies often sound balanced and symmetrical because they are frequently made up of two phrases of the same length. The second phrase, in such melodies, may begin like the first, but it ends more conclusively. Such a melodic type, which may be diagrammed a a', is easy to sing (it is frequently found in nursery tunes such as *Mary Had a Little Lamb*). Baroque melodies, on the contrary, tend to be less symmetrical, more elaborate, and harder to sing.

Dynamics and the Piano

The classical composers' interest in expressing shades of emotion led to the widespread use of gradual dynamic change—crescendo and decrescendo. They did not restrict themselves to the terraced dynamics (abrupt shifts from loud to soft) characteristic of baroque music. Both crescendos and decrescendos were an electrifying novelty; audiences sometimes rose excitedly from their seats.

During the classical period, the desire for gradual dynamic change led to the replacement of the harpsichord by the piano. By varying the finger pressure on the keys, a pianist can play more loudly or softly. Although the piano was invented around 1700, it began to replace the harpsichord only around 1775. Almost all the mature keyboard compositions of Haydn, Mozart, and Beethoven were written for the piano, rather than for harpsichord, clavichord, and organ, which were featured in baroque music.

The End of the Basso Continuo

The basso continuo was gradually abandoned during the classical period. In Haydn's or Mozart's works, a harpsichordist did not need to improvise an accompaniment. One reason why the basso continuo became obsolete was that more and more music was written for amateurs, who could not master the difficult art of improvising from a figured bass. Also, classical composers wanted more control; they preferred to specify an accompaniment rather than trust the judgment of improvisers.

THE CLASSICAL ORCHESTRA

A new orchestra evolved during the classical period. Unlike the baroque orchestra, which could vary from piece to piece, it was a standard group of four sections: strings, woodwinds, brass, and percussion. In the late instrumental works of Mozart and Haydn, an orchestra might consist of the following:

Strings: 1st violins, 2d violins, violas, cellos, double basses
Woodwinds: 2 flutes, 2 oboes, 2 clarinets, 2 bassoons
Brass: 2 French horns, 2 trumpets
Percussion: 2 timpani

Notice that woodwind and brass instruments are paired and that clarinets have been added. Trombones were also used by Haydn and Mozart, but only in opera and church music, not in solely instrumental works.

The number of musicians in a classical orchestra was greater than in a baroque group, but practice varied considerably from place to place. Haydn directed a private orchestra of only twenty-five players from 1761 to 1790. But for public concerts in London in 1795, he led a large orchestra of sixty musicians.

Classical composers exploited the individual tone colors of orchestral instruments. Unlike baroque composers, they did not treat one instrument like another. Classical composers would not let an oboe duplicate the violin melody for the entire length of a movement. A classical piece has greater variety of tone color, and more rapid changes of color. A theme might begin in the full orchestra, shift to the strings, and then continue in the woodwinds.

Each section of the classical orchestra had a special role. The strings were the most important section, with the first violins taking the melody most of the time and the lower strings providing an accompaniment. The woodwinds added contrasting tone colors and were often given melodic solos. Horns and trumpets brought power to loud passages and filled out the harmony, but they did not usually play the main melody. Timpani were used for rhythmic bite and emphasis. As a whole, the classical orchestra had developed into a flexible and colorful instrument to which composers could entrust their most powerful and dramatic musical conceptions.

CLASSICAL FORMS

Instrumental compositions of the classical period usually consist of several movements that contrast in tempo and character. There are often four movements, arranged as follows:

1. Fast movement
2. Slow movement
3. Dance-related movement
4. Fast movement

Classical symphonies and string quartets usually follow this four-movement pattern, while classical sonatas may consist of two, three, or four movements. A *symphony* is written for orchestra; a *string quartet* for two violins, viola, and cello; and a *sonata* for one or two instruments. (The classical symphony, string quartet, and sonata are more fully described in Sections 3 to 7 and 9.)

In writing an individual movement of a symphony, string quartet, or sonata, a classical composer could choose from several different forms. One movement of a composition might be in A B A form, while another might be a theme and variations. The sections that follow will describe some forms used in classical movements, but now let's look at a few general characteristics of classical form.

Classical movements often contrast themes vividly. A movement may contain two, three, or even four or more themes of different character. This use of contrasting themes distinguishes classical music from baroque music, which often uses only one main theme. The classical composer sometimes signals the arrival of a new theme with a brief pause.

The larger sections of a classical movement balance each other in a satisfying and symmetrical way. Unstable sections that wander from the tonic key are balanced by stable sections that confirm it. By the end of a classical movement, musical tensions have been resolved.

Though we speak of the classical style, we must remember that Haydn, Mozart, and Beethoven were three individuals with dissimilar personalities. While Haydn's and Mozart's works at first may sound similar, deeper involvement reveals striking personal styles. Beethoven's music seems more powerful, violent, and emotional when compared with the apparently more restrained and elegant works of the earlier masters. But Haydn and Mozart also composed music that is passionate and dramatic. We'll see that all three composers employed similar musical procedures and forms, yet their emotional statements bear the particular stamp of each.

COMPOSER, PATRON, AND PUBLIC IN THE CLASSICAL PERIOD

CLASSICAL

2

Haydn, Mozart, Beethoven—three of the world's greatest composers— worked during a time of violent political and social upheaval. The seventy-year period from 1750 to 1820 was convulsed by the American and French revolutions and by the Napoleonic Wars. Political and economic power shifted from the aristocracy and the church to the middle class. Social mobility increased to a point where Napoleon could become emperor of France through his own genius rather than as a birthright. "Subversive" new slogans like *Liberty, equality, fraternity!* sprang from the people's lips. All established ideas were being reexamined, including the existence of God.

Most of Haydn's music was composed for a wealthy aristocratic family. Shown here is a performance of a Haydn comic opera in 1775 at the palace Eszterháza.

SOCIAL TRENDS AND CLASSICAL COMPOSITION

Like everyone else, musicians were strongly affected by such changes, and in the careers of the three classical masters we can trace the slow emancipation of the composer. First came Joseph Haydn (1732–1809), content to spend most of his life serving a wealthy aristocratic family. His contract of employment (1761) shows that he was considered a skilled servant, like a gardener or gamekeeper. He had to wear a uniform and "compose such music as His Highness shall order"—and was warned to "refrain from vulgarity in eating, drinking, and conversation." Wolfgang Amadeus Mozart (1756–1791), born just twenty-four years later, could not bear being treated as a servant; he broke from his court position and went to Vienna to try his luck as a free-lance musician. But his personality was unsuited to the struggles of such a career, and he died tragically in poverty. Ludwig van Beethoven (1770–1827) succeeded where Mozart failed. Only a few years after Mozart's death, Beethoven was able to work as an independent musician in Vienna. His success was gained through a wider middle-class market for music and a commanding personality that prompted the nobility to give him gifts and treat him as an equal.

As the eighteenth century advanced, more people made more money. Merchants, doctors, and government officials could afford larger homes, finer clothes, and better food. But the prospering middle class wanted more than material goods; it also sought aristocratic luxuries like theater, literature, and music. In fact, during the classical period, the middle class had a great influence on music. Because palace concerts were usually closed to townspeople, they organized public concerts where, for the price of admission, they could hear the latest symphonies and concertos. Following the success of a famous concert series in Paris, the *Concert spirituel* (1725), public concerts mushroomed throughout Europe. But merchants and lawyers were not content to hear music only in concerts. They wanted to be surrounded by music at home. They felt that their sons and daughters deserved music lessons as much as the children of aristocrats did. Indeed, if middle-class children played instruments well enough, they might be invited to palaces and eventually marry into the aristocracy. In any event, the demand for printed music, instruments, and music lessons had vastly increased.

Composers in the classical period took middle-class tastes into account. They wrote pieces that were easy for amateur musicians to play and understand. They turned from serious to comic opera, from heroic and mythological plots dear to the nobility to middle-class subjects and folklike tunes. Their comic operas sometimes even ridiculed the aristocracy, and their dance movements became less elegant and courtly, more vigorous and rustic.

Serious composition was flavored by folk and popular music. The classical masters sometimes used familiar tunes as themes for symphonies and variations. Mozart was delighted that people danced to waltzes arranged from melodies in his operas. Haydn, Mozart, and Beethoven all wrote dance music for public balls in Vienna.

VIENNA

Vienna was one of the music centers of Europe during the classical period, and Haydn, Mozart, and Beethoven were all active there. As the seat of the Holy Roman Empire (which included parts of present-day Austria, Germany, Italy, Hungary, and Czechoslovakia), it was a bustling cultural and commercial center with a cosmopolitan character. Its population of almost 250,000 (in 1800) made Vienna the fourth largest city in Europe. All three classical masters were born elsewhere, but they were drawn to Vienna to study and to seek recognition. In Vienna, Haydn and Mozart became close friends and influenced each other's musical style. Beethoven traveled to Vienna at sixteen to play for Mozart; at twenty-two, he returned to study with Haydn.

Aristocrats from all over the empire spent the winter in Vienna, sometimes bringing their private orchestras. Music was an important part of court life, and a good orchestra was a symbol of prestige. Many of the nobility were excellent musicians. For instance, Empress Maria Theresa had sung in palace musicales when she was young, Emperor Joseph II was a competent cellist, and Archduke Rudolf was Beethoven's long-time student of piano and composition.

Much music was heard in private concerts, where aristocrats and wealthy commoners played alongside professional musicians. Mozart and Beethoven often earned money by performing in these intimate concerts. The nobility frequently hired servants who could double as musicians. An advertisement in the *Vienna Gazette* of 1789 reads: "Wanted, for a house of the gentry, a manservant who knows how to play the violin well."

In Vienna there was also outdoor music, light and popular in tone. Small street bands of wind and string players played at garden parties or under the windows of people likely to throw down money. A Viennese almanac reported that "on fine summer nights you may come upon serenades in the streets at all hours." Haydn and Mozart wrote many outdoor entertainment pieces, which they called *divertimentos* or *serenades.* Vienna's great love of music and its enthusiastic demand for new works made it the chosen city of Haydn, Mozart, and Beethoven.

CLASSICAL 3

SONATA FORM

An astonishing amount of important music from the classical period to the twentieth century is composed in sonata form (sometimes called *sonata-allegro form*). The term **sonata form** refers to the form of a *single* movement. It should not be confused with the term *sonata,* which is used for a whole composition made up of *several* movements. The opening fast movement of a classical symphony, sonata, or string quartet is usually in sonata form. This form is also used in slow movements and in fast concluding movements.

A sonata-form movement consists of three main sections: the exposition, where the themes are presented; the development, where themes are treated in new ways; and the recapitulation, where the themes return. These three main sections are often followed by a concluding section, the coda (Italian for *tail*). Remember that these sections are all within *one movement*. A *single* sonata-form movement may be outlined as follows:

Exposition
First theme in tonic (home) key
Bridge containing modulation from home key to new key
Second theme in new key
Closing section in key of second theme

Development
New treatment of themes; modulations to different keys

Recapitulation
First theme in tonic key
Bridge
Second theme in tonic key
Closing section in tonic key

(Coda)
In tonic key

A fast movement in sonata form is sometimes preceded by a slow introduction that creates a strong feeling of expectancy.

EXPOSITION

The *exposition* sets up a strong conflict between the tonic key and the new key, between the first theme (or group of themes) and the second theme (or group of themes). It begins with the first theme in the tonic, or home, key. There follows a *bridge*, or *transition*, leading to the second theme, which is in a new key. The modulation from the home key to a new key creates a feeling of harmonic tension and forward motion. The second theme often contrasts in mood with the first theme. A closing section ends the exposition in the key of the second theme. At the end of a classical exposition there is usually a repeat sign (:‖) to indicate that the whole exposition is to be repeated.

DEVELOPMENT

The *development* is often the most dramatic section of the movement. The listener may be kept off balance as the music moves restlessly through several different keys. Through these rapid modulations, the harmonic tension is heightened.

In this section, themes are *developed*, or treated in new ways. They are broken into fragments, or **motives**, which are short musical ideas developed within a composition. A motive may take on different and unexpected emotional meanings. One fragment of a comic theme, for example, may be made to sound aggressive and menacing through changes of melody, rhythm, or dynamics. Themes can be combined with new ideas or changed in texture. A complex polyphonic texture can be woven by shifting a motive rapidly among different instruments. The harmonic and thematic searching of the development builds a tension that demands resolution.

RECAPITULATION

The beginning of the **recapitulation** brings resolution, as we again hear the first theme in the tonic key. In the recapitulation, the first theme, bridge, second theme, and concluding section are presented more or less as they were in the exposition, with one crucial difference: all the principal material is now in the tonic key. Earlier, in the exposition, there was strong contrast between the first theme in the home key and the second theme and closing section in a new key; that basis for tension is resolved in the recapitulation by presenting the first theme, second theme, and closing section all in the tonic key.

CODA

An even more powerful feeling of conclusion is attained by following the recapitulation with yet another section. The **coda** rounds off a movement by repeating themes or developing them further. It always ends in the tonic key.

The amazing durability and vitality of sonata form result from its capacity for drama. The form moves from a stable situation toward conflict (in the exposition), to heightened tension (in the development), and then back to stability and resolution of conflict. The illustration on the opposite page shows an outline.

Sonata form is exceptionally flexible and subject to endless variation. It is not a rigid mold into which musical ideas are poured. Rather, it may be viewed as a set of principles that serve to shape and unify contrasts of theme and key. Haydn, Mozart, and Beethoven repeatedly used sonata form, yet each maintained individuality. Movements in sonata form may differ radically in character, in length, and in the number and treatment of themes. Sonata form is so versatile that it is no surprise to find its use spanning more than two centuries.

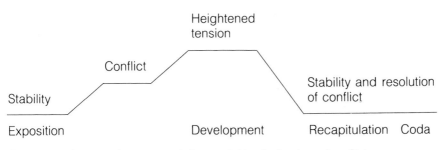

A movement in sonata form proceeds from a stable situation toward conflict, to heightened tension, and then back to stability.

SYMPHONY NO. 40 IN G MINOR, K. 550, BY WOLFGANG AMADEUS MOZART

Fourth Movement:

Allegro assai (very fast)

The rapid sonata-form last movement from Mozart's Symphony No. 40 in G Minor, K. 550, conveys a feeling of controlled tension. The opening theme, in the tonic key of G minor, offers brusque contrasts of dynamics and rhythm. A soft upward arpeggio (broken chord) alternates repeatedly with a loud rushing phrase.

Side 6, band 5
CD 3 [43]

Excitement is maintained throughout the long bridge, which is based on the loud rushing phrase of the first theme. The bridge ends clearly with a brief pause, as do other sections in this movement.

The tender second theme, in the new key of B flat major, is a lyrical contrast to the brusque opening theme. It is softer, flows more smoothly, and uses longer notes.

Mozart weaves almost the entire development section from the upward arpeggio of the first theme. During the opening few seconds, there is an eruption of violence as the orchestra in unison plays a variation of the arpeggio and a series of jagged downward leaps. As the development continues, the texture becomes polyphonic and contrasts with the homophony of the exposition. Arpeggios press upon each other in quick imitation. Rapid shifts of key create restless intensity.

In the recapitulation, both the first and second themes are in the tonic key, G minor. This minor key now adds a touch of melancholy to the tender second theme, which was heard in major before. The passion and violence of this movement foreshadow the romantic expression to come during the nineteenth century.

Listening Outline   To be read while music is heard

SYMPHONY NO. 40 IN G MINOR, K. 550 (1788),
BY WOLFGANG AMADEUS MOZART

Fourth Movement: Allegro assai (very fast)

Sonata form, duple meter ($\frac{2}{2}$), G minor

Flute, 2 oboes, 2 clarinets, 2 bassoons, 2 French horns, 1st violins, 2d violins, violas, cellos, double basses

(Duration, 4:59)

EXPOSITION
First theme
43 0:00   1. Upward arpeggio, *p*, explosive rushing phrase, *f*, minor key.

High repeated tones, *f*, upward arpeggio, *p*, rushing phrase, *f*, leads into

Bridge
44 0:28   2. Long passage of continuously rushing notes, strings, *f*.

Second
theme
45 1:05   3. *a.* Tender melody in violins, *p*, major key.

1:20   *b.* Clarinet, *p,* tender melody somewhat varied.

Closing section
46 1:35   4. Suddenly loud, continuously rushing notes in strings, *f.*

DEVELOPMENT
47 1:57   1. Orchestra in unison, *f,* upward arpeggio, jagged downward leaps.

2:06   2. Suddenly soft, upward arpeggio lightly tossed between violins and woodwinds.
2:18   3. Suddenly loud, string arpeggios interwoven with rushing notes. Arpeggios press upon each other in quicker imitation. Woodwinds rejoin imitative dialogue.

RECAPITULATION
First theme
48 3:14   1. Upward arpeggio, *p,* explosive rushing phrase, *f* minor key. High repeated tones, *f,* upward arpeggio, *p,* rushing phrase, *f,* leads into

Bridge
3:28   2. Passage of continuously rushing notes, strings, *f.*

Second theme
49 3:52   3. *a.* Tender melody in violins, *p,* minor key.
4:06   *b.* Woodwinds, *p,* tender melody somewhat varied.

Closing section
4:21   4. Suddenly loud, continuously rushing notes, full orchestra. Cadence.

BASIC TERMS

sonata form (page 208)   motive (210)
exposition (209)   recapitulation (210)
bridge (transition) (209)   coda (210)
development (209)

THEME AND VARIATIONS

CLASSICAL

4

The form called *theme and variations* is widely used in the classical period, either as an independent piece or as one movement of a symphony, sonata, or string quartet. In a ***theme and variations,*** a basic musical idea—the theme—is repeated over and over and is changed each time. This form may be outlined as theme (A)–variation 1 (A′)–variation 2 (A″)–variation 3 (A‴), and so on; each prime mark indicates a variation of the basic idea.

Each variation is usually about the same length as the theme. Changes of melody, rhythm, harmony, accompaniment, dynamics, or tone color may be used to give a variation its own identity. The core melody may appear in the bass, or it may be repeated in a minor key instead of a major key. It may be heard together with a new melody. Each variation is unique and may differ in mood from the theme. The variations may be connected to each other or separated by pauses. For the theme itself, a composer may invent an original melody or borrow someone else's. Beethoven once borrowed a little waltz tune and put it through thirty-three brilliant variations. More modest examples of theme and variations have as few as three variations.

SYMPHONY NO. 94 IN G MAJOR *(SURPRISE)*, BY JOSEPH HAYDN

Second Movement:

Andante

Side 5, band 1
CD 3 1

The second movement (andante) of Haydn's Symphony No. 94 in G major (the *Surprise* Symphony) is a theme and variations. The folklike, staccato theme begins softly but is punctuated by a sudden loud chord. This is the "surprise" of the symphony. There are four variations, in which the theme is changed in tone color, dynamics, rhythm, and melody. Sometimes the original melody is accompanied by a new one called a ***countermelody.*** Such combinations of two distinctive melodies result in a polyphonic texture. In one variation the theme is presented in minor instead of major. The last variation is followed by a closing section in which a gently dissonant accompaniment momentarily darkens the mood of the carefree theme.

The theme is composed of two parts, sections a and b, each of which is repeated. This pattern is usually retained in the variations.

Listening Outline
To be read while music is heard

SYMPHONY NO. 94 IN G MAJOR *(SURPRISE;* 1791),
BY JOSEPH HAYDN (1732–1809)

Second Movement: Andante

Theme and variations, duple meter ($\frac{2}{4}$), C major

2 flutes, 2 oboes, 2 bassoons, 2 French horns, 2 trumpets, timpani, 1st violins, 2d violins, violas, cellos, double basses

(Duration, 6:14)

THEME
Section a

1 | 0:00   Violins, *p,* staccato theme.

Section b

    Section a repeated, *pp,* with pizzicato string accompaniment. Surprise chord, *ff.*
Violins, *p,* continuation of theme.

    Section b repeated with flute and oboe.

VARIATION 1

2 | 1:07   *a.* Theme begins, *f,* higher countermelody in violins, *p.* Section a repeated.

    b. Violins, *p,* continuation of theme and higher countermelody. Section b repeated.

VARIATION 2

3 | 2:12   *a.* Theme in minor, *ff,* violin phrase in major, *p.* Section a repeated.

b. Violins, *f,* rapid downward scales, orchestra *f.* Violins alone, *p,* lead into

VARIATION 3

[4] 3:20   *a.* Oboe, *p,* theme in faster repeated notes, major key.

Flute and oboe, *p,* legato countermelody above staccato theme in violins, *p.*

b. Continuation of theme and countermelody. Section b repeated.

VARIATION 4

[5] 4:23   *a.* Theme in brasses and woodwinds, *ff,* fast notes in violins, *ff.* Violins, *p,* legato version of theme, dotted rhythm (long-short).

b. Violins, *p,* continuation of theme, dotted rhythm. Full orchestra, *ff,* triumphant continuation of theme leads to suspenseful chord, *ff,* sudden *p.*

CLOSING SECTION

[6] 5:45   Theme in oboe, *p,* gently dissonant chords in strings, flute joins, *pp* conclusion.

BASIC TERMS

216   theme and variations (page 214)   countermelody (214)

MINUET AND TRIO

The form known as **minuet and trio,** or **minuet,** is employed as the third movement of classical symphonies, string quartets, and other works. Like the movements of the baroque suite, the minuet originated as a dance. It first appeared at the court of Louis XIV of France around 1650 and was danced by aristocrats throughout the eighteenth century. The minuet was a stately, dignified dance in which the dancing couple exchanged curtsies and bows.

The minuet movement of a symphony or string quartet is written for listening, not dancing. It is in triple meter ($\frac{3}{4}$) and usually in a moderate tempo. The movement is in A B A form: minuet (A), trio (B), minuet (A). The trio (B) is usually quieter than the minuet (A) section and requires fewer instruments. It often contains woodwind solos. The trio section got its name during the baroque period, when a set of two dances would be followed by a repetition of the first dance. The second dance was known as a "trio" because it was usually played by three instruments. Classical composers did not restrict themselves to three instruments in the B sections of their minuets, but the name *trio* remained.

The A (minuet) section includes smaller parts a, b, and a' (variation of a). In the opening A (minuet) section, all the smaller parts are repeated, as follows: a (repeated) ba' (repeated). (In the musical score, the repeat sign :‖ indicates each repetition.) The B (trio) section is quite similar in form: c (repeated) dc' (repeated). At the close of the B (trio) section, the repetition of the entire A (minuet) section is indicated by the words **da capo** *(from the beginning).* This time, however, the minuet is played straight through without the repetitions: a ba'. The whole movement can be outlined like this:

Minuet	Trio	Minuet
A	B	A
a (repeated) ba' (repeated)	c (repeated) dc' (repeated)	a ba'

With its A B A form and its many repeated parts, the minuet is structurally the simplest movement of a symphony or string quartet.

In many of Beethoven's compositions, the third movement is not a minuet but a related form called a *scherzo.* Like a minuet, a **scherzo** is usually in A B A form and triple meter, but it moves more quickly, generating energy, rhythmic drive, and rough humor. (*Scherzo* is Italian for *joke.*)

EINE KLEINE NACHTMUSIK (A LITTLE NIGHT MUSIC), K. 525, BY WOLFGANG AMADEUS MOZART

Third Movement:

Minuet (Allegretto)

Side 5, band 2
CD 3 7

Mozart's *Eine kleine Nachtmusik* is a **serenade,** a work that's usually light in mood, meant for evening entertainment. It is written for a small string orchestra or for a string quartet plus a double bass. (The double bass plays the cello part an octave lower.) The third movement is a courtly minuet in A B A form. The A (minuet) section is stately, mostly loud and staccato, with a clearly marked beat. In contrast, the B (trio) section is intimate, soft, and legato. Its murmuring accompaniment contributes to the smooth flow of the music.

Listening Outline   To be read while music is heard

EINE KLEINE NACHTMUSIK, K. 525 (1787),
BY WOLFGANG AMADEUS MOZART

Third Movement: Minuet (Allegretto)

A B A form, triple meter ($\frac{3}{4}$), G major

1st violins, 2d violins, violas, cellos, double bass

(Duration, 2:03)

MINUET (A)
7 0:00   1. Stately melody, *f*, predominantly staccato. Repeated.

Legato phrase, *p*, leads to stately staccato phrase, *f*. Repeated.

TRIO (B)
8 0:42   2. Gracious legato melody, *p*, murmuring accompaniment. Repeated.

Climbing legato phrase, *f,* leads to legato melody, *p.* Repeated.

MINUET (A)
[9] 1:37

3. Stately melody, *f,* predominantly staccato.
Legato phrase, *p,* leads to stately staccato phrase, *f.*

BASIC TERMS

minuet and trio (minuet) (page 217)
da capo (217)
scherzo (217)
serenade (218)

RONDO

Many classical movements are in rondo form. A ***rondo*** features a tuneful main theme (A) which returns several times in alternation with other themes. Common rondo patterns are A B A C A and A B A C A B A. The main theme is usually lively, pleasing, and simple to remember, and the listener can easily recognize its return. Because the main theme is usually stated in the tonic key, its return is all the more welcome. The rondo can be used either as an independent piece or as one movement of a symphony, string quartet, or sonata. It often serves as a finale, because its liveliness, regularity, and buoyancy bring a happy sense of conclusion.

Rondo form is often combined with elements of sonata form to produce the sonata-rondo. The ***sonata-rondo*** contains a development section like that in sonata form and is outlined A B A–development section–A B A.

The popularity of the rondo did not end with the classical period. It has been used by twentieth-century composers such as Igor Stravinsky and Arnold Schoenberg.

219

STRING QUARTET IN C MINOR, OP. 18, NO. 4, BY LUDWIG VAN BEETHOVEN

Fourth Movement:

Rondo (Allegro)

Side 8, band 1
CD 4 [26]

The exciting rondo movement from Beethoven's String Quartet in C minor, Op. 18, No. 4, may be outlined A B A C A B A. Its main theme, A, is a lively gypsy dance made up of two repeated parts: a a b b. An unexpected held tone in part b suggests the improvisatory playing of a gypsy fiddler. The main theme, in minor, contrasts with the other themes, which are in major. Theme B is a lyrical legato melody, while theme C is playful, with quick upward rushes. At its final return, the main theme (A) has a faster tempo, prestissimo, and leads into a frenzied concluding section.

Listening Outline To be read while music is heard

STRING QUARTET IN C MINOR, OP. 18, NO. 4 (1798–1800), BY LUDWIG VAN BEETHOVEN

Fourth Movement: Rondo (Allegro)

Duple meter ($\frac{2}{2}$), C minor

1st violin, 2d violin, viola, cello

(Duration, 4:18)

A

[26] 0:00   1. Lively main theme in 1st violin, minor key.

B

[27] 0:32   2. Lyrical melody, legato, major key.

A	**28** 1:16	3. Lively main theme, minor key. Theme becomes more agitated.
C	**29** 1:46	4. Upward rushes in each instrument, playful downward phrase in 1st violin, major key.
A	2:10	5. Lively main theme, minor key. Crescendo to held chord, *ff*.
B	2:48	6. Lyrical melody, legato, major key. Melody repeated an octave higher. Playful phrases in violins, crescendo to *f*, sustained tones in 1st violin.
A	3:31	7. Lively main theme, *ff*, faster tempo (prestissimo), minor key. Concluding section builds, downward staccato scale, high repeated tones, *p*. Upward rushes, *ff*, at end.

BASIC TERMS

rondo (page 219)
sonata-rondo (219)

THE CLASSICAL SYMPHONY

CLASSICAL

7

The great contribution of the classical period to orchestral music is the symphony. Haydn wrote at least 104 symphonies, Mozart over forty, and Beethoven nine. Most of Haydn's symphonies were composed for his employers, who required a steady flow of works for their palace concerts. Beethoven, on the other hand, wrote a symphony only when inspired. His symphonies are longer than Haydn's or Mozart's and were conceived for performance in large concert halls.

A *symphony* is an extended, ambitious composition typically lasting between 20 and 45 minutes, exploiting the expanded range of tone color and dynamics of the classical orchestra. A classical symphony usually consists of four movements which evoke a wide range of emotions through contrasts of tempo and mood. A typical sequence is (1) a vigorous, dramatic fast movement; (2) a lyrical slow movement; (3) a dancelike movement (minuet or scherzo); and (4) a brilliant or heroic fast movement.

The opening movement is almost always fast and in sonata form. It is usually the most dramatic movement and stresses an exciting development of short motives. Sometimes a slow introduction leads to the opening fast movement and creates a feeling of anticipation.

221

It is in the slow second movement that we are most likely to find broad, songlike melodies. This movement, by and large, is either in sonata form, A B A form, or theme-and-variations form. Unlike the other movements in the symphony, the slow movement is generally *not* in the tonic key. For example, if the first, third, and fourth movements are in the tonic key of C major, the second movement may be in F major. The new key points up the expressive contrast of the slow movement.

In the symphonies of Haydn and Mozart, the third movement is generally a minuet and trio, which may be in a moderate or fairly quick tempo. This movement varies in character from a courtly dance to a peasant romp or a vigorous piece that is hardly dancelike. Beethoven liked fast, energetic scherzos for his third movements.

The fourth, concluding movement of a Haydn or Mozart symphony is fast, lively, and brilliant, but somewhat lighter in mood than the opening movement. (The agitated final movement of Mozart's Symphony No. 40 in G minor is not typical.) Beethoven's concluding movement tends to be more triumphant and heroic in character and sometimes is meant as the climax of the whole symphony. The final movement of a classical symphony is most often in sonata or sonata-rondo form.

In most classical symphonies, each movement is a self-contained composition with its own set of themes. A theme in one movement will only rarely reappear in a later movement. (Beethoven's Fifth and Ninth Symphonies are exceptions.) But a symphony is unified partly by the use of the same key in three of its movements. More important, the movements balance and complement each other both musically and emotionally.

The importance of the symphony has lasted into the middle of the twentieth century. Its great significance is reflected in such familiar terms as *symphonic music, symphony hall,* and *symphony orchestra.*

BASIC TERM

symphony (page 221)

symphony (page 221)

[CLASSICAL **8**] THE CLASSICAL CONCERTO

A classical *concerto* is a three-movement work for an instrumental soloist and orchestra. It combines the soloist's virtuosity and interpretive abilities with the orchestra's wide range of tone color and dynamics. Emerging from this encounter is a contrast of ideas and sound that is dramatic and satisfying. The soloist is very much the star, and all of his or her musical talents are needed in this challenging dialogue.

THE CLASSICAL PERIOD

The Interrupted Sleep (1750), by François Boucher. During the early eighteenth century, the heavy monumental baroque style gave way to a more intimate style, the rococo, with light colors, curved lines, and graceful ornaments. The French rococo painter Boucher chose subjects that were decorative and sweetly sensuous.

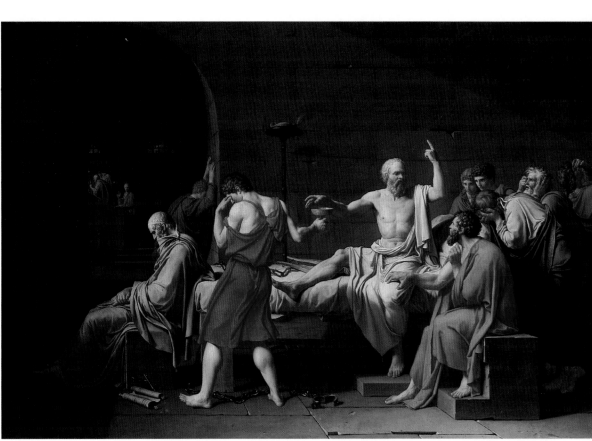

Above: *Death of Socrates* (1787), by Jacques-Louis David. By the late eighteenth century, the rococo style had been superseded by the neoclassical style, which attempted to recapture the "noble simplicity and calm grandeur" of ancient Greek and Roman art. Neoclassical artists such as the French painter David emphasized firm lines, clear structures, and moralistic subjects.

Opposite page: *Napoleon at St. Bernard* (1800), by Jacques-Louis David. Beethoven originally planned to name his Third Symphony *(Eroica;* 1803–1804) "Bonaparte," because he saw Napoleon as the embodiment of heroism; but when he learned that Napoleon had proclaimed himself emperor, he tore out the title page and later renamed the symphony "Heroic Symphony composed to celebrate the memory of a great man."

The Third of May, 1808 (1814), by Francisco Goya. The classical period was a time of violent political and social upheaval, witnessing the American Revolution, the French Revolution, and the Napoleonic wars. The Spanish painter Goya vividly showed the execution of Spanish hostages by soldiers of Napoleon's army.

The classical love of balance can be seen in the concerto, for soloist and orchestra are equally important. Between them, there's an interplay of melodic lines and a spirit of give-and-take. One moment the soloist plays the melody while the orchestra accompanies. Then the woodwinds may unfold the main theme against rippling arpeggios (broken chords) played by the soloist. Mozart and Beethoven—the greatest masters of the classical concerto—often wrote concertos for themselves to play as piano soloists; the piano is their favored solo instrument. But other solo instruments used in classical concertos include violin, cello, horn, trumpet, clarinet, and bassoon.

Like symphonies, concertos can last anywhere from 20 minutes to 45 minutes. But instead of the symphony's four movements, a classical concerto has three: (1) fast, (2) slow, and (3) fast. A concerto has no minuet or scherzo.

In the first movement and sometimes in the last movement, there is a special unaccompanied showpiece for the soloist, the **cadenza** (Italian for *cadence*). Near the end of the movement, the orchestra suspends forward motion by briefly sustaining a dissonant chord. This is indicated in the score by a *fermata* (⌒), a sign meaning *pause*, which is placed over the chord. The suspense announces the entry of the soloist's cadenza. For several minutes, the soloist, *without orchestra*, displays virtuosity by playing dazzling scale passages and broken chords. Themes of the movement are varied and presented in new keys. At the end of a cadenza, the soloist plays a long trill followed by a chord that meshes with the reentrance of the orchestra.

In the classical era, the soloist, who was often the composer, generally improvised the cadenzas. In this case, the score contained only the fermata, indicating where the cadenza should be inserted. But after the eighteenth century, the art of improvisation declined, and composers began to write cadenzas directly into the score. This gave them more control over their compositions.

Today, performers of eighteenth-century concertos may have a choice of cadenzas. For some concertos, composers wrote cadenzas for their own performance or for that of a student. Also, many nineteenth- and twentieth-century musicians later provided cadenzas for classical concertos. These are best when their style matches that of the concerto. For example, the cadenzas Beethoven composed for Mozart's D Minor Piano Concerto are so strong and so much in the spirit of the work that pianists today still use them.

A classical concerto begins with a movement in sonata form of a special kind, containing *two* expositions. The first is played by the orchestra, which presents several themes in the home key. This opening section sets the mood for the movement and leads us to expect the soloist's entrance. The second exposition begins with the soloist's first notes. Music for the solo entry may be powerful or quiet, but its effect is dramatic because suspense has been built. Together with the orchestra, the soloist explores themes from the first exposition and introduces new ones. After a modulation from the home key to a new key, the second exposition then moves to a development section, followed by the recapitulation, cadenza, and coda. The slow middle movement may take any one of several forms, but the finale is usually a quick rondo or sonata-rondo.

BASIC TERMS

concerto (page 222)
cadenza (223)

9 CLASSICAL CHAMBER MUSIC

CLASSICAL

Classical *chamber music* is designed for the intimate setting of a room (chamber) in a home or palace, rather than for a public concert hall. It is performed by a small group of two to nine musicians, with one player to a part. Chamber music is lighter in sound than classical orchestral music. During the classical period, it was fashionable for an aristocrat or a member of the well-to-do middle class to play chamber music with friends and to hire professional musicians to entertain guests after dinner.

Chamber music is subtle and intimate, intended to please the performer as much as the listener. A chamber music group is a team. Each member is essential, and each may have an important share of the thematic material. Therefore much give-and-take is called for among the instruments. Classical chamber music does not need a conductor; instead, each musician must be sensitive to what goes on and coordinate dynamics and phrasing with the other musicians. In this respect, a chamber ensemble is like a small jazz group.

The most important form in classical chamber music is the *string quartet,* written for two violins, a viola, and a cello. Haydn, Mozart, and Beethoven wrote some of their most important music in this form. The string quartet can be compared to a conversation among four lively, sensitive, and intelligent people. And it's not surprising that the string quartet evolved when conversation was cultivated as a fine art.

Like the symphony, the string quartet usually consists of four movements: (1) fast, (2) slow, (3) minuet or scherzo, (4) fast. (Sometimes the second movement is a minuet or a scherzo and the slow movement is third.)

Other popular forms of classical chamber music are the sonata for violin and piano, the piano trio (violin, cello, and piano), and the string quintet (two violins, two violas, and cello).

Today, as in the eighteenth century, much chamber music is performed by amateurs. By consulting the directory *Amateur Chamber Music Players,* one can find partners for chamber music almost anywhere in the United States.

BASIC TERMS

chamber music (page 224)
string quartet (224)

JOSEPH HAYDN

The first of the three classical masters, Joseph Haydn (1732–1809), was born in a tiny Austrian village called Rohrau. His father made wagon wheels, and until he was six, Haydn's musical background consisted of folk songs his father loved to sing and the peasant dances that whirled about him on festive occasions. (This early contact with folk music later had an influence on his style.) Haydn's eager response to music was recognized, and he was sent to live with a relative who gave him basic music lessons for two years. At the age of eight, he went to Vienna to serve as a choirboy in the Cathedral of St. Stephen. There, though his good voice was appreciated, he had no chance for composition lessons or for perfecting an instrumental technique. And when his voice changed, Haydn was dismissed from St. Stephen's and turned out on the street without a penny. "I barely managed to stay alive by giving music lessons to children for about eight years," he wrote. Throughout those years he struggled to teach himself composition and also took odd jobs, including playing violin in the popular Viennese street bands that offered evening entertainment.

Gradually, aristocratic patrons of music began to notice Haydn's talent. For a brief time he was music director at the court of a Bohemian count, but the orchestra was dissolved because of his patron's financial problems. When he was twenty-nine, Haydn's life changed for the better, permanently.

In 1761, Haydn entered the service of the Esterházys, the richest and most powerful of the Hungarian noble families. For almost thirty years,

(Royal College of Music)

Joseph Haydn.

from 1761 to 1790, most of his music was composed for performance in the palaces of the family. Haydn spent much of his time at Eszterháza, a magnificent but isolated palace in Hungary that contained an opera house, a theater, two concert halls, and 126 guest rooms.

As a highly skilled servant, Haydn was to compose all the music requested by his patron, conduct the orchestra of about twenty-five players, coach singers, and oversee the condition of instruments and the operation of the music library. He was also required to "appear daily in the antechamber before and after midday and inquire whether His Highness is pleased to order a performance of the orchestra." The amount of work demanded of Haydn as assistant music director and later as music director was staggering; there were usually two concerts and two opera performances weekly, as well as daily chamber music in the prince's apartment. Since Nicholas Esterházy played the baryton (a complicated string instrument now obsolete), Haydn wrote over 150 pieces with a baryton part.

Though today it seems degrading for a genius to be dependent on the will of a prince, in the eighteenth century patronage was taken for granted. Composers found definite advantages in it: they received a steady income and their works were performed. And though Haydn felt restricted by his job from time to time, he later wisely said, "Not only did I have the encouragement of constant approval, but as conductor of an orchestra I could make experiments, observe what produced an effect and what weakened it, and was thus in a position to improve, alter, make additions or omissions, and be as bold as I pleased. I was cut off from the world; there was no one to confuse or torment me, and I was forced to become original."

Despite an unhappy marriage, Haydn was good-humored and unselfish. He was conscientious about professional duties, and he cared about the personal interests of his musicians. Prince Nicholas loved Eszterháza and once stayed at the palace longer than usual. The orchestra members came to Haydn and asked to return to Vienna; they were tired of being isolated in the country, away so long from their wives and children. Haydn obliged by composing his Symphony in F Sharp Minor, now known as the *Farewell*. At its first performance for the prince, the musicians followed the indications in the score: during the last movement, one after another stopped playing, put out his candle, and quietly left the hall. By the time that only Haydn and the first violinist remained, Nicholas took the hint; the next day he ordered the household to return to Vienna.

Haydn met the younger Mozart in the early 1780s and they became close friends. To someone finding fault with one of Mozart's operas, Haydn replied, "I cannot settle this dispute, but this I know: Mozart is the greatest composer the world possesses now.'

Over a period of twenty years, word spread about the Esterházys' composer, and Haydn's music became immensely popular all over Europe. Publishers and concert organizations sent commissions for new works. After the death of Prince Nicholas Esterházy in 1790, Haydn was free to go to London, where a concert series was planned around his compositions. He'd been asked by the concert manager Johann Peter Salomon to write and conduct new symphonies for performance at public concerts. Six were composed for a first visit in 1791–1792 and six more for a second visit in 1794–1795. The twelve became known as the *Salomon* or *London* symphonies.

Reports of the time say that Haydn's appearances were triumphs. By the end of the eighteenth century, London was the largest and richest city in the world. Its concert life was unusually active and attracted many foreign musicians. The acclaim at Haydn's concerts was so overwhelming that some movements of his symphonies had to be repeated. One listener noted that there was "an electrical effect on all present and such a degree of enthusiasm as almost amounted to a frenzy."

And so a servant became a celebrity. Haydn was wined and dined by the aristocracy, given an honorary doctorate at Oxford, and received by members of the royal family. And, as though to balance out earlier personal unhappiness, he had a love affair with a rich English widow. After his thirty years of service to the Esterházys, Haydn's reception by the English moved him to write, "How sweet is some degree of liberty. The consciousness of no longer being a bond servant sweetens all my toil."

(Vienna City Museum)

A performance of Haydn's oratorio *The Creation* at the University of Vienna in 1808.

Haydn returned to Vienna in 1795, rich and honored, and maintained good relations with Eszterháza. The new prince, Nicholas II, did not have his father's wide musical interests and liked only religious music. Haydn's agreement specified that he would compose a mass a year. He wrote six, and all reflect the mature, brilliant writing of the London symphonies. In this period, when he was in his late sixties, Haydn composed two oratorios, *The Creation* (1798) and *The Seasons* (1801). They were so popular that choruses and orchestras were formed at the beginning of the nineteenth century for the sole purpose of performing them.

Haydn died in 1809, at the age of seventy-seven, while Napoleon's army was occupying Vienna. The wide recognition he had attained could be seen in a memorial service held for him: joining the Viennese were French generals and an honor guard of French soldiers.

HAYDN'S MUSIC

Haydn was a pathfinder for the classical style, a pioneer in the development of the symphony and string quartet. Both Mozart and Beethoven were influenced by his style. Haydn's music, like his personality, is robust and direct; it radiates a healthy optimism.

Haydn never forgot the peasant dances and songs of his childhood in a small village, and many of his works have a folk flavor. He quoted actual peasant tunes and composed original melodies in a folklike style. The minuets often romp and stomp rather than bow and curtsy. *The Creation* (1798) and *The Seasons* (1801), his late oratorios, reflect Haydn's love of nature. There are vivid and humorous musical descriptions of storms, hail, animals, birds, and fish.

Haydn was a master at developing themes. He would split them into small fragments to be repeated quickly by different instruments. His skill at development made it possible for him to build a whole movement out of a single main theme. In such movements, contrast of mood results from changes in texture, key, rhythm, dynamics, and orchestration. The contagious joy that springs from his lively rhythms and vivid contrasts makes it clear why London went wild.

"I prefer to see the humorous side of life," Haydn once said. He produced comic effects from unexpected pauses and tempo changes and from sudden shifts in dynamics and pitch. We've heard one of his musical jokes in the second movement of the *Surprise* Symphony, where a soft theme is suddenly punctuated by a loud chord.

Haydn's enormous output revolves around his 104 symphonies, which span a period of over forty-five years, from about 1758 to 1795. For a long time, the last twelve symphonies (Nos. 93 to 104), composed for public concerts in London during the 1790s, were the only ones regularly performed. Now, thanks to venturesome scholars and performers, the earlier symphonies composed for Eszterháza and other castles are heard more often. Many of Haydn's popular symphonies have nicknames, such as *Surprise* (No. 94), *Military* (No. 100), *Clock* (No. 101), and *Drum Roll* (No. 103).

Haydn's symphonies and his sixty-eight string quartets are considered his most important works. Some scholars believe Haydn invented the string quartet form. He began writing string quartets for good reason—only three other musicians were on hand during the summer of 1757, when he was invited to take part, as violist, in chamber music performances at a castle. The steward of the aristocratic host and the parish priest each played a violin, and there was a cellist named Albrechtsberger. Spurred by necessity, the twenty-five-year-old Haydn wrote the first of his lifelong series of string quartets.

Haydn's output also includes piano sonatas, piano trios, divertimentos, operas, and masses. The variety in his works is astounding. He was a great innovator and experimenter who hated arbitrary "rules" of composition. "What is the good of such rules? Art is free, and should be fettered by no such mechanical regulations. The educated ear is the sole authority in all these questions, and I think that I have as much right to lay down the law as anyone."

SYMPHONY NO. 94 IN G MAJOR (*SURPRISE*; 1791)

Haydn composed his most famous symphony, the Symphony No. 94 in G Major (*Surprise*), in 1791, during his first visit to London. It was performed at a public concert on March 23, 1792, by an orchestra of forty players, a large group for the time. The London *Diary* reported that the new symphony was "of extraordinary merit. It was simple, profound and sublime. The andante movement was particularly admired."

The nickname *Surprise*, coined by Haydn's contemporaries, comes from the sudden loud chord that punctuates the soft theme of the andante (as we've seen on page 214). "It was my wish to surprise the public with something new," Haydn once explained, "and to make a debut in a brilliant manner." Typical of Haydn are the musical surprises, folklike tunes, and vivid contrasts of tone color and dynamics in Symphony No. 94.

First Movement:

Adagio (slow introduction); Vivace assai (very lively)

Supplementary sets:
Side 3, band 1
CD 2 [1]

The slow introduction to the first movement begins with a peaceful melody that is divided between woodwinds and strings:

The mood soon becomes serious, as a pulsating rhythm, a crescendo, and chromatic harmonies create a momentary feeling of uncertainty.

The uncertainty of the introduction is resolved in the vivace assai, a very rapid, joyful movement in sonata form.

[2] 1:12

The first theme is a brief dance tune that is played softly by the violins:

It is followed by a section for full orchestra that's loud and energetic. After a restatement of the soft opening theme, the exposition continues with a long and powerful bridge section for full orchestra. During the bridge, the soft opening theme is heard once again, this time slightly varied and in a new key:

1:41

[3] 2:00

A carefree waltz melody serves as the second theme of the exposition:

4 2:15

It begins with a syncopated repetition of a single tone and is played softly by the violins with an "oom-pah-pah" accompaniment in the other strings. Haydn rounds off the exposition with a gracious closing theme that is introduced by the strings and continued by the woodwinds:

5 2:32

Soon the remaining instruments join in and bring the exposition to a rousing finish. The exposition is repeated.

Repeat of exposition
6 3:10

The development begins softly as Haydn reveals the potential of his lilting first theme. In the agitated continuation of the development, tension is built through motives from the bridge section which move restlessly through minor keys. After a sudden *p*, the development concludes with repeated notes that lead into the recapitulation.

Development
7 5:08

For a while, all is "normal" in the recapitulation; we hear the first theme, a shortened form of the bridge, and the second theme. But before letting us hear the closing theme, Haydn expands the recapitulation through a rich polyphonic development of the first theme. The return of the closing theme brings a feeling of relaxation, and the movement ends jubilantly.

Recapitulation
8 6:08

Second Movement:

Andante

The second movement of the symphony is the well-known theme and variations already discussed in Section 4.

Side 5, band 1
CD 3 1

Third Movement:

Minuet (Allegro molto)

Supplementary sets:
Side 3, band 2
CD 2 9

With its heavily marked "oom-pah-pah" beat and unusually fast tempo, the minuet of Symphony No. 94 sounds more like a boisterous peasant romp than an elegant court dance. This movement is written in the customary A B A minuet form:

Section A (minuet)
9 0:00
Section B (trio)
10 2:28
Repeat of A (minuet)
11 3:33

Minuet	Trio	Minuet
A	B	A
a (repeated) ba' (repeated)	c (repeated) dc' (repeated)	a ba'

The high-spirited A (minuet) section is mostly loud and played by the full orchestra, but there are softer interludes played by strings and woodwinds.

The minuet section concludes with a soft flute phrase that is repeated loudly by the whole orchestra.

In contrast to the A section, the trio (B) section is intimate, with softer dynamics, fewer instruments (only strings and bassoon), and a less strongly emphasized beat.

232

Fourth Movement:
Finale (Allegro di molto)

The symphony's very rapid and brilliant finale is a sonata-rondo. It imaginatively combines the thematic development typical of sonata form with the recurring main theme found in rondo form. The movement may be outlined as A B A' (shortened)–development section–A' (shortened)–development section–A B coda. Its playful main theme, A, is soft but lively:

Supplementary sets:
Side 3, band 3
CD 2 [12]

[12] 0:00

Theme B is a gentle, lilting melody:

[13] 1:06

At its first two returns the main theme is shortened and leads immediately into a bustling development section. With great wit, Haydn prepares for the second return of the main theme by repeating its upbeat beginning over and over.

[14] 2:05

The *Surprise* Symphony is an example of Haydn's genius at making rich, complex music from the simplest phrases and themes.

TRUMPET CONCERTO IN E FLAT MAJOR (1796)

Haydn's Trumpet Concerto in E Flat Major has a remarkable history. After its premiere in 1800, it was forgotten for almost 130 years. It was first published only in 1929, and in the 1930s a phonograph recording brought the work to a wide audience. Now, it may well be Haydn's most popular work.

233

Haydn wrote the concerto in 1796 for a friend, a trumpeter at the Viennese court who had recently invented a keyed trumpet that could produce a complete chromatic scale. The keyed trumpet was intended to replace the natural trumpet, which could produce only a restricted number of tones. But the keyed trumpet had a dull sound and was supplanted by the valve trumpet around 1840. Today, the concerto is performed on a valve trumpet. Like most concertos, it has three movements:

1. fast
2. slow
3. fast

We'll examine the third movement.

Third Movement:
Allegro

Side 4, band 9
CD 2 [37]

The third movement is a dazzling sonata-rondo in which Haydn gives the trumpeter's virtuosity free rein. The movement combines the recurring main theme characteristic of rondo form with the development section found in sonata form. It may be outlined as A B A B′ A–development section–A B″–coda. Themes A and B are introduced by the orchestra and are then presented mainly by the trumpet, with orchestral support. The main theme, A, is a high-spirited melody that is well suited to the trumpet. Theme B is playful; it contains a short, downward-moving phrase that is repeated several times. Haydn's fondness for musical surprises is reflected in the coda, which contains sudden changes of dynamics, unexpected harmonic twists, and a suspenseful long pause.

Listening Outline   To be read while music is heard

TRUMPET CONCERTO IN E FLAT MAJOR (1796),
BY JOSEPH HAYDN

Third Movement: Allegro

Sonata-rondo form, duple meter ($\frac{2}{4}$), E flat major

Solo trumpet, 2 flutes, 2 oboes, 2 bassoons, 2 French horns, 2 trumpets, timpani, 1st violins, 2d violins, violas, cellos, double basses

(Duration, 4:26)

A

37 0:00   1. *a.* Main theme in violins, *p.*

              b. Main theme in full orchestra, *f,* violins, running notes and rising scale lead
                  to

B

38 0:22   *c.* Violins, *f,* downward short phrase, repeated *p,*

              orchestra, *f,* brass fanfares, cadence, pause.

A

39 0:38   2. Main theme in trumpet, strings accompany, trumpet repeats main theme,
                  orchestra, *f,* violins, *p,* lead to

B′

40 1:07   3. Trumpet, held tone, ushers in downward short phrases, upward phrases with
                  trills, downward legato phrases, trumpet trill to cadence, trumpet fanfares,
                  orchestra, *f.*

A

41 1:46   4. *a.* Trumpet, held tone, ushers in main theme.
                  b. Main-theme phrase in full orchestra, *f.*

DEVELOPMENT

42 2:04   5. Trumpet, main-theme phrases, *p,* violins, *p,* main-theme phrases in minor with
                  trumpet fanfares, running notes in violins, *f,* trumpet and brasses join, suddenly
                  soft, violins introduce

A

43 2:36   6. *a.* Trumpet, held tone, ushers in main theme.
                  b. Orchestra, *f,* running notes and rising scale lead to

B″

       2:54   7. *a.* Trumpet, downward short phrases, downward broken chords, octave leaps,
                  trill to cadence.
                  b. Violins, *p,* high woodwinds, *p,* trumpet fanfares, violins, *p,* lead to

CODA

       3:27   8. *a.* Trumpet, main-theme phrase, strings, *p,* trumpet, downward chain of trills.
                  b. Suddenly loud, full orchestra, sudden *pp,* string tremolos, suddenly loud, full
                  orchestra, repeated notes in trumpet, long pause.
                  c. Trumpet, main-theme phrases, orchestra, *p,* crescendo to *ff,* repeated notes
                  in trumpet, closing chords in orchestra.

11 WOLFGANG AMADEUS MOZART

Wolfgang Amadeus Mozart (1756–1791), one of the most amazing child prodigies in history, was born in Salzburg, Austria. By the time he was six, he could play the harpsichord and violin, improvise fugues, write minuets, and read music perfectly at first sight. At the age of eight, he wrote a symphony; at eleven, an oratorio; and at twelve, an opera. By his early teens, Mozart had behind him many works that would have brought credit to a composer three times his age.

Mozart's father, Leopold, who was a court musician, was understandably eager to show him off and went to great lengths to do so. Mozart spent almost half the time between the ages of six and fifteen on tour in Europe and England. He played for Empress Maria Theresa in Vienna, for Louis XV at Versailles, for George III in London, and for innumerable aristocrats along the way. On his trips to Italy he was able to study and master the current operatic style, which he later put to superb use. Mozart was in Rome during Holy Week when he was fourteen, and he went to hear the famous choir of the Sistine Chapel performing a work that was its treasured property. Anyone caught copying this choral piece was to be punished by excommunication. Mozart heard it once, wrote it out afterward almost completely, returned with his manuscript to make a few additions— and was discovered. For anyone to copy the music was a crime; for anyone to hear it and remember it so accurately seemed incredible. Mozart not only escaped punishment but was knighted by the pope for his musical accomplishments.

When he was fifteen, Mozart returned to Salzburg, which was ruled by a new prince-archbishop, Hieronymus Colloredo. The archbishop was a tyrant who did not appreciate Mozart's genius, and he refused to grant him more than a subordinate seat in the court orchestra. With his father's help, Mozart tried repeatedly over the next decade to find a suitable position elsewhere, but with no success.

The tragic irony of Mozart's life was that he won more acclaim as a boy wonder than as an adult musician. His upbringing and personality were partly to blame. In his childhood, his complete dependence on his father gave him little opportunity to develop initiative. Even when Mozart was twenty-two, his mother tagged along when he went to Paris to seek recognition and establish himself. A Parisian observed that Mozart was "too good-natured, not active enough, too easily taken in, too little concerned with the means that may lead him to good fortune."

Unlike Haydn, Mozart began his professional life as an international celebrity, pampered by kings. He could not tolerate being treated like a

(Austrian Information Service, New York)

Wolfgang
Amadeus Mozart.

servant and eating with valets and cooks, and his relations with his patron
went from bad to worse. Mozart became totally insubordinate when the
prince-archbishop forbade him to give concerts or perform at the houses of
the aristocracy. After an ugly confrontation, Mozart wrote: "He lied to my
face that my salary was five hundred *gulden*, called me a scoundrel, a

rascal, a vagabond. At last my blood began to boil, I could no longer contain myself, and I said, 'So Your Grace is not satisfied with me?' " He was answered with, "What, you dare to threaten me—you scoundrel? There is the door!" On his third attempt to request dismissal, Mozart was thrown out of the room by a court official and given a kick.

By 1781, when he was twenty-five, Mozart could stand it no longer. He broke free of provincial Salzburg and traveled to Vienna, intending to be a free-lance musician. To reassure his father, he wrote: "I have the best and most useful acquaintances in the world. I am liked and respected in the best houses, and all possible honors are given me, and moreover I get paid for it. I guarantee you I'll be successful."

Indeed, Mozart's first few years in Vienna were successful. His German opera *Die Entführung aus dem Serail* (*The Abduction from the Seraglio*, 1782) was acclaimed. Concerts of his own music were attended by the emperor and nobility. Pupils paid him high fees, his compositions were published, and his playing was heard in palace drawing rooms. He even went against his father's wishes by marrying Constanze Weber, who had no money and was as impractical as he. Contributing to the brightness of these years was Mozart's friendship with Haydn, who told Leopold, "Your son is the greatest composer that I know, either personally or by reputation; he has taste and, what is more, the most profound knowledge of composition."

Then, in 1786, came Mozart's opera *Le Nozze di Figaro* (*The Marriage of Figaro*). Vienna loved it, and Prague was even more enthusiastic. "They talk about nothing but *Figaro*. Nothing is played, sung, or whistled but *Figaro*," Mozart joyfully wrote. This success led an opera company in Prague to commission *Don Giovanni* the following year. *Don Giovanni* was a triumph in Prague, but it pushed the Viennese too far. Emperor Joseph II acknowledged that it was a masterwork, but not appropriate for his pleasure-loving subjects. Dark qualities and dissonance did not appeal to them.

Mozart's popularity in Vienna began to decline. It was a fickle city; one was society's darling for a few seasons and then was suddenly ignored. And Mozart's music was considered complicated and hard to follow, too "highly spiced" with dissonance. A publisher warned him: "Write in a more popular style, or else I can neither print nor pay for any more of your music!" His pupils dwindled, and the elite snubbed his concerts. In desperate financial straits, he wrote to friends, "Great God, I would not wish my worst enemy to be in this position. . . . I am coming to you not with thanks but with fresh entreaties."

Many of Mozart's letters have been published. These span his life, and it is sad to move from the colorful, witty, and keenly observant notes of a prodigy on tour through his initial optimism about Vienna to the despair of "I cannot describe what I have been feeling. . . . A kind of longing that is never satisfied."

During his last year, Mozart was happier and more successful. He was delighted to receive a commission from a Viennese theater for a German comic opera, *Die Zauberflöte (The Magic Flute)*. While hard at work, Mozart was visited by a stranger who carried an anonymous letter commissioning a requiem, a mass for the dead. Mozart could not begin the Requiem because he had to finish *The Magic Flute* and compose another opera, *La Clemenza di Tito*, which was performed in Prague on September 6, 1791. On September 30, two months before his death, *The Magic Flute* was premiered to resounding praise in Vienna. Its success probably would have brought large financial rewards, but it came too late. Mozart died of rheumatic fever on December 5, 1791, shortly before his thirty-sixth birthday, leaving the Requiem unfinished. On the day of his burial, a Vienna newspaper reported that "his works, which are loved and admired everywhere, are proof of his greatness—and they reveal the irreplaceable loss which the noble art of music has suffered through his death."

MOZART'S MUSIC

Mozart was among the most versatile of all composers; he wrote masterpieces in all the musical forms of his time. His symphonies are as profound as his string quartets, his piano concertos as dramatic and lyrical as his operas. All his music sings: even his instrumental melodies seem to grow out of the human voice. His works convey a feeling of ease, grace, and spontaneity, as well as balance, restraint, and perfect proportion. Yet mysterious harmonies bring dark moods that contrast with the lyricism. Mozart fuses power and elegance in a unique way. However passionate and intense, his works are always sensuous and beautiful. He believed that music "must never offend the ear, but must please the hearer, or in other words, must never cease to be *music*."

Not only do Mozart's compositions sound effortless; they were created with miraculous ease and rapidity. For example, he completed his last three symphonies in only six weeks! And he composed extended works completely in his mind. He could even converse while notating a score.

Mozart's more than 600 compositions were catalogued during the nineteenth century by Ludwig von Köchel. Hence, it is customary to refer to a Mozart work by the "K." number that indicates its chronological place in his output. For example, his Piano Concerto in D Minor (1785) is K. 466, and his Symphony No. 40 in G Minor (1788)—composed three years later—is K. 550.

In Mozart's hands, the classical concerto was raised to its highest level. Many of his concertos are among his greatest works. Particularly important are the more than twenty piano concertos that Mozart—a brilliant virtuoso—composed mainly for his own performances. He also wrote several violin concertos and horn concertos, two flute concertos, and one concerto each for bassoon, oboe, and clarinet. The concertos, as well as his other works, show a sensitivity to woodwind tone colors that is unmatched by earlier composers. The clarinet, especially, came into its own through

Mozart. The Concerto for Clarinet, K. 622 (1791), written in the last year of his life, remains the finest ever composed for that instrument.

Mozart was a master of opera; few composers have matched his ability to coordinate music and stage action. His dramatic works reveal a keen sense of theater, an inexhaustible gift of melody, and a genius for creating characters through tone. Most of his operas are comedies, composed to librettos in German or in Italian, which was the international language of music in Mozart's time. While the Italian operas are entirely sung, the German operas include spoken dialogue, as was customary in German opera at the time. Mozart's three masterpieces of Italian comic opera are *The Marriage of Figaro* (1786), *Don Giovanni* (1787), and *Così fan tutte* (1790); they were all composed to librettos by Lorenzo da Ponte. Mozart's finest opera in German is *The Magic Flute* (1791); its wide range of style embraces folk song and fugue, farcical comedy, and solemn hymns about the brotherhood of man.

The comic operas contain both humorous and serious characters. The major characters are not mere stereotypes but are human beings who think and feel. Even when six characters sing together in a complex ensemble, the individuality of each shines through. Mozart once tried to explain how he depicted emotion in an aria: "Would you like to know how I have expressed it—and even indicated his throbbing heart? By two violins playing octaves. You feel the trembling—the faltering—you see how his throbbing breast begins to swell; this I have expressed by a crescendo. You hear the whispering and sighing—which I have indicated by the first violins with mutes and a flute playing in unison." Emotions in Mozart's arias and ensembles are not static; they continuously evolve and change. A character may feel one way at the beginning of an ensemble and a different way at its end. In a duet from *Don Giovanni*, for example, the feelings of a peasant girl change as she gradually gives in to the charm of the aristocrat Don Giovanni.

Throughout his life, Mozart learned from other composers. As a boy, he was influenced by Italian operas and the graceful style of one of Bach's sons, Johann Christian Bach. The strongest influence on his later works came from J. S. Bach, dead and nearly forgotten, and from Haydn, the most famous composer at the time. From Bach, Mozart learned to write intricate polyphonic textures that flow smoothly. He arranged Bach's and Handel's works for performances at private concerts sponsored by Baron Gottfried van Swieten, a Viennese who was a passionate music lover. From Haydn's works, he learned ways to develop themes. But his musical relationship with Haydn was not one-sided. Some compositions by Haydn show traces of Mozart's melodic and orchestral style.

"I am never happier," Mozart once wrote his father, "than when I have something to compose, for that, after all, is my sole delight and passion." Mozart's "delight and passion" are communicated in his works, which represent late eighteenth-century musical style at its highest level of perfection.

DON GIOVANNI (1787)

Don Giovanni (Don Juan) is a unique blend of comic and serious opera, combining seduction and slapstick with violence and the supernatural. The old tale of Don Juan, the legendary Spanish lover, had attracted many playwrights and composers before Mozart. Mozart's Don Giovanni is an extremely charming but ruthless nobleman who will stop at nothing to satisfy his sexual appetite. Don Giovanni's comic servant, Leporello, is a grumbling accomplice who dreams of being in his master's place.

The Don attempts to rape a young noblewoman, Donna Anna; her father, the Commendatore (Commandant), challenges him to a duel. Don Giovanni kills the old man, causing Donna Anna and her fiancé, Don Ottavio, to swear revenge. Pursued by his enemies, the Don deftly engages in new amorous adventures. During one of them, he hides in a cemetery, where he sees a marble statue of the dead Commandant. The unearthly statue utters threatening words, but Don Giovanni brazenly invites it to dinner. When the statue appears at the banquet hall, it orders the Don to repent. Don Giovanni defiantly refuses and is dragged down to hell.

Overture

Mozart plunges us into a dark atmosphere at the beginning of the overture with awesome D minor chords, anxious syncopations, and sinister scale passages; there is a hair-raising effect when this slow, ominous music returns at the end of the opera for the statue's confrontation with Don Giovanni in the banquet hall. The overture continues with a fast sonata-form movement in D major, which has the energy and swagger of the opera's leading character. This contrast of minor and major, mystery and brilliance, foretells the tremendous range of emotions to come.

Act I:

Introduction

The overture leads directly into the action-packed opening scene. In breathless succession we witness Leporello keeping guard, Don Giovanni struggling with Donna Anna, the Commandant dueling with the Don, and the Commandant's agonized last gasps. Mozart's music vividly depicts the characters and pushes the action forward. (In the excerpt from the libretto that follows, braces indicate that characters sing at the same time. *Etc.* indicates that previous lines of text are repeated.)

Side 5, band 4
CD 3 |17|

|17| 0:00
Orchestral introduction, molto allegro; sudden fortes suggest pacing and abrupt turns.

(Late evening outside the Commandant's palace in Seville. Don Giovanni, concealing his identity, has stolen into Donna Anna's room for an amorous adventure. Leporello paces back and forth.)

Leporello

Notte e giorno faticar,	Night and day I slave
Per chi nulla sa gradir;	For one who does not appreciate it.
Piova e vento sopportar,	I put up with wind and rain,
Mangiar male e mal dormir!	Eat and sleep badly.
Voglio far il gentiluomo,	I want to be a gentleman
E non voglio più servir,	And to give up my servitude.
No, no, no, no, no, no,	No, no, no, no, no, no,
Non voglio più servir!	I want to give up my servitude.
O che caro galantuomo!	Oh, what a fine gentleman!
Voi star dentro colla bella	You stay inside with your lady
Ed io far la sentinella!	And I must play the sentinel!
Voglio far il gentiluomo, ecc.	Oh, what a fine gentleman, etc.
Ma mi par che venga gente . . .	But I think someone is coming!
Non mi voglio far sentir, ecc.	I don't want them to hear me, etc.

1:39
Orchestral
crescendo.

(Leporello hides to one side. Don Giovanni and Donna Anna come down the palace stairs struggling. The Don hides his face to prevent her from recognizing him.)

Donna Anna

Non sperar, se non m'uccidi.	There's no hope, unless you kill me
Ch'io ti lasci fuggir mai!	That I'll ever let you go!

Don Giovanni

Donna folle, indarno gridi:	Idiot! You scream in vain.
Chi son io tu non saprai.	Who I am you'll never know!

Donna Anna

Non sperar, ecc.	There's no hope, etc.

Don Giovanni

Donna folle! ecc.	Idiot! etc.

Leporello

Che tumulto! Oh ciel, che gridi!	What a racket! Heaven, what screams!
Il padron in nuovi guai.	My master in another scrape.

Donna Anna

Gente! Servi! Al traditore!	Help! Everyone! The betrayer!

Don Giovanni

Taci, e trema al mio furore!	Keep quiet! Beware my wrath!

Donna Anna

Scellerato!	Scoundrel!

Don Giovanni

Sconsigliata! Fool!

Donna Anna

Scellerato! Scoundrel!

Don Giovanni

Sconsigliata! Fool!

Leporello

Sta a veder che il malandrino We will see if this rascal
Mi farà precipitar. Will be the ruin of me!

Donna Anna

Gente! Servi! Help! Everyone!

Don Giovanni

Taci, e trema! Keep quiet!

Donna Anna

Come furia disperata Like a desperate fury
Ti saprò perseguitar! ecc. I'll know how to pursue you! etc.
Scellerato! Gente! Servi! Scoundrel! Help! Everyone!
Come furia disperata, ecc. Like a desperate fury, etc.

Don Giovanni

Questa furia disperata This desperate fury
Mi vuol far precipitar! ecc. Is aimed at destroying me!
Sconsigliata! Taci, e trema! Fool! Keep quiet!
Questa furia disperata, ecc. This desperate fury, etc.

Leporello

Che tumulto! Oh ciel, che gridi! What a racket! Heavens, what
screams!

Sta a veder che il malandrino, ecc. We will see if this rascal, etc.

(Donna Anna hears the Commandant: she leaves Don Giovanni and goes into the house. The Commandant appears.)

18 3:05
String tremolo, *ff*,
shift to minor key.

Commandant

Lasciala, indegno! Battiti meco! Leave her alone, wretch, and defend
yourself.

Don Giovanni

Va, non mi degno di pugnar teco. Go away! I disdain to fight with you.

Commandant

Così pretendi da me fuggir?   Thus you think to escape me?

Potessi almeno di qua partir.

Leporello

If I could only get out of here!

Don Giovanni

Va, non mi degno, no!   Go away! I disdain you!

Commandant

Così pretendi da me fuggir?   Thus you think to escape me!

Leporello

Potessi almeno di qua partir!   If I could only get out of here!

Commandant

Battiti!   Fight!

Don Giovanni

Misero! Attendi, se vuoi morir!   So be it, if you want to die!

Dueling music,
upward sweeps in
strings.
Death blow,
suspenseful, held
chord.

(They duel. The Commandant is fatally wounded.)

19 4:09
Andante, *pp*,
pathetic minor
phrases.

Commandant

Ah, soccorso! son tradito!   Help! I've been betrayed!
L'assassino m'ha ferito,   The assassin has wounded me!
E dal seno palpitante   And from my heaving breast
Sento l'anima partir.   I feel my soul escaping!

Don Giovanni

Ah! già cade il sciagurato!   Ah, already the wretch has fallen,
Affannosa e agonizzante   And he gasps for air.
Già dal seno palpitante   From his heaving breast I already
Veggo l'anima partir, ecc.   See his soul escaping, etc.

Leporello

Qual misfatto! Qual eccesso!   What a misdeed! What a crime!
Entro il sen dallo spavento   I can feel my heart
Palpitar il cor mi sento!   Beating hard from fright!
Io non sò che far, che dir, ecc.   I don't know what to do or say, etc.

(The Commandant dies.)

Don Giovanni

20 5:19
Recitative,
harpsichord
accompanies.

Leporello, ove sei? Leporello, where are you?

Leporello

Son qui, per mia disgrazia. E voi? I'm here, unfortunately, and you?

Don Giovanni

Son qui. Over here.

Leporello

Chi è morto, voi, o il vecchio? Who's dead, you or the old man?

Don Giovanni

Che domanda da bestia! Il vecchio. What an idiotic question! The old
man.

Leporello

Bravo! Due imprese leggiadre, Well done! Two misdeeds!
Storzar la figlia, ed ammazzar il padre! First you raped the daughter then
murdered the father!

Don Giovanni

L'ha voluto, suo danno. It was his own doing: too bad for
him.

Leporello

Ma Donn'Anna cosa ha voluto? And Donna Anna, did she ask for it
too?

Don Giovanni

Taci, non mi seccar! Keep quiet and don't bother me.
Vien meco, se non vuoi qualche cosa Now come along, unless you're
ancor tu. anxious for something for yourself.

Leporello

Non vo' nulla, signor, non parlo più. I have no desires, sir, and no more to
say.

Act I:

Leporello's catalog aria *(Madamina)*

Not long after the opening scene, Leporello sings his famous "catalog" aria
(Madamina) to Donna Elvira, a woman whom Don Giovanni had earlier
seduced and deserted and who has now appeared on the scene. In

Side 5, band 5
CD 3 21

mocking "consolation," Leporello tells her that she is but one of many and displays a fat catalog of his master's conquests. The music bubbles with Leporello's delight as he reels off the amazing totals: 640 in Italy, 231 in Germany, 100 in France, 91 in Turkey, and in Spain, 1,003! Mozart makes the most of comic description as Leporello proceeds to list the Don's seduction techniques for different types of women:

21 0:00 Allegro	*Madamina, il catalogo è questo* *Delle belle, che amò il padron mio;*	My dear lady, this is a list Of the beauties my master has loved,
	Un catalogo egli è, che ho fatt'io, *Osservate, leggete con me.*	A list which I have compiled. Observe, read along with me.
0:22 Staccato woodwind chuckles.	*In Italia seicento e quaranta,*	In Italy, six hundred and forty;
	In Almagna duecento a trentuna,	In Germany, two hundred and thirty-one;
	Cento in Francia, in Turchia novantuna,	A hundred in France; in Turkey ninety-one.
0:39 Longer notes.	*Ma in Ispagna son già mille e tre!*	In Spain already one thousand and three!
0:57 Shorter notes.	*V'han fra queste contadine,* *Cameriere, cittadine,* *V'han contesse, baronesse,* *Marchesine, principesse,* *E v'han donne d'ogni grado,* *D'ogni forma, d'ogni età!* *In Italia seicento e quaranta, ecc.*	Among these are peasant girls Maidservants, city girls, Countesses, baronesses, Marchionesses, princesses, Women of every rank, Every shape, every age. In Italy six hundred and forty, etc.
22 2:12 Andante con moto, courtly minuet.	*Nella bionda egli ha l'usanza* *Di lodar la gentilezza;*	With blondes it is his habit To praise their kindness;
2:32 Mock-heroic flourish.	*Nella bruna, la costanza;*	In brunettes, their faithfulness;
2:42 Suave melodic phrase	*Nella bianca la dolcezza;*	In the very blonde, their sweetness.
	Vuol d'inverno la grassotta, *Vuol d'estate la magrotta;*	In winter he likes fat ones, In summer he likes thin ones.

È la grande maestosa,	He calls the tall ones majestic.	3:05 Crescendo, melody slowly rises to high held tone.
La piccina è ognor vezzosa;	The little ones are always charming.	3:28 Sprightly quick notes
Delle vecchie fa conquista *Pel piacer di porle in lista.* *Sua passion predominante* *È la giovin principiante.* *Non si picca se sia ricca,* *Se sia brutta, se sia bella,* *Se sia ricca, brutta, se sia bella;* *Purchè porti la gonnella,* *Voi sapete quel che fa!* *Purchè porti la gonnella, ecc.*	He seduces the old ones For the pleasure of adding to the list. His greatest favorite Is the young beginner. It doesn't matter if she's rich, Ugly or beautiful; If she is rich, ugly or beautiful. If she wears a petticoat, *You* know what he does. If she wears a petticoat, etc.	

Act I:

Duet: *Là ci darem la mano (There you will give me your hand)*

The Don's seduction technique is put to use in the lovely duet *Là ci darem la mano*. Don Giovanni persuades the pretty peasant girl Zerlina to come to his palace, promising to marry her and change her life. The music magically conveys his persuasiveness and her gradual surrender, as the voices become more and more intertwined. Forgetting her fiancé, Masetto, Zerlina throws herself into the Don's arms and they sing together, "Let us go, my beloved."

Side 5, band 6
CD 3 [23]

Don Giovanni		[23] 0:00
Là ci darem la mano,	There you will give me your hand,	Andante, $\frac{2}{4}$, legato melody.
Là mi dirai di sì. *Vedi, non è lontano;* *Partiam, ben mio, da qui*	There you will tell me "yes." You see, it is not far; Let us leave, my beloved.	
Zerlina		
Vorrei e non vorrei;	I'd like to, but yet I would not.	Legato melody repeated.
Mi trema un poco il cor. *Felice è ver, sarei,* *Ma può burlarmi ancor.*	My heart trembles a little. It's true I would be happy, But he may just be tricking me.	

247

(Photo by Jack Vartoogian)

Samuel Ramey as Don Giovanni and Dawn Upshaw as Zerlina in the Metropolitan Opera's production of *Don Giovanni*.

	Don Giovanni	
Vieni, mio bel diletto!	Come, my dearly beloved!	24 0:42 Quicker interchange between voices.

	Zerlina	
Mi fa pietà Masetto!	I'm sorry for Masetto.	

Don Giovanni

Io cangierò tua sorte. I will change your life!

Zerlina

Presto, non son più forte! Soon I won't be able to resist.

Don Giovanni

Vieni! Vieni! Come! Come!

Là ci darem la mano! There you will give me your hand.

25 1:07
Legato melody now shared by both voices.

Zerlina

Vorrei, e non vorrei! I'd like to, but yet I would not.

Don Giovanni

Là mi dirai di sì. There you will tell me "yes."

Zerlina

Mi trema un poco il cor! My heart trembles a little.

Don Giovanni

Partiam, mio ben, da qui! Let us leave, my beloved.

Zerlina

Ma può burlarmi ancor! But he may just be tricking me.

Don Giovanni

Vieni, mio bel diletto! Come, my dearly beloved!

Zerlina

Mi fa pietà Masetto! I'm sorry for Masetto. Voices overlap.

Don Giovanni

Io cangierò tua sorte. I will change your life.

Zerlina

Presto, non son più forte! Soon I won't be able to resist.

Don Giovanni

Andiam! Andiam!   Let us go!

Zerlina

Andiam!   Let us go!

Allegro, ⁶⁄₈; together
they sing a new,
joyous tune.

Don Giovanni and Zerlina

Andiam, andiam, mio bene,   Let us go, let us go, my beloved,
A ristorar le pene   To soothe the pangs
D'un innocente amor! ecc.   Of an innocent love, etc.

Act II:

Finale

The finale of Act II, the concluding section of the opera, opens as Don Giovanni enjoys good food and good music; it closes with a sextet celebrating his horrible punishment. Mozart's genius fuses these dissimilar events into a coherent whole. Don Giovanni dines in his banquet hall while watching Leporello's comic antics and listening to his private band play three hit tunes. The third tune is from Mozart's *Marriage of Figaro,* and Leporello comments, "This I know only too well." The frivolous mood evaporates when Donna Elvira bursts in and begs the Don to mend his ways. Terror strikes as the Commandant's marble statue enters, accompanied by the awesome opening of the overture, in D minor. Mozart uses this return to weld a powerful sense of unity within the opera. As the orchestra plays the dueling music from Act I, the statue commands, "Repent, change your life, it is your last moment!" Defiant to the end, Don Giovanni shouts, "No, no I do not repent!" Flames and smoke surround the Don. He cries out in agony as a chorus of demons sing of his eternal damnation. With a hideous shriek, Don Giovanni is engulfed by the flames of hell.

An epilogue in a lighter mood follows this scene of terror. The other characters, learning of Don Giovanni's fate, form a sextet and jubilantly sing a moral to the audience: "This is how evildoers end up!" This moral ending fools no one: Mozart's music has made a sinner seem very attractive.

SYMPHONY NO. 40 IN G MINOR, K. 550 (1788)

The Symphony No. 40 in G minor is the most passionate and dramatic of Mozart's symphonies. Although the work is classical in form and technique, it is almost romantic in emotional intensity. It staggers the imagination that Mozart could compose the G minor and two other great symphonies—No. 39 in E Flat and No. 41 in C *(Jupiter)*—during the short period of six weeks. They are his last three symphonies.

Like most classical symphonies, the Symphony No. 40 in G minor has four movements: (1) fast, (2) slow, (3) minuet, (4) fast.

First Movement:
Molto allegro

A quiet but agitated opening theme in the violins sets the mood for the entire first movement, which is in sonata form. A throbbing accompaniment in the violas contributes to the feeling of unrest. Dominating the violin melody is the rhythmic pattern short-short-long, first heard in the opening three-note motive.

Side 6, band 2
CD 3 28

The persistence of this rhythmic pattern gives the music a sense of urgency. Yet the melody is balanced and symmetrical. Questioning upward leaps are answered by downward scales, and the second phrase of the melody is a sequential repetition of the first, one step lower. The exposition continues with a bridge section that presents a new staccato motive played loudly by the violins.

The lyrical second theme, in B flat major, contrasts completely with the agitated G minor opening. Mozart exploits the expressive resources of tone color by dividing the theme between strings and woodwinds. In the closing section of the exposition, Mozart uses a fragment from the opening theme to achieve a different emotional effect. The three-note motive now sounds gentle and plaintive as it is passed between clarinet and bassoon against a sighing string background.

In the development, the movement becomes feverish. The opening theme is led into different keys and is cut into smaller and smaller pieces. The development begins mysteriously as the opening phrase ends in an unexpected way and sinks lower and lower. Then a sudden explosion of polyphonic texture increases the excitement and complexity. Mozart brusquely shifts the opening phrase between low and high strings while combining it with a furious staccato countermelody. Soon after, he demolishes the opening phrase: we hear the beginning of the theme without its upward leap.

Then the final note is lopped off.

Finally, we are left with the irreducible minimum of the original theme, the three-note motive.

The tension resolves only with the entrance of the entire opening theme in the tonic key.

In the recapitulation, exposition material is given new expressive meaning. The bridge is expanded and made more dramatic. The lyrical second theme, now in G minor, is touching and sad.

Listening Outline   To be read while music is heard

SYMPHONY NO. 40 IN G MINOR, K. 550 (1788),
BY WOLFGANG AMADEUS MOZART

First Movement: Molto allegro

Sonata form, duple meter ($\frac{2}{2}$), G minor

Flute, 2 oboes, 2 clarinets, 2 bassoons, 2 French horns, 1st violins, 2d violins, violas, cellos, double basses

(Duration, 8:20)

EXPOSITION

First theme
☐28 0:00

1. *a.* Main theme in violins, *p,* throbbing accompaniment in violas, minor key.

Molto allegro
Violins

p

b. Full orchestra, *f.*

Bridge
☐29 0:24

2. *a.* Violins, *p,* main theme takes new turn to
   b. Full orchestra, *f,* major key, staccato motive and insistent upward scales in violins. Pause.

Second theme
☐30 0:53

3. *a.* Lyrical melody, *p,* major key, strings and woodwinds.

p

1:02

   b. Woodwinds and strings, *p,* lyrical melody somewhat varied. Crescendo in full orchestra.
   c. Staccato phrase, *f,* downward scale to

Closing section
☐31 1:29

4. *a.* String sighs, *p,* three-note motive in woodwinds, violins, *f.* Varied repetition of string sighs and three-note motive.
   b. Downward scales, *f,* full orchestra, cadence in major key.

☐32 2:04 Exposition is repeated.

DEVELOPMENT

☐33 4:09

1. *a.* High woodwinds, *p,* lead to
   b. Violins, *p,* main-theme phrase repeated on lower pitches.

4:24

2. Sudden *f,* full orchestra, main-theme phrase combined with rapid countermelody.

4:53

3. *a.* Sudden *p,* high violins and woodwinds, three-note motive.
   b. Sudden *f,* full orchestra, three-note motive.
   c. Sudden *p,* high flutes and clarinets, three-note motive carried down to

RECAPITULATION

First theme
☐34 5:26

1. *a.* Main theme in violins, *p,* throbbing accompaniment in violas, minor key.
   b. Full orchestra, *f.*

Bridge
5:50

2. *a.* Violins, *p,* main theme takes new turn to
   b. Full orchestra, *f,* staccato motive in violins and cellos. Insistent upward scales in violins, *f.* Pause.

3. *a.* Lyrical melody, *p,* minor key, strings and woodwinds.
   b. Woodwinds and strings, *p,* lyrical melody somewhat varied. Crescendo in full orchestra.
   c. Staccato phrase, *f,* downward scale to

4. *a.* String sighs, *p,* three-note motive in woodwinds, violins, *f.* Varied repetition of string sighs and three-note motive.
   b. Downward scales, *f,* full orchestra.

1. *a.* Sudden, *p,* main-theme motive in strings.
   b. Full orchestra, *f,* cadence in minor key.

Second Movement:

Andante

The mood of the andante hovers between gentleness and longing. The andante is written in sonata form and is the only movement of this symphony in major (it is in E flat). This movement develops from a series of gently pulsating notes in the opening theme.

As the theme continues, the violins introduce an airy two-note rhythmic figure that will appear—with changes of dynamics and orchestration—in almost every section of the andante. The rhythmic figure will be, at different times, graceful, insistent, and forceful.

Later, Mozart uses the airy figures as a delicate countermelody to the repeated-note idea. Floating woodwinds interwoven with strings reveal Mozart's sensitivity to tone color as an expressive resource.

Third Movement:

Menuetto (Allegretto)

The minuet, in G minor, is serious and intense; it does not sound like an aristocratic dance. The form of the minuet is A B A:

Side 6, band 4
CD 3 40

Minuet	Trio	Minuet
A	B	A
A (repeated) ba' (repeated)	c (repeated) dc' (repeated)	a ba'

Powerful syncopations give a fierce character to the A section (the minuet), which is predominantly loud and in minor.

Section A
40 0:00

Later, Mozart increases the tension through polyphonic texture and striking dissonances. At the end of the A section, there is a sudden drop in dynamics; the flute, supported by oboes and a bassoon, softly recalls the opening melody of the minuet.

The trio section (B) brings a shift from minor to major, from fierce energy to graceful relaxation.

Section B
41 1:51

This change of mood is underscored by a soft dynamic level and pastoral woodwind interludes. After the trio, a sudden forte announces the return of the fierce A section.

Return of section A
42 3:48

Fourth Movement:

Allegro assai

Mozart ends the symphony with the tense movement already described in Section 3.

Side 6, band 5
CD 3 43

PIANO CONCERTO NO. 23 IN A MAJOR, K. 488

The Piano Concerto in A Major—completed on March 2, 1786—dates from a very productive and successful period in Mozart's life. Between October 1785 and May 1786, he taught piano and composition, conducted operas, performed in concerts, and composed *The Marriage of Figaro,* the comic one-act opera *The Impressario,* two other great piano concertos (K. 482 in E Flat and K. 491 in C Minor), a Quartet for Piano and Strings (K. 478), and the *Masonic Funeral Music* (K. 477).

Mozart thought highly of the A Major concerto. In a letter to the court chamberlain of a prospective patron, he included it among "the compositions which I keep for myself or for a small circle of music-lovers and connoisseurs. . . ." Today, it is one of the best known of his piano concertos.

Like all classical concertos, this one has three movements. The grace of the opening movement and the high spirits of the finale contrast with the melancholy of the middle movement. This concerto stresses poetry and delicacy rather than pianistic virtuosity or orchestral power. It is scored for an orchestra without trumpets or timpani and highlights the clarinets, flute, and bassoon. Mozart associated its key—A major—with tenderness, lyricism, and elegance. (He also used this key for the Clarinet Concerto and the duet between Don Giovanni and Zerlina in *Don Giovanni.*)

In our recording the soloist Malcolm Bilson plays a modern replica of Mozart's concert fortepiano. The late-eighteenth-century *fortepiano*—an early piano—weighed much less than the modern piano and had thinner strings held by a frame made of wood, rather than metal. Its pitch range was smaller, and its tone was softer and lasted a shorter time.

First Movement:

Allegro

Side 5, band 3
CD 3 [10]

The gentle opening movement blends lyricism with a touch of sadness owing to many shifts between major and minor. Two main lyrical themes introduced by the orchestra in the first exposition are restated by the piano and orchestra in the second exposition. The development section is based on a new legato theme that is unexpectedly introduced by the orchestra after a dramatic pause. (In the listening outline, this is called the *development theme.*) Mozart creates a dramatic confrontation by juxtaposing fragments of this new theme, played by the woodwinds, with restless ideas in the piano and orchestra.

Toward the end of the allegro is a cadenza—an unaccompanied show-piece for the soloist. Exceptionally, Mozart notated the cadenza directly into the score, instead of leaving it to be improvised by the soloist. With its rapid sweeps up and down the keyboard, its alternation between brilliant and tender passages, and its concluding trill, this cadenza gives us some idea of how Mozart himself must have improvised.

Listening Outline To be read while music is heard

PIANO CONCERTO NO. 23 IN A MAJOR, K. 488 (1786),
BY WOLFGANG AMADEUS MOZART

First Movement: Allegro

Sonata form, quadruple meter ($\frac{4}{4}$), A major

Solo piano, flute, 2 clarinets, 2 bassoons, 2 French horns, 1st violins, 2d violins, violas, cellos, double basses

(Duration, 10:34)

FIRST
EXPOSITION
First theme

[10] 0:00   1. *a.* Strings, *p,* gracious main melody, legato, major key,

        staccato ascent.
        b. Winds, *p,* repeat opening of main melody an octave higher. Strings, *f,* answered by winds; cadence to

Bridge

[11] 0:32   2. *a.* Full orchestra, *f,* vigorous bridge theme,

        running notes in violins, *f.* Brief pause.

Second
theme
group

[12] 0:55   3. *a.* Violins, *p,* tender second theme, repeated notes in dotted rhythm.

       ..*b.* Violins and bassoon, *p,* repeat second theme, flute joins.

                                c. Agitated rhythms in minor lead to

1:25   *d.* Full orchestra, *f,* major; sudden *p,* winds alternate with violins, minor, crescendo to

        e. Full orchestra, *f,* major, cadence. Brief pause.

        f. High woodwind phrase, *p,* orchestral chords, *f.* Brief pause.

SECOND EXPOSITION

First theme

[13] 2:03   1. *a.* Piano solo, main melody, low strings join, violins introduce

        b. Piano, varied repetition of main melody, rapid downward and upward scales.

Bridge

2:31   2. *a.* Full orchestra, *f,* bridge theme.

        b. Piano, running notes, with string accompaniment. High staccato violins, high staccato winds, downward scale in piano. Brief pause.

Second theme group

2:59   3. *a.* Piano solo, second theme, dolce.

        b. Violins and flute repeat second theme, piano joins.

3:29   *c.* Piano and orchestra, minor; sudden *f,* in piano, major.

3:39   *d.* Sudden *p,* violins and piano, repeated figure, minor.

3:46   *e.* Sudden *f* in piano, major. Long passage of running notes in piano culminating in short trill closing into

4:09   4. Full orchestra, opening of bridge theme. Sudden pause.

DEVELOPMENT

[14] 4:22   1. *a.* Strings, *p,* legato development theme.

        b. Piano solo, development theme embellished by rapid notes.

4:44   2. *a.* Clarinet, fragment of development theme in minor, answered by piano and staccato strings.

4:52   *b.* Flute, fragment of development theme in major, answered by piano and staccato strings.

4:59   *c.* High woodwinds, development theme fragment in minor answered by piano, strings join with development theme fragment.

5:10   3. Piano continues with running notes; clarinet and flute, imitations of development theme fragment.

5:25   4. Strings, minor, repeatedly alternate with piano and woodwinds.

5:39   5. Piano solo, orchestra joins. Long descents and ascents, rising chromatic scale leads into

RECAPITULATION

First theme

[15] 6:02   1. *a.* Strings, *p,* main melody, woodwinds join.

        b. Piano *p,* with woodwinds, ornamented repeat of main melody in higher octave; piano scales lead to

Bridge
6:29

2. *a.* Full orchestra, *f*, bridge theme.

b. Piano, running notes, strings accompany; staccato violins, high staccato winds, upward scale in piano. Brief pause.

Second
theme
group

6:56

3. *a.* Piano solo, second theme.

b. Winds repeat second theme an octave higher, piano joins.

7:24   *c.* Piano and orchestra, minor; sudden *f* in piano, major.

7:35   *d.* Sudden *p*, violins and piano, repeated figure, minor.

7:42   *e.* Sudden *f* in piano, major, running-note passage interrupted by brief pause.

7:56   4. *a.* Piano alone, development theme.

b. Clarinets and bassoons repeat development theme, accompanied by running notes in piano, staccato winds join, piano trill meshes with entrance of

8:36   5. *a.* Full orchestra, *f*, bridge theme; sudden brief pause.

8:49   *b.* Strings and winds, *p*, development theme. Full orchestra, *f*, dotted rhythm, briefly held chord.

CADENZA

[16] 9:03   *c.* Extended piano solo; long trill closes into

CODA

10:02   6. *a.* Full orchestra, *f*, cadence.

b. High woodwind phrase, *p*; sudden *f*, full orchestra; sudden *p* ending, trills in flutes and violins.

Second Movement:

Adagio

The extraordinary melancholy of this adagio is matched by its even more unusual key, F sharp minor. It is in three-part form: A(minor)–B (major)–A'(minor)-coda. The piano alone introduces a sad main theme characterized by the dotted rhythmic pattern long-short-long and by expressive upward and downward leaps.

Supplementary sets:
Side 3, band 4
CD 2 [15]
[15] 0:00

The orchestra continues with a minor-key theme of its own, imitated between the clarinet, bassoon, and flute.

Rounding off the A section is a touching piano melody that grows out of the themes heard earlier.

16 2:23

The sad mood of the second movement is somewhat lightened by its middle section, which begins with a gracious new theme in major played by the flute and clarinets.

17 3:31

A varied return of the opening section (A′) is followed by a reflective coda in which pizzicato strings accompany a piano melody that shifts expressively between high and low pitches.

Third Movement:

Allegro assai

Supplementary sets:
Side 3, band 5
CD 2 18

The melancholy of the adagio is immediately dispelled by the exhilarating opening of the very rapid finale, which brings a return to major. This movement is in a special type of rondo form favored by Mozart: A B A′ (highly abridged) C B A. Each large section (A, B, and C) contains a rich variety of musical ideas and begins with a theme introduced by the piano and continued by the orchestra.

18 0:00

The exuberant main theme of section A opens with a three-note idea (short-short-long) that leaps downward and then upward.

In Sections B and C there are delightful shifts between major and minor, piano and orchestra; and there are tuneful themes and running passages. Woodwinds are often given virtuoso passages.

19 0:55

Section B contrasts a graceful opening idea in major presented by the piano with a wistful contrasting theme in minor, introduced by the flute and bassoon. 20 1:34

Section C begins with a stormy piano passage in minor, but the mood changes when we hear a new playful theme in major, as though a comic character has come on stage. 21 3:24
22 3:53

The movement concludes brilliantly with a long-awaited return of A, in which the piano is more active. It is typical for late-eighteenth-century music to end happily.

REQUIEM IN D MINOR, K. 626 (1791)

Although Mozart did not live to complete his monumental Requiem—a *requiem* is a mass for the dead—it is one of the finest sacred choral works of the classical period. It was commissioned anonymously by an unscrupulous nobleman who meant to claim the work as his own composition. In the last two months of his life, Mozart composed nine movements of the Requiem and part of a tenth. Reportedly, as his health grew worse, Mozart came to believe that the Requiem was for himself and tried to finish it on his deathbed. After Mozart died, his friend and pupil Franz Xaver Süssmayr filled out the often sketchy orchestration, completed the fragmentary section, and added four other movements. We do not know to what extent these additions represent the intentions of the dying Mozart. Süssmayr may have used sketches by Mozart which have not survived.

Mozart associated the Requiem's key of D minor with moods of foreboding, conflict, and tragedy. (He had used it in *Don Giovanni* for the somber opening of the overture and for the appearance of the statue of the Commandant at the end of the opera.) The solemnity is deepened by the dark colors in the orchestra, which is restricted to basset horns (low clarinets), bassoons, trumpets, trombones (traditional in sacred music), timpani, strings, and organ—with no lighter-sounding woodwinds such as flutes or clarinets. Mozart's Requiem includes movements for chorus, for soloists, and for a combination of both. It draws on a wide range of styles, from baroque fugues to almost operatic solos and ensembles.

We'll focus on the third movement, the *Dies irae* in D minor for chorus and orchestra.

Dies irae

Side 6, band 1
CD 3 27

The dramatic *Dies irae (Day of wrath)* is based on a thirteenth-century text which vividly describes the last judgment. Enormous tension is created by the key of D minor, by stormy rushing notes in the violins, and by the distinctive rhythmic pattern (long-long-short-short) of the opening phrase, which intensifies the word *irae (wrath)*.

Most of the *Dies irae* is homophonic in texture, with all the voices singing in the same rhythm simultaneously. As the movement progresses, however, Mozart uses a change of texture to heighten the tension. A trill-like idea in the basses of the chorus in unison with the orchestra, representing the fearful trembling of *Quantus tremor est futurus (How great the trembling shall be)* is answered by the three higher voices in chords on *Dies irae (Day of wrath)*.

Though it could have been written by no one but Mozart, the *Dies irae* has a baroque flavor and reflects his great admiration for Handel, whose *Messiah* he conducted and reorchestrated.

Latin	English	Description
Dies irae, dies illa	Day of wrath, day of mourning	Chorus.
Solvet seculum in favilla: *Teste David cum Sibylla.*	Earth in smouldering ashes lying: So spake David and the Sybil.	
		Orchestra briefly alone.
Quantus tremor est futurus. *Quando judex est venturus,* *Cuncta stricte discussurus!*	How great the trembling shall be when the judge shall come by whose sentence all shall be bound!	
		Orchestra alone.
Dies irae, dies illa *Solvet seculum in favilla:* *Teste David cum Sibylla.*	Day of wrath, day of mourning Earth in smouldering ashes lying: So spake David and the Sybil.	
		Orchestra briefly alone.
Quantus tremor est futurus. *Quando judex est venturus,* *Cuncta stricte discussurus!*	How great the trembling shall be when the judge shall come by whose sentence all shall be bound!	
Quantus tremor est futurus.	How great the trembling shall be	Basses, "trembling" figure twice answered by higher voices.
Dies irae, dies illa *Quantus tremor est futurus,*	Day of wrath, day of mourning, How great the trembling shall be,	Basses answered by full chorus, "trembling" figure.
Quantus tremor est futurus, *Quanto judex est venturus,* *Cuncta stricte discussurus!* *Cuncta stricte discussurus!*	How great the trembling shall be when the judge shall come by whose sentence all shall be bound! by whose sentence all shall be bound!	Syncopated phrase exchanged between high and low voices. Agitated orchestral close.

Apart from Mozart's Requiem, the best-known requiem masses were written in the nineteenth century by the French composers Hector Berlioz and Gabriel Fauré, and the Italian composer Giuseppe Verdi. The term *requiem* has also been applied to choral works which honor the dead but are not masses, such as Johannes Brahms's *A German Requiem* (1868), which will be discussed in Part VI (Section 16); and Benjamin Britten's *War Requiem* (1962).

263

[CLASSICAL [**12**]] LUDWIG VAN BEETHOVEN

For many people, Ludwig van Beethoven (1770–1827) represents the highest level of musical genius. His unique stature is comparable to Shakespeare's in literature and Michelangelo's in painting and sculpture. He opened new realms of musical expression and profoundly influenced composers throughout the nineteenth century.

Beethoven was born on December 16, 1770, in Bonn, Germany. Like Bach and Mozart before him, he came from a family of musicians. His grandfather, also named Ludwig, was music director at the court at Bonn. His father, Johann, was a tenor who held a low position in the court and who saw his talented son as a profitable prodigy like Mozart. It's told that Johann Beethoven and a musician friend would come home from the local tavern late at night, rouse young Ludwig from sleep, and make him practice at the keyboard until morning. At the age of eleven, Beethoven served as assistant to the court organist, and at twelve he had several piano compositions published.

Beethoven went to Vienna when he was sixteen to improvise for Mozart. Mozart reportedly said, "Keep your eyes on him; some day he will give the world something to talk about." Beethoven then returned to Bonn, because his mother was critically ill. She died shortly after. His father, who had become an alcoholic, was soon dismissed from the court choir. Beethoven, at eighteen, became the legal guardian of his two younger brothers. By now, Beethoven had become a court organist and violist and was responsible for composing and performing; suddenly, he was also head of a family.

Shortly before his twenty-second birthday, Beethoven left Bonn to study with Haydn in Vienna, where he spent the rest of his life. In 1792, Haydn was at the height of his fame, too busy composing to devote much time or energy to teaching. As a result, he overlooked errors in Beethoven's counterpoint exercises, and Beethoven felt forced to go secretly to another teacher. (Haydn never learned of this.) Beethoven's drive for thoroughness and mastery—evident throughout his life—is shown by his willingness to subject himself to a strict course in counterpoint and fugue even after he had composed fine works.

Beethoven's first seven years in Vienna brought hard work, growing confidence, a strong sense of identity, and public praise. His letters of introduction from members of the aristocracy in Bonn opened the doors of the social and cultural elite in this music-loving city. People were dazzled by his piano virtuosity and moved by his improvisations. "He knew how to produce such an impression on every listener," reports a contemporary, "that frequently there was not a single dry eye, while many broke out into loud sobs, for there was a certain magic in his expression." Beethoven rebelled against social convention, asserting that an artist deserved as much respect as the nobility. Once, while playing in an aristocratic drawing room, he was disturbed by the loud conversation of a young count. Beethoven jumped up from the piano, exclaiming, "I will not play for such swine!" For a long time he was a guest of Prince Karl von Lichnowsky, who told his personal servant that if ever he and Beethoven rang at the same time, Beethoven should be served first. Aristocrats showered Beethoven with gifts, and he earned good fees from piano lessons and private concerts. Publishers were quick to buy his compositions, even though some critics complained that they were "bizarre" and "excessively complicated."

Disaster struck during his twenty-ninth year: Beethoven felt the first symptoms of deafness. Doctors could do nothing to halt its progress or to relieve Beethoven's physical and emotional torment. In 1801 he wrote despairingly, "For two years I have avoided almost all social gatherings because it is impossible for me to say to people 'I am deaf.' If I belonged to any other profession it would be easier, but in my profession it is a terrible handicap." On October 6, 1802, Beethoven was in Heiligenstadt, a village outside Vienna where he sought solitude during the summer. That day he expressed his feelings in what is now known as the Heiligenstadt testament, a long, agonized letter addressed to his brothers. Beethoven wrote, "I would have ended my life—it was only my art that held me back. Ah, it seemed to me impossible to leave the world until I had brought forth all that I felt was within me."

Beethoven's victory over despair coincided with an important change in his musical style. Works that he created after his emotional crisis have a new power and heroism. From 1803 to 1804, he composed the gigantic Third Symphony, the *Eroica*, a landmark in music history. At first, he planned to name it *Bonaparte*, after Napoleon, the first consul of the French Republic. Beethoven saw Napoleon as the embodiment of heroism and the champion of the principles underlying the French Revolution. *Liberty, equality, fraternity* were stirring words that expressed Beethoven's democratic ideals. But when he learned that Napoleon had proclaimed himself

Beethoven opened new realms of musical expression that profoundly influenced composers throughout the nineteenth century.

emperor of the French, Beethoven "flew into a rage and cried out, 'He too is nothing but an ordinary man! Now he will trample under foot all the rights of man and only indulge his ambition. He will exalt himself above all others and become a tyrant!'" Seizing his score, Beethoven tore out the title page bearing Napoleon's name and threw it on the floor. On a new title page, later, Beethoven wrote, "Heroic Symphony composed to celebrate the memory of a great man."

In 1812, Beethoven met Johann Wolfgang von Goethe, the great German poet he had long worshiped. He played for Goethe, and the two artists walked and talked together. Shortly after this meeting, Goethe described Beethoven to a friend as "an utterly untamed personality." To his wife, the poet wrote, "Never before have I seen an artist with more power of concentration, more energy, more inwardness."

Despite such descriptions by people who knew him, Beethoven remains a mystery. He was self-educated and had read widely in Shakespeare and the ancient classics, but he was weak in elementary arithmetic. He claimed the highest moral principles, but he was often unscrupulous in dealing with publishers. Although orderly and methodical when composing, Beethoven dressed sloppily and lived in incredibly messy apartments. During his thirty-five years in Vienna, he changed dwellings about forty times.

Beethoven fell in and out of love with several women, mostly of noble birth, but was never able to form a lasting relationship. He wrote a passionate letter to a woman referred to as the "immortal beloved"; it was found in a drawer after his death. Only recently has a Beethoven scholar established her identity as the Viennese aristocrat Antonie Brentano. Beethoven took consolation from nature for disappointments in his personal life. Ideas came to him while he walked through the Viennese countryside. His Sixth Symphony, the *Pastoral*, beautifully expresses his recollections of life in the country.

Beethoven was never in the service of the Viennese aristocracy. A growing musical public made it possible for him to earn a fairly good income by selling compositions to publishers. His stature was so great that when he threatened to accept a position outside Austria in 1809, three nobles made a special arrangement to keep him in Vienna. Prince Kinsky, Prince Lobkowitz, and Archduke Rudolf—the emperor's brother and Beethoven's pupil—committed themselves to give Beethoven an annual income. Their only condition was that Beethoven continue to live in the Austrian capital—an unprecedented arrangement in music history.

As Beethoven's hearing weakened, so did his piano playing and conducting. By the time he was forty-four, this once brilliant pianist was forced to stop playing in public. But he insisted on conducting his orchestral works long after he could do it efficiently. The players would become confused by his wild gestures on the podium, and performances were often chaotic. His sense of isolation grew with his deafness. Friends had to communicate with him through an ear trumpet, and during his last eight years he carried notebooks in which people would write questions and comments.

In 1815, his brother Caspar died, leaving a nine-year-old son, Karl, to whom Beethoven and Caspar's widow became coguardians. Young Karl was the object of a savage tug-of-war. For five years, Beethoven fought legal battles for exclusive custody of his nephew; he finally won. This "victory" was a disaster for everyone. Growing up in the household of a deaf, eccentric bachelor uncle is not easy at best, and for Karl it was complicated by Beethoven's craving for love and companionship. The young man attempted suicide, and Beethoven, whose health was already poor, was shattered.

During the first three years of legal battles over Karl, Beethoven composed less, and the Viennese began to whisper that he was finished. Beethoven heard the rumor and said, "Wait a while; they'll soon learn differently!" And they did. After 1818, Beethoven's domestic problems did not prevent a creative outburst that produced some of his greatest works: the late piano sonatas and string quartets, the *Missa solemnis,* and the Ninth Symphony—out of total deafness, new realms of sound.

BEETHOVEN'S MUSIC

"I must despise the world which does not know that music is a higher revelation than all wisdom and philosophy." For Beethoven, music was not mere entertainment, but a moral force capable of creating a vision of higher ideals. His music directly reflects his powerful, tortured personality. In both art and life, his heroic struggle resulted in victory over despair.

Beethoven's demand for perfection meant long and hard work. Unlike Mozart, he couldn't dash off three great symphonies in six weeks. Sometimes he worked for years on a single symphony, writing other works during the same period of time. He carried music sketchbooks everywhere, jotting down new ideas, revising and refining old ones. These early notes often seem crude and uninspired when compared with the final versions of his works, which were often hammered out through great labor.

Beethoven mostly used classical forms and techniques, but he gave them new power and intensity. The musical heir of Haydn and Mozart, he bridged the classical and romantic eras. Many of his innovations were used by composers who came after him.

In his works, great tension and excitement are built up through syncopations and dissonances. The range of pitch and dynamics is greater than ever before, so that contrasts of mood become more pronounced. Accents and climaxes seem titanic. Tiny rhythmic ideas are often repeated over and over to create momentum. Greater tension called for a larger musical framework, and so Beethoven expanded his forms. For example, the Third Symphony *(Eroica)* is far longer than any symphony by Haydn or Mozart; it takes almost 50 minutes to perform. Beethoven was a musical architect who was unsurpassed in his ability to create large-scale structures in which every note seems inevitable. In describing Beethoven's music, it is perhaps too easy to give the impression that all of it is stormy and powerful. A lot is; but much is gentle, humorous, noble, or lyrical. His range of expression is enormous. Tempo, dynamic, and expressive indications are marked far more extensively in his scores than in those of earlier composers. For example, one direction reads, "Somewhat lively and with deepest feeling." Characteristic of his explicit dynamic markings is $\textfeatured{\;\diagup\!\!<}\; p$, a gradual increase in loudness followed by a sudden softness.

More than his predecessors, Beethoven tried to unify the contrasting movements of a symphony, sonata, or string quartet. Musical continuity is heightened in his works in several ways. Sometimes one movement leads directly into the next, instead of ending with a pause, as was traditional. In the Fifth Symphony, for example, the last two movements are linked by a suspenseful bridge section. A musical bond between different movements of the same work is also created when their themes resemble each other. In a few compositions (the Fifth and Ninth Symphonies, for example), a theme from one movement is quoted in a later movement.

Like Haydn and Mozart, Beethoven wrote many movements in sonata form. In his works, however, the development section is greatly expanded and becomes even more dramatic. It often contains a powerful crescendo that leads to a climactic return of the first theme at the start of the recapitulation. The coda is also expanded and serves to develop themes still further. Its length balances what has come before and affirms the victory of the tonic key over the many new keys in the development section.

As the third movement of a symphony or string quartet, Beethoven most often used a scherzo rather than the traditional minuet. Where earlier composers had used a courtly dance, Beethoven composed a rapid movement with rhythmic drive. The character of the scherzo in Beethoven is flexible. In the Fifth Symphony, it's an ominous force, but in the Sixth Symphony *(Pastoral)*, it depicts peasants' merrymaking. Beethoven's works often have climactic, triumphant finales, toward which the previous movements seem to build. These mark an important departure from the light, relaxed ending movement favored by Haydn and Mozart.

Beethoven's most popular works are the nine symphonies, which were conceived for larger orchestras than Haydn's or Mozart's. For greater power and brilliance, Beethoven sometimes added the trombone, piccolo, and contrabassoon—instruments that had not previously been used in symphonies. All the orchestral instruments have to play difficult music.

For example, the French horn has prominent melodies, and the timpani participate in the musical dialogue, rather than merely mark the beat.

Each of Beethoven's symphonies is unique in character and style. There is a curious alternation of mood between his odd-numbered symphonies (Symphonies No. 3, 5, 7, and 9), which tend to be forceful and assertive, and his even-numbered ones (Symphonies No. 4, 6, and 8), which are calmer and more lyrical. In the finale of the Ninth Symphony (Choral), Beethoven took the unprecedented step of using a chorus and four solo vocalists. They sing the text of Schiller's Ode to Joy, a poem about human brotherhood.

A hint of the virtuosity and improvisation that so astounded the Viennese can be gotten from Beethoven's thirty-two piano sonatas, which are far more difficult than the sonatas of Haydn and Mozart. They exploit the stronger, tonally improved piano of Beethoven's time. Beethoven drew many new effects from the piano, ranging from massive chords to the hollow, mystical sounds produced when the right and left hands play far apart on the keyboard. The piano sonatas were experimental grounds for the compositional techniques he later expanded in the symphonies and string quartets.

Beethoven's sixteen string quartets, which span his entire career, are among the greatest music composed. They are unsurpassed in sheer invention, thematic treatment, and heart-rending expressiveness. In three of the last quartets, Beethoven again stepped beyond the conventions of classical form: he used five, six, and seven movements (in Op. 132, Op. 130, and Op. 131 respectively), which he connected in subtle ways. He also wrote five superb piano concertos, each remarkable in its individuality. In the Fourth and Fifth Piano Concertos, the opening movement begins with a brief piano solo rather than the traditional orchestral exposition.

While most of Beethoven's important works are for instruments, his sense of drama was also expressed in vocal music. In his only opera, Fidelio, a wife's heroism enables justice to triumph over tyranny. Beethoven also composed two masses. The Missa solemnis (Solemn Mass, 1819–1823) is one of the most monumental and expressive settings of this sacred text.

Beethoven's total output is usually divided into three periods: early (up to 1802), middle (1803–1814), and late (1815–1827). The music of Haydn and Mozart influences some works of the early period, but other pieces clearly show Beethoven's personal style. The compositions of the middle period are longer and tend to be heroic in tone. And the sublime works of the last period well up from the depths of a man almost totally deaf. During this period Beethoven often used the fugue to express new musical conceptions. The late works contain passages that sound surprisingly harsh and "modern." When a violinist complained that the music was very difficult to play, Beethoven reportedly replied, "Do you believe that I think of a wretched fiddle when the spirit speaks to me?"

PIANO SONATA IN C MINOR, OP. 13 *(PATHÉTIQUE;* 1798)

The title *Pathétique,* coined by Beethoven, suggests the tragically passionate character of his famous Piano Sonata in C Minor, Op. 13. Beethoven's
impetuous playing and masterful improvisational powers are mirrored in
the sonata's extreme dynamic contrasts, explosive accents, and crashing
chords. At the age of twenty-seven, during his early period, Beethoven
had already created a powerful and original piano style that foreshadowed
nineteenth-century romanticism.

First Movement:

Grave (solemn, slow introduction);
Allegro molto e con brio (very fast and brilliant allegro)

The *Pathétique* begins in C minor with an intense, slow introduction, dominated by an opening motive in dotted rhythm: long-short-long-short-long-
long.

Side 8, band 2
CD 4 [30]

30 0:00

This six-note idea seems to pose a series of unresolved questions as it is
repeated on higher and higher pitch levels. The tragic mood is intensified
by dissonant chords, sudden contrasts of dynamics and register, and
pauses filled with expectancy. The slow introduction is integrated into the
allegro that follows it in imaginative and dramatic ways.

The tension of the introduction is maintained in the allegro con brio, a
breathless, fast movement in sonata form. The opening theme, in C minor,
begins with a staccato idea that rapidly rises up a 2-octave scale. It is ac-

31 1:34

companied by low broken octaves, the rapid alternation of two tones an octave apart.

1:54

Growing directly out of the opening theme is a bridge that is also built from a climbing staccato motive.

This bridge motive has an important role later in the movement.

32   2:08

The contrasting second theme, which enters without a pause, is spun out of a short motive that is repeatedly shifted between low and high registers.

33   3:03

This restless idea begins in E flat minor but then moves through different keys. The exposition is rounded off by several themes, including a high running passage and a return of the opening staccato idea in E flat major.

The development section begins with a dramatic surprise: Beethoven 34 3:25 brings back the opening bars of the slow introduction. This reappearance creates an enormous contrast of tempo, rhythm, and mood. After four bars of slow music, the fast tempo resumes as Beethoven combines two differ- 4:01 ent ideas: the staccato bridge motive and a quickened version of the intro- duction motive. The introduction motive is presented in a rhythmically altered form: short-short-short-long-long.

The bridge motive is then developed in the bass, played by the pianist's left hand while the right hand has high broken octaves. After several high accented notes, the brief development concludes with a running passage that leads down to the recapitulation.

For a while, the recapitulation runs its usual course as themes from the Recapitulation 35 4:50 exposition are presented in the tonic key of C minor. But Beethoven has one more surprise for the coda—after a loud dissonant chord and a brief pause, he again brings back the opening of the slow introduction. This 36 6:25 time the slow music is even more moving, as it is punctuated by moments of silence. Then the fast tempo resumes, and the opening staccato idea and powerful chords bring the movement to a decisive close.

Second Movement:

Adagio cantabile (lyrical adagio)

The second movement, in A flat major, is slow, intimate, and songlike. It is Side 8, band 3 CD 4 37 in rondo form and may be outlined A B A C A–coda. The legato main theme (A), played in the piano's rich middle register, is one of Beethoven's Section A 37 0:00 most lyrical melodies.

This melody is immediately repeated an octave higher with fuller har- mony.

Section B is also legato and maintains the opening mood while introducing a new accompaniment of repeated chords. Section C is a duet between tender legato phrases in the top part and more animated staccato replies in the bass. This section brings some contrast with a shift to minor, a powerful crescendo, and a triplet rhythm in the accompaniment. On its last return, the main melody sounds more flowing, because it is now accompanied by a rocking figure in triplet rhythm. The movement is rounded off by a poetic coda that descends leisurely to soft concluding chords.

Third Movement:

Rondo (Allegro)

The last movement, in C minor, is a rapid and energetic rondo. It is outlined A B A C A B A–coda. The lively main theme (A), in minor, contrasts with the other sections, which are in major.

Section B
[42] 0:29

Section C
[43] 1:38

End of coda
[44] 4:15

The B section includes several lyrical themes, while the C section is polyphonic and contains ideas that are shifted from one hand to the other. Sections B and C both end with a sustained dominant chord that creates expectancy for the return of the main theme and key. Toward the end of the stormy coda, a sustained chord is followed unexpectedly by the opening notes of the main theme, in major rather than minor.

But the consolation of major is brief, as a rapid downward scale brings the movement to a powerful close in C minor.

SYMPHONY NO. 5 IN C MINOR, OP. 67 (1808)

The Fifth Symphony opens with one of the most famous rhythmic ideas in all music, a short-short-short-long motive. Beethoven reportedly interpreted this four-note motive as "fate knocking at the door." It dominates the first movement and plays an important role later in the symphony, too.

The entire work can be seen as an emotional progression from the conflict and struggle of the first movement, in C minor, to the exultation and victory of the final movement, in C major. The finale is the climax of the symphony; it is longer than the first movement and more powerful in sound.

Through several different techniques, Beethoven brilliantly welds four contrasting movements into a unified work. The basic rhythmic motive of the first movement (short-short-short-long) is used in a marchlike theme in the third movement. And this third-movement theme is later quoted dramatically within the finale. The last two movements are also connected by a bridge passage.

Beethoven jotted down a few themes for the Fifth Symphony in 1804, but mainly worked on it during 1807 and 1808, an amazingly productive period when he also composed the Mass in C Major; the Sonata for Cello and Piano, Op. 69; and the Sixth Symphony.

First Movement:

Allegro con brio (allegro with vigor)

The allegro con brio is an enormously powerful and concentrated movement in sonata form. Its character is determined by a single rhythmic motive, short-short-short-long, from which Beethoven creates an astonishing variety of musical ideas. Tension and expectation are generated from the very beginning of the movement. Three rapid notes of the same pitch are followed by a downward leap to a held, suspenseful tone. This powerful idea is hammered out twice by all the strings in unison; the second time, it is a step lower in pitch.

Side 7, band 1
CD 4 [1]

As the opening theme continues in C minor, Beethoven maintains excitement by quickly developing his basic idea. He crowds varied repetitions of the motive together and rapidly shifts the motive to different pitches and instruments.

The second theme, in E flat major, dramatically combines different ideas. It begins with an unaccompanied horn call that asserts the basic motive in a varied form (short-short-short-long-long-long).

This horn-call motive announces a new legato melody which is calm and contrasts with the preceding agitation. Yet even during this lyrical moment, we are not allowed to forget the basic motive; now it is muttered in the background by cellos and double basses.

Beethoven generates tension in the development section by breaking the horn-call motive into smaller and smaller fragments until it is represented by only a single tone. Supported by a chord, this tone is echoed between woodwinds and strings in a breathtaking decrescendo. The recapitulation comes as a tremendous climax as the full orchestra thunders the basic motive. The recapitulation also brings a new expressive oboe solo at the end of the first theme. The heroic closing section of the recapitulation, in C major, moves without a break into a long and exciting coda in C minor. This coda is like a second development section in which the basic motive creates still greater power and energy.

Listening Outline To be read while music is heard

SYMPHONY NO. 5 IN C MINOR, OP. 67 (1808),
BY LUDWIG VAN BEETHOVEN

First Movement: Allegro con brio

Sonata form, duple meter ($\frac{2}{4}$), C minor

2 flutes, 2 oboes, 2 clarinets, 2 bassoons, 2 French horns, 2 trumpets, timpani, 1st violins, 2d violins, violas, cellos, double basses

(Duration, 7:33)

EXPOSITION
First theme
☐1 0:00

1. *a.* Basic motive, *ff*, repeated a step lower, strings in unison.

0:08

b. Sudden *p,* strings quickly develop basic motive, minor key, powerful chords, high held tone.

Bridge

2 0:21

0:25

2. *a.* Basic motive, *ff*, orchestra in unison.
   b. Sudden *p,* strings quickly develop basic motive, crescendo, *ff*, powerful
      chords.

Second theme

3 0:46

3. *a.* Solo French horns, *ff*, horn-call motive.

0:49

   b. Violins, *p,* lyrical melody in major. Basic motive accompanies in low strings.

Crescendo to

4 1:09

4. *a.* Triumphant melody, *ff*, violins.

1:19

   b. Woodwinds and horns, basic motive rushes downward. Cadences in basic
      rhythm. Pause.

5 1:28

Exposition is repeated.

DEVELOPMENT

6 2:57

1. *a.* Basic motive, *ff*, horns, strings.
   b. Sudden *p,* strings and woodwinds, basic motive quickly developed. Motive
      climbs to rapidly repeated chords, *ff*.

3:33

2. *a.* Violins, *ff*, horn-call motive, low strings, descending line.

3:43　　　　　　　*b.* High woodwinds, *ff*, in dialogue with lower strings, *ff*. Horn-call motive
　　　　　　　　　broken into tiny fragments. Decrescendo to *pp*.

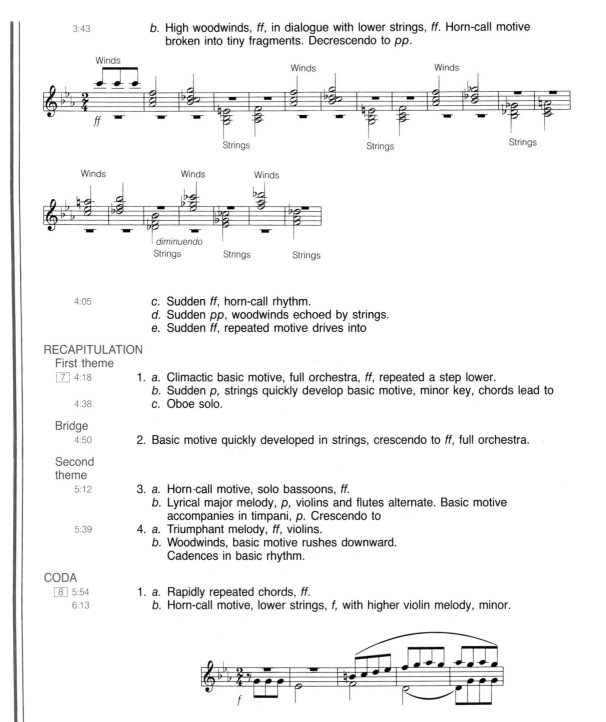

4:05　　　　　　　*c.* Sudden *ff*, horn-call rhythm.
　　　　　　　　　d. Sudden *pp*, woodwinds echoed by strings.
　　　　　　　　　e. Sudden *ff*, repeated motive drives into

RECAPITULATION
First theme
　7　4:18　　　　1. *a.* Climactic basic motive, full orchestra, *ff*, repeated a step lower.
　　　　　　　　　　　b. Sudden *p,* strings quickly develop basic motive, minor key, chords lead to
　4:38　　　　　　　*c.* Oboe solo.

Bridge
　4:50　　　　　2. Basic motive quickly developed in strings, crescendo to *ff*, full orchestra.

Second
theme
　5:12　　　　　3. *a.* Horn-call motive, solo bassoons, *ff*.
　　　　　　　　　　　b. Lyrical major melody, *p*, violins and flutes alternate. Basic motive
　　　　　　　　　　　　accompanies in timpani, *p*. Crescendo to
　5:39　　　　　4. *a.* Triumphant melody, *ff*, violins.
　　　　　　　　　　　b. Woodwinds, basic motive rushes downward.
　　　　　　　　　　　　Cadences in basic rhythm.

CODA
　8　5:54　　　　1. *a.* Rapidly repeated chords, *ff*.
　6:13　　　　　　　*b.* Horn-call motive, lower strings, *f,* with higher violin melody, minor.

Descending violin melody, staccato, leads to

6:29   2. *a.* New, rising theme in strings, legato and staccato.

6:39   *b.* High woodwinds, *ff*, answered by lower strings in powerful interchange. Rapidly repeated notes lead to
7:05   3. *a.* Basic motive, *ff*, repeated a step lower, full orchestra.
              b. Sudden *p*, basic motive quickly developed in strings and woodwinds.
              c. Sudden *ff*, powerful concluding chords.

Second Movement:

Andante con moto (moderately slow but not too slow)

The second movement, in A flat major, is mostly relaxed and lyrical, but it includes moments of tension and heroism. It is an extended set of variations based on two themes. The main theme (A), softly introduced by the cellos and violas, is a long, legato melody of great nobility. The second theme (B) begins very gently in the clarinets but soon brings a startling contrast of mood. The full orchestra suddenly bursts in, and the clarinet melody is transformed into a triumphant trumpet fanfare. A hushed transitional passage then leads back to the main theme, presented now in quicker notes.

Side 7, band 2
CD 4 9

After several variations, there is a middle section in which fragments of the themes are treated in new ways. Woodwind instruments are featured, and there is a brief episode in minor. The movement concludes with a final variation of the main melody—now majestically proclaimed by the full orchestra—and a coda that poetically recalls what has come before.

Listing Outline To be read while music is heard

SYMPHONY NO. 5 IN C MINOR, OP. 67 (1808), BY LUDWIG VAN BEETHOVEN

Second Movement: Andante con moto

Theme and variations, triple meter ($\frac{3}{8}$), A flat major

2 flutes, 2 oboes, 2 clarinets, 2 bassoons, 2 French horns, 2 trumpets, timpani, 1st violins, 2d violins, violas, cellos, double basses

(Duration, 10:19)

THEME A

9 0:00

1. Lyrical melody, violas and cellos, *p.*

Melody continues in higher register, violins alternate with flute.

THEME B

10 0:56

2. *a.* Clarinets, *p,* rising phrases.

1:18

Violins, *pp,* sudden *ff,* full orchestra.
b. Trumpets, *ff,* rising phrases.

Violins, *pp,* sustained notes.

VARIATION A¹

11 2:03

3. Violas and cellos, *p,* lyrical melody in even-flowing rhythm.

Melody continues in higher register, violins alternate with flute.

VARIATION B¹

2:56

4. *a.* Clarinets, *p,* rising phrases. Violins, *pp,* sudden *ff,* full orchestra.
   b. Trumpets, *ff,* rising phrases. Violins, *pp,* sustained notes, cellos, low repeated notes.

VARIATION A²

12 4:05

5. *a.* Violas and cellos, *p,* lyrical melody decorated by quick, even-flowing notes.

b. Violins, *pp*, repeat decorated melody in higher register.
c. Loud repeated chords, decorated melody in cellos and double basses. Upward scales lead to high held tone.

MIDDLE
SECTION

[13] 5:09   6. Sudden *pp*, repeated string chords, clarinet phrase passed to bassoon and flute. High woodwind interlude leads to

6:07   7. *a.* Full orchestra, *ff*, rising phrases, timpani rolls.
6:32   *b.* Strings, *p*, repeated short figure.
6:53   8. *a.* Woodwinds, *p*, staccato variation of lyrical melody, minor key.
            b. Rising scales in flute, strings. Crescendo.

VARIATION A³

[14] 7:36   9. Full orchestra, *ff*, lyrical melody in high register, major key, rising scales. Flute and violins, *p*, continue melody.

CODA

8:28   10. *a.* Più mosso (faster tempo), bassoon, *p*, variation of lyrical phrase. Violins, crescendo.
8:56   *b.* Original tempo, flute and strings, *p*, conclusion of lyrical melody.
9:29   *c.* Clarinets, *p*, variation of lyrical phrase, low strings, crescendo. Cadence in full orchestra, *ff*.

Third Movement:

Allegro (scherzo)

The rapid third movement is a scherzo, in C minor, composed of three sections: A (scherzo) B (trio) A′ (scherzo). The scherzo opens with a hushed, mysterious theme played by cellos and double basses in a low register.

Side 7, band 3
CD 4 [15]
Section A
[15] 0:00

Soon, in sharp contrast, a bold repeated-note theme is hammered out loudly by the horns.

This theme is dominated by the rhythmic pattern short-short-short-long and recalls the basic motive of the first movement.

The B section (trio), in major, brings a gruff, hurried theme, played by cellos and double basses.

Section B
16 1:44

This theme is imitated, in the style of a fugue, by each of the higher strings. The bustling rhythmic motion of the B section has a feeling of energy and rough humor.

Section A'
17 3:08

When the scherzo section (A') returns, it is hushed and ominous throughout, sounding like a ghost of its former self. The mysterious opening theme is now played pizzicato rather than legato. The repeated-note theme is completely transformed in mood; it is no longer proclaimed by horns but is whispered by clarinets, plucked violins, and oboe.

One of the most extraordinary passages in the symphony follows the scherzo section (A'): a bridge leading from the dark, mysterious world of the scherzo to the bright sunlight of the finale. It opens with a feeling of suspended animation as the timpani softly repeat a single tone against a sustained chord in the strings. Over the timpani pulsation, the violins hesitantly play a fragment of the mysterious scherzo theme. Tension mounts as this fragment is carried higher and higher, until a sudden crescendo climaxes with the heroic opening of the finale.

Bridge
18 4:16

Fourth Movement:

Allegro

The fourth movement, in sonata form, is the climax of the symphony. It brings the victory of C major over C minor, of optimism and exultation over struggle and uncertainty. For greater power and brilliance, Beethoven enlarged the orchestra in the finale to include three trombones, a piccolo, and a contrabassoon. Brass instruments are especially prominent and give a marchlike character to much of the movement.

Side 7, band 3
(continued)
CD 4 19

The exposition is rich in melodic ideas; even the bridge has a theme of its own, and there is also a distinctive closing theme. The triumphant opening theme begins with the three tones of the C major triad, brilliantly proclaimed by the trumpets.

19 0:00

A bridge theme, similar in mood to the opening theme, is announced by the horns and continued by the violins.

20 0:36

Triplets lend a joyous quality to the second theme, which contrasts loud and soft phrases.

21 1:04

Two powerful chords and a brief pause announce the closing theme of the exposition. This melody, composed of descending phrases, is first played by the strings and woodwinds and then forcefully repeated by the entire orchestra.

22 1:33

The exposition is repeated.

The development focuses mainly on the second theme and its triplet rhythm. A huge climax at the end of the development is followed by one of the most marvelous surprises in all music. Beethoven dramatically quotes the whispered repeated-note theme (short-short-short-long) of the preceding scherzo movement. This ominous quotation is like a sudden recollection of past anxiety, and it creates a connection between the last two movements. Leading into the powerful recapitulation of the fourth movement, it prepares the renewal of the victory over uncertainty.

23 2:05
24 4:17
25 5:54
Recapitulation
6:25

During the long coda of the finale, earlier themes are heard in altered and quickened versions. Several times, the music keeps going even though the listener thinks it's coming to an end. Over and over, Beethoven affirms the tonic key and resolves the frenzied tensions built up during the symphony. Such control over tension is an essential element of Beethoven's genius.

STRING QUARTET IN F MAJOR, OP. 18, NO. 1 (1798–1800)

"Accept this quartet as a small token of our friendship, and whenever you play it remember the days we spent together," wrote Beethoven to a violinist friend after completing the String Quartet in F Major in 1799. But two years later Beethoven wrote to his friend, "Do not lend your copy of the quartet to anybody, because I have greatly changed it, having just learned how to write quartets properly." It is the second version of the String Quartet in F Major that was published as Op. 18, No. 1, and became the best-known of Beethoven's early string quartets. In this work each instrumental part is given important thematic material and demands virtuosity from the player.

The opening movement, in F major (which we'll focus on), is a brilliant allegro in sonata form. It is followed by a highly emotional slow movement, in D minor, that is also in sonata form. This second movement, marked *adagio affettuoso ed appassionato (tender and impassioned adagio),* was inspired by the burial vault scene in Shakespeare's *Romeo and Juliet.* The very rapid third movement, in F major, is a scherzo in A B A form. The whirlwind finale, in sonata-rondo form, has an extended, mostly polyphonic development section.

First Movement:

Allegro con brio

Supplementary sets:
Side 4, band 1
CD 2 23

The first movement, allegro con brio, is built from transformations of its brief opening motive. As in the opening movement of Beethoven's Fifth Symphony, an amazing variety of musical material is drawn from a single rhythmic idea. At the beginning of the first movement of the quartet, the basic rhythmic motive is presented twice, softly, by all four string instruments in unison; the second time, its last note is a step higher in pitch.

A lyrical answering phrase, in homophonic texture, begins with a variation of the basic motive.

After a forte return of the basic motive in all four instruments in unison, intensity is generated when the motive is harmonized by dissonant chords.

As the first theme continues, sudden accents, rapid imitations, and additional dissonances make the motive sound even more tense. After a cadence comes the bridge section, which begins with a graceful violin melody set against the basic motive in the cello.

The second theme contrasts with the first theme and the bridge owing to its even rhythms and long phrases. It is ushered in by a syncopated repetition of a single tone in the first violin and continues with a flowing melody that is passed from the first violin to each of the other instruments.

The closing theme begins with a flowing upward phrase that resembles the second theme and ends with a dramatic surprise: after the rising phrase comes a long, questioning silence that is followed by the basic motive played softly. The rising phrase is then repeated in a high register, but now the silence is answered by brusque heavy chords in a low register instead of the soft basic motive. Such abrupt contrasts of register, dynamics, and mood are characteristic of Beethoven.

In the development section, the texture becomes polyphonic as the basic motive is quickly tossed from one instrument to the other. Sharp accents, dissonances, and rapid changes of key create excitement. A change to homophonic texture occurs when a pulsating accompaniment supports descending repetitions of the main motive in the violins. After a suspenseful passage of rapid scales, the recapitulation comes as a triumphant climax when the first theme returns fortissimo.

In the recapitulation, a shortened version of the first theme and bridge is followed by the second and closing themes. The coda begins with a powerful new ascending scale idea that is soon combined with a playful transformation of the basic motive.

Listening Outline To be read while music is heard

STRING QUARTET IN F MAJOR, OP. 18, NO. 1 (1798–1800),
BY LUDWIG VAN BEETHOVEN

First Movement: Allegro con brio

Sonata form, triple meter ($\frac{3}{4}$), F major

1st violin, 2d violin, viola, cello

(Duration, 8:58)

EXPOSITION
First theme
23 0:00   1. *a.* Basic motive, *p,* strings in unison, answered by lyrical phrase, *p.*

b. Basic motive, *f,* rising basic motive, *p,* dissonant chords, cadence.
c. Rising basic motive imitated, accented dissonant chords, high 1st violin
ascends, powerful cadence, *f.*

Bridge
24 0:37   2. *a.* Pulsating accompaniment, *p,* 1st violin, graceful melody with trills, cello,
basic motive.

b. Viola, *p,* basic motive, 1st violin, graceful melody varied, crescendo to
c. Rapid rising scales in violin and cello, *p,* crescendo, unison scale, *ff,* leads
to

Second
theme
25 1:09   3. *a.* 1st violin, single tone repeated, solo flowing melody, *p,* answered in viola,
cello.

Crescendo to cadence.

b. Pulsating accompaniment, *p,* basic motive tossed between high cello and 1st violin, running notes in 1st violin, unison strings, crescendo to *f,* trill, cadence.

Closing
theme
26 1:45

4. *a.* Rising phrase, *p,* pause,

basic motive, cadence.
b. Rising phrase octave higher, *p,* pause, low accented chords, cadence.
c. Pulsating accompaniment, *p,* cello, basic motive, violin melody with trill, rapid descending scales in 1st violin and unison strings, crescendo, repeated chords, *f,* pause.

27 2:24
Exposition is repeated.

DEVELOPMENT
28 4:45
1. Rapid descending scales in 1st violin, *f,* unison strings, cello, basic motive, answered by running notes in high 1st violin, 2d violin, lyrical basic motive echoed in higher register by higher 1st violin, *pp.*

5:02
2. Cello, *f,* basic motive, quickly imitated by other instruments, sudden accents, dissonances, rapid changes of key.

5:29
3. Pulsating accompaniment, *p,* violin, basic motive successively repeated on lower pitches.

5:48
4. Rapid descending scales in 1st violin, cello, rising accented violin melody, crescendo, rapid ascent to

RECAPITULATION
First theme
29 6:02
1. *a.* Basic motive, *ff,* unison strings, answered by lyrical phrase, *p,* 1st violin, lyrical phrase imitated an octave lower by 2d violin, crescendo.

Bridge
6:28
b. Viola, *p,* basic motive, 1st violin, graceful melody with trills, crescendo.
c. Rapid rising scales in 1st violin and cello, *p,* crescendo, unison scale, *ff,* leads to

Second
theme
6:50
3. *a.* 1st violin, single tone repeated, solo flowing melody, *p,* answered in viola, cello, crescendo to cadence.

b. Pulsating accompaniment, *p,* basic motive tossed between high cello and 1st violin, running notes in 1st violin, unison strings, crescendo to *f,* trill, cadence.

4. *a.* Rising phrase, *p,* pause, basic motive, cadence.
   b. Rising phrase octave higher, *p,* pause, low accented chords, *ff,* cadence.
   c. Pulsating accompaniment, *p,* cello, basic motive, violin melody with trill, rapid descending scales in 1st violin and unison strings, crescendo to

1. *a.* Unison staccato scale, *ff,* rises to sustained tone, repeated at lower pitch.

b. Violin, *pp,* playful variation of basic motive, rising scale accompanies, *pp,* crescendo, rising basic motive, dissonant chords, sudden *pp,* cadence to
c. Cello, *pp,* basic motive, 1st violin, basic motive rises, crescendo, varied and accented basic motive descends to closing chords, *f.*

288

VI

THE ROMANTIC PERIOD

VI

Emotional subjectivity was a basic quality of romanticism.
Théodore Géricault's *Portrait of a Young Man in an Artist's Studio*
(1819) depicts the artist's suffering and isolation.

ROMANTICISM IN MUSIC (1820–1900)

The early nineteenth century brought the flowering of romanticism, a cultural movement that stressed emotion, imagination, and individualism. In part, romanticism was a rebellion against the neoclassicism of the eighteenth century and the age of reason. Romantic writers broke away from time-honored conventions and emphasized freedom of expression. Painters used bolder, more brilliant colors and preferred dynamic motion to gracefully balanced poses.

But romanticism was too diverse and complex to be defined by any single formula. It aimed to broaden all human horizons and encompass the totality of our experience. The romantic movement was international in scope and influenced all the arts.

Emotional subjectivity was a basic quality of romanticism in art. "All good poetry is the spontaneous overflow of powerful feelings," wrote William Wordsworth, the English romantic poet. And "spontaneous overflow" made much romantic literature autobiographical; authors projected their personalities in their work. Walt Whitman, the American poet, expressed this subjective attitude beautifully when he began a poem, "I celebrate myself, and sing myself."

In exploring their inner lives, the romantics were especially drawn to the realm of fantasy: the unconscious, the irrational, the world of dreams. Romantic fiction includes tales of terror and the supernatural, such as *The Cask of Amontillado,* by Edgar Allan Poe; and *Frankenstein,* by Mary Wollstonecraft Shelley. The writer Thomas De Quincey vividly describes his drug-induced dreams in the *Confessions of an English Opium-Eater:* "I was buried, for a thousand years, in stone coffins, with mummies and sphinxes. I was kissed, with cancerous kisses, by crocodiles." The visual arts also depict nightmarish visions. In an etching called *The Sleep of Reason Breeds Monsters,* the Spanish painter Francisco Goya shows batlike monsters surrounding a sleeping figure. The realm of the unknown and the exotic also interested the French artist Eugène Delacroix, who often depicted violent scenes in far-off lands.

The romantic fascination with fantasy was paired with enthusiasm for the Middle Ages, that time of chivalry and romance. Whereas neoclassicists had thought of the medieval period as the "dark ages," the romantics cherished it. They were inspired by medieval folk ballads, by tales of fantasy and adventure. Romantic novels set in the Middle Ages include *Ivanhoe* (1819), by Sir Walter Scott; and *The Hunchback of Notre Dame* (1831), by the French writer Victor Hugo. Gothic cathedrals, which had long gone unappreciated, now seemed picturesque and mysterious. A "gothic revival" in architecture resulted in the construction of buildings such as

Eugène Delacroix's painting *The Bark of Dante* (1822) depicts the agony of the damned in hell. The romantics were drawn to the realm of the supernatural and drew inspiration from medieval literary works such as Dante's *Inferno*.

the Houses of Parliament in London (1836–1852) and Trinity Church in New York (1839–1846).

Of all the inspirations for romantic art, none was more important than nature. The physical world was seen as a source of consolation and a mirror of the human heart. Wordsworth, for example, thought of nature as "the nurse,/the guide, the guardian of my heart, and soul." One of his poems begins:

> There was a time when meadow, grove, and stream,
>   The earth, and every common sight,
>   To me did seem
>   Apparelled in celestial light,
> The glory and the freshness of a dream.

293

The Hay Wain (1821), by John Constable. Of all the sources of inspiration for romantic art, none was more important than nature.

The romantic sensitivity to nature is revealed in landscape painting, which attained new importance. Artists like John Constable and William Turner in England were masters in conveying the movement of nature: rippling brooks, drifting clouds, stormy seas. In Turner's seascapes, the sweep of waves expresses not only the grandeur of nature, but human passion as well.

Romanticism coincided with the industrial revolution, which caused vast social and economic changes. Many writers and painters recorded the new social realities of their time. The novels of Charles Dickens and the paintings of Honoré Daumier reflect an interest in the working class and the poor.

Subjectivity, fantasy, and enthusiasm for nature and the Middle Ages are only a few aspects of romanticism in literature and painting. We'll now focus on romanticism in music.

THE ROMANTIC PERIOD IN MUSIC

The romantic period in music extended from about 1820 to 1900. Among the most significant romantic musicians were Franz Schubert, Robert Schumann, Clara Wieck Schumann, Frédéric Chopin, Franz Liszt, Felix Mendelssohn, Hector Berlioz, Peter Ilyich Tchaikovsky, Bedřich Smetana, Antonin Dvořák, Johannes Brahms, Giuseppe Verdi, Giacomo Puccini, Richard Wagner, and Gustav Mahler. The length of this list—and some important composers have been omitted from it—testifies to the richness and variety of romantic music and proves its continuing impact on today's concert and operatic repertory.

Composers of the romantic period continued to use the musical forms of the preceding classical era. The emotional intensity associated with romanticism was already present in the work of Mozart and particularly in that of Beethoven, who greatly influenced composers after him. The romantic preference for expressive, songlike melody also grew out of the classical style.

Nonetheless, there are many differences between romantic and classical music. Romantic works tend to have greater ranges of tone color, dynamics, and pitch. Also, the romantic harmonic vocabulary is broader, with more emphasis on colorful, unstable chords. Romantic music is linked more closely to the other arts, particularly to literature. New forms developed, and in all forms there was greater tension and less emphasis on balance and resolution. But romantic music is so diverse that generalizations are apt to mislead. Some romantic composers, such as Mendelssohn and Brahms, created works that were deeply rooted in classical tradition; other composers, such as Berlioz, Liszt, and Wagner, were more revolutionary.

CHARACTERISTICS OF ROMANTIC MUSIC

Individuality of Style

Romantic music puts unprecedented emphasis on self-expression and individuality of style. There is "not a bar which I have not truly felt and which is not an echo of my innermost feelings," wrote Tchaikovsky of his Fourth Symphony. "A new world of music" was the goal of the young Chopin. Many romantics created music that sounds unique and reflects their personalities. Robert Schumann observed that "Chopin will soon be unable to write anything without people crying out at the seventh or eighth bar, 'That is indeed by him.'" And today, with some listening experience, a music lover can tell within a few minutes—sometimes within a few seconds—whether a piece is by Schumann or Chopin, Tchaikovsky or Brahms.

Romantic music puts unprecedented emphasis on individuality of style. Eugène Delacroix's *Paganini* (1832) conveys the intensity of a performance by the most famous violinist of the nineteenth century.

Expressive Aims and Subjects

The romantics explored a universe of feeling that included flamboyance and intimacy, unpredictability and melancholy, rapture and longing. Countless songs and operas glorify romantic love. Often the lovers are unhappy and face overwhelming obstacles. Fascination with the fantastic and diabolical is expressed in music like the *Dream of a Witches' Sabbath* from Berlioz's *Symphonie fantastique (Fantastic Symphony)*. All aspects of nature attracted romantic musicians. In different sections of Part VI we'll study music that depicts shepherds' pipes and distant thunder (Berlioz's *Fantastic Symphony*), a wild horseback ride on a stormy night (Schubert's *Erlkönig*, or *Erlking*), the flow of a river (Smetana's *Moldau*), and a trout swimming in a brook (Schubert's *Die Forelle*). Romantic composers also dealt with subjects drawn from the Middle Ages and from Shakespeare's plays.

Nationalism and Exoticism

Nationalism was an important political movement that influenced nineteenth-century music. Musical *nationalism* was expressed when romantic composers deliberately created music with a specific national identity, using the folk songs, dances, legends, and history of their homelands. This national flavor of romantic music—whether Polish, Russian, Bohemian (Czech), or German—contrasts with the more universal character of classical music.

Fascination with national identity also led composers to draw on colorful materials from foreign lands, a trend known as musical *exoticism.* For instance, some wrote melodies in an Asian style or used rhythms and instruments associated with distant lands. The French composer Georges Bizet wrote *Carmen*, an opera set in Spain; the Italian Giacomo Puccini evoked Japan in *Madame Butterfly*; and the Russian Rimsky-Korsakov suggested an Arabian atmosphere in his orchestral work *Scheherazade*. Musical exoticism was in keeping with the romantics' attraction to things remote, picturesque, and mysterious.

Program Music

The nineteenth century was the great age of *program music,* instrumental music associated with a story, poem, idea, or scene. Usually the nonmusical element is specified by a title or by explanatory comments called a *program.* A programmatic instrumental piece can represent the emotions, characters, and events of a particular story, or it can evoke the sounds and motions of nature. For example, in Tchaikovsky's *Romeo and Juliet,* an orchestral work inspired by Shakespeare's play, agitated music depicts the feud between the rival families, a tender melody conveys young love, and a funeral-march rhythm suggests the lovers' tragic fate. And in _The Moldau,_ an orchestral work glorifying the main river of Bohemia, Smetana uses musical effects that call to mind a flowing stream, a hunting scene, a peasant wedding, and the crash of waves.

Program music in some form or another has existed for centuries, but it became particularly prominent in the romantic period, when music was closely associated with literature. Many composers—Berlioz, Schumann, Liszt, and Wagner, for example—were prolific authors as well. Artists in all fields were intoxicated by the concept of a "union of the arts." Poets wanted their poetry to be musical, and musicians wanted their music to be poetic.

Expressive Tone Color

Romantic composers reveled in rich and sensuous sound, using tone color to obtain variety of mood and atmosphere. Never before had timbre been so important.

In both symphonic and operatic works, the romantic orchestra was larger and more varied in tone color than the classical orchestra. Toward the end of the romantic era, an orchestra might include close to 100 musicians. (There were twenty to sixty players in the classical ensemble.) The constant expansion of the orchestra reflected composers' changing needs as well as the growing size of concert halls and opera houses. The brass, woodwind, and percussion sections of the orchestra took on a more active role. Romantic composers increased the power of the brass section to something spectacular, calling for trombones, tubas, and more horns and trumpets. In 1824, Beethoven broke precedent by asking for nine brasses in the Ninth Symphony; and in 1894, the Austrian composer Gustav Mahler demanded twenty-five brass instruments for his Second Symphony. The addition of valves had made it easier for horns and trumpets to cope with intricate melodies.

The woodwind section took on new tone colors as the contrabassoon, bass clarinet, English horn, and piccolo became regular members of the orchestra. Improvements in the construction of instruments allowed woodwind players to perform more flexibly and accurately. Orchestral sounds became more brilliant and sensuously appealing through increased use of cymbals, the triangle, and the harp.

New sounds were drawn from all instruments of the nineteenth-century orchestra. Flutists were required to play in the breathy low register, and violinists were asked to strike the strings with the wood of their bows. These demands compelled performers to attain a higher level of technical virtuosity.

New ways of blending and combining tone colors were sought to achieve the most poignant and intense sound. In 1844, Hector Berlioz's

Treatise on Modern Instrumentation and Orchestration signaled the recognition of orchestration as an art in itself.

The piano, the favorite instrument of the romantic age, was improved vastly during the 1820s and 1830s. A cast-iron frame was introduced to hold the strings under greater tension, and the hammers were covered with felt. Thus the piano's tone became more "singing." Its range was also extended. With a stronger instrument, the pianist could produce more sound. And use of the damper ("loud") pedal allowed a sonorous blend of tones from all registers of the piano.

Colorful Harmony

In addition to exploiting new tone colors, the romantics explored new chords and novel ways of using familiar chords. Seeking greater emotional intensity, composers emphasized rich, colorful, and complex harmonies. There was more prominent use of *chromatic harmony*, which employs chords containing tones not found in the prevailing major or minor scale. Such chord tones come from the chromatic scale (which has twelve tones), rather than from the major or minor scales (which have seven different tones). Chromatic chords add color and motion to romantic music. Dissonant, or unstable, chords were also used more freely than during the classical era. By deliberately delaying the resolution of dissonance to a consonant, or stable, chord, romantic composers created feelings of yearning, tension, and mystery.

A romantic piece tends to have a wide variety of keys and rapid modulations, or changes from one key to another. Because of the nature and frequency of these key shifts, the tonic key is somewhat less clear than in classical works. The feeling of tonal gravity tends to be less strong. By the end of the romantic period, even more emphasis was given to harmonic instability and less to stability and resolution.

Expanded Range of Dynamics, Pitch, and Tempo

Romantic music also calls for a wide range of dynamics. It includes sharp contrasts between faint whispers and sonorities of unprecedented power. The classical dynamic extremes of *ff* and *pp* didn't meet the needs of romantics, who sometimes demanded *ffff* and *pppp*. Seeking more and more expressiveness, nineteenth-century composers used frequent crescendos and decrescendos, as well as sudden dynamic changes.

The range of pitch was expanded, too, as composers reached for extremely high or low sounds. In search of increased brilliance and depth of sound, the romantics exploited instruments like the piccolo and contrabassoon, as well as the expanded keyboard of the piano.

Mood changes in romantic music are often underlined by accelerandos, ritardandos, and subtle variations of pace: there are many more fluctuations in tempo than there are in classical music. To intensify the expression of the music, romantic performers made use of **rubato,** the slight holding back or pressing forward of tempo.

Form: Miniature and Monumental

The nineteenth century was very much an age of contradictions. Romantic composers characteristically expressed themselves both in musical miniatures and in monumental compositions. On the one hand are piano pieces by Chopin and songs by Schubert that last but a few minutes. Such short forms were meant to be heard in the intimate surroundings of a home; they met the needs of the growing number of people who owned pianos. The romantic genius for creating an intense mood through a melody, a few chords, or an unusual tone color found a perfect outlet in these miniatures. On the other hand, there are gigantic works by Berlioz and Wagner that call for a huge number of performers, last for several hours, and were designed for large opera houses or concert halls.

Romantic composers continued to write symphonies, sonatas, string quartets, concertos, operas, and choral works, but their individual movements tended to be longer than Haydn's and Mozart's. For example, a typical nineteenth-century symphony might last about 45 minutes, as opposed to 25 minutes for an eighteenth-century symphony. And as the romantic period drew to a close, compositions tended to become ever more extended, more richly orchestrated, and more complex in harmony.

New techniques were used to unify such long works. The same theme or themes might occur in several different movements of a symphony. Here composers followed the pioneering example of Beethoven's Fifth Symphony, where a theme from the scherzo is quoted within the finale. When a melody returns in a later movement or section of a romantic work, its character may be transformed by changes in dynamics, orchestration, or rhythm—a technique known as **thematic transformation.** A striking use of thematic transformation occurs in Berlioz's *Symphonie fantastique (Fantastic Symphony, 1830),* where a lyrical melody from the opening movement becomes a grotesque dance tune in the finale.

Different movements or sections of a romantic work can also be linked through transitional passages; one movement of a symphony or concerto may lead directly into the next. Here, again, Beethoven was the pioneer. And nineteenth-century operas are unified by melodic ideas that reappear in different acts or scenes, some of which may be tied together by connecting passages.

In dealing with an age that so prized individuality, generalizations are especially difficult. The great diversity found in romantic music can best be appreciated, perhaps, by approaching each piece as its composer did—with an open mind and heart.

BASIC TERMS

nationalism (page 297)   chromatic harmony (298)
exoticism (297)   rubato (300)
program music (297)   thematic transformation (300)
program (297)

ROMANTIC COMPOSERS AND THEIR PUBLIC

ROMANTIC

2

The composer's role in society changed radically during Beethoven's lifetime (1770–1827). In earlier periods, part of a musician's job had been the composition of works for a specific occasion and audience. Thus Bach wrote cantatas for weekly church services in Leipzig, and Haydn composed symphonies for concerts in the palaces of the Esterházy family. But Beethoven, as we have seen, was one of the first great composers to work as a free-lance musician outside the system of aristocratic or church patronage.

The image of Beethoven as a "free artist" inspired romantic musicians, who often composed to fulfill an inner need rather than a commission. Romantic composers were interested not only in pleasing their contemporaries, but also in being judged favorably by posterity. The young Berlioz wrote to his father, "I want to leave on this earth some trace of my existence." It became common for romantics to create extended works with no immediate prospects for performance. For example, Wagner wrote *Das Rheingold (The Rhine Gold)*, a 2½-hour opera, and then had to wait fifteen years before seeing its premiere.

Sometimes the romantic composer was a "free artist" by necessity rather than choice. Because of the French Revolution and the Napoleonic Wars (from 1789 to 1814), many aristocrats could no longer afford to maintain private opera houses, orchestras, and "composers in residence." Musicians lost their jobs when many of the tiny princely states of Germany were abolished as political units and merged with neighboring territories. (In Bonn, Germany, the court and its orchestra were disbanded; Beethoven could not have returned to his position there even if he had wanted to.) Many composers who would have had modest but secure incomes in the past had to fight for their livelihood and sell their wares in the marketplace.

Romantic composers wrote primarily for a middle-class audience whose size and prosperity had increased because of the industrial revolution. During the nineteenth century, cities expanded dramatically, and a sizable number of people wanted to hear and play music.

301

Romantic composers wrote primarily for a middle-class audience. In this picture by Moritz von Schwind, Franz Schubert is shown at the piano accompanying the singer Johann Michael Vogl.

The needs of this urban middle class led to the formation of many orchestras and opera groups during the romantic era. Public concerts had developed during the eighteenth century, but only in the nineteenth century did regular subscription concerts become common. The London Philharmonic Society was founded in 1813, the Paris Société des Concerts du Conservatoire in 1828, and the Vienna Philharmonische Konzerte and the New York Philharmonic in 1842.

The first half of the nineteenth century also witnessed the founding of music conservatories throughout Europe. In the United States, conservatories were founded in Chicago, Cleveland, Boston, Oberlin (Ohio), and Philadelphia during the 1860s. More young men and women than ever before studied to be professional musicians. At first women were accepted only as students of performance, but by the late 1800s they could study musical composition as well.

The nineteenth-century public was captivated by virtuosity. Among the musical heroes of the 1830s were the pianist Franz Liszt and the violinist Niccolò Paganini, who toured Europe and astonished audiences with their feats. Never before had instrumental virtuosity been so acclaimed. After one concert by Liszt in Budapest, Hungarian nobles presented him with a jeweled sword, and a crowd of thousands formed a torchlight parade to escort him to his dwelling. Following Liszt's example, performers like the pianist Clara Schumann and the violinist Joseph Joachim began to give solo recitals in addition to their customary appearances with orchestras.

Private music making also increased during the romantic era. The piano became a fixture in every middle-class home, and there was great demand for songs and solo piano pieces. Operas and orchestral works were transcribed, or arranged, so that they could be played on pianos in the home.

Romantic composers came from the social class that was their main audience. Berlioz was the son of a doctor; Schumann was a bookseller's son; and Mendelssohn was the son of a banker. This was a new situation. In

The needs of the urban middle class led to the formation of many orchestras during the romantic era. This engraving shows Louis Jullien conducting an orchestra and four military bands at Covent Garden Theatre in London in 1846.

(Southhampton University Library)

earlier periods, music, like cabinetmaking, had been a craft passed from one generation to another. Bach, Mozart, and Beethoven were all children of musicians. But the romantics often had to do a great deal of persuading before their parents permitted them to undertake a musical career. Berlioz wrote to his reluctant father in 1824: "I am voluntarily driven towards a magnificent career (no other term can be applied to the career of an artist) and I am not in the least headed towards damnation. . . . This is the way I think, the way I am, and nothing in the world will change me."

Middle-class parents had reason for concern when their children wanted to be musicians. Few romantic composers were able to support themselves through composition alone. Only a very successful opera composer like Verdi could become wealthy by selling music to opera houses and publishers. Most composers were forced to work in several areas at once. Some were touring virtuosos like Paganini and Liszt. Many taught. Chopin charged high fees for piano lessons he gave to rich young women in Paris. Music criticism was a source of income for Berlioz and Schumann. (And Berlioz bitterly resented having to waste time reviewing compositions by nonentities.) Some of the finest conductors of the romantic period were composers, among them Mendelssohn and Mahler. And last, a few fortunates, such as Tchaikovsky and Wagner, had wealthy patrons to support them while they created.

[ROMANTIC]
[**3**]

THE ART SONG

One of the most distinctive forms in romantic music is the ***art song,*** a composition for solo voice and piano. Here, the accompaniment is an integral part of the composer's conception, and it serves as an interpretive partner to the voice. Although they are now performed in concert halls, romantic songs were written to be sung and enjoyed at home.

Poetry and music are intimately fused in the art song. It is no accident that this form flowered with the emergence of a rich body of romantic poetry in the early nineteenth century. Many of the finest song composers— Schubert, Schumann, and Brahms, for example—were German or Austrian and set poems in their native language. Among the poets favored by these composers were Johann Wolfgang von Goethe (1749–1832) and Heinrich Heine (1797–1856). The German word *Lied (song)* is commonly used for a song with German text. (*Lied* is pronounced *leet;* its plural, *Lieder,* is pronounced *leader.*)

Yearning—inspired by a lost love, nature, legend, or other times and places—haunted the imagination of romantic poets. Thus art songs are filled with the despair of unrequited love, the beauty of flowers, trees, and brooks, and the supernatural happenings of folk tales. There are also songs of joy, wit, and humor. But by and large, romantic song was a reaching out of the soul.

Song composers interpreted a poem, translating its mood, atmosphere, and imagery into music. They created a vocal melody that was musically satisfying and perfectly molded to the text. Important words were emphasized by stressed tones or melodic climaxes.

The voice shares the interpretive task with the piano. Emotions and images of the text get added dimension from the keyboard commentary. Arpeggios in the piano might suggest the splashing of oars or the motion of a mill wheel. Chords in a low register might depict darkness or a lover's torment. The mood is often set by a brief piano introduction and summed up at the end by a piano section called a *postlude.*

STROPHIC AND THROUGH-COMPOSED FORM

When a poem has several stanzas, the musical setting must accommodate their total emotional impact. Composers can use *strophic form,* repeating the same music for each stanza of the poem. This makes the song easy to remember. Strophic form is used in almost all folk songs. Or composers might use *through-composed form,* writing new music for each stanza. (*Through-composed* is a translation of the German term *durchkomponiert.*) Through-composed form allows music to reflect a poem's changing moods.

The art song is not restricted to strophic or through-composed form. There are many ways that music can be molded to the structure and feeling of a poem. A three-stanza poem is frequently set as follows: A (stanza 1)–B (stanza 2)–A (stanza 3). This might be called a *modified strophic form,* since two of the three stanzas are set to the same music.

THE SONG CYCLE

Romantic art songs are sometimes grouped in a set, or *song cycle.* A cycle may be unified by a story line that runs through the poems, or by musical ideas linking the songs. Among the great romantic song cycles are *Die Winterreise* (*The Winter Journey,* 1827) by Schubert, and *Dichterliebe* (*Poet's Love,* 1840) by Schumann.

In their art songs, romantic composers achieved a perfect union of music and poetry. They created an intensely personal world with a tremendous variety of moods. These miniatures contain some of the most haunting melodies and harmonies in all music.

BASIC TERMS

art song (page 304)	through-composed form (305)
postlude (305)	modified strophic form (305)
strophic form (305)	song cycle (305)

[4] FRANZ SCHUBERT

The career of Franz Schubert (1797–1828), the earliest master of the romantic art song, was unlike that of any great composer before him. He never held an official position as musical director or organist, and he was neither a conductor nor a virtuoso. He was the first Viennese composer whose income came entirely from musical composition. "I have come into the world for no other purpose but to compose," he told a friend. The full measure of his genius was recognized only years after his tragically early death.

Schubert was born in Vienna, the son of a schoolmaster. Even as a child, he had astounding musical gifts. "If I wanted to instruct him in anything new," recalled his amazed teacher, "he knew it already. Therefore I gave him no actual instructions but merely talked to him and watched him in silent astonishment." At eleven, Schubert became a choirboy in the court chapel and won a scholarship to the Imperial Seminary, an exclusive boarding school, where he played first violin and occasionally conducted the orchestra. Schubert so loved music that he once sold his schoolbooks to buy a ticket for a performance of Beethoven's opera *Fidelio*.

Schubert managed to compose an extraordinary number of masterpieces in his late teens while teaching at his father's school, a job he hated. His love of poetry led him to the art song, a form that Haydn, Mozart, and Beethoven had only touched on. Inflamed by the poetry and passion of Goethe's *Faust*, seventeen-year-old Schubert composed his first great song, *Gretchen am Spinnrade (Gretchen at the Spinning Wheel)*. The next year he composed 143 songs, including *The Erlking*. When he was nineteen, his productivity rose to a peak: he composed 179 works, including two symphonies, an opera, and a mass.

When he was twenty-one, Schubert gave up teaching school to devote himself entirely to music. He associated with a group of Viennese poets and artists who admired his compositions. "We often wandered about town until three in the morning," recalled a friend. "One of us not seldom would sleep in the apartment of another. We were not particular about comfort in those days. Whoever happened to have money paid for us all." Schubert often lived with friends because he did not have money to rent a room of his own.

Working with incredible speed, Schubert turned out one piece after another. He worked from seven o'clock in the morning until one or two in the afternoon; then he spent his afternoon in cafes, drinking coffee, playing billiards, reading newspapers, and talking with friends. His evenings were spent at "Schubertiads," parties where only his music was played. He accompanied the songs and played his delightful waltzes while friends danced. Most of his works were composed for performances in the homes

(Omikron/Photo Researchers)

Franz Schubert did not mingle with the aristocracy, preferring instead the company of poets, painters, and other musicians.

of Vienna's cultivated middle class. Unlike Beethoven, Schubert did not mingle with the aristocracy.

At the age of twenty-five, Schubert contracted venereal disease, becoming moody and prone to despair. "Think of a man," he wrote of himself, "whose health can never be restored, . . . of a man whose brightest hopes have come to nothing, to whom love and friendship are but torture. . . . " He applied for musical positions several times during his last years but never received them. The publication and performance of his songs brought some recognition, but his two most important symphonies, the

Unfinished and the *Great* C Major, were not performed in public during his lifetime.

Schubert was thirty-one when he died of syphilis in 1828, a year after Beethoven's funeral. His reputation was mainly that of a fine song composer, until the *Unfinished* Symphony was performed almost forty years later. Then the world began to recognize Schubert's comprehensive greatness.

SCHUBERT'S MUSIC

It is amazing how original, varied, and numerous are the works of this composer who died at thirty-one. Along with over 600 songs, Schubert left symphonies, string quartets, chamber music for piano and strings, piano sonatas, short piano pieces for two and four hands, masses, and operatic compositions.

The songs embrace an enormous variety of moods and types. Some are very short, others very long; their forms include strophic, modified strophic, and through-composed. Many deal with nature—the flow of a brook, the mystery of the night—or with unhappy love. The songs amply display Schubert's melodic genius. His melodies range from simple, folk-like tunes to complex lines that suggest impassioned speech. His piano accompaniments are equally rich and evocative. Many songs draw emotional power from the relentless repetition of a rhythmic idea or from a shattering climax.

Schubert's imaginative harmonies provide some of the most poetic moments in music. He uses unexpected dissonances to capture a mood, and he shifts abruptly to contrasting keys. In Schubert's hands, even the simple change from minor to major can evoke a sudden thought of love or an illusion of light breaking through clouds.

The spirit of song permeates Schubert's instrumental music, too. Many of his symphonies and chamber works have long, lyrical melodies, and often Schubert writes variations on his own songs. For instance, the fourth movement of the *Trout* Quintet, for piano and strings, is a set of variations on his song *Die Forelle (The Trout)*. And his short piano pieces such as the *Moments musicaux (Musical Moments)* and *Impromptus* are true "songs without words."

Schubert wrote a number of symphonies and chamber works that are comparable in power and emotional intensity to those of his idol, Beethoven. The *Unfinished* Symphony (1822) and the *Great* C Major Symphony (1825–1826) employ French horns, trombones, and woodwinds with a new feeling for their poetic capacities. The *Unfinished* Symphony, Schubert's most popular orchestral work, was written six years before his death; we probably will never learn why it contains two rather than the usual four movements. The *Great* C Major Symphony was discovered ten years after

Schubert's death by Robert Schumann, who was ecstatic about the work. "It is not possible to describe it to you," he wrote to his fiancée. "All the instruments are human voices; . . . and this length, this heavenly length. . . ." Reviewing the first public performance of this symphony, Schumann made an observation that is true of much of Schubert's music: "It bears within it the seeds of everlasting youth."

ERLKÖNIG (THE ERLKING; 1815)

Schubert's song *Erlkönig (The Erlking)* is one of the earliest and finest examples of musical romanticism. A friend of Schubert's tells how he saw the eighteen-year-old composer reading Goethe's narrative ballad of the supernatural. "He paced up and down several times with the book; suddenly he sat down, and in no time at all (just as quickly as he could write) there was the glorious ballad finished on the paper." Goethe's ballad, in dialogue almost throughout, tells of a father riding on horseback through a storm with his sick child in his arms. The delirious boy has visions of the legendary Erlking, the king of the elves who symbolizes death.

Side 8, band 5
CD 4 45

Schubert employs a through-composed setting to capture the mounting excitement of the poem. The piano part, with its rapid octaves and menacing bass motive, conveys the tension of the wild ride.

The piano's relentless triplet rhythm unifies the episodes of the song and suggests the horse's gallop.

By imaginatively varying the music, Schubert makes one singer sound like several characters in a miniature drama. The terrified boy sings in a high register in minor. Three times during the poem, he cries out, "My father, my father." Each time, the boy sings a musical outcry that is intensified through dissonant harmonies.

Mein Va - ter, mein Va - ter,

To convey mounting fear, Schubert pitches the boy's outcry higher and higher each time. The reassuring father sings in a low register that contrasts with the high-pitched outcries of his child. The Erlking, who tries to entice the boy, has coy melodies in major keys.

"Du lie - bes Kind, komm, geh mit mir! gar schö - ne Spie - le spiel' - ich mit dir;

The deeply moving climax of *The Erlking* comes when father and son arrive home and the galloping accompaniment gradually comes to a halt. In a bleak, heartbreaking recitative that allows every word to make its impact, the narrator tells us, "In his arms the child was dead!"

45 0:00
Piano
introduction, rapid
octaves, *f*, bass
motive, minor key.

Narrator

Wer reitet so spät durch Nacht und Wind?	Who rides so late through the night and the wind?
Es ist der Vater mit seinem Kind;	It is the father with his child;
Er hat den Knaben wohl in dem Arm,	he folds the boy close in his arms,
Er fasst ihn sicher, er hält ihn warm.	he clasps him securely, he holds him warmly.

46 0:56
Low register.

Father

"Mein Sohn, was birgst du so bang dein Gesicht?"	"My son, why do you hide your face so anxiously?"

47 1:04
Higher register.

Son

"Siehst, Vater, du den Erlkönig nicht?	"Father, don't you see the Erlking?

Den Erlenkönig mit Kron' und Schweif?''

The Erlking with his crown and his train?''

Father

''Mein Sohn, es ist ein Nebelstreif.''

"My son, it is a streak of mist."

Low register.

Erlking

48 1:29

''Du liebes Kind, komm, geh mit mir!

"Dear child, come, go with me!

Coaxing tune, *pp*, higher register, major.

Gar schöne Spiele spiel' ich mit dir,

I'll play the prettiest games with you.

Manch bunte Blumen sind an dem Strand,

Many colored flowers grow along the shore;

Meine Mutter hat manch gülden Gewand.''

My mother has many golden garments."

Son

49 1:54

''Mein Vater, mein Vater, und hörest du nicht,

"My father, my father, and don't you hear

Outcry, *f*, minor.

Was Erlenkönig mir leise verspricht?''

the Erlking whispering promises to me?"

Father

2:07

''Sei ruhig, bleibe ruhig, mein Kind:

"Be quiet, stay quiet, my child;

Low register.

In dürren Blättern säuselt der Win''

the wind is rustling in the dead leaves."

Erlking

2:17

''Willst, feiner Knabe, du mit mir gehn?

"My handsome boy, will you come with me?

Playful tune, *pp*, major.

Meine Töchter sollen dich warten schön;

My daughters shall wait upon you;

Meine Töchter führen den nächtlichen Reihn

my daughters lead off in the dance every night,

Und wiegen und tanzen und singen dich ein.''

and cradle and dance and sing you to sleep."

Son

50 2:36

''Mein Vater, mein Vater, und siehst du nicht dort.

"My father, my father, and don't you see there

Outcry, *f*, higher than before, minor.

Erlkönigs Töchter am düstern Ort?''

the Erlking's daughters in the shadows?"

Father

2:48

''Mein Sohn, mein Sohn, ich seh' es genau:

"My son, my son, I see it clearly;

Lower register.

	Es scheinen die alten Weiden so grau."	the old willows look so gray."

Erlking

	"Ich liebe dich, mich reizt deine schöne Gestalt;	"I love you, your beautiful figure delights me!
	Und bist du nicht willig, so brauch' ich Gewalt."	And if you are not willing, then I shall use force!"

Son

3:18 Outcry, *f*, highest yet.	*"Mein Vater, mein Vater, jetzt fasst er mich an!*	"My father, my father, now he is taking hold of me!
	Erlkönig hat mir ein Leids getan!"	The Erlking has hurt me!"

Narrator

3:31	*Dem Vater grauset's, er reitet geschwind,*	The father shudders, he rides swiftly on;
	Er hält in Armen das ächzende Kind,	he holds in his arms the groaning child,
	Erreicht den Hof mit Mühe und Not;	he reaches the courtyard weary and anxious:
Piano stops. Recitative.	*In seinen Armen das Kind war tot.*	in his arms the child was dead.

DIE FORELLE (THE TROUT; 1817)

Side 8, band 6
CD 4 51

One of Schubert's most famous songs, *Die Forelle (The Trout)* reflects the romantics' attraction to nature and to folklike simplicity. The text—by Christian Daniel Schubart (1739–1791)—tells of a trout that swims merrily in a brook but is then caught by a clever fisherman. *Die Forelle* is in modified strophic form: A (stanza 1)–A (stanza 2)–BA′ (stanza 3). It begins with a short piano introduction, which reappears as an interlude after the first and second stanzas and as a postlude after the third stanza. The first two stanzas of the poem, which describe the fish happily swimming, are both sung to the same lighthearted melody (A). Repeated-note patterns (as on *einem* and *Bächlein*) contribute to the melody's folklike quality.

The piano accompaniment is pervaded by a short ascending figure which depicts the trout's leaps and twists.

New music (B) is used for most of the last stanza, which tells how the trout is caught.

Doch end - lich ward dem Die - be die Zeit zu lang,

The change to a more dramatic mood is conveyed by a momentary shift from major to minor and the appearance of a more agitated accompaniment in place of the repeated rising "trout" figure. To round off the song, Schubert brings back the last phrase (A') of the opening melody for the concluding line, *Und ich mit regem Blute /Sah die Betrogne an (and I, with my pulse beating high, watched the betrayed one.)*

51 0:00
Piano
introduction,
major
A

In einem Bächlein helle,
Da schoss in froher Eil'
Die launischer Forelle
Vorüber wie ein Pfeil.
Ich stand an dem Gestade,
und sah in süsser Ruh'
Des muntern Fischleins Bade
Im klaren Bächlein zu.

In a clear brooklet,
with happy haste,
a capricious trout
darted about like an arrow.
I stood on the bank
and contentedly watched
the merry fish bathe
in the clear brooklet.

Piano
interlude
0:39

Ein Fischer mit der Rute
Wohl an dem Ufer stand,
Und sah's mit kaltem Blute,
Wie sich das Fischlein wand.
So lang dem Wasser helle,
So dacht' ich, nicht gebricht,
So fängt er die Forelle
Mit seiner Angel nicht.

A fisherman with his rod
stood on the bank
and looked on heartlessly
as the fish wriggled about.
So long as the clear water,
I thought, is not disturbed,
he will not catch the trout
with his hook.

A

52 1:12

Doch endlich ward dem Diebe
Die Zeit zu lang. Er macht
Das Bächlein tückisch trübe,

But suddenly the thief
got tired of waiting. He
slyly muddied up the brook,

B, minor

1:31

Side 8, band 7
CD 4 [53]

A', major

Piano
postlude

Und eh' ich es gedacht;	and before I realized it
So zuckte seine Rute,	he jerked his rod
Das Fischlein zappelt dran,	and the fish struggled on the line,
Und ich mit regem Blute	and I, with my pulse beating high,
Sah die Betrogne an.	watched the betrayed one.

PIANO QUINTET IN A MAJOR (*TROUT*; 1819)

Fourth Movement

Among the best-loved of all chamber works is the *Trout* Quintet, which was commissioned in 1819 by an amateur cellist who admired Schubert's song *Die Forelle (The Trout)* and asked the composer to write variations on it. The theme and variations is the fourth of five movements in this quintet, which is scored for the unusual combination of piano, violin, viola, cello, and double bass. Schubert gives each player a chance to present the main melodic line.

The strings alone introduce the theme, a charming melody in D major marked *andantino (moderately slow)*. The six variations that follow embellish the theme and combine it with countermelodies. The first three variations build in rhythmic animation and brilliance of sound, but in them the original melody is altered very little. Variation 4 is a dramatic climax: the key shifts to D minor and the theme is changed radically in melody, rhythm, and dynamics. Variation 5 is in the new key of B flat major, and the theme is transformed into an intense legato melody that sounds almost new. The concluding variation brings back the original D major melody in a faster tempo (allegretto). The music sounds fresh and sparkling as Schubert introduces a new accompaniment figure that he had used in the original song to suggest the brook trout's leaps and twists.

The theme is in the two-part form aa b. This pattern is retained in most of the variations.

Listening Outline To be read while music is heard

PIANO QUINTET IN A MAJOR *(TROUT; 1819),*
BY FRANZ SCHUBERT

Fourth Movement: Andantino

Theme and variations, duple meter ($\frac{2}{4}$), D major

Piano, violin, viola, cello, double bass

(Duration, 8:12)

THEME
(andantino)

53 0:00 — Violin, *pp,* theme, strings accompany.

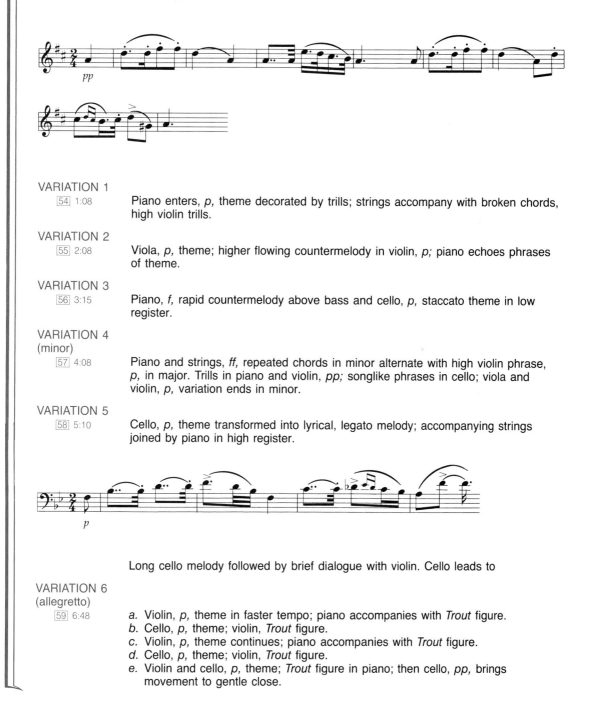

pp

VARIATION 1

54 1:08 — Piano enters, *p,* theme decorated by trills; strings accompany with broken chords, high violin trills.

VARIATION 2

55 2:08 — Viola, *p,* theme; higher flowing countermelody in violin, *p;* piano echoes phrases of theme.

VARIATION 3

56 3:15 — Piano, *f,* rapid countermelody above bass and cello, *p,* staccato theme in low register.

VARIATION 4
(minor)

57 4:08 — Piano and strings, *ff,* repeated chords in minor alternate with high violin phrase, *p,* in major. Trills in piano and violin, *pp;* songlike phrases in cello; viola and violin, *p,* variation ends in minor.

VARIATION 5

58 5:10 — Cello, *p,* theme transformed into lyrical, legato melody; accompanying strings joined by piano in high register.

p

Long cello melody followed by brief dialogue with violin. Cello leads to

VARIATION 6
(allegretto)

59 6:48
a. Violin, *p,* theme in faster tempo; piano accompanies with *Trout* figure.
b. Cello, *p,* theme; violin, *Trout* figure.
c. Violin, *p,* theme continues; piano accompanies with *Trout* figure.
d. Cello, *p,* theme; violin, *Trout* figure.
e. Violin and cello, *p,* theme; *Trout* figure in piano; then cello, *pp,* brings movement to gentle close.

5 ROBERT SCHUMANN

Robert Schumann (1810–1856) in many ways embodied musical romanticism. His works are intensely autobiographical, and they are usually linked with descriptive titles, texts, or programs. He expressed his essentially lyrical nature in startlingly original piano pieces and songs. As a gifted writer and critic, he also discovered and made famous some of the leading composers of his day.

Schumann was born in Zwickau, Germany. His father was a bookseller, from whom he acquired a love of literature. As a youth, Schumann wrote poetry, composed short pieces, and played the piano fairly well. To please his mother, he studied law at Leipzig University; but he rarely attended lectures and devoted his time instead to literature and music.

Schumann decided to become a piano virtuoso at the late age of twenty. Around that time, he developed serious problems with the fingers of his right hand. In search of a cure, he used a mechanical gadget designed to stretch and strengthen the fingers. But neither this device nor various medical treatments alleviated his condition: one finger was permanently crippled, and his hopes of becoming a virtuoso were dashed. "Don't worry about my finger," he wrote his mother. "I can compose without it." Indeed, in his twenties he composed many poetic piano works which are a basic part of the pianist's repertory even today. In Schumann's time, however, many considered his compositions too unconventional, too personal. Schumann admitted that his works were autobiographical: "I am affected by everything that goes on in the world—politics, literature, people—I think it over in my own way, and then I long to express my feelings in music."

During his twenties, too, Schumann founded and edited the twice-weekly *New Journal of Music* to promote musical originality and combat the commercial trash that flooded the market. In his essays, Schumann invented an imaginary "league of David" fighting against musical "philistines," lovers of the conventional. He often signed his articles "Florestan" or "Eusebius," names of imaginary characters who represented, respectively, the outgoing and introspective sides of his personality. The *New Journal* grew to be influential and contained Schumann's appreciative reviews of young "radical" composers like Chopin and Berlioz.

While studying piano, Schumann became acquainted with his teacher's daughter and prize pupil, Clara Wieck. Schumann was eighteen when they met, and Clara was a nine-year-old prodigy who was already a well-known pianist. The two were engaged when Clara was seventeen, despite bitter opposition from her father, who did not want his daughter's brilliant career to be hampered by marriage to an impoverished musician. Since

Robert Schumann's works are intensely autobiographical and are usually linked with descriptive titles, texts, or programs.

Clara was not of age, the couple fought bitter court battles against Wieck before they could be married. Their marriage turned out to be a happy one that produced eight children. Clara, herself a composer, was the ideal interpreter of her husband's piano works and introduced many of them to the public.

Schumann was temperamentally ill-suited for a regular musical position. He taught in the newly established Leipzig Conservatory of Music, but only for a short time. He was a failure as municipal music director at Düsseldorf because of his inability to control an orchestra and chorus. During later years his mental and physical health progressively deteriorated, and in 1854 he attempted suicide by throwing himself from a bridge into the Rhine. At his own request, he was committed to an asylum, where he died two years later.

SCHUMANN'S MUSIC

Schumann's genius is most characteristically expressed in his songs and short piano pieces, both of which he usually organized into sets or cycles. The titles of these sets—*Carnaval (Carnival)*, *Kinderscenen (Scenes of Childhood)*, *Nachtstücke (Night Pieces)*, *Dichterliebe (Poet's Love)*, *Fantasiestücke (Fantasy Pieces)*—provide insight into his imagination. Schumann thought of music in emotional, literary, and autobiographical terms; his work is full of extramusical references.

During the first ten years of his creative life, Schumann published only piano pieces. His basic musical style seems to grow out of piano improvisation, and these short pieces are like mosaics of vivid musical fragments. Each expresses a single mood through an intensely sensitive melody. Dance rhythms such as the waltz are prominent, as are syncopations and dotted rhythms. Schumann's cycles of short pieces are unified through a story, through a title, or through thematic connections.

In 1840, the year of his marriage, Schumann composed many art songs. The songs, like the piano pieces, reveal Schumann's great gift for melody. Many of the songs have piano postludes which sum up the message of the text. Schumann's song texts suit his feelings, and he often changes a poem by repeating words, lines, and even whole stanzas.

After 1840, Schumann turned to symphonies and chamber music. This direction may well have resulted from Clara's influence, for she wrote in her diary, "I am infinitely delighted that Robert has at last found the sphere for which his great imagination fits him." Schumann's four symphonies are romantic in their emphasis on lyrical second themes, in their use of thematic transformation, and in their connections between movements.

AUFSCHWUNG (SOARING), FROM *FANTASIESTÜCKE (FANTASY PIECES),* OP. 12 (1837)

Side 9, band 2
CD 5 2

Aufschwung (Soaring) is one of the *Fantasiestücke (Fantasy Pieces)*, a set of eight short piano pieces with titles like *Des Abends (Evening)*, *Grillen (Whims)*, *In der Nacht (In the Night)*, and *Träumes Wirren (Dream Visions)*. Like many other romantics, Schumann was especially drawn to the world of fantasy and linked his works with definite images or poetic ideas.

A   2 0:00

Soaring is passionate and impulsive, with a very fast tempo, driving rhythms, and rapid changes of musical ideas. It may be outlined A B A C A B A. The restless main theme, A, is loud, with powerful accents and dotted rhythms.

Theme B is lyrical and continuously flowing. Both a melody and a rapid accompanying figure are played by the pianist's right hand.

B   ③ 0:16

The extended middle section, C, brings a more relaxed mood and flexible tempo. Near the end of section C, a crescendo creates tension and prepares for the return of the impulsive main theme.

C   ④ 1:00

Soaring vividly expresses the outgoing side of Schumann's musical personality. *Im wonderschönen Monat Mai*, which we'll study next, seems to express his inward side.

IM WUNDERSCHÖNEN MONAT MAI (IN THE LOVELY MONTH OF MAY), FROM DICHTERLIEBE (POET'S LOVE), OP. 48 (1840)

Im wunderschönen Monat Mai (In the lovely month of May) opens *Dichterliebe (Poet's Love)*, a cycle of sixteen songs set to poems by the great German romantic poet Heinrich Heine. Schumann composed the cycle in 1840, his "song year," during a difficult period of separation from Clara and legal battles against her father. The title *Poet's Love* doubtless refers to Schumann's own feelings for his bride-to-be.

Side 9, band 1
CD 5 ①

A mood of tenderness and longing is beautifully conveyed in *Im wunder-schönen Monat Mai*, which is just 1½ minutes long. The song is in strophic form, with each of its two stanzas sung to the same melody (A A). Schumann probably decided on a strophic setting because of the similarity between the two stanzas, which open with the same words *(In the lovely month of May, when all . . . ")*. Like Schubert's *Die Forelle*, this song has a piano introduction that reappears as an interlude between stanzas and as a postlude at the end.

Schumann creates a sense of longing by wavering between several different keys and by avoiding a feeling of conclusion. The piano introduction sounds as though it will lead to a cadence in a minor key.

Yet the vocal melody that follows is in major.

The melodic ascent (from *da ist)* to the voice's concluding high note expresses the idea of love breaking forth. Dissonances on the accented syllables of *Herzen (heart)* and *aufgegangen (broke forth)* contribute to the emotional intensity of this phrase. Most remarkably, the piano postlude ends the song inconclusively on an unstable chord that remains unresolved, a poignant expression of "longing and desire."

Im wunderschönen Monat Mai,	In the lovely month of May,	**1** 0:00 Piano introduction A
Als alle Knospen sprangen,	when all the buds were bursting,	
Da ist in meinem Herzen	then within my heart	
Die Liebe aufgegangen.	love broke forth.	
Im wunderschönen Monat Mai,	In the lovely month of May,	Piano interlude A
Als alle Vögel sangen,	when all the birds were singing,	
Da hab' ich ihr gestanden	then I confessed to her	
Mein Sehnen und Verlangen.	my longing and desire.	
		Piano postlude, ends on unstable chord.

CLARA WIECK SCHUMANN (1819–1896) [ROMANTIC **6**]

One of the leading concert pianists of the nineteenth century, Clara Wieck Schumann premiered many works by her husband Robert and by her close friend Johannes Brahms. Born in Leipzig, Germany, she was the daughter of Marianne Wieck, a singer and pianist; and Friedrich Wieck, a well-known piano pedagogue. Her father trained her to be a child prodigy who would both earn money and demonstrate the superiority of his teaching methods. Between the ages of twelve and twenty she performed throughout Europe to great acclaim, usually programming one or more of her own compositions.

(Bettmann Archive)

Clara Wieck Schumann was one of the leading concert pianists of the nineteenth century and a composer of songs, piano pieces, and chamber music.

Clara Wieck married Robert Schumann the day before her twenty-first birthday, despite her father's opposition. During their fourteen-year marriage she continued to concertize and compose—though on a reduced scale—while caring for seven children (one of the Schumanns' children had died in infancy) and catering to the needs of her hypersensitive husband. The year 1853 was particularly important for Clara Schumann. The twenty-year-old composer Johannes Brahms came to play his works for the Schumanns, beginning a friendship with Clara that lasted until her death in 1896. In the same year, she also met the famous violinist Joseph Joachim, with whom she would often give chamber music concerts.

After her husband's death Clara Schumann expanded her performing activities, became renowned as a teacher, and edited his collected works. She helped refine the tastes of concert audiences by performing serious works by earlier composers like Bach, Mozart, and Beethoven as well as those by her late husband and her friend Brahms.

Clara Schumann considered herself primarily a performing artist. "I feel I have a mission to perform beautiful works, Robert's above all," she once wrote. "The practice of my art . . . is the very air I breathe." She was less confident about her creative ability and stopped composing when she was thirty-six, after she had become a widow. Her self-doubts were perhaps influenced by the predominantly negative attitude toward woman composers and by her relationship with overwhelming geniuses like Robert Schumann and Brahms.

Until recently, Clara Schumann was known mainly as a famous pianist who had been the wife of one great composer and the close friend of another. But in the last decade, her compositions have been increasingly recorded and performed. These include songs, lyrical and virtuoso piano pieces; a piano concerto; a trio for piano, violin, and cello; and three Romances for Violin and Piano, one of which will be studied here.

ROMANCE IN G MINOR FOR VIOLIN AND PIANO, OP. 22, NO. 2 (1853)

Clara Schumann composed her Romances for Violin and Piano in 1853, during a creative spurt that was inspired by her husband's forty-third birthday. They were dedicated to Joseph Joachim, who performed them for his employer, King George V of Hannover, Germany. The music-loving king was reportedly "completely ecstatic" about the Romances and was eager to experience such "marvelous, heavenly pleasure again."

Side 9, band 3
CD 5 ⑤

In the nineteeth century, the term *romance* (*Romanze* in German) was often used for short, lyrical pieces for piano or solo instrument with piano accompaniment. The Romance in G Minor displays Clara Schumann's gifts as a melodist. Marked *Allegretto, to be performed tenderly*, it is in A B A' form. Sweet melancholy is created in the outer (A) sections by the minor key and by a violin melody that repeatedly leaps upward an octave to a syncopated tone. A transition smoothly links A to the middle section. It uses a two-note figure, repeated in gradually quickening rhythms until it blossoms into the trill and the soaring phrase that open section B.

The more extended middle section (B) brings a shift from minor to major, from sweet melancholy to relaxed playfulness. Its mood is lightened by a staccato "chirping" idea that is tossed between violin and piano. As in the opening section, a transition using the two-note figure smoothly links B with the concluding A′ section, which is in minor. At the end of A′, we hear a very brief recollection of the opening phrase of B, now sounding melancholy because it is minor instead of major. The Romance ends unexpectedly on a pizzicato major chord, perhaps to recall the playfulness of its middle section.

Listening Outline   To be read while music is heard

ROMANCE IN G MINOR FOR VIOLIN AND PIANO, OP. 22, NO. 2 (1853), BY CLARA WIECK SCHUMANN

Allegretto, duple meter ($\frac{2}{4}$), ABA′ form

Violin, piano

(Duration, 2:45)

A (minor)
 5 0:00   1. *a.* Main violin melody, *p*, minor, syncopated upward octave leap.

                   Melody descends from high tone.
 0:18   *b.* Main melody repeated, syncopated leaps in violin, tempo slows slightly.
 6 0:37   *c.* Long trills in violin, melody in piano; two-note figure, repeated in ever-quicker rhythms,

                   introduces

B (major)
 7 0:47   2. *a.* New soaring phrase in major, beginning with short trill, *p*.

8 0:56 b. Playful phrase with trill; staccato "chirping" idea tossed from violin to piano.

1:04   c. Violin trill, soaring phrase returns, shift from major to minor, melody in low register in violin and piano, *mf*. Staccato "chirping" idea and trill bring return to major.

1:33   d. Violin trill, soaring phrase, *p*, playful phrase with trills.

1:46   e. Two-note figure repeated in ever-quicker rhythms introduces

A′ (minor)

9 1:53   3. a. Main violin melody, minor; piano immediately imitates violin. Melody descends from high tone.

2:10   b. Main melody repeated, syncopated leaps in violin, tempo slows slightly.

2:30   c. Long trills in violin; melody in piano leads to soaring phrase, now in minor;

ascent from low register to high; pizzicato major ending, *p*.

BASIC TERM

romance (page 323)

FRÉDÉRIC CHOPIN

ROMANTIC

7

Frédéric Chopin (1810–1849), called the poet of the piano, was the only great composer who wrote almost exclusively for the piano.

Chopin was brought up in Warsaw, the son of a Polish mother and a French father. When he was very young, his highly original style of playing and composing astonished the Polish aristocracy. After graduating from the Warsaw Conservatory, he toured Austria and Germany, playing his own compositions. While he was away, the Poles revolted against the Russians. Upon learning that the Russians had conquered Warsaw, Chopin was filled with despair and guilt: "They have burnt down the town, . . . and here I am—doing nothing, only heaving sighs and pouring out my grief at the piano."

325

A portrait of Chopin by Eugène Delacroix. Chopin was a shy, reserved man who disliked crowds and preferred to play in salons rather than in public concert halls.

In 1831, the twenty-one-year-old Chopin arrived in Paris, which would be his home for the rest of his short life. In the 1830s Paris was a center of romanticism and the artistic capital of Europe. Chopin met such writers as Victor Hugo, Balzac, and Heine. The painter Delacroix was a close friend, as were Liszt and Berlioz. Chopin's playing quickly gained him access to the aristocratic salons of Paris. Liszt provides a vivid description of the kind of people who attended Chopin's rare concerts: "Numerous carriages brought . . . the most elegant ladies, the most fashionable of young men, the richest financiers, the most illustrious great lords, . . . an entire aristocracy of birth, fortune, and beauty."

Chopin was a shy, reserved man who disliked crowds and preferred to play in salons rather than in public concert halls. It was for such intimate gatherings that he conceived short pieces like the nocturnes, preludes, and waltzes.

Chopin's frail physique made it difficult for him to draw big sounds from the piano. The fascination of his playing lay, rather, in his beautiful tone, rhythmic flexibility, atmospheric use of the pedal, and poetic subtleties of dynamics. Chopin is the only pianist in history to have achieved a legendary reputation on the basis of only thirty or so public performances. He earned a good living by teaching piano to the daughters of the rich. Chopin was an elegant and fashionable man of the world and lived in luxury.

Chopin's life took an increasingly productive turn after he met Aurore Dudevant, a well-known novelist whose pen name was George Sand. She was a feminist who often wore men's clothing, smoked cigars, and fought for sexual freedom. Chopin and Sand became lovers when he was twenty-eight and she thirty-four. He thrived on the care she provided, composing many of his greatest works during the nine years they lived together. After they separated, his health declined rapidly and he composed very little.

Before dying of tuberculosis at thirty-nine, Chopin asked that Mozart's Requiem be played at his funeral. The mourners also heard Chopin's own *Funeral March* from the Piano Sonata in B Flat Minor.

CHOPIN'S MUSIC

By the age of eighteen, Chopin had evolved an utterly personal and original style. Compared with other great composers, he wrote relatively few works, but almost all of them remain in the pianist's repertory. Most of his pieces are short. But in these exquisite miniatures, Chopin evokes an infinite variety of moods, from melancholy to heroism. His music is always elegant and graceful. Even the virtuoso passages are melodic, not intended merely for display.

Chopin expressed his love of Poland in mazurkas and polonaises. In these stylized dances, he captured the spirit of the Polish people without actually using folk tunes. Unlike Schumann, Chopin did not attach literary programs or titles to his pieces.

No composer has made the piano sound as beautiful as Chopin. His unique melodic gift creates the illusion that the piano is singing. In repeating a melody, Chopin adds delicate and graceful ornamental tones, similar to the vocal decorations heard in the Italian opera of his time. Many of Chopin's most poetic effects come from the sensitive exploitation of the damper ("loud") pedal. He blends harmonies like washes of color. The pedal connects widely spaced tones in the left-hand accompaniment. Chopin's treatment of harmony was highly original and influenced later composers.

Chopin's compositions allow a pianist to heighten expression by slightly speeding up or slowing down the tempo, or by holding a note longer than the music actually indicates. This use of rubato lends a poetic and improvisatory quality to his music.

NOCTURNE IN E FLAT MAJOR, OP. 9, NO. 2 (1830–1831)

Side 9, band 5
CD 5 14

14 0:00

Chopin composed his popular Nocturne in E Flat Major, Op. 9, No. 2, when he was about twenty. A **nocturne**, or *night piece*, is a slow, lyrical, intimate composition for piano. Like much of Chopin's music, the Nocturne in E Flat Major is tinged with melancholy. It opens with a legato melody containing graceful upward leaps which become increasingly wide as the line unfolds.

This main melody is heard again three times during the piece. With each repetition—the first of these is shown below—it is varied by ever more elaborate decorative tones and trills.

First repetition
15 0:25

16 0:51

A sonorous foundation for the melody is provided by the widely spaced notes in the accompaniment that are connected by the damper ("loud") pedal. The nocturne also includes a subordinate melody, which is played with rubato—slight fluctuations of tempo.

The music is reflective in mood until near the end, when it suddenly becomes passionate. The melody rises to a high register and is played forcefully in octaves. Then, after a brilliant trill-like passage, the excitement subsides, and the nocturne ends calmly.

ÉTUDE IN C MINOR, OP. 10, NO. 12 (*REVOLUTIONARY*; 1831?)

Supplementary sets:
Side 4, band 2
CD 2 31

The Russian takeover of Warsaw in 1831 may have inspired Chopin to compose the blazing and furious *Revolutionary* Étude in C Minor, Op. 10, No. 12. An *étude* is a study piece designed to help a performer master specific technical difficulties. The *Revolutionary* Étude, for example, develops speed and endurance in a pianist's left hand, which must play rapid passages throughout. Chopin's études reach beyond mere exercises in technique to become masterpieces of music, exciting to hear as well as to master.

The *Revolutionary* Étude begins with a dramatic outburst. High, dissonant chords and downward rushing passages lead to the main melody, marked *appassionato (impassioned)*, which is played in octaves by the right hand. Tension mounts because of the melody's dotted rhythms and its tempestuous accompaniment. Toward the end of the piece, after a climax, the tension momentarily subsides. Then a torrential passage sweeps down the keyboard to come to rest in powerful closing chords.

329

POLONAISE IN A FLAT MAJOR, OP. 53 (1842)

Side 9, band 4
CD 5 [10]

The *polonaise,* a piece in triple meter, originated as a stately processional dance for the Polish nobility. Chopin's heroic polonaises evoke the ancient splendor of the Polish people.

The Polonaise in A Flat Major is majestic and powerful, with moments of lyrical contrast. It may be outlined as follows: introduction–A B A'–coda. Its main theme makes a grand entrance.

Introduction
[10] 0:00
Section A
[11] 0:32

Section B
[12] 3:02

Section A'
[13] 5:20

The majesty of this theme is enhanced by intervals of thirds in the right hand and by the resonant, wide-ranging accompaniment. After the main theme is repeated twice with an even richer texture, Chopin offers the contrasting middle section (B). This is a marchlike melody accompanied by relentlessly repeated rapid octaves in the left hand. This section tests a pianist's strength and endurance. Powerful crescendos bring mounting excitement. Then Chopin gradually relaxes the mood to prepare for the final return of the heroic main theme (A').

BASIC TERMS

nocturne (page 328)
étude (329)
polonaise (330)

FRANZ LISZT

During the 1840s, a handsome, long-haired, magnetic young man performed superhuman feats at the piano and overwhelmed the European musical public. Irresistible to women and an incredible showman, Franz Liszt (1811–1886) left a trail of broken hearts from Paris to Moscow. Musicians were as impressed as the concertgoing public. Brahms said, "Whoever has not heard Liszt cannot speak of piano playing." Chopin wished he could play his own piano études the way Liszt did. Schumann wrote that Liszt "enmeshed every member of the audience with his art and did with them as he willed. Within a few seconds tenderness, boldness, exquisiteness, wildness succeed one another; the instrument glows and flashes under the master's hands."

Franz Liszt, an outstanding pacesetter in the history of music, was born in Hungary. His father was an administrator for the same Esterházy family that Haydn had served. As a boy of eleven, Liszt studied in Vienna, where he met Schubert and Beethoven.

Paris, a city where romanticism flourished and a mecca for virtuoso performers, was Liszt's home during his teens and twenties. When he was nineteen and already acclaimed as a brilliant pianist, Liszt was overwhelmed by the virtuosity of the great violinist Paganini. The unheard-of effects Paganini drew from his violin drove audiences into a frenzy; people half suspected he had been taught by the devil. Young Liszt was determined to become the Paganini of the piano. He withdrew from the concert stage for a few years, practiced from eight to twelve hours a day, and emerged as probably the greatest pianist of his time.

To display his own incomparable piano mastery, Liszt composed his *Transcendental Études* and made piano transcriptions of Paganini's violin pieces. "My piano," he wrote, "is my very self, my mother tongue, my life. . . . A man's ten fingers have the power to reproduce the harmonies which are created by hundreds of performers." Following an orchestral performance of a movement from Berlioz's *Fantastic Symphony*, Liszt played his own piano arrangement of the movement and made a more powerful effect than the entire orchestra. He toured Europe tirelessly between 1839 and 1847, playing mainly his own piano music and receiving unprecedented public adulation.

But Liszt wanted recognition as a serious composer, too. At thirty-six, he abandoned his career as a traveling virtuoso to become court conductor for the grand duke in Weimar. He composed many orchestral pieces during the years that followed and developed a new form of program music that influenced later composers. Weimar had become a center for modern music, and Liszt conducted works by such contemporaries as Berlioz, Schumann, and Wagner. One of the most unselfish and generous musi-

Franz Liszt—handsome, long-haired, magnetic—performed superhuman feats at the piano and overwhelmed the European musical public.

cians who ever lived, he provided musical and financial support crucial to Wagner's success. Hundreds of gifted pianists flocked to Weimar, and he taught them free of charge.

Liszt was also an active writer about music, publishing music criticism as well as books on Chopin and gypsy music. His literary efforts were aided by two women with whom he had long-term relationships. Both were aristocrats and writers. The first, Countess Marie d'Agoult, left her husband to live with Liszt. (One of their three children, Cosima, later left her own husband to marry Richard Wagner.) Liszt's companion in Weimar was the Russian Princess Carolyne Sayn-Wittgenstein, a deeply religious woman who wrote a twenty-four-volume study entitled *Interior Causes of the External Weakness of the Church.*

Liszt's many-sided career took another abrupt turn in 1861. Dissatisfied with conditions at Weimar, he resigned and went to Rome to pursue religious studies. In 1865 he took minor holy orders, becoming Abbé Liszt. Contemporaries were stunned by the seeming incongruity: a notorious Don Juan and diabolical virtuoso had become a churchman. In Rome, Liszt composed oratorios and masses, feeling a mission to reform and renew church music.

During the last seventeen years of his life, Liszt traveled between Rome, Weimar, and Budapest, where he was president of the new Academy of Music. Now he began to write curious, experimental piano pieces that foreshadowed features of twentieth-century music. Though these late works went unappreciated, Liszt had become a living legend. The grand duke who had once employed him said, "Liszt *was* what a prince *ought* to be."

LISZT'S MUSIC

Liszt's music is controversial. Some consider it vulgar and bombastic; others revel in its extroverted romantic rhetoric. Yet few would deny Liszt's originality, influence, and importance as the creator of the symphonic poem.

Liszt found new ways to exploit the piano; under his hands it could give the impression of an entire orchestra. In the *Hungarian Rhapsodies,* which influenced a generation of nationalist composers, Liszt made the piano sound at times like a cimbalom (a Hungarian instrument in which strings are struck by hammers held in the hand) and at other times like an entire gypsy band. Liszt's piano works demand an unprecedented range of dynamics, from a whispered *ppp* to a thunderous *fff*. He requires a pianist to play rapid octaves and daring leaps. Lyrical melodies are embellished with rapid runs, and melodies in the middle register are sometimes surrounded by garlands of arpeggios which create the impression that three hands are playing, not two. Before the age of phonograph records and frequent concerts, Liszt's transcriptions of operas and symphonies made it possible for people to play great orchestral works on their own pianos.

Liszt created the symphonic poem, or tone poem, a one-movement orchestral composition based to some extent on literary or pictorial ideas (see Section 10). In his symphonic poems and other works, Liszt unified contrasting moods through thematic transformation: a single musical idea recurs throughout a work but is varied so that its character is transformed. For example, in his most famous symphonic poem, *Les Préludes*, a basic motive is treated as a majestic melody in one section, a love theme in another, and a march in the concluding section. Liszt's music can stand by itself without a program, as can most program music. However, he no doubt felt that particular influences from literature should be cited to make his musical processes very clear. Liszt broke away from the standard four-movement symphony and from the sonata form as it was used by the classical masters.

Among Liszt's favorite inspirations were the literary works of Goethe (on which he based his *Faust* Symphony, 1854) and Dante (which inspired the *Dante* Symphony, 1856). Many of his compositions are concerned with the devil or death and bear titles like *Mephisto Waltz*, *Totentanz (Dance of Death)*, or *Funérailles*. Constant changes of tempo and mood and alternations between diabolical fury and semireligious meditation contribute to a feeling of improvisation.

Liszt's music influenced many composers, including Wagner, who admitted to him: "When I compose and orchestrate, I always think only of you." As a stupendous performer, innovative composer, and charismatic personality, Liszt typified the romantic movement.

TRANSCENDENTAL ÉTUDE NO. 10 IN F MINOR

Side 9, band 6
CD 5 17

As dazzling, passionate, and poetic as Liszt himself, the *Transcendental Étude* No. 10 in F Minor is one of the finest virtuoso pieces of the romantic era. Liszt had written an early, simpler version of this piece in 1824, when he was only thirteen, and included it in a group of twelve studies. Fifteen years later, at the peak of his career as a virtuoso, he published a revised version that demanded transcendent, almost superhuman technical skill from the pianist. (Schumann was so overwhelmed by Liszt's études that he described them as "studies in storm and dread meant to be played by, at most, ten or twelve players in the world.") In 1851, after retiring from the concert stage, Liszt dedicated a third and final version—which we'll study—to his piano teacher Carl Czerny "as a token of esteem, gratitude and friendship."

The étude taxes the player with left-hand passages that require rapid skips and changes of hand position. Though written in A–B–A'–coda form, it almost seems like an improvisation, owing to its frequent alternations between brilliant, virtuoso passages and more melodic ideas. The A section contains three themes: the first, in minor, is fragmentary and syncopated. The second, in major, is more lyrical and in a high register, with dotted rhythms, and rapid notes in the accompaniment. The third, which has a processional character, is a transformation of the second. (In the listening outline, this is called the *processional theme*.) A melody that was introduced in major in a high register is now presented in minor, in a low register set against higher arpeggios. Yet another thematic transformation takes place in the coda, which is based on a speeded-up variant of the syncopated main theme.

Listening Outline To be read while music is heard

TRANSCENDENTAL ÉTUDE NO. 10 IN F MINOR (1851),
BY FRANZ LISZT

Allegro agitato molto (very agitated allegro), duple meter ($\frac{2}{4}$), ABA'-coda form, F minor

Piano

(Duration, 4:44)

A

17 0:00   1. *a.* Rapid falling chords and syncopated fragment, *p*; rapid falling chords, syncopated main theme.

                 Gradual ascent and crescendo to

0:17   *b.* Abrupt outbursts, *f*, alternating with upward sweeps; descent to rapid falling chords, decrescendo, slight ritard.

0:29   *c.* Syncopated main theme, ascent and crescendo to

18 0:42   2. *a.* Very high lyrical theme in octaves, *ff*, major, dotted rhythm, rapid accompaniment.

                 High syncopated octaves in melody, close into

1:00   *b.* Abrupt outbursts, *f*, alternating with upward sweeps, *ff*, slight ritard.

19 1:14
3. Low "processional theme," *ff,* in minor, against higher rapid arpeggios.

B

20 1:26
4. *a.* Sudden *p,* syncopated main theme varied, crescendo, ascending phrases lead to *ff* climax, downward sweeps, slight ritard.
1:49
   b. Breathless staccato syncopated chords, ascent with crescendo and accelerando to high chord, *ff.* Rapid falling chords, decrescendo, and ritard introduce

A'

21 2:04
5. Syncopated main theme, *p,* gradual ascent, crescendo and ritard to high octaves.
2:22
6. *a.* Very high lyrical theme in minor, *p,* accompanied by rapid arpeggios; gradual crescendo builds to high repeated octaves, *ff,* climax on
3:04
   b. Syncopated octave descending melody in minor, *ff,* ritard; cadence to
3:22
   c. Abrupt outbursts, *f,* alternating with upward sweeps, *ff;* high broken octaves descend to
3:36
7. *a.* Low minor "processional theme," *ff,* against higher rapid arpeggios; ascent to dissonant held chord.
   b. High broken chords ascend chromatically. Brief pause.

Coda

22 4:05
8. *a.* Faster tempo, furiously syncopated octaves,

crescendo, close into
   b. Rising octave leaps, concluding massive chords.

ROMANTIC

9

FELIX MENDELSSOHN

Felix Mendelssohn (1809–1847) was a romantic whose music was rooted deeply in classical tradition. He was born in Hamburg, Germany, to a wealthy and famous family. His father was a banker, and his grandfather was the distinguished Jewish philosopher Moses Mendelssohn. Felix, a brother, and two sisters were raised in the Protestant faith.

Besides his musical achievements, Felix Mendelssohn was a talented painter,
a fine writer, and a brilliant conversationalist in four languages.

Mendelssohn's talent was as phenomenal and precocious as Mozart's. By the age of nine, he was a brilliant pianist; and by thirteen, he had written symphonies, concertos, sonatas, and vocal works. And the quality of this youthful work is even more astounding than its quantity. His Overture to *A Midsummer Night's Dream* (1826), which he composed when he was seventeen, is a masterpiece of startling originality. As a teenager, Mendelssohn tried out his compositions with a private orchestra in the family dining room at a series of Sunday musicales. These gatherings were attended by the intellectual and artistic elite of Berlin, where the Mendelssohns had settled.

In 1829, at twenty, Mendelssohn conducted Bach's *St. Matthew Passion* in its first performance since the composer's death. This historic concert rekindled interest in Bach's music and earned an international reputation for Mendelssohn. He often performed as pianist, organist, and conductor in Germany and in England, where his music was especially popular. When only twenty-six, Mendelssohn became conductor of the Leipzig Gewandhaus Orchestra and transformed it into one of the finest performing groups in Europe. He directed the posthumous premiere of Schubert's *Great* C Major Symphony, which his friend Robert Schumann had discovered, as well as the first performances of two Schumann symphonies. As though all these accomplishments weren't enough, Mendelssohn founded the Leipzig Conservatory when he was thirty-three.

Besides his musical achievements, Mendelssohn was a talented painter, a fine writer, and a brilliant conversationalist in four languages. He was extremely polished and charming and felt at ease in aristocratic salons. In England, he often visited the young Queen Victoria, who sang his songs while Mendelssohn accompanied her on the piano. His personal life was more conventional than that of many romantics; he was happily married and the father of four children.

The high point of Mendelssohn's career was the triumphant premiere of his oratorio *Elijah* in Birmingham, England, in 1846. The London *Times* reported that "the last note of 'Elijah' was drowned in a long-continued unanimous volley of plaudits, vociferous and deafening." But constant travel and exhausting work sapped Mendelssohn's strength. The death of a beloved sister in 1847 was a violent shock, and he died five months later at the age of thirty-eight.

MENDELSSOHN'S MUSIC

Mendelssohn's music radiates the elegance and balance of his personality. It evokes a variety of moods but avoids emotional extremes. His pieces typically convey an elfin quality through rapid movement, lightness, and transparent orchestral texture. He was a musical landscapist who could depict a particular atmosphere in orchestral program works. For example, the *Hebrides* Overture (1830–1832; also called *Fingal's Cave*) suggests an agitated sea through swells and surges of sound. But even when Mendelssohn evokes something extramusical, his compositions have a logical form, and we can enjoy them without knowing their sources of inspiration.

Mendelssohn wrote an enormous amount of music in all the forms of his day except opera. Today, only a few of his works are in the concert repertory, but these are extremely popular. Among his best-known compositions are the Violin Concerto—which we'll study—the *Midsummer Night's Dream* and *Hebrides* overtures, the *Italian* and *Scotch* symphonies (1833, 1842), the oratorio *Elijah*, and the Trio in D Minor for Violin, Cello, and Piano (1839). His collection of short piano pieces *Songs without Words* (1829–1845) has now returned to favor after a period of neglect. These pieces convey youthful dash and vigor as well as lyricism tinged with melancholy, basic qualities of Mendelssohn's art.

CONCERTO FOR VIOLIN AND ORCHESTRA IN E MINOR, OP. 64

The Violin Concerto in E Minor, Op. 64, was inspired by Mendelssohn's friendship with the concertmaster of his orchestra, the famous violinist Ferdinand David. "I should like to make a violin concerto for you next winter," Mendelssohn wrote. "One in E minor runs in my head and its beginning gives me no rest." With David as soloist, the Violin Concerto met great success at its premiere in 1845. Ever since, its unique fusion of lyricism and virtuosity has made it one of the best-loved concertos.

The concerto's three movements are played without pause, in a characteristic linking technique used by romantic composers. Mendelssohn's love of balance is reflected in the cooperation and interplay between soloist and orchestra. Themes pass from one to another, producing a beautiful contrast of tone color and expression. At one moment, the violinist plays a melody while the orchestra discreetly accompanies; at another, the woodwinds present thematic fragments while the soloist has dazzling running passages.

First Movement:
Allegro molto appassionato (very impassioned allegro)

Though Mendelssohn is usually considered a conservative composer, a "classical romantic," his opening movement departs from classical concerto form. Traditionally, the opening movement of a concerto began with an extended section for orchestra. But Mendelssohn's first movement begins with the soloist, who presents the main theme. This ardent, expansive melody is heard high above a murmuring string accompaniment. The orchestra then expands the violin's theme and introduces a new, flowing

Side 9, band 7
CD 5 23

melody that begins the bridge section of this sonata-form movement. Toward the end of the bridge the excitement is gradually relaxed to prepare for the second theme, a tranquil woodwind melody which the soloist accompanies with a single sustained tone. This unusual combination of instruments produces a delicate, intimate sound. Following this, the violin reclaims the spotlight and sings the tranquil theme while the woodwinds support.

The cadenza has a new function in this movement. In classical concertos, the cadenza was improvised by the soloist and played near the end of the movement. Here, the composer has written it out and placed it at the end of the development section as a transition to the recapitulation. Mendelssohn wanted the cadenza to be an integral part of the movement, not merely something tacked on to display the soloist's virtuosity. Listen for the magical moment when the violinist's rapid arpeggios are joined by the orchestra softly playing the first theme of the recapitulation.

Listening Outline To be read while music is heard

CONCERTO FOR VIOLIN AND ORCHESTRA IN E MINOR, OP. 64 (1844),
BY FELIX MENDELSSOHN

First Movement: Allegro molto appassionato

Sonata form, duple meter ($\frac{2}{2}$), E minor

Solo violin, 2 flutes, 2 oboes, 2 clarinets, 2 bassoons, 2 French horns, 2 trumpets, timpani, 1st violins, 2d violins, violas, cellos, double basses

(Duration, 12:01)

EXPOSITION
First theme
23   0:00

1. *a.* Strings, *p*, introduce solo violin. Main melody in minor, high register, legato.

0:29   *b.* Running notes in solo violin. Crescendo, climbing phrases.
0:56   *c.* Orchestra, *ff*, main melody. Increased rhythmic motion leads to cadence.

Bridge

`24` 1:27   2. *a.* Violins, flowing bridge theme. Solo violin repeats bridge theme an octave higher.

1:42   *b.* Solo violin phrases sweep downward and upward through wide range. Flute joins. Crescendo. Running passage rises and falls. Decrescendo, mood calms.

Second theme

`25` 2:47   3. *a.* Clarinets and flutes, *pp*, calm melody in major. Solo violin accompanies with sustained tone.

3:00   *b.* Solo violin, *pp*, calm theme expanded. Woodwinds, then strings accompany.

3:58   4. *a.* Main melody in solo violin, major. Brilliant running passages, pizzicato accompaniment. Crescendo.

4:47   *b.* Climactic orchestral trills alternate with solo violin, opening of main melody. Decrescendo.

DEVELOPMENT

`26` 5:09   1. *a.* Solo violin, *p*, flowing bridge theme. Violins, *f*.

5:22   *b.* Running passage in solo violin and fragments of main melody in orchestra.

5:50   2. Solo violin, *p*, main melody varied. Decrescendo. Violin melody slowly descends. Orchestral crescendo to *ff*.

CADENZA

`27` 6:40   3. Unaccompanied solo violin, broken chords. Ascents to high tones, trills, fragment of main melody. Rapid broken chords lead into

RECAPITULATION

First theme

8:02   1. Main melody in orchestra, *p*. Broken chords continue in solo violin. Crescendo.

Bridge

    2. *a.* Orchestra, *ff*, bridge theme.

8:20   *b.* Solo violin, *mf,* bridge theme carried downward. Decrescendo.

3. *a.* Woodwinds, *pp,* calm melody in major. Solo violin accompanies with sustained tone.
   b. Solo violin, *pp,* calm theme expanded. Woodwinds, then strings accompany.
4. *a.* Brilliant running passages in solo violin. Pizzicato accompaniment. Crescendo.
   b. Climactic orchestral trills alternate with solo violin, opening of main melody. Decrescendo.

5. Solo violin, bridge theme. Tempo becomes faster. Crescendo. Brilliant running passages. Full orchestra, *ff.*

Second Movement:

Andante

A single bassoon tone links the brilliant opening movement with the hushed introduction to the slow second movement. The C major andante is a songlike, intimate piece in A B A' form. Its opening section (A) features a warm, expansive melody in the solo violin's high register; a string accompaniment gently emphasizes the $\frac{6}{8}$ meter (1–2–3–4–5–6). The middle section (B) becomes more agitated, and the accompaniment is rhythmically more active. The orchestra plays a more important role as it engages in dialogue with the soloist. Mendelssohn requires the solo violinist to play both a melody and a trembling accompaniment figure at the same time. The soloist also presents the melody in full-sounding octaves. The transition to the concluding A' section is very smooth because the trembling accompaniment figure is maintained. The andante ends quietly with a tender epilogue for solo violin and woodwinds.

Third Movement:

Allegretto non troppo (transitional section);
Allegro molto vivace (very lively allegro)

A pensive transitional section for solo violin and strings connects the andante with the concluding movement of the concerto. The very rapid finale, in sonata form, creates the lightness, joy, and brilliance so typical of Mendelssohn's art. Forceful chords in the woodwinds and upward solo figures usher in the playful and mostly staccato opening theme of the exposition; it is presented by the solo violin and high woodwinds.

A dazzling series of running passages and a long upward scale lead directly into the second theme, which is also a carefree one. With great effect, it combines a loud, marchlike phrase by the full orchestra with a softer motive from the opening theme.

Second theme
28 1:54

ff   p

In the development, the woodwinds softly present the marchlike phrase while the soloist plays brilliant running passages. A highlight of the development comes when the violinist presents a new legato melody which the strings lightly accompany with fragments of the opening theme.

29 3:08

Solo violin

Then there is a reversal of roles: the strings sing the lyrical melody while the soloist gracefully presents the fragment of the opening theme.

At the beginning of the recapitulation, the two themes are combined once again. The French horn and lower strings play the warm, legato melody while the soloist brings back the sparkling first theme. After a return of the second theme, the movement builds to an exciting climax in the coda, which is fuller in sound than anything that has come before.

Recapitulation
30 3:44

PROGRAM MUSIC $\left[\substack{\text{ROMANTIC} \\ \textbf{10}}\right]$

Romantic composers were particularly attracted to *program music*—instrumental music associated with a story, poem, idea, or scene. Programmatic orchestral works such as Berlioz's *Fantastic Symphony*, Tchaikovsky's *Romeo and Juliet*, and Smetana's *Moldau* depict the emotions, characters, and events of particular stories or the sounds and motions of nature. Such nonmusical ideas are usually specified by the title or by the composer's explanatory comments *(program)* in the concertgoer's program.

343

Program music draws on music's capacity to suggest and evoke. It is obvious that music can imitate certain sounds—bird songs, the rumble of thunder, the clang of bells, or the howling of the wind. But "sound effects" are only part of the descriptive resources of music. A composer can also exploit the correspondence between musical rhythm and objects in motion. A continuous flow of rapid notes, for example, can evoke a running stream or the rise and fall of waves. Most important, though, is the ability of music to create mood, emotion, and atmosphere. An agitated theme can represent a feud between rival families, just as a lyrical melody can symbolize youthful love.

Apart from the sound effects just described, music alone makes no definite reference to ideas, emotions, and objects. Music cannot identify anything. It is the title or a verbal explanation that lets us fully grasp a composer's source of inspiration. We know that the agitated theme in Tchaikovsky's *Romeo and Juliet* is meant to suggest the feud between rival families, but in another piece, the same theme could as easily evoke a king's rage or a cavalry charge.

The aim of most program music is expression more than mere description. Beethoven explicitly stated this aim when he referred to his *Pastoral* Symphony (his Symphony No. 6) as "an expression of feeling rather than painting." Even the most "realistic" episodes in program music can also serve a purely musical function, as in the slow movement of the *Pastoral, By the Brook,* where the songs of a nightingale, quail, and cuckoo are realistically imitated. (The names of these birds are even written in the score.) These bird calls provide a point of rest near the end of the movement and flow logically from what has come before.

Generally, one can appreciate a descriptive piece as pure music, without knowing its title or program. We can enjoy the lyrical theme of Tchaikovsky's *Romeo and Juliet,* for example, without associating it with young love. The forms used for program music are similar to those used for nonprogram music, or ***absolute music.*** A programmatic work can be heard simply as an example of rondo, fugue, sonata form, or theme and variations. But our pleasure may be greater when we can relate music to literary or pictorial ideas. Romantic composers were well aware that verbal explanations helped listeners follow the flow of music. Occasionally, they even added titles or programs to finished works. Musicians and audiences in the romantic period liked to read stories into all music, whether intended by the composer or not.

Clearly, the distinction between program music and absolute music is not always useful. A composition entitled simply Symphony No. 6 might have a program that its composer chooses not to reveal. Here are Tchaikovsky's comments about his Sixth Symphony *(Pathétique):* "This time a program symphony—but with a program which shall remain an enigma for everyone—let them puzzle their heads over it. This program is subjective through and through, and during my journey, while composing it in my mind, I often wept bitterly."

Most romantic program music was written for piano or for orchestra. Schumann's *Carnival* (1835) and Mussorgsky's *Pictures at an Exhibition* (1874)—each a set of short pieces—are well-known descriptive compositions for piano. But program music found its most varied expression in the coloristic resources of the romantic orchestra. The main forms of orchestral program music are the program symphony, the concert overture, the symphonic poem (tone poem), and incidental music.

A *program symphony* is a composition in several movements—as its name implies, a symphony with a program. Each movement usually has a descriptive title. For example, Berlioz's *Fantastic Symphony* has five movements: (1) *Reveries, Passions,* (2) *A Ball,* (3) *Scene in the Country,* (4) *March to the Scaffold,* and (5) *Dream of a Witches' Sabbath.* (This work is discussed in Section 11.)

A *concert overture* has one movement, usually in sonata form. The romantic concert overture was modeled after the opera overture, a one-movement composition that establishes the mood of an opera. But the concert overture is *not* intended to usher in a stage work; it is an independent composition. Well-known concert overtures include Mendelssohn's *Hebrides* Overture and Tchaikovsky's *Overture 1812* and *Romeo and Juliet* Overture, which is studied in Section 13.

A *symphonic poem,* or *tone poem,* is also a one-movement composition. Symphonic poems take many traditional forms—sonata form, rondo, or theme and variations—as well as irregular forms. This flexibility of form separates the symphonic poem from the concert overture, which usually is in sonata form. Franz Liszt developed the symphonic poem in the late 1840s and 1850s, and it became the most important type of program music after 1860. Well-known tone poems include *Les Préludes,* by Liszt; *Don Juan* (1888) and *Till Eulenspiegel* (1895), by Richard Strauss; and *The Sorcerer's Apprentice* (1897), by Paul Dukas. During the late nineteenth century, symphonic poems became an important means of expression for nationalism in music. In Section 14, we'll consider a nationalistic tone poem, Smetana's *Moldau,* which depicts the longest river of Bohemia (in Czechoslovakia) as it winds through the countryside.

Incidental music is music that is intended to be performed before and during a play. It is "incidental" to the staged drama, but it sets the mood for certain scenes. Interludes, background music, marches, and dances are all incidental music (as are today's movie scores). Mendelssohn's incidental music for *A Midsummer Night's Dream* includes his famous *Wedding March.*

BASIC TERMS

program music (page 343)
program (343)
absolute music (344)
program symphony (345)

concert overture (345)
symphonic poem (tone poem) (345)
incidental music (345)

[11] HECTOR BERLIOZ

Hector Berlioz (1803–1869), one of the first French romantic composers and a daring creator of new orchestral sounds, was born in a small town near Grenoble. Berlioz was twenty before he could devote himself to music. His father, a physician, sent him to Paris to study medicine, but Berlioz was "filled with horror" by the dissecting room. He shocked his parents by abandoning his medical studies to pursue a career in music.

It did not take long for Berlioz to fill the gaps in his musical knowledge. He studied at the Paris Conservatory, analyzed musical scores, haunted the opera house, and composed. He memorized many operas and became furious if a conductor tampered with the orchestration. This fiery young fanatic would stand during a performance and shout, "Not two flutes, you scoundrels! Two piccolos! Two piccolos!"

When he was twenty-three, Berlioz was overwhelmed with the works of Shakespeare. He also fell madly in love with Harriet Smithson, a Shakespearean actress whose portrayals of Ophelia and Juliet had captivated the Parisian public. Berlioz wrote Harriet letters that were so wild and impassioned that she thought he was a lunatic and refused to see him. He grieved: "If she could for one moment conceive all the poetry, all the infinity of such a love, she would fly into my arms." Instead, Harriet Smithson left Paris without meeting Berlioz. That came later.

To depict his "endless and unquenchable passion," Berlioz wrote the *Symphonie fantastique (Fantastic Symphony)* in 1830. Parisians were startled by the sensationally autobiographical program for the symphony, its amazingly novel orchestration, and its vivid depiction of the weird and diabolical. At twenty-six, Berlioz had become the musical counterpart of such revolutionary French romantics as Victor Hugo and Delacroix.

In 1830, too, Berlioz won the Prix de Rome (the Rome Prize), the highest award of the Paris Conservatory. The prize subsidized two years' study in Rome. When he returned to Paris from his studies in Rome, Berlioz presented a concert featuring his *Fantastic Symphony*. In the audience was Harriet Smithson. When she realized that Berlioz's music depicted her, "she felt the room reel about her; she heard no more but sat in a dream." The next day, they met, and a year later they were married. Alas, the fantasy was more successful than reality—they separated after only a few years.

Berlioz's unconventional music irritated the directors of the main Paris opera house and concert society. To get a hearing for his works, Berlioz had to arrange concerts at his own expense. This involved hiring a hall, rounding up hundreds of musicians, writing publicity, getting the music copied, and countless other petty chores; it drained Berlioz financially,

The French composer Hector Berlioz was a daring creator of new orchestral sounds and one of the first great orchestra conductors.

physically, and emotionally. "The main reason for the long war against me," he wrote when he was fifty-four, "lies in the antagonism existing between my musical feeling and that of the great mass of the Parisian public." He complained that "all music off the beaten track . . . seemed to these people the music of madness." Berlioz was not completely unappreciated in Paris. He had a following of about 1,200 who faithfully bought tickets to his concerts. Nevertheless, this was not enough support for a composer of difficult and monumental works requiring much rehearsal time and hundreds of performers. To support his family, Berlioz turned to musical journalism. He was one of the most brilliant and witty music critics who ever lived. He made it his mission to convince the Parisian public that music was not merely a form of entertainment but a dramatic emotional expression.

Outside France, Berlioz's stock was higher. Liszt directed a German orchestra in several "Berlioz weeks," performing nothing but Berlioz's works. After 1840, Berlioz was in demand throughout Europe, conducting his own music and that of others. As one of the first great orchestral conductors, he influenced a whole generation of musicians. In 1860, Wagner wrote to Liszt, saying that the three greatest composers of the time were Wagner, Liszt, and Berlioz.

Berlioz's later years were bitter. He was repeatedly passed over for important conducting positions and academic honors. He composed very little during the six years before his death at sixty-five.

BERLIOZ'S MUSIC

"The prevailing qualities of my music," wrote Berlioz, "are passionate expressiveness, inner fire, rhythmic drive, and unexpectedness." Above all, Berlioz's music sounds unique. It includes abrupt contrasts between high woodwinds and low strings, snarling brass, and rumbling percussion. The dynamics fluctuate constantly, and the tempo changes many times.

Berlioz was extraordinarily imaginative in treating the orchestra, creating tone colors never before heard. At a time when the average orchestra contained about sixty players, Berlioz often assembled hundreds of musicians to achieve an enormous range of power and instrumental timbre. More than any earlier composer, he made tone color a basic part of his musical language. A list of orchestral effects in the *Fantastic Symphony* alone would include four kettledrums combining to play a chord, bells combined with brasses, and violinists striking the strings with the bow stick.

Berlioz's compositions are full of long melodies that take unexpected turns and are irregular and asymmetrical in construction. To critics who complained that his works lacked melodies, Berlioz replied, "To deny their existence is unfair and absurd. But as they are often on a large scale, an immature or unappreciative mind cannot appreciate their forms."

Most of Berlioz's works are for orchestra, or for orchestra with chorus and vocal soloists. All his major works are dramatic in nature and relate either to a literary program or to a text. He invented new forms: his "dramatic symphony" *Romeo and Juliet* (1839) is for orchestra, chorus, and vocal soloists, and his "dramatic legend" *The Damnation of Faust* (1846) combines opera and oratorio. Berlioz wrote three operas, *Benvenuto Cellini* (1838), *The Trojans* (1856–1858), and *Beatrice and Benedict* (1860–1862). Some of his works are grandiose and monumental, such as his Requiem (1837). He knew he was a pioneer in this territory: "In the Requiem, for example, I employ four distinct brass orchestras, answering each other at certain distances around the main orchestra and chorus. The result of this immensity of form is that one either entirely misses the drift of the music or is crushed by a tremendous emotion. . . . I have seen one man listening in terror, shaken to the depths of his soul, while his next neighbor could not catch an idea, though trying with all his might to do so."

SYMPHONIE FANTASTIQUE (FANTASTIC SYMPHONY; 1830)

The astonishing *Symphonie fantastique (Fantastic Symphony)*, a five-movement program symphony, is a romantic manifesto. Both the symphony and Berlioz's program reflect the twenty-six-year-old composer's unrequited passion for the actress Harriet Smithson:

> A young musician of extraordinary sensibility and abundant imagination, in the depths of despair because of hopeless love, has poisoned himself with opium. The drug is too feeble to kill him but plunges him into a heavy sleep accompanied by weird visions. His sensations, emotions, and memories, as they pass through his affected mind, are transformed into musical images and ideas. The beloved one herself becomes to him a melody, a recurrent theme (*idée fixe*) which haunts him continually.

A single melody, which Berlioz called the **idée fixe,** or *fixed idea*, is used to represent the beloved. It appears in all five movements and unifies the contrasting episodes of the symphony. This recurrence of the same theme in every movement of a symphony was a striking novelty in Berlioz's day. The theme changes in character during the work, sounding, in turn, exultant, waltzlike, and vulgar.

Another innovation in the symphony is its requirement of a very large and colorful orchestra: piccolo, 2 flutes, 2 oboes, English horn, 2 clarinets, 4 bassoons, 4 French horns, 2 cornets, 2 trumpets, 3 trombones, 2 tubas, 4 timpani, bass drum, snare drum, cymbals, bells, 2 harps, and strings. (Beethoven, for one, had not used the English horn, tuba, bells, cornet, or harp in his symphonies.) Berlioz saves the heaviest orchestration for the last two movements, where he depicts the fantastic and diabolical. Though the macabre and supernatural had long been dealt with in opera (for example, in Mozart's *Don Giovanni*), this is its first expression in an important symphony.

First Movement: *Reveries, Passions*
Largo (slow introduction);
Allegro agitato e appassionato assai
(agitated and very impassioned allegro)

> First he remembers that weariness of the soul, that indefinable longing, that somber melancholia and those objectless joys which he experienced before meeting his beloved. Then, the volcanic love with which she suddenly inspired him, his delirious suffering, his return to tenderness, his religious consolations.

The symphony opens with an extended slow introduction—almost a movement in itself—in which fluctuations of tempo and mood help create a dreamlike atmosphere. A long muted violin melody expresses, in Berlioz's words, "the overpowering sadness of a young heart first caught in the toils of a hopeless love."

Supplementary sets:
Side 4, band 3
CD 2 ⃞32
Idée fixe

The allegro movement following the introduction is written in a modified sonata form. Its first theme, played by the violins and flutes, is the *idée fixe (fixed idea)*. Berlioz described this expansive, upward-groping melody as "passionate but at the same time noble and shy."

In the development, Berlioz uses a fragment of the *idée fixe* and builds tension through rising and falling chromatic scales played by staccato strings. A shattering climax is followed by a pregnant moment of silence. Yet another climax occurs toward the end of the movement when the full orchestra plays the *idée fixe* in a hysterically jubilant transformation. The movement concludes with slow chords that evoke the "religious consolations" mentioned in the program.

THE ROMANTIC PERIOD

The Large Enclosure Near Dresden (1832), by the German painter Caspar David Friedrich. Romantic sensitivity to nature was revealed in landscape painting, which attained new importance. In Friedrich's landscapes, mystical feelings are often conveyed by a distant horizon.

Liberty Leading the People (1830), by Eugène Delacroix. Romantic painters and musicians often saw political revolution as a reflection of their own struggle for artistic freedom. Delacroix combined a realistic description of street fighting in Paris in the July Revolution of 1830 with a symbolic representation of liberty.

Slave Ship (1839), by Joseph Turner. In the seascapes of the English painter Turner, the sweep of waves expressed not only the power of nature but human passion as well.

Third-Class Carriage (1863–1865), by the French lithographer and painter Honoré Daumier. The industrial revolution caused vast social and economic changes and spurred interest in the poor. Daumier sympathetically portrayed people of the working class in a crowded train compartment.

Second Movement: *A Ball*
Allegro non troppo

He finds his beloved again at a ball in the midst of the tumult of a brilliant party.

The second movement is a waltz, the most popular dance of the romantic era. Its form may be outlined as introduction–A B A'–coda. A shimmering atmosphere is created in the introduction by string tremolos and delicate harp arpeggios. The lilting waltz theme (the A section) is introduced by the violins.

The B section brings a return of the *idée fixe,* now transformed into a waltz played by woodwinds.

The *idée fixe* is soon joined by an oom-pah-pah accompaniment and intertwined with fragments of the lilting waltz theme.

In the coda, Berlioz builds to a climax that is suddenly interrupted by yet another reminiscence of the *idée fixe*—this time played soulfully by a solo clarinet. The movement concludes brilliantly.

Third Movement: *Scene in the Country*
Adagio

On a summer evening in the country, he hears two herders calling each other with their shepherd melodies. The pastoral duet in such surroundings, the gentle rustle of the trees softly swayed by the wind, some reasons for hope which had come to his knowledge recently—all unite to fill his heart with a rare tranquillity and lend brighter colors to his ideas. But his beloved appears anew, spasms contract his heart, and he is filled with dark premonitions. What if she were deceiving him? One of the shepherds resumes his rustic tune, the other does not reply. The sun sets. Far away there is rumbling thunder—solitude—silence.

Like the preceding waltz movement, the adagio has the form introduction—A B A'—coda. In the introduction, Berlioz evokes a mood of loneliness in the midst of nature: a solo English horn is echoed by an oboe an octave higher. No previous symphonic movement had ever begun with a duet between these two instruments. The A section opens with an extended melody for flute and violins—"delightful reverie."

The *idée fixe* returns in the B section. It is now played by the oboe and flute against an agitated low countermelody in the cellos and basses. This combination of contrasting melodies in widely separated registers and different tone colors is a typically brilliant stroke. At the end of the coda, we again hear the English horn solo, but this time the oboe does not answer. Instead, four timpani suggest the rumbling of distant thunder. Berlioz explains that his aim is not merely to imitate thunder, "but rather to make silence more perceptible, and thus to increase the impression of uneasy sadness and painful isolation."

Fourth Movement: *March to the Scaffold*
Allegretto non troppo

> He dreams that he has murdered his beloved, that he has been condemned to death and is being led to execution. A march that is alternately somber and wild, brilliant and solemn, accompanies the procession. . . . The tumultuous outbursts are followed without transition by the muffled sound of heavy steps. At the end, the fixed idea returns for a moment, like a last thought of love interrupted by the death blow.

Side 10, band 1
CD 5 [28]

Introduction
   [28] 0:00

First theme
   [29] 0:27

"The March to the Scaffold is fifty times more frightening than I expected," Berlioz gleefully observed after the first rehearsals of the *Fantastic Symphony*. It is not until this fiendish fourth movement that all the brass and percussion instruments enter the action. Berlioz creates a menacing atmosphere with the opening orchestral sound, a unique combination of muted French horns, timpani tuned a third apart, and basses playing pizzicato chords. The first theme, stated by the cellos and basses, moves steadily downward for two octaves.

This idea is repeated several times with countermelodies in the bassoons. Then we hear a syncopated march tune blared by the brasses and wood-winds.

March tune
30 1:36

At the end of the march a solo clarinet begins to play the *idée fixe* but is savagely interrupted by a very loud chord representing the fall of the guil-lotine's blade.

Idée fixe
31 6:19

Fifth Movement: *Dream of a Witches' Sabbath*
Larghetto; Allegro

> He sees himself at a witches' sabbath in the midst of a hideous crowd of ghouls, sorcerers, and monsters of every description, united for his funeral. Strange noises, groans, shrieks of laughter, distant cries, which other cries seem to answer. The melody of the loved one is heard, but it has lost its character of nobleness and timidity; it is no more than a dance tune, ignoble, trivial, and grotesque. It is she who comes to the sabbath! . . . A howl of joy greets her arrival. . . . She participates in the diabolical orgy. . . . The funeral knell, burlesque of the *Dies irae*. Witches' dance. The dance and the *Dies irae* combined.

The *Dream of a Witches' Sabbath* is the most "fantastic" movement of the symphony; it depicts a series of grotesque events. Its slow, hushed introduction (larghetto) immediately draws the listener into the realm of the macabre and supernatural, evoking "strange noises, groans, shrieks of laughter" and "distant cries." Eerie tremolos in high muted strings and menacing low tones of cellos and basses begin a succession of fragmentary ideas in starkly contrasting tone colors, registers, and dynamics. In the exploratory spirit of his romantic age, Berlioz dared to create sounds that are weird rather than conventionally pleasing.

Side 10, band 2
CD 5 32
Introduction
32 0:00

In the allegro section, the beloved is revealed to be a witch. Her theme, the once "noble and timid" *idée fixe,* is transformed into a dance tune that is "trivial and grotesque." Played shrilly by a high-pitched clarinet, the tune moves in quick notes decorated by trills.

2:59

A "funeral knell" of sonorous bells lends an awesome atmosphere to the next part of the movement. Tubas and bassoons intone a solemn low melody in long, even notes.

This melody is the medieval chant *Dies irae (Day of wrath),* traditionally sung in the mass for the dead. (We studied Mozart's setting of the *Dies irae* in Part V.) Berlioz quotes it here as a symbol of eternal damnation. Soon the chant melody is shifted up to a high register and played by woodwinds and pizzicato strings in a quick dancelike rhythm.

Thus Berlioz dared to parody a sacred chant by transforming it into a trivial tune, as he had just done moments earlier with the *idée fixe*.

Berlioz conveys the frenzy of a witches' dance in a fuguelike section. The fugue subject (the witches' dance) is introduced by the lower strings and then imitated by other instruments.

Fugue subject
36 5:21

37 8:06

A crescendo builds to a powerful climax in which the rapid witches' dance, played in the strings, is set against the slower-moving *Dies irae*, proclaimed by the brasses and woodwinds. This musical nightmare ends in an orgy of orchestral power.

BASIC TERM

idée fixe (page 349)

NATIONALISM IN NINETEENTH-CENTURY MUSIC

ROMANTIC

12

During the nineteenth century, Europeans felt strongly that their homelands merited loyalty and self-sacrifice. These nationalistic feelings were awakened during the upheavals of the French Revolution and the Napoleonic Wars (1789–1814), when French armies invaded much of Europe. In many countries, military resistance to Napoleon aroused the citizens' sense of national identity. Common bonds of language, culture, and history were strengthened, since now battles were fought by soldiers drawn from the general population, not by mercenaries, as in the past. Patriotic feeling was intensified, too, by romanticism, which glorified love for one's national heritage.

As a revolutionary political movement, nationalism led to the unification of lands—like Germany and Italy—that had previously been divided into tiny states. It spurred revolts in countries under foreign rule, such as Poland and Bohemia (now part of Czechoslovakia).

Nationalism was a potent cultural movement, as well, particularly regarding language. In lands dominated by foreign powers, the national language was used increasingly in textbooks, newspapers, and official documents. For example, in Bohemia there was a revival of the Czech language, which before 1800 had lost ground to the German spoken by Austrian rulers. By the 1830s and 1840s, important textbooks on astronomy and chemistry were written in Czech, and there were many collections of Czech folk poetry. In every land, the "national spirit" was felt to reside in the "folk," the peasantry. The national past became a subject of intense historical investigation, and there was new enthusiasm for folk songs, dances, legends, and fairy tales.

Nationalism influenced romantic music, as composers deliberately gave their works a distinctive national identity. They used folk songs and dances and created original melodies with a folk flavor. Nationalist composers wrote operas and program music inspired by the history, legends, and landscapes of their native lands. Their works bear titles like *Russian Easter* Overture (Rimsky-Korsakov), *Finlandia* (Sibelius), and *Slavonic Dances* (Dvořák). But a genuine feeling of national style does not come merely through the use of folk songs or patriotic subjects. A piece of music will *sound* French, Russian, or Italian when its rhythm, tone color, texture, and melody spring from national tradition. There were regional traits in music before the romantic period, but never had differences of national style been emphasized so strongly or consciously.

In these revolutionary times, musical compositions symbolized nationalist yearnings and sometimes stirred audiences to violent political demonstrations. The Italian opera composer Giuseppe Verdi deliberately chose librettos that fanned public hatred for Austrian overlords; censors constantly pressured him to change scenes that might be interpreted as anti-Austrian or antimonarchical. A twentieth-century parallel occurred when the Nazis banned performances of Smetana's symphonic poem *The Moldau* in Prague, the composer's home city.

The strongest impact of nationalism was felt in lands whose own musical heritage had been dominated by the music of Italy, France, Germany, or Austria. During the romantic period, Poland, Russia, Bohemia, and the Scandinavian countries produced important composers whose music had a national flavor. Early in the nineteenth century, Chopin transformed his native Polish dances into great art. After about 1860, groups or "schools" of composers consciously declared their musical independence and established national styles. Among the leading musical nationalists were Mussorgsky, Rimsky-Korsakov, and Borodin from Russia; Smetana and Dvořák from Bohemia; Grieg from Norway; and Sibelius from Finland. We will focus on the most important of the national schools, the Russian.

THE RUSSIAN FIVE

The most distinctive national music arose in Russia, where folk songs pervaded everyday life. "Every muzhik, carpenter, bricklayer, doorkeeper, cabman; every peasant woman, laundry-maid and cook, every nurse and wet-nurse—all bring the folk songs of their villages with them to Petersburg, Moscow, to each and every city, and we hear them the whole year round," wrote a Russian music critic of the nineteenth century. The folk music of Russia sounds different from that of western Europe. It is often based on ancient church modes, rather than on major or minor scales. (Like major and minor scales, church modes consist of eight tones within an octave, but they have different patterns of whole and half steps.) Russian folk tunes also tend to be irregular in meter. A measure may contain 5 beats ($\frac{5}{4}$ time), instead of the customary 2, 3, 4, or 6. And the meter may change within a song so that two bars in $\frac{3}{4}$ time will be followed by one in $\frac{5}{4}$. Russian nationalist composers thus were able to draw on folk music that was both distinctive and highly varied.

Before 1800, there were no important Russian composers of art music. Tsars imported Italian and German composers to provide music at the court. But in the early 1800s a composer emerged who is considered the father of Russian music—Mikhail Glinka (1804–1857). His opera *A Life for the Tsar* (1836) incorporated peasant and folk tunes in a convincing way and laid the groundwork for a national style.

But it was only in the 1860s that a true "school" of national music came into being. (This decade also saw the appearance of the great Russian novels *Crime and Punishment*, by Dostoyevsky; and *War and Peace*, by Tolstoy.) Five young men, whom we now know as the "Russian five," met together in St. Petersburg (later Leningrad, and now St. Petersburg again) with the aim of creating a truly Russian music. They criticized each other's works and asserted the necessity of breaking from some of the traditional techniques of German, Italian, and French composers. Remarkably, all but one began as amateurs; most had nonmusical jobs and could compose only in their spare time. At first, the only professional musician was Mily Balakirev (1837–1910). The other members were César Cui (1835–1918), an army engineer; Alexander Borodin (1833–1887), a chemist; Nikolai Rimsky-Korsakov (1844–1908), a naval officer; and Modest Mussorgsky (1839–1881), a civil servant. Mussorgsky was the most original and probably the greatest of the Russian five. We'll focus on his opera *Boris Godunov*, a masterpiece of musical nationalism.

BORIS GODUNOV (1874), BY MODEST MUSSORGSKY

The son of a wealthy landowner, Modest Mussorgsky (1839–1881) was educated in a military academy and became an army officer when he was seventeen. After two years he left the army to devote himself to music. But the emancipation of the Russian serfs in 1861 caused financial hardship to his family, and Mussorgsky had to find a job. He became a government clerk in St. Petersburg and remained in that position for most of his life.

Though a competent pianist, Mussorgsky had little training in composition. He taught himself, except for occasional advice from Balakirev—one of the Russian five. Mussorgsky was plagued by severe psychological problems and eventually became an alcoholic. When he died at forty-two, he left relatively few compositions. These include *Boris Godunov,* some songs, the symphonic poem *Night on Bald Mountain,* and the piano piece *Pictures at an Exhibition,* which Maurice Ravel later arranged for orchestra.

Mussorgsky's highly original music is imbued with the spirit of Russian folk music. His melodies reflect the rhythms, accents, and pitch fluctuations of Russian speech. "I should like to make my characters speak on the stage exactly as they do in real life," he wrote. Contemporaries condemned his unconventional chord progressions as "crude" and "incorrect." Today, we can appreciate their color, strength, and originality.

Mussorgsky adapted the libretto of *Boris Godunov* (1874) from a drama by Alexander Pushkin, the Russian romantic poet. The opera deals with a violent chapter in Russian history and centers on the powerful personality of Tsar Boris, who reigned from 1598 to 1605. Boris gained the throne by causing the murder of its rightful heir, the child Dimitri. In a series of episodes, Mussorgsky vividly depicts Boris's coronation, his anguished feelings of guilt, his political enemies, his love of family and country, and his tragic death.

The opera's central character is Tsar Boris, but the Russian people emerge as its real "hero." In 1873, Mussorgsky wrote, "It is the people I want to depict. When I sleep I see them, when I eat I think of them, when I drink—I can visualize them, integral, big, untainted, and without any tinsel." Through massive choruses and vocal solos, he offers realistic portraits of the Russian peasant, aristocrat, nursemaid, soldier, police officer, vagabond monk, and village idiot. In this "musical folk-drama" (as *Boris* is subtitled), Mussorgsky's aim was not merely to create a work of art, but to reveal the depth and variety of the Russian character.

Boris was acclaimed by the Russian public during Mussorgsky's lifetime, but it was dropped from the repertory not long after his death in 1881. In 1896 and again in 1908, the score was revised by Rimsky-Korsakov, who edited and published Mussorgsky's works. Rimsky changed many passages and made the orchestration more brilliant. Though scholars debate the merits of Rimsky's revision, it is the one usually performed today. We'll focus on the spectacular *Coronation* Scene from the Prologue to Act I.

Prologue to Act I: *Coronation* Scene

Supplementary sets:
Side 4, band 4
CD 2 [33]

The dazzling *Coronation* Scene from the Prologue to Act I, which is set in the courtyard of the Kremlin in Moscow, calls up the splendor, pageantry, and religious fervor of ancient Russia.

The Cathedral of the Archangels, burial place of tsars, is on one side of the stage; on the other side is the Cathedral of the Assumption, where tsars are crowned. The courtyard is filled with a mass of common people, kneeling; they are being watched by police.

In a brilliant and highly original orchestral introduction, Mussorgsky depicts the tolling of all the great bells of the Kremlin. Bells were a characteristic feature of ancient Russia and were linked with events that marked the passing of time—births, deaths, weddings, and coronations. The orchestral introduction is built entirely from the repeated alternation of just two dissonant chords:

This particular succession of chords was highly unusual in Mussorgsky's day; furthermore, no other composer had thought of repeating such an unusual progression to create a special atmosphere. Mussorgsky's technique of repetition was to have a profound influence on twentieth-century composers such as Igor Stravinsky.

A procession of nobles moves toward the cathedral for the coronation of Boris. From the porch of the cathedral, Prince Shuisky, Boris's adviser, exclaims, "Long live Tsar Boris." Then the chorus sings an exultant hymn of praise which Mussorgsky based on a Russian folk song.

To the sun in all splen - dor ris - en be glo - ry, glo - ry!

As the tsar's procession emerges from the cathedral, the music builds to a climax. When Boris appears, the mood changes dramatically. Clad in magnificent royal garb and followed by his two children, Boris at first voices "dark foreboding" about his fate and prays for God's blessing. Then he invites everyone present—nobles and lowly poor—to a feast, and his melody becomes powerful and determined. The bell chords and choral hymn of praise recur as Boris's procession continues to the cathedral to pay homage before the tombs of Russia's tsars.

33 0:00
Extended orchestral
introduction, bells.

Prince Shuisky

Da zdrávstvuyet Tsar Borís Feódorovich!   Long life Tsar Boris Feodorovich!   1:36

Chorus

Zhiví i zdrávstvui, Tsar násh bátyushka!   Long live the Tsar, our little father!

Prince Shuisky

Slávte!	Glory to you!

Chorus

34 1:58

Uzh kák na nébe sólntsu krásnomu,	Even as glory to the radiant sun in the sky,
Sláva!	Glory!
Uzh i sláva no Rusí Tsaryú Borísu!	So glory to Tsar Boris in Russia!
Sláva!	Glory!

(An imperial procession from the Cathedral. Police officers keep the people in line on both sides of the procession.)

Zhivi i zdrávstvui! Ráduisya, veselísya pravoslávnyi lyud! Velichái Tsaryá Borísa i sláv!	Long live the Tsar! Rejoice and make merry, all ye faithful of the Russian church, and glory to the great Tsar Boris.

Nobles
(From the porch)

Da zdrávstvuyet Tsar Boris Feódorovich!	All hail to Tsar Boris Feodorovich!

Chorus

Da zdrávstvuyet!	All hail!

(Boris now appears and crosses the stage.)

Uzh, kák na Rusí tsaryú Borísu!	Glory to Tsar Boris in all Russia!
Sláva, sláva, Tsaryú! Sláva, sláva, sláva!	Glory, glory to the Tsar! Glory, glory, glory!

Boris

35 4:00

Skorbít dushá! Kakói-to strákh nevólnyi Zlovéschim predchúvstviyem Skovál mne sérdtse. O právednik, o mói otéts derzhávnyi! Vozzrí s nebés na slyózy vérnykh slug I nisposhlí ty mné svyaschénnoye na vlást Blagoslovénye. Da búdu blag i práveden kak tý, Dá v sláve právlyu svói naród. Tepér poklónimsya pochíyuschim Vlastítelyam Rusíyi. A tám szyvát naród na pir, Vsekh, ot boyár do nischevo sleptsá, Vsem vólnyi vkhod, vse gósti dorogíye.	My soul is torn with anguish! Involuntary fears and sinister forebodings clutch my heart. Oh, righteous and sovereign Father, look down from heaven and behold the tears of these your faithful servants! Bestow Thy sacred blessings upon me and my dominion! Help me to be kind and just like Thyself, and rule over my people in glory! And now let us bow in homage to the great departed rulers of Russia. Then let us summon the people, from the noble to the blind beggar, to a feast. All are free to come and be my dear and welcome guests.

(Bells are rung on stage as the procession continues to the cathedral.)

Chorus

Zhiví zdrávstvui Tsár nash bátyushka.	Long live the Tsar, our little father!

(Police officers try to restore order, but the people break away and dash towards the Archangels Cathedral.)

Uzh kák na nébe sólntsu krásnomu,	Even as glory to the radiant sun in the sky,
Sláva, sláva!	Glory, Glory!
Uzh, kák na Rusí Tsaryú Borísu,	So glory to Tsar Boris in Russia!
Sláva, sláva, i mnógaya léta!	Glory, glory and a long life!

(Great commotion. The police officers struggle with the people. Boris emerges from the Archangels Cathedral and proceeds to his chambers.)

BASIC TERM

nationalism (page 356)

PETER ILYICH TCHAIKOVSKY

ROMANTIC
13

Peter Ilyich Tchaikovsky (1840–1893), the most famous Russian composer, came from the small town of Votkinsk, where his father was a mining inspector. When he was ten, he and his family moved to St. Petersburg, where he studied at the School of Jurisprudence. After graduating at nineteen, Tchaikovsky became a government clerk. He began to study music theory at the relatively late age of twenty-one. While keeping his government position, he entered the newly established St. Petersburg Conservatory, the first college-level music school in Russia. Two days after the opening of the conservatory, he wrote to his sister: "Sooner or later I shall abandon my present job for music. . . . Of course, I won't resign from my present job till I'm certain that I'm no longer a clerk, but a musician." The next year he did just that. So rapid was his progress in music that after graduating he became professor of harmony at the new Moscow Conservatory, a position he held for twelve years. As though to make up for his late start, Tchaikovsky composed furiously; a symphony, an opera, and a tone poem flowed from his pen, and by the age of thirty, he had composed his first great orchestral work, *Romeo and Juliet*.

Peter Ilyich Tchaikovsky was the most famous Russian composer of the nineteenth century.

The year 1877 was bitterly dramatic. Tchaikovsky took the disastrous step of marrying a twenty-eight-year-old conservatory student who adored him and his music. Tchaikovsky seems to have married only to conceal his homosexuality. A few days after the wedding, he was writing of "ghastly spiritual torture." Two weeks later he waded into the icy Moscow River, intending to commit suicide by getting pneumonia. But a strong constitution saved him, and he fled to St. Petersburg, where a nervous collapse put him into a coma for two days. He separated from his wife, never seeing her again.

In 1877 Tchaikovsky also acquired a benefactress, Nadezhda von Meck, a very rich widow of forty-six with eleven children. Madame von Meck passionately loved Tchaikovsky's music. She gave him an annuity that allowed him to quit his conservatory position and devote himself to composition. For fourteen years they corresponded, but they agreed never to meet. "I prefer to think of you from afar," she wrote, "to hear you speak in your music and to share your feelings through it." After so many years of this curious but intimate friendship, Tchaikovsky was deeply hurt when she abruptly cut off the annuity and stopped corresponding. "This situation lowers me in my own eyes," he wrote to her son-in-law; "it makes the memory of the money I accepted from her almost unbearable. . . ."

During these years, Tchaikovsky conducted his own works more and more, achieving success throughout Europe. Yet success did not bring spiritual peace. His brother observed, "The weariness and suffering which sprang up in Tchaikovsky's soul . . . reached their greatest intensity at the moment of his greatest triumphs." In 1891 he was invited to the United States, where he participated in four concerts inaugurating Carnegie Hall in New York and two concerts of his music in Baltimore and Philadelphia.

On October 28, 1893, Tchaikovsky conducted the premiere of his last great work, the Symphony No. 6 *(Pathétique)*, which ends unconventionally with a slow, despairing finale. Nine days later, he died at the age of fifty-three.

TCHAIKOVSKY'S MUSIC

"I grew up in the backwoods, filling myself from earliest childhood with the inexplicable beauty of the characteristic traits of Russian folk music. . . . I passionately love the Russian element in all its manifestations." Tchaikovsky thought of himself as *"Russian* in the fullest sense of the word." But Russian folk song was only one influence on his art. His style also contains elements of French, Italian, and German music.

Tchaikovsky's works are much more in the western tradition than are the compositions of his contemporaries, the Russian five. He fused national and international elements to produce intensely subjective and passionate music. "At the moment of composing," Tchaikovsky wrote, "when I am aglow with emotion, it flashes across my mind that all who will hear my music will experience some reflection of what I am feeling myself." And indeed, the brooding melancholy that plagued Tchaikovsky is a prominent feature in much of his music.

Tchaikovsky was a prolific composer of both instrumental and vocal works. Among his most popular orchestral compositions are the Fourth, Fifth, and Sixth *(Pathétique)* Symphonies (1877, 1888, and 1893), the Piano

Concerto No. 1 in B Flat Minor (1875), the Violin Concerto (1878), and the overture-fantasy *Romeo and Juliet* (1869), which we'll study. Tchaikovsky wrote some of his best music for ballet: *Swan Lake* (1876), *The Sleeping Beauty* (1889), and *The Nutcracker* (1892). He reworked these ballet scores into concert suites, of which the suite from *The Nutcracker* is best known. The spirit of ballet permeates much of Tchaikovsky's music. Of his eight operas, *Eugene Onegin* (1877–1878) and *Pique Dame* (*The Queen of Spades;* 1890) are performed with some frequency. There also are the orchestral showpieces *Marche slave (Slavic March)* and *Overture 1812*.

All of Tchaikovsky's music contains beautiful melodies that stretch and leap widely, like dancers. He repeats melodies over and over, sometimes transforming an intimate, lyrical utterance into an intense outcry by means of louder dynamics and fuller orchestration. His treatment of the orchestra is extremely colorful, marked by striking contrasts and alternations of strings, woodwinds, and brasses. The emotional quality of his music results from sharp contrasts of tempo, dynamics, and thematic material, as well as from powerful climaxes.

ROMEO AND JULIET, OVERTURE-FANTASY

Side 10, band 3
CD 5 [38]

Romantic composers felt an artistic kinship to Shakespeare because of his passionate poetry, dramatic contrasts, and profound knowledge of the human heart. Some of Shakespeare's plays inspired many of the finest nineteenth-century compositions. Among these were *Macbeth* and *Othello,* set as operas by Verdi; and *A Midsummer Night's Dream,* depicted in incidental music by Mendelssohn. *Romeo and Juliet* inspired both a "dramatic symphony" by Berlioz and a concert overture by Tchaikovsky.

Tchaikovsky composed *Romeo and Juliet* at twenty-nine, near the beginning of his musical career. Now one of the best-loved works, *Romeo and Juliet* was a dismal failure at its premiere in 1870. "After the concert we dined. . . . No one said a single word to me about the overture the whole evening. And yet I yearned so for appreciation and kindness." Tchaikovsky decided to revise the overture. He composed a new theme to represent Friar Laurence, adopting a suggestion of his friend Balakirev. Despite this, the work remained unappreciated. Only about twenty years later, after further revisions, did *Romeo and Juliet* achieve worldwide popularity.

Like Shakespeare's play, Tchaikovsky's *Romeo and Juliet* glorifies a romantic love powerful enough to triumph over death. He captures the essential emotions of Shakespeare's play without defining the characters or the exact course of events. Highly contrasted themes are used to express the conflict between family hatred and youthful love. Tchaikovsky also depicts the gentle and philosophical Friar Laurence, intermediary between the lovers and the harsh outside world.

Romeo and Juliet is a concert overture consisting of a slow introduction followed by a fast movement in sonata form. (Tchaikovsky's title—

Overture-Fantasy—implies that he treated the musical material in a free and imaginative way.) We can enjoy *Romeo and Juliet* as an exciting orchestral piece without knowing the play. However, a new dimension is added to our listening experience when we associate the music with the drama.

Tchaikovsky opens the overture with the Friar Laurence theme, a solemn, hymnlike melody. As the slow introduction unfolds, brooding strings set an atmosphere of impending tragedy. The clash of swords and the anger of the feud between the Montagues and the Capulets are suggested by the violent first theme of the allegro. Syncopations, rushing strings, and massive sounds create enormous excitement. The second theme of the exposition, a tender love theme, is expressively scored for English horn and muted violas. When the love theme returns in the recapitulation, it has a new exultant character, as Tchaikovsky envelops the listener in opulent sound. There are long crescendos as the melody is led higher and higher to ever more passionate orchestral climaxes.

In the coda, Tchaikovsky transforms the love theme into a song of mourning, while timpani softly beat the rhythm of a funeral march. Then, a new hymn and a tender reminiscence of the love theme suggest that Romeo and Juliet are reunited in death.

Listening Outline To be read while music is heard

ROMEO AND JULIET, OVERTURE-FANTASY (1869), BY PETER ILYICH TCHAIKOVSKY

Andante non tanto quasi moderato (andante, almost a moderate tempo, slow introduction); Allegro giusto (moderate allegro)

Sonata form, quadruple meter ($\frac{4}{4}$), B minor

Piccolo, 2 flutes, 2 oboes, English horn, 2 clarinets, 2 bassoons, 4 French horns, 2 trumpets, 3 trombones, tuba, timpani, cymbals, bass drum, harp, 1st violins, 2d violins, violas, cellos, double basses.

(Duration, 18:38)

INTRODUCTION
Andante non
tanto quasi
moderato

38 0:00   1. *a.* Low clarinets and bassoons, *p,* hymnlike Friar Laurence theme.

0:34	*b.* Strings and French horns, *p,* sustained tones. Basses.
1:05	*c.* Woodwinds and strings, crescendo. Harp, *mf,* flutes, *p.*
2:00	2. *a.* Pizzicato strings accompany high woodwinds, *p,* Friar Laurence theme.
2:34	*b.* Strings and French horns, *p,* sustained tones. Basses.
3:03	*c.* Strings and woodwinds, crescendo. Harp, *mf,* violins, *p.*
3:57	3. *a.* Strings answered by high woodwinds, *mf.* Crescendo to *ff,* full orchestra, accelerando. Timpani roll, decrescendo, much slower tempo.
4:51	*b.* Strings, *p,* answered by woodwind chords, *pp.* Crescendo and accelerando to

Allegro giusto

EXPOSITION
First theme
39 5:01   1. *a.* Orchestra, *f,* feud theme, minor.

5:17	*b.* Cellos imitated by piccolo, *f,* feud motive.
5:47	*c.* Cymbal crashes against rushing notes in strings. Crescendo to *ff.*
5:59	*d.* Full orchestra, *ff,* feud theme. Cymbal crashes.

Bridge
40 6:19   2. Suddenly soft, woodwinds. Basses and French horns, *pp,* rhythm slows.

Second
theme
41 6:58   3. *a.* English horn and muted violas, love theme, major.

42 7:13   *b.* Muted violins, *pp,* gently pulsating melody.

Crescendo.

          c. High woodwinds, *p,* love theme extended.

Closing
section   4. Harp, *p,* accompanies muted strings, bassoon, English horn, *p.*

DEVELOPMENT

43 9:52   1. Strings, woodwinds, *p,* feud motive. Crescendo, rushing notes in strings, *f.*

    2. *a.* French horns, *p,* Friar Laurence theme, strings accompany. Violins, *pp,* high repeated notes, brass, woodwind chords, *pp.*
       b. Horns, *p,* Friar Laurence theme. Crescendo, rushing notes in strings, *f.*
       c. Horns, *p,* Friar Laurence theme, strings accompany. Violins, *pp,* high repeated notes, brass, woodwind chords, *pp.*
       d. Horns, *p,* Friar Laurence theme.
    3. Low strings, *f,* answered by woodwinds, *f,* feud motive. Crescendo to *ff,* cymbal crashes.
    4. *a.* Trumpets, *ff,* Friar Laurence theme.
       b. Strings, *ff,* rushing notes, cymbal crashes.

RECAPITULATION
First theme

44 11:58   1. Full orchestra, *ff,* feud theme, minor, cymbal crashes. Downward rushing notes in strings, decrescendo.

Second
theme

45 12:21   2. Oboes, *p,* gently pulsating melody, major. Violins accompany *pp.* Crescendo.
46 12:58   3. *a.* Strings, *f,* love theme extended. Crescendo to *ff.* Love theme repeated. Decrescendo.
       b. Cellos, woodwinds, *mf,* love-theme phrases. French horn. Crescendo.
       c. Strings, *ff,* love theme. Feud motive, cymbal crashes.
    4. *a.* Full orchestra, *ff,* feud theme, cymbal crashes.
       b. Brasses, *ff,* Friar Laurence theme.
       c. Full orchestra, *ff,* feud theme, cymbal crashes.
       d. Brasses, *ff,* Friar Laurence theme.
       e. Full orchestra, *ff,* cymbal crashes. Cellos and basses, timpani roll, decrescendo to *p.*

CODA

47 15:53   1. Timpani, *p,* funeral-march rhythm. Strings, *mf,* love theme transformed into song of mourning. Very moderate tempo.

    2. Woodwinds, *pp,* hymnlike melody. Harp.
    3. Violins, *mf,* love theme varied. Timpani roll, crescendo.
    4. Full orchestra, *ff,* repeated chords.

367

[14] BEDŘICH SMETANA

Bedřich Smetana (1824–1884) was the founder of Czech national music. His works are steeped in the folk songs, dances, and legends of his native Bohemia (now part of Czechoslovakia). When Smetana was growing up, Bohemia was under Austrian domination and the official language in Prague schools and government bureaus was German, not Czech. The young Smetana's feelings of national identity were inflamed during the revolutions of 1848, when Czech radicals fought for political freedom and the abolition of serfdom. As a member of the armed Citizen Corps, he was probably on the barricades when the Austrians bombarded Prague. The insurrection was a failure and resulted in a harsh reaction from Austria; censorship was increased and patriots were imprisoned.

In this repressive atmosphere, Smetana's musical nationalism could make little headway. Though he was recognized as a pianist, his compositions were scorned by those opposed to nationalism or "modernity" of any variety. In 1856, Smetana emigrated to Sweden, where he taught, conducted, and composed symphonic poems in the style of Franz Liszt. He returned to Prague only in 1862, when Austria's military defeats had resulted in some liberal concessions. Political prisoners were released, Czech-language newspapers were established, and Czech theaters for drama and opera were allowed to open. It was for one of these theaters that Smetana wrote *The Bartered Bride,* his most famous opera, based on Bohemian legend and folk material. Smetana was active in Prague not only as a composer, but as a pianist, conductor, teacher, and tireless propagandist for Czech musical nationalism.

At the age of fifty, Smetana suffered the same fate as Beethoven—he became completely deaf. Yet some of his finest works followed, including *Má Vlast (My Country;* 1874–1879), a cycle of six symphonic poems glorifying Bohemian history and legend, the fertile Czech countryside, and peasant songs and dances. Smetana passed his last ten years in acute physical and mental torment caused by syphilis. He died in an insane asylum at the age of sixty.

THE MOLDAU

"Today I took an excursion to the St. John Rapids where I sailed in a boat through huge waves. . . . The view of the landscape was both beautiful and grand." Smetana's trip inspired his famous symphonic poem *The Moldau,* which depicts Bohemia's main river as it flows through the countryside. This orchestral work, part of the cycle *Má Vlast (My Country),* is both a romantic representation of nature and a display of Czech nationalism. *The Moldau* was written in three weeks shortly after Smetana became deaf, but its fresh, optimistic mood gives no hint of the composer's anguish and despair. Smetana wrote the following program to preface his score:

> The composition depicts the course of the river, beginning from its two small sources, one cold the other warm, the joining of both streams into one, then the flow of the Moldau through forests and across meadows, through the countryside where merry feasts are celebrated; water nymphs dance in the moonlight; on nearby rocks can be seen the outline of ruined castles, proudly soaring into the sky. The Moldau swirls through the St. John Rapids and flows in a broad stream toward Prague. It passes Vyšehrad [where an ancient royal castle once stood], and finally the river disappears in the distance as it flows majestically into the Elbe.

The Moldau falls into contrasting musical sections that represent different scenes and episodes described in the program. Hunting along the river bank is suggested by horn fanfares; a peasant wedding by a rustic polka, the Bohemian dance; and a moonlit night by shimmering woodwinds and a serene melody in high muted strings. An expansive folklike theme that recurs several times symbolizes the river. Smetana unifies the symphonic poem by running notes evoking the movement of water, sometimes rippling, sometimes turbulent.

Listening Outline To be read while music is heard

THE MOLDAU (1874), BY BEDŘICH SMETANA

Allegro commodo non agitato (unhurried allegro, not agitated), sextuple meter ($\frac{6}{8}$), E minor

Piccolo, 2 flutes, 2 oboes, 2 clarinets, 2 bassoons, 4 French horns, 2 trumpets, 3 trombones, tuba, timpani, bass drum, triangle, cymbals, harp, 1st violins, 2d violins, violas, cellos, double basses

(Duration, 11:54)

Two springs

    ⬚ 0:00   1. *a.* Flutes, *p*, running notes. Harp, pizzicato violins.

                    Clarinets, *p*, join, running notes.
             b. Lower strings, *p*, running notes lead to

The river
2 1:00

2. Violins, songlike river theme, minor key. Running-note accompaniment in strings.

p ——— < *sf* > — *p* < *diminuendo*

1:28

River theme extended.

Forest hunt
3 2:50

3. *a.* French horns and trumpets, *f,* hunting calls. Strings, running notes. Crescendo to *ff.*
   b. Decrescendo to *ppp.*

Peasant wedding
4 3:54

4. *a.* Strings, *p,* polka.

mf

Crescendo to *f,* triangle strokes.
   b. Decrescendo to *ppp,* melody descends.

Moonlight: dance of water nymphs
5 5:20
5:42
6:53

5. *a.* Woodwinds, *pp,* sustained tones. Flutes, *p,* running notes lead to
   b. High muted violins, *pp,* serene legato melody. Harp, *p.*
   c. Brasses, *pp.* Staccato chords join accompaniment to violin melody.
   d. Crescendo. Woodwinds, running notes lead to

The river
7:55

6. Violins, river theme. Running-note accompaniment in strings.

The rapids
6 8:46

7. *a.* Full orchestra, *ff.* Brasses, timpani roll, piccolo, cymbal crashes.
   b. Strings, *pp.* Quick crescendo.

The river at its widest point
7 10:00

8. Full orchestra, *ff,* river theme in major key. Faster tempo.

Vyšehrad, the ancient castle

9. *a.* Brasses and woodwinds, *ff,* hymnlike melody. Cymbal crashes.
   b. Decrescendo. Violins, *ppp.* Full orchestra, *ff,* closing chords.

ANTONIN DVOŘÁK

Antonin Dvořák (1841–1904) followed Smetana as the leading composer of Czech national music. He infused his symphonies and chamber music with the spirit of Bohemian folk song and dance.

Dvořák's father was a poor innkeeper and butcher in a small town near Prague. After working in his father's butcher shop, Dvořák left home at the age of sixteen to study music in Prague. For years he earned a meager living by playing in an opera orchestra under Smetana's direction. He was little known as a composer until his works came to the attention of the German master Brahms, who recommended Dvořák to his own publisher: "I took much pleasure in the works of Dvořák of Prague. If you play them through, you will enjoy them as much as I have done. Decidedly he is a very talented man."

From this time on—Dvořák was then about thirty-six—his fame spread rapidly. He was invited several times to England, where the melodiousness of his symphonies, chamber music, Slavonic dances, and choral works appealed to the English love for folk music and the countryside. Although Dvořák rarely quoted actual folk tunes, his works breathe a folk quality and express a cheerful and direct personality.

In 1892, Dvořák went to New York, where he was to spend almost three years as the director of the National Conservatory of Music. He received a salary of $15,000, about twenty times what he was earning as a professor at the Prague Conservatory. Dvořák encouraged American composers to write nationalistic music. Besides his urban impressions, Dvořák learned about the American heartland by spending a summer in Spillville, Iowa, where there was a colony of Czechs.

Dvořák soon became interested in American Indian melodies and African American spirituals, which he learned about from his student Henry T. Burleigh, a black composer and baritone. Dvořák told a reporter from the New York *Herald* that in the spirituals he had "found a secure basis for a new national musical school. America can have her own music, a fine music growing up from her own soil and having its own character—the natural voice of a free and great nation." In 1895 Dvořák returned to his homeland and rejoined the faculty of the Prague Conservatory, becoming its director six years later.

SYMPHONY NO. 9 IN E MINOR *(FROM THE NEW WORLD)*

Dvořák wrote his *New World* Symphony, the Symphony No. 9 in E Minor, during his first year in the United States. One of the best known of all symphonies, it glorifies the American and the Czech folk spirit. Its popular character grows out of Dvořák's use of syncopations, **pentatonic** (five-note) **scales,** and modal scales often found in folk music. Colorful orchestration and melodious thematic material add to the *New World* Symphony's attractiveness. The symphony's four contrasting movements are unified through quotation of thematic material: themes from the first movement are recalled in the second and third movements, and the finale brings back themes from all three preceding movements.

First Movement:
Adagio (slow introduction); Allegro molto

Supplementary sets:
Side 5, band 1
CD 3 ☐1

The slow introduction to the first movement builds great tension and contains an ominous bass motive that foreshadows the opening theme of the energetic allegro that follows. In the exposition of this sonata-form movement, there are three distinctive themes. The first begins in minor with a syncopated arpeggio motive that dominates the entire symphony. The dancelike second theme, also in minor, is gentler than the first and narrower in range. Dvořák shifts to a major key for the third theme, a gracious melody which resembles the spiritual *Swing Low, Sweet Chariot*. (In the listening outline this is called the *Swing Low theme,* but with no implication that Dvořák meant it to recall the spiritual.) Between these themes come beautiful bridge passages that rise to a climax and then calm down to usher in new melodic material. In his development, Dvořák concentrates on the first and third themes, which he varies and combines. The recapitulation of all three themes is followed by a coda, which brings the first movement to a climactic close.

Listening Outline   To be read while music is heard

SYMPHONY NO. 9 IN E MINOR *(FROM THE NEW WORLD;* 1893), BY ANTONIN DVOŘÁK

First Movement: Adagio (slow introduction); Allegro molto

Sonata form, duple meter ($\frac{2}{4}$), E minor

Piccolo, 2 flutes, 2 oboes, 2 clarinets, 2 bassoons, 4 French horns, 2 trumpets, 3 trombones, timpani, 1st violins, 2d violins, violas, cellos, double basses

(Duration, 9:19)

Adagio
(slow
introduction)
    ☐1 0:00   1. *a.* Cellos, *pp*, downward phrases. French horns.

0:32	b. Flute, *p*, downward phrases.
0:53	2. a. Strings, *ff*, alternate with timpani, woodwinds, horns, *ff*.
	b. Cellos and basses, *pp*.
	c. High woodwinds alternate with low strings, bass motive.
	d. Full orchestra, crescendo, timpani roll, violin tremolo, *pp*.

Allegro molto

EXPOSITION
First theme
2 1:48

1. a. Horns, arpeggio motive. Woodwinds, *p*, playful rhythm, minor key.

b. Oboes, arpeggio motive. Woodwinds, playful rhythm.
c. Strings, *ff*, arpeggio motive developed. Crescendo.

Bridge
3 2:21

2. Brasses, *ff*, arpeggio motive. Strings, playful rhythm developed. Decrescendo.

Second
theme

4 2:52

3. a. Flute and oboe, *p*, dancelike tune.

b. Violins, *ppp*, dancelike tune developed, crescendo to *f*. Decrescendo.

Third theme
5 3:57

4. a. Flute, *p*, *Swing Low* theme, major.

b. Violins, *Swing Low* theme. Crescendo to *ff*, full orchestra.

DEVELOPMENT

⑥ 4:29	1. Strings, decrescendo.
4:41	2. *a.* Horn, *p, Swing Low* motive, piccolo. Crescendo.
	b. Trumpets, *f, Swing Low* motive. Trombones, *f,* arpeggio motive. Horns, *ff.* Strings, *ff.*
	c. Trombones, *ff,* arpeggio motive. High violins, *ff.* Rhythm quickens.
5:50	3. Oboes, *p,* arpeggio motive, flute. Crescendo

RECAPITULATION

First theme

⑦ 6:06	1. *a.* Horns, *mf,* arpeggio motive. Woodwinds, *p,* playful rhythm, minor.
	b. Oboes, arpeggio motive. Woodwinds, *p,* playful rhythm.
	c. Strings, *ff,* arpeggio motive developed. Decrescendo.

Second theme

6:44	2. *a.* Flute, *p,* dancelike tune.
	b. Woodwinds, *p,* dancelike tune. Strings, dancelike tune developed, crescendo to *ff.* Decrescendo.

Third theme

7:48	3. *a.* Flute, *p, Swing Low* theme, major.
	b. Violins, *Swing Low* theme. Crescendo.

CODA

8:17	1. Full orchestra, *fff. Swing Low* and arpeggio motives, minor.
	2. Repeated chords, *ff,* at end.

Second Movement:

Largo

Supplementary sets:
Side 5, band 2
CD 3 ⑧

After several introductory chords, we hear the famous largo melody, which has a nostalgic quality heightened by the timbre of the English horn. Dvořák uses tone color expressively throughout the second movement, frequently passing musical ideas among different instruments. The largo is in the form A B–bridge–A'. Its gentle mood is broken only in the bridge, which contains a climactic quotation of motives from the first movement.

Listening Outline   <small>To be read while music is heard</small>

SYMPHONY NO. 9 IN E MINOR *(FROM THE NEW WORLD;* 1893), BY ANTONIN DVOŘÁK

Second Movement: Largo

A B–bridge–A' form, quadruple meter ($\frac{4}{4}$), D flat major

2 flutes, 2 oboes, English horn, 2 clarinets, 2 bassoons, 4 French horns, 2 trumpets, 3 trombones, tuba, timpani, 1st violins, 2d violins, violas, cellos, double basses

(Duration, 11:48)

INTRODUCTION

8 0:00   1. Brasses and woodwinds, *pp*, solemn chords. Crescendo and decrescendo.
    2. Muted strings, *ppp*.

A

0:36   1. *a.* English horn, *p*, main melody, major key.

        b. Clarinet, *pp*, repeats ending notes of melody.

2:06   2. High woodwinds, *pp*, solemn chords, crescendo. Brasses, timpani, *ff*, decrescendo.

2:37   3. Muted strings, *ppp*, extension of main melody.

3:29   4. *a.* English horn, *p*, concluding phrases of main melody. Clarinet, violins softly repeat ending notes of melody.
        b. Muted French horns, *p*, opening notes of melody.

B

9 4:35   1. Oboe and flute, *pp*, minor melody, a little faster tempo than before. Tremolo strings accompany.

10 5:07   2. *a.* Clarinets, *pp*, hymnlike minor melody, a little slower tempo. Pizzicato basses accompany.

        b. Flutes and oboes, *p*, hymnlike melody continued. Pizzicato basses accompany.

5:55   3. Muted violins, *pp*, minor melody, a little faster tempo. Countermelody in oboe and flute. Strings, decrescendo.

6:58   4. Muted violins, *pp*, hymnlike minor melody, a little slower tempo. Tremolo strings accompany. Strings, *pp*, major chord.

Bridge

11 8:06   5. *a.* Staccato oboe, *p*, flute trills, *p*.
        b. Crescendo to *ff*, full orchestra. Arpeggio and *Swing Low* motives from first movement combined with opening of largo melody. Decrescendo.

A'

12 8:56

9:55
10:10

10:59

1. *a.* English horn, main melody, original tempo, major.
   b. Muted strings, *pp*, main melody broken up by pauses.
   c. Solo violin and solo cello, *pp*.
   d. Strings, concluding phrases of main melody. Clarinet, *p*, repeats ending notes of melody. Violins, decrescendo to *ppp*.
2. Brasses, *pp*, solemn chords. Crescendo. Decrescendo. Strings, *pp*, melody rises to high, sustained chord, *pp*. Ending chords in double basses, *pp*.

Third Movement:

Scherzo (Molto vivace)

Supplementary sets:
Side 5, band 3
CD 3 13

Section A
13 0:00

The exciting scherzo breathes the spirit of dancing. Its form is outlined as A (scherzo)–bridge–B (trio)–bridge–A (scherzo)–coda. Motives from the first movement are recalled in the bridge to the trio and in the coda. The opening part of the scherzo (A) section, in minor, has great rhythmic drive and features a short motive which chases itself in close imitation.

14 1:32

Dvořák then relaxes the tension with a lilting legato melody in a major key; the charm is heightened by delicate strokes of the triangle.

15 2:44

Section B
16 3:03

In the bridge to the trio (B), the cellos recall the arpeggio motive from the first movement.

The trio (B) section, in major, features two staccato dance tunes that might be performed by a town band. The first is softly played by the wood-winds with the triangle accompanying.

376

The second tune, graced by delightful trills, alternates between violins and woodwinds.

17 3:35

The scherzo section (A) is played again, and then we hear a dramatic string tremolo that ushers in the coda. Horns vigorously recalling the arpeggio motive are whimsically answered by woodwinds, *p*, playing the scherzo motive. The movement fades into silence before ending with a powerful chord for full orchestra.

Return of section A
18 5:10
Coda
7:07

Fourth Movement:

Allegro con fuoco (allegro with fire)

The *New World* Symphony ends with a sonata-form finale of great power and splendor. Dvořák skillfully combines the themes of the finale with motives from the three earlier movements.

After a brief string introduction, the horns and trumpets proclaim the first theme, which sounds like a proud march song.

Supplementary sets:
Side 6, band 1
CD 3 19

Introduction
19 0:00
First theme
0:15

A solo clarinet presents the yearning second theme, accompanied by a cello countermelody in faster time values.

20 1:54

21 2:45

The third theme, jubilant and folklike, ends with a three-tone descending figure that resembles *Three Blind Mice*.

Dvořák plays with the three-tone figure, shifting it from low to high instruments and embellishing it with humorous variations.

Largo melody
22 4:42

In the development, motives from preceding movements are quoted and varied. Flutes and clarinets softly recall the largo melody, which is combined with the marchlike finale theme and reminiscences of the scherzo. A crescendo builds to the opening of the recapitulation, as brasses proclaim the marchlike theme. The remainder of the recapitulation is subdued in dynamics, and from it the coda emerges as a passionate and triumphant summary of the whole symphony.

BASIC TERM

pentatonic scale (page 372)

ROMANTIC 16

JOHANNES BRAHMS

Johannes Brahms (1833–1897) was a romantic who breathed new life into classical forms. He was born in Hamburg, Germany, where his father made a precarious living as a string bass player. At thirteen, Brahms led a double life: during the day he studied piano, music theory, and composition; at night he played dance music for prostitutes and their clients in waterfront bars. Brahms's first concert tour, when he was twenty, gave him a chance to meet two of the greatest composers then living—Liszt and Schumann. The contact with Liszt was not helpful. Brahms, a product of a conservative musical education, was repelled by what he considered the bombast and lack of form in Liszt's music. Schumann, on the other hand, was to shape the course of Brahms's artistic and personal life.

Moments after presenting himself at Schumann's home, Brahms began to play one of his own piano sonatas. At the end of the first movement, Schumann called his wife Clara, the famous piano virtuoso, and they listened enthusiastically to Brahms's music for hours. Four weeks later, Schumann published a magazine article hailing young Brahms as a musical messiah "called to give ideal expression to his time." Brahms was both overjoyed and apprehensive about his overnight fame. "The open praise which you gave me," he wrote Schumann, "has probably excited the expectations of the public to such a degree that I don't know how I can come anywhere near fulfilling them."

As Brahms was preparing new works for an eager publisher, Schumann had a recurrence of his nervous illness and tried to drown himself. He was committed to an asylum, leaving Clara Schumann with seven children to support. Brahms rushed to her aid and helped care for the children while she went on concert tours to earn money. For two years Brahms lived in the Schumann home, becoming increasingly involved with Clara, who was fourteen years older. The conflict between his loyalty to Robert and his passion for Clara may well have accounted for the stormy music he wrote at the time. Robert Schumann's death left Brahms and Clara Schumann free to marry, yet they did not. Since they destroyed many of their letters, we'll never know what passed between them. A few months later they separated, although they remained lifelong intimate friends. Brahms never married; for him, Clara Schumann was "the most beautiful experience of my life."

Brahms desperately wanted to become conductor of the Philharmonic Orchestra in Hamburg, his birthplace. When he was passed over for the post in 1862, the disappointment was overwhelming. "For me this was much sadder even than you can possibly imagine," he wrote Clara Schumann, "perhaps even sadder than you can understand." He left his native city to settle in Vienna, where he spent the last thirty-five years of his life. For several years he conducted a Viennese musical society and introduced many forgotten masterpieces by Bach, Handel, and Mozart to the public. Brahms had a wide knowledge of older music; he edited baroque and classical compositions, and he was an ardent collector of music manuscripts.

His intimate knowledge of past masterpieces made Brahms extremely critical of his own work. Once, after a violinist had played a Bach piece, he threw his own music to the floor, exclaiming, "After that, how could anyone play such stuff as this!" Brahms was obsessed by Beethoven. "You have no idea," he told a friend, "how the likes of us feel when we hear the tramp of a giant like him behind us." He worked at his First Symphony on and off for twenty years and completed it only when he was forty-three. Brahms endlessly revised compositions and sent them to friends for advice and criticism. He sent some songs to Clara Schumann with the request, "Write me if possible one short word about each, . . . such as: Op. 10, No. 5, bad; No. 6, shameful; No. 7, ridiculous."

In 1879, an honorary doctoral degree from Breslau University calling Brahms "the first among today's masters" provoked a venomous attack from Richard Wagner, who sneered, "Compose, compose, even if you don't have the slightest of ideas!" Music critics of the time pitted Brahms's fondness for traditional forms against Wagner's innovative music dramas.

(Bettmann Archive)

Brahms was a romantic who breathed new life into classical forms.

Actually, their musical paths hardly ever crossed; Brahms never ventured into opera, Wagner's special territory.

Brahms always lived frugally, even though he earned a good income from publishers and from playing and conducting his works. He hid a shy, sensitive nature behind a mask of sarcasm and rudeness. On leaving a party, he reportedly announced, "If there is anyone here I have not insulted, I apologize!" Yet this gruff bear could be extremely generous to talented young musicians. He helped Dvořák find a publisher, and the grateful Czech composer wrote: "I am so overcome by his kindness that I cannot help but love him! What a warm heart and great spirit there is in that man!"

When Brahms's beloved Clara Schumann lay dying in 1896, his grief found expression in the haunting *Four Serious Songs*, set to biblical texts. Not long after, it was discovered that he had cancer. On March 7, 1897, he dragged himself to hear a performance of his Fourth Symphony; the audience and orchestra gave him a tremendous ovation. Less than a month later, at the age of sixty-four, he died.

BRAHMS'S MUSIC

Brahms created masterpieces in all the traditional forms except opera. His varied output includes four symphonies, two concertos for piano and one for violin, short piano pieces, over two hundred songs, and some magnificent choral music, such as the *German Requiem* (1868; we'll study its fourth movement). Some of Brahms's finest music may be found in the two dozen chamber works written for many different instrumental combinations, including duo sonatas for cello and piano (Op. 38 and Op. 99), a trio for violin, horn, and piano (Op. 40), and a quintet for clarinet and strings (Op. 115).

Brahms's works, though very personal in style, are rooted deeply in the music of Haydn, Mozart, and Beethoven. They reinterpret classical forms while using the harmonic and instrumental resources of Brahms's own time. Brahms was the greatest master of theme-and-variations form since Beethoven. He wrote variations that sound completely different from their thematic source, while retaining the theme's basic structure. We'll study this aspect of Brahms's art as represented in the last movement of the Fourth Symphony.

Brahms's music embraces a range of moods, but particularly it has an autumnal or mellow feeling and a sense of lyrical warmth. Lyricism pervades even the rich polyphonic textures he was so fond of. One Brahms scholar has aptly observed, "It is possible to sing every Brahms movement from beginning to end as though it were a single, uninterrupted melody. Through all its polyphonic intricacies, the clear flow of invention always remains distinctly recognizable."

Among romantics, Brahms is outstanding in his ability to make intricate polyphonic texture sound natural and spontaneous. When he was in his twenties, he and a violinist friend gave each other difficult contrapuntal exercises to correct. "Why shouldn't we two serious and intelligent people," Brahms wrote, "be able to teach each other better than some professor could?"

All of Brahms's music is rhythmically exciting. Contrasting rhythmic patterns are set against one another; one instrument plays two even notes to the beat, while another plays three. The use of "2 against 3," as this rhythmic technique is called, is one of Brahms's trademarks. He also delights in all sorts of syncopations and in phrases of irregular length that push against the prevailing meter.

The quality of sound in Brahms's music is very special. He liked rich, dark tone colors. In his orchestral music, he usually blended the different instrumental choirs, favoring mellow instruments like the viola, clarinet, and French horn. (It's characteristic of Brahms's feeling for tradition that he preferred the old-fashioned hunting-type horn to the modern horn with valves.) The rich sound often results from his practice of doubling melodies in thirds and sixths; the same melody is duplicated at the interval of a third or sixth.

All of Brahms's music radiates the security and solidity of a complete master. He justified Schumann's prediction of greatness for the "young eagle."

SYMPHONY NO. 4 IN E MINOR, OP. 98

Brahms composed his Fourth Symphony during the summers of 1884 and 1885 in the tiny Austrian town of Mürzzuschlag. At its Vienna premiere in 1886, the Fourth Symphony bewildered the audience; some even hissed. Yet this work grew on the Viennese and was responsible for Brahms's greatest triumph in Vienna, less than a month before his death. At a concert of the Viennese Philharmonic Orchestra on March 7, 1897, tremendous applause broke out after every movement of the symphony. "Tears ran down his cheeks," a biographer of Brahms writes, "as he stood there, shrunken in form, with lined countenance, strained expression, white hair hanging lank, and through the audience there was a feeling as of a stifled sob, for each knew that he was saying farewell. Another outburst of applause and yet another; one more acknowledgment from the master; and Brahms and his Vienna had parted forever."

The Fourth Symphony combines strength and lyricism with the autumnal melancholy that is so typical of Brahms's music. The first movement, in sonata form, is dominated by its expansive opening theme. Listen for the magical moment when the first two phrases of the theme are presented in long notes to usher in the recapitulation. The slow second movement is based upon a pair of songlike themes that are stated and then recapitulated with imaginative changes in orchestration. The rapid third movement is a scherzo in sonata form.

Fourth Movement

The monumental fourth movement, marked *allegro energico e passionato (energetic and impassioned allegro)*, is the climax of the symphony. It is a type of theme and variations related to the baroque ground-bass form (also called **passacaglia**) that we've heard in Purcell's *Dido's Lament* and Bach's *Crucifixus*. Brahms's use of a baroque variation form is unique in the romantic symphonic literature and reflects his strong attachment to the musical past.

Side 11, band 2
CD 6 8

The movement, in E minor, consists of a theme, thirty variations, and an extended coda. Brasses and woodwinds introduce the theme, a solemn eight-note melody that steadily ascends by step before coming to a cadence.

Brahms borrowed the theme from Bach's Cantata No. 150, *Unto Thee, O Lord, I Lift Up My Soul,* but enhanced it harmonically and dramatically by inserting a new chromatic note into the original melody.

The variations embrace a wide range of moods: some are impassioned; others are lyrical or playful. Like the baroque masters he revered, Brahms focuses the listener's attention on the ever-changing melodic and rhythmic ideas rather than on the repeated theme. Some variations sound completely new, even though most tones of the theme are retained. Brahms's delight in disguising a theme was noted by his contemporaries. When he grew a beard one summer, a friend joked that Brahms's face was now as hard to recognize under the beard as the theme in his variations.

The variations are connected to each other and maintain the theme's 8-bar form and triple meter. In variations 1 to 3, the theme is heard in the top or middle part; but from variation 4 to variation 11, the theme is presented in the bass, with countermelodies above it. From variation 12 on, the theme appears either in the top, middle, or bass part.

The movement is composed of three large sections and a coda:

A	B	A'	Coda
Theme, variations 1–11	Variations 12–15	Variations 16–30	

The rapid A section, in minor, is mostly forceful and intense. The B section brings a more relaxed mood, a slower tempo, and a major key in three of its four variations. Section A′ returns to the quick tempo, minor key, and energetic mood of the opening section and is treated somewhat like a recapitulation. The opening variation of A′, variation 16, is very similar to the original theme, and variations 24 and 25 are based on variations 1 and 2. Sections A, B, and A′ all contain subgroups of variations that belong together because of similarities in melody, rhythm, texture, or orchestration. In the listening outline, these subgroups are indicated by brackets.

The impassioned coda begins with a climactic reappearance of the main theme in the woodwinds and brasses. Then Brahms abandons the strict succession of 8-bar units and treats the theme more freely, presenting it in accelerated transformations in the trombones, woodwinds, and full orchestra.

Listening Outline To be read while music is heard

SYMPHONY NO. 4 IN E MINOR (1885),
BY JOHANNES BRAHMS

Fourth Movement: Allegro energico e passionato

Theme and variations (ground-bass or passacaglia form), triple meter ($\frac{3}{4}$ and $\frac{3}{2}$), E minor

2 flutes, 2 oboes, 2 clarinets, 2 bassoons, contrabassoon, 4 French horns, 2 trumpets, 3 trombones, timpani, 1st violins, 2d violins, violas, cellos, double basses

(Duration, 10:18)

A

THEME
   8 0:00   Brasses and woodwinds, *f*, ascending theme, minor key.

VARIATION 1
   9 0:17   Timpani rolls and horns, *f*, answered by syncopated theme in pizzicato violins, decrescendo.

VARIATION 2
       0:32   Oboe, *mp*, legato melody, against theme in pizzicato cellos, *mp*, flutes join, crescendo.

VARIATION 3
       0:48   Woodwinds, *f*, staccato melody, brasses, *f*, timpani roll.

VARIATION 4

1:03   Violins, *f,* lyrical melody, against theme in cellos and basses.

VARIATION 5

1:20   Violins, varied lyrical melody, against theme in pizzicato basses.

VARIATION 6

1:32   Violins continue melody against legato theme in basses, melody rises, crescendo to

VARIATION 7

1:48   High violin melody, *f,* forceful dotted rhythm (short-long, short-long), melody descends.

VARIATION 8

2:03   Rushing notes in violins, *f,* against theme in bass, decrescendo.

VARIATION 9

2:18   Suddenly loud, faster rushing notes in strings, suddenly soft, woodwinds, descending chromatic scale.

VARIATION 10

2:35   Sustained chords, *p,* strings answered by woodwinds.

VARIATION 11

2:57   Violins, *p,* staccato phrases, flutes *pp,* descending chromatic scale.

B

VARIATION 12

10 3:17   Extended legato flute solo, slower tempo, strings accompany, *p,* melody descends, decrescendo.

VARIATION 13

4:01   Clarinet phrases, *p,* answered by oboe, low strings, *pp,* major key, flute, descending oboe phrase introduces

VARIATION 14

4:40   Trombones, *pp,* slow chords, strings accompany, descending horn phrase introduces

VARIATION 15

5:20   Oboe and brasses, *pp,* slow chords, strings accompany, descending flute phrase, ritardando, pause.

A′

VARIATION 16

11 6:05   Brasses and woodwinds, *ff,* original theme and tempo, minor key, high violins, *ff,* descending scale.

VARIATION 17

6:18   String tremolo, *p,* woodwinds, *mf.*

VARIATION 18

6:28   Horns and high woodwinds, *f,* ascending melody, crescendo.

VARIATION 19
  6:40   Violins, *f,* staccato phrases, answered by woodwinds, *f.*
VARIATION 20
  6:51   Violins and brasses, *f,* rapid staccato notes.
VARIATION 21
  7:03   Timpani rolls, upward rushes in violins, *ff,* answered by trombones, *ff.*
VARIATION 22
  7:16   Suddenly soft, woodwinds, staccato phrases, staccato strings, *pp.*
VARIATION 23
  7:27   Suddenly loud, horns, ascending theme.
VARIATION 24
  7:39   Timpani and brasses, *ff,* answered by high violins, *ff,* theme.
VARIATION 25
  7:52   High violin tremolo, *ff,* legato melody punctuated by repeated chords in orchestra, *ff.*
VARIATION 26
  8:05   Suddenly soft, melody in horns, *p,* oboes and violas continue, *p.*
VARIATION 27
  8:18   Woodwind sighs, *p,* accompanied by flowing phrases in strings.
VARIATION 28
  8:30   High woodwinds, lilting melody, strings accompany, *p.*
VARIATION 29
  8:42   Flute, *p,* rising phrases, pizzicato strings, violins, legato phrase.
VARIATION 30
  8:55   Suddenly loud, cellos and violins, downward phrase in imitation, crescendo timpani rolls, tempo slows.

CODA
  9:15   *a.* Brasses and woodwinds, *ff,* theme, faster tempo, woodwinds answered by brass chords.
  9:35   *b.* Trombones, *ff,* accelerated ascending theme, staccato, timpani rolls.

marcato

  9:43   *c.* Violins, *p,* crescendo.
  9:50   *d.* Woodwinds, *f,* accelerated ascending theme answered by orchestra, *ff.*
  9:57   *e.* Orchestra, *ff,* accelerated ascending theme, powerful ending chords.

EIN DEUTSCHES REQUIEM (A GERMAN REQUIEM; 1868)

A masterpiece of romantic choral music, the *German Requiem* established Brahms, at thirty-four, as a leading composer of his time. Scored for chorus, baritone and soprano soloists, and orchestra, it consists of seven movements and lasts more than an hour. Brahms entitled the work *Ein Deutsches Requiem—A German Requiem*—because he had chosen texts relating to death and resurrection from Luther's German translation of the Bible. He meant to distinguish his composition from the Latin requiem, or mass for the dead, which includes a vivid depiction of the last judgment (as in the *Dies irae* from Mozart's Requiem, studied in Section 11 of Part V).

Fourth Movement: *How Lovely Is Thy Dwelling Place*
Chorus and orchestra

Side 11, band 3
CD 6 12

Brahms sent the manuscript of this movement to his close friend Clara Schumann, who wrote back that "the chorus from the Requiem pleases me very much; I imagine it must sound beautiful." The predominantly lyrical music subtly reflects the text, which is from Psalm 84, verses 2, 3, and 5. For example, the word *lieblich (lovely)* is increasingly emphasized within the movement, and the excitement of *Meine Seele verlanget und sehnet (My soul longs and faints)* is expressed through quicker rhythms and polyphonic imitations.

Like the rest of the *German Requiem*, this movement shows Brahms's masterful vocal writing, gained from his wide experience as a choral conductor performing works by Bach and Handel. The rich variety of choral colors in the *German Requiem* is created by skillful alternation among homophonic, monophonic, and polyphonic textures. There is frequent interplay between chorus and orchestra. For example, the fourth movement opens with an introductory downward phrase in the high woodwinds, which is immediately inverted, or turned upside-down, to become the magical rising opening phrase with which the sopranos enter.

Soon after, a second idea in long notes is introduced by the violins and immediately imitated by the tenors.

12 0:00

Woodwinds, *p*,
downward phrase
introduces
sopranos, upward
phrase.

Wie lieblich sind deine Wohnungen Herr Zebaoth!

How lovely is thy dwelling place, O Lord of Hosts!

Woodwinds repeat
upward phrase.

0:27

deine Wohnungen Herr Zebaoth!

thy dwelling place O Lord of Hosts!

0:38

High violins, long-
note theme, imitated
by tenors, basses,
sopranos; *lieblich
(lovely)* emphasized.

Wie lieblich sind deine Wohnungen,

How lovely is thy dwelling place,

Herr Zebaoth!

O Lord of Hosts!

Wie lieblich sind deine Wohnungen, Herr Zebaoth!

How lovely is thy dwelling place, O Lord of Hosts!

1:13

Pizzicato strings
introduce chorus.

1:19

Imitation, basses,
tenors, altos,
sopranos; quicker
notes; crescendo
to *f*.

Meine Seele verlanget und sehnet sich

My soul longs and faints

P, homophonic,
pizzicato
accompaniment.

Oboe echo.

nach den Vorhöfen des Herrn.

for the courts of the Lord.

1:51

String accents.

Mein Leib und Seele freuen sich in dem lebendigen Gott.

My body and soul rejoice in the living God.

Mein Leib und Seele freuen sich in dem lebendigen Gott.

My body and soul rejoice in the living God.

388

		2:22
Wie lieblich sind deine Wohnungen, Herr Zebaoth!	How lovely is thy dwelling place O Lord of Hosts!	Violins, woodwinds, *p*, downward phrase introduces sopranos, *p*; upward phrase.
		Woodwinds, upward phrase.
deine Wohnungen, Herr Zebaoth!	is thy dwelling place O Lord of Hosts!	
		3:01 High violins, long-note theme.
Wohl denen,	Blessed are those	
Wohn denen, die in deinem Hause wohnen,	Blessed are those who dwell in thy house	3:15 Chorus, *p*, long-note theme, crescendo.
die loben dich immerdar,	who praise Thee evermore.	3:38 Extended fugal imitation, *f*; quicker rhythms, staccato strings.
immerdar.	evermore.	4:08 Sudden *p*, low, extended tones.
		4:14 Woodwinds, downward phrase.
Wie lieblich	How lovely	Sopranos, tenors imitated by altos, basses.
Wie lieblich sind deine Wohnungen!	How lovely is thy dwelling place!	Sopranos, *p*, rise to *f* peak and gently descend.
		Soft orchestral close.

BASIC TERM

passacaglia (page 383)

389

[**17**] GIUSEPPE VERDI

Giuseppe Verdi (1813–1901), the most popular of all opera composers, was born in a tiny Italian village. His father was a poor tavern keeper who could neither read nor write. At the age of ten, Verdi went to live in a nearby town, Busseto, to study music and go to school. Every Sunday for nine years, he walked three miles barefoot to serve as church organist in his own village, carrying his shoes to preserve them. A wealthy music patron took Verdi into his home and later supported his studies in Milan. After finishing his music education at twenty-two, Verdi returned to Busseto and became municipal music director. Thus assured of a regular income, he was able to marry his patron's daughter, a young woman he had known and loved since childhood.

But the small town couldn't fulfill Verdi's needs for long. After three years he returned to Milan with the score of his first opera, *Oberto* (1839). With the help of an influential friend, the young provincial's work was produced at La Scala, the most important opera house in Italy. Though the response to *Oberto* was only modest, it was enough to win Verdi a contract for three more operas. Just when Verdi's future seemed bright, however, disaster struck. While he was working on his next opera—a comedy—his wife fell ill and died. This tragedy completed the destruction of his family, since two infant children had died within the previous two years. Verdi managed to complete the opera, but it understandably lacked inspiration and was greeted by boos and hisses. In despair, he vowed to compose no more.

He changed his mind after reading a libretto about the ancient Jews exiled from their homeland. Verdi was an ardent nationalist who yearned to see the Italian people free from Austrian domination and unified into one nation. For him, the ancient Jews symbolized the enslaved Italians. He quickly composed *Nabucco* (*Nebuchadnezzar*, king of Babylon), which was an enormous success. One melody, *Oh, my country so beautiful and lost!* became a national liberation hymn sung by all Italian patriots. From that time on, Verdi and his operas symbolized a free and united Italy. A poet wrote that "the very soul of Italy . . . has today its voice in the name of Giuseppe Verdi." As Italy approached war with Austria, the cry *Viva Verdi* stood also for the patriotic slogan, *Vittorio Emmanuele, Re D'Italia* (*Victor Emmanuel, king of Italy*).

In his late thirties, Verdi composed *Rigoletto* (1851), *Il Trovatore* (1853), and *La Traviata* (1853), the first of his operas which are now universally known. Although the public loved these works, critics were often scandalized by their subject matter. *Rigoletto* seemed to condone rape and suicide, and *La Traviata* apparently glorified free love and made a heroine out of a

(Brown Brothers)

Guiseppe Verdi was one of the greatest opera composers and an ardent Italian nationalist.

kept woman. But Verdi was a fiercely independent man who himself lived openly with his second wife for ten years before marrying her.

After these successes had made him wealthy, Verdi bought an estate at Busseto. In 1861 he was elected deputy to the first Italian parliament to convene after Italy had become a nation. Verdi was Italy's most famous native son when he wrote *Aïda* (1871), an opera commissioned to commemorate the opening of the Suez Canal. In 1887, Verdi, then seventy-three, had a triumphant success with *Otello*, one of his greatest operas. Even this masterpiece did not still his creative urge. Remarkably, at the age of seventy-nine, Verdi completed *Falstaff* (1893), his only comedy since the failure of his second opera fifty years earlier.

VERDI'S MUSIC

"In the theater," Verdi once wrote, "lengthy is synonymous with boring, and of all styles the boring style is the worst." He composed not for the musical elite, but for a mass public whose main entertainment was opera. Verdi wanted subjects that were "original, interesting . . . and passionate; passions above all!" An aria "needs the greatest variety of mood; irony, contempt, rage, all thrown into sharp profile." Almost all of Verdi's mature works are serious and end unhappily. The operas move fast and involve characters who are plunged quickly into extremes of hatred, love, jealousy, and fear. His powerful music summons up heroes and villains and vividly underlines dramatic situations.

Expressive vocal melody is the soul of a Verdi opera. No matter how elaborate or atmospheric the orchestral part, the musical center lies in the voice. There are many duets, trios, and quartets, in which each character is given melodies superbly tailored to the emotions depicted. Choruses—of gypsies, Egyptian priests, conspirators, and monks, for example—play an important role in his operas.

In the course of his long life, Verdi's style became less conventional, more subtle and flexible. His later works have greater musical continuity. He used fewer pauses between sections and lessened the difference between aria and recitative. His orchestration became more imaginative and the accompaniments richer.

Verdi's last three operas are perhaps his greatest. *Aïda* is a true "grand opera" with spectacular pageants, ballets, and choruses. Yet for all its spectacle, there are many scenes of tender and intimate beauty. *Otello* and *Falstaff*, the operas of Verdi's old age, have marvelous librettos based on plays by Shakespeare. The librettist was Arrigo Boito, himself a gifted opera composer. For *Otello*, the seventy-three-year-old Verdi wrote sensuous, overpowering music that completely fuses with the poetry and action. The opera rivals Shakespeare's play in its dramatic force and lyricism. Verdi's last opera, *Falstaff*, is incomparably witty, imaginative, and sparkling. The aged composer ended this comic masterwork with a carefree fugue to the words *All the world's a joke!*

RIGOLETTO (1851)

Verdi dared to create an operatic hero out of a hunchbacked court jester named Rigoletto, whose only redeeming quality is an intense love for his daughter Gilda. Rigoletto's master, the licentious Duke of Mantua, has won Gilda's love while posing as a poor student. He seduces the innocent girl, causing Rigoletto to plot his death. Gilda loves the Duke even after learning about his dissolute character, and she ultimately sacrifices her own life to save his. Vice triumphs in this powerful drama.

Act III:

La donna è mobile and Quartet

Act III of *Rigoletto* contains two of the most popular pieces in opera, the Duke's aria *La donna è mobile* and the Quartet. The scene is a run-down inn where the Duke has come to meet Maddalena, the voluptuous sister of the cutthroat Sparafucile.

Side 11, band 4
CD 6 [13]

The carefree and tuneful *La donna è mobile (Woman is fickle)* perfectly expresses the Duke's pleasure-loving personality. Even before the premiere of *Rigoletto*, which was to take place in Venice, Verdi knew that *La donna è mobile* would be a hit. Afraid that his catchy tune would leak out during rehearsals and be sung by every Venetian gondolier, he waited until the last possible moment before giving the manuscript to the tenor who was to sing the aria.

The Quartet is sung as Rigoletto and Gilda peer through a crack in the wall of the inn, observing the Duke flirting with Maddalena. Verdi projects four conflicting emotions at one time, characterizing each singer with an appropriate melodic line. The Duke attempts to seduce Maddalena with a suave and ardent legato melody. Maddalena coquettishly repels his advances with quick, staccato laughs. Outside the inn, Gilda laments her fate with anguished sobs punctuated by rests, while Rigoletto curses and mutters threats of vengeance in repeated notes. Verdi lets us hear each of the four voices separately before combining them in a glorious ensemble.

[13] 0:00
Aria. Orchestra
introduces Duke's
melody.

Duke	
La donna è mobile	Woman is fickle
Qual piuma al vento,	Like a feather in the wind,
Muta d'accento	She changes her words
E di pensiero.	And her thoughts.

La don-na_è mo - bi-le   qual piu-ma_al ven - to,

mu - ta d'ac-cen - to   e di pen - sie - ro.

Sempre un amabile	Always a lovable
Leggiadro viso,	And lovely face,
In pianto o in riso,	Weeping or laughing,
È menzognero.	Is lying.
La donna è mobile, ecc.	Woman is fickle, etc.

1:05

Orchestra.

Duke's melody
repeated with
different words.

È sempre misero	The man's always wretched
Chi a lei s'affida,	Who believes in her,
Chi le confida	Who recklessly entrusts
Mal cauto il core!	His heart to her!
Pur mai non sentesi	And yet one who never
Felice appieno	Drinks love on that breast
Chi su quel seno	Never feels
Non liba amore!	Entirely happy!
La donna è mobile, ecc.	Woman is fickle, etc.

2:18

Duke's melody in
orchestra,
decrescendo.

(Sparafucile comes back in with a bottle of wine and two glasses, which he sets on the table; then he strikes the ceiling twice with the hilt of his long sword. At this signal, a laughing young girl, in a Gypsy dress, leaps down the stairs: the Duke runs to embrace her, but she escapes him. Meanwhile Sparafucile has gone out into the road, where he says softly to Rigoletto:)

Sparafucile

È là vostr'uomo . . .	Your man is there . . .
Viver dee o morire?	Must he live or die?

Rigoletto

Più tardi tornerò l'opra a compire.	I'll return later to complete the deed.

Brief pause.

(Sparafucile goes off behind the house toward the river. Gilda and Rigoletto remain in the street, the Duke and Maddalena on the ground floor.)

14 3:00

Allegro.

Duke

Un dì, se ben rammentomi,	One day, if I remember right,
O bella, t'incontrai . . .	I met you, O beauty . . .
Mi piacque di te chiedere,	I was pleased to ask about you,
E intesi che qui stai.	And I learned that you live here.
Or sappi, che d'allora	Know then, that since that time
Sol te quest'alma adora!	My soul adores only you!

| | **Gilda** | |
| *Iniquo!* | Villain! | |

	Maddalena	
Ah, ah! . . . e vent'altre appresso	Ha, ha! . . . And does it now perhaps	
Le scorda forse adesso?	Forget twenty others?	
Ha un'aria il signorino	The young gentleman looks like	
Da vero libertino . . .	A true libertine . . .	

	Duke	
	(starting to embrace her)	
Si . . . un mostro son . . .	Yes . . . I'm a monster . . .	

| | **Gilda** | |
| *Ah padre mio!* | Ah, Father! | |

| | **Maddalena** | |
| *Lasciatemi, stordito.* | Let me go, foolish man! | |

| | **Duke** | |
| *Ih, che fracasso!* | Ah, what a fuss! | |

| | **Maddalena** | |
| *Stia saggio.* | Be good. | |

	Duke	
E tu sii docile,	And you, be yielding,	
Non fare tanto chiasso.	Don't make so much noise.	
Ogni saggezza chiudesi	All wisdom concludes	Rhythm slows.
Nel gaudio e nell'amore.	In pleasure and in love.	

| | (He takes her hand.) | |
| *La bella mano candida!* | What a lovely, white hand! | Quick rhythm resumes. |

| | **Maddalena** | |
| *Scherzate voi, signore.* | You're joking, sir | |

| | **Duke** | |
| *No, no.* | No, no. | |

| | **Maddalena** | |
| *Son brutta.* | I'm ugly. | |

| | **Duke** | |
| *Abbracciami.* | Embrace me. | |

| | **Gilda** | |
| *Iniquo!* | Villain! | |

Maddalena

Ebro!   You're drunk!

Duke

D'amor ardente!   With ardent love!

Maddalena

Signor l'indifferente,   My indifferent sir,
Vi piace canzonar?   Do you enjoy teasing?

Duke

No, no, ti vo'sposar.   No, no, I want to marry you.

Maddalena

Ne voglio la parola.   I want your word.

Duke
                           (ironic)
Amabile figliuola!   Lovable maiden!

Rigoletto
                           (to Gilda, who has seen and heard all)
E non ti basta ancor?   Isn't that enough for you yet?

Gilda

Characters sing   *Iniquo traditor!*   Villainous betrayer!
simultaneously.

Maddalena

Ne voglio la parola.   I want your word.

Duke

Amabile figliuola!   Lovable maiden!

Rigoletto

E non ti basta ancor?   Isn't that enough for you yet?

Short pause.

15 4:33   **Duke**
Quartet, andante.
Bella figlia dell'amore,   Beautiful daughter of love,
Schiavo son de' vezzi tuoi;   I am the slave of your charms;
Con un detto sol tu puoi   With a single word you can
Le mie pene consolar.   Console my sufferings.

Duke

Bel - la fi - glia del - l'a - mo — re,   schia - vo son de' vez - zi tuo - i; con un det-to, un det - to sol tu

puo - i le mie pe - ne le mie pe - ne con - so - lar.

Vieni, e senti del mio core	Come, and feel the quick beating
Il frequente palpitar . . .	Of my heart . . .
Con un detto sol tu puoi	With a single word you can
Le mie pene consolar.	Console my sufferings.

Maddalena

Ah! ah! rido ben di core,	Ha! Ha! I laugh heartily,
Chè tai baie costan poco.	For such tales cost little.

Maddalena

Ah! ah! ri - do ben di co - re, chè tai ba - ie cos-tan po - co;

Gilda

Ah! così parlar d'amore . . .	Ah! To speak thus of love . . .

Gilda

Ah!_____ co - si___ par-lar___ d'a - mo - re!

Maddalena

Quanto valga il vostro gioco,	Believe me, I can judge
Mel credete, so apprezzar.	How much your game is worth.

Gilda

. . . a me pur l'infame ho udito!	. . . I too have heard the villain so!

Rigoletto
(to Gilda)

Taci, il piangere non vale.	Hush, weeping is of no avail.

Rigoletto

Ta - ci, il pian-ge - re non va - le;

	Gilda
Infelice cor tradito,	Unhappy, betrayed heart.
Per angoscia non scoppiar. Ah, no!	Do not burst with anguish. Ah, no!
	Maddalena
Son avvezza, bel signore,	I'm accustomed, handsome sir,
Ad un simile scherzare.	To similar joking.
Mio bel signor!	My handsome sir!
	Duke
Bella figlia dell'amore, ecc.	Beautiful daughter of love, etc.
Vieni!	Come!
	Rigoletto
Ch'ei mentiva sei sicura.	You are sure that he was lying.
Taci, e mia sarà la cura	Hush, and I will take care
La vendetta d'affrettar.	To hasten vengeance.
Sì, pronto fia, sarà fatale,	Yes, it will be swift and fatal,
Io saprollo fulminar.	I will know how to strike him down.
Taci taci . . .	Hush, hush . . .

[ROMANTIC **18**] GIACOMO PUCCINI

Some of the best-loved operas were created by Giacomo Puccini (1858–1924), who succeeded Verdi as the most important Italian opera composer of his time. Puccini came from a long line of composers and church organists. During his student years at the Milan Conservatory (1880–1883), he lived a hand-to-mouth existence, usually eating on credit at a restaurant fittingly named *Aïda*. The success of Puccini's first opera, written shortly after his graduation, brought him to the attention of Italy's leading music publisher, who commissioned new works and gave him an annual income.

In 1893 Puccini became well known throughout Italy for his opera *Manon Lescaut;* and after 1896, he was wealthy and world-famous from the enormous success of *La Bohème*, which portrays a "bohemian" life similar to Puccini's as an impoverished music student. *La Bohème,* along with two other very popular operas, *Tosca* (1900) and *Madame Butterfly* (1904), was written in collaboration with the librettists Luigi Illica and Giuseppe Giacosa. Puccini was very much concerned with the literary and dramatic qualities of his librettos, often demanding endless changes from his collaborators. He spent as much time polishing the librettos as he did composing the music. His last opera, *Turandot,* was based on a Chinese fairy tale. He died before finishing it; the work was completed from Puccini's sketches by a friend, Franco Alfano.

Puccini's marvelous sense of theater has given his operas lasting appeal. He knew just when to introduce new musical material or a moment of silence, and he was able to provide smooth transitions from one scene or mood to another. His melodies have short, easily remembered phrases and are intensely emotional. He used the orchestra to reinforce the vocal melody and to suggest atmosphere, landscape, and mood. As Verdi did in his late works, Puccini minimized the difference between aria and recitative, thus creating a continuous flow of music. He achieved unity and continuity also by using the same material in different acts, particularly at moments when his characters reflect on past events or emotions.

Some of Puccini's operas—notably *Tosca*—reflect an artistic trend of the 1890s known as *verismo, realism,* or the quality of being "true to life." Operas coming out of this realistic movement deal with ordinary people rather than kings, gods, or great heroes and often contain many shockingly violent scenes set to music of raw emotional power. *Cavalleria rusticana (Rustic Chivalry,* 1890), by Pietro Mascagni, and *I Pagliacci (The Clowns,* 1892), by Ruggiero Leoncavallo, are other famous examples of *verismo.* Puccini's operas also feature exoticism. Not only is *Madame Butterfly* set in Japan and *Turandot* in China, but Puccini used melodic and rhythmic elements in these operas derived from Japanese and Chinese music. His melodies cast a romantic glow over any subject matter, whether realistic or exotic.

LA BOHÈME (1896)

La Bohème (Bohemian Life) takes place in the Latin Quarter of Paris around 1830. Its hero is Rodolfo, a young poet who shares a garret with Marcello, a painter; Colline, a philosopher; and Schaunard, a musician. Mimi, the heroine, is a poor, tubercular seamstress who lives in the same building. The simple, touching plot has been aptly summarized as "boy meets girl, boy loses girl, boy and girl are reunited as girl dies of consumption in boy's arms and curtain falls." Everyone can relate to the characters and emotions of this enchanting opera. Though there are many realistic touches in this picture of bohemian life, it is seen through a romantic haze.

Act I:
Scene between Rodolfo and Mimi
Toward the end of Act I, Mimi and Rodolfo meet and fall in love. Her candle has blown out, and she knocks on his door asking for a light. After a short musical conversation, Mimi realizes she has lost her key, and they both search for it in the dark. When their hands touch, Rodolfo sings the aria *Che gelida manina (What a cold little hand).* He sings about himself, his dreams and his fantasies. Mimi responds with a poetic description of her simple life in the aria *Mi chiamano Mimi (They call me Mimi).* Under the spell of their new-found love, they join in a duet which closes the act.

Side 12, band 1
CD 6 [16]

Ilona Tokodny as Mimi and Dennis O'Neill as Rodolfo in a performance of *La Bohème* at the San Diego Opera.

Puccini's sensuous melody casts a glow over the entire scene. His music has an improvisatory quality that is due to the many fluctuations of tempo. When Mimi enters, the orchestra murmurs a touching phrase, Mimi's theme, which suggests her fragility and tenderness. Each of the two arias begins simply, almost in conversation. Then the melody grows warmer until it reaches a climax in a broad, passionate phrase. The climactic phrase of Rodolfo's aria, sung to the words *Talor dal mio forziere (My hoard of treasure is robbed by two thieves: a pair of beautiful eyes)*, is the love theme of the whole opera. Mimi's emotional high point is reached when she dreams about the end of winter *(ma quando vien la sgelo)*, when "the first kiss of April" is hers. Returning to reality at the end of her aria, she sings in conversational repeated tones. The tension breaks momentarily as Rodolfo goes to the window and has a brief exchange with his friends in the court-yard—an example of Puccini's great theatrical timing, for he provides a moment of relaxation before the lovers join in the closing duet. First, Rodolfo sings alone, then both voices beautifully unite in a declaration of love.

(Rodolfo closes the door, sets his light on the table, and tries to write. But he tears up the paper and throws the pen down.)

16 0:00 Flute melody.

Rudolfo

Non sono in vena.   I'm not in the mood.

(A timid knock at the door.)

Chi è la?   Who's there?   Speechlike.

Mimi

Scusi.   Excuse me . . .

Rudolfo

Una donna!   A woman!

Mimi

Di grazia, mi si è spento   I'm sorry . . . my light   Mimi's theme, *pp*,
in orchestra.

Il lume.   Has gone out.

Rudolfo

Ecco.   (opens) Here.

Mimi
(in the doorway, with a candlestick and a key)

Vorrebbe . . .?   Would you . . .?

Rudolfo

S'accomodi un momento.   Come in for a moment.

Mimi

Non occorre.   There's no need.

Rudolfo

La prego, entri.   Please . . . come in.

(Mimi enters, has a fit of coughing.)

Rudolfo

Si sente male?   You're not well?

Mimi

No . . . nulla.   No . . . it's nothing.

Rudolfo

Impallidisce!   You're pale!   401

Mimi

È il respir . . . quelle scale . . .   I'm out of breath . . . the stairs . . .

1:04
Oboe.

(She faints, and Rodolfo is just in time to support her and help her to a chair. The key and the candlestick fall from her hands.)

Rudolfo

Ed ora come faccio?   Now what shall I do?

(He gets some water and sprinkles her face.)
Così.   So.
Che viso d'ammalata!   How ill she looks!

1:28
Staccato muted
strings.

(Mimi comes to.)

Si sente meglio?   Are you better now?

Mimi

Sì.   Yes.

Rudolfo

Qui c'è tanto freddo.   It's so cold here.
Segga vicino al fuoco.   Come and sit by the fire.

(He helps her to a chair by the stove.)
Aspetti . . . un po' di vino.   Wait . . . some wine.

Mimi

Grazie.   Thank you.

Rudolfo

A lei.   Here.

Mimi

Poco, poco.   Just a little.

Rudolfo

Così.   There.

Mimi

Grazie.   Thank you.

Rudolfo

402   *Che bella bambina!*   What a lovely creature!

Mimi	
Ora permetta	Now, please,
Che accenda il lume.	Relight my candle.
È tutto passato.	I'm better now.

Rudolfo

Tanta fretta.   Such a hurry.

Mimi

Sì.   Yes.

(Rodolfo lights her candle for her.)

Mimi

Grazie. Buona sera.   Thank you. Good evening.

Rudolfo

Buona sera.   Good evening.

(Mimi goes out, then reappears at the door.)

Mimi

		2:28
Oh! sventata, sventata,	Oh! foolish me! . . .	A little faster.
La chiave della stanza	Where have I left	Tuneful vocal
Dove l'ho lasciata?	The key to my room?	melody.

Rudolfo

Non stia sull'uscio: Don't stand in the door:
Il lume vacilla al vento.   The wind makes your light flicker.

(Her candle goes out.)

Mimi

Oh Dio! Torni ad accenderlo.   Heavens! Will you relight it?

(Rodolfo rushes to her with his light, but when he reaches the door, his candle goes out, too. The room is dark.)

Rudolfo

Oh Dio! Anche il mio s'è spento.   There . . . Now mine's out, too.

Mimi

Ah! E la chiave ove sarà?   Ah! And where can my key be?

Rudolfo

Buio pesto!   Pitch dark!

Disgraziata!

Mimi
Unlucky me!

Ove sarà?

Rudolfo
Where can it be?

Importuna è la vicina . . .

Mimi
You've a bothersome neighbor . . .

Ma le pare!

Rudolfo
Not at all.

Importuna è la vicina . . .

Mimi
You've a bothersome neighbor . . .

Cosa dice, ma le pare!

Rudolfo
What do you mean? Not at all.

Cerchi.

Mimi
Search.

Cerco.

Rudolfo
I'm searching.

(They both grope on the floor for the key.)

Ove sarà?

Mimi
Where can it be?

Ah!

Rudolfo
Ah! (finds the key, pockets it)

L'ha trovata?

Mimi
Did you find it?

No.

Rudolfo
No.

Mi parve . . .

Mimi
I thought . . .

In verità!

Rudolfo
Truthfully!

Cerca?

Mimi
Are you hunting?

Rudolfo

Cerco.	I'm hunting for it.	

(Guided by her voice, Rodolfo pretends to search as he draws closer to her. Then his hand meets hers, and he holds it.)

3:50
Orchestra alone,
tempo slows.

Mimi

Ah!	(Surprised) Ah!

(They rise. Rodolfo continues to hold Mimi's hand.)

Rudolfo

17 4:14
Rodolfo's aria.

Che gelida manina,	What a cold little hand,
Se la lasci riscaldar.	Let me warm it.

pp Che ge - li - da ma - ni - na, se la la - sci ri - scal - dar.

Cercar che giova? Al buio	What's the use of searching?	
Non si trova. Ma per fortuna	We'll never find it now.	Harp.
È una notte di luna,	But luckily there's a moon,	
E qui la luna l'abbiamo vicina.	And she's our neighbor here.	
Aspetti, signorina,	Just wait, my dear young lady,	
Le dirò con due parole chi son,	And meanwhile I'll tell you	
Chi son, e che faccio, come vivo.	In a word who and what I am.	
Vuole?	Shall I?	

(Mimi is silent.)

Chi son? Chi son? Son un poeta.	Who am I? I'm a poet.
Che cosa faccio? Scrivo.	My business? Writing.
E come vivo? Vivo.	How do I live? I live.
In povertà mia lieta	In my happy poverty
Scialo da gran signore	I squander like a prince
Rima ed inni d'amore.	My poems and songs of love.
Per sogni e per chimere	In hopes and dreams
E per castelli in aria	And castles in air,
L'anima ho milionaria.	I'm a millionaire in spirit.
Talor dal mio forziere	My hoard of treasure

6:42
Love theme.

Ruban tutti i gioielli	Is robbed by two thieves:
Due ladri: gli occhi belli.	A pair of beautiful eyes.

Ta - lor dal mio for - zie - re_____ ru - ban tut - ti i gio-

iel - li due la - dri: gli oc - chi bel - li.

Ventrar con voi pur ora	They came in now with you
Ed i miei sogni usati,	And all my lovely dreams,
Ed i bei sogni miei	My dreams of the past,
Tosto si dileguar!	Were soon stolen away.
Ma il furto non m'accora	But the theft doesn't upset me,
Poichè, poichè v'ha preso stanza	Since the empty place was filled
La speranza.	With hope.
Or che mi conoscete	Now that you know me,
Parlate voi. Deh parlate.	It's your turn to speak.
Chi siete? Vi piaccia dir?	Tell me, please, who are you?

18 8:49

Mimi's aria.

Mimi

Sì.	Yes.
Mi chiamano Mimí,	They call me Mimi,
Ma il mio nome è Lucia.	But my real name is Lucia.

Andante lento

Mi chia - ma - no Mi - mì, ma il mio no - me è Lu - ci - a_____

La storia mia è breve.	My story is brief.
A tela o a seta	I embroider silk and satin
Ricamo in casa e fuori.	At home or outside.
Son tranquilla e lieta,	I'm tranquil and happy,
Ed è mio svago	And my pastime
Far gigli e rose.	Is making lilies and roses.
Mi piaccion quelle cose	I love all things
Che han si dolce malia,	That have a gentle magic,
Che parlano d'amor, di primavere,	That talk of love, of spring,
Che parlano di sogni e di chimere,	That talk of dreams and fancies—
Quelle cose che han nome poesia . . .	The things called poetry . . .
Lei m'intende?	Do you understand me?

Rudolfo

Sì.	Yes.

Mi chiamano Mimí.	They call me Mimi—	10:49
Il perchè non so.	I don't know why.	
Sola, mi fo il pranzo	I live all by myself	
Da me stessa.	And I eat all alone.	
Non vado sempre a messa,	I don't often go to church,	
Ma prego assai il Signor.	But I like to pray.	
Vivo sola, soletta,	I stay all alone	
Là in una bianca cameretta;	In my tiny white room,	
Guardo sui tetti e in cielo.	I look at the roofs and the sky.	
Ma quando vien lo sgelo	But when the thaw comes	
Il primo sole è mio,	The first sunshine is mine,	
Il primo bacio	The first kiss	
Dell'aprile è mio!	Of April is mine!	
Il primo sole è mio!	The first sunshine is mine!	
Germoglia in un vaso una rosa.	A rose blossoms in my vase,	
Foglia a foglia l'aspiro.	I breathe in its perfume,	
Così gentil è il profumo d'un fior.	Petal by petal. So lovely,	
Ma i fior ch'io faccio, ahimè,	So sweet is the flower's perfume.	
I fior ch'io faccio,	But the flowers I make,	
Ahimè non hanno odore.	Alas, have no scent.	
Altro di me non le saprei narrare.	What else can I say?	
Sono la sua vicina	I'm your neighbor,	
Che la vien fuori d'ora a importunare.	Disturbing you at this impossible hour.	

Schaunard
(from below)

Eh! Rodolfo!	Hey! Rodolfo!

19 14:03

Colline

Rodolfo!	Rodolfo!

Marcello

Olà! Non senti?	Hey! Can't you hear?
Lumaca!	You snail!

Colline

Poetucolo!	You fake!

Schaunard

Accidenti al pigro!	To hell with that lazy one!

(Rodolfo, impatient, goes to the window to answer. When the window is opened, the moonlight comes in, lighting up the room.)

Rudolfo

Scrivo ancora tre righe a volo.	I've a few more words to write.

407

Mimi

Chi son?   Who are they?

Rudolfo

Amici.   Friends.

Schaunard

Sentirai le tue.   You'll hear about this.

Marcello

Che te ne fai lì solo?   What are you doing there alone?

Rudolfo

Non son solo. Siamo in due.   I'm not alone. There's two of us.
Andate da Momus, tenete il posto. Go to Momus and get a table.
Ci saremo tosto.   We'll be there soon.

Marcello, Schaunard, Colline

Momus, Momus, Momus,   Momus, Momus, Momus.
Zitti e discreti audiamocene via. Quietly, discreetly, we're off.
Momus, Momus, Momus.   Momus, Momus, Momus.
Trovò poesia.   He's found his poem at last.

(Turning, Rodolfo sees Mimi wrapped in a halo of moonlight. He contemplates her, in ecstasy.)

14:48

Duet.

Rudolfo

O soave fanciulla, o dolce viso   Oh! lovely girl, oh! sweet face
Di mite circonfuso alba lunar,   Bathed in the soft moonlight.
In te, ravviso il sogno   I see in you the dream
Ch'io vorrei sempre sognar!   I'd dream forever!

Voices unite, love
theme.

Fremon già nell'anima   Already I taste in spirit
Le dolcezze estreme,   The heights of tenderness!
Amor nel bacio freme!   Love trembles in our kiss!

Mimi

Ah, tu sol comandi, amore. . . . Ah! Love, you rule alone. . . .
Oh! come dolci scendono   How sweet his praises
Le sue lusinghe al core. . . .   Enter my heart. . . .
Tu sol comandi, amore!   Love, you alone rule!

(Rodolfo kisses her.)

Mimi

No, per pietà!   No, please!

Rudolfo

Sei mia!   You're mine!

	Mimi
V'aspettan gli amici. . . .	Your friends are waiting.

	Rudolfo
Già mi mandi via?	You send me away already?

	Mimi
Vorrei dir . . . ma non oso.	I daren't say what I'd like . . .

	Rudolfo
Di'.	Tell me.

	Mimi
Se venissi con voi?	If I came with you?

	Rudolfo
Che? Mimí!	What? Mimí!
Sarebbe così dolce restar qui.	It would be so fine to stay here.
C'è freddo fuori.	Outside it's cold.

	Mimi
Vi starò vicina!	I'd be near you!

	Rudolfo
E al ritorno?	And when we come back?

	Mimi
Curioso!	Who knows?

	Rudolfo	
Dammi il braccio, o mia piccina . . .	Give me your arm, my dear . . .	Melody from Rodolfo's aria.

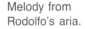

	Mimi
Obbedisco, signor!	Your servant, sir . . .

	Rudolfo
Che m'ami . . . di' . . .	Tell me you love me!

	Mimi
Io t'amo.	I love you.

	Rudolfo
Amor!	My love!

	Mimi
Amor!	My love!

	Rodolfo and Mimi
Amor!	Beloved!

[19] RICHARD WAGNER

Few composers have had so powerful an impact on their time as Richard Wagner (1813–1883). During the last decades of the nineteenth century, his operas and artistic philosophy influenced not only musicians, but also poets, painters, and playwrights. Such was his preeminence that an opera house of his own design was built in Bayreuth, Germany, solely for performances of his music dramas.

Wagner was born in Leipzig and grew up in a theatrical atmosphere. Both his stepfather and two of his sisters were actors, and another sister was an opera singer. His boyhood dream was to be a poet and playwright. But at fifteen he was overwhelmed by the power of Beethoven's music, and he decided to become a composer. The young Wagner taught himself by studying scores. He never tried to master an instrument, though he did have almost three years of formal training in music theory.

When he was seventeen, Wagner enrolled in Leipzig University, where he was more interested in riotous student club life than in academic studies. His family thought him good for nothing because of his dueling, drinking, and gambling. The pattern continued throughout his life; Wagner shamelessly lived off other people and accumulated enormous debts that he never repaid.

During his early twenties, Wagner conducted in small German theaters, wrote several operas, and married Minna Planer, a beautiful and well-known actress. In 1839 he decided to try his luck in Paris, then the center of grand opera. Unpaid debts prevented his getting a passport, and so he and Minna crossed the frontier illegally. Their two years in Paris were miserable. Unable to get an opera performed, Wagner was reduced to musical hackwork. He ran up so many bills that he was briefly confined to a debtors' prison.

Wagner returned to Germany in 1842 to supervise the production of his opera *Rienzi* at the Dresden opera. The work was immensely successful, and Wagner was appointed conductor of the Dresden opera; the job paid a good salary and was to have been a lifetime position. He spent six years there, becoming famous both as an opera composer and as a great conductor. Wagner demanded that his orchestra play with enormous dynamic subtlety and rhythmic freedom. "When he conducts," a musician observed, "he is almost beside himself with excitement. . . . Every sinew in his body speaks. His whole appearance is of arrogance and despotism personified."

The revolutions of 1848 swept across Europe like a forest fire and marked an important turning point in Wagner's career. His life in Dresden had become increasingly difficult because of debts he had again accumulated

(Bettmann Archive)

Richard Wagner's operas and artistic philosophy had a powerful impact on musicians, poets, painters, and playwrights.

(he owed more than ten times his annual salary). Hoping that a new society would wipe out his debts and produce conditions favorable to his art, Wagner participated in the Dresden insurrection. He ordered hand grenades and tried to incite disobedience among the king's soldiers. When a warrant was issued for his arrest, Wagner fled to Switzerland.

For several years Wagner did no composing; instead he worked out theories of art in essays such as *Art and Revolution* (1849), *The Art Work of the Future* (1850), and *Opera and Drama* (1851). More important, he completed the librettos to *Der Ring des Nibelungen (The Ring of the Nibelung)*, a set of four operas based on Nordic mythology. The *Ring* was to occupy Wagner for a quarter of a century. He began the text in 1848 and finished the music in 1874. Wagner's amazing self-confidence and belief in his greatness enabled him to compose one gigantic opera after another, with no prospect for performance. He composed the first opera of the *Ring* cycle, *Das Rheingold* (*The Rhine Gold*, 1853–1854); the second, *Die Walküre* (*The Valkyrie*, 1854–1856); and the first two acts of the third, *Siegfried* (1856–1857)—and then he interrupted his work to compose *Tristan and Isolde* (1857–1859), which he hoped would have a better chance for performance. In this opera, sexual passion is presented musically with unprecedented power and vividness.

Wagner had several bad years after finishing *Tristan*. His opera *Tannhäuser* was a failure in a revival at the Paris Opera in 1861, and *Tristan* was abandoned by the Vienna Opera after many rehearsals. Creditors pounded on his door, demanding payment for the silks, satins, laces, and perfumes he "needed" as part of his lifestyle.

In 1864 Wagner was rescued from his desperate situation by King Ludwig of Bavaria, an eighteen-year-old fanatical Wagnerite who was determined to help Wagner produce his operas and complete the *Ring*. All the resources of the Munich Opera were put at Wagner's disposal. *Tristan* and *Die Meistersinger von Nürnberg* (*The Mastersingers of Nuremberg*, 1862–1867) were lavishly produced in Munich. Wagner completed *Siegfried* (1869–1870) and composed the final opera of the *Ring*, *Götterdämerung* (*The Twilight of the Gods*, 1869–1874).

During this period, Wagner fell in love with Cosima von Bülow. She was Liszt's daughter and the wife of Hans von Bülow, Wagner's close friend and favorite conductor. Cosima gave birth to two of Wagner's children while still married to Von Bülow. Shortly after Wagner's first wife died, he married Cosima.

In Richard Wagner, towering musical genius was allied with utter selfishness, ruthlessness, and an absolute conviction about his place in history. He was a rabid German nationalist; he wrote in his diary, "I am the most German of beings. I am the German spirit." He bent people to his will. Indeed, he forged an audience for his complex music dramas from a public accustomed to conventional opera.

Wagner designed a theater to suit performances of the *Ring*. With the help of King Ludwig and contributions from Wagner clubs which had been formed all over Germany, Wagner's festival theater was constructed in Bayreuth, a small Bavarian town. The premiere of the *Ring* cycle in 1876 was perhaps the single most important musical event of the century. Sixty newspaper correspondents from all over the world attended, including two from the United States. Though some critics still found his music too dissonant, heavily orchestrated, and long-winded, Wagner was generally acclaimed the greatest composer of his time. A year after completing *Parsifal* (1877–1882), his last opera, Wagner visited Venice, where he died at the age of sixty-nine.

WAGNER'S MUSIC

For Wagner, an opera house was a temple in which the spectator was to be overwhelmed by music and drama. He wrote his own librettos, which he based on medieval Germanic legends and myths. His characters are usually larger than life—heroes, gods, demigods.

Wagner called his works *music dramas* rather than operas, to emphasize the close relationship in them between music and drama. He envisioned music drama as a "universal art work" (*Gesamtkunstwerk* in German) in which all the arts—music, drama, dance, painting—are fused. Today, however, many people find Wagner's music more exciting than his rather static drama. For long stretches of time his characters exult, lament, or relate what has happened to them.

Within each act, there is a continuous musical flow, which Wagner described as "unending melody." The music is not broken into traditional arias, recitatives, and duets. He achieves musical and dramatic continuity by smoothly connecting each section to the next. There are no breaks where applause can disturb the listener's concentration. Wagner conceived his vocal line as a "speech song" combining the speechlike quality of a recitative with the lyricism of an aria. The vocal line is inspired by rhythms and pitch fluctuations in the German text.

Wagner revolutionized opera by shifting the musical center of gravity from the voice toward the orchestra. His expanded and colorful orchestration brilliantly expresses the drama and reveals characters' thoughts and feelings. He treats the orchestra symphonically, constantly developing, transforming, and intertwining musical ideas. Many long orchestral interludes graphically depict scenic effects such as floods, sunrises, and flames.

Wagner loved to exploit the rich power of the brasses. The *Ring* calls for eight horns and four new brass instruments (called *Wagner tubas*) that he designed. The orchestral sound is so full that only singers with unusually powerful voices, such as a "Wagnerian soprano" or a "heroic tenor," can cut through it.

Wagner spins an orchestral web out of recurrent musical ideas called *leitmotifs,* or *leading motives.* A **leitmotif** is a short musical idea associated with a person, object, or thought in the drama. When the text refers to Siegfried, for example, his leitmotif is usually heard in the orchestra. These motives are sometimes in the vocal parts, too. They are varied and transformed to convey the evolving dramatic situation and changes of character. When Siegfried is murdered, his leitmotif is set against strident dissonant harmonies. As Wagner develops his leitmotifs, he sets one against another to suggest the clash of two persons or ideas. The leitmotifs unify Wagner's greatly extended music dramas.

The emotional tension of Wagner's music is heightened by chromatic and dissonant harmonies. He creates motion and color through rapid shifts from one key to another and through many chromatic chords in each key.

The listener often expects a resolution to a stable chord, only to hear yet another dissonance. Wagner's chromatic harmony ultimately led to the breakdown of tonality and to the new musical language of the twentieth century.

DIE WALKÜRE (THE VALKYRIE; 1856)

Die Walküre (The Valkyrie) is the second and most widely performed of the four music dramas in Wagner's gigantic cycle *Der Ring des Nibelungen (The Ring of the Nibelung)*. Despite its gods, giants, dwarfs, and magic fire, the *Ring* is really about Wagner's view of nineteenth-century society. He uses Nordic mythology to warn that society destroys itself through lust for money and power. It is fitting that Wagner first sketched the plot of the *Ring* in 1848, the year that brought Marx's *Communist Manifesto* and revolutions throughout Europe.

Act I:

Love scene (conclusion)

Side 12, band 2
CD 6 [20]

Wagner builds the first act of *Die Walküre* to an overwhelming climax in the passionate love scene which concludes it. To grasp this scene fully, it's helpful to know what has happened earlier in *The Ring*.

A Nibelung dwarf, Alberich, has stolen gold belonging to the Rhinemaidens, mermaids in the Rhine River. From this gold, the dwarf fashions a ring that can bestow immense power on anyone who wears it and is willing to renounce love. The dwarf, in turn, is robbed of his prize by Wotan, king of the gods. (*Wednesday* comes from *Wotan's day*.) Soon Wotan himself is forced to give up the ring; he then lives in fear that Alberich will get it back amd use it to destroy him. Hoping to protect himself, he surrounds his castle, Valhalla, with a bodyguard of heroes. His daughters, goddesses called *Valkyries*, swoop over battlefields on horseback and bear away the dead bodies of the bravest warriors. The Valkyrie of the opera's title is Brünnhilde, Wotan's favorite daughter.

Seeking to create a hero who can help him regain the ring, Wotan takes a human wife and fathers the Volsung twins—a son, Siegmund; and a daughter, Sieglinde. The twins know their father as Wälse, unaware that he is the god Wotan. They are separated as children when a hostile clan kidnaps Sieglinde and kills their mother. Siegmund becomes an outlaw and Sieglinde is eventually forced to marry the warrior-chief Hunding, whom she hates. During the wedding feast in Hunding's home, Wotan appears, disguised as an old man dressed in gray. He thrusts a magic sword into the tree around which the house is built, and proclaims that the weapon belongs to the one can draw it out. Hunding and his followers try but are unable to withdraw the sword.

The first act of *Die Walküre* begins as Siegmund, weaponless and pursued by enemies, unwittingly takes refuge in the house of Hunding, who is away hunting. Sieglinde and Siegmund almost immediately fall in love, unaware that they are brother and sister. Hunding returns and soon realizes that the stranger—who identifies himself as *Wehwalt (Woeful)*—is an enemy of his clan. He says that Siegmund is his guest for the night, but the next day they must do battle. Sieglinde gives her husband a sleeping potion and tells Siegmund that her shame and misery will be avenged by the hero who can withdraw the sword from the tree. As they embrace passionately, the door of the hut suddenly opens, allowing the moonlight of a beautiful spring night to shine upon them.

The following excerpt occurs at the end of the love scene, when Siegmund and Sieglinde gradually become aware of their amazing resemblance to each other and finally realize that they are brother and sister. Since her beloved no longer wants to be called *Wehwalt*, Sieglinde renames him *Siegmund (Victor)*. With a powerful effort, Siegmund withdraws the sword from the tree and the lovers rapturously embrace. (The offspring of this unlawful union will be Siegfried, the human hero of the *Ring* cycle. In the mythology and folklore of many lands, heros are often born of incestuous love.)

In the excerpt which we'll study, Wagner creates a continuous musical flow that depicts the surging passions of the lovers through frequent changes of tempo, dynamics, and orchestral color. Typically, the vocal lines range from speechlike to highly melodic and closely reflect the inflections and meaning of the text. For example, the word *Notung (Needful)*—the name of the sword—is powerfully emphasized when it is sung to the downward leap of an octave.

Several leitmotifs are heard, sometimes together. In this excerpt, the leitmotif *Valhalla*—Wotan's castle—is first presented when Sieglinde looks at Siegmund and later returns when she recalls how their father (Wotan disguised as the old man) gazed at her during her marriage feast. The very important *Sword* leitmotif is barely noticeable when it first appears, as Sieglinde refers to the fire in Siegmund's eyes. It is presented *pp*, in combination with the leitmotif *Volsung* (the people to which Siegmund and Sieglinde belong). Later, the sword motive is very prominent when it is proclaimed by the brasses as Siegmund draws the sword out of the tree and as the lovers embrace during the orchestral conclusion of the act. Other leitmotifs heard in our excerpt are *love* and *spring*.

(Beth Bergman)

Jeannine Altmeyer as Sieglinde and Peter Hoffmann as Siegmund in the love scene from Act I of *Die Walküre*.

(Sieglinde pushes Siegmund's hair back from his brow and looks at him with astonishment.)

Sieglinde

Wie dir die Stirn so offen steht,	Look how your forehead broadens out,	20 0:00
der Adern Geäst in den Schläfen sich schlingt!	and the network of veins winds into your temples.	
Mir zagt es vor der Wonne, die mich entzückt!	I tremble with the delight that enchants me.	

20 0:20

Valhalla, French horns, *p*.

Ein Wunder will mich gemahen:	It brings something strange to my mind:
den heut zuerst ich erschaut,	though I first saw you today,
mein Auge sah dich schon!	I've set eyes on you before.

Siegmund

Ein Minnetraum gemahnt auch mich:	A dream of love comes to my mind as well:
in heissem Sehnen sah ich dich schon!	burning with longing I have seen you before.

Sieglinde

Im Bach erblickt' ich mein eigen Bild	In the stream I've seen my own likeness;
und jetzt gewahr ich es wieder:	and now I see it again.
wie einst dem Teich es enttaucht,	As once it appeared in the water
bietest mein Bild mir nun du!	so now you show me my likeness.

Siegmund

Du bist das Bild, das ich in mir barg.	You are the likeness that I hid in myself.	22 1:26

Love, voice.

	Sieglinde	
Love, French horn, *p*.	*O still! Lass mich der Stimme lauschen: mich dünkt, ihren Klang hört' ich als Kind.*	Hush! let me listen to your voice. Its sound, I fancy, I heard as a child,
	Doch nein! Ich hörte sie neulich, als meiner Stimme Schall mir widerhallte der Wald.	but no! I heard it recently— when the echo of my voice sounded back through the forest.

	Siegmund	
	O lieblichste Laute, denen ich lauschte!	O loveliest sound for me to hear!

23 2:19

Volsung, low strings, *pp*, together with *Sword*, bass trumpet, *pp*.

	Sieglinde	
2:28	*Deines Auges Glut erglänzte mir schon:*	The fire in your eyes has blazed at me before,
Valhalla, French horns, *pp*, then strings, *pp*.	*so blickte der Greis grüssend auf mich,*	So the old man gazed at me in greeting
	als der Traurigen Trost er gab.	when to my sadness he brought comfort.
	An dem Blick erkannt' ihn sein Kind, schon wollt' ich beim Namen ihn nennen!	By his look his child recognized him, I even wanted to call him by name.
Pause.	*Wehwalt heisst du fürwahr?*	Are you really called Woeful?

	Siegmund	
	Nicht heiss ich so, seit du mich liebst:	I am not called that since you love me:
	nun walt ich der hehrsten Wonnen!	Now I am full of purest rapture.

	Sieglinde	
	Und Friedmund darfst du froh dich nicht nennen?	And "Peaceful" may you not, being happy, be named?

	Siegmund	
	Nenne mich du, wie du liebst, dass ich heisse:	Name me what you love to call me.
418	*den Namen nehm ich von dir!*	I take my name from you.

Sieglinde

Doch nanntest du Wolfe den Vater?   But did you name Wolf as your
                                       father?

Siegmund

Ein Wolf war er feigen Füchsen!   A Wolf he was to craven foxes!
Doch dem so stolz strahlte das Auge, But he whose proud eyes shone
wie, Herrliche, hehr dir es strahlt, as grandly as yours, you marvel,
der war: Wälse genannt.   his name was "Volsa."

Sieglinde

War Wälse dein Vater, und bist du ein If "Volsa" was your father and you
Wälsung,   are a "Volsung,"
stiess er für dich sein Schwert in den it was for you he thrust his sword in
Stamm,   the tree—
so lass mich dich heissen, wie ich dich so let me call you by the name I love:
liebe:
Siegmund: so nenn ich dich!   Siegmund (Victor)—so I name you.

Siegmund

Siegmund heiss ich und Siegmund bin   Siegmund I am called and Siegmund I
ich!   am,
Bezeug es dies Schwert, das zaglos ich let this sword, which I fearlessly hold,
halte!   bear witness.
Wälse verhiess mir, in höchster Not   Volsa promised me that in deepest
                                         distress
fänd' ich es einst: ich fass en nun!   I should one day find it. Now I grasp
                                         it.

Heiligster Minne höchste Not,   Holiest love's deepest distress,   4:47
sehnender Liebe sehrende Not,   yearning love's scorching desire,
brennt mir hell in der Brust,   burn bright in my breast,
drängt zu Tat und Tod: urge me to deeds and death.

                                                                                   24 5:13
Notung! Notung! so nenn ich dich,   "Needy," "Needy," I name you,   Voice, downward
                                                                                   octave leaps.

Schwert.   sword.
Notung, Notung! neidlicher Stahl!   "Needy," "Needy," precious blade,
Zeig deiner Schärfe schneidenden Zahn: show your sharpness and cutting
                                         edge:
heraus aus der Scheide zu mir!   come from your scabbard to me!

                                                                                   25 5:42
(With a powerful effort, Siegmund pulls the sword from the tree, showing it to   *Sword*, trumpets, *ff.*
the astonished and delighted Sieglinde.)

Volsung, trumpets,
pp.

Siegmund, den Wälsung, siehst du, Weib!	You see Siegmund, the Volsung, woman!
Als Brautgabe bringt er dies Schwert:	As wedding gift he brings this sword;
so freit er sich	so he weds
die seligste Frau;	the fairest of women;
dem Feindeshaus entführt er dich so.	he takes you away from the enemy's house.

26 6:29

Spring, voice.

Fern von hier folge mir nun,	Now follow me far from here,
fort in des Lenzes lachendes Haus:	out into springtime's smiling house.

fort   in   des   Len - zes   la - chen-des   Haus;

dort schützt dich Notung, das Schwert,	For protection you'll have "Needy" the sword,
wenn Siegmund dir liebend erlag!	even if Siegmund expires with love.

Sieglinde

Bist du Siegmund, den ich hier sehe,	Are you Siegmund whom I see here?
Sieglinde bin ich, die dich ersehnt:	I am Sieglinde who longed for you:
die eigne Schwester	your own sister
gewannst du zu eins mit dem Schwert!	you have won and the sword as well.

Siegmund

Braut und Schwester bist du dem Bruder,	Wife and sister you'll be to your brother.
so blühe denn Wälsungen-Blut!	So let the Volsung blood increase.

27 7:29

Sword, brasses, *ff.*
Passionate
orchestral
conclusion.

(He draws her to him with passionate fervor.)

BASIC TERM

leitmotif (page 413)

GUSTAV MAHLER

Gustav Mahler (1860–1911) was the last great Austrian romantic composer. He opened new realms of orchestral sound that influenced composers of the early twentieth century, but his works were not fully appreciated until a half-century after his death.

Mahler was born in Bohemia and grew up in a small town where his father was a tavern keeper. His musical environment included Bohemian peasant songs and dances, and marches played by a local military band. (This early contact with folk music and marches later had an influence on his style.) As a boy, he studied piano and composed constantly. At fifteen, he entered the Vienna Conservatory, where he studied for three years. He also took courses in history, Greek art, and ancient literature at the University of Vienna. At twenty he began his conducting career, directing musical comedies at a summer resort. In the years that followed, Mahler steadily gained in professional status, working as an opera conductor in several theaters, each more important than the last. By the time he was twenty-eight, he was director of the Budapest Opera. Brahms heard one of his performances there and declared that to hear "the true *Don Giovanni*" you had to go to Budapest. Mahler's ambition as a performer was to direct the Vienna Opera, but there was one obstacle: he was Jewish. However, in 1897, at thirty-seven, he converted to Roman Catholicism and became director of the Vienna Opera, a position he held for ten years. Mahler brought the Vienna Opera to new heights of excellence, supervising every aspect of its performances: music, acting, costumes, and scenery. He was uncompromising in artistic matters, with the result that many performers regarded him as a tyrant.

Although Mahler quickly won fame as a conductor, he had to struggle for recognition as a composer. Performances of his symphonies often met with mixed receptions. Critics would acknowledge his talent but complain about his harsh dissonances, overelaborate orchestration, and confusing shifts of mood. Mahler composed much of his music during summer vacations, since he was preoccupied by his feverish activity as a conductor during most of the year. In addition to his directorship of the Vienna Opera, he also conducted the Vienna Philharmonic orchestra.

At the age of forty-two, Mahler married the beautiful and musically talented Alma Schindler, who was nineteen years his junior. Two daughters were born to the couple within the first two years of their marriage. Tragically, Maria ("Puzi"), the older daughter, died of scarlet fever at the age of four, leaving Mahler a broken man.

In 1908, Mahler traveled to the United States to become principal conductor of the Metropolitan Opera in New York. The next year he was elected director of the New York Philharmonic orchestra. Mahler's experiences in New York were not happy. His own works were received coolly, he aroused the dislike of many of his players, and he was unable to get along with the socialites who supported the orchestra. In 1911 he became seriously ill and returned to Europe. He died in Vienna at the age of fifty.

Mahler was a passionately intense man, full of conflicts and contradictions. He was an active leader and administrator, but he often craved solitude. His moods frequently shifted from exaltation to despair. He could be cruel to his players, and yet he gave generous support to young musicians such as Bruno Walter and Arnold Schoenberg.

MAHLER'S MUSIC

Mahler's music is often programmatic and reflects his constant search for the meaning of life. His output consists basically of nine symphonies (plus an unfinished Tenth Symphony that is also performed) and several song cycles for voice and orchestra, including *Des Knaben Wunderhorn* (*The Boy's Magic Horn*, 1888) and his monumental masterpiece *Das Lied von der Erde* (*The Song of the Earth*, 1908). "The symphony is the world!" Mahler once explained. "The symphony must embrace everything." Following the example of Beethoven's Ninth Symphony, Mahler used voices in four of his symphonies. And his symphonies are often monumental in length and in their performing forces. His Eighth Symphony (*Symphony of a Thousand*, 1907), for example, lasts about an hour and a half and calls for eight vocal soloists, a boys' choir, two choruses, and a gigantic orchestra. Yet Mahler often uses his gigantic orchestra to achieve delicate chamber music effects in which only a few instruments are heard at a time. He created polyphonic textures in which several themes are presented simultaneously in contrasting tone colors. His use of unconventional instruments—including cowbells, celesta, guitar, and mandolin—influenced twentieth-century Viennese composers such as Arnold Schoenberg, Anton Webern, and Alban Berg.

Mahler's instrumental music, like that of Schubert—whose music was a source of inspiration—is permeated with the spirit of song. Many of Mahler's symphonic movements are based on themes from his own songs. Mahler loved to use folklike tunes and march music, perhaps remembering his childhood in a small Bohemian town. But sometimes he parodies a tune by giving it an unusual twist or grotesque glissando, and there are many sudden and extreme shifts of mood in his music—an intensely emotional section may be interrupted by something light and frivolous.

SYMPHONY NO. 1 IN D MAJOR

Mahler's popular First Symphony, composed between 1885 and 1888, shows most of the features of his mature style. The first and third of the symphony's four movements (in an early version there were five movements) use themes from songs Mahler had composed earlier. The first movement, in sonata form, beautifully evokes the sounds of nature through distant trumpet fanfares and bird calls. The second movement is a folklike scherzo. The third movement, which we'll study, is a funeral march. The last movement, also in sonata form, is by far the most extended; it thematically transforms material from the opening movement.

Third Movement *(Funeral March)*

The third movement, a funeral march, is the most strikingly original in the symphony. Mahler wrote that it was inspired by a satirical engraving, *The Hunter's Funeral Procession*, well known to all Austrian children from an old book of fairy tales. "The forest animals accompany the dead hunter's coffin to the grave. Hares carry the banner, before them march a band of Bohemian musicians, accompanied by singing cats, toads, crows, etc. Stags, deer, foxes, and other four-legged and feathered animals accompany the funeral procession in all kinds of farcical postures. The music is intended to express alternating moods of ironical gaiety and uncanny gloom."

Supplementary sets:
Side 4, band 5
CD 2 36

A source of inspiration for the funeral march movement of Mahler's First Symphony was *The Hunter's Funeral Procession*, by the German romantic artist Moritz von Schwind.

The funeral march is in three sections (A B A') that contain extraordinary contrasts of sound and theme. The weird procession is depicted by a distorted, minor-key version of the round *Frère Jacques (Are You Sleeping, Brother John?)*. The tune is introduced by a solo muted double bass straining in its top register, and then it is imitated by other instruments.

A relentless funeral-march beat in the timpani accompanies sounds that are, in Mahler's words, "dull and muffled, as if shadows were passing by." The *Frère Jacques* round is soon joined by a staccato oboe countermelody that seems like a mocking commentary. A feeling of even greater mockery comes with the appearance of two deliberately banal tunes—one minor and the other major—scored to sound like a Bohemian village band (complete with bass drum and cymbals).

The middle section (B) brings a shift to a lyrical, dreamlike mood as Mahler quotes part of the last song in his cycle *Songs of a Wayfarer*. Its major key, muted strings and harp, and expansive legato melody offer a striking contrast to the minor keys, brass sounds, and staccato phrases heard earlier.

The third section (A') is a condensed and varied return of the opening. The *Frère Jacques* round is now in a somewhat faster tempo, beginning with woodwinds instead of a solo double bass. After the return of one of the "village band" themes, there is a moment of agitation as the tempo quickens and several contrasting themes are presented simultaneously. The processional mood and tempo soon return, and the funeral march gradually fades into silence.

Listening Outline   To be read while music is heard

SYMPHONY NO. 1 IN D MAJOR (1885–1888),
BY GUSTAV MAHLER

Third Movement: Moderate and solemn, not too slow

Quadruple meter ($^4_4$), D minor

4 flutes, 2 oboes, English horn, 4 clarinets, bass clarinet, 2 bassoons, 7 French horns, 2 trumpets, 3 trombones, tuba, timpani, bass drum, gong, cymbals, harp, 1st violins, 2d violins, violas, cellos, double basses

(Duration, 10:58)

A

36 0:00   1. *a.* Muted timpani, *pp*, funeral-march beat. Solo muted double bass in high register, *Frère Jacques* in minor. *Frère Jacques* imitated as a round by bassoon, cellos, tuba, *pp*.

p

37 1:09   *b.* Oboe, *p,* staccato countermelody enters as *Frère Jacques* round continues.

p

1:47   *c.* Oboe and clarinet, *p,* repeat staccato countermelody. *Frère Jacques* round fades away, tempo slows.

38 2:25   2. *a.* Oboes, *p,* legato minor tune in dotted rhythm; pizzicato strings accompany, *p.*

pp   *p subito*

39 2:54   *b.* Clarinets, *mf,* major tune; bass drum and cymbal, "oom-pah" accompaniment, *pp.*

mf

3:12   *c.* Violins, *pp,* legato minor tune an octave higher; pizzicato strings accompany, *p.*

3:42   *d.* Clarinets, *p,* repeat major tune; bass drum and cymbal, "oom-pah" accompaniment, *pp.* High woodwinds, *pp,* lead to

4:05   *e.* High violin melody, *pp,* timpani, *pp,* funeral-march beat. Oboe, *p,* repeats violin melody.

4:46   *f.* Cellos and violas, *pp,* staccato countermelody in low register accompanied by bassoon, *p,* fragment of *Frère Jacques.* Funeral march, in low register, gradually fades away.

B

40 5:23   3. *a.* Harp, *p,* introduces muted violins, *pp,* tender song theme in major, slightly slower tempo. Song theme continued in turn by flutes, solo violins, and clarinets.

pp

6:19   *b.* Oboe, *p,* continues song theme; harp, *p,* in background. Violins, *pp,* melody slowly descends. Bass drum and gong, *pp.* High flutes, *pp.*

41 7:35

4. *a.* Funeral-march beat; *Frère Jacques* round in woodwinds and horns, *pp,* low register, minor key, slightly faster tempo, as at beginning.

7:54

b. Clarinet, *p,* staccato countermelody, joins *Frère Jacques* round. Staccato countermelody continued by solo violins and flute.

42 8:16

c. Trumpets, *p,* new legato melody; staccato countermelody and *Frère Jacques* in background.

8:43

d. Clarinets, *p,* major tune; bass drum and cymbal, "oom-pah" accompaniment, *pp.* High woodwinds lead to

9:05

e. *Frère Jacques* and trumpet melody, suddenly faster and louder; lively melody in high woodwinds. Decrescendo and ritardando to original tempo.

9:25

f. Oboe, *p,* legato minor melody; timpani, *pp,* funeral-march beat. Decrescendo, strings, *p,* woodwinds, *p,* melody moves downward.

10:16

g. Low bassoon, *p,* staccato countermelody; timpani, *pp,* funeral-march beat. Funeral march fades away with faint sounds from gong and brass drum.

VII

THE
TWENTIETH
CENTURY

VII

Twentieth-century painters distorted human figures and objects with extraordinary daring. In *The Juggler* (1943), by Marc Chagall, a man with wings and a bird's head holds a clock case bent into a semicircle.

1 MUSICAL STYLES: 1900–1950

The years 1900 to 1913 brought radical new developments in science and art. During the period preceding World War I, discoveries were made that overturned long-held beliefs. Sigmund Freud explored the unconscious and developed psychoanalysis, and Albert Einstein revolutionized the view of the universe with his theory of relativity. Pablo Picasso's painting and sculpture distorted human figures and objects with unprecedented daring, showing them from several angles at one time; Wassily Kandinsky's abstract paintings no longer tried to represent the visual world.

In music, too, the early twentieth century was a time of revolt. The years following 1900 saw more fundamental changes in the language of music than any time since the beginning of the baroque era. There were entirely new approaches to the organization of pitch and rhythm and a vast expansion in the vocabulary of sounds used, especially percussive sounds. Some compositions broke with tradition so sharply that they were met with violent hostility. The most famous riot in music history occurred in Paris on May 29, 1913, at the premiere of Igor Stravinsky's ballet *Le Sacre du printemps (The Rite of Spring).* Police had to be called in as hecklers booed, laughed, made animal noises, and actually fought with those in the audience who wanted to hear Stravinsky's evocation of primitive rites. One music critic complained that *The Rite of Spring* produced a "sensation of acute and almost cruel dissonance" and that "from the first measure to the last, whatever note one expects is never the one that comes. . . ." Another wrote, "To say that much of it is hideous in sound is a mild description. . . . It has no relation to music at all as most of us understand the word."

Today, we are amused by the initial failure of some music critics to understand this composition, now recognized to be a masterpiece. Chords, rhythms, and percussive sounds that were baffling in 1913 are now commonly heard in jazz, rock, and music for movies and television. But the hostile critics of the early 1900s were right in seeing that a great transformation in musical language was taking place.

From the late 1600s to about 1900, musical structure was governed by certain general principles. As different as the works of Bach, Beethoven, and Brahms may be, they share fundamental techniques of organizing pitches around a central tone. After 1900, however, no single system governs the organization of pitch in all musical compositions. Each piece is more likely to have its own unique system of pitch relationships.

In the past, composers depended on the listener's awareness—conscious or unconscious—of the general principles underlying the inter-

(Collection, Museum of Modern Art, New York, Mrs. Simon Guggenheim Fund)

Three Musicians, by Pablo Picasso. In this cubist painting of 1921, the musicians and their instruments are flattened into planes. The year before, Picasso had designed the costumes for *Pulcinella* (1920), a ballet with music by his friend Igor Stravinsky. Picasso's portrait of Stravinsky is shown on page 462.

relationship of tones and chords. For example, they relied on the listener's expectation that a dominant chord would normally be followed by a tonic chord. By substituting another chord for the expected one, the composer could create a feeling of suspense, drama, or surprise. Twentieth-century music relies less on preestablished relationships and expectations. Listen-

431

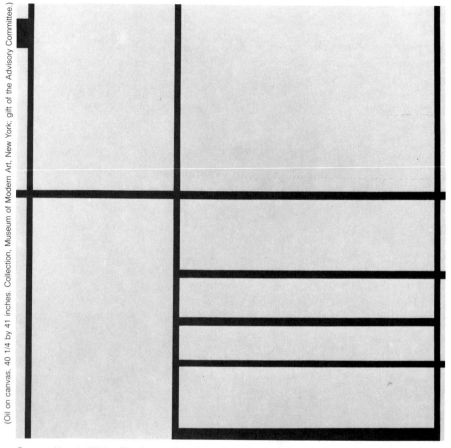

Composition in White, Black, and Red (1936), by Piet Mondrian. Abstract paintings do not try to represent the visual world.

ers are guided by musical cues contained only within an individual composition. This new approach to the organization of sound makes twentieth-century music fascinating. When we listen openly, with no assumptions about how tones "should" relate, modern music is an adventure.

1900–1950: AN AGE OF MUSICAL DIVERSITY

The range of musical styles during the first half of the twentieth century was vast. The stylistic diversity in the works of Claude Debussy, Maurice Ravel, Igor Stravinsky, Arnold Schoenberg, Alban Berg, Anton Webern, Béla Bartók, Charles Ives, George Gershwin, and Aaron Copland—to name only composers studied here—is a continuation and intensification of the diversity we've seen in romantic music. During the twentieth century, differences among styles have been so great that it seems as though composers use different musical languages, not merely different dialects of the same musical language. Radical changes of style occur even within the works of individual composers.

This great variety of musical styles reflected the diversity of life during the early twentieth century. More people were free to choose where to live, how to earn a living, and how to spend their time. The automobile, airplane, telephone, phonograph, movies, and radio all made the world more accessible and expanded the range of experiences.

Through the work of scholars and performers, a wider range of music became available. Composers drew inspiration from an enormous variety of sources, including folk and popular music from all over the world, the music of Asia and Africa, and European art music from the Middle Ages through the nineteenth century.

Elements of folk and popular music were often incorporated within personal styles. Composers were attracted especially to unconventional rhythms, sounds, and melodic patterns that deviated from the common practice of western music. Folk music was studied more systematically than before, and scholars could now record the actual sounds of peasant songs. One of the greatest twentieth-century composers, Béla Bartók, was also a leading scholar of the peasant music of his native Hungary and other parts of eastern Europe. "Studies of folk music in the countryside," he wrote, "are as necessary to me as fresh air is to other people." Bartók's imagination was fired by Hungarian, Bulgarian, and Rumanian folk songs, and he believed that peasant music provided "the ideal starting point for a musical renaissance." Other composers stimulated by folklore were Stravinsky, who drew upon the folk songs of his native Russia, and Charles Ives, who used American revival hymns, ragtime, and patriotic songs.

During the early twentieth century, non-European music had a deep influence on the music of the west. Composers and painters were more receptive and sympathetic to Asian and African cultures than they had been earlier. For example, in 1862, Hector Berlioz could say that "the Chinese sing like dogs howling, like a cat screeching when it has swallowed a toad." But in 1889, Debussy was delighted by the Javanese music he heard at the Paris International Exhibition. "If we listen without European prejudice to the charm of their percussion," he wrote later, "we must confess that our percussion is like primitive noises at a country fair." Echoes of the gamelan (Indonesian orchestra) can be heard in the bell-like sounds and five-tone melodic patterns of Debussy's piano piece *Pagodes* (*Pagodas,* 1903). Another composer who was influenced by Asian culture is the Frenchman Olivier Messiaen (b. 1908); Messiaen's novel rhythmic procedures grew out of his study of Indian music.

American jazz is another non-European influence on twentieth-century composers. Musicians were fascinated by its syncopated rhythms and improvisational quality, as well as by the unique tone colors of jazz bands. Unlike a string-dominated symphony orchestra, a jazz band emphasizes woodwinds, brasses, and percussion.

Jazz elements were used in works as early as Debussy's *Golliwogg's Cake-Walk* (from the suite *Children's Corner*, 1908) and Stravinsky's *Ragtime* (from *The Soldier's Tale*, 1918). But the peak of jazz influence came during the "jazz age" of the 1920s, with works such as the ballet *La Création du monde* (*The Creation of the World*, 1923) by the French composer Darius Milhaud and the Piano Concerto (1926) by the American composer Aaron Copland. For Americans, jazz idioms represented a kind of musical nationalism, a search for an "American sound." For European composers, the incorporation of jazz rhythms and tone colors represented a kind of musical exoticism. During the 1920s and 1930s, popular composers such as George Gershwin (1898–1937) used jazz and popular elements within "classical" forms. Gershwin's *Rhapsody in Blue* (1924) and his opera *Porgy and Bess* (1934–1935) are well known.

Modern composers can also draw inspiration from a wider historical range of music. During the twentieth century, music from remote times has been unearthed by scholars and then published, performed, and recorded. There has been a rediscovery of earlier masters such as Perotin and Machaut from the medieval period, Josquin Desprez and Gesualdo from the Renaissance, and Purcell and Vivaldi from the baroque. Some important modern composers have been music historians, like Anton Webern, or experts in the performance of "old" music, like Paul Hindemith.

Music from the past is a fruitful source of forms, rhythms, tone colors, textures, and compositional techniques. Baroque dances like the gavotte and gigue and forms like the passacaglia and concerto grosso are being used again. The long-forgotten harpsichord has been put to new use in compositions such as Elliott Carter's Sonata for Flute, Oboe, Cello, and Harpsichord (1952), which we'll study. In the *Classical Symphony* (1917) by the Russian composer Sergei Prokofiev (1891–1953), a classical orchestra is used, and the texture is light and transparent like much late eighteenth-century music. Occasionally a twentieth-century composer uses themes of earlier composers, as Benjamin Britten did in *The Young Person's Guide to the Orchestra*, which is based on a theme by Henry Purcell (about 1659–1695).

Modern compositions may be inspired by older music, but this does not mean that they simply imitate past styles. Instead, a traditional form might be used with harmonies, rhythms, melodies, and tone colors that would have been inconceivable before the twentieth century.

Modern composers were also influenced by the music of the immediate past. Nineteenth-century composers such as Wagner, Brahms, Mahler, Richard Strauss, and Mussorgsky were musical points of departure for composers of the early twentieth century. Wagner's music, in particular, was as potent an influence as Beethoven's was for romantic musicians. Composers took Wagner's style as a point of departure, or else they violently reacted against all he stood for.

Having reviewed some of the sources of inspiration for twentieth-century music, let's now examine some of its musical characteristics.

CHARACTERISTICS OF TWENTIETH-CENTURY MUSIC

Tone Color

During the twentieth century, tone color has become a more important element of music than it ever was before. It often has a major role, creating variety, continuity, and mood. In Webern's Orchestral Piece, Op. 10, No. 3 (1913), for example, the use of eerie, bell-like sounds at the beginning and end is vital to the form. If this composition were altered in tone color—say, by being played on a piano—it would lose much. An orchestral work from an earlier period, like Beethoven's Fifth Symphony, suffers less in a piano arrangement.

In modern music, noiselike and percussive sounds are often used, and instruments are played at the very top or bottom of their ranges. Uncommon playing techniques have become normal. For example, the *glissando,* a rapid slide up or down a scale, is more widely used. Woodwind and brass players are often asked to produce a fluttery sound by rapidly rolling their tongues while they play. And string players frequently strike the strings with the stick of the bow, rather than draw the bow across the strings.

Percussion instruments have become prominent and numerous, reflecting the twentieth-century interest in unusual rhythms and tone colors. Instruments that have become standard during the 1900s include the xylophone, celesta, and wood block, to name a few. Composers occasionally call for noisemakers—typewriters, sirens, and automobile brake drums. A piano is often used to add a percussive edge to the sound of an orchestra. Modern composers often draw hard, drumlike sounds from the piano, in contrast to the romantics, who wanted the instrument to "sing." Besides expanding the percussion section of the orchestra, early twentieth-century composers wrote works for unconventional performing groups in which percussion plays a major role. Well-known examples are Stravinsky's Les Noces (*The Wedding,* 1914–1923), for vocal soloists, chorus, four pianos, and percussion; Bartók's Music for Strings, Percussion, and Celesta (1936); and Varèse's Ionisation (1931), which was one of the first works for percussion ensemble.

Modern orchestral and chamber works often sound transparent; individual tone colors are heard clearly. To bring out the individuality of different melodic lines that are played simultaneously, a composer will often assign each line to a different timbre. In general, there is less emphasis on blended sound than there was during the romantic period. Many twentieth-century works are written for nonstandard chamber groups made up of instruments with sharply contrasting tone colors. Stravinsky's *L'Histoire du soldat* (*The Soldier's Tale*, 1918), for example, is scored for violin, double bass, clarinet, bassoon, cornet, trombone, and percussion. Even orchestral works often sound as though they are scored for a group of soloists.

Harmony

Consonance and dissonance

The twentieth century brought fundamental changes in the way chords are treated. Up to about 1900, chords were divided into two opposing types: consonant and dissonant. A consonant chord was stable; it functioned as a point of rest or arrival. A dissonant chord was unstable; its tension demanded onward motion, or resolution to a stable, consonant chord. Traditionally, only the triad, a three-tone chord, could be consonant. All others were considered dissonant. In the nineteenth century, composers came to use ever more dissonant chords, and they treated dissonances with increasing freedom. By the early twentieth century, the traditional distinction between consonance and dissonance was abandoned in much music. A combination of tones that earlier would have been used to generate instability and expectation might now be treated as a stable chord, a point of arrival. In Stravinsky's words, dissonance "is no longer tied down to its former function. Having become an entity in itself, it frequently happens that dissonance neither prepares nor anticipates anything. Dissonance is thus no more an agent of disorder than consonance is a guarantee of security."

This "emancipation of the dissonance" does not prevent composers from differentiating between chords of greater or lesser tension. Relatively mild-sounding chords may be goals of motion, while harsher chords are used for transitional sounds. But no longer is there a general principle that determines whether a chord is stable or not. It is now entirely up to the composer's discretion. "We find ourself confronted with a new logic of music that would have appeared unthinkable to the masters of the past," wrote Stravinsky. "This new logic has opened our eyes to riches whose existence we never suspected."

New chord structures

Before 1900, there were general principles governing chord construction: certain combinations of tones were considered chords, while others were not. At the core of traditional harmony is the triad. A triad might be made up of alternate tones of a major scale, such as the first *(do)*, third *(mi)*, and fifth *(sol)*. Within a triad, there are two intervals of a third.

Although the triad often appears in twentieth-century music, it no longer is so fundamental.

Some twentieth-century composers create fresh harmonies by placing one traditional chord against another. Such a combination of two chords heard at the same time is called a *polychord.*

Copland, *Appalachian Spring*

A polychord can be heard either as a single block of sound or as two distinct layers, depending on whether the two combined chords contrast in tone color and register.

Another development in twentieth-century music is the use of chordal structures *not* based on triads. One used commonly is the *fourth chord,* in which the tones are a fourth apart, instead of a third. (From *do* to *fa,* or from *re* to *sol,* is an interval of a fourth.)

Ives, *The Cage*

Harmonic resources have been extended also through the *tone cluster,* a chord made up of tones only a half step or a whole step apart. A tone cluster can be produced on a piano by striking a group of adjacent keys with the fist or forearm.

Ives, *The Majority*

Alternatives to the Traditional Tonal System

In addition to creating new chord structures, twentieth-century composers explored alternatives to the traditional tonal system. This system of tonal gravity, known as *tonality* or *key*, governed the organization of pitch from the 1600s to about 1900. By the late nineteenth century, the gravitational pull of a central tonality had been weakened by rapid and frequent key shifts. After 1900, some composers continued to use the traditional system, but others modified it greatly and still others discarded it entirely.

Before looking at new approaches to pitch organization, recall the basic principles of the traditional tonal system. As we saw in Part I (Elements), *tonality*, or *key*, refers to the use of a central tone, scale, and chord within a composition. The central tone, called the *tonic* or *keynote (do)*, is the composition's resting point. The tonic major or minor scale and the tonic triad are built on this tone. Since the tonic triad is stable and restful, compositions almost always ended with it. Next in importance to the tonic triad is the *dominant chord*, which is built on the fifth tone *(sol)* of the tonic scale. There is a special gravitational pull from the dominant chord toward the tonic chord, and the motion from dominant to tonic is the essential chord progression of the tonal system. This cadence provides a strong sense of conclusion, and traditionally it was used to round off melodies, sections, and entire pieces. In summary, the tonal system is based on a central tone, a major or minor scale, and a triad; and there is a special relationship between the tonic and dominant chords.

After 1900, this system was modified in many different ways. The new techniques of pitch organization are so varied as to resist easy generalization. Some compositions have a central tone but are missing other traditional elements, such as the tonic triad, the central major or minor scale, or the dominant-tonic relationship.

This modified approach to tonality is reflected even in the titles of compositions, which are less likely to include the terms *major* or *minor*. For example, one Stravinsky piano piece is entitled *Serenade in A* to show that it revolves around the tone A but is not in a major or minor key.

To create fresh sounds, composers used scales other than major or minor. For example, they breathed new life into the ancient church modes, scales that had been used widely before 1600, as well as in folk songs of every period. Other scales were borrowed from the musical tradition of lands outside western Europe, and still others were invented by composers.

Twentieth-century compositions are often organized around a central chord other than the triad. Thus, the basic chord may well be one that was considered a dissonance earlier. In some works, the traditional relationship between dominant and tonic triads is replaced by other chord relationships. Melodies, sections, or entire pieces are rounded off not by the usual dominant-tonic cadence, but by other chord progressions.

Another twentieth-century approach to pitch organization is the use of two or more keys at one time: *polytonality.* When only two different keys are used at once—as is most common—the technique is called **bitonality.** A famous bitonal passage occurs in Stravinsky's ballet *Petrushka,* when one clarinet plays in C major and another plays in F sharp major:

In general, the greater the contrast of tone color, register, and rhythm between the different layers of sound, the more we can hear the different keys.

A further departure from tradition is *atonality,* the absence of tonality or key. Atonality was foreshadowed in nineteenth-century works such as Wagner's *Tristan and Isolde,* where the pull of a central key is weakened by frequent modulations and by liberal use of all twelve tones in the chromatic scale. Arnold Schoenberg wrote the first significant atonal pieces around 1908. He avoided traditional chord progressions in these works and used all twelve tones without regard to their traditional relationship to major or minor scales. But atonality is not a specific technique of composition; each atonal work is structured according to its needs. (Though the word *atonality* is imprecise and negative, no other term has yet come into general use.)

Before long, Schoenberg felt the need for a more systematic approach to atonal composition, and during the early 1920s he developed the *twelve-tone system,* a new technique of pitch organization. This system gives equal prominence to each of the twelve chromatic tones, rather than singling out one pitch, as the tonal system does. For about twenty years, only Schoenberg and a few disciples used the twelve-tone system, but during the 1950s it came to be used by composers all over the world.

Rhythm

The new techniques of pitch organization were accompanied by new ways to organize rhythm. The rhythmic vocabulary of music was expanded, with increased emphasis on irregularity and unpredictability. Rhythm is one of the most striking elements of twentieth-century music; it is used to generate power, drive, and excitement.

In the twentieth century, new rhythmic procedures are drawn from many sources, including folk music from all over the world, jazz, and European art music from the Middle Ages through the nineteenth century. Béla Bartók used the "free and varied rhythmic structures" of east European peasant music. The syncopations and complex rhythmic combinations of jazz fired the imagination of Stravinsky and Copland. And irregular phrase structures in Brahms's music inspired rhythmic innovations in Schoenberg's works.

Rapidly changing meters are characteristic of twentieth-century music, whereas baroque, classical, and romantic music maintain a single meter throughout a movement or section. Before the twentieth century, beats were organized into regularly recurring groups; the accented beat came at equal time intervals. Rhythmic irregularities such as syncopations or accents on weak beats were heard against a pervasive meter. But in many twentieth-century compositions, beats are grouped irregularly, and the accented beat comes at unequal time intervals. In some modern music the meter changes with almost every bar, so that we might count *1–2–3, 1–2–3–4–5, 1–2–3–4–5, 1–2–3, 1–2–3–4, 1–2–3–4–5, 1–2–3–4–5–6, 1–2–3–4–5, 1–2, 1–2–3–4–5–6:*

Stravinsky, *Ritual of Abduction* from *The Rite of Spring*

Count this again quickly and experience some of the rhythmic excitement of twentieth-century music, which often has a rapid and vigorous beat with jolting accents at unexpected times.

The rhythmic resources of twentieth-century music have also been expanded through the use of unconventional meters. Along with traditional meters such as duple and triple, modern composers use meters with five or seven beats to the measure. The pulses within a measure of any length may be grouped in irregular, asymmetrical ways. For example, eight quick pulses in a measure may be subdivided 3 + 3 + 2, or *1–2–3–4–5–6–7–8, 1–2–3–4–5–6–7–8.* This meter, common in east European folk music, is used by Bartók in one of his *Six Dances in Bulgarian Rhythm:*

Twentieth-century music often uses two or more contrasting and independent rhythms at the same time, a procedure called *polyrhythm.* Each part of the musical texture goes its own rhythmic way, often creating accents that are out of phase with accents in the other parts. Different meters are used at the same time. For example, one instrument may play in duple meter (*1–2, 1–2*) while another plays in triple meter (*1–2–3, 1–2–3*). Although polyrhythm occasionally occurs in classical and romantic music, it became both more common and more complex after 1900. The polyrhythms of jazz strongly influenced composers in the 1920s and 1930s.

Rhythmic repetition of a group of pitches is a widely used unifying technique in twentieth-century music. Many modern compositions contain an *ostinato,* a motive or phrase that is repeated persistently at the same pitch throughout a section. The ostinato may occur in the melody or in the accompaniment. (The accompaniment for the example from Bartók's *Six Dances* has an eight-note ostinato: **1**–*2–3–4–5–6–7–8.*) Ostinatos can be found in music from various periods and cultures. In twentieth-century music, they usually serve to stabilize particular groups of pitches.

Melody

The new techniques of pitch and rhythmic organization that we've surveyed had a strong impact on twentieth-century melody. Melody is no longer necessarily tied to traditional chords or to major and minor keys. It may be based on a wide variety of scales, or it may freely use all twelve chromatic tones and have no tonal center. Melody today often contains wide leaps that are difficult to sing. Rhythmic irregularity and changing meters tend to make twentieth-century melodies unpredictable. They often consist of a series of phrases that are irregular in length. In general, twentieth-century music relies less than classical and romantic music on melodies that are easy to sing and remember. Melody is as rich and varied as twentieth-century music itself; neither can be classified easily.

BASIC TERMS

glissando (page 435)
polychord (437)
fourth chord (437)
tone cluster (437)
polytonality (439)
bitonality (439)
atonality (439)
polyrhythm (441)
ostinato (441)

[2] MUSIC AND MUSICIANS IN SOCIETY

The twentieth century has seen dramatic changes in how music reaches its listeners. The living room has become the new "concert hall" through recordings, radio, and television. These technological advances have brought music to a larger audience than ever before, besides vastly increasing the range of music available. Today's repertory of recorded music includes not only familiar classics, but also Renaissance, early baroque, non-western, and unconventional twentieth-century works—music not often played in concert. Recordings of such lesser-known music multiplied with the appearance of long-playing disks in 1948. But as early as 1904, composers' interpretations of their own works were recorded, giving composers an unprecedented opportunity to communicate precisely their intentions about phrasing, dynamics, and tempo.

Radio broadcasts of live or recorded music began to reach a large audience during the 1920s. In the 1930s, radio networks in several countries formed orchestras specifically to broadcast live music. The best-known American ensemble of this kind was the NBC Symphony Orchestra, directed by Arturo Toscanini. In addition to such radio-sponsored groups, regular broadcasts of the Saturday matinee performances of the Metropolitan Opera have made opera available to millions of people.

With television, broadcast music performances can be seen as well as heard. Christmas Eve, 1951, brought the premiere of the first opera created for television, *Amahl and the Night Visitors*, by the Italian-American composer Gian-Carlo Menotti. Other television highlights included appearances of Leonard Bernstein conducting the New York Philharmonic Orchestra. Apart from such notable exceptions, commercial television has devoted little time to opera and symphonic music. Public television, however, has brought a wide range of music to home viewers; successful music programming has included *Live from Lincoln Center* and *Live from the Met*. In addition, music videos of operas, symphonies, and solo performances are becoming popular.

In the first half of the twentieth century, the concert and operatic repertory was dominated by music from earlier periods rather than by contemporary works. This was a new situation in music history. In Mozart's time, for instance, audiences demanded and got the latest music, not operas by Handel or cantatas by Bach. Even during the romantic period, when interest in past music was high, concert programs consisted mainly of recent works.

After 1900, however, listeners and performers were often baffled by the dissonances, percussive sounds, and irregular rhythms in some of the new music. (Remember the riot at the first performance of Stravinsky's *Rite of Spring*.) To avoid alienating audiences, many conductors chose not to perform "difficult" contemporary works, but favored works that were relatively accessible in style. One result was that some of the most innovative twentieth-century composers—Ives, Webern, and Varèse, for example—were neglected.

After World War I, organizations were formed for the specific purpose of giving the public a greater opportunity to hear new music. The International Society for Contemporary Music was the most influential, with branches in many countries.

Starting in the 1950s, major orchestras and opera companies began to program more twentieth-century music. Long-playing recordings gave listeners access to works that had seemed incomprehensible; they could now be played repeatedly until they were understood and enjoyed. Musicians themselves grew more accustomed to intricate modern rhythms and thus were better able to perform them.

Many modern compositions were commissioned by ballet and opera companies, foundations, orchestras, performers, film studios, and wealthy music lovers. Developments in dance had an especially strong impact on twentieth-century music. A single company, Sergei Diaghilev's Russian Ballet, provided the impetus for masterpieces such as Stravinsky's *Petrushka* (1911), Ravel's *Daphnis et Chloé* (1912), and Debussy's *Jeux* (1913). Films provided a new stimulus for music, too. Though most film scores were merely background music, some, like Prokofiev's *Lieutenant Kije* (1934), were enjoyed apart from the movie. Philanthropic foundations have become significant music patrons in our time. One, most active in the field of chamber music, was established by Elizabeth Sprague Coolidge in 1925 at the Library of Congress in Washington. Her generosity spurred the creation of many fine compositions, including Bartók's Fifth String Quartet (1934) and Schoenberg's Fourth String Quartet (1936). Yet, however important commissions have been in our century, few serious musicians can live on them alone. Most modern composers are also teachers, conductors, or performers. Recently, some are "composers in residence" with symphony orchestras. They advise music directors on the contemporary repertory and compose works for performance by the host orchestra.

In the twentieth century, more women have been active as composers, virtuoso soloists, and music educators than ever before. Among the most noted women among American composers are Amy Beach (1867–1944), Ruth Crawford-Seeger (1901–1953), Miriam Gideon (b. 1906), Vivian Fine (b. 1913), Pauline Oliveros (b. 1932), Joan Tower (b. 1938), Ellen Taaffe Zwilich (b. 1939), and Barbara Kolb (b. 1940), to name only a few. The

French musician Nadia Boulanger (1887–1979) was among the most important teachers of musical composition in the twentieth century. And since World War II (1939–1945), women have functioned in professional orchestras as performers and conductors.

Like all people, musicians have been affected by the political, economic, and social upheavals of the twentieth century. Hitler's rise to power in Germany in 1933 had an especially dramatic impact on the lives and careers of musicians. Avant-garde, socialist, and Jewish musicians were abruptly ousted from their jobs, and their works were no longer performed. Dictatorship, persecution, and the onset of World War II led to the largest migration of artists and intellectuals in history. Many composers, including Stravinsky, Bartók, Schoenberg, and Hindemith, left Europe for the United States. Such distinguished refugees made enormous contributions to American musical culture. Schoenberg and Hindemith, for example, taught in universities and helped train some of the finest composers in the United States.

During the twentieth century, the United States became a potent force in music. American jazz and popular music swept the world. After 1920 the country produced a large group of composers representing a wide spectrum of contemporary styles. In addition, the United States now has more first-rank symphony orchestras than any other country.

American colleges and universities have played an unusually vital role in our musical culture. They have trained and employed many of our leading composers, performers, and scholars. Music courses have expanded the horizons and interests of countless students. And since the middle of the century, many universities have sponsored performing groups specializing in twentieth-century music. In addition, they have housed most of the electronic music studios. Thus, American colleges and universities have indirectly become patrons of music, much as the church and nobility were in earlier times.

3 IMPRESSIONISM AND SYMBOLISM

TWENTIETH CENTURY

Many different musical styles coexisted around the turn of the century. Among the most important was impressionism, best represented by the music of the French composer Claude Debussy (1862–1918). We'll look closely at musical impressionism in Section 4; first, two related, but slightly earlier, artistic movements in France demand our attention: impressionist painting and symbolist poetry.

La Grenouillère (1869), by Claude Monet. Impressionist painters were concerned primarily with effects of light, color, and atmosphere.

FRENCH IMPRESSIONIST PAINTING

In 1874, a group of French painters including Claude Monet (1840–1926), Auguste Renoir (1841–1919), and Camille Pissarro (1830–1903) had an exhibition in Paris. One Monet painting entitled *Impression: Sunrise*—a misty scene of boats in port—particularly annoyed an art critic, who wrote, "Wallpaper in its embryonic state is more finished than that seascape." Using Monet's title, the critic mockingly called the entire show "the exhibition of the impressionists." The term *impressionist* stuck, but it eventually lost its derisive implication.

Today most of us appreciate impressionist paintings, which colorfully depict the joys of life and the beauties of nature. But during the 1870s, they were seen as formless collections of tiny colored patches—which they are

445

when viewed closely. From a distance, however, the brush strokes blend and merge into recognizable forms and shimmering colors. Impressionist painters were concerned primarily with effects of light, color, and atmosphere—with impermanence, change, and fluidity. Monet created a series of twenty paintings (1892–1894) showing Rouen Cathedral at different times of the day, from dawn to dusk. In this series, the cathedral's stone facade is desolidified and looks like colored mist. Many impressionist painters preferred to work in the open air rather than in a studio. They were fascinated by outdoor scenes from contemporary life, picnics in the woods, and crowds on Parisian boulevards. But most of all, the impressionists were obsessed with water. Using light, pastel colors, they depicted the ripples and waves of the ocean and sailboats on the river Seine.

FRENCH SYMBOLIST POETRY

As impressionist painters broke from traditional depictions of reality, writers called *symbolists* rebelled against the conventions of French poetry. Like the painters, poets such as Stéphane Mallarmé (1842–1898), Paul Verlaine (1844–1896), and Arthur Rimbaud (1854–1891) emphasized fluidity and suggestion. "To *name* an object," insisted Mallarmé, "is to suppress three-quarters of the enjoyment of a poem, which is made up of gradually guessing; the dream is to *suggest* it." Symbolist writers emphasized the purely musical, or sonorous, effects of words.

Claude Debussy was a close friend of many symbolist poets, especially Mallarmé, whose poem *L'Après-midi d'un faune (The Afternoon of a Faun)* inspired Debussy's most famous orchestral work. Many poems by Verlaine became texts for Debussy's songs. (And, more personally, Verlaine's mother-in-law was Debussy's first piano teacher.) Both impressionist painting and symbolist poetry were catalysts for many developments during the twentieth century. Section 4 describes their effect on music.

CLAUDE DEBUSSY

The French impressionist composer Claude Debussy (1862–1918) linked the romantic era with the twentieth century. He was born in St. Germain-en-Laye, a small town near Paris. At the early age of ten, he entered the Paris Conservatory, where he studied until he was twenty-two. (While Debussy was at the Conservatory, the impressionists were exhibiting their paintings in Paris.) Debussy's teachers regarded him as a talented rebel who improvised unorthodox chord progressions of dissonances that did not resolve.

IMPRESSIONISM

Impression, Sunrise (1874), by Claude Monet. At an exhibition in Paris in 1874, this painting annoyed a critic who viewed it as a formless collection of tiny colored patches. Using Monet's own title, he mockingly called the entire show the "exhibition of the impressionists." Like the impressionist painters, the French composer Claude Debussy was a master at evoking a fleeting mood and misty atmosphere.

THE TWENTIETH CENTURY

Street Scene, Dresden (1907), by Ernst Ludwig Kirchner. German expressionist painters used deliberate distortions and violent colors to communicate the tension and anguish of the human psyche. Expressionist composers include Arnold Schoenberg, Alban Berg, and Anton Webern.

Painting No. 198 (above) and *Painting No. 200* (right), by
Wassily Kandinsky (1914). Kandinsky stated that his
abstract paintings were a "graphic representation of a
mood and not of objects."

Girl before a Mirror (1932), by Pablo Picasso. The young girl on the left looks at an older, troubled reflection of herself. Picasso reinterpreted the traditional theme of a woman seeing a death's head in her mirror. Twentieth-century composers such as Stravinsky have also reinterpreted earlier musical forms and styles.

Synthetic polymer on canvas, 124 by 140 inches. Collection of Whitney Museum of American Art, New York, Purchase, with funds from the Friends of the Whitney Museum of American Art. Photo, Geoffry Clements.)

Flood (1967), by Helen Frankenthaler. Working without a brush, Frankenthaler allows paint to soak and stain an unprimed canvas stretched on the floor.

Marilyn, from *Ten Marilyns* (1967), by Andy Warhol. Pop artists like Warhol use ordinary subjects from everyday life and mass media.

Hundred-Yard Dash (1969), by Alexander Calder. Calder created stabiles—large stable sculptures. He was also the originator of the mobile—a sculpture that moves with the aid of air currents.

Thrusting Rocks (1990), by David Hockney. One of the best-known contemporary painters, Hockney is also a leading designer of operatic sets and costumes.

In his late teens, Debussy worked summers as pianist for Mme. von Meck, the Russian patroness of Tchaikovsky. During these stays in Russia, Debussy's lifelong interest in Russian music took root. In 1884, he won the highest award in France for composers, the Prix de Rome, which subsidized three years of study in Rome. But he left Italy after only two years, because he lacked musical inspiration away from his beloved Paris.

When Debussy returned to Paris in 1887, the music and ideas of Richard Wagner were having a profound influence on French composers and writers. Many of Debussy's friends wrote articles for *La Revue Wagnérienne (The Wagnerian Review)*, a periodical devoted to the German master. During the summers of 1888 and 1889, Debussy traveled to Bayreuth, Germany, to hear Wagner's music dramas. They were memorable events for Debussy, who was both attracted and repelled by Wagner's music.

The Asian music performed at the Paris International Exposition of 1889 also had a strong impact on Debussy. "Do you not remember the Javanese music," he wrote a friend, "able to express every shade of meaning, . . . which makes our tonic and dominant seem like ghosts?"

For years, Debussy led an unsettled life, earning a small income by teaching piano. His friends were mostly writers, such as Stéphane Mallarmé, whose literary gatherings Debussy attended regularly. In cafes and cabarets he mingled with jockeys and entertainers like those immortalized in the paintings of Toulouse-Lautrec. Until the age of thirty-one, Debussy was little known to the musical public and not completely sure of himself. "There are still things that I am not able to do—create masterpieces, for example," he wrote in 1893. But that same year Debussy did complete a masterpiece, his String Quartet. And in 1894 he created another, the tone poem *Prelude to "The Afternoon of a Faun,"* which has become his most popular orchestral work.

A dramatic turning point in Debussy's career came in 1902, with his opera *Pelléas et Mélisande*. Critics were sharply divided. Some complained about the absence of melody and the harmonies that broke traditional rules; others were delighted by the poetic atmosphere and subtle tone colors. The opera soon caught on, however, and Debussy was recognized as the most important living French composer. Musicians all over the world imitated his style.

This artistic triumph contrasted with a personal life filled with financial and emotional crises. Debussy constantly borrowed money for luxuries he craved: fine food, beautiful clothes, and art works. The attempted suicides of two women in his life were major scandals in Paris. His longtime mistress shot herself when he left her for Rosalie Texier, a milliner who became his first wife. Then Rosalie Texier, in turn, shot herself when Debussy left *her* for Emma Bardac, an intelligent, talented, and rich society woman.

Debussy's marriage to Emma Bardac necessitated his undertaking concert tours to maintain their high standard of living. Though he was not gifted as a conductor and hated appearing in public, he presented his

(Culver Pictures)

The impressionist composer Claude Debussy was a master at evoking a fleeting mood and misty atmosphere.

music throughout Europe. The onset of World War I in 1914 heightened his sense of nationalism, and he began to sign his works "Claude Debussy, French musician." He had developed cancer at the age of fifty, and he died in Paris on March 25, 1918, while the city was being shelled by German artillery.

DEBUSSY'S MUSIC

Like the French impressionist painters and symbolist poets, Debussy was a master at evoking a fleeting mood and misty atmosphere. His interest in the effects of fluidity, intangibility, and impermanence is mirrored even in his titles: *Reflets dans l'eau (Reflections in the Water), Nuages (Clouds),* and *Les Sons et les parfums tournent dans l'air du soir (Sounds and Perfumes Swirl in the Evening Air).* Literary and pictorial ideas often inspired Debussy, and most of his compositions have descriptive titles. His music sounds free and spontaneous, almost improvised. He once wrote, "I am more and more convinced that music is not, in essence, a thing which can be cast into a traditional and fixed form. It is made up of colors and rhythms." This stress on tone color, atmosphere, and fluidity is characteristic of *impressionism* in music.

Tone color truly gets unprecedented attention in Debussy's works. His subtle changes of timbre are as crucial to his music as thematic contrasts are to earlier music. The sound he sought is sensuous and beautiful—never harsh. The entire orchestra seldom plays together to produce massive sound. Instead, there are brief but frequent instrumental solos. The woodwinds are especially prominent and are used in unusual registers. (The velvety low register of the flute is featured in the *Prelude to "The Afternoon of a Faun."*) Strings and brasses are often muted; their sound seems to come from far off. Atmosphere is created through the shimmer of a string tremolo or the splash of a harp.

Debussy wrote some of his finest music for piano, again creating new sonorities. His frequent use of the damper pedal, which allows a pianist to sustain tones after the keys are released, results in hazy sounds. Chords are often blended together, and the pianist is directed to let the sounds vibrate. The rich variety of bell and gong sounds in Debussy's piano works may reflect the influence of Asian music he heard at the Paris International Exposition in 1889.

Debussy's treatment of harmony was a revolutionary aspect of musical impressionism. He tends to use a chord more for its special color and sensuous quality than for its function in a standard harmonic progression. He uses successions of dissonant chords that do not resolve. (When young, Debussy was asked which harmonic rules he followed; he replied, simply, "My pleasure.") He freely shifts a dissonant chord up or down the scale; the resulting parallel chords characterize his style.

Debussy, *La Cathédrale engloutie (The Sunken Cathedral)**

Debussy's harmonic vocabulary is large. Along with traditional three- and four-note chords, he uses five-note chords with a lush, rich sound. Chord progressions that were highly unorthodox when Debussy wrote them soon came to seem mild and natural.

"One must drown the sense of tonality," Debussy wrote. Although he never actually abandoned tonality, Debussy weakened it by deliberately avoiding chord progressions that strongly affirm the key. The traditional dominant-tonic cadence is relatively rare in his music. He also "drowns" tonality by using scales in which the main tone is less emphasized than in major or minor scales. He turned to the medieval church modes, which he knew from Gregorian chant. He also used the *pentatonic,* or five-tone, scales heard in Javanese music. These pentatonic scales lend an Asian atmosphere to some of Debussy's music. (A pentatonic scale is produced by five successive black keys of the piano: F♯–G♯–A♯–C♯–D♯.)

Debussy's most unusual and tonally vague scale is the *whole-tone scale,* made up of six different notes each a whole step away from the next (C–D–E–F♯–G♯–A♯–C). Unlike major and minor, the whole-tone scale has no special pull from *ti* to *do,* since its tones are all the same distance apart. And because no single tone stands out, the scale creates a blurred, indistinct effect.

The pulse in Debussy's music is sometimes as vague as the tonality. "Rhythms cannot be contained within bars," he wrote. He avoids recurring strong accents that coincide with the bar line. His rhythmic flexibility reflects the fluid, unaccented quality of the French language. In fact, few composers have set French to music as sensitively as Debussy. He composed fifty-nine art songs, many of which are set to symbolist poems by Charles Baudelaire, Paul Verlaine, and Stéphane Mallarmé. His only opera, *Pelléas et Mélisande,* is an almost word-for-word setting of a symbolist play by the Belgian poet Maurice Maeterlinck. This great and highly original opera is the essence of musical impressionism. Its vague, mysterious plot includes characters who barely communicate with each other.

There are no arias, and the melodic line is almost entirely speechlike. The play's dreamlike atmosphere is magically evoked by an orchestral accompaniment that is discreet and understated; it's as though Debussy had consciously sought to avoid the powerful sound of Wagner's orchestral parts.

Although not large, Debussy's output is remarkably varied. Along with his opera, he contributed masterpieces to the literature of the piano, orchestra, chamber ensemble, and art song. We have seen that Debussy's music is tonally vague and has an improvisational, floating quality. It's not surprising, then, that he avoided sonata form, which traditionally calls for a clear contrast of keys and systematic development of themes. One section of Debussy's music melts into the next; melodic lines tend to be brief and fragmentary.

Echoes of Debussy's music can be heard in the works of many composers during the first two decades of the twentieth century. However, no other important musician can so fairly be described as an impressionist. Even the composer most similar to Debussy, his younger French contemporary Maurice Ravel (1875–1937), wrote music with greater clarity of form. Debussy's impressionist style was both a final expression of romanticism and the beginning of a new era. His use of tone color as a vital element of form and his novel harmonic techniques made him the immediate forerunner of later twentieth-century musicians. Igor Stravinsky was perceptive when he remarked, "I and the members of my generation owe most to Debussy."

PRÉLUDE À "L'APRÈS-MIDI D'UN FAUNE" (PRELUDE TO "THE AFTERNOON OF A FAUN")

"The music of this Prelude," wrote Debussy regarding his *Prelude to "The Afternoon of a Faun,"* "is a very free illustration of the beautiful poem by Stéphane Mallarmé, *The Afternoon of a Faun.*" This poem evokes the dreams and erotic fantasies of a pagan forest creature who is half man, half goat. While playing a "long solo" on his flute, the intoxicated faun tries to recall whether he actually carried off two beautiful nymphs or only dreamed of doing so. Exhausted by the effort, he falls back to sleep in the warm sunshine.

Side 13, band 3
CD 7 [5]

Debussy intended his music to suggest "the successive scenes through which pass the desires and dreams of the faun in the heat of this afternoon." The subtle, sensuous timbres of this miniature tone poem were new in Debussy's day. Woodwind solos, muted horn calls, and harp glissandos create a rich variety of delicate sounds. The dynamics are usually subdued, and the entire orchestra—from which trombones, trumpets, and timpani are excluded—rarely plays at one time. The music often swells sensuously, only to subside in voluptuous exhaustion.

The prelude begins with an unaccompanied flute melody; its vague pulse and tonality make it dreamlike and improvisatory. This flute melody is heard again and again, faster, slower, and against a variety of lush chords. Though the form of the prelude may be thought of as A B A', one section blends with the next. It has a continuous ebb and flow. The fluidity and weightlessness typical of impressionism are found in this music. We are never tempted to beat time to its subtle rhythms. The prelude ends magically with the main melody, played by muted horns, seeming to come from far off. The bell-like tones of antique cymbals finally evaporate into silence. With all its new sounds and musical techniques, the piece has aptly been described as a "quiet revolution" in the history of music.

Listening Outline   To be read while music is heard

PRÉLUDE À "L'APRÈS-MIDI D'UN FAUNE"
(*PRELUDE TO "THE AFTERNOON OF A FAUN,"* 1894),
BY CLAUDE DEBUSSY

At a very moderate tempo, A B A' form, E major

3 flutes, 2 oboes, 1 English horn, 2 clarinets, 2 bassoons, 4 French horns, 2 harps,
antique cymbals, 1st violins, 2d violins, violas, cellos, double basses

(Duration, 10:21)

A

| 5 | 0:00 | 1. *a.* Solo flute, *p*, main melody. |

			Harp glissando; soft horn calls. Short pause. Harp glissando; soft horn calls.
6	0:54	*b.*	Flute, *p*, main melody; tremolo strings in background. Oboe, *p*, continues melody. Orchestra swells to *f*. Solo clarinet fades into
7	1:57	*c.*	Flute, *p*, main melody varied and expanded; harp and muted strings accompany. Flute melody comes to quiet close.

3:12   2. *a.* Clarinet; harp and cellos in background.

[8] 3:41   *b.* New oboe melody.

Violins take up melody, crescendo and accelerando to climax. Excitement subsides. Ritardando. Clarinet, *p,* leads into

B

[9] 4:56   3. *a.* Woodwinds, *p,* legato melody in long notes. Crescendo.

5:31   *b.* Strings repeat melody; harps and pulsating woodwinds in background, crescendo. Decrescendo. Horns, *p,* solo violin, *p,* clarinet, oboe.

A'

[10] 6:46   4. *a.* Harp accompanies flute, *p,* main melody in longer notes. Oboe, staccato woodwinds.

7:21   *b.* Harp accompanies oboe, *p,* main melody in longer notes. English horn, harp glissando.

[11] 8:03   5. *a.* Antique cymbals, bell-like tones. Flutes, *p,* main melody. Solo violins, *pp,* in high register.

8:48   *b.* Flute and solo cello, main melody; harp in background.

9:15   *c.* Oboe, *p,* brings melody to close. Harps, *p.*

9:46   *d.* Muted horns and violins, *ppp,* beginning of main melody sounding far off. Flute, antique cymbals, and harp; delicate tones fade into silence.

VOILES (SAILS), FROM PRELUDES FOR PIANO, BOOK I (1910)

In this short piano piece, Debussy exploits the blurred and tonally vague quality of the whole-tone scale to suggest the gentle rocking of sails in the wind. (However, Debussy's title may also refer to veils, a second meaning of the French word *voiles.*) *Voiles* is subdued in dynamics, moderate in tempo, and played "in a rhythm that is caressing and not strict." Debussy uses the piano's damper pedal to create lingering vibrations that suggest a misty atmosphere. Contributing to the impression of motion in place is a low repeated tone, B flat, that serves as a pedal point in all three sections of the piece.

Supplementary sets:
Side 8, band 1
CD 4 [21]

453

Debussy, *Voiles (Sails)**

The opening section, which is longest, uses the whole-tone scale almost exclusively. It is based on three main ideas. One is a short melodic figure in parallel thirds that is first presented alone, and then with accompaniment. (This is called the *sails* motive in the listening outline.)

The second idea is a stepwise melody that is first heard in soft octaves in a low register

and later in a high register doubled by parallel chords in a middle register.

This use of chords moving in parallel motion—with the same chord structure shifted to different pitch levels—is characteristic of impressionist style.

The third idea of the opening section is a figure that turns around a single note.

pp

In the brief but animated middle section, contrast is created by a shift from the whole-tone to the pentatonic (five-tone) scale: E♭–G♭–A♭–B♭–D♭. This scale is used for rapid upward rushes.

En animant

p

The concluding section brings a return of the whole-tone scale, the stepwise melody, and the *sails* motive. But now the upward melody is presented in a high register, in single notes—rather than in octaves or chords—and accompanied by gliding upward whole-tone-scale figures. At the end of *Voiles* there is no sense of harmonic resolution; we are left drifting in a sonorous haze.

Listening Outline To be read while music is heard

VOILES (SAILS) FROM PRELUDES FOR PIANO, BOOK I (1910), BY CLAUDE DEBUSSY

Piano

Moderate tempo, duple meter ($\frac{2}{4}$)

(Duration, 4:25)

21 0:00	1.	a. *Sails* motive, *pp,* in thirds, high register; melodic line gradually descends.
0:13		b. Low repeated tones, *pp,* introduce
22 0:18		c. Stepwise melody in octaves, in middle register, *pp,* joined by *sails* motive in higher register.
0:45		d. Opening *sails* motive repeated, accompanied by low repeated tones and gentle rising chords. Melodic line in thirds slowly rises; bell-like octaves, *pp.*

BASIC TERMS

impressionism (page 449)
pentatonic scale (450)
whole-tone scale (450)

TWENTIETH CENTURY

5

MAURICE RAVEL

The French composer Maurice Ravel (1875–1937) was a master of orchestral and pianistic tone color. Like Debussy, who was his older contemporary, Ravel grew up in Paris and studied piano and composition for many years at the Paris Conservatory. But unlike Debussy, Ravel never succeeded in winning the Prix de Rome, despite five attempts. His last failure—at age thirty, when he was already a recognized composer—caused a scandal that led to a change of administration at the Conservatory. It was perhaps owing to lingering resentment at the musical establishment that he refused the Legion of Honor when it was offered to him, as France's most famous living composer, in 1920.

Though he is often described as an impressionist and paired with Debussy, Ravel does not fit neatly into any stylistic category. It is true that some of his music—such as the piano piece *Jeux d'eaux* (*Fountains,* 1901) and the ballet *Daphnis and Chloé* (1909–1912)—has the fluid, misty, atmospheric quality associated with impressionism. And subtle changes of tone color are indeed extremely important in Ravel's works, as in the impressionist music of Debussy. Yet much music by Ravel is too clearly defined in form and tonality and classically balanced in phrase structure to be considered impressionist. His lyrical melodic lines, though individual in style, are closely related to melodies by nineteenth-century French composers such as Georges Bizet. However, Ravel's melodies are often based on modes, which sometimes make them suggest music from a foreign land or from the distant past. His music is often characterized by a clear beat, and rhythmic patterns are often obsessively repeated.

Above all, Ravel was a master craftsman who once said, "My objective is technical perfection." He worked unceasingly to produce a relatively small number of vocal and instrumental works (for piano, orchestra, and chamber groups) that are almost all widely performed and recorded. His highly original piano pieces contain novel sonorities and extend the virtuoso style of Liszt. They were a proving ground for compositional procedures he later used in orchestral compositions. In fact, a considerable proportion of his orchestral works—including *Alborada del Gracioso* and *Le Tombeau de Couperin (The Tomb of Couperin)*—are orchestrations of piano pieces; and his orchestral transcription of Mussorgsky's piano piece *Pictures at an Exhibition* is very popular. Ravel was extremely sensitive to the technical and expressive capacities of orchestral instruments and created many fresh combinations of tone colors.

Ravel had a taste for exotic musical idioms. Many of his works have a Spanish flavor; examples are the one-act opera *L'Heure espagnole (The Spanish Hour,* 1907–1909) and the orchestral works *Rhapsodie espagnole (Spanish Rhapsody,* 1908) and *Bolero.* The rhythms and tone colors of American jazz are exploited in such works of the 1920s as the Piano Concerto in G major, the Piano Concerto for the Left Hand (commissioned by the one-armed pianist Paul Wittgenstein), and the *Blues* movement of the Sonata for Violin and Piano. Ravel was also fascinated by the dance and wrote several ballets including *Daphnis and Chloé,* which he later arranged as two concert suites for orchestra. Stylized dance rhythms pervade much of his music: the Renaissance pavane in *Pavane pour une infante défunte (Pavane for a Dead Princess,* 1899); the baroque forlane, rigaudon, and minuet in *Le Tombeau de Couperin* (1914–1917); the Viennese waltz in *Valses nobles et sentimentales (Noble and Sentimental Waltzes,* 1911) and *La Valse (The Waltz,* 1919–1920); and the Spanish bolero in *Bolero.*

BOLERO

One of the best known of all orchestral works, *Bolero* reflects Ravel's fascination with tone color, Spanish music, and obsessive rhythmic repetition. It originated as a ballet commissioned by the dancer Ida Rubinstein and was introduced by her at the Paris Opera in 1928. Set in a dimly lit Spanish cafe, the ballet centers on a young Gypsy woman dancing a bolero on a table surrounded by men. Her movements become increasingly lively, and the excitement and tension of the onlookers culminate in violence. The ballet was a success, but soon *Bolero* became more famous internationally as a concert piece. After its American premiere by Arturo Toscanini and the New York Philharmonic in 1929, a critic wrote that *"Bolero* brought shouts and cheers from the audience."

Side 13, band 4
CD 7 [12]

Ravel modestly described *Bolero* as an "experiment" consisting of "one long, very gradual crescendo." Its theme and rhythm "were deliberately given a Spanish character" and "repeated to the point of obsession." *Bolero* is unusual in form, consisting of an extended, exotic-sounding theme that is heard over and over with increasingly rich and brilliant orchestration. Ravel creates movement and growth through changes of tone color, as Stravinsky did in the *Firebird* Suite and *The Rite of Spring*. The theme is first presented by solo woodwind instruments, including the unusual oboe d'amore, which is lower than the oboe but higher than the English horn. As the volume gradually increases, brass instruments and tenor and sopranino saxophones—rare in a symphony orchestra—are given the theme. Novel tone colors result from unusual doublings, such as muted trumpet and flute, as though Ravel were inventing new instruments. Sometimes the melody is doubled at different pitch levels, a device which results in sliding parallel chords.

Only after the dynamic level has reached *f* is the melody presented by the violins and doubled by woodwinds and brasses.

Bolero's accompaniment is even more obsessive than its melody. From beginning to end, a two-bar bolero rhythmic pattern is repeated in the snare drum, which is progressively doubled by more and more instruments. Moreover, in the bass of virtually every bar we hear a three-note ostinato played pizzicato by the lower strings. Also contributing to the hypnotic effect is the insistence on the key of C major, which persists until an electrifying climax—resulting from a sudden, momentary upward shift to the brighter key of E major—and a violently dissonant ending.

The theme of *Bolero* is made up of two extended parts which are each heard twice with varied orchestration: A A B B. This A A B B pattern is presented four times, gradually building in power. Finally, Ravel compresses the theme to A B. Thus, *Bolero* can be outlined as A A B B–A A B B–A A B B–A A B B–A B. The bolero rhythmic pattern and accompanying bass ostinato are presented alone—without the melody—as an introduction to each A and B, with gradually increasing volume and richness of sound.

In part A, the melody is fairly narrow in range and uses only the notes of the C major scale. It has two phrases, the first ending with a questioning upward skip to an incomplete cadence, and the second ending with a complete cadence as if giving an answer.

Part B of the theme is also made up of two phrases, but it is wider in range and darker in mood because it combines elements of major, minor, and modal scales. After ascending to a climactic tone that is repeated with hypnotic insistence, the melody gradually moves downward a long distance until it reaches a cadence.

Listening Outline To be read while music is heard

BOLERO (1928), BY MAURICE RAVEL

Tempo di bolero, moderato assai (tempo of a bolero, very moderate), triple meter ($\frac{3}{4}$)

2 piccolos, 2 flutes, 2 oboes (one doubling on oboe d'amore), English horn, E-flat clarinet, 2 B-flat clarinets, bass clarinet, 3 saxophones (sopranino, soprano, tenor), 2 bassoons, contrabassoon, 4 French horns, 1 small trumpet in D, 3 trumpets, 3 trombones, tuba, harp, 3 timpani, cymbals, tam-tam, celesta, 2 snare drums, 1st violins, 2d violins, violas, cellos, double basses

(Duration, 15:02)

12 0:00   1. a. Bolero rhythm in snare drum, *pp,* accompanied by ostinato in pizzicato violas and cellos.

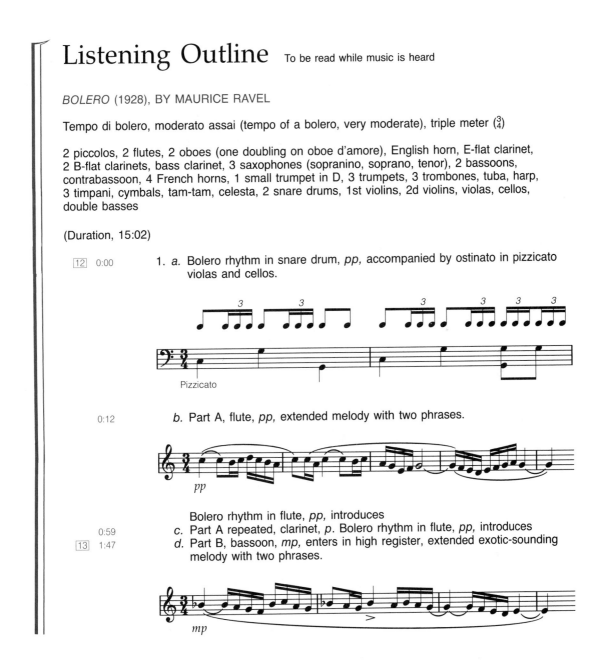

0:12   b. Part A, flute, *pp,* extended melody with two phrases.

Bolero rhythm in flute, *pp,* introduces
0:59   c. Part A repeated, clarinet, *p.* Bolero rhythm in flute, *pp,* introduces
13 1:47   d. Part B, bassoon, *mp,* enters in high register, extended exotic-sounding melody with two phrases.

Harp, *pp,* and bolero rhythm in flute, *pp,* introduce

2:36   *e.* Part B, repeated an octave higher, high (E-flat) clarinet, *p.* Bolero rhythm in high bassoon, *mp,* introduces

[14] 3:24   2. *a.* Part A, oboe d'amore, *mp.* Bolero rhythm in French horn, *p,* introduces

4:12   *b.* Part A repeated, muted trumpet, *mp,* doubled an octave higher by flute, *p.* Pizzicato violins, bolero rhythm in muted trumpet, *mp,* introduce

[15] 5:00   *c.* Part B, tenor saxophone, *mp,* melody decorated by slides. Pizzicato violins, bolero rhythm in muted trumpet, *mp,* introduce

5:48   *d.* Part B repeated an octave higher, sopranino saxophone, *mf.* Harp, bolero rhythm in French horn, *mf,* introduce

6:36   3. *a.* Part A, French horn, *mf,* doubled at higher pitches by piccolos. Pizzicato strings, bolero rhythm in muted trumpets, *mf,* introduce

7:24   *b.* Part A repeated in woodwinds, *mf.* Harp, bolero rhythm in violas and French horns, *mf,* introduce

8:11   *c.* Part B, trombone, *mf,* melody decorated by slides. Bolero rhythm in trumpets, *f,* introduces

8:59   *d.* Part B repeated in high woodwinds, *mf,* with melody in parallel chords, *f.* Bolero rhythm in French horns, *f,* introduces

9:47   4. *a.* Part A, violins, *f,* and woodwinds. Bolero rhythm in French horns, *f,* introduces

10:35   *b.* Part A, repeated in violins, *f,* and woodwinds, with melody in parallel chords. Bolero rhythm in French horns, *f,* introduces

11:20   *c.* Part B, violins, woodwinds, and trumpet, *f.* Bolero rhythm in strings, woodwinds, and French horns, *f,* introduces

12:08   *d.* Part B repeated in strings, woodwinds, and trombone, *f,* with melody in parallel chords. Bolero rhythm in strings, woodwinds, and French horns, *ff,* introduces

12:55   5. *a.* Part A, violins, trumpets, and woodwinds, *ff,* with melody in parallel chords. Bolero rhythm in strings, woodwinds, and French horns, *ff,* introduces

13:42   *b.* Part B, violins, woodwinds, and brasses, *ff,* with melody in parallel chords; melody changes with shift to new key, closes with return to original key. Bolero rhythm in whole orchestra; percussion, *ff,* cymbal crashes, dissonant concluding chords.

TWENTIETH
CENTURY

6 NEOCLASSICISM

From about 1920 to 1950, the music of many composers, including Igor Stravinsky and Paul Hindemith, reflected an artistic movement known as *neoclassicism.* Neoclassicism is marked by emotional restraint, balance, and clarity; neoclassical compositions use musical forms and stylistic features of earlier periods, particularly of the eighteenth century. Stravinsky summed it up: "I attempted to build a new music on eighteenth-century classicism." Neoclassical music is not merely a revival of old forms and styles; it uses earlier techniques to organize twentieth-century harmonies and rhythms.

"Back to Bach" was the slogan of this movement that reacted against romanticism and impressionism. (Since many neoclassical compositions were modeled after Bach's music, the term *neobaroque* might have been more appropriate.) Neoclassical composers turned away from program music and the gigantic orchestras favored at the turn of the century. They preferred absolute (nonprogrammatic) music for chamber groups. This preference for smaller performing groups partly reflected economic necessity: during the post-World War I period, economic conditions were so bad in parts of Europe that there was little money to hire large orchestras. Favoring clear polyphonic textures, composers wrote fugues, concerti grossi, and baroque dance suites. Most neoclassical music was tonal and used major and minor scales. Still, neoclassicism was more an attitude than a style. Schoenberg wrote minuets and gigues using his twelve-tone system. And though neoclassical composers referred to many past styles, their works sound completely modern. They play on the delightful tension between our expectations about old forms and styles and the novel harmonies and rhythms. In Section 7, we'll study a neoclassical work by Stravinsky, the *Symphony of Psalms* (1930).

Neoclassicism was an important trend in other arts, too. The poet T. S. Eliot often quoted and alluded to earlier writers. Picasso, who designed sets for Stravinsky's first neoclassical work, *Pulcinella* (1920), went through a phase during which he created paintings that show the influence of ancient Greek art. Picasso described the neoclassical attitude by saying that artists "must pick out what is good for us where we find it. When I am shown a portfolio of old drawings, for instance, I have no qualms about taking anything I want from them."

BASIC TERM

neoclassicism (page 460)

IGOR STRAVINSKY

Even before his death at the age of eighty-eight, Igor Stravinsky (1882–1971) was a legendary figure and was regarded as the world's greatest composer. His once revolutionary works were modern classics; he was a restless innovator who influenced three generations of composers and inspired many painters, writers, and choreographers. Cultural giants like Picasso and T. S. Eliot were his friends; President John F. Kennedy honored him at a White House dinner in his eightieth year.

Igor Stravinsky, in a sketch by Picasso.

Stravinsky, who was born in a small town near St. Petersburg, Russia, grew up in a musical atmosphere. His father was a leading singer at the St. Petersburg opera. Despite Stravinsky's obvious talent, his parents insisted that he study law at the University of St. Petersburg. Soon he began to neglect his studies and devote himself to composition. At the age of twenty-one, he became a private student of Nikolai Rimsky-Korsakov.

Stravinsky's life took a sudden turn in 1909, when the great impresario Sergei Diaghilev heard his music at a concert in St. Petersburg. Diaghilev was director of the Russian Ballet. This troupe, based in Paris, had a powerful impact not only on Stravinsky but on the entire cultural scene in Europe from 1909 to 1929. It employed great masters in all arts. Its dancers included Vaslav Nijinsky, and the choreographers Michel Fokine and George Balanchine created works for the troupe. It commissioned stage designs from great painters like Picasso and ballet music from outstanding musicians like Stravinsky, Debussy, Ravel, and Prokofiev. Diaghilev asked the twenty-six-year-old Stravinsky to orchestrate piano pieces by Chopin as ballet music for the first season of the Russian Ballet in 1909. In 1910, Stravinsky was commissioned to compose an original ballet, *The Firebird*. The immense success of this ballet, which was based on a Russian fairy tale, immediately established Stravinsky as a leading young composer. His second ballet, *Petrushka* (1911), was performed a year later, and at the age of twenty-nine Stravinsky was hailed as a modern master. His incisive rhythms, witty musical satire, and brilliant orchestral colors delighted sophisticated Parisians.

A now-legendary riot erupted in the audience when Stravinsky's third ballet, *The Rite of Spring*, was performed in Paris in 1913. Spectators hissed and booed at the music's "primitive" evocation of pagan fertility rites, its harshly insistent dissonance, its percussiveness, and its pounding rhythms. One member of the audience reported that someone excitedly "began to beat rhythmically on top of my head with his fists. My emotion was so great that I did not feel the blows." Soon after, however, the ballet was recognized as a masterpiece; it influenced composers all over the world.

The outbreak of World War I in 1914 forced Stravinsky to seek refuge in neutral Switzerland, where he lived for six years with his wife and children. Since the Russian Revolution of 1917 ended his private income, he met financial difficulties for the first time in his life. To "escape from this alarming situation," Stravinsky wrote *The Soldier's Tale* (1918), a theatrical work that required few performers and was easy to present under wartime conditions.

After the armistice in 1918, Stravinsky moved to France, his home until the onset of World War II. Now Stravinsky was an international figure, constantly touring Europe and the United States to play and conduct his music. His voluntary exile from Russia coincided with his turning away from Russian folk music as a source of inspiration. Stravinsky's works in the 1920s and 1930s seemed excessively cool and objective to some music lovers, who preferred the early, Russian-flavored ballets.

Unlike his great contemporaries Schoenberg and Bartók, Stravinsky got well-paying commissions for his work and was an astute businessman. He described himself as composing "every day, regularly, like a man with banking hours." Stravinsky's love of order and discipline was reflected in his studio, which had, in the words of a friend, "all the instruments needed for writing, copying, drawing, pasting, cutting, clipping, filing, sharpening, and gluing that the combined effects of a stationery and hardware store can furnish."

World War II caused Stravinsky to settle in yet another country, the United States. He lived outside Los Angeles, not far from Arnold Schoenberg, but the two never visited. Their different musical philosophies created an unbridgeable gulf, and each had his own group of loyal disciples.

In 1948, Stravinsky engaged Robert Craft, a twenty-four-year-old conductor, as his musical assistant. Craft encouraged Stravinsky to become more familiar with the works of Schoenberg, Berg, and Webern. By the 1950s, all three composers were dead, and Stravinsky astonished his followers by adopting Schoenberg's twelve-tone system. And in his seventies and eighties, despite physical pain, this incredible man toured the world from Chile to Tahiti, conducting his rich and intense late works. He also, for the first time in fifty years, returned to Russia and bared his soul to a group of Soviet composers: "The smell of the Russian earth is different. . . . A man has one birthplace, one fatherland, one country."

STRAVINSKY'S MUSIC

Stravinsky had an enormous influence on twentieth-century music. His innovations in rhythm, harmony, and tone color inspired musicians throughout the world. No contemporary contributed so many masterpieces to the international repertory. Stravinsky's extensive output includes music of almost every kind, for both voices and instruments. His many works for the stage include thirteen ballet scores.

Like his friend Picasso, Stravinsky's development shows dramatic changes of style. His three early ballets—*The Firebird* (1910), *Petrushka* (1911), and *The Rite of Spring* (1913)—call for very large orchestras and draw upon Russian folklore and folk tunes. During World War I, Stravinsky abandoned the large orchestra and wrote for small chamber groups with unconventional combinations of instruments. Ragtime rhythms and popular dances (for example, the tango) were used in such works as *The Soldier's Tale* (1918). During the period from about 1920 to 1951 (described earlier, in Section 6, as the era of neoclassicism), he gradually turned from Russian folklore and drew inspiration largely from eighteenth-century music. First came the ballet *Pulcinella* (1920), based partly on the music of Giovanni Battista Pergolesi, an Italian composer of the early eighteenth century; the period ended with his opera *The Rake's Progress* (1951), modeled after Mozart's operas. Emphasizing emotional restraint, balance, and wit, Stravinsky's work at this time was far removed from the violence and "primitivism" of *The Rite of Spring*. Many pieces feature woodwind and brass instruments, which Stravinsky felt to be less "romantic" in sound than strings. Some works are based on subjects from antiquity, like the opera-oratorio *Oedipus Rex* (1927); others were inspired by sacred texts, like the *Symphony of Psalms* (1930).

Whatever Stravinsky's current style, he had always written music with a clear tonal center, and so the musical world was startled when he shifted from tonality to the twelve-tone system. This dramatic change of approach came during the 1950s, when Stravinsky was in his seventies. Taking inspiration from the music of Anton Webern (1883–1945), Stravinsky now wrote brief works in which melodic lines were "atomized" into brief fragments in constantly changing tone colors and registers.

Despite such stylistic changes, all of his music has an unmistakable "Stravinsky sound." His tone colors tend to be dry and clear, while the beat is strong and regular.

Stravinsky's rhythmic imagination was one of the most fertile in the twentieth century. His music abounds in changing and irregular meters; sometimes several meters are heard at once. Ostinatos, or repeated rhythmic patterns, frequently unify sections of a piece. They also accompany melodies with highly irregular phrase structures.

Stravinsky's treatment of musical form is also unique. Rather than connecting themes with bridge passages, he shifts abruptly from one section to the next. One idea is repeated and varied for a while, only to be broken off by something new. "Here, you see, I cut off the fugue with a pair of scissors," he remarked of a fugue that is repeatedly punctuated by contrasting material. But despite all the sudden changes, Stravinsky's music sounds unified and continuous.

Tone color is an integral part of his work. The effectiveness of his rhythms, chords, and melodies depends largely on how they are orchestrated. Much of his music is scored for unconventional groups of instruments. Highly contrasting tone colors are often combined: a vioin is set against a trumpet, or a piano against a trombone. Instruments play in unusual registers, too. For example, *The Rite of Spring* opens with the highest tones of a solo bassoon. Stravinsky uses percussion instruments imaginatively, often giving them solo roles. (He even acquired percussion instruments so that he could personally try out his drum parts.) The writer with whom he collaborated on *The Soldier's Tale* reported that he and Stravinsky met almost daily "in the blue room, . . . surrounded by side drums, kettle drums, bass drums, and every kind of percussion instrument."

Stravinsky's music has rich, novel harmonies, such as the famous "Petrushka chord," a bitonal combination of a C major triad with an F sharp major triad. He makes even conventional chords sound unique through spacing, doubling, and the orchestration of their tones. The spirit of this composer's approach is seen in his exclamation about one such novel-sounding harmony: "How happy I was when I discovered this chord!"

Stravinsky often used known material to create original music. He drew on a vast range of styles, from Russian folk songs to baroque melodies, from Renaissance madrigals to tango rhythms. Sometimes he gave another composer's melody new harmonies and orchestration. But more often, the music is entirely Stravinsky's, while vaguely suggesting a past style. Stravinsky spoke of a "lifelong need for outside nourishment." He believed that tradition is "a living force that animates and informs the present. . . . It appears as an heirloom, a heritage that one receives on condition of making it bear fruit before passing it on to one's descendants."

PETRUSHKA (1911)

Petrushka was Stravinsky's second ballet score for the Russian Ballet in Paris. It is a fantasy that unfolds against the backdrop of a Russian street fair during the St. Petersburg Carnival in the 1830s. Its main characters are three life-sized puppets—Petrushka, the Moor, and the Ballerina—who are brought to life by an old magician. In Stravinsky's words, Petrushka is "the immortal and unhappy of every fair in all countries." In a way, he's the Russian counterpart of the puppet Pinocchio. Petrushka competes with the Moor for the affection of the Ballerina. In the fourth and last scene of the ballet, the Moor strikes Petrushka with a sword and kills him, to the crowd's astonishment.

Petrushka's music is, by turns, brilliant, grotesque, and humorous. It perfectly matches the story line. Stravinsky uses Russian folk songs as well as popular songs and dances to capture the atmosphere of the Russian street fair. The sheer color and imagination of the score make *Petrushka* as popular in the concert hall as it is in the theater. We'll now focus on the ballet's opening scene, which is divided into three sections: (1) *The Crowds*, (2) *The Magic Trick*, and (3) *The Russian Dance*.

Opening Scene

Supplementary sets:
Side 7, band 1
CD 4 [1]

The curtain rises on a street fair with booths, a puppet theater, and a milling crowd. Soon an organ grinder and a street dancer compete with a music-box player and another dancer for the crowd's attention. The music is marvelously descriptive; trills and running notes match the lively activity on stage. The general confusion of a crowd is suggested through use of polyrhythm—the double basses play in one meter, while piccolos play in another. Woodwinds imitate the sound of a barrel organ amazingly closely.

The most important borrowed melody in the first section is an Easter song from the Smolensk region of Russia. The tune begins with a tone that is repeated several times. After its introduction by the double basses, the melody is played by the full orchestra as a group of drunken merrymakers dance across the stage. There are two different barrel-organ tunes. The second was originally a French music-hall favorite, *She Had a Wooden Leg*, which Stravinsky actually heard outside his window while he was composing this scene.

The opening section of *Petrushka* is in three-part form: A (crowd) B (soloists: barrel organ and music box) A' (crowd). The two outer sections are more complex musically, with the many abrupt changes characteristic of Stravinsky—rapidly changing meters, irregular rhythms, and twentieth-century chord structures. In the contrasting middle section (B), the harmo-

A scene from the original production of *Petrushka* (1911) by the Russian Ballet in Paris.

nies and rhythms are conventional, in keeping with the humble folk instruments shown playing them on stage.

The second and third sections of this scene—*The Magic Trick* and *The Russian Dance*—are much shorter than the first. An old magician appears at the puppet theater and brings the three puppets to life by playing a magic flute. The puppets then do a frantic Russian dance, first dangling on their strings in the theater and then out in the street amidst the amazed crowd.

Stravinsky uses a descending figure in the bassoon to represent the old magician. Strange chromatic harmonies and wisps of sound from the celesta and harp create a mysterious atmosphere.

The Russian Dance suggests the puppets' jerky movements by a rapid, powerful beat and bright, percussive tone colors. Piano, xylophone, and woodwinds often have solo parts. The main theme has a narrow range and is spun out of a small group of tones; these are repeated again and again with slight rhythmic variations. Repeated rhythmic figures also occur in the accompaniment.

467

Listening Outline
To be read while music is heard

OPENING SCENE FROM *PETRUSHKA* (ORIGINAL 1911 VERSION), BY IGOR STRAVINSKY

2 piccolos, 2 flutes, 4 oboes, English horn, 4 clarinets, bass clarinet, 4 bassoons, contrabassoon, 4 French horns, 2 cornets, 2 trumpets, 3 trombones, tuba, timpani, bass drum, cymbals, gong, triangle, tambourine, snare drum, xylophone, glockenspiel, 2 harps, piano, celesta, 1st violins, 2d violins, violas, cellos, double basses

(Duration, 9:39)

SECTION I: CROWDS
(Vivace)

Bustling crowd.
  ☐1 0:00   1. *a.* High flute, crowd theme; accompanying trills in clarinets and French horns.

  ☐2 0:18   *b.* Low basses, opening of Russian tune.

                  c. High flute, crowd theme; accompanying trills in clarinets and horns.
      0:29   *d.* Low basses, Russian tune. High piccolos join Russian tune in faster notes. Crescendo, trumpets.

A group of drunken merrymakers pass by, dancing.
  ☐3 0:50   2. *a.* Full orchestra, *fff*, Russian tune; powerful beat, cymbals.

                  b. Suddenly softer, Russian tune in woodwinds and violins, pizzicato. Brass chord crescendo.

The old showman of the fair entertains the crowd from the height of his booth.
      1:19   3. *a.* Timpani; staccato repeated notes in strings; irregular accents. Staccato brasses, *f.*
                  b. High piccolos, crowd theme.

An organ-grinder with a street dancer appears in the crowd.

              c. Timpani. Clarinets, opening of first barrel-organ tune.

              d. Timpani; staccato repeated notes in strings. Staccato brasses, *ff.*

              e. High violins, crowd theme.

Organ-grinder begins to play.

    4 1:59   **4.** *a.* Clarinets, first barrel-organ tune; slow "oom-pah-pah" accompaniment.

The street dancer dances, beating time on the triangle.

    5 2:14   *b.* Triangle accompanies second barrel-organ tune in flutes and clarinets.

Trumpet joins. Violins, crowd theme bursts in.

The organ-grinder, continuing to turn the crank with one hand, plays the cornet with the other. On the other side of the stage a music box begins to play. Another street dancer dances around it.

    2:37   *c.* Glockenspiel (bells), music-box tune; clarinets, first barrel-organ tune. Triangle accompanies second barrel-organ tune in flutes and clarinets. High violins, crowd theme bursts in.

The barrel organ and the music box stop playing. The old showman again entertains the crowd.

              d. Timpani; staccato repeated notes in strings; irregular accents.

    3:27   **5.** High crowd theme with bustling accompaniment. Piccolos and trumpets join, crescendo.

The drunken merrymakers return.

    3:40   **6.** *a.* Russian tune, orchestra, *fff,* powerful beat; cymbals.

              b. Suddenly softer, Russian tune in woodwinds and violins, pizzicato. Brass chord crescendo.

    4:09   **7.** *a.* Timpani; staccato repeated notes in strings, irregular accents. Staccato brasses, *f.*

              b. High piccolo, crowd theme.

              c. Timpani; staccato repeated notes in strings, irregular accents. Staccato brasses, *f.*

              d. High piccolo, crowd theme. Trumpets join, crescendo to *fff* climax.

Two drummers standing in front of the little theater attract the attention of the crowd by their drum rolls.

    5:04   *e.* Drum rolls.

SECTION II: THE MAGIC TRICK
(Lento)

Out of the little theater steps the old magician.

[6] 5:26   1. Solo bassoon, *p*, slow descending figure. High, mysterious sounds in celesta, harp, and violins. Chord in strings.

The magician plays the flute.

     2. Solo flute, *p*, upward and downward arpeggios.

The curtain of the little theater opens, and the crowd sees three puppets: Petrushka, the Moor, and the Ballerina.

     3. Violins, *pp*, high descending figure. Mysterious sounds in celesta, harps, and woodwinds.

The magician animates them by touching them with his flute.

     Solo flute, piccolo (two tones for each puppet).

SECTION III: THE RUSSIAN DANCE
(Allegro, in strict time)

Petrushka, the Moor, and the Ballerina began to dance together, to the great surprise of all.

[7] 7:10   1. *a.* Main theme, *f*. Upward glissando to

     b. Brief solos by cornet, clarinet, and oboe. Other instruments join on melody, crescendo.

7:46   2. *a.* Main theme, *ff*, full orchestra.

     b. Oboe solo punctuated by loud percussive sounds.

8:09   3. *a.* Piano solo, second theme. Solo violin takes second theme. Xylophone, main theme.

     b. Clarinet and English horn, *p*, main theme in slower tempo.

8:58   4. Solo piano, *f*, main theme in fast tempo. Other instruments join. Running notes punctuated by loud chords. Abrupt concluding cadence, cornet, sustained tone.

LE SACRE DU PRINTEMPS
(THE RITE OF SPRING, 1913)

Few compositions have had so powerful an impact on twentieth-century music as *Le Sacre du printemps (The Rite of Spring)*, Stravinsky's third ballet score for the Russian Ballet. Its harsh dissonances, percussive orchestration, rapidly changing meters, violent offbeat accents, and ostinatos fired the imaginations of many composers. The idea for *The Rite of Spring* came to Stravinsky as a "fleeting vision," while he was completing *The Firebird* in St. Petersburg in 1910. "I saw in imagination a solemn pagan rite: wise elders, seated in a circle, watching a young girl dance herself to death. They were sacrificing her to propitiate the god of spring." Later in life,

470

Les Demoiselles d'Avignon (1907), by Picasso, reflects the influence of African sculpture.

Stravinsky revealed that the "most wonderful event" of every year of his childhood was the "violent Russian spring that seemed to begin in an hour and was like the whole earth cracking."

Stravinsky's interest in a so-called primitive or nonliterate culture was shared by many artists and scholars in the early 1900s. In 1907, Picasso's violent and path-breaking painting *Les Demoiselles d'Avignon* reflected the influence of African sculpture. In 1913—the same year as *The Rite of Spring*—Freud published *Totem and Taboo*, a study of "resemblances between the psychic lives of savages and neurotics." But ***primitivism***—the deliberate evocation of primitive power through insistent rhythms and percussive sounds—did not have a lasting impact on early twentieth-century music. Stravinsky never again wrote anything like *The Rite of Spring;* and with the exception of works like *Allegro barbaro* (1911), a piano piece by Bartók, few primitivistic compositions have entered the repertory.

The Rite of Spring consists of two large parts which are subdivided into sections with varying speeds. These subsections follow each other without pause. The titles of the dances suggest their primitive subject matter: Part I, *The Adoration of the Earth:* (1) *Introduction;* (2) *Omens of Spring: Dances of the Youths and Maidens;* (3) *Ritual of Abduction;* (4) *Spring Rounds;* (5) *Games of the Rival Tribes;* (6) *Procession of the Wise Elder;* (7) *Adoration of the Earth;* (8) *Dance of the Earth.* Part II, *The Sacrifice:* (1) *Introduction;* (2) *Mysterious Circles of the Young Girls;* (3) *Glorification of the Chosen Maiden;* (4) *Evocation of the Ancestors;* (5) *Ritual of the Ancestors;* (6) *Sacrifical Dance.* Each of the two large parts begins with a slow introduction and ends with a frenzied, climactic dance.

The Rite of Spring is written for an enormous orchestra including eight horns, four tubas, and a very important percussion section made up of five timpani, bass drum, tambourine, tam-tam, triangle, antique cymbals, and a guiro (a notched gourd scraped with a stick). The melodies of *The Rite of Spring* are folklike. Like ancient Russian folk tunes, they have narrow ranges, and they are made up of fragments that are repeated with slight changes in rhythm and pitch. Many individual chords are repeated, and each change of harmony produces a great impact. This melodic and harmonic repetition gives the music a ritualistic, hypnotic quality. Rhythm is a vital form-building element in *The Rite of Spring;* it has a life of its own, almost independent of melody and harmony. Today, *The Rite of Spring* is performed more frequently as a concert piece than as a ballet.

We'll now take a closer look at four sections of *The Rite of Spring:* the *Introduction, Dances of the Youths and Maidens,* and *Ritual of Abduction,* which open Part I; and the *Sacrificial Dance,* which concludes Part II.

Part I: *Introduction*

Side 12, band 3
CD 6 [28]

[28] 0:00

For Stravinsky, the *Introduction* to Part I represented "the awakening of nature, the scratching, gnawing, wiggling of birds and beasts." It begins with the strangely penetrating sound of a solo bassoon straining at the top of its register. As though improvising, the bassoon repeats a fragment of a Lithuanian folk tune in irregular ways.

Soon other woodwind instruments join the bassoon with repeated fragments of their own. The impression of improvisation is strengthened by the absence of a clearly defined pulse or meter. Dissonant, unconventional chord structures are used. Toward the end of the *Introduction,* different layers of sounds—mostly from woodwinds and brasses—are piled on top of each other, and the music builds to a piercing climax. But suddenly, all sound is cut off; only the solo bassoon forlornly repeats its opening melody. Then the violins, playing pizzicato, introduce a repeated four-note figure.

Solo bassoon
2:29
[29] 2:40

This figure later serves as an ostinato in the *Dances of the Youths and Maidens,* which immediately follows the Introduction.

Part I: *Omens of Spring—Dances of the Youths and Maidens*

Sounding almost like drums, the strings pound out a dissonant chord. There are unexpected and irregular accents whose violence is heightened by jabbing sounds from the eight horns. This is the way the passage might be counted (with a rapid pulse): 1–2–3–4, 1–2–3–4, 1–**2**–3–**4**, 1–2–3–4, 1–2–3–4, **1**–2–3–4, 1–2–3–4, 1–2–3–4. The unchanging dissonant harmony is a polychord that combines two different traditional chords.

Side 12, band 3
(continued)
CD 6 [30]
[30] 3:00

A succession of melodic fragments soon join the pounding chord and other repeated figures. The melodic fragments, played by brass and woodwind instruments, are narrow in range and are repeated over and over with slight variations.

[31] 3:48

a Bassoons

32 4:45

b Horn

mp

33 5:21

c Trumpets

mp

The rhythmic activity is constant and exciting, and gradually more and more instruments are added.

It's interesting to contrast Stravinsky's musical techniques in *Dances of the Youths and Maidens* with those of a classical movement in sonata form. A classical movement grows out of conflicts between different keys; this section of *The Rite of Spring* is based almost entirely on the repetition of a few chords. The themes in a classical movement are developed through different keys, varied, and broken into fragments that take on new emotional meanings. In *Dances of the Youths and Maidens*, Stravinsky simply repeats melodic fragments with relatively slight variation. His novel techniques grew out of the Russian musical tradition of the nineteenth century. The *Coronation* Scene from *Boris Godunov* (1874), by Mussorgsky, also uses just a few chords that are repeated throughout a section. Like some of his Russian forebears, Stravinsky relies on variations of rhythm and tone color to create movement and growth.

Part I: *Ritual of Abduction*

Side 12, band 3
(continued)
CD 6 34 6:21
35 7:13

The frenzied *Ritual of Abduction* grows out of the preceding section and is marked by violent strokes on the timpani and bass drum. Enormous tension is generated by powerful accents and rapid changes of meter (see the music example on page 440). This section of *The Rite of Spring* closes with high trills in the strings and flutes.

Part II: *Sacrificial Dance*

Side 13, band 1
CD 7 1

Section A
1 0:00

The *Sacrificial Dance* is the overwhelming climax of the work. It consists of sections that can be outlined as follows: A B A' C A" (very brief) C A'''. In the opening section (A), explosive, percussive chords fight brutal blows on the timpani. The time signature changes with almost every bar: $\frac{3}{16}$ $\frac{2}{16}$ $\frac{3}{16}$ $\frac{2}{8}$ $\frac{2}{16}$ $\frac{3}{16}$. The rapid pulse and irregular, jolting accents create intense excitement.

Section B
2 0:30

The second section (B) begins with a sudden drop in dynamic level as a single chord is repeated obsessively. Brief silences between these repeated chords urge the listener to supply accents.

Section C features brasses and percussive sounds from five timpani, a tam-tam (gong), and a bass drum. The *Sacrificial Dance* glorifies the power of rhythm, as does the entire *Rite of Spring*.

Section C
3 2:29

SYMPHONY OF PSALMS (1930)

The *Symphony of Psalms*, a masterpiece from Stravinsky's "neoclassical period," was written for the fiftieth anniversary of the Boston Symphony Orchestra in 1930. It has three movements and is scored for chorus and orchestra. The Latin text is taken from three psalms in the Vulgate Bible. Stravinsky chose the Latin version to evoke the feeling of an ancient and solemn ritual. An austere, archaic quality is also communicated through chantlike melodies that are sometimes restricted to one or two tones.

The neoclassical features of the *Symphony of Psalms* include its use of tonality, major and minor triads, and fugue; and its deliberate evocation of the past. Yet the music sounds completely of this century. As in many works by Stravinsky, the orchestra is highly unconventional. There are no violins, violas, or clarinets; the sounds of woodwinds, brasses, and two pianos predominate. Stravinsky intended the voices and instruments to "be on an equal footing, neither of them outweighing the other." He uses the term *symphony* not in its usual sense, but simply to indicate a work in several movements that calls for an orchestra. The three movements are related motivically and are performed without interruption. We'll focus on the first movement.

First Movement: Psalm 38 (Vulgate), Verses 13–14*

The brief opening movement, based on a psalm beginning "Hear my prayer, O Lord," is a prelude to the successively longer movements that follow. First, a staccato orchestral chord repeatedly punctuates woodwind solos. Although it is a standard E minor triad, this chord sounds unique because its tones are spaced and orchestrated in a novel way. After this orchestral introduction, the alto voices of the chorus sing a chantlike melody composed of just two notes that alternate.

Side 13, band 2
CD 7 4

Altos
mf

E - xau - di___ o - ra - ti - o - nem me-am, Do - mi - ne,___

---

*Psalm 38 in the Vulgate is Psalm 39 in the King James version.

This chantlike theme is supported by ostinatos in the woodwinds.

The first part of the movement is marked by abrupt contrasts between the staccato chord, woodwind interludes, and brief passages for chorus and orchestra. The second part of the movement is more continuous as the chorus and orchestra are always heard together. The movement ends in triumph, with a sustained G major triad that has a great impact because it is the movement's only *major* triad; it vividly contrasts with the staccato minor triads heard earlier.

		4
		Orchestral introduction; loud staccato chord punctuates solos by oboe, bassoon.
Exaudi orationem meam, Domine,	Hear my prayer, O Lord,	Piano. High cello. Altos, chantlike theme.
et deprecationem meam;	and my supplication;	Full chorus. Oboe.
auribus percipe lacrymas meas.	give ear to my tears.	Altos, chantlike theme.
Ne sileas,	Be not silent:	Staccato chord. Tenors and altos, *f;* staccato chord,
quoniam advena ego	for I am a stranger	Altos, basses.
sum apud te, et peregrinus	with thee, and a sojourner	Other voices join.
sicut omnes patres mei.	as all my fathers were.	Crescendo to *ff.*
Remitte mihi, (remitte mihi,)	O forgive me, (O forgive me,)	Suddenly softer, chantlike theme in tenors and sopranos.
ut refrigerer priusquam abeam et amplius non ero.	that I may be refreshed, before I go hence, and be no more.	Major chord, *ff.*

BASIC TERM
primitivism (page 471)

EXPRESSIONISM

Much twentieth-century music reflects *expressionism,* an artistic movement which stressed intense, subjective emotion. It was largely centered in Germany and Austria from 1905 to 1925. Painters, writers, and composers explored inner feelings rather than depicting outward appearances. They used deliberate distortions to assault and shock their audience, to communicate the tensions and anguish of the human psyche. Expressionism grew out of the same intellectual climate as Freud's studies of hysteria and the unconscious. The German expressionist painters were reacting against French impressionism, with its pleasant subjects, delicate pastel colors, and shimmering surfaces.

The expressionists rejected conventional prettiness. Their works may seem "ugly" in their preoccupation with madness and death. Expressionist painters such as Ernst Ludwig Kirchner, Emil Nolde, Edvard Munch, and Oskar Kokoschka often use jarring colors and grotesquely distorted shapes. Expressionist art is fragmentary; the scenes of an expressionist play may be episodic and discontinuous. Expressionism is an art concerned with social protest. It movingly conveyed the anguish felt by the poor and oppressed. Many expressionists opposed World War I and used art to depict their horror of bloodshed.

There was close communication between expressionist writers, painters, and musicians. Many were creative in different areas. The painter Wassily Kandinsky wrote essays, poetry, and plays; the composer Schoenberg painted and even participated in the shows of expressionist artists.

Twentieth-century musical expressionism grows out of the emotional turbulence in the works of late romantics like Wagner, Richard Strauss, and Mahler. In Sections 9, 10, and 11, we'll study four expressionistic compositions: Five Pieces for Orchestra, Op. 16 (1909), and *A Survivor from Warsaw,* Op. 46 (1947), by Schoenberg; the opera *Wozzeck* (1917–1922) by Alban Berg; and Five Pieces for Orchestra, Op. 10 (1911–1913), by Anton Webern. These works all stress harsh dissonance and fragmentation, and exploit extreme registers and unusual instrumental effects. All four avoid tonality and traditional chord progressions. Both *A Survivor from Warsaw* and *Wozzeck* depict a nightmarish world and express a profound empathy with the poor and tormented.

BASIC TERM
expressionism (page 477)

477

(Oslo kommunes kunstsamlinger)

The Scream (1893), by the Norwegian expressionist Edvard Munch. Expressionist painters reacted against French impressionism; they often used jarring colors and grotesquely distorted shapes to explore the subconscious.

ARNOLD SCHOENBERG

Arnold Schoenberg (1874–1951) was born in Vienna, the city of Mozart, Beethoven, and Brahms. Unlike such earlier masters, he was an almost entirely self-taught musician. "I began studying the violin at eight and almost immediately started composing," he later recalled. Schoenberg acquired his profound knowledge of music by studying scores, by playing in amateur chamber groups, and by going to concerts. His first musical hero was Brahms, then considered the greatest living German composer. He soon became "an equally confirmed addict" of Wagner; he saw each of Wagner's operas from twenty to thirty times.

When Schoenberg was sixteen, his father died, and he had to work for several years as a bank clerk. When he lost that job at twenty-one, he decided to devote himself to music. He earned a poor living by conducting a choir of metalworkers in an industrial center outside Vienna. He also orchestrated operettas written by popular composers of the time. Performances of his own early works met with hostility from the conservative Viennese public. One music critic suggested that Schoenberg be put in an insane asylum without music paper.

Schoenberg began to teach music theory and composition in Vienna in 1904. His personality inspired love and loyalty among his students. Two of his disciples, Alban Berg and Anton Webern, themselves became leading composers.

Around 1908 Schoenberg took the revolutionary step of abandoning the traditional tonal system. "I already feel the opposition that I shall have to overcome," he wrote in a program note for his first atonal works. Schoenberg was a man possessed. "I have a mission. I have a task. . . . I am but the loudspeaker of an idea." His productivity between 1908 and 1915 was incredible. Besides creating many dazzlingly original works at lightning speed, he published a harmony textbook, wrote his own librettos, and entered his paintings in exhibitions of the German expressionists.

Following this fertile period came a span of eight years, encompassing World War I and the difficult postwar period, when Schoenberg published nothing. He searched for a way to organize the new musical resources he had discovered. Finally, in the summer of 1921, he told a student, "I have made a discovery which will ensure the supremacy of German music for the next hundred years." From 1923 to 1925 Schoenberg published compositions using his newly developed twelve-tone system. Although his music did not find a large audience, many important musicians respected it. At the age of fifty-one, Schoenberg received an important academic post: director of the master class in musical composition at the Prussian Academy of Arts in Berlin.

This period of official recognition was cut short in 1933, when the Nazis

(Photo Researchers)

Arnold Schoenberg developed the twelve-tone system, which offers the composer a new way of organizing pitch in a composition.

seized power in Germany. Schoenberg was dismissed from the faculty of the Prussian Academy. This shattering experience caused him to return to Judaism. (He had converted to Protestantism when he was eighteen.) The same year, he and his family left Germany for the United States, where he soon joined the music faculty at the University of California in Los Angeles. But Schoenberg felt neglected in his adopted country. His music was rarely performed, and he was refused a grant from the Guggenheim Foundation. At the age of seventy he was forced to retire from UCLA with a pension of less than $40 a month. "I am quite conscious," he wrote in 1947, "that a full understanding of my work cannot be expected before some decades, . . . and I know that—success or not—it is my historic duty to write what my destiny orders me to write." But appreciation came earlier than Schoenberg had anticipated. After his death in 1951, the twelve-tone system was adopted increasingly by composers throughout the world. It remains an important influence to this day.

SCHOENBERG'S MUSIC

"I claim the distinction of having written a truly new music which, based upon tradition as it is, is destined to become tradition." This proud assertion by Schoenberg contains a great deal of truth. His musical language was indeed new, yet it was rooted in the past and resulted from a gradual stylistic evolution. And his musical system *was* eventually adopted by many other composers.

Schoenberg's point of departure was the music of Wagner, Brahms, and Mahler. His early works, like the string sextet *Verklärte Nacht* (*Transfigured Night*, 1899), show many features of the late romantic style. The music is emotionally intense and often has a literary program. Some early compositions use the gigantic orchestras favored by late nineteenth-century composers. For example, the immense cantata *Gurrelieder* (*Songs of Gurre*, 1901; orchestration, 1911) calls for five vocal soloists, a speaker-narrator, four choruses, and a greatly expanded orchestra including about fifty woodwind and brass players. A feeling of subjectivity is generated through dissonances that resolve in unexpected ways and through angular melodies that have wide ranges and big leaps. There is prominent use of chromatic harmony, or chords with tones that do not belong to the prevailing major or minor scale. The pull of a central tonality is weakened because the music rapidly moves through keys remote from the main one.

During the years 1903 to 1907, Schoenberg moved farther from the harmonic language of the late romantics. In compositions such as the *Chamber Symphony*, Op. 9 (1906), for fifteen solo instruments, he uses whole-tone scales and fourth chords.

Atonality

Around 1908, Schoenberg finally began to write atonal music. Although it was a revolutionary development, *atonality*—the absence of key— evolved from Schoenberg's earlier emphasis on chromatic harmony and liberal use of all twelve tones in the chromatic scale. But in his atonal works, all twelve tones are used without regard for their traditional relationship to major or minor scales. Dissonances are "emancipated" from the necessity of resolving to consonances. Schoenberg explained atonality as a style based on "emancipation of the dissonance"; it "treats dissonances like consonances and renounces a tonal center. By avoiding the establishment of a key, modulation is excluded, since modulation means leaving an established tonality and establishing another tonality." In Schoenberg's atonal music from 1908 to 1914, triads and the traditional vocabulary of chord progressions are deliberately avoided, as are major and minor scales. But the word *atonality* does not imply a single system of composition. Each atonal composition has its own means of achieving unity. A piece usually grows out of a few short motives that are transformed in many different ways.

Among the best-known of Schoenberg's atonal compositions are Five Pieces for Orchestra, Op. 16 (1909); and *Pierrot lunaire, Op.* 21 *(Moonstruck Pierrot,* 1912), a setting of twenty-one poems. The jagged melodies, novel instrumental effects, and extreme contrasts of dynamics and register in Schoenberg's music are like the distorted figures and shocking colors in expressionist paintings. The texture is polyphonic and very complex. Phrases are of irregular length, and melodic repetition is avoided. *Pierrot lunaire* and other works by Schoenberg call for an unusual style of vocal performance halfway between speaking and singing. This is called **Sprechstimme,** which literally means *speech-voice* in German. The vocal part is written in music notation, but small *x*'s on the note stems indicate that the pitches are only approximate.

Schoenberg's atonal language was soon adopted by his students Berg and Webern. Their early atonal works, like Schoenberg's, tended to be extremely emotional and very short. Without a musical system like tonality, the three composers could create extended compositions only when they had a long text to serve as an organizing force.

The Twelve-Tone System

During the years 1914 to 1920, Schoenberg finished very few works as he tried to develop a more systematic method of organizing atonal music. In the early 1920s, he finally developed what he called the "method of composing with twelve tones." He partly applied this new technique in the Five Piano Pieces, Op. 23, and the Serenade, Op. 24, and then fully elaborated it in the Suite for Piano, Op. 25. All were composed from 1920 to 1923. These and some other works of the 1920s are less subjective and expressionistic than Schoenberg's earlier and later music. They use traditional forms (such as sonata form) and eighteenth-century dance types (the minuet and trio, the gavotte, and the gigue).

The twelve-tone system enabled Schoenberg to write more extended compositions than he had written when using free atonality. In 1928 he composed the monumental Variations for Orchestra, and in the years 1930 to 1932 he wrote the opera *Moses und Aron (Moses and Aaron).* Though he never finished the third act of this great masterpiece, the opera has an overwhelming impact. From the time of his arrival in the United States in 1933 to his death in 1951, Schoenberg used the twelve-tone system in many rich and varied works, including the Violin Concerto, Op. 36 (1936), the Fourth String Quartet, Op. 37 (1936), the Piano Concerto, Op. 42 (1942), and the cantata *A Survivor from Warsaw,* Op. 46 (1947).

The *twelve-tone system* offers the composer a new way of organizing pitch in a composition. It is a twentieth-century alternative to tonality. The twelve-tone system gives equal importance to each of the twelve chromatic tones, rather than emphasizing one central tone as the tonal system does. The twelve-tone method is a systematized form of atonality. It grew out of Schoenberg's desire to structure his music "*consciously* on a unifying idea."

In a twelve-tone composition, all pitches are derived from a special ordering of the twelve chromatic tones. This ordering or unifying idea is called a *tone row, set,* or *series.** The composer creates a unique tone row for each specific piece. (Schoenberg's opera *Moses and Aaron* is based entirely on a single tone row.) The choice of rows is practically limitless, since there are 479,001,600 possible arrangements of the twelve chromatic tones. The tone row must be constructed with great care because it vitally affects the total sound and is the source of every melody and chord in a piece. Here is an example of a row, the one used by Schoenberg in his Suite for Piano, Op. 25:

E	F	G	Db	Gb	Eb	Ab	D	B	C	A	Bb
1	2	3	4	5	6	7	8	9	10	11	12

Notice that no pitch occurs more than once within a row. This prevents any single tone from receiving too much emphasis.

An entire composition is built by manipulating a single twelve-tone row. The row may be presented in four basic forms: forward (original form), backward (retrograde), upside down (inversion), and backward and upside down (retrograde inversion). The retrograde (backward) form simply presents the original tone row in reverse (see the illustration on page 484). The inverted (upside down) form keeps the original sequence of intervals between tones, but the intervals move in the opposite direction. For example, the original row begins by moving *up* a half step from E to F. The inversion begins by moving *down* a half step from E to E flat.

Original

E F G Db Gb Eb Ab D B C A Bb

Inversion

E Eb Db G D F C F# A G# B Bb

*Because of its systematic use of a *series* of tones, the twelve-tone method is also referred to as *serial technique.*

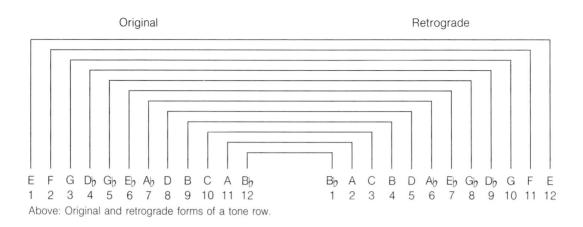

Original   Retrograde

E	F	G	D♭	G♭	E♭	A♭	D	B	C	A	B♭		B♭	A	C	B	D	A♭	E♭	G♭	D♭	G	F	E
1	2	3	4	5	6	7	8	9	10	11	12		1	2	3	4	5	6	7	8	9	10	11	12

Above: Original and retrograde forms of a tone row.

Below: Inversion and retrograde inversion of a tone row.

Inversion   Retrograde inversion

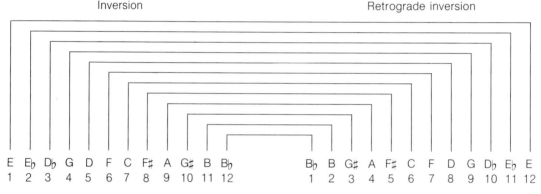

E	E♭	D♭	G	D	F	C	F♯	A	G♯	B	B♭		B♭	B	G♯	A	F♯	C	F	D	G	D♭	E♭	E
1	2	3	4	5	6	7	8	9	10	11	12		1	2	3	4	5	6	7	8	9	10	11	12

The retrograde inversion (backward and upside down) presents the tones of the inversion in reverse (see the illustration).

A tone row may be shifted to any pitch level. That is, it may begin on any of the twelve chromatic tones while keeping the original pattern of intervals. This applies to all four forms of the row: original, retrograde, inversion, and retrograde inversion. Since a row may begin on any one of twelve pitches and exist in four forms, there are forty-eight (twelve times four) possible versions of a row. This gives the composer a great deal of flexibility.

Each tone of a row may also be placed in any register, allowing an infinite variety of melodic shapes to be drawn from a single row. For example, given a row that begins with tones E–F–G, a composer could have the tones move upward by step or could have the E leap up to a high F and the F leap down to a low G.

484

This further increases the flexibility of the system and may partially explain why so many twelve-tone melodies have unusually wide leaps. The tones of a row may be presented one after another, to form a melodic line, or at the same time, to form chords. Here is the same row treated in two different ways.

We'll now study two works by Schoenberg: the "freely" atonal *Five Pieces for Orchestra*, Op. 16 (1909); and the twelve-tone cantata, *A Survivor from Warsaw*, Op. 46 (1947), composed almost forty years later.

FIVE PIECES FOR ORCHESTRA, OP. 16 (1909)

"I can promise you something really colossal, especially in sound and mood," wrote Schoenberg to the composer and conductor Richard Strauss after completing his Five Pieces for Orchestra, Op. 16, in 1909. These revolutionary pieces were the first atonal works for full orchestra. Though Schoenberg calls for an especially large orchestra, he treats it as a group of soloists. (In 1949, Schoenberg rearranged the Five Pieces for a conventional orchestra.) Many novel orchestral effects are exploited, and instruments are often used at the top or bottom of their ranges. The pieces, especially the third, embody Schoenberg's concept of a **tone-color melody** (*Klangfarbenmelodie*, in German), a succession of varying tone colors used as a musical idea in a composition. The third piece, *Summer Morning by a Lake: Colors* (also called *The Changing Chord*), is based on subtly shifting tone colors of a gradually changing chord. Schoenberg wrote in the score that

"the change of harmonies should occur gently, without emphasis on instrumental entries, so that only a difference in tone color is perceived."

Schoenberg added descriptive titles after he composed the music. Each
piece is quite brief; at the time, Schoenberg unconsciously felt the need to
"counterbalance extreme emotionality with extraordinary shortness." The
first piece is called *Vorgefühle (Premonitions)*.

Vorgefühle (Premonitions)

Side 14, band 1
CD 7 16

An amazing amount of musical activity takes place in the 2-minute span of
Premonitions. It is "just an uninterrupted change of colors, rhythms, and
moods," according to Schoenberg. The constant intensity and desperate
energy of *Premonitions* are typically expressionistic.

16 0:00

The piece consists of two connected sections: an introductory part lasting
about ½ minute, and a main part three times as long. The introduction
sounds fragmentary and has a bewildering succession of musical ideas in
different tempos, tone colors, dynamics, and registers. As though holding
his full resources in reserve, Schoenberg uses only a few instruments at
any one time. First, muted cellos introduce an abrupt upward motive
(short-long-long, short-long-long):

The entire piece is built from rhythmic and melodic transformations of this
idea.

The second part of *Premonitions* is rhythmically more continuous; it becomes increasingly complex in both texture and sound.

17 0:27

The cellos begin with a steady succession of rapid notes. They have a
three-note figure that is repeated as a background ostinato throughout the
piece.

The sound becomes increasingly loud and dense as more and more melodic fragments are piled on top of one another. After an ear-splitting climax, the texture thins and the volume decreases. *Premonitions* ends with a
snarling chord played by trombones and tuba. (The effect results from
flutter-tonguing; each brass player rapidly rolls the tongue as if pronounc-
ing *d-r-r-r*.) This chord is sustained in the background throughout most of
Premonitions, and it unifies the flow of free associations in the piece.

A SURVIVOR FROM WARSAW, OP. 46 (1947)

A Survivor from Warsaw, a dramatic cantata for narrator, male chorus, and orchestra, deals with a single episode in the murder of 6 million Jews by the Nazis during World War II. Schoenberg wrote the text himself, partly basing it on a direct report by one of the few survivors of the Warsaw ghetto. Over 400,000 Jews from this ghetto died in extermination camps or of starvation; many others perished during a heroic revolt against the Nazis in 1943. The narrator's text is spoken in English, except for some terrifying Nazi commands, which are shouted in German. The narrator's part is a kind of *Sprechstimme*, the novel speech-singing developed by Schoenberg. The rhythms of the spoken words are precisely notated, but their pitch fluctuations are indicated only approximately.

Side 14, band 2
CD 7 [18]

Besides English and German, the text includes Hebrew. These were the three languages of Schoenberg's life: German, his native tongue; English, his adopted language in the United States; and Hebrew, the language of the faith to which he returned. The 6-minute cantata builds to an overwhelming conclusion when the male chorus sings in unison the Hebrew words of the prayer *Shema Yisroel (Hear, O Israel).* For centuries this has been the prayer of Jewish martyrs in their last agonized moments.

A Survivor from Warsaw is a twelve-tone composition written in 1947, when Schoenberg was seventy-two. Its tense, expressionistic style recalls the composer's orchestral piece *Premonitions*, written almost forty years earlier. The music vividly sets off every detail in the text.

A Survivor from Warsaw opens with a brief orchestral introduction that captures the nightmarish atmosphere that prevailed as Nazi soldiers awakened the Warsaw Jews for transport to death camps. We hear a weirdly shrill reveille in the trumpet and fragmentary sounds in the military drum and high xylophone.

During the narrator's opening lines, Schoenberg already prepares for the concluding Hebrew prayer. As the narrator speaks of "the old prayer they had neglected for so many years," a French horn softly intones the beginning of the melody that is later proclaimed by the chorus.

An especially vivid musical description comes when the narrator describes how the Nazis counted their victims: "They began again, first slowly: One, two, three, four, became faster and faster. . . ." The music itself becomes faster and louder, building to the powerful entrance of the chorus.

The sung Hebrew contrasts dramatically with the spoken English and German that comes before, and it is the first extended melody in the work.

Orchestral
introduction
18 0:00

I cannot remember everything. I must have been unconscious most of the time; I remember only the grandiose moment when they all started to sing, as if prearranged, the old prayer they had neglected for so many years—the forgotten creed!

But I have no recollection how I got underground to live in the sewers of Warsaw so long a time.

The day began as usual. Reveille when it still was dark—get out whether you slept or whether worries kept you awake the whole night: you had been separated from your children, from your wife, from your parents, you don't know what happened to them; how could you sleep?

They shouted again: "Get out! The sergeant will be furious!" They came out; some very slow, the old ones, the sick men, some with nervous agility. They fear the sergeant. They hurry as much as they can. In vain! Much too much noise, much too much commotion and not fast enough!

The Feldwebel shouts: *"Achtung! Still gestanden! Na wird's mal, oder soll ich mit dem Gewehrkolben nachhelfen? Na jut; wenn Ihr's durchaus haben wollt!"* ("Attention! Stand still! How about it, or should I help you along with the butt of my rifle? Oh well, if you really want to have it!")

The sergeant and his subordinates hit everyone: young or old, strong or sick, guilty or innocent—it was painful to hear the groaning and moaning.

I heard it though I had been hit very hard, so hard that I could not help falling down. We all on the ground who could not stand up were then beaten over the head.

I must have been unconscious. The next thing I knew was a soldier saying, "They are all dead!" Whereupon the sergeant ordered to do away with us.

There I lay aside half conscious. It had become very still—fear and pain— Then I heard the sergeant shouting: *"Abzählen!"* ("Count Off!")

[19] 3:45

They started slowly, and irregularly: One, two, three, four, *"Achtung."* The sergeant shouted again: *"Rascher! Nochmals von vorn anfangen! In einer Minute will ich wissen wieviele ich zur Gaskammer abliefere! Abzählen!"* ("Faster! Once more, start from the beginning! In one minute I want to know how many I am going to send off to the gas chamber! Count off!")

They began again, first slowly: one, two, three, four, became faster and faster, so fast that it finally sounded like a stampede of wild horses, and all of a sudden, in the middle of it, they began singing the *Shema Yisroel.*

Shema Yisroel Adonoy elohenoo Adonoy ehod. Veohavto es Adonoy eloheho behol levoveho oovehol nafsheho oovehol meodeho. Vehoyoo haddevoreem hoelleh asher onohee metsavveho hayyom al levoveho. Veshinnantom levoneho vedibbarto bom beshivteho beveteho oovelehteho baddereh ooveshohbeho oovekoomeho. ("Hear, O Israel, the Lord our God, the Lord is One! And thou shalt love the Lord thy God with all thy heart, and with all thy soul, and with all thy might. And these words, which I command thee this day, shall be in thy heart. And thou shalt teach them diligently unto thy children, and speak of them when thou sittest in thy house, and when thou goest on the way, and when thou liest down, and when thou risest up.")

BASIC TERMS

atonality (page 481)   tone row (set, series) (483)
Sprechstimme (482)   tone-color melody (485)
twelve-tone system (483)

ALBAN BERG [TWENTIETH CENTURY **10**]

Alban Berg (1885–1935), a student of Schoenberg, wrote music that is a unique synthesis of traditional and twentieth-century elements. He combines romantic sounds and time-honored forms with the techniques of free atonality and the twelve-tone system. A wide audience has been attracted by the lyrical warmth, vivid tone colors, and theatrical qualities of Berg's compositions.

Like his teacher, Berg was born in Vienna. He began studying privately with Schoenberg at nineteen and continued working with him from 1904 to 1911. After serving in the Austrian army during World War I, he became codirector (with Schoenberg) of the Society for Private Musical Performances in Vienna. The goal of the society, which lasted from 1918 to 1921, was to "give artists and music-lovers a real and exact knowledge of modern music" through repeated and well-rehearsed performances.

Berg first attracted international attention in 1925, when his opera *Wozzeck* premiered in Berlin. Though the opera's atonality baffled many critics, *Wozzeck* made such a powerful impression on the public that it was soon performed throughout Europe and in the United States.

Perhaps because of chronic ill health, Berg did not perform or conduct, and he composed relatively few works. From the time he finished *Wozzeck* (1922) until his death at the age of fifty, his works include the *Chamber Concerto*, for piano, violin, and thirteen winds (1925); the *Lyric Suite*, for string quartet (1926); the opera *Lulu* (1929–1935, orchestration not completed); and the Violin Concerto (1935).

WOZZECK (1917–1922)

Wozzeck is the tragic story of a soldier who is driven to murder and madness by a hostile society. An antihero obsessed by strange visions, Wozzeck is persecuted by his sadistic captain, used as a guinea pig by a half-demented doctor, and betrayed by his mistress, Marie. Wozzeck stabs Marie to death and drowns while trying to wash her blood from his hands.

Berg's musical imagination was fired in 1914 when he saw *Woyzeck*, a play by the German dramatist and revolutionary Georg Büchner (1813–1837). Though written in the early 1830s, the play is amazingly modern in its starkly realistic dialogue and disconnected scenes. Berg adapted the play into an opera while in the Austrian army in World War I. His traumatic army experiences may well have deepened his sympathy for Wozzeck.

The opera's nightmarish atmosphere makes it a musical counterpart of expressionist painting and literature. Berg conveys the tensions and torments of the unconscious through harsh dissonances and grotesque distortions. The range of emotions and styles in the music is tremendous. Though most of *Wozzeck* is freely atonal—it does not use the twelve-tone system—major and minor keys occasionally add contrast. The vocal line includes speaking, shrieking, *Sprechstimme*, distorted folk songs, and melodies with wide leaps that are difficult to sing. The gigantic orchestra closely parallels the dialogue and stage action. Descriptive effects include vivid orchestral depiction of the moon rising, frogs croaking, and water engulfing the drowning Wozzeck. Berg's music rapidly shifts between very high and very low registers, between *ffff* and *pppp*.

Wozzeck has three acts, each with five scenes. Connecting the scenes are short orchestral interludes that comment musically on the preceding action and serve as preparation for what is to come. As in the music dramas of Wagner, there is a continuous musical flow within each act, and characters are associated with specific musical ideas. A novel feature of *Wozzeck* is that the music for each scene is a self-contained composition with a particular form (passacaglia, sonata form, etc.) or of a definite type (military march, lullaby). The five scenes of the last act—we'll study scenes 4 and 5—are organized as (1) variations on a theme, (2) variations on a single tone, (3) variations on a rhythmic pattern, (4) variations on a chord, and (5) variations on continuous running notes. But Berg did not intend for the listener to concentrate on or even be aware of these unifying techniques. He wanted the audience to be caught up in the opera's dramatic flow.

In Act II, Wozzeck has been driven to desperation by Marie's infidelity and by a savage beating from the man who has slept with her. Near the beginning of Act III, Wozzeck stabs Marie to death as they walk along a forest path near a pond.

Act III: Scenes 4 and 5

Scene 4: A path near a pond

Wozzeck returns to the scene of the crime to dispose of his knife. Berg's orchestra vividly evokes the dark forest scene as a background to Wozzeck's anguished shrieks. Rising harp tones suggest the blood-red moon coming up through the clouds. Wozzeck goes mad and drowns in the pond while trying to wash the blood from his hands. Soft chromatic slides depict the engulfing water as the Captain and the Doctor, Wozzeck's tormentors, indifferently comment that someone is drowning. As Wozzeck drowns, the slides become slower and narrower in range.

Side 14, band 3
CD 7 [20]

The long orchestral interlude that follows is a deeply moving expression of grief for Wozzeck's tragic fate. It recalls the musical themes associated with his life. Berg described it as "a confession of the author stepping outside the dramatic events of the theater and appealing to the public as representing mankind." For this outpouring of compassion, Berg returns to tonality (the interlude is in D minor) and the musical language of late romanticism.

Scene 5: A street before Marie's door

Children are playing in front of Marie's house; bright sunshine brings a glaring contrast to the darkness of the preceding scenes. One of the children cruelly tells Wozzeck's son: "Hey! Your mother is dead." The boy rides off on his hobby horse with the other children to see the body. The orchestra is reduced in size to produce delicate sounds that match the children's high voices, and a continuous rhythm symbolizes their utter indifference.

Side 14, band 3
(continued)
CD 7 [24]

The opera does not end with a conclusive chord. It simply breaks off as though to suggest that the tragedy could begin again.

Scene 4

(Forest path by the pond. Moonlit night as before. Wozzeck staggers on hastily, and then stops as he searches for something.)

[20] 0:00

Winds, *p*, repeated chord.

Wozzeck

Spoken
(Sprechstimme).

Das Messer? Wo ist das Messer? Ich hab's dagelassen . . . Näher, noch näher. Mir graut's! Da regt sich was.

Where is it? Where has the knife gone? Somewhere here I left it . . . Somewhere here, somewhere. Oh! Horror! There something moved!

Shouted.

Still! Alles still und tot . . . Mörder! Mörder! Ha! Da ruft's. Nein, ich selbst.

Still! All is still and dead! . . . Murder! Murder! Ah, who cried? No, 'twas me.

(Still searching, he staggers forward a few more steps, and comes on the corpse.)

Marie! Marie! Was hast Du für eine rote Schnur um den Hals? Hast Dir das rote Halsband verdient, wie die Ohrringlein, mit Deiner Sünde! Was hängen Dir die schwarzen Haare so wild? Mörder! Mörder! Sie werden nach mir suchen . . . Das Messer verrät mich! Da, da ist's. So! Da hinunter. Es taucht ins dunkle Wasser wie ein Stein.

Marie! Marie! What is that so like a crimson cord round your neck? And was that crimson necklace well earned, like the gold earrings: the price of sinning! Why hangs your fine black hair so wild on your head? Murder! Murder! For me they'll soon be searching . . . That knife will betray me! *(Seeks it feverishly.)* Ah! It's here! *(At the pond.)* Down to the bottom! *(Throws the knife in.)* It sinks through deep dark water like a stone.

21 1:44

Rising harp tones,
pp.

(The moon comes up blood-red through the clouds.)

Aber der Mond verrät mich . . . der Mond ist blutig. Will denn die ganze Welt es ausplaudern?!—Das Messer, es liegt zu weit vorn, sie finden's beim Baden oder wenn sie nach Muscheln tauchen. Ich find's nicht . . . Aber ich muss mich waschen. Ich bin blutig. Da ein Fleck . . . und noch einer. Weh! Weh!

See how the moon betrays me . . . the moon is bloody! Must then the whole wide world be blabbing it?— The knife there, too near to the shore! They'll find it when bathing, maybe when they are mussel-gathering. *(He wades into the pond.)* It's gone now. I ought to wash my body. I am bloody. Here's a spot . . . and here . . . something. Woe! Woe!

Ich wasche mich mit Blut! Das Wasser ist Blut . . . Blut . . .
(He drowns.)

I wash myself with blood! The water is blood . . . blood . . .

22 2:38

Water music.
Upward orchestral
slides, *pp.*
Rhythm gradually
slows.

(After a short time the Doctor enters, followed by the Captain.)

Captain

Spoken.

Halt!

Stop!

Doctor
(Stands still.)

Hören Sie? Dort!   Do you hear? There!

Captain
(Stands still.)

Jesus! Das war ein Ton.   Heavens! There was a sound.

Doctor
(Pointing to the pond.)

Ja, dort!   Yes, there!

Captain

Es ist das Wasser im Teich. Das Wasser   It is the water in the pond. The water
ruft. Es ist schon lange Niemand   calls. It is a long time since anyone
ertrunken. Kommen Sie, Doktor! Es ist   was drowned. Come, Doctor, this is
nicht gut zu hören.   not good to hear.

(He tries to drag off the Doctor.)

Doctor
(Stands still and listens.)

Das stöhnt . . . als stürbe ein Mensch.   It groans . . . like a dying man.
Da ertrinkt Jemand!   There's someone drowning!

Captain

Unheimlich! Der Mond rot und die   It's uncanny! The moon is red, and   Celesta.
Nebel grau. Hören Sie? . . . Jetzt wieder   the mist is grey. Do you hear? . . .
das Ächzen.   That groaning again.

Doctor

Stiller, . . . jetzt ganz still.   It's getting softer . . . and now quite
          gone.

Captain

Kommen Sie! Kommen Sie schnell.   Come away! Quick!

(Drags the Doctor off with him.)

23 4:21
Extended orchestral
interlude.

Scene 5

(Street before Marie's door. Bright morning. Sunshine. Children are playing and
shouting. Marie's child is riding a hobby-horse.)

Children

Ringel, Ringel, Rosenkranz,   Ring-a-ring-a-roses, all fall down!   24 7:53
Ringelreih'n!

Ringel, Ringel, Rosenkranz, Rin . . .   Ring-a-ring-a-roses, all . . .

(They stop, and other children come rushing on.)

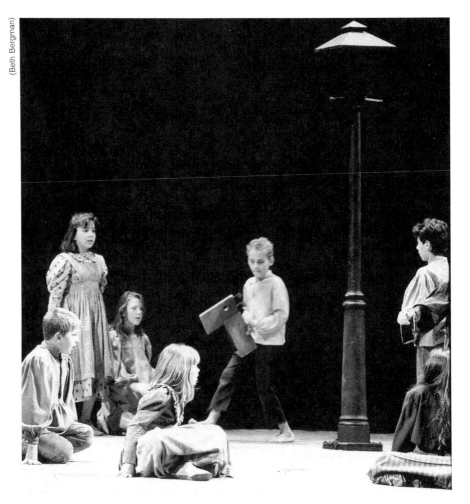

(Beth Bergman)

The concluding scene of *Wozzeck* in a production by the Metropolitan Opera.

One of them

Du Käthe! . . . Die Marie . . .   Katie! . . . Marie . . .

Second Child

Was is?   What is it?

First Child

Weisst' es nit? Sie sind schon Alle'naus.   Don't you know? They've all gone out there.

Third Child
(To Marie's child.)

Du! Dein Mutter ist tot!   Hey! Your mother is dead.

Marie's Child
(Still riding his horse.)

Hopp, hopp! Hopp, hopp! Hopp, hopp!   Hop, hop! Hop, hop! Hop, hop!

Second Child

Wo is sie denn?   Where is she now?

First Child

Draus' liegt sie, am Weg, neben dem   Out there, on the path by the pond.
Teich.

Third Child

Kommt, anschaun!   Let's go and look!

(All the children run off.)

Marie's Child
(Continues to ride.)

Hopp, hopp! Hopp, hopp! Hopp, hopp!   Hop, hop! Hop, hop! Hop, hop!

(He hesitates a moment, and then rides off after the other children.)   Music breaks off.

ANTON WEBERN

Neglected during his lifetime, Anton Webern (1883–1945) did not live to see his music influence composers throughout the world during the 1950s and 1960s.

Webern was born in Vienna, the son of a mining engineer. As a young man, he composed constantly and studied piano, cello, and music theory. At eighteen, he entered the University of Vienna, and later he earned a doctorate in music history. While at the university, he studied composition privately with Arnold Schoenberg.

After finishing his studies with Schoenberg, Webern earned a modest living conducting various orchestras and choruses. His career was solid but unspectacular. His most important position was as director of the Vienna Workers' Symphony Concerts, where traditional and contemporary compositions were performed for a working-class audience. The rare performances of his own works were usually met with ridicule.

Webern was a shy man, devoted to his wife and children. He was a Christian mystic who loved to commune with nature while mountain-climbing in the Austrian Alps. "It is not the beautiful landscape, the beautiful flowers in the usual romantic sense, that moves me," he wrote to his friend Alban Berg. "My object is the deep, bottomless, inexhaustible meaning in all. I love all nature, but most of all that which is found in the mountains."

With the rise of Nazism in Austria in 1934, Webern's orchestra and chorus—which had been sponsored by the Social Democratic party—were dissolved. In 1938, when Nazi Germany annexed Austria, Webern lost his job with the government radio, and his music was banned. He was forced to earn a living by proofreading for his Viennese publisher.

Webern's life seems ordinary enough, but his death was a bizarre tragedy. Toward the end of World War II, he took refuge from the bombing of Vienna in the small Austrian town of Mittersill. His daughter lived there with her husband and three children. In 1945, victorious American soldiers occupied the town; on the night of September 15 they arrested Webern's son-in-law, who was suspected of dealing in the black market. During the questioning, Webern and his wife—who were unaware of their son-in-law's activities—went into the bedroom, where their grandchildren were sleeping. Later, Webern stepped outside the house to smoke a cigar without disturbing the children. Minutes later, an American soldier left the house and bumped into Webern in the darkness. Nervous because he was in a hostile foreign country, the soldier mistakenly thought he was being attacked. He fired three shots, and Webern was dead.

WEBERN'S MUSIC

Poetic lyricism pervades Webern's music, which is amazingly original in its brevity, quietness, and concentration. Webern distills a musical universe into miniatures lasting only two or three minutes; every single tone is of crucial importance, so that the listener experiences time with a new intensity. Schoenberg aptly observed that Webern "expressed a novel in a single gesture, a joy in a breath."

Rarely has a composer achieved such worldwide influence on the basis of so little music; virtually all of Webern's mature music can be played in less than 3½ hours. Choral works and songs make up about half of his output. The rest is music written for chamber orchestra or small chamber groups (as in the Quartet for Clarinet, Tenor Saxophone, Violin, and Piano, Op. 22, 1930). Webern's first atonal works date from 1908 to 1909, around the same time as Schoenberg's. He adopted the twelve-tone system in the late 1920s, not long after his teacher had developed it.

Webern exploited Schoenberg's idea of a "melody built of tone colors." His melodic lines are "atomized" into two- or three-note fragments which are presented in constantly changing tone colors and registers. He forces us to focus on the tone color, dynamic level, and register of each note. At first his music may seem like isolated wisps of sound, but repeated hearings reveal that the fragments add up to a unified whole.

The texture of Webern's music is delicate and transparent; usually not more than a few solo instruments play at once. In his twelve-tone works, there is often strict polyphonic imitation among the lines of the texture. This technique may well reflect Webern's profound knowledge of Renaissance choral music, in which polyphonic imitation is so important. Texture, tone color, and dynamics play a crucial role in creating form in Webern's music.

Composers in the 1950s and 1960s used Webern's special way of manipulating a tone row as a musical point of departure. They were fascinated by his use of texture, tone color, dynamics, and register as unifying elements, and they often imitated the deceptively "cool" sound of his later music. Works that appealed to very few during Webern's lifetime have become a source of inspiration after his death.

FIVE PIECES FOR ORCHESTRA, OP. 10 (1911–1913)

Webern's unique style is fully revealed in his early, atonal Five Pieces for Orchestra, Op. 10, composed before he adopted the twelve-tone system. These five "expressions of musical lyricism," as Webern called them, are among the shortest orchestral compositions ever written. The fourth piece is only 6⅓ measures long and lasts less than thirty seconds. Webern's chamber orchestra of eighteen soloists includes unconventional instruments like the mandolin, guitar, cowbells, and harmonium (a small organ with metal reeds). Each piece (we'll consider the third) is scored for a different number and combination of instruments.

Melodic fragments are whispered by ever-changing solo instruments and framed by poetic silences. Tone-color melodies replace "tunes" in this music. There are few notes, but each is crucial. The tempo constantly fluctuates. Brasses and strings are usually muted.

Third Piece:
Very slow and extremely calm

With its bell sounds coming as though from far off, the third piece has a feeling of solitude and eerie stillness. The dynamics never rise above pp. The sustained bell-like sounds—produced by mandolin, celesta, guitar, harp, glockenspiel, cowbells, chimes, and harmonium—are heard both at the beginning and at the ending. This creates a vague A B A′ effect. Melodic fragments in ever-changing solo instruments are set apart from one another by brief moments of near silence.

Side 14, band 4
CD 7 25

Listening Outline To be read while music is heard

THIRD PIECE (1913) FROM FIVE PIECES FOR ORCHESTRA,
OP. 10 (1911–1913), BY ANTON WEBERN

Clarinet, muted French horn, muted trombone, harmonium, mandolin, guitar, celesta, harp,
bass drum, snare drum, chimes, cowbells, violin, muted viola, muted cello.

Very slow and extremely calm

(Duration, 1:28)

25 0:00
1. *a.* Pulsating bell-like sounds, *ppp.*
   b. Violin, *pp*, pulsating bell-like sounds, *ppp.*
   c. Muted horn, *pp*, chimes, *ppp.*

0:38
2. Quicker notes in clarinet. Muted viola.

0:47
3. *a.* Pulsating bell-like sounds, *ppp.*
   b. Muted trombone, *ppp*; pulsating bell-like sounds, *ppp.* Snare-drum roll,
   extremely soft.

TWENTIETH
CENTURY

12 BÉLA BARTÓK

Béla Bartók (1881–1945), whose music is infused with the spirit of east
European folk song, was born in the Hungarian town of Nagyszentmiklós.
When Bartók was seven, his father died; his mother was forced to move
with her son from town to town while she earned a living as a school-
teacher. She gave him his first lessons on the piano, an instrument which
played an important role in his career. For twenty-seven years (1907–1934),
Bartók taught piano at his alma mater, the Budapest Academy of Music,
and gave recitals throughout Europe.

During the early 1900s, Bartók was influenced by the nationalist movement that swept Hungary. He came to love the music of Hungarian peasants, and he spent most of his free time in tiny villages recording folk songs
on a cylinder phonograph. Bartók became a leading authority on the peasant music of the Magyars, Rumanians, Slovaks, and Turks, and the Arabs
of north Africa. Soon his own music was profoundly affected by the folk
music he knew so well.

Though Bartók was recognized early as an important composer abroad,
he was neglected in Hungary. For a time after 1911, he even refused to play
in Hungary because of the "indifference and animosity" of the Hungari-
ans. It was only after the successful Budapest premiere of his ballet *The
Wooden Prince* in 1917 that Bartók's music gained acceptance in his home-

Caught up in the nationalist movement that swept Hungary, Bartók spent most of his free time in tiny villages recording folk songs on a cylinder phonograph.

land. During a tour of the United States he made in 1927 to 1928, one newspaper headline warned readers: "Hungarian modernist advances upon Los Angeles to convince scoffers." By 1939 he was able to report gleefully to his son, "Since 1934, I have worked almost exclusively upon commissions!"

Hitler's rise posed a serious problem for Bartók, who was violently anti-Nazi. After the annexation of Austria by Germany in 1938, Bartók wrote a friend: "There is the imminent danger that Hungary will also surrender to this system of robbery and murder. How I could then continue to live or—which amounts to the same thing—work in such a country is quite inconceivable." Bartók did not allow his music to be performed in Germany or on any radio station that could be heard in Germany or Italy.

In 1940, Bartók finally emigrated to the United States, where he was to spend the last five years of his life. This was a bleak period for him; he had little money, he was in poor health, and he felt isolated and neglected.

499

"My career as a composer is as much as finished," he wrote in 1942. "The quasi boycott of my works by the leading orchestras continues. . . ." For three years he stopped composing. He held a position as a research scholar in folk music at Columbia University, but his grant ended before he could finish his work. In 1943, his health declined alarmingly. After his weight fell to 87 pounds, he entered a New York hospital; while there, he unexpectedly received a commission for the Concerto for Orchestra, which is now his best-known work. The success of its first performance in 1944 resulted in a series of commissions for the once-ignored composer. Tragically, Bartók had only a year to live and could write just two more compositions, the Sonata for Solo Violin (1944) and the Third Piano Concerto (1945).

Soon after his death in New York in 1945, Bartók became one of the most popular twentieth-century composers.

BARTÓK'S MUSIC

"I do not reject any influence," wrote Bartók, "whether its source be Slovak, Rumanian, Arab, or some other; provided this source be pure, fresh and healthy." But he emphasized that the "Hungarian influence is the strongest." Bartók evolved a completely individual style that fused folk elements, classical forms, and twentieth-century sounds. He believed that peasant music helped liberate him from the "exclusive rule of the major or minor system." Most folk melodies, he observed, "adhere to the old church modes or the ancient Greek modes and certain still older modes (especially pentatonic), and moreover display extremely free and varied rhythmic structures and changes of meter. . . ." Bartók arranged many Hungarian and Rumanian folk tunes, often giving them highly dissonant accompaniments. In most of his works, however, Bartók does not quote folk melodies; he uses original themes that have a folk flavor. His aim was to "assimilate the idiom of peasant music so completely" that he could "forget all about it and use it as his mother tongue."

Bartók's genius found its most characteristic expression in instrumental music. He wrote many works for piano solo, six string quartets, other chamber music, three concertos for piano, one concerto for violin, and several compositions for orchestra. Bartók's music embraces a wide range of emotions and is deeply expressive. Fast movements can convey a primitive brutality or the vitality and swing of a peasant dance. Slow movements often suggest feelings of bleakness and profound pessimism. They frequently contain atmospheric, almost impressionistic music suggesting nocturnal insect noises and the chirping of birds. Such mysterious passages are known as Bartók's "night music."

Bartók revitalized and reinterpreted traditional forms such as the rondo, fugue, and sonata form. He unifies the contrasting movements of a composition by bringing back a theme in transformed versions. He also creates formal unity by beginning and ending a movement in the same way. For example, the second movement of the Concerto for Orchestra (1943) opens and closes with a solo on the side drum. Polyphonic imitation and motivic development often generate tension and excitement.

Bartók always organized his works around a tonal center. Within this tonal framework, he often used harsh dissonances, polychords, and tone clusters—although in some of his late works, he returned to a more traditional and less dissonant vocabulary. Bartók's music is rhythmically characterized by a powerful beat, unexpected accents, and changing meters. The irregular meters and asymmetrical rhythmic patterns of east European folk music are used imaginatively. (See the example from Bartók's *Six Dances in Bulgarian Rhythm* in Section 1, page 440.)

Bartók was also imaginative in his use of tone colors, particularly of percussion instruments. In works such as Music for Strings, Percussion and Celesta (1936) and the Sonata for Two Pianos and Percussion (1937), he drew unusual sounds from the xylophone and timpani. Bartók was especially fond of glissandos on the timpani (this sliding effect is produced by a pedal mechanism). Like many twentieth-century composers, Bartók drew percussive, drumlike sounds from the piano as well.

Bartók's six string quartets are widely thought to be the finest since those of Beethoven. The works abound in exciting glissandos and in pizzicatos that produce a "snap" when the string rebounds against the fingerboard. But Bartók's string quartets are more than a collection of novel sounds; they reflect the composer's profundity and nobility of spirit.

CONCERTO FOR ORCHESTRA (1943)

The commission which led to the Concerto for Orchestra was offered to Bartók in 1943, while he was hospitalized in New York City. Serge Koussevitzky, the conductor of the Boston Symphony Orchestra, offered him a $1,000 commission for a new work. While recuperating at Saranac Lake, New York, Bartók was able to work "practically day and night" on his new composition. He finished it in six weeks. The Concerto for Orchestra was an enormous success at its premiere in Boston in 1944 and has since become Bartók's most popular work.

"The general mood of the work," wrote Bartók, "represents, apart from the jesting second movement, a gradual transition from the sternness of the first movement and the lugubrious death-song of the third, to the life-assertion of the last one." Bartók explained that the unusual title reflects the work's "tendency to treat the single orchestral instruments in a *concertant* or soloistic manner."

Indeed, the Concerto for Orchestra is a showpiece for an orchestra of virtuosos. It is romantic in spirit because of its emotional intensity, memorable themes, and vivid contrasts of mood. Though its melodies were original with Bartók, they have a distinct folk flavor. The concerto is an example of Bartók's mellow "late" style, which is characterized by more frequent use of traditional chords. In all five movements, time-honored procedures like A B A form, sonata form, and fugue are fused with twentieth-century rhythms and tone colors.

First Movement: *Introduction*

Andante non troppo; Allegro vivace

Side 14, band 5
CD 7 [26]

The concerto begins with an extended slow introductory section based on two melodic ideas that grow in intensity as they are varied. Low cellos and double basses mysteriously introduce the first idea, a short phrase that climbs and then falls. This phrase returns twice, each time ascending higher before it descends. The flute then softly introduces the second thematic idea, an exotic-sounding figure that circles around a single tone. This theme also returns twice. First it is varied and expanded by the trumpets playing very softly, and then it is transformed into a passionate outcry by the strings.

The allegro vivace is in a kind of sonata form. Themes are broken into fragments that are shifted among different instruments. In this movement there are frequent alternations between fast, powerful sections featuring strings and brasses and slower, calmer sections in which woodwinds are most prominent.

The assertive opening theme of the exposition is marked by the rapidly changing meter so typical of twentieth-century music.

Its descending second phrase is an inversion, or upside-down form, of the ascending first phrase.

Before the contrasting second theme enters, the trombone plays a somber phrase. This has an important role later in the movement. The atmosphere of the middle east is evoked by the plaintive second theme, which is first played by the oboe. It features an alternation between two tones, and it has a static, dronelike accompaniment that is common in folk music.

In the development section, the trombone motive from the exposition grows into an exciting brass fanfare. It is polyphonically imitated among the trombones, trumpets, French horns, and tuba. The recapitulation of the movement is unusual because the second theme comes before—rather than after—the first theme. The allegro vivace ends decisively with the trombone motive, played in unison by all the brasses.

Listening Outline To be read while music is heard

CONCERTO FOR ORCHESTRA (1943), BY BÉLA BARTÓK

First Movement: *Introduction* (Andante non troppo; Allegro vivace)

Sonata form

Piccolo, 3 flutes, 3 oboes, English horn, 3 clarinets, bass clarinet, 3 bassoons, 4 French horns, 3 trumpets, 3 trombones, tuba, timpani, cymbals, 2 harps, 1st violins, 2d violins, violas, cellos, double basses

(Duration, 9:00)

Andante non troppo (slow introduction)

26 0:00

1. *a.* Low strings, *p*, ascending and descending phrase. High string tremolo, *pp*, flutes.

Cellos and basses

p   legato

0:34

b. Low strings, *p*, phrase ascends higher, then descends. High string tremolo, *pp*, flutes.

1:04

c. Low strings, phrase ascends still higher, then descends.

27 1:22

2. *a.* Flute, *p*, new phrase. Strings, *p*.

Flute

p

1:48

b. Trumpets, *pp*, new phrase varied and extended. Strings in background.

2:19

c. Violins, *f*, new phrase transformed into forceful melody.

28 2:36

d. Crescendo, bass motive repeated faster and faster, leading into

Allegro vivace

EXPOSITION
First theme

29 3:04

1. *a.* Violins, *f*, main theme. Fast tempo. Violin melody becomes slightly softer. Crescendo to *f*.

f

|30| 3:48   *b.* Trombone motive, *mf.* Flute, *p,* descending melody.

Second theme
|31| 4:04   2. *a.* Oboe, *p,* folklike melody, slower tempo. Strings and harp accompany.

4:24   *b.* Folklike melody repeated and extended by clarinets, flutes, *p.* Strings and
                            harp accompany.

DEVELOPMENT
|32| 5:17   1. Orchestra, *f,* fragments of main theme in imitation. Allegro vivace. Crescendo
                            to *ff.*
5:48   2. Clarinet, *p,* new legato melody, slower tempo. Melody extended by English
                            horn, flute, *p.*
|33| 6:24   3. Strings, *ff.* Brasses, trombone motive in imitation. Allegro vivace. Orchestra, *fff,*
                            high sustained tone.

RECAPITULATION
Second theme
|34| 7:19   1. *a.* Clarinet, *p,* folklike melody, slower tempo. Strings and harp accompany.
7:44   *b.* Folklike melody repeated and extended by flutes, oboe, *p.* Strings and harp
                            accompany.
8:20   *c.* Low strings alternate with higher woodwinds. Crescendo and accelerando to

First theme
8:38   2. Orchestra, *ff,* main theme. Allegro vivace. Brasses, *ff,* trombone motive ends
                            movement.

Second Movement: *Game of Pairs*
Allegretto scherzando

Supplementary sets:
Side 7, band 2
CD 4 |8|

The jesting second movement, *Game of Pairs,* which is in A B A' form, is a
"game" involving different pairs of woodwind and brass instruments. The
melodic lines of each pair are in parallel motion and are separated by a
distinctive pitch interval.

In the opening section (A), a chain of five melodies are played consecutively by pairs of bassoons, oboes, clarinets, flutes, and muted trumpets. The contrasting middle section (B) is a hymnlike melody softly played by brass instruments. When the opening section returns (A'), it has a more active accompaniment. The incisive sound of a side drum (without snares) is prominent throughout the movement. It plays syncopated solos at the beginning and the end, as well as in the hymnlike middle section.

Listening Outline   To be read while music is heard

CONCERTO FOR ORCHESTRA (1943), BY BÉLA BARTÓK

Second Movement: *Game of Pairs* (Allegretto scherzando)

A B A' form, duple meter ($\frac{2}{4}$)

2 flutes, 2 oboes, 2 clarinets, 3 bassoons, 4 French horns, 2 trumpets, 2 trombones, tuba, timpani, side drum, 2 harps, 1st violins, 2d violins, violas, cellos, double basses

(Duration, 6:05)

A

8	0:00	1. Solo side drum (without snares), *mf.*
	0:11	2. Two bassoons, *p,* accompanied by pizzicato strings.
9	0:33	3. *a.* Two oboes, *p,* in higher register. Pizzicato strings accompany.
		b. Low strings, pizzicato, while oboes sustain tones.
10	1:01	4. *a.* Two clarinets.
		b. Low strings, accented notes.
11	1:22	5. *a.* Two flutes, *mf,* in higher register.
		b. Low strings, pizzicato, while flutes sustain tones.
12	2:04	6. Two muted trumpets, *p.* Muted string tremolos, *pp,* in background.

B

13	2:50	1. *a.* Brasses, *mf,* hymnlike legato melody. Side drum accompanies.
		b. French horns, *p,* conclude hymnlike melody and sustain chord.
		2. Oboe, flute, and clarinet, *p,* lead to

A'

14	3:51	1. Two bassoons, *p,* opening melody. Staccato third bassoon in background.
	4:13	2. *a.* Two oboes, *p,* in higher register. Clarinets and strings in background.
		b. Low strings, pizzicato, while oboes sustain tones.
	4:36	3. *a.* Two clarinets. Flutes and strings in background.
		b. Low strings, accented notes.
	4:56	4. *a.* Two flutes, *mf,* in higher register. Woodwinds and strings in background.
		b. Low strings, pizzicato, while flutes sustain tones.
	5:18	5. Two muted trumpets, *mf.* Harp glissandos and muted string tremolos in background.
	5:55	6. Woodwinds, *p,* repeated chord; solo side drum, decrescendo, ends *Game of Pairs.*

Third Movement: *Elegy*
Andante, non troppo

Bartók thought of the deeply moving music of the third movement *(Elegy)* as a "death song." It is based largely on themes from the slow introduction to the first movement. Mysterious opening bars—similar to those of the introduction—lead into a section of "night music." A misty, nocturnal atmosphere is evoked by soft harp glissandos, splashes of woodwind sound, chirps from the piccolo, and a mournful oboe line.

The central section of the *Elegy* is louder and more melodic than the rest. High violins proclaim a theme that was played softly by trumpets in the slow introduction to the first movement. A folklike melody is then introduced by violas and repeated, at a higher pitch, by woodwinds. The *Elegy* ends as it began, with misty "night music" and faint chirps from a piccolo.

Fourth Movement: *Interrupted Intermezzo*
Allegretto

There is an amusing story behind the title of the fourth movement. While working on the Concerto for Orchestra, Bartók heard a radio broadcast of the Seventh Symphony by the Soviet composer Dimitri Shostakovich. Bartók considered one of its themes so silly that he decided to parody it. In the middle of the movement, which is outlined A B A–interruption–B A, we hear this tune in the clarinet mocked by vulgar and noisy "interruptions" from the entire orchestra.

The *Interrupted Intermezzo* begins with a wistful folklike melody (A) played by the oboe.

Constant alternation between $\frac{2}{4}$ and $\frac{5}{8}$ meters makes the tune delightfully irregular. The strings play an ardent, expansive melody (B). After the "interruption," there is a return of both melodies in reverse order, and the movement ends abruptly and humorously.

Fifth Movement: *Finale*
Presto

The *Finale,* in sonata form, sounds like a frenzied dance. An opening horn motive introduces a fiery "perpetual motion" theme in the violins. Tension drops when Bartók introduces a quiet woodwind episode, and the tempo slows. But the dancelike mood and rapid tempo are soon resumed when a trumpet introduces a fanfare theme with staccato repeated notes.

The fanfare theme is immediately imitated by a second trumpet, but in inverted, or upside-down, form. After a gentle harp passage, the fanfare theme is further developed in a fuguelike section, first by the strings, then by the whole orchestra. The shortened recapitulation ends with brasses proclaiming a slowed-down form of the fanfare theme.

CHARLES IVES

TWENTIETH
CENTURY

13

The American composer Charles Ives (1874–1954) wrote startlingly original music that was far ahead of its time. He was born in Danbury, Connecticut, the son of a bandmaster who loved to experiment with unusual sounds. "Pa taught me what I know," Ives later recalled. He learned to play many instruments and to follow the "rules" of harmony and counterpoint. But when Charles was ten, his father also encouraged his independence of mind and ear by instructing him to sing a tune in one key while being accompanied in another. At thirteen, Ives held a regular job as church organist, and his compositions were performed publicly. Still, he was prouder of his ability as a baseball player than of his musical skill. When asked what he played, he gruffly replied "Shortstop!"

When he was twenty, Ives entered Yale University to study musical composition. His conservative teacher, Horatio Parker, frowned on his musical experimentation. Faced with choosing a profession on graduating, Ives decided that he could keep his music "stronger, cleaner, bigger, and freer"

(Omikron/Photo Researchers)

The American composer Charles Ives knew that his unconventional music would not be popular, and he became a businessman so that his family would not "starve on his dissonances."

if he did not try to make a living out of it. He knew that his unconventional music would not be popular, and he did not want to raise a family that might "starve on his dissonances." Ives therefore went into the insurance business, starting out as a clerk in a New York firm. Eventually he founded a successful insurance agency and became very wealthy. Ives, a creative businessman, invented the concept of estate planning and wrote a text-book widely used by insurance agents.

Ives composed furiously each day after business until two or three in the morning, and on weekends and holidays as well. During the years he composed, he was isolated from the music world; none of his major works was publicly performed. Musicians for whom he occasionally played his compositions commented: "It is not music," "It makes no sense," or "How can you like horrible sounds like that?" They urged him to write more conventionally. His wife—a clergyman's daughter appropriately named Harmony—believed in his genius and supported his refusal to compromise. Completely unknown, his scores accumulated in the barn of his Connecticut farm.

The participation by the United States in World War I from 1917 to 1918 dampened Ives's creative urge. "I did practically nothing in music. I did not seem to feel like it," he recalled. "We were very busy at the office at this time with the extra Red Cross and Liberty Loan drives, and all the problems that the War brought on." Then, in October 1918, shortly before the end of the war, the forty-four-year-old Ives had a heart attack from which he never completely recovered. He composed almost nothing after 1921. Instead, he began to make his compositions known to the public.

From 1920 to 1922, Ives privately printed his monumental *Concord* Sonata for piano, his explanatory *Essays before a Sonata,* and his collection 114 Songs and sent them to musicians, critics, and libraries. At first, the volumes aroused little more than ridicule. ("It was the fate of many of them," wrote Henry Cowell, Ives's biographer, "to be used to adjust the height of the piano bench" in the studio of more than one well-known musician.) Gradually a few young composers and performers recognized that Ives was enormously original. In 1939, when Ives was sixty-four, his *Concord* Sonata (1909–1915) aroused an ovation at its first complete New York performance. By the 1940s, many thought Ives to be the first great composer from the United States. In 1947 he won a Pulitzer Prize for his Third Symphony (1904–1911), written some forty years earlier. Newspapers and magazines all over the country took up the story of the businessman who had lived a secret life as a composer. Ives's typically gruff reaction to the Pulitzer Prize was "Prizes are for boys. I'm grown up."

A few years before his death, Ives received a letter from Arnold Schoenberg's widow, who had found the following note among her husband's papers: "There is a great Man living in this Country—a composer. He has solved the problem how to preserve one's self and to learn. He responds to negligence by contempt. He is not forced to accept praise or blame. His name is Ives."

IVES'S MUSIC

Though experimental and far ahead of their time, Ives's compositions are rooted deeply in the folk and popular music he knew as a boy: revival hymns and ragtime, village bands and church choirs, patriotic songs and barn dances. Ives was inspired by the "unconventional" features of the American tradition: the village fiddler playing slightly out of tune, the cornetist a fraction ahead of the rest of the band, the church organist accidentally holding one chord while the choir sings another. Earlier American composers had made folk material conform to academic "rules," but Ives reveled in its irregular rhythms and asymmetrical melodies. His polyrhythms, polytonality, and tone clusters grew out of the music he knew.

To evoke nostalgic memories, Ives often quotes snatches of familiar tunes—*Yankee Doodle; Columbia, the Gem of the Ocean; America*—along with revival hymns and college songs. These snatches are not merely quoted but are developed and integrated within his music. Even the titles of his works evoke Ives's New England heritage: the Second Piano Sonata is subtitled *Concord, Mass. 1840–60;* its movements are *Emerson, Hawthorne, The Alcotts,* and *Thoreau.* We'll study one movement from a set of orchestral pieces entitled *Three Places in New England.* His large and varied output includes five symphonies and other orchestral music; music for piano, chorus, and chamber ensembles; and over two hundred songs. Many of his instrumental works have philosophical or descriptive programs. *The Unanswered Question,* for example—a work for chamber orchestra—depicts a search for the meaning of life.

A boyhood incident seems to have had an important influence on Ives. Two bands playing different music passed each other as they marched by him in different directions. Their dissonant clash fascinated the young boy. In later works Ives simultaneously presents musical events that seem unrelated: two bands play in different keys; consonant chords are set against dissonant chords; conflicting meters and rhythmic patterns are intertwined.

Ives's music shows a wide range of emotions, styles, and musical techniques. It includes mild-sounding consonant chords and earsplitting dissonances that caused his contemporaries to think of him as a crank. Ives scorned those who couldn't take dissonance. "Beauty in music," he wrote, "is too often confused with something that lets the ears lie back in an easy chair." Once, when dissonant music of his friend Carl Ruggles was hissed at a concert, Ives jumped up and shouted, "You goddamn sissy. . . . When you hear strong masculine music like this, get up and use your ears like a man!" Interested only in satisfying his inner ear, Ives created music that is extraordinarily difficult to perform. "The impossibilities of today are the possibilities of tomorrow," he wrote.

PUTNAM'S CAMP, REDDING, CONNECTICUT (1912), FROM *THREE PLACES IN NEW ENGLAND* (1908–?1914)

Side 14, band 6
CD 7 [35]

Putnam's Camp, Redding, Connecticut, is part of *Three Places in New England,* a set of three movements for orchestra evoking American history, life, and landscape. Though completed around 1914, *Three Places in New England* was not performed until 1930, when it was booed and hissed at its premiere in Boston. Today, it is one of Ives's most popular works and a landmark in American music.

The daring and brilliant second movement, *Putnam's Camp,* is a child's impression of a Fourth of July picnic. Ives recaptures his boyhood memory of two marching bands clashing dissonantly as they play different tunes. He quotes many fragments from once well-known marches by John Philip Sousa (1854–1932), the American composer nicknamed the "march king." Snatches of patriotic songs and folklike tunes written by Ives contribute to the piece's popular flavor.

In his preface to this score, Ives wrote, "Near Redding Center, Conn., is a small park preserved as a Revolutionary Memorial; for here General Israel Putnam's soldiers had their winter quarters in 1778–1779." One Fourth of July, "a child went there on a picnic held under the auspices of the First Church and the Village Cornet Band." The child wanders "away from the rest of the children past the camp ground into the woods. As he rests on the hillside of laurel and hickories, the tunes of the band and the songs of the children grow fainter. . . ." He falls asleep and dreams of the discouraged American soldiers breaking camp, marching out "with fife and drum to a popular tune of the day. Suddenly a new national note is heard. Putnam is coming over the hills from the center,—the soldiers turn back and cheer. The little boy awakes, he hears the children's songs and runs down past the monument to 'listen to the band' and join in the games and dances."

Putnam's Camp is in three sections (A B A') that parallel the descriptive program. The first, marked *quick step time*, captures the gaiety and confusion of a Fourth of July picnic in a nineteenth-century town. After a raucous, highly dissonant introduction, the strings play the main theme, a vigorous march that begins with conventional harmonies.

Introduction
35   0:00
Main theme
0:11

Such abrupt shifts between harsh dissonances and mild-sounding consonances are typical of Ives and are heard throughout *Putnam's Camp*. The piano, woodwinds, and brasses begin to compete for the listener's attention, and soon it sounds as though two bands are playing against each other. The mood becomes even more comic when a parody of the opening phrase of *Yankee Doodle* is quickly played by the trumpet, the flute, and the violins.

36   1:06

After more orchestral confusion, the music gradually becomes softer and slows to a halt, depicting the child as he falls asleep.

Middle section
37 2:17

A mysterious high chord in the strings ushers in the middle section, which depicts the child's dream. Repeated piano and drum beats that seem out of phase with the rest of the orchestra begin one of the boldest parts of the score. Ives creates the impression of two bands playing at different tempos. (One band employs strings and woodwinds; the other has piano, drums, and trumpet.) Here the conductor must beat four bars with one hand against three bars in the other. The bands merge, and we hear a flute playing *The British Grenadiers*, a favorite tune of the Revolutionary army. A sentimental tune in the strings then ushers in the riotous concluding section. In this conclusion Ives creates deliberate melodic and rhythmic confusion as the main march theme is combined with *The British Grenadiers* and other fragments. *Putnam's Camp* ends with an earsplitting dissonant chord.

Concluding section
38 4:37

GEORGE GERSHWIN

Popular songs and musical comedies as well as jazz-flavored orchestral works and opera won world fame for the American composer George Gershwin (1898–1937). Born in Brooklyn of Russian-Jewish immigrant parents, he grew up on the lower east side of Manhattan. "Music never really interested me," said Gershwin of his childhood. "I spent most of my time with the boys in the street, skating and, in general, making a nuisance of myself." His first attraction to music came when he was ten, while he was standing outside Public School 25 and heard, through an open window, Dvořák's *Humoresque* played by a young violinist at a school assembly. Possibly inspired by this "flashing revelation of beauty," he taught himself to play hit tunes of the day on a neighbor's piano. Another musical turning point came three years later, when Gershwin began studying with a teacher who recognized his amazing talent and introduced him to piano works ranging from Bach to Liszt and Debussy.

When he was fifteen, Gershwin left high school to become a "piano pounder," a pianist demonstrating new songs in the salesrooms of a Tin Pan Alley publisher. (Tin Pan Alley was the name for the neighborhood in Manhattan where the popular music business was centered, and for the type of music it represented.) The young Gershwin saw no contradiction in his love for both "popular" and "classical" music. Once, while practicing some Bach preludes and fugues during a break from demonstrating songs,

George Gershwin wrote jazz-flavored orchestral works and an opera as well as popular songs and musical comedies.

he was asked, "Are you studying to be a concert pianist?" "No," he answered, "I'm studying to be a great popular songwriter." Gershwin's drive for musical mastery was evident throughout his life. Even at the height of his fame, he seized every opportunity to take lessons in music theory, composition, and orchestration.

After three years of "piano pounding" for the music publisher, Gershwin quit his job to make a career as a songwriter. Success came quickly. In 1919, at the age of twenty, he wrote *La, La, Lucille*, his first complete Broadway musical. In 1920, his song *Swanee* was a tremendous hit; the recording by the singer Al Jolson sold millions of copies. During the 1920s and 1930s—usually collaborating with his brother Ira, who wrote the lyrics—Gershwin wrote one brilliant musical after another, including *Lady, Be Good* (1924), *Funny Face* (1927), and the political satire *Of Thee I Sing* (1931). He was an important figure in the "golden era" of the American musical (which we'll study in Part IX); and hit tunes from his shows, like *The Man I Love, I Got Rhythm, Embraceable You,* and *Someone to Watch Over Me,* proved to be of lasting appeal.

Gershwin's career as a composer of music for the concert hall was launched in 1924 by the triumphant premiere of *Rhapsody in Blue.* One of the listeners captivated by the work was the conductor Walter Damrosch, who commissioned Gershwin to write a piano concerto for the New York Symphony Orchestra. In 1925, Gershwin gave the first performance of his Concerto in F with the orchestra at Carnegie Hall in New York and later performances in six other cities. In that same year, he was the first American-born musician to appear on the cover of *Time* magazine.

During the 1920s, Gershwin made several trips to Europe, where he heard performances of his own works and met other composers—among them Alban Berg, in Vienna; and Maurice Ravel and Igor Stravinsky, in Paris. On one visit to Paris, he composed part of the symphonic poem *An American in Paris* (1928), which includes four taxi horns in its colorful orchestration.

In 1934 Gershwin began to write his most extended work, the opera *Porgy and Bess* (1935), which deals with the lives of poor black people in Charleston, South Carolina. Part of the opera was composed during a summer on Folly Island, near Charleston, from which Gershwin visited nearby islands to hear music in isolated African American communities. *Porgy and Bess* was premiered in Boston in 1935, played sixteen weeks in the Alvin Theater in New York, and then went on a three-month road tour. It was not revived during Gershwin's lifetime, but it has since had performances all over the world, including a production at the Metropolitan Opera.

Gershwin was an outgoing person, a sportsman, and irresistible to women. He enjoyed attending parties, where he would play the piano for hours. Royalties, concert fees, and the salary from his nationally broadcast weekly radio show *Music by Gershwin* made him wealthy. He had an outstanding art collection and was himself a talented painter.

Gershwin spent the last year of his life in Hollywood, where he wrote the music for several movies and played tennis with the composer Arnold Schoenberg in his spare time. During the spring of 1937, he began to experience dizziness and fumbled passages when performing his works. One day he fell into a coma and was rushed to a hospital, where it was found that he had a brain tumor. His doctors wanted a famous neurosurgeon to operate, but the surgeon was vacationing on a yacht in Chesapeake Bay. Friends called the White House, and the Coast Guard was sent to locate him. But before he could fly to Gershwin in California, an emergency operation had to be performed. It was not a success, and Gershwin died at the age of thirty-eight.

RHAPSODY IN BLUE (1924)

Rhapsody in Blue, Gershwin's most famous work, was commissioned by the bandleader Paul Whiteman for a special concert to be given on Lincoln's birthday in 1924. The concert was intended to prove that jazz—or, more accurately, the popular music Whiteman considered jazz—merited serious attention. At first, Gershwin was reluctant to take the commission, because the concert was only five weeks away and he was busy preparing his musical comedy *Sweet Little Devil* for its Boston tryout. But Whiteman's persuasiveness and Gershwin's own eagerness to write jazz-flavored concert music won out. The twenty-five-year-old composer accepted the commission for a new composition for piano and jazz band and agreed to appear as soloist.

Supplementary sets:
Side 7, band 3
CD 4 15

During a trip to Boston, Gershwin decided on the form for *Rhapsody in Blue*. "It was on the train, with its steely rhythms, its rattlety-bang, . . . that I suddenly heard—and even saw on paper—the complete construction of the *Rhapsody*, from beginning to end," he later recalled. "I heard it as a sort of musical kaleidoscope of America—of our vast melting pot, of our unduplicated national pep, of our blues, our metropolitan madness. By the time I reached Boston, I had a definite *plot* of the piece. . . ." After only three weeks of work, Gershwin finished a two-piano version of the *Rhapsody* that was orchestrated for the Whiteman band by its arranger, Ferde Grofé.

The well-publicized concert took place in New York, in the prestigious Aeolian Hall, before an audience of celebrities that included Tin Pan Alley songwriters as well as the violinists Jascha Heifetz and Fritz Kreisler, the conductors Walter Damrosch and Leopold Stokowski, and the composers Sergei Rachmaninoff and Ernest Bloch. The earlier pieces on the program were received with indifference, but *Rhapsody in Blue* electrified the audience with its novelty, its memorable melodies, its distinctive American flavor, and—not least—Gershwin's brilliant piano playing. So great was its success that it was soon heard in concert halls around the world and earned the composer $250,000 within a decade. In an era when composers such as Stravinsky, Ravel, and Copland were incorporating jazz elements into their compositions, this concert work by a songwriter had the most lasting impact and the widest appeal. It is heard most often in a version by Ferde Grofé that is scored for piano and full symphony orchestra. (For his later orchestral works, Gershwin did his own scoring.)

The title *Rhapsody in Blue* reflects the music's free, rhapsodic form and its blues flavor. The term *blues* refers to a style of vocal music originating among blacks that involves "bent" notes and slides of pitch. "Blue" notes are produced by slightly lowering, or flatting, the third, fifth, and seventh notes of the major scale. (The blues will be discussed more fully on pages 562–566.) *Rhapsody in Blue* is not true jazz; but it employs jazzlike rhythms

515

and melodies, and the orchestration suggests the distinctive sounds of jazz by such effects as a clarinet glissando, or slide, and brass instruments played with a "wha-wha" mute.

Rhapsody in Blue is a one-movement work consisting of three main sections and a coda. Each main section includes at least one extended piano solo in which varied repetitions of the main themes are combined with Lisztian virtuoso passages. The solos reflect Gershwin's own dazzling pianism and his genius as an improvisor. The piece opens with a now-famous clarinet solo that starts from a low trill, climbs the scale, and then slides up to a high "wailing" tone. The clarinet slide, or glissando—a novel effect at the time—was improvised during rehearsals by the clarinetist of the Whiteman band, and Gershwin incorporated it into the score. The blueslike opening theme, which grows out of the clarinet slide, is marked by the syncopations so typical of Gershwin's style. It is followed by a repeated-note theme, presented by French horns, which reappears many times. A new jazzlike theme, introduced in the low register, begins the lively second section, marked *con moto*. The moderately slow third section is based on a lyrical, romantic melody first presented by the violins. This memorable tune is combined with a countermelody played by the French horns. The rapid coda is ushered in by an accelerated transformation of the romantic melody.

Listening Outline   To be read while music is heard

RHAPSODY IN BLUE (1924), BY GEORGE GERSHWIN

B flat major

Solo piano, 2 flutes, 2 oboes, 2 clarinets, bass clarinet, 2 bassoons, 2 alto saxophones, tenor saxophone, 3 French horns, 3 trumpets, 3 trombones, tuba, timpani, bass drum, snare drum, cymbals, gong, triangle, 1st violins, 2d violins, violas, cellos, double basses

(Duration, 15:56)

15 0:00   1. *a.* Clarinet, *p*, trill, upward scale and slide (glissando) to blues theme, *mf*, moderate tempo.

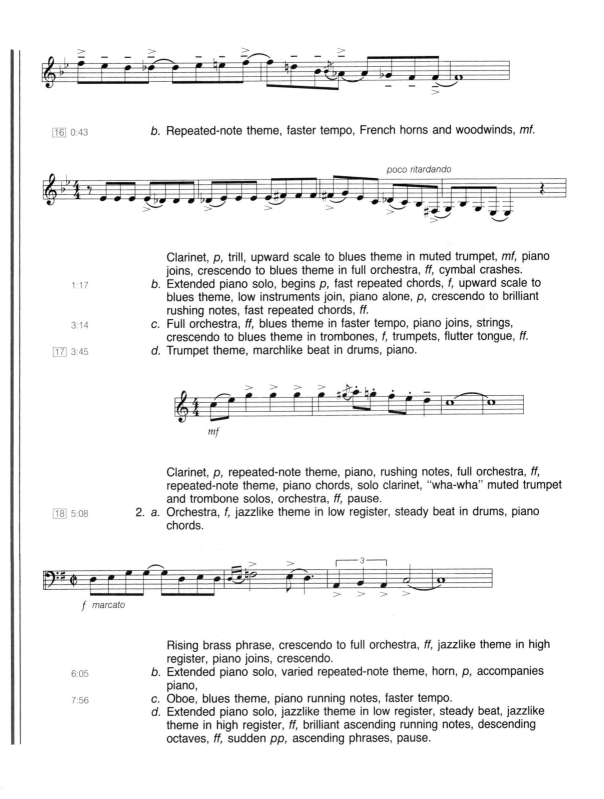

16 0:43   *b.* Repeated-note theme, faster tempo, French horns and woodwinds, *mf.*

Clarinet, *p,* trill, upward scale to blues theme in muted trumpet, *mf,* piano joins, crescendo to blues theme in full orchestra, *ff,* cymbal crashes.

1:17   *b.* Extended piano solo, begins *p,* fast repeated chords, *f,* upward scale to blues theme, low instruments join, piano alone, *p,* crescendo to brilliant rushing notes, fast repeated chords, *ff.*

3:14   *c.* Full orchestra, *ff,* blues theme in faster tempo, piano joins, strings, crescendo to blues theme in trombones, *f,* trumpets, flutter tongue, *ff.*

17 3:45   *d.* Trumpet theme, marchlike beat in drums, piano.

Clarinet, *p,* repeated-note theme, piano, rushing notes, full orchestra, *ff,* repeated-note theme, piano chords, solo clarinet, "wha-wha" muted trumpet and trombone solos, orchestra, *ff,* pause.

18 5:08   2. *a.* Orchestra, *f,* jazzlike theme in low register, steady beat in drums, piano chords.

Rising brass phrase, crescendo to full orchestra, *ff,* jazzlike theme in high register, piano joins, crescendo.

6:05   *b.* Extended piano solo, varied repeated-note theme, horn, *p,* accompanies piano,

7:56   *c.* Oboe, blues theme, piano running notes, faster tempo.

        d. Extended piano solo, jazzlike theme in low register, steady beat, jazzlike theme in high register, *ff,* brilliant ascending running notes, descending octaves, *ff,* sudden *pp,* ascending phrases, pause.

19 10:22 **3. *a.*** Strings, *p,* romantic theme, horns, *p,* moderate tempo, high violin solo.

b. Full orchestra, *ff,* romantic theme, drumrolls, cymbals, piano joins, bells introduce

12:07   **c.** Extended piano solo, romantic theme, very fast repeated notes, brilliant ascending scale to

20 14:00 **4. *a.*** Brasses and piano, accelerated romantic theme, brass swells and sustained dissonant chord, *fff.*

b. Piano and orchestra, rising chromatic scale, crescendo, ritardando.
c. Piano and orchestra, *ff,* repeated-note theme, ritardando.
d. Full orchestra, *fff,* blues theme, cymbal crashes, piano chords, crescendo to final orchestral chord, *ff.*

AARON COPLAND

Aaron Copland (1900–1990), a leading American composer who recently died at the age of ninety, was born in Brooklyn of Russian-Jewish immigrant parents. "No one ever talked music to me or took me to a concert," he recalled of his boyhood. "Music as an art was a discovery I made all by myself." At the age of fifteen he decided to become a composer. He studied with a competent but conservative teacher who discouraged contact with "modern" music. This only made the forbidden fruit more attractive. Copland showed only his academic exercises to his teacher, keeping his more original efforts to himself.

In 1921 Copland went to France, where he was the first American to study composition with Nadia Boulanger. This extraordinary woman was sympathetic to modern musical trends and became the teacher of several generations of American composers. Both Boulanger's teaching and the stimulating atmosphere of Paris—where the expatriates Picasso, Stravinsky, and Ernest Hemingway, among others, felt at home—were to have a lasting influence on Copland's music.

When he returned to New York after three years in Paris, Copland was "anxious to write a work that would immediately be recognized as American in character." For Copland in 1925, *American* meant jazz. In his *Music for the Theater* (1925), a work for small orchestra, elements of blues and ragtime are combined with an approach to rhythm and harmony that is like Stravinsky's. Copland's "jazz period" lasted only a few years. During the early 1930s he composed serious, highly dissonant works that were accessible only to sophisticated listeners. His compositions of the time, such as the highly regarded *Piano Variations* (1930), convey starkness, power, percussiveness, and intense concentration.

In the late 1930s, Copland modified his style again, writing more accessible works for a larger audience. To understand this shift, recall that the 1930s brought the great depression; artists throughout the world were appalled by the economic misery surrounding them. To many composers, it seemed futile to write merely for a sophisticated elite, and they simplified their music to reach a wider audience. "I began to feel an increasing dissatisfaction with the relations of the music-loving public and the living composer," Copland later explained. Most concertgoers, he felt, could not grasp complex, highly dissonant music and wanted to hear only familiar music such as the works of Beethoven and Brahms. "It made no sense to ignore them and to continue writing as if they did not exist. I felt that it was worth the effort to see if I couldn't say what I had to say in the simplest

Aaron Copland drew on American folklore for his ballets *Billy the Kid*, *Rodeo*, and *Appalachian Spring*.

possible terms." Copland drew on American folklore for his ballets *Billy the Kid* (1938), *Rodeo* (1942), and *Appalachian Spring* (1944). The use of jazz, revival hymns, cowboy songs, and other folk tunes helped make Copland's name synonymous with American music. His scores for films such as *Of Mice and Men* (1939) and *Our Town* (1940) brought his music before a mass public, as did patriotic works such as *A Lincoln Portrait* (1942).

Copland accomplished the difficult feat of writing simple yet highly professional music (in this he resembles Leonard Bernstein, whose work we'll study in Part IX). The texture of his music is clear and transparent. There are slow-moving, almost motionless harmonies that seem to evoke the openness of the American landscape. Though strongly tonal, his works embody twentieth-century techniques such as polychords, polyrhythm, changing meters, and percussive orchestration. After 1950, Copland used serial technique—the manipulation of a tone row or series—in such works as *Connotations* for orchestra (1962). This composition recalls the austere, uncompromising style of Copland's music during the early 1930s. Like

Stravinsky, who also turned to serial technique during the 1950s, Copland used a tone row to create music that is completely personal in style.

Aside from his numerous compositions, Copland made many other valuable contributions to music in America. He directed composers' groups, organized concerts of American music, lectured around the country, and wrote books and magazine articles. At the request of the State Department, he was a musical ambassador to South America, where he talked with many composers and listened to their works. For twenty-five years, he taught young composers every summer at the Berkshire Music Center at Tanglewood. When he was fifty, Copland began yet another career, that of conductor; he conducted many orchestras—primarily in his own music—throughout the world.

APPALACHIAN SPRING (1943–1944)

Appalachian Spring originated as a ballet score for Martha Graham, the great modern dancer and choreographer. It took Copland about a year to finish the music. While composing *Appalachian Spring*, he thought, "How foolhardy it is to be spending all this time writing a thirty-five-minute score for a modern-dance company, knowing how short-lived most ballets *and* their scores are." But Copland arranged parts of the ballet as a suite for full orchestra (originally, the ballet used only thirteen instrumentalists) that won important prizes and brought his name to a large public. Today, *Appalachian Spring* is widely performed both as a ballet and as a concert piece.

The ballet concerns a "pioneer celebration in spring around a newly built farmhouse in the Pennsylvania hills" in the early 1800s. Its characters include a bride and groom, a neighbor, and a revivalist preacher with his followers. The rhythms and melodies are American-sounding and suggest barn dances, fiddle tunes, and revival hymns. But Copland uses only one actual folk tune in the score—a Shaker melody entitled *Simple Gifts*. (The Shakers were a religious sect established in America around the time of the Revolution. They expressed religious fervor through shaking, leaping, dancing, and singing.) *Appalachian Spring* is bright and transparent, has a clear tonality, and is basically tender and calm in mood. The score's rhythmic excitement comes from delightful syncopations and rapid changes of meter. As in many twentieth-century works, the orchestra contains a piano and a large percussion section.

The ballet suite has eight sections, including a duo for the bride and groom, a fast dance for the revivalist preacher and his followers with "suggestions of square dances and country fiddlers," and a finale in which the couple are left "quiet and strong in their new house." We'll focus on Section 7, which originally accompanied "Scenes of daily activity for the Bride and her Farmer-husband."

(Arnold Eagle)

A scene from the original production of *Appalachian Spring*.

Section 7:
Theme and Variations on *Simple Gifts*

Side 15, band 1
CD 8 [1]

Section 7 is a theme and five variations on the Shaker tune *Simple Gifts*. The melody's folklike simplicity reflects the Shaker text, which opens as follows:

> 'Tis the gift to be simple, 'tis the gift to be free,
> 'Tis the gift to come down where we ought to be.

In each variation, Copland brings the tune back unadorned, creating variety and contrast through changes of tempo, tone color, dynamics, register, accompaniment, and key. Variation 2 sounds thoughtful and lyrical, as the tune is played more slowly, in a lower register, with polyphonic imitations. Variation 3 brings a brilliant contrast, as *Simple Gifts* is presented faster and staccato by trumpets and trombones. In each of the last two variations, Copland uses only part of the tune: its second part in the pastoral variation 4, and its first part in the majestic closing variation.

522

Listening Outline   To be read while music is heard

APPALACHIAN SPRING (1943–1944; ORCHESTRAL ARRANGEMENT, 1945),
BY AARON COPLAND

Section 7: Theme and Variations on *Simple Gifts*

Theme and variations, duple meter ($\frac{2}{4}$), A flat major

2 flutes, 2 oboes, 2 clarinets, 2 bassoons, 2 French horns, 2 trumpets, 2 trombones, timpani, triangle, glockenspiel, harp, piano, 1st violins, 2d violins, violas, cellos, double basses

(Duration, 2:58)

THEME
1 0:00   Clarinet, *p, Simple Gifts,* legato.

VARIATION 1
2 0:36   Oboe, *mp,* and bassoon, *mp, Simple Gifts,* slightly faster, in higher register.

VARIATION 2
3 1:02   High harp, piano, glockenspiel, *p,* introduce *Simple Gifts,* violas and trombone, *mf,* played half as fast, in lower register. *Simple Gifts* imitated in violins, *f,* then in cellos and basses, *f.* Woodwinds, *p,* brief transition to

VARIATION 3
4 1:50   Trumpets and trombones, *f, Simple Gifts,* twice as fast, staccato.

VARIATION 4
5 2:14   Woodwinds, *mf,* second part of *Simple Gifts,* slightly slower than variation 3, gentle and legato.

VARIATION 5
6 2:31   Full orchestra, *fff,* first part of *Simple Gifts,* played slowly and majestically, in high register.

[16] MUSICAL STYLES SINCE 1950

Since World War II, we have lived with instant communication—television, computers, and space satellites provide access to a virtually unlimited flow of information. Not only have we been bombarded by an incredible variety of stimuli, but there has also been a constant demand for novelty. New styles in fashion and the visual arts spread rapidly and then disappear.

In music as well, emphasis has been on novelty and change. Musical innovations since 1950 have been even more far-reaching than those of the earlier 1900s. There have been many new directions, and the range of musical styles and systems is wider than ever. As the American composer Hugo Weisgall observed, "Many composers today change their musical points of view with astonishing rapidity, composing this way and that, moving easily from complete traditionalism into the 'avant' *avant garde.*"

CHARACTERISTICS OF MUSIC SINCE 1950

Accurately describing the relatively recent past is a difficult task. Yet any overview of music since 1950 must include the following major developments:

1. Increased use of the *twelve-tone system*
2. *Serialism*—use of the techniques of the twelve-tone system to organize rhythm, dynamics, and tone color
3. *Chance music,* in which a composer chooses pitches, tone colors, and rhythms by random methods, or allows a performer to choose much of the musical material
4. *Minimalist music,* characterized by a steady pulse, clear tonality, and insistent repetition of short melodic patterns
5. Works containing deliberate *quotations* from earlier music; and a *return to tonality* by some composers
6. *Electronic music*
7. *"Liberation of sound"*—greater exploitation of noiselike sounds
8. *Mixed media*
9. New concepts of *rhythm* and *form*

Since 1950, long-playing records, audiotape, and compact disks have spread these new musical ideas far and wide.

(Collection Norman Breman, Miami)

In Black and White No. 2 (1975), by Robert Motherwell. Since 1950, there have been many new styles in the visual arts.

Increased Use of the Twelve-Tone System

A striking development after World War II (1945) was the gradual abandonment of tonality in favor of the twelve-tone system. From the early 1920s—when Schoenberg invented the system—to about 1950, most composers still wrote music with a tonal center. Few were attracted to the new method, because it was associated with Schoenberg's expressionist style, which had gone out of fashion. During the 1950s, however, the twelve-tone system was adopted by many composers, including Stravinsky, who had been the leading composer of tonal music.

What contributed to this dramatic shift? In Europe, the end of the war brought a strong desire for new musical beginnings. During the Nazi years, composers had been denied access to the twelve-tone works of Schoenberg and Webern; when peace came, they were eager to explore unfamiliar musical territory. In the United States, twelve-tone music was now available on long-playing records, and complex scores became easier to study.

But the most important reasons for the shift to the twelve-tone system were the resources of the system itself. Composers discovered that it was a compositional technique rather than a special musical style. Musicians as different as Bach, Mozart, and Chopin had all used the tonal system; a comparable diversity of style was possible within the twelve-tone system. The new method also had the advantage of stimulating unconventional approaches to melody, harmony, and form. As Aaron Copland once expressed it, "I began to hear chords that I wouldn't have heard otherwise. Heretofore I had been thinking tonally, but this was a new way of moving tones about. It freshened up one's technique and one's approach."

Many composers of the 1950s and 1960s chose to write music that was stylistically reminiscent of Anton Webern, Schoenberg's disciple. They created "pointillist" music in which melodic lines are "atomized" into tiny fragments that are heard in widely separated registers and framed by moments of silence. Webern's style answered the needs of the post-World War II generation: his music had a lean, "modern" sound, whereas Schoenberg's was considered too "romantic" and traditional in form. The French composer Pierre Boulez (b. 1925) spoke for many of his generation in 1952 when he unfavorably compared Schoenberg's alliance with "the decadence of the great German Romantic tradition" and Webern's reaction "against all inherited rhetoric."

Extensions of the Twelve-Tone System: Serialism

During the late 1940s and early 1950s, the techniques of the twelve-tone system came to be used to organize dimensions of music other than pitch, such as rhythm, dynamics, and tone color. Recall that in early twelve-tone music the system was used primarily to order *pitch* relationships. All the pitches of a twelve-tone composition would be derived from a single tone row, or series. After 1950, a series of durations (rhythmic values), dynamic levels, or tone colors also could serve as a unifying idea. A rhythmic or dynamic series might be manipulated like the series of twelve tones. The use of a series, or ordered group of musical elements, to organize several dimensions of a composition is called *serialism.* The proponents of serialism include Milton Babbitt (b. 1916), in the United States, Karlheinz Stockhausen (b. 1928), in Germany, and Olivier Messiaen and Pierre Boulez, in France. Their methods lead to a totally controlled and organized music, but the actual sound—in certain cases—might seem random and chaotic. The complex relationships in the music are often difficult to perceive.

Chance Music

The 1950s witnessed not only serialism but an opposite approach known as *chance,* or *aleatory, music* (from the Latin *alea,* or *game of chance).* In chance music, composers choose pitches, tone colors, and rhythms by random methods such as throwing coins. They may also ask performers to choose the ordering of the musical material, or even to choose much of the material itself. For example, a composer might write out brief passages of a composition but ask the performer to play them in any desired order. Or a composer might indicate a group of pitches but direct the performer to invent rhythmic patterns.

The most famous and influential creator of chance music is the American John Cage. At the very beginning of this book, a reference was made to Cage's silent "composition" entitled 4'33" (1952), which requires the performer *not* to make a sound for 4 minutes and 33 seconds. The "music" is made up of the unintentional sounds that an audience might produce in this time span. "I try to arrange my composing means," explains Cage, "so

(Oil and enamel paint on canvas, 8 feet 10 inches by 17 feet 5 inches. Collection, The Museum of Modern Art, New York; Sidney and Harriet Janis Collection Fund)

Chance effects are incorporated into *One* (Number 31, 1950), by the abstract expressionist painter Jackson Pollock. The artist dripped, poured, and flung paint onto an enormous canvas tacked to the floor.

that I won't have any knowledge of what might happen. . . . My purpose is to eliminate purpose." For Cage, "The purpose of this purposeless music would be achieved if people learned to listen. Then when they listened they might discover that they preferred the sounds of everyday life to the ones they would presently hear in the musical program. . . . That was all right as far as I was concerned." Cage's approach is also illustrated by his *Imaginary Landscape No. 4* (1951), for twelve radios. The score gives precise directions to the performers—two at each radio—for manipulating the dials affecting wavelength and volume. Yet all the indications in the score were chosen by chance means. They show no regard for local station wavelengths or the time of performance. "At the actual performance of *Imaginary Landscape*," reported one member of the audience, "the hour was later than anticipated before the work's turn came on the program, so that the instruments were unable to capture programs diversified enough to present a really interesting result." This is not surprising, since Cage chose the wavelengths and dynamics by throwing dice.

With Cage's work as an example, serial composers such as Pierre Boulez and Karlheinz Stockhausen introduced elements of chance into their compositions during the mid-1950s. Stockhausen's Piano Piece No. 11 (1956) has nineteen short segments of music printed on a large roll of paper that measures 37 by 21 inches. The segments can be played in any order, and the performer is instructed to begin with the fragment that first catches the eye. The piece is likely to be different each time it is played.

527

Chance music makes a complete break from traditional values in music. It asserts, in effect, that one sound or ordering of sounds is as meaningful as another. To most listeners, a piece of chance music is more often significant as an idea than as a collection of actual sounds. Some composers may be attracted by the sheer novelty of chance music, by its ability to shock and attract attention. Others are influenced by Asian philosophies such as Zen Buddhism, which is not structured according to western concepts of logic. Finally, some composers may want to give performers a major part in the creative process.

Minimalist Music

The mid-1960s saw the development of an artistic movement called *minimalism*, which was partly a reaction against the complexity of serialism and the randomness of chance music. **Minimalist music** is characterized by its steady pulse, clear tonality, and insistent repetition of short melodic patterns. Its dynamic level, texture, and harmony tend to stay constant for fairly long stretches of time, creating a trancelike or hypnotic effect. Leading minimalist composers, such as Terry Riley (b. 1935), Steve Reich (b. 1936), Philip Glass (b. 1937), and John Adams (b. 1947) have been profoundly influenced by nonwestern thought; many have studied African, Indian, or Balinese music. Minimalist music grew out of the same intellec-

Untitled (1966–1967), by Ronald Bladen, is a minimalist sculpture in three identical parts.

(Painted and burnished aluminum in three slanted parts, each 10 feet by 48 inches by 24 inches, spaced 9 feet 4 inches apart, overall length 24 feet 4 inches. Collection, The Museum of Modern Art, New York; James Thrall Soby Fund)

tual climate as minimalist art, which features simple forms, clarity, and understatement. Indeed, in the 1960s, minimalist musicians were appreciated more by painters and sculptors than by their fellow composers. "I gravitated towards artists because they were always more open than musicians, and I liked looking at what they did," Philip Glass has said.

Minimalist composers have generally tried to bring their music to the widest possible audience. "One mode of feedback I rely on most," writes Steve Reich, "is the popular naive reactions. . . . My work, and that of Glass and Riley, comes as a breath of fresh air to the new music world. . . . This feeling is very healthy. It's a feeling of moving back away from a recondite and isolated position, toward a more mainstream approach." Both Reich and Glass have ensembles which perform their music in auditoriums and rock clubs. An important turning point in the public acceptance of minimalist music came in 1976, when Reich's *Music for 18 Musicians* received an ovation in Town Hall in New York and—also in New York— Glass's opera *Einstein on the Beach* (created in collaboration with the playwright-director Robert Wilson) sold out the Metropolitan Opera House. After the early 1970s, minimalist music became progressively richer in harmony, tone color, and texture, as is exemplified in Adams's opera *Nixon in China*, which we'll study.

Musical Quotation and the Return to Tonality

Since the mid-1960s, many composers have written works in which they deliberately make extensive use of quotations from earlier music, usually fairly familiar works of the eighteenth, nineteenth, and twentieth centuries. Like minimalist music, *quotation music* often represents a conscious break with serialism, as well as an attempt to improve the communication between composer and listener. The quoted material usually either conveys a symbolic meaning or is varied, transformed, and juxtaposed with other music. For example, in the outer movements of *Concerto Grosso 1985*, which we'll study, Ellen Taaffe Zwilich juxtaposes parts of a Handel sonata with original passages. In *Sinfonia* (1968), a composition for voices and orchestra by the Italian composer Luciano Berio (b. 1925), the third section is based on the scherzo from Mahler's Second Symphony; on this quoted material from Mahler, Berio superimposes fragments of music by Bach, Debussy, Ravel, Berlioz, Schoenberg, and other composers, creating a musical collage. Like Charles Ives early in the twentieth century, composers since the 1960s have often juxtaposed heterogeneous material. The American composer George Crumb (b. 1929) explained that in writing his song cycle *Ancient Voices of Children*, which we'll study, he "was conscious of an urge to fuse various unrelated stylistic elements, . . . a suggestion of Flamenco with a Baroque quotation . . . or a reminiscence of Mahler with a breath of the orient."

Occasionally, modern composers not only quote earlier composers but also imitate their styles. In the String Quartet No. 3 (1972) by the American composer George Rochberg (b. 1918), there are sections of atonal music and passages in the styles of Beethoven and Mahler.

Paralleling the use of musical quotation is the return to tonality in some recent music. Some works are entirely tonal, while others are basically atonal but contain traditional chord progressions that provide a fleeting sensation of stability. Tonality could be a fascinating "new" option for composers trained in the twelve-tone system. "For me," explained the American composer David Del Tredici (b. 1937), "tonality was actually a daring discovery. I grew up in a climate in which, for a composer, only dissonance and atonality were acceptable. Right now, tonality is exciting for me."

Electronic Music

Since the development of tape studios, synthesizers, and computers in the 1950s and 1960s, composers have had potentially unlimited resources for the production and control of sound. Electronic music is as diverse as nonelectronic music. Its spectrum includes rock, chance music, and serial compositions.

Electronic instruments let composers control tone color, duration, dynamics, and pitch with unprecedented precision. Composers are no longer limited by human performers. For the first time, they can work *directly* in their own medium—sound. There is no more need for intermediaries, that is, performers. The audiotape of a composition *is* the composition. Thus, a composer alone is now responsible for putting into music the subtle variations of rhythm, tone color, and dynamics that once rested with the performer.

Many composers have felt a need to "humanize" their electronic music by combining it with live performers. This can be done in several ways. Some pieces use one or more live performers and taped sounds. The taped sounds may be electronic pitches or noises, or they may be previously recorded sounds of live performers. In some cases, performers may be involved in a duet with themselves, or with electronically manipulated versions of their own performances. In combining live performers with taped sounds, composers face the problem of synchronizing sounds that change from performance to performance—those of the live musicians— and the taped sounds, which don't vary. Recently, some composers have dealt with this problem by creating interactive works for performers and computer. In such compositions, the computer is programmed by the composer to respond in musically meaningful ways to the live performance.

There are also works for traditional instruments and digital synthesizers and samplers that are performed "live." In addition, traditional instruments may also be "electrified" through amplification. Composers use "electric" pianos and violins, for instance.

Electronic music is important not only in itself, but in its influence on musical thought in general. Electronic instruments have suggested new sounds and new forms of rhythmic organization. "These limitless electronic media," said Milton Babbitt, "have shown us new boundaries and new limits that are not yet understood—the very mysterious limits, for example, of the human capacity to hear, to conceptualize, and to perceive. Very often we will specify something and discover that the ear can't take in what we have specified. . . . The human organism simply cannot respond quickly enough, cannot perceive and differentiate as rapidly and precisely as the synthesizer can produce it and as the loudspeaker can reproduce it."

"Liberation of Sound"

Composers today use a wider variety of sounds than ever, including many that were once considered undesirable noises. Composers have achieved what Edgard Varèse called "the liberation of sound . . . the right to make music with any and all sounds. . . ." Electronic music may include environmental sounds, such as thunder, or electronically generated hisses and blips. But composers also may draw novel sounds from voices and non-electronic instruments. Singers are asked to scream, whisper, laugh, groan, sneeze, cough, whistle, and click their tongues. They may sing phonetic sounds rather than words. Composers may treat their vocal text merely as a collection of sounds and not attempt to make the meaning of the words clear to the audience.

Wind and string players tap, scrape, and rub the bodies of their instruments. A brass or woodwind player may hum while playing, thus creating two pitches at once. A flutist may click the keys of the instrument without producing a tone; a pianist may reach inside the piano to pluck a string and then run a chisel along it, creating a sliding sound. To communicate their intentions to performers, composers may devise new systems of music notation, because standard notation makes no provision for many noiselike sounds. Recent music scores contain graphlike diagrams, new note shapes and symbols, and novel ways of arranging notation on the page (see the illustration on page 532). But composers are not the only ones to invent unusual sounds. Often the players themselves discover new possibilities for their instruments. Many modern works have been inspired by the discoveries of inventive performers.

The greatest expansion and experimentation have involved percussion instruments. In many recent compositions, percussion instruments outnumber strings, woodwinds, and brasses. Traditional percussion instruments are struck with new types of beaters made of glass, metal, wood, and cloth. Unconventional instruments now widely used include tomtoms, bongos, slapstick, maracas, guiro, and vibraphone.

In the search for novel sounds, increased use has been made of

Scores for recent music often contain notes in new shapes, or new symbols, as well as novel ways of arranging notation on the page. Here is a page from the score of *Ancient Voices of Children,* by George Crumb.

(Pablo Delano)

The New Music Consort. Percussion instruments are imaginatively exploited in much recent music.

microtones, intervals smaller than the half step. Small intervals like quarter tones have long been used in nonwestern music, but they have only recently become an important resource for western composers. Electronic instruments have stimulated this development, since they are not restricted to conventional scales and do not force players to unlearn performance habits.

Composers such as Krzysztof Penderecki (b. 1933) create sounds bordering on electronic noise through tone clusters—closely spaced tones played together. Clusters are unlike traditional chords in that one usually does not hear individual tones but hears a mass, block, or band of sound. Composers may achieve a sense of growth or change by widening or narrowing such a band, or by making it more or less dense.

The directional aspect of sounds—how they are projected in space—has taken on new importance. Loudspeakers or groups of instruments may be placed at opposite ends of the stage, in the balcony, or at the back and sides of the auditorium. In electronic compositions like Edgard Varèse's *Poème électronique* (1958) and nonelectronic works like Elliott Carter's Double Concerto for harpsichord and piano with two chamber orchestras (1961), sounds are made to travel gradually in space, passing from one loudspeaker or player to another.

Mixed Media

Electronic music is often presented together with visual counterparts such as slide projections, films, light shows, gestures, and theatrical actions. One such mixed-media presentation was Varèse's *Poème électronique*, which combined electronic sounds with images projected on walls. But multimedia works are not confined to electronic music. Chance music and other types of recent music sometimes require performers to function as actors as well as sound producers, as in *Ancient Voices of Children* (1970), by George Crumb. Mixed-media presentations generally are intended to break down the ritual surrounding traditional concerts and to increase communication between composer and audience.

Rhythm and Form

Rhythm and form have undergone some of the most striking changes in music since 1950. Earlier in the century, composers often changed meters or used unconventional meters such as $\frac{7}{8}$ and $\frac{5}{8}$. Today, some composers abandon the concepts of beat and meter altogether. This is a natural outcome of electronic music, which needs no beat to keep performers together. In nonelectronic music, too, the composer may specify duration in absolute units such as seconds rather than in beats, which are relative units. In some recent music, there may be several different speeds at the same time.

More than ever, each piece of music follows its own laws, and its form grows out of its material. Many composers no longer write music in the traditional forms, such as A B A, sonata form, or rondo. Indeed, form may unfold with little or no obvious repetition of material.

BASIC TERMS

serialism (page 526)
chance music (aleatory music) (526)
minimalist music (528)
quotation music (529)
microtone (533)

MUSIC SINCE 1950: SEVEN REPRESENTATIVE PIECES $\begin{bmatrix} 17 \end{bmatrix}$

SONATA FOR FLUTE, OBOE, CELLO, AND HARPSICHORD (1952), BY ELLIOTT CARTER

Elliott Carter (b. 1908) is an American composer who is recognized as a major figure in contemporary music. He first attracted international attention when his String Quartet No. 1 (1951) won first prize at a composition contest held by the city of Liège in Belgium in 1953. Since then, he has produced an imposing series of instrumental works, including two other string quartets (1959, 1972), Variations for Orchestra (1955), the Double Concerto (1961), the Piano Concerto (1966), Concerto for Orchestra (1969), *Symphony of Three Orchestras* (1977), *Night Fantasies* for solo piano (1980), and *Enchanted Preludes* for Flute and Cello (1988).

In Carter's works, several highly contrasting ideas are often presented simultaneously. These superimposed ideas may differ in melodic character, rhythm, meter, and tempo. Carter's music has many tempo changes that are precisely regulated. He developed a technique called *metrical modulation*, which has been defined as "a means of going smoothly, but with complete accuracy, from one absolute metronomic speed to another, by lengthening or shortening the value of the basic note unit." Carter does not belong to any compositional "school" but has evolved a personal style; that style is illustrated in his Sonata for Flute, Oboe, Cello, and Harpsichord (1952).

"The Sonata," Carter explains, "was commissioned by the Harpsichord Quartet of New York. My idea was to stress as much as possible the vast and wonderful array of tone-colors available on the modern harpsichord. . . . This aim of using the wide variety of the harpsichord involved many tone colors which can only be produced very softly and therefore conditioned very drastically the type and range of musical expression, all the details of shape, phrasing, rhythm, texture, as well as the large form." Carter has said that at the time he was composing the sonata in 1952, "it seemed very important to have the harpsichord speak in a new voice, expressing characters unfamiliar to its extensive Baroque repertory."

Each of the four instrumental parts has a separate, highly individual identity, like a character in a drama. As Carter put it, "I regard my scores as scenarios, auditory scenarios, for performers to act out with their instru-

535

ments, dramatizing the players as individuals and participants in the ensemble. . . ." The three movements of the sonata are not in traditional forms; they have a feeling of purposeful improvisation. We'll focus on the first movement.

First Movement:

Risoluto (determined)

Supplementary sets:
Side 8, band 2
CD 4 26

26 0:00

"The music starts, *Risoluto*," writes Carter, "with a splashing dramatic gesture whose subsiding ripples form the rest of the movement." This 3-minute movement consists of a furiously energetic opening half and a calmer second half that contains a gradual decrescendo. The opening is mostly loud, with complex rhythms and polyphonic texture; several different, apparently unrelated things go on at once. Each of the simultaneous instrumental parts has individualized rhythms and melodic gestures, the flute and cello playing in their highest registers. Near the beginning of the first section comes a brief moment of relative calm when the harpsichord plays a succession of even eighth notes while the other instruments comment with short phrases.

27 1:21

This contrast between a steady mechanical pulse in the harpsichord and more fluid, impulsive rhythms in the other instruments becomes the basis of the second part of the movement, which is marked *tempo giusto (moderate tempo)*. This part begins with a harpsichord phrase in even quarter notes.

Tempo giusto

The harpsichord phrase returns several times, each time varied, expanded, and with different responses from the other instruments. Usually only one other instrument is heard with the harpsichord, so that the texture is less dense than that of the opening section. The movement's last "subsiding ripples" result from the soft dynamic level and the ever-widening distance between low and high harpsichord tones.

THRENODY: TO THE VICTIMS OF HIROSHIMA, BY KRZYSZTOF PENDERECKI

Supplementary sets:
Side 8, band 3
CD 4 28

During the late 1950s, a group of avant-garde composers unexpectedly emerged in Poland. For years, all artistic experimentation had been actively discouraged by the Soviet government and by other regimes in eastern Europe. However, after the revolt against Stalinism in 1955–1956, the new Polish government encouraged cultural independence and free artistic expression in films, painting, theater, and music. Composers had at their disposal well-trained performing groups and electronic music studios. The best-known Polish composer today is Krzysztof Penderecki (b. 1933).

Penderecki was a young boy when the Nazis occupied Poland and massacred most of its Jewish population. Although not threatened personally, Penderecki felt great compassion for the victims. "That great war crime," he wrote, "has undoubtedly been in my subconscious mind since the war, when, as a child, I saw the destruction of the ghetto in my small native town of Debica." His compassion for human suffering has been expressed in such works as *Dies irae* (1967), to the memory of the victims of Auschwitz; and *Threnody: To the Victims of Hiroshima*. In these works, and in his well-known *St. Luke Passion* (1963–1965), Penderecki draws spectacular and novel sounds from voices and conventional instruments. He often calls for tone clusters, glissandos, noiselike and percussive effects, and choral hissing, laughing, shouting, and whistling.

Penderecki's *Threnody*, or song of mourning, is an almost unbearably intense work; its sounds are not intended to be "pleasant." Fifty-two string instruments—violins, violas, cellos, and double basses—produce a wide variety of noiselike sounds that often seem to come from electronic generators. Many of these sounds are tone clusters. At the beginning of this 9-minute work, shrill clusters are produced by ten groups of instruments playing "the highest note of the instrument (no definite pitch)." At the end of the piece, a huge cluster that sounds like the roar of a jet engine is produced by all fifty-two strings playing pitches a quarter tone apart. Penderecki often uses slides or glissandos to make the clusters expand and contract. Noiselike sounds are also produced by tapping on the body of the instrument and bowing on the tailpiece.

There is no feeling of beat in this music. The duration of its various musical events is indicated in seconds at the bottom of the score. *Threnody* is divided into six sections. Some feature sustained sounds; others contain a variety of rapid percussive attacks. Noiselike sounds are so predominant that the definite pitch heard at the beginning of section 2 is very striking. An overall sense of coherence is produced by the general similarity of the first and last sections, as well as by the climactic character of section 4.

Listening Outline To be read while music is heard

THRENODY: TO THE VICTIMS OF HIROSHIMA FOR 52 STRINGS (1960), BY KRZYSZTOF PENDERECKI

24 violins, 10 violas, 10 cellos, 8 double basses

(Duration, 8:57)

28 0:00
1:07
1:24
1:54
2:27
2:39
3:34
4:02
4:51
5:06
5:31
6:25
7:28
8:25

1. *a.* Shrill, sustained clusters, one entering after the other.
   b. Suddenly soft.
   c. Pizzicatos. Soft, rapid squeaks. Increased rhythmic activity.
   d. Clusters fade out, squeaks and pizzicatos remain.
2. *a.* Sustained tone.
   b. Upward and downward glissandos (slides). Single, sustained tones expand into clusters, clusters contract into single tones.
   c. High sustained tone together with clusters; brief silence.
3. *a.* Low, sustained cluster, *p.* Higher sustained cluster, *f.* Other clusters join, *ff.*
   b. Glassy sounds slide upward. Decrescendo into silence.
4. *a.* Quick attacks of single tones build to very wide and loud cluster.
   b. Low, roaring cluster. Slides. Low cluster narrows to single sustained cello tone. Decrescendo into 10-second pause.
5. Disconnected pizzicatos, tremolos, blips, scratches at various dynamics and registers. Percussive sounds lead to
6. *a.* Sustained clusters in various registers. Momentarily soft, high squeaks and clusters, crescendo to brief silence.
   b. Sustained cluster like jet roar. Sound gradually fades into silence.

POÈME ÉLECTRONIQUE (ELECTRONIC POEM), BY EDGARD VARÈSE

Side 15, band 2
CD 8 7

Edgard Varèse (1883–1965), one of the great innovators of twentieth-century music, was born in France but spent most of his life in the United States. As early as 1916, he dreamed of freeing music from the limitations of traditional instruments and expanding the vocabulary of sounds. During the 1920s and 1930s, Varèse pioneered in the exploration of percussive and noiselike sounds, and he wrote the first important work for percussion ensemble *(Ionisation*, 1931).

But it was the new electronic developments of the 1950s that enabled Varèse to realize his vision of the "liberation of sound." In 1958, at the age of seventy-five, he composed *Poème électronique,* one of the earliest master-pieces of electronic music created in a tape studio. The 8-minute work was designed to be heard within the pavilion of the Philips Radio Corporation at the 1958 Brussels World Fair. Varèse obtained unique spatial effects by projecting sound from 425 loudspeakers placed all over the interior surfaces of the pavilion. The composer worked in collaboration with the architect Le Corbusier, who selected a series of images—photographs, paintings, and writing—that were projected on the walls as the music was heard. But there was no attempt to synchronize the sounds with the images, which included "birds and beasts, fish and reptiles, . . . masks and skeletons, idols, girls clad and unclad, cities in normal appearance and then suddenly askew," as well as atomic mushroom clouds.

Varèse's raw sound material—tones and noises—came from a wide variety of sources, including electronic generators, church bells, sirens, organs, human voices, and machines. The sounds are often electronically

538

processed in a such a way that they cannot be precisely identified. In the listening outline, the effect of such sounds is conveyed by words placed in quotation marks; for example, "wood blocks" or "animal noises." Varèse organized his sounds into an electronic poem that seems weird, yet is amazingly logical and compelling.

Poème électronique is subdivided into two main sections, the first lasting 2 minutes and 36 seconds and the second 5 minutes and 29 seconds. Each section begins with low bell tolls and ends with sirens. Heard several times during the *Poème* is a distinctive group of three rising tones. Human voices and recognizable organ tones appear only during the second section. Varèse once remarked about the female voice heard toward the end of the *Poème:* "I wanted it to express tragedy—and inquisition."

Because it was created in a tape studio, *Poème électronique* exists in only a single "performance" whose duration is fixed on audiotape.

Listening Outline To be read while music is heard

POÈME ÉLECTRONIQUE (ELECTRONIC POEM; 1958),
BY EDGARD VARÈSE (1883–1965)

Tape studio

(Duration, 8:05)

7	0:00	1. a.	Low bell tolls. "Wood blocks." Sirens. Fast taps lead into high, piercing sounds. 2-second pause.
	0:43	b.	"Bongo" tones and higher grating noises. Short "squawks." Three-tone group stated three times.
	1:11	c.	Low sustained tones with grating noises. Sirens. Short "squawks." Three-tone group. 2-second pause.
	1:40	d.	Short "squawks." High "chirps." Variety of "shots," "honks," "machine noises." Sirens. Taps lead to
	2:36	2. a.	Low bell tolls. Sustained electronic tones. Repeated "bongo" tones. High and sustained electronic tones. Low tone, crescendo. Rhythmic noises lead to
	3:41	b.	Voice, "Oh-gah." 4-second pause. Voice continues softly.
	4:17	c.	Suddenly loud. Rhythmic percussive sounds joined by voice. Low "animal noises," scraping, shuffling, hollow vocal sounds. Decrescendo into 7-second pause.
	5:47	d.	Sustained electronic tones, crescendo and decrescendo. Rhythmic percussive sounds. Higher sustained electronic tones, crescendo. "Airplane rumble," "chimes," jangling.
	6:47	e.	Female voice. Male chorus. Electronic noises, organ. High taps. Swooping organ sound. Three-note group stated twice. Rumble, sirens, crescendo.

COMPOSITION FOR SYNTHESIZER (1960–1961), BY MILTON BABBITT

The American Milton Babbitt (b. 1916) is a leading composer and theorist of twelve-tone music and a major figure in the development of electronic music. A brilliant teacher who is now Conant Professor of Music (Emeritus) at Princeton University, Babbitt has profoundly influenced many young composers. He was the first composer to extend serial principles of organization to all musical dimensions—rhythm, dynamics, and tone color, as well as pitch. Not only are all the pitches in a Babbitt work derived from a tone row, but all the rhythms are drawn from a "durational row," a series of rhythmic values. His earliest works to use such techniques of serialism date from the late 1940s: *Three Compositions for Piano* (1947), *Composition for Four Instruments* (1947–1948), and *Composition for Twelve Instruments* (1948).

Babbitt's desire to control every aspect of his music attracted him to the possibilities of electronic music. From 1959 to 1979, he made extensive use of the RCA Mark II synthesizer, an enormous machine filling an entire wall at the Columbia-Princeton Electronic Music Center in New York City. "If you know how to specify it, any sound that can be passed by a loudspeaker can be created by this machine," Babbitt once explained. "I could synthesize the equivalent of a recorded violin sound if I knew exactly what the relevant dimensions of such a violin sound are." With the RCA synthesizer, composers could precisely control the pitch, duration, tone color, and dynamic level of sounds. Using a mechanism similar to a typewriter, composers could punch their musical specifications into a wide roll of paper fed into the synthesizer. The sounds produced could then be recorded on audiotape. The RCA synthesizer is very complex, and although it is still in existence today, it is no longer used. In fact, few composers other than Babbitt—who is a trained mathematician—ever used it. The synthesizer was not "played" as one plays an organ or a piano; composers might spend many hours with the machine to produce a few minutes of music. Babbitt used the RCA synthesizer to produce works such as *Vision and Prayer*, for soprano and synthesized accompaniment (1961); *Philomel*, for soprano, recorded soprano, and synthesized tape (1964); *Ensembles for Synthesizer* (1962–1964); and *Composition for Synthesizer* (1960–1961), which we'll now study.

In *Composition for Synthesizer*, both pitch and rhythm are governed by serial organization. Here is the basic twelve-tone row: G–E–A♭–E♭–B–C–D–A–B♭–D♭–F–G♭. Babbitt has written that the piece is less concerned with "new sounds and timbres" than with the control and specification of rhythm made possible by the RCA synthesizer. Electronic music, he explains, provides "a means of controlling rhythm in all its aspects, including speed and flexibility of pitch succession and time rate of change of dynamics, something that was never afforded a composer before." Though some noiselike sounds are heard in *Composition for Synthesizer*, most of the sounds have definite pitches.

The opening clearly shows Babbitt's skillful use of contrasting textures and registers. In the first 45 seconds, there is a regular alternation between gonglike chords and melodic fragments, which are shifted to different registers, changed in speed, and presented in backward (retrograde) and upside-down (inverted) form. The texture becomes more and more complex as the number of melodic lines increases from one to four. This increasing complexity can be seen in the following outline:

Side 15, band 3
CD 8 8

1. *a.* Gonglike sustained chord stated twice.
   b. One staccato melody.
2. *a.* Sustained chord stated twice.
   b. Two staccato melodies.
3. *a.* Sustained chord.
   b. Low legato melody joined by two higher staccato melodies.
4. *a.* Sustained chord.
   b. Two very low melodies joined by two higher staccato melodies.

Many trill-like figures are heard in the section that follows. Their speed and evenness could be achieved only through electronic means.

ANCIENT VOICES OF CHILDREN (1970), BY GEORGE CRUMB

During the late 1960s, the American composer George Crumb (b. 1929) became prominent as the result of a series of works that were acclaimed highly by both audiences and critics. His music is personal and emotionally intense; it is distinguished by an imaginative use of novel and delicate tone colors. Currently, Crumb teaches composition at the University of Pennsylvania.

Like much of his music, Crumb's *Ancient Voices of Children* is set to poetry by Federico García Lorca, the great Spanish writer who was murdered in 1936 during the civil war in Spain. "I have sought musical images," wrote Crumb, "that enhance and reinforce the powerful, yet strangely haunting imagery of Lorca's poetry. I feel that the essential meaning of this poetry is concerned with the most primary things: life, death, love, the smell of the earth, the sounds of the wind and the sea."

Ancient Voices of Children is a cycle of five songs with two instrumental interludes. The work is written for mezzo-soprano, boy soprano, oboe, mandolin, harp, percussion, and "electric piano." (A normal grand piano is amplified by means of contact microphones attached to its sounding board.) Three percussionists command a variety of instruments, including

541

such unconventional ones as tuned tom-toms, Tibetan prayer stones, and Japanese temple bells. The pianist also plays a toy piano (in the fourth song); the oboist, a harmonica (also in the fourth song); and the mandolinist, a "musical saw" (an ordinary saw played with a double-bass bow).

"Perhaps the most characteristic vocal effect in *Ancient Voices*," writes Crumb, "is produced by the mezzo-soprano singing a kind of fantastic vocalise (on purely phonetic sounds) into an amplified piano, thereby producing a shimmering aura of echoes." (A *vocalise* is an extended melody sung without a text, only on vowels.) Gradually fading sounds are produced by gongs, harp, vibraphone, and marimbas—among other instruments—and contribute to the vaguely Asian atmosphere. (A ***vibraphone*** is a percussion instrument with tuned metal bars and tubular metal resonators that produce a vibrato by means of motor-driven metal revolving vanes; a ***marimba*** is a large xylophone with resonators.) The composer wants us to savor individual tone colors; in many passages, only a single instrument or voice is heard.

Ancient Voices is theatrical in character and has already been used as ballet music by several companies. A boy soprano singing offstage heightens the drama. Even the instrumentalists play a dramatic role; they are occasionally required to sing, shout, or whisper. We'll focus on the third song of the cycle.

From Where Do You Come, My Love, My Child?
(Dance of the Sacred Life-Cycle)

Side 15, band 4
CD 8 9

The most spectacular part of *Ancient Voices of Children* is the central song, which uses the characteristic rhythm of a bolero, the Spanish dance which also inspired Ravel's *Bolero* (see Section 5). The song opens with a soprano solo on phonetic sounds, sung into the amplified piano. During this solo, the singer is required to trill the tongue and make laughing sounds. Then the percussionists begin an ostinato in bolero rhythm that continues throughout the piece. They make a gradual crescendo and decrescendo, and progress from whispering to shouting, then back to whispering. Each of the poem's three stanzas has a half-sung question and answer by the two vocalists, a decorative oboe phrase, and an exuberant soprano melody. (Crumb's special music notation for this song is shown on page 532.)

9	
¿De dónde vienes, amor, mi niño?	From where do you come, my love, my child?
De la cresta del duro frío.	From the ridge of hard frost.
¿Qué necesitas, amor, mi niño?	What do you need, my love, my child?
La tibia tela de tu vestido.	The warm cloth of your dress.

¡Que se agiten las ramas al sol	Let the branches ruffle in the sun
y salten las fuentes alrededor!	and the fountains leap all around!
En el patio ladra el perro,	In the courtyard a dog barks,
en los árboles canta el viento.	in the trees the wind sings.
Los bueyes mugen al boyero	The oxen low to the ox-herd
y la luna me riza los cabellos.	and the moons curls my hair.
¿Qué pides, niño, desde tan lejos?	What do you ask for, my child,
	from so far away?
Los blancos montes que hay en tu pecho.	The white mountains of your breast.
¡Que se agiten las ramas al sol	Let the branches ruffle in the sun
y salten las fuentes alrededor!	and the fountains leap all around!
Te diré, niño mío, que sí,	I'll tell you, my child, yes,
tronchada y rota soy para ti.	I am torn and broken for you.
¡Cómo me duele esta cintura	How painful is this waist
donde tendrás primera cuna!	where you will have your first cradle!
¿Cuándo mi niño, vas a venir?	When, my child, will you come?
Cuando tu carne huela a jazmín.	When your flesh smells of jasmine
	flowers.
¡Que se agiten las ramas al sol	Let the branches ruffle in the sun
y salten las fuentes alrededor!	and the fountains leap all around!*

CONCERTO GROSSO 1985
(TO HANDEL'S SONATA IN D MAJOR
FOR VIOLIN AND CONTINUO, FIRST MOVEMENT),
BY ELLEN TAAFFE ZWILICH

The American composer Ellen Taaffe Zwilich (b. 1939) won the 1983 Pulitzer Prize for Music for her Symphony No. 1. Zwilich was born in Miami, Florida, the daughter of an airline pilot. She studied at Florida State University and at the Juilliard School and played for several years as a professional violinist in the American Symphony Orchestra under the direction of Leopold Stokowski. She has composed an impressive series of widely performed instrumental works, including the String Quartet (1974), Chamber Symphony (1979), String Trio (1982), Double Quartet for Strings (1984), Symphony No. 2 (1985), Concerto for Piano and Orchestra (1986), and *Symbolon*, an orchestral work that was premiered by the New York Philharmonic Orchestra during its tour of the Soviet Union in 1988.

Ellen Taaffe Zwilich.

Concerto Grosso 1985 was commissioned by the Washington Friends of Handel to commemorate Handel's three-hundredth birthday. Each of its five movements uses thematic material drawn from the opening movement of Handel's Sonata for Violin and Continuo in D Major. Zwilich has said: "I performed the [Handel] many years ago, and I especially love the opening theme of the first movement. . . . Throughout [*Concerto Grosso 1985*], I found myself using compositional techniques typical of the baroque period, including terraced dynamics, repeated phrases . . . techniques I would not normally use, but I felt inspired to do so because of the fact that this piece was based on Handel." Like the concerti grossi of Handel and Bach, Zwilich's *Concerto Grosso 1985* is written for a small orchestra including a harpsichord and gives solo instruments prominent roles. Its five movements are arranged symmetrically: the finale is similar to the opening movement, and the fourth movement parallels the second. The outer two movements include entire passages from the Handel sonata, whereas the inner three movements employ no quotations but freely develop its opening melodic motive. We'll focus on the first movement, a clear example of "quotation music."

First Movement:

Maestoso (majestic)

The maestoso repeatedly alternates quotations from Handel with passages that could have been written only in the twentieth century. Though abrupt, these contrasts somehow add up to a unified whole. Partly, this is because the newly composed sections are often based on a speeded-up variation of Handel's opening four-note motive.

Side 15, band 5
CD 8 [10]

In addition, Zwilich's own music uses compositional techniques associated with the baroque. Long pedal points in the bass give a firm definition of key to melodic lines that use dissonances freely in a twentieth-century manner. And these melodic lines include the repeated rhythmic pattern short-short-long, short-short-long found in music by Bach and Handel.

Listening Outline   To be read while music is heard

CONCERTO GROSSO 1985 (TO HANDEL'S SONATA IN D MAJOR FOR VIOLIN AND CONTINUO, FIRST MOVEMENT), BY ELLEN TAAFFE ZWILICH

Maestoso (majestic), quadruple meter ($\frac{4}{4}$), D major

Flute, 2 oboes, bassoon, 2 French horns, harpsichord, 1st violins, 2d violins, violas, cellos, double basses

(Duration, 2:45)

1. *a.* Orchestra in unison, *f*, single sustained tone presented three times.
   b. Violins, *f*, vigorous phrase, short-short-long rhythm, sustained tone in bass;

vigorous phrase repeated softly.
   c. Handel quotation, strings and harpsichord, *mp*,

interrupted by

2. *a.* Vigorous phrase developed in strings and woodwinds; crescendo to *f;* short string phrases with abrupt pauses.
   b. Handel quotation continued, oboe *mf*, accompanied by harpsichord and strings.
3. *a.* Vigorous phrase in violins, *f*, imitated in flute, *f;* vigorous phrase in violins, *f*.
   b. Handel quotation continued, *f;* trills in strings and woodwinds; harpsichord; melody closes.
4. *a.* Vigorous phrase in violins, flute, and oboes; crescendo to *ff*,
   b. Woodwinds, high sustained dissonant chords; low strings, fragments of vigorous string phrase, *ff*. Ends on sustained dissonant chord, *f*.

0:55

1:31

2:03
2:13

NIXON IN CHINA (1987), BY JOHN ADAMS

John Adams (b. 1947) is a leading American composer who has described himself as "a minimalist bored with minimalism." Like other minimalists, he writes music with a steady, driving pulse, clear tonality, constant repetition of melodic and rhythmic patterns, and a slow rate of change. But his works are enriched by lyrical, expressive melodies and varied orchestral colors. A conductor as well as composer, he taught and directed the New Music Ensemble at the San Francisco Conservatory of Music from 1972 to 1982 and was composer in residence with the San Francisco Symphony Orchestra during 1982–1985. His works include *Harmonium* (1980), for chorus and orchestra; *Light over Water* (Symphony for Brass and Synthesizers,

President Richard Nixon, Chairman Mao Tse-Tung, and Mao's three secretaries in Act I, scene 2, of *Nixon in China*, as performed by the Houston Grand Opera.

1983); *Harmonielehre* (1985) for orchestra; and the operas *Nixon in China* (1987), which we'll study, and *The Death of Klinghoffer* (1991).

Nixon in China takes place from February 21 to 25, 1972, when Richard Nixon, then president of the United States, made a historic trip to Beijing to meet the Chinese leader, Chairman Mao Tse-Tung, and work toward the establishment of diplomatic relations between the two countries. The opera is extraordinary because it deals with a media event involving famous people contemporary with the composer. Its libretto, by Alice Goodman, is written in eight-syllable couplets and is based on news reports, television broadcasts, biographies, and memoirs. The main characters are the two leaders; their wives, Pat Nixon and Chiang Ch'ing; the American Secretary of State, Henry Kissinger, who is a former Harvard professor; and the Chinese Prime Minister, Chou En-Lai.

547

Act I: Opening of Scene 2 (Chairman Mao's Study)

Side 15, band 6
CD 8 [12]

In this scene, Nixon, Kissinger, Mao, and Chou En-Lai chat about such topics as Chiang Kai-shek (then head of the Chinese government in exile on Taiwan), Mao's books (which are "read at Harvard"), and Kissinger's reputation in "foreign affairs."

The opening orchestral passage, heard while the leaders enter Mao's study, is a characteristic example of minimalist music, with high repeated rhythmic figures pulsating over low, syncopated notes played on a Yamaha HX-1 synthesizer. Rhythmic pulsations in the orchestra accompany the singers throughout the scene. To convey the effect of a simultaneous translation, every word that Mao sings is also sung at the same time by his three female secretaries, who are given different melodies with slower rhythms.

[12]

Orchestral introduction, high pulsations over low, syncopated tones of synthesizer.

Mao
I can't talk very well. My throat—

Nixon
I'm nearly speechless with delight
Just to be here.

Mao
We're even then.
That is the right way to begin.
Our common old friend Chiang Kai-shek
With all his virtues would not look
Too kindly on all this. We seem
To be beneath the likes of him.
You've seen his latest speech?

Nixon
    You bet.
It was a scorcher. Still, he's spit
Into the wind before, and will
Again. That puts it into scale.
You shouldn't despise Chiang.

Mao
     No fear
Of that. We've followed his career
For generations. There's not much
Beneath our notice.

Chou
We will touch
On this in our communiqué.

Mao
(addressing Kissinger)
Ah, the philosopher! I see
Paris can spare you then.

Kissinger
The Chair-
Man may be gratified to hear
He's read at Harvard. I assign
All four volumes.

Mao
Those books of mine
Aren't anything. Incorporate
Their words within a people's thought
As poor men's common sense and try
Their strength on women's nerves, then say
They live.

Nixon
The Chairman's books enthralled
A nation, and have changed the world.

Mao
I could not change it. I'd be glad
To think that in the neighborhood
Of Peking something will remain.

Nixon
Let us turn our talk towards Taiwan,
Vietnam and the problems there.
Japan—

Mao
Save that for the Premier.
My business is philosophy.
Now Doctor Kissinger—

Kissinger
Who me?

Mao
—Has made his reputation in
Foreign affairs.

Nixon
My right hand man.
You'd never think to look at him
That he's James Bond.

Chou
And all the time
He's doing undercover work.

Kissinger
I had a cover.

Mao
In the dark
All diplomats are gray.

Chou
Or *gris* [*gray* in French]
When their work takes them to *Paris*.

Kissinger
I pull the wool over their—

Mao
He pulls the wool over their lap.

Nixon
He's a consummate diplomat.
Girls think he's lukewarm when he's hot.

Sung
simultaneously.

Mao
You also dally with your girls?

Nixon
His girls, not mine.

Kissinger
He never tells.

Chou
And this is an election year.

BASIC TERMS

vibraphone (page 542)
marimba (542)

VIII

JAZZ

VIII

Louis Armstrong had a worldwide impact on jazz.

1 JAZZ STYLES: 1900–1950

JAZZ

At about the time when Schoenberg and Stravinsky were changing the language of music in Europe, a new musical style called *jazz* was being developed in America.* It was created by musicians—predominantly African Americans—performing in the streets, bars, brothels, and dance halls of New Orleans and other southern cities. *Jazz* can be described generally as music rooted in improvisation and characterized by syncopated rhythm, a steady beat, and distinctive tone colors and techniques of performance. Although the term *jazz* became current in 1917, the music itself was probably heard as early as 1900. We do not know exactly when early jazz started or how it sounded, because this new music existed only in performance, not musical notation. Moreover, very little jazz was captured on recordings before 1923, and none at all before the Original Dixieland Jazz Band recorded in 1917.

Since its beginnings, jazz has developed a rich variety of substyles such as New Orleans style (or Dixieland), swing, bebop, cool, free jazz, and jazz rock. It has produced such outstanding figures as Louis Armstrong, Duke Ellington, Benny Goodman, Charlie Parker, and John Coltrane. Its impact has been enormous and worldwide, affecting not only many kinds of popular music, but the music of such composers as Maurice Ravel, Darius Milhaud, and Aaron Copland.

ROOTS OF JAZZ

Early jazz blended elements from many musical cultures, including west African, American, and European. Most American slaves originally came from west Africa, an area that today includes Ghana, Nigeria, and several other countries. West African elements that influenced jazz include its emphasis on improvisation, drumming, percussive sounds, and complex rhythms. Another feature of jazz that was probably derived from west Africa is known as *call and response*. In much west African vocal music, a soloist's phrases are repeatedly answered by a chorus. In jazz, **call and response** occurs when a voice is answered by an instrument, or when one instrument (or group of instruments) is answered by another instrument (or group). The call-and-response pattern of jazz was derived more directly from African American church services in which the congregation vocally responds to the preacher's "call." In America, blacks developed a rich

---

*An excellent recorded anthology of jazz is the *Smithsonian Collection of Classic Jazz,* available from Smithsonian Books and Recordings (P.O. Box 10229, Des Moines, Iowa 50381–0229) as a set of seven records (no. 1846), five cassettes (no. 1847), or five compact disks (no. 1848).

554

(Photo Files)

One major source of jazz was the American band tradition.

body of music that became a vital source for jazz. This music included work songs, spirituals, gospel hymns, and such dances as the cakewalk. Much of this music was never written down and is now lost to us. But it was probably performed in a way that created sounds and rhythms similar to those of early jazz.

Black music influenced and was influenced by the music of white America, which included hymns, popular songs, folk tunes, dances, marches, and piano pieces. In origin, this repertory was partly American and partly written or influenced by European composers. Nineteenth-century American and European musical traditions provided melodies, harmonies, and forms that became elements in the background of jazz.

One major source of jazz was the American band tradition. Bands—both black and white—played an important role in American life during the late nineteenth and early twentieth centuries. Virtually every village had its band and bandstand; bands performed at picnics, parades, political rallies, dances, and carnivals. Many of the instruments used in marching bands—the trumpet, cornet, trombone, tuba, clarinet, and drums—were also used in early jazz bands. Band music also influenced the forms and rhythms of early jazz.

Along with band music, the immediate sources of jazz were ragtime and the blues. Ragtime is a style of syncopated piano music that was popular from the 1890s to about 1915. The term *blues* refers to, among other things, a style of black vocal music involving ''bent'' notes and slides of pitch. Ragtime and the blues will be discussed more fully in Sections 2 and 3.

JAZZ IN SOCIETY

The world of jazz has witnessed many changes since its beginnings at the turn of our century. Geographically, its center has shifted from New Orleans to Chicago, Kansas City, and New York. Today, it is hard to speak of *a* jazz center, since good jazz is heard worldwide, from Paris to Tokyo. Jazz has changed in function, too. For a long time, it was basically music for dancing; but since the 1940s, many newer jazz styles have been intended for listening. Now we are as likely to hear jazz in a concert hall or college classroom as in a bar or nightclub. The image of jazz has also changed. It was originally condemned for its emphasis on sexuality, but it has long since become respectable. Since the 1960s, jazz has even been heard in American houses of worship.

ELEMENTS OF JAZZ

Like other music of the twentieth century, jazz is too diverse and complex to be defined by any single formula. We'll now consider some of the elements of jazz that was created before 1950. Jazz after 1950 is discussed in Section 7.

Tone Color

Jazz is generally played by a small group (or *combo*) containing from three to eight players, or by a "big band" with ten to fifteen musicians. The backbone of a jazz ensemble is its rhythm section, which is comparable to the basso continuo in baroque music. The *rhythm section,* usually made up of piano, plucked double bass (bass), percussion, and—sometimes—banjo or guitar, maintains the beat, adds rhythmic interest, and provides supporting harmonies. Modern percussionists produce a variety of sounds from several drums and cymbals, using sticks, mallets, wire brushes, and bare hands.

The main solo instruments of jazz include the cornet, trumpet, saxophone (soprano, alto, tenor, baritone), piano, clarinet, vibraphone, and trombone. Jazz emphasizes brasses, woodwinds, and percussion rather than the bowed strings that dominate symphonic music. Brass players produce a wide variety of tone colors by using different mutes and muting techniques. A jazz performance usually involves both solo and ensemble sections. For example, a full ensemble might be followed by a trumpet solo and then by a clarinet solo or a duet for saxophone and trumpet.

Compared with "classical" musicians, who strive for an ideal sound, jazz performers aim for more individuality of sound and tone color. For example, it is usually easier to distinguish between two jazz trumpet players than between two "classical" trumpeters. Although jazz is basically

The rhythm section of a jazz ensemble usually includes piano, bass, and percussion. The singer Ella Fitzgerald is accompanied here by Paul Smith, Keter Betts, and Bobby Durham.

instrumental music, its players try to match the personal quality of singing. In all, the distinctive sounds of jazz are easy to recognize but hard to describe. A jazz sound results from the particular way tones are attacked, "bent," and released; from the type of vibrato employed; and from a variety of pitch inflections that might be described as "smears," "scoops," "falloffs," and "shakes."

Improvisation

At the heart of jazz lies improvisation. Jazz musicians create a special electricity as they simultaneously create and perform, making decisions at lightning speed. The fertility of great improvisers is staggering. Their recorded performances represent only a tiny fraction of the music they create almost nightly.

Of course, not all jazz is improvised, and most contains both improvised and composed sections. Yet it is improvisation that contributes most to the freshness and spontaneity of jazz. The reputations of jazz performers rest mainly on the originality of their improvisations.

557

A jazz improvisation is usually in theme-and-variations form. The theme is often a popular song melody made up of 32 **bars,** or measures. The improviser varies this original melody by adding embellishments and changing its pitches and rhythms. Some improvised variations are similar to the original theme, but others are so different that the tune may be difficult to recognize. Often, jazz improvisations are based not on a melody but on a harmonic pattern, or series of chords. This harmonic pattern will be repeated over and over while the improviser creates melodies above it. In jazz, each statement of the basic harmonic pattern or melody is called a *chorus.* For example, a jazz performance that is based on a 32-bar melody might be outlined as follows:

Chorus 1 (32 bars)   Theme
Chorus 2 (32 bars)   Variation 1
Chorus 3 (32 bars)   Variation 2
Chorus 4 (32 bars)   Variation 3

A jazz performance usually includes improvised solos by various members of the ensemble. In addition, there may be sections of *collective* improvisation, during which several musicians make up different melodies simultaneously. Their music is held together by the underlying chords. Until the introduction of long-playing records in 1948, most recorded jazz performances were about 3 minutes in length, the duration of one side of a 78 rpm record.

Rhythm, Melody, and Harmony

Syncopation and rhythmic swing are two of the most distinctive features of jazz. We say that jazz performers *"swing"* when they combine a steady beat with a feeling of lilt, precision, and relaxed vitality. In most jazz styles, the beat is provided by the percussionist (on drums or cymbals) and by the bass player. There are usually four beats to the bar. Accents often come on the weak beats: 1-**2**-3-**4.** Many kinds of syncopated rhythms result when accented notes come *between* the beats. Jazz musicians also create a swing feeling by playing a series of notes slightly unevenly. For example, the second note of a pair of eighth notes will be shorter than the first:

But the rhythms of jazz are so irregular that it is difficult to notate them accurately. A performer must deviate from the notated rhythms to get a true jazz feeling. And as jazz has evolved, rhythms have become ever more irregular and complex.

Jazz melodies are as flexible in pitch as in rhythm. They employ a major scale in which the third, fifth, and seventh notes are often lowered, or flatted. These "bent," or "blue," notes came into jazz through the vocal blues, as you'll see in Section 3. Jazz uses chord progressions like those of the traditional tonal system. But over the years, the harmonic vocabulary of jazz—like its rhythm—has become increasingly complex and sophisticated.

BASIC TERMS

jazz (page 554)
call and response (554)
rhythm section (556)
bar (558)
chorus (558)
swing (558)

RAGTIME [JAZZ **2**]

Ragtime is a style of composed piano music that flourished from the 1890s to about 1915. It was developed primarily by African American pianists who traveled in the midwest and south playing in saloons and dance halls. Not long after it originated, ragtime became a nationally popular style that reached millions of people—both black and white—through sheet music, player pianos, ragtime songs, and arrangements for dance and marching bands.

Ragtime piano music is generally in duple meter ($\frac{2}{4}$) and is performed at a moderate march tempo. The pianist's right hand plays a highly syncopated melody, while the left hand steadily maintains the beat with an "oom-pah" accompaniment. A ragtime piece usually consists of several melodies that are similar in character. It takes such forms as AA BB A CC DD or introduction–AA BB CC DD EE. Although the forms derive from European marches and dances, the rhythms of ragtime are rooted in African American folk music.

Early jazz musicians often used ragtime melodies as a springboard for their improvisations. The syncopations, steady beat, and piano style of ragtime were an important legacy for jazz.

(Photo Researchers)

Scott Joplin was the leading ragtime composer.

SCOTT JOPLIN

The acknowledged "king of ragtime" was Scott Joplin (1868–1917), a composer and pianist whose father had been a slave. Joplin was trained in "classical" music and wrote a ballet and two operas, as well as many piano rags. His most famous piano piece was *Maple Leaf Rag*, named after the saloon in Sedalia, Missouri, where he worked as a pianist. After it was published in 1899, *Maple Leaf Rag* sold hundreds of thousands of copies. This success allowed Joplin to quit his saloon job and move to St. Louis, where he taught and composed.

In 1909, Joplin settled in New York City, where he spent the last years of his life. This was a bleak period for him: his health was poor, and he was unsuccessful in his desperate attempts to get a professional production of his opera *Treemonisha* (1911). Finally, in 1915, he mounted the opera himself in Harlem—without scenery, costumes, or orchestra. The failure of this endeavor led Joplin to a physical and mental breakdown. He was confined to a hospital in 1916 and died the following year. Only recently has *Treemonisha* been revived, and with great success.

MAPLE LEAF RAG (1899)

Maple Leaf Rag is a classic example of ragtime; it lasts about 3 minutes and has the standard ragtime form AA BB A CC DD. Each section is exactly 16 bars in length. The opening melody (A), marked *tempo di marcia (march tempo)*, features the right-hand syncopations so typical of the style:

Side 15, band 7
CD 8 [13]

[13] 0:00

The second melody (B) begins in a higher register than A and moves steadily downward.

[14] 0:44

15 1:48 Section C modulates to a new key and has the "oom-pah" accompaniment in the left hand characteristic of ragtime. The accompaniment includes low octaves followed by higher chords:

16 2:30 The final section (D) returns to the home key and ends with a decisive cadence.

BASIC TERMS

ragtime (page 559)

[3] JAZZ

THE BLUES

Among the most important sources of jazz is a type of music known as the *blues.* The term refers to a form of vocal and instrumental music and to a style of performance. The blues grew out of African American folk music, such as work songs, spirituals, and the field hollers of slaves. It is uncertain exactly when the blues originated, but by around the 1890s they were sung in rural areas of the south. The original "country blues," which were usually performed with a guitar accompaniment, were unstandardized in form or style.

The poetic and musical form of the blues crystallized around 1910 and gained popularity through the publication of *Memphis Blues* (1912) and *St. Louis Blues* (1914), by W. C. Handy (1873–1958). During the 1920s, the blues became a national craze among African Americans. Records by such blues singers as Bessie Smith sold in the millions. The 1920s also saw the blues become a musical form widely used by jazz instrumentalists as well as blues singers. Since then, jazz and the blues have been intertwined. The continuing impact of the blues is apparent in such popular styles as rhythm and blues, rock and roll, and soul.

Vocal blues are intensely personal; they often contain sexual references and deal with the pain of betrayal, desertion, and unrequited love. The lyrics consist of several 3-line stanzas, each in the same poetic and musical form. The first line is sung and then repeated to roughly the same melodic phrase (a a'); the third line has a different melodic phrase (b).

> a : I'm going to leave baby, ain't going to say goodbye.
> a': I'm going to leave baby, ain't going to say goodbye.
> b : But I'll write you and tell you the reason why.

A blues stanza is set to a harmonic framework that is usually 12 bars in length. This harmonic pattern, known as the *12-bar blues,* involves only three basic chords: the tonic (I), the subdominant (IV), and the dominant (V). (The *subdominant* is the triad based on the fourth note—*fa*—of the scale.) The specific ordering of these chords can be outlined as follows: tonic (4 bars)-subdominant (2 bars)-tonic (2 bars)-dominant (2 bars)-tonic (2 bars). Here is how the 3-line stanza is set to this chord progression:

	Line 1 (a)				Line 2 (a')				Line 3 (b)			
Bars	1	2	3	4	5	6	7	8	9	10	11	12
Chords	I				IV		I		V		I	

Each stanza of the text is sung to the same series of chords, although other chords may be inserted between the basic ones of the 12-bar blues. Singers either repeat the same basic melody for each stanza or improvise new melodies to reflect the changing moods of the lyrics. The music is in quadruple meter ($\frac{4}{4}$), and so each bar contains 4 beats.

The 12-bar blues is divided into three phrases, each of which is 4 bars long. The soloist takes only about 2 bars to sing a line. This leaves the remainder of the 4-bar phrase to be filled in by the supporting instrument or instruments. In blues recordings of the 1920s and 1930s, instrumental responses to the singer's lines were often improvised by leading jazz musicians. The following example shows how the vocal lines and instrumental responses fit into the 12-bar blues pattern (some pitches and rhythms are approximate):

Bessie Smith, *Lost Your Head Blues,* fourth stanza

Blues singers have a special style of performance involving "bent" notes, microtonal shadings, and vocal scoops and slides. Their melodies contain many "blue" notes, which are produced by slightly lowering or flatting the third, fifth, and seventh tones of a major scale. Blues rhythm is also very flexible. Performers often sing "around" the beat, accenting notes either just before or after it.

Jazz instrumentalists imitate the performing style of blues singers and use the harmonic pattern of the 12-bar blues as a basis for improvisation. This 12-bar pattern is repeated over and over while new melodies are improvised above it. As with the baroque ground bass, the repeated chord progression provides unity while the free flow of improvised melodic lines contributes variety. Music in this 12-bar form can be happy or sad, fast or slow, and in a wide range of styles. In Section 4, we'll consider an instrumental blues, *Dippermouth Blues*, which is an example of New Orleans jazz. Now we'll study a vocal blues by Bessie Smith.

LOST YOUR HEAD BLUES (1926), BY BESSIE SMITH

Side 15, band 8
CD 8 [17]

Bessie Smith (1894–1937), known as the "empress of the blues," was the most famous blues singer of the 1920s. Her *Lost Your Head Blues* is a well-known example of blues form and performance style. The lyrics express the feelings of a woman who plans to leave her man because she's "been treated wrong." Each of the poem's five stanzas is set to the 12-bar blues pattern. Typically, a cornet response follows each line that is sung (see the example above).

Bessie Smith was one of the most influential blues singers.

Lost Your Head Blues begins with a 4-bar introduction by the accompanying cornet (Joe Smith) and piano (Fletcher Henderson). Bessie Smith then sings a melody that she'll repeat—with extensive variations of pitch and rhythm—in each stanza. Her "blue" notes, microtonal shadings, and slides between pitches are essential to the effect of the song. Notice the eloquent slides up to *I* in her singing of *I was with you baby,* as well as the ornamental quiver on *down* when she sings the words *your good gal down.* There are many syncopated rhythms, since words are often sung just before or after the beat. Bessie Smith's vocal melody is highly sensitive to the words. For example, the long high notes at the beginning of the last stanza ("*Days* are lonesome, *nights* are long") produce a wonderful climax. Throughout the song, Bessie Smith's vocal inflections are perfectly matched by the cornet's improvised responses and echoes.

I was with you baby when you did not have a dime.
I was with you baby when you did not have a dime.
Now since you got plenty money you have throw'd your good gal down.

Once ain't for always, two ain't for twice.
Once ain't for always, two ain't for twice.
When you get a good gal you better treat her nice.

When you were lonesome I tried to treat you kind.
When you were lonesome I tried to treat you kind.
But since you've got money, it's done changed your mind.

I'm going to leave baby, ain't going to say goodbye.
I'm going to leave baby, ain't going to say goodbye.
But I'll write you and tell you the reason why.

Days are lonesome, nights are long.
Days are lonesome, nights are so long.
I'm a good old gal, but I've just been treated wrong.

BASIC TERMS

blues (page 562)   12-bar blues (563)   subdominant (563)

[4] JAZZ 4 NEW ORLEANS STYLE

From about 1900 to 1917, jazz developed in a number of American cities, but the major center was New Orleans. The city was the home of such important jazz musicians as Ferdinand "Jelly Roll" Morton, Joseph "King" Oliver, and Louis Armstrong.

Around the turn of the century, New Orleans was a major port and a thriving cultural and commercial center with a cosmopolitan character. Its diverse population included people of African, French, Spanish, Portuguese, English, Italian, and Cuban ancestry. A particular group in New Orleans made up of people of mixed African, French, and Spanish descent maintained its own ethnic identity. This diversity of population was mirrored in the rich musical life of New Orleans. It included opera and chamber music as well as folk, popular, dance, and sacred music of all kinds. The tradition of marching bands and dance bands was particularly strong. There were frequent competitions between bands to see which could play more loudly or more brilliantly. Some band musicians were trained in classical music and could read musical notation; others played by ear and relied on improvisation. Many were only part-time performers who worked full time at other trades, such as bricklaying, carpentry, and cigar making.

Band music—including early jazz—was heard at picnics, parades, and political meetings and in dance halls. African American bands often played jazz during funeral processions. In the words of one New Orleans musician: "You'd march to the graveyard playing very solemn and very slow, then on the way back all hell would break loose! . . . We didn't know what a sheet of music was. Just six or seven pieces, half a dozen men pounding it out all together, each in his own way and yet somehow fitting in all right with the others."

But the main home of early jazz was Storyville, a red-light district of brothels, gambling joints, saloons, and dance halls. These establishments often employed a piano player or small band. Storyville provided not only employment but an atmosphere in which musicians felt free to improvise. When Storyville was closed down in 1917 on orders of the Navy Department, many jazz musicians left New Orleans. The center of jazz soon shifted from the Crescent City to Chicago, Kansas City, and New York.

Jazz in *New Orleans style* (or *Dixieland*) was typically played by a small group of from five to eight performers. The melodic instruments, or *front line,* included the cornet (or trumpet), clarinet, and trombone. The front-line players would improvise several contrasting melodic lines at once, producing a kind of polyphonic texture. This collective improvisation was the most distinctive feature of New Orleans jazz. Each instrument had a special role. The cornet was the leader, playing variations of the main melody. Above the cornet, the clarinet wove a countermelody, usually in a faster rhythm. The trombone played a bass line that was simpler than the upper lines, but melodically interesting nevertheless. The syncopations and rhythmic independence of the melodic instruments created a marvelous sense of excitement.

The front-line instruments were supported by a rhythm section that clearly marked the beat and provided a background of chords. This section usually included drums, chordal instruments (banjo, guitar, piano), and a single-line low instrument (plucked bass or tuba).

New Orleans style (or Dixieland) was typically played by five to eight performers. King Oliver (standing, at left rear) is shown here with his Creole Jazz Band in 1923. The band included Louis Armstrong (seated, center) and Lil Hardin (at the piano).

New Orleans jazz was usually based on a march or church melody, a ragtime piece, a popular song, or the 12-bar blues. Some well-known tunes associated with this style are *When the Saints Go Marching In* and *Oh, Didn't He Ramble?* One or more choruses of collective improvisation generally occurred at the beginning and end of a piece. In between, individual players were featured in improvised solos, accompanied by the rhythm section or by the whole band. Sometimes there were brief unaccompanied solos, called *breaks.* The band's performance might begin with an introduction and end with a brief coda, or *tag.*

As the New Orleans style evolved during the 1920s—mainly in Chicago—solo playing came to be emphasized more than collective improvisation. Soloists began to base their improvisations less on the original melody than on its harmonies. In addition, the trumpet gradually replaced the cornet, and the saxophone became a member of the band.

568

DIPPERMOUTH BLUES (1923), BY KING OLIVER'S CREOLE JAZZ BAND

Dippermouth Blues, as performed in 1923 by King Oliver's Creole Jazz Band, is a fine example of the New Orleans style. It is based on the chord progression of the 12-bar blues. Nine choruses of 12-bar blues are preceded by an introduction and followed by a brief tag (coda). Choruses 1, 2, 5, and 9 are for full ensemble and illustrate a style of collective improvisation that is typical of New Orleans jazz. Choruses 3 and 4 feature a clarinet solo with an accompaniment in repeated rhythm. The climax of *Dippermouth Blues* is Joe "King" Oliver's muted cornet solo (in choruses 6 to 8), which is heard against a background of improvisation by the other instruments. Oliver's solo, with its "blue" notes and swinging syncopations, was widely imitated by other jazz musicians.

Side 16, band 1
CD 8 [18]

Listening Outline To be read while music is heard

DIPPERMOUTH BLUES (1923),
BY KING OLIVER'S CREOLE JAZZ BAND

2 cornets (Joe "King" Oliver, Louis Armstrong), clarinet (Johnny Dodds), trombone (Honoré Dutrey), piano (Lil Hardin), banjo and voice (Bud Scott), drums (Baby Dodds)

Fast tempo, quadruple meter ($\frac{4}{4}$)

Introduction—nine choruses of 12-bar blues—tag

(Duration, 2:32)

Introduction (4 bars) [18] 0:00	1. *a.* Cornets introduce.
Choruses 1–2 (12 + 12 bars)	*b.* All instruments.
Choruses 3–4 (12 + 12 bars) 0:37	2. High clarinet melody, chordal accompaniment in repeated rhythm. Clarinet melody repeated.
Chorus 5 (12 bars) 1:09	3. All instruments.

569

Choruses 6–8
(12 + 12 + 12
bars)
   1:25

Chorus 9
(12 bars +
2-bar tag)
   2:13

4. Muted cornet melody with "blue" notes; other instruments in background.
   Voice: "Oh play that thing."

5. All instruments.

LOUIS ARMSTRONG

As both a trumpeter and a singer, Louis "Satchmo" Armstrong (1900–1971) had a worldwide impact on jazz. He was born on the Fourth of July in a poor black section of New Orleans, and he learned to play the cornet in a reformatory (where he was sent at the age of thirteen for shooting a gun into the air during a New Year's celebration). Upon his release after one year of confinement, Armstrong was soon playing in honky-tonks at night (he drove a coal wagon during the day). His musical ambitions were encouraged by the cornetist King Oliver, who took a fatherly interest in the young boy and gave him some lessons. When Oliver left for Chicago in 1918—after Storyville was closed down—Armstrong took his place in the famous Kid Ory Band. Four years later, Armstrong himself went to Chicago to be second cornetist in King Oliver's Creole Jazz Band.

In 1925, he started to make a series of recordings with bands known as Louis Armstrong's Hot Five and Louis Armstrong's Hot Seven. The Hot Five included three New Orleans musicians—Johnny Dodds (clarinet), Kid Ory (trombone), and Johnny St. Cyr (banjo)—along with Lil Hardin (piano), whom Armstrong had married a year earlier. These recordings established Armstrong's reputation as the leading jazz trumpeter. After 1930 he appeared with a wide variety of groups, made many tours, and was featured in many films. In the 1950s and 1960s Armstrong served as a "goodwill ambassador" for the United States. And at age sixty-four, he had his greatest popular success, the hit recording of *Hello, Dolly!*

Armstrong was one of the greatest jazz improvisers; he was able to invent extraordinary solos and to transform even ordinary tunes into swinging melodies through changes of rhythm and pitch. He revealed new dimensions of the trumpet, showing that it could be played in a higher register than was thought possible. His playing style featured "rips" up to high pitches, along with a tone that was both beautiful and alive. One jazz expert has singled out the "subtly varied repertory of vibratos and shakes with which Armstrong colors and embellishes individual notes." Armstrong also introduced *scat singing,* vocalization of a melodic line with nonsense syllables. His gravel-throated voice was not conventionally "beautiful," but it conveyed the same jazz feeling as his trumpet playing.

570

Hotter Than That, in a rendition by Louis Armstrong and His Hot Five, was used as an example in Part I, Section 1. It shows how the New Orleans style developed in Chicago during the 1920s (see the listening outline on page 9). The emphasis is on improvisatory solos. Collective improvisation—so important in earlier New Orleans style—is restricted to the introduction and closing chorus (items 1 and 6*b* in the listening outline). Listen for the exciting vocal and instrumental breaks (items 2, 3, 4, and 6*a*), the syncopations of Armstrong's vocal melody (item 4), and the dissonant guitar chord that gives *Hotter Than That* an unusual, inconclusive ending.

Side 1, band 4
CD 1 [10]

BASIC TERMS

New Orleans style (Dixieland) (page 567)
front line (567)
break (568)
tag (568)
scat singing (570)

SWING [JAZZ 5]

A new jazz style called *swing* developed in the 1920s and flourished from 1935 to 1945, a decade nicknamed the "swing era." (In this section, the term *swing* will refer to a specific style rather than to the rhythmic vitality characteristic of all jazz.)

Swing was played mainly by *big bands,* whose powerful sound could fill the large dance halls and ballrooms that mushroomed across the country, particularly after the repeal of prohibition in 1933. There were hundreds of "name" bands—both black and white—like those of Duke Ellington, Count Basie, Glenn Miller, Tommy Dorsey, and Benny Goodman (the "king of swing"). Some bands included such leading musicians as the saxophonists Coleman Hawkins and Lester Young and featured singers like Billie Holiday, Ella Fitzgerald, and Frank Sinatra. During the 1930s and 1940s, the big band was as important as the rock group has been since the 1950s. Swing became a truly popular music, reaching millions of people. Benny Goodman's band, for example, was heard coast to coast on a weekly radio show called *Let's Dance.* The kind of music once associated with honky-tonks and brothels had achieved a new respectability, symbolized by Benny Goodman's historic jazz concert at Carnegie Hall in 1938.

In Section 4, we noted that New Orleans jazz was performed by small groups of from five to eight musicians and featured collective improvisation by several soloists. The typical *swing band* included about fourteen or

Typically, a swing band included about fifteen musicians. The Benny Goodman Band was one of the leading swing ensembles.

fifteen musicians grouped into three sections: saxophones (three to five players, some doubling on clarinet), brasses (three or four each of trumpet and trombone), and rhythm (piano, percussion, guitar, and bass). A band that size needed music that was more composed than improvised and was also *arranged*, or notated in written-out parts from which the musicians could read. With swing, the arranger became an important figure in jazz.

In the swing band, melodies were often performed by entire sections, either in unison or in harmony. Thus, in ensemble playing, it was usually necessary to rely on arrangements instead of improvising. What solo improvisations there were tended to be restricted in length. The main melody was frequently accompanied by saxophones playing sustained chords, or by saxophones and brasses playing short, repeated phrases called *riffs.* Arrangers often used a rapid alternation of brass and sax riffs to create tension and excitement. Each band took pride in the distinctiveness of its sound, which it owed to its arrangers as well as its players.

Not only was the swing band larger and more dependent on arrangements than the New Orleans-style band; it also had other distinctive features. For example, the saxophone became one of the most important solo

572

instruments during the swing era. In addition, percussionists—such as Gene Krupa—had a more prominent role, often taking spectacular solos. They also kept the beat in a new way. While they continued to maintain the pulse on the bass drum, percussionists now used the cymbals to stress the second and fourth beats of the bar:

The harmonic vocabulary of swing was richer and more varied than that of earlier jazz, but its forms were essentially the same. As before, jazz performances were usually based on the 12-bar blues or on a 32-bar popular song melody. Such melodies can usually be outlined A A B A. An 8-bar phrase is stated and then repeated (A A); a contrasting 8-bar phrase (B) follows; then there's a return to the opening phrase (A). The song *Blue Skies*, by Irving Berlin, is in A A B A form. We'll now see how it was performed by the Benny Goodman Band, one of the leading swing ensembles.

BLUE SKIES, BY IRVING BERLIN, AS PERFORMED BY THE BENNY GOODMAN BAND (1938)

One very popular recording of the swing era is *Blue Skies*, as arranged by Fletcher Henderson and performed by the Benny Goodman Band. The version in our recording is a "live" performance from the historic Benny Goodman jazz concert at Carnegie Hall in 1938. The band's playing is smooth, polished—and swinging. The piece consists of an 8-bar introduction and four choruses in A A B A form (32 bars each). The following outline will clarify the form of each chorus:

Side 16, band 2
CD 8 19

Introduction	(band)	
Chorus 1	A A (band)–B (saxes, trombone solo)–A (saxes)	19 0:00
Chorus 2	A A (trumpets)–B A (tenor sax solo)	0:10
Chorus 3	A A (trumpets solo)–B A (band)	0:56
Chorus 4	A A (clarinet solo and band)–B (saxes)–A (band)	1:42
		2:29

Only the soloists have an opportunity to improvise. Typically, their solos are quite short, lasting less than the length of a full chorus. Some soloists stay close to the original melody; others depart from it almost completely, following only the original harmonies. Listen for the great variety of tone color as the melody is played by the full band, by sections, or by soloists. Often the melody is accompanied by chords or riffs in the saxophone section. Benny Goodman's clarinet solos are followed by responses from the band. This is the typical jazz pattern of call and response.

Duke Ellington and his orchestra in 1943. Ellington was perhaps the most important swing composer, arranger, and conductor.

DUKE ELLINGTON

Edward Kennedy "Duke" Ellington (1899–1974) was perhaps the most important swing-band composer, arranger, and conductor; he certainly ranks among the leading figures in the history of jazz. Ellington's works, which span half a century, include hundreds of 3-minute band pieces, as well as music for film, television, ballet, theater, and church. He was among the first jazz composers to break the 3-minute "sound barrier" imposed by the 78 rpm record, creating extended jazz compositions such as *Black, Brown and Beige*. Ellington accomplished all this while playing the piano, touring the world, and writing such hit songs as *Satin Doll*, *Sophisticated Lady*, and *In a Sentimental Mood*.

Ellington's music—sometimes created in collaboration with his arranger Billy Strayhorn—is the product of constant experimentation and improvisation. "There is no set system," he once observed. "Most times I write it and arrange it. Sometimes I write it and the band and I collaborate on the arrangement. . . . When we're all working together, a guy may have an idea and he plays it on his horn. Another guy may add to it and make something out of it. Someone may play a riff and ask, 'How do you like this?'"

"My band is my instrument," Ellington once remarked. His arrangements are outstanding for their rich variety of sensuous tone colors and for their exploitation of the distinctive sounds of individual musicians. "You've got to write with certain men in mind," he once explained. "I know what Tricky Sam can play on a trombone and I know what Lawrence Brown can play on the trombone, and it is not the same." Ellington's com-

574

positions include miniature "concertos" built around individual performers. (We'll study his *Concerto for Cootie*, written for the trumpeter Cootie Williams.) With his respect for their talents, it's no wonder that many of Ellington's musicians remained in the band for long periods of time.

Ellington's works are richer in harmony and more varied in form than those of this contemporaries. Their variety of mood may be sampled in such works as *Ko-ko, Harlem Air Shaft, In a Mellotone,* and *Blue Serge* (all included in *The Smithsonian Collection of Classic Jazz).*

CONCERTO FOR COOTIE (1940), BY DUKE ELLINGTON

Concerto for Cootie was designed to display the great variety of tone colors that the trumpeter Cootie Williams could draw from his instrument. Although the trumpet is the star of this piece, the band accompaniment adds much by discreetly responding to the soloist's phrases and by linking one section to the next. Several years after writing *Concerto for Cootie*, Ellington adapted it into the hit song *Do Nothin' Till You Hear from Me.*

Side 16, band 3
CD 8 [20]

Concerto for Cootie consists of an introduction and three main sections. The opening section has the standard A A B A form of popular songs, but its phrases are irregular in length. (The A phrases are 10 bars long instead of 8.) The main melody (A) consists of a repeated idea that is narrow in range, winding around a single tone. This is always played with a mute, but the soloist uses a variety of vibratos and muting techniques so that the melody sounds different each time. Listen for the subtlety of Ellington's orchestration: the bass, which provides much of the relaxed swing of this piece, enters only after the soloist is well into the melody. The middle section (C) is a striking contrast to the opening, because now the trumpeter plays an expansive new melody in a higher register and without a mute. *Concerto for Cootie* is rounded off by a brief third section in which a shortened and varied return of A is followed by a coda.

Listening Outline To be read while music is heard

CONCERTO FOR COOTIE (1940), BY DUKE ELLINGTON

Trumpet solo (Cootie Williams), piano (Duke Ellington), trumpet (Wallace Jones), cornet (Rex Stewart), 2 trombones (Joe Nanton, Lawrence Brown), valve trombone (Juan Tizol), clarinet, tenor saxophone (Barney Bigard), 2 alto saxophones (Otto Hardwicke, Johnny Hodges), tenor saxophone (Ben Webster), baritone saxophone (Harry Carney), guitar (Fred Guy), bass (Jimmy Blanton), percussion (Sonny Greer)

Moderate tempo, quadruple meter ($\frac{4}{4}$), F major

(Duration, 3:17)

INTRODUCTION

[20] 0:00   1. *a.* Solo muted trumpet, *p,* main motive; saxophones respond, *p;* brasses join, crescendo.

A

0:17   *b.* Trumpet, *p,* main melody, "shake" on held tones;

band responses, *p;* saxophones, *p,* lead to

A'

B

0:42   *c.* Trumpet, *p,* varies main melody; saxophone responses, *p;* band leads to

1:08   *d.* Trumpet, *mf,* "growling" phrases; saxophones, *p,* respond.

A''

1:26   *e.* Trumpet, *pp,* main melody, muffled sound; saxophone responses, *p;* brasses, *mf,* bridge to

C

1:57   2. Open trumpet, *f,* contrasting high melody, band in background. Trumpet repeats melody. Band bridge to

A'''

2:38   3. *a.* Muted trumpet, *p,* main melody shortened and varied; band responses, *p.*

CODA   *b.* Full band, *f;* trumpet, *f,* joins; high repeated notes, sustained tones at cadence.

BASIC TERMS

swing (page 571)
swing band (571)
riff (572)

[6] JAZZ BEBOP

The early 1940s saw the development of *bebop* (or *bop),* a complex style of music usually for small jazz groups. In part, bebop was a rebellion by creative improvisers against the commercialism and written arrangements of swing bands. The new music was meant for attentive listening, not dancing, and its sophisticated harmonies and unpredictable rhythms bewildered many listeners. Bop performers were a special "in" group who sometimes drove other jazz musicians from the bandstand by using complex melodies and unusual chord progressions. "We knew that they couldn't make those chord changes," one bop drummer recalled. "We kept the riff-raff out and built our clique on new chords."

Bebop performers also differentiated themselves by their goatees, berets, and special "hip" language. The bebop center in the early 1940s was a Harlem club called Minton's Playhouse, where young innovators—like the alto saxophonist Charlie Parker, the trumpeter Dizzy Gillespie, and the pianist Thelonious Monk—came to participate in jam sessions.

BEBOP STYLE

A typical bebop group might include a saxophone and a trumpet supported by a rhythm section of piano, bass, and percussion. The role of bebop rhythm instruments was different from that in earlier jazz. For example, the bass drum no longer marked the beat but was reserved for occasional irregular accents called "bombs." Similarly, the pianist's left hand no longer helped emphasize the basic pulse but joined with the right hand to play complex chords at irregular intervals. Both hands were needed to perform bebop's dense chord structures. The beat, then, was marked mainly by the pizzicato bass.

The rhythms in bop melodies were more varied and unpredictable than those in earlier jazz. In an improvised solo by Charlie Parker, for example, accented notes might come on weak or strong beats, or at varying points within the beat. Bop melodies often contained a stream of short notes with accents on the offbeats.

The new style may well have gotten its name from a vocalization of the two fast notes (be-bop) that often end phrases. The melodic phrases themselves were often varied and irregular in length. A two- or three-note fragment would be followed by a melodic unit lasting several bars. And the harmonies of bop were as complex as its rhythms. Performers often built melodies on chords containing six or seven notes rather than on the four- or five-note chords used in earlier jazz.

A bop performance generally began and ended with a statement of the main theme by one soloist, or by two soloists in unison. The remainder of the piece was made up of solo improvisations based on the melody or harmonic structure. As in earlier jazz, bebop musicians used popular song melodies and the 12-bar blues as a springboard for improvisation. Often, however, they composed *new* tunes to fit the basic harmonies of familiar melodies. As an "in" joke, a bop musician would give a tune a new title so that only sophisticated listeners could guess its origin, as in Charlie Parker's *KoKo*, which we'll study.

CHARLIE "BIRD" PARKER

Charlie Parker (1920–1955), the alto saxophonist, was a towering figure among bebop musicians and one of the greatest of all jazz improvisers. His enormous influence was felt not only by other alto saxophonists but by performers of many other instruments.

(Bettmann Archive)

Bebop was a complex style of music usually for small jazz groups. Charlie Parker (alto saxophone) is shown with Tommy Potter (bass), Miles Davis (trumpet), and Duke Jordon (piano).

Parker was born in Kansas City, Kansas, and grew up in Kansas City, Missouri. As a youngster, he roamed the streets listening outside nightclub doors to the jazz of Lester Young and the Count Basie Band. He was a professional musician by the age of fifteen, having dropped out of school. In his twenties, Parker lived in New York and participated in Harlem jam sessions. He made his first bebop recordings in 1944, and by the late 1940s he was a featured soloist in jazz clubs.

Parker became a prominent musician despite severe personal problems, including drug addiction, alcoholism, ulcers, and emotional illness. But after 1950, his playing declined along with his physical and emotional health. He died in 1955 at the age of thirty-four.

All the style characteristics of bebop were embodied in Parker's improvisations. He was able to control a rich flow of ideas at either slow or very rapid tempos. His amazing technique enabled him to create lightning-fast melodies that sound jagged and angular because of frequent changes of direction. Unlike earlier saxophonists, whose tone was lush and sweet, Parker produced a sound that was rather hard and dry. It perfectly matched the nervous intensity of his melodic lines.

KOKO (1945), BY CHARLIE PARKER

Side 16, band 4
CD 8 [21]

Bebop style and Parker's improvisatory genius are both illustrated in *KoKo*, which is performed here by a group of four outstanding musicians. Parker based the melody of *KoKo* on the harmonies of the popular song *Cherokee*, a big-band standard of the swing era. "I'd been getting bored with the stereotyped [chord] changes that were being used all the time," said Parker about the composition of *KoKo*. "I kept thinking that there's bound to be something else. I could hear it sometimes but I couldn't play it. Well, that night, I was working over *Cherokee*, and as I did, I found that by using the higher intervals of the chord as a melody line and backing them with appropriately related changes, I could play the things I'd been hearing. I came alive."

    KoKo consists of a 16-bar introduction, two choruses (32 bars each) of alto saxophone solo (by Charlie Parker), a drum solo (by Max Roach), and a 16-bar coda that recalls the introduction. The tempo is extremely fast, and the beat is usually marked by the pizzicato bass and by the "ride" cymbal played with brushes. Notice the "bombs," or irregular accents, in the bass drum. The introduction begins with a short melody played by the saxophone and the trumpet (Dizzy Gillespie) in unison and continues with two brief solos played at breakneck speed by these instruments. Parker's extended solo is a torrential flow of rapid notes with asymmetrical phrases and unexpected accents and rests. Only in this solo is the full rhythm section heard. In the spectacular drum solo, the beat is obscured by the complex rhythms.

Listening Outline   <small>To be read while music is heard</small>

KOKO (1945), BY CHARLIE PARKER

Alto saxophone (Charlie Parker), trumpet and piano (Dizzy Gillespie), bass (Curley Russell), percussion (Max Roach)

Introduction—two choruses in A A B A form—coda

(Duration, 2:51)

INTRODUCTION
(16 bars)

[21] 0:00

1.   *a.* Unison alto saxophone and muted trumpet, short melody, drum accompaniment.
      b. Fast trumpet solo, drum accompaniment.
      c. Fast alto saxophone solo, drum accompaniment.
      d. Alto saxophone and trumpet in thirds, brief melody, drum accompaniment.

    0:25   2. Alto saxophone, extended solo with asymmetrical phrases and unexpected accents and rests, accompanied by pizzicato bass, piano, and percussion.

    2:06   3. Drum solo, snare drum and bass drum.

CODA
(16 bars)

    2:29   4. *a.* Unison alto saxophone and muted trumpet, short melody, brushed cymbal accompaniment.
                     b. Fast trumpet solo, brushed cymbal accompaniment.
                     c. Fast alto saxophone solo, brushed cymbal accompaniment.
                     d. Alto saxophone and trumpet in thirds, brief melody, brushed cymbal accompaniment.

BASIC TERMS

bebop (bop) (page 576)

JAZZ 7 | JAZZ STYLES SINCE 1950

Since 1950, there have been many innovations and new directions in jazz. The range of styles is wider than ever. But as new styles proliferate, older jazz—from Dixieland to bebop—remains very much alive.

The introduction of long-playing records in 1948 inspired more extended jazz compositions and improvisations. Typically, a jazz performance on a long-playing record might last from 5 to 15 minutes, compared with the 3 minutes permitted by 78 rpm records before 1948. Also, more jazz now was meant for listening than for dancing. It was often heard at concerts on college campuses. Increasingly, jazz musicians studied at colleges and music schools and became familiar with much music other than jazz.

Since 1950, there has been an expansion in the musical resources used in jazz. New meters, rhythms, harmonies, forms, and tone colors have been explored. Orchestral instruments, such as the flute, French horn, and cello, have become a part of jazz. Since the 1960s, synthesizers and the electric piano and bass have come to be used more and more. Also, some musicians of the 1960s created *free jazz*, which discarded many of the forms and basic chord patterns of earlier jazz. Performers drew inspiration from a great variety of sources, including Bach, rock, and the music of Africa, Asia, and Latin America. The interaction between jazz and rock has led to a style known as *jazz rock*. Some musicians, such as Gunther Schuller (b. 1925), created a *third stream* style that is not quite jazz or "classical" but a blend of both. Among all these recent developments, we will consider three of the most important: cool jazz, free jazz, and jazz rock.

COOL JAZZ

During the late 1940s and early 1950s, a jazz style emerged that was related to bop but was far more calm and relaxed in character. It was called *cool jazz* (in contrast to the "hot jazz" of an earlier era). The leaders of the cool jazz movement were Lester Young (1909–1959) and Stan Getz (b. 1927), tenor saxophonists; Lennie Tristano (1919–1978), a pianist; and Miles Davis (1926–1991), a trumpeter and bandleader who started out as a bebop musician and was also an important figure in jazz during the 1960s, 1970s, and 1980s. Performers of cool jazz played in a relatively subdued manner, with a gentle attack and little vibrato. Cool jazz pieces tended to be longer than bebop works and relied more heavily on arrangements. They sometimes used instruments that were new to jazz, including the French horn, flute, and cello.

One of the finest works in cool jazz style is *Boblicity* (1949), by Miles Davis and the arranger Gil Evans (included in *The Smithsonian Collection of Classic Jazz*). It is scored for an unusual ensemble of nine different instruments: trumpet, trombone, French horn, tuba, alto and baritone saxophones, piano, bass, and drums. The smooth, mellow, and blended sound of this ensemble is typical of cool jazz.

Some cool jazz groups, such as the Modern Jazz Quartet, were influenced by the works of Bach and favored polyphonic textures and imitation. Another prominent group that was influenced by "classical" music was the Dave Brubeck Quartet. It pioneered in the use of meters that had been considered unusual in jazz, such as $\frac{3}{4}$, $\frac{5}{4}$ (in *Take Five*), and $\frac{7}{4}$ (in *Unsquare Dance*, studied in Part I, Section 3).

Side 1, band 7
CD 1 [21]

FREE JAZZ:
ORNETTE COLEMAN AND JOHN COLTRANE

Until about 1960, jazz improvisations tended to be quite regular in form. That is, improvised variations kept the original theme's length and chord structure, even if they abandoned the original melody. During the 1960s, some musicians broke from this tradition and created *free jazz*, a style that was not based on regular forms and established chord patterns.

"If I'm going to follow a preset chord sequence, I may as well write out my solo," commented Ornette Coleman (b. 1930), an alto saxophonist and a major composer of free jazz. In 1960 Coleman assembled eight musicians in a recording studio to improvise individually and collectively with almost no guidelines of melody, form, or harmony. The result was *Free Jazz*, a performance whose apparent randomness can be compared to the chance music created during the same period by John Cage and his followers. (An excerpt from *Free Jazz* is included in *The Smithsonian Collection of Classic Jazz*.) "I don't tell the members of my group what to do," Coleman has explained. "I let everyone express himself just as he wants to." Nevertheless, many performances by Coleman are structured more highly than *Free Jazz*, since they begin and end with a composed theme. (One example is *Lonely Woman*, also included in *The Smithsonian Collection of Classic Jazz.*) Like other free-jazz improvisers, Coleman develops melodic and rhythmic ideas from the theme. In many of his performances, a steady beat and tempo are emphasized much less than in earlier jazz, and his bass and percussion players are given more melodic and rhythmic freedom.

Another musician searching for rhythmic and harmonic freedom during the 1960s was John Coltrane (1926–1967), who was extremely influential as an improviser, tenor and soprano saxophonist, and composer. Coltrane's tone was large, intense, and equally powerful in all registers—an unusual trait. He could play higher than the normal top range of his instrument, and his arpeggios were flung at such lightning speed that they became "sheets of sound." The fury and passion of his improvisations sometimes led to sounds that might be described as "cries," "wails," and "shrieks."

Coltrane's style evolved steadily from the late 1950s, when he worked with Miles Davis, to his untimely death at the age of forty in 1967. His early performances—such as the pathbreaking *Giant Steps* of 1959—feature many complex chords that change very rapidly. His later works, on the other hand, are often based on a background of only two or three chords, each sustained in the accompaniment for many bars. Coltrane's pianist, McCoy Tyner, often sustained a single tone in the bass as a drone, or pedal point, while Coltrane improvised on modes, or scales, other than the conventional major or minor. Coltrane's growing use of drones and unusual scales may well have been influenced by his deep interest in Indian and Arabic music.

A drone accompaniment is used in Coltrane's meditative work *Alabama* (1963), for tenor saxophone, piano, bass, and drums (this too is in the *Smithsonian Collection of Classic Jazz.*) This short piece is in A B A' form. In the opening section, the saxophone melody is accompanied only by a sustained low broken chord in the piano. The contemplative melody conveys little sense of beat or meter. It is only in the middle section that a definite beat is heard. When the opening section returns (A'), there is a more active accompaniment as the bass and drums play complex rhythms.

JAZZ ROCK (FUSION)

Rock music became a potent influence on jazz during the late 1960s, the 1970s, and the 1980s. This influence led to *jazz rock*, or *fusion*, a new style combining the jazz musician's improvisatory approach with rock rhythms and tone colors. Jazz rock achieved a popularity unmatched by any other jazz style since the swing of the 1930s and 1940s.

A jazz rock group typically includes acoustic instruments along with

Weather Report is a leading jazz rock (fusion) group.

synthesizers and electric piano, guitar, and bass. Acoustic instruments are often used with electric attachments that expand the range of tonal effects. The percussion section is larger than that in earlier jazz groups and frequently includes instruments from Africa, Latin America, or India. Jazz rock groups produce a remarkable variety of tone colors, partly as a result of their imaginative use of synthesizers. The emphasis is often on the group sound rather than on the individuality of any single player. Other distinctive features of jazz rock are the melodic role of the electric bass and the insistent repetition of rhythmic figures.

A major figure in the development of jazz rock was Miles Davis, whose albums of 1969 *In a Silent Way* and *Bitches Brew* pointed the way to much of the music of the next decade. Many musicians who played with Davis on these recordings—including the pianists Herbie Hancock, Chick Corea, and Joe Zawinul and the saxophonist Wayne Shorter—became pacesetters of jazz rock during the 1970s and 1980s.

Jazz rock was only one of the substyles that could be heard during the 1970s, 1980s, and early 1990s. Every kind of jazz we've studied—New Orleans, swing, bebop, cool jazz, and free jazz—had its fans and devoted performers. As they have done since the early days, jazz musicians continue to explore new resources to further the development of their art.

BASIC TERMS

cool jazz (page 581)
free jazz (581)
jazz rock (fusion) (582)

THE
AMERICAN
MUSICAL

IX

The musical is one of the most important American contributions to twentieth-century popular culture. Shown here is *Jerome Robbins' Broadway*.

[1] MUSICAL THEATER

Along with jazz and rock, the musical is one of the most important American contributions to twentieth-century popular culture. Musical shows like *Oklahoma!, South Pacific, West Side Story,* and *My Fair Lady* are performed and enjoyed all over the world.

ELEMENTS OF THE MUSICAL

A *musical,* or *musical comedy,* is a type of theater that aims to entertain through fusion of a dramatic script, acting, and spoken dialogue with music, singing, and dancing and with scenery, costumes, and spectacle. Most musicals are in fact comedies, but some are serious, with unhappy endings. Although many musicals have been written by New Yorkers and produced in Broadway theaters (hence the term *Broadway musical*), successful ones reach nationwide and even worldwide audiences: the original production is likely to be taken "on the road," and there will be new productions and revivals over the years. Many musicals also become musical films.

Generally, a musical is in two acts, of which the second is shorter and brings back some of the melodies heard earlier. Traditionally, the songs consisted of an introductory section (called the *verse)* and a main section (called the *chorus)* in A A B A form (32 bars). Hit tunes from musicals, like *Ol' Man River* (from *Showboat)* or *Some Enchanted Evening* (from *South Pacific),* have often had lasting appeal, detached from their original theatrical context.

The American musical embraces a variety of styles, yet it is a distinct type of musical theater, separate from opera. In contrast to opera, it tends to use simpler harmonies, melodies, and forms, and it contains more spoken dialogue. Its songs tend to be narrower in pitch range than operatic arias because popular singers and opera singers employ different vocal techniques. Also, the musical is even more of a collaborative effort. In opera, one composer writes and orchestrates the music, and one librettist—occasionally two—is responsible for the entire text. In a musical, one composer creates the songs, but other musicians are responsible for the orchestration, the overture, the connective musical passages, and the ballets. The book and song lyrics are usually divided among two or more writers. Despite these differences between musicals and operas, certain works, such as George and Ira Gershwin's *Porgy and Bess* (1935), fall somewhere between the two categories. And shows originally produced as musicals, like *Porgy and Bess* and Leonard Bernstein's *West Side Story,* are sometimes later performed in opera houses and recorded by opera singers.

DEVELOPMENT OF THE MUSICAL

Sources of the Musical

The American musical has drawn on a variety of musical and dramatic sources from the late nineteenth and early twentieth centuries, including operetta, vaudeville, and the revue.

Operetta, or *comic opera,* combines song, spoken dialogue, and dance; employs quite sophisticated musical techniques; and is generally set outside the United States. The operettas of the Englishmen W. S. Gilbert and Arthur Sullivan, such as *The Mikado* (1885), were widely performed in the United States around the turn of the century. The best-known American operettas were those by Victor Herbert, such as *Babes in Toyland* (1903) and *Naughty Marietta* (1910).

A more popular antecedent of the musical was *vaudeville,* a variety show with songs, comedy, juggling, acrobats, and animal acts, but no plot. About 10,000 vaudeville theaters dotted the United States during the first two decades of the century.

Also in the background of the modern musical was the *revue,* a variety show without a plot but with a unifying idea. Revues in the first decades of the century were often satirical and featured pretty, scantily clad young women ("chorus girls") who sang and danced, and comedians who performed sketches.

The Golden Era of the American Musical (1920–1960)

A golden era in American musical theater was created from about 1920 to 1960 by such songwriters and composers as Irving Berlin (1888–1989), Jerome Kern (1885–1945), George Gershwin (1898–1937), Cole Porter (1893–1964), Richard Rodgers (1902–1979), Frank Loesser (1910–1969), and Leonard Bernstein (1919–1990). During this period, plots of musicals became more believable, and the range of subject matter expanded. Song and dance were more closely integrated into the story, and composers increasingly borrowed sophisticated musical techniques from opera and operetta.

During the 1920s and the 1930s, musicals were usually based on unrealistic "boy meets girl" stories, but the lyrics were clever and witty, as in Cole Porter's song *You're the Top* (1934).

> You're the top! You're the Colosseum.
> You're the top! You're the Louvre Museum.
> You're a melody from a symphony by Strauss.
> You're a Bendel bonnet, a Shakespeare sonnet, you're Mickey Mouse.
> You're the Nile, you're the Tow'r of Pisa,
> You're the smile on the Mona Lisa.
> I'm a worthless check, a total wreck, a flop,
> But, if, baby, I'm the bottom, You're the top!

Oklahoma! was a landmark in the history of American musical theater. Shown here is the 1950 touring production.

A pathbreaking musical of the 1920s with an unusually serious plot was *Show Boat* (1927), with music by Jerome Kern and lyrics by Oscar Hammerstein II. *Show Boat* brought interracial romance to the American musical stage for the first time. Its songs—including the well-known *Ol' Man River* and *Why Do I Love You?*—revealed character and were smoothly woven into the action. In the 1930s, some musicals satirized social and political institutions, perhaps in reaction to the great depression. A prominent instance was George and Ira Gershwin's *Of Thee I Sing* (1931), which poked fun at American presidential elections and was the first musical to win a Pulizer Prize for drama for its librettist. An important development of the late 1930s was the increased significance of ballet, which was used to carry the action forward. For example, the climax of the musical *On Your Toes* (1936) was a ballet by George Balanchine (1904–1989) called *Slaughter on Tenth Avenue*, in which the hero must keep dancing to avoid being killed by mobsters.

A landmark in the integration of dance, songs, and plot came in 1943 with *Oklahoma!*—the first in a memorable series of musicals by Richard Rodgers and the lyricist Oscar Hammerstein II. For this show, Agnes de

Mille created ballets (inspired by square dances) that were important for the progress of the story.

Like most musicals, *Oklahoma!* was set in the United States. After World War II, however, an increasing number of shows were set in foreign lands, such as Siam (*The King and I;* 1951), France (*Fanny;* 1954), England (*My Fair Lady;* 1956), and Russia (*Fiddler on the Roof;* 1964). Even when set in the United States, postwar musicals began to explore new kinds of serious subject matter, such as teenage gang warfare in *West Side Story* (1957).

The Musical after 1960

After 1960, some composers of Broadway shows continued to write songs fairly similar to those of the 1940s and 1950s. This conservative trend was also reflected in the many revivals of classic musicals like *Oklahoma!* (in 1979). However, other composers departed from the traditional A A B A form; and often the songs were so closely integrated with the plot and production that they were unlikely to become hits on their own. Unlike jazz, the musical was relatively unaffected by the "rock revolution" of the 1960s. One of the few rock musicals was *Hair* (1967), which reflected the hippie movement and had a scene of total nudity. Rock elements were also

Sunday in the Park with George (1984), by the composer-lyricist Stephen Sondheim—perhaps the most original contributor to American musical theater since the 1960s.

(Martha Swope)

incorporated in *Jesus Christ Superstar* (1971), by the British musician Andrew Lloyd Webber (b. 1948), who also created *Cats* (1982) and *Phantom of the Opera* (1987). The unusual prominence of English composers on the American musical scene is also reflected in the shows *Les Misérables* (1986) and *Miss Saigon* (1989).

Perhaps the most original contributions to American musical theater since the 1960s have been made by the composer-lyricist Stephen Sondheim (b. 1930), who first became known as the lyricist for *West Side Story*. Many of his works are "concept musicals," based more on an idea than on a traditional linear plot. For example, *Company* (1970) deals with the theme of marriage; *Sunday in the Park with George* (1984) deals with the theme of artistic creativity as exemplified by a painting: Georges Seurat's *Sunday on the Grande-Jatte—1884.* Sondheim's most ambitious work— *Sweeney Todd, the Demon Barber of Fleet Street* (1979), about a bloodthirsty psychopath—blurs the boundary between the musical and opera. It includes arias, duets, trios, complex choruses, and musical themes associated with characters and elements of the plot. Sondheim's musical style fuses elements of the traditional Broadway song with elements of Stravinsky, Copland, and Bernstein. His work reflects the continued vitality and stylistic inventiveness of the American musical.

AMERICAN MUSICAL 2 — LEONARD BERNSTEIN

One of the landmark popular musicals, *West Side Story* (1957), was composed by the extraordinarily versatile Leonard Bernstein (1918–1990), a twentieth-century culture hero who was a leading conductor, a concert pianist, a composer of orchestral and vocal works, and an author-lecturer whose appearances on television broadened the musical knowledge of millions. Bernstein was born in Lawrence, Masssachusetts; graduated from Harvard University; and studied piano and conducting at the Curtis Institute in Philadelphia. In 1943, he was appointed assistant conductor of the New York Philharmonic Orchestra. Not long after, a guest conductor, Bruno Walter, became ill and the twenty-five-year-old Bernstein took his place on the podium with no rehearsal and only a few hours' notice. This successful concert on nationwide radio was hailed as "a dramatic musical event" on the front page of the *New York Times* and launched Bernstein's spectacular career.

"I have a deep suspicion that every work I write, for whatever medium, is really theater music in some way." Bernstein's characterization indeed fits not only his musicals, operas, and ballets and his theater piece *Mass*

(Bernstein: 1947 Photo by William Gottlieb/Retna)

The versatile American musician Leonard Bernstein was a composer of musicals and symphonic works, as well as an outstanding conductor, concert pianist, and author-lecturer.

(1971), but also his choral work *Chichester Psalms* (1965) and his three programmatic symphonies—*Jeremiah* (1942), *The Age of Anxiety* (1949), and *Kaddish* (1963)—two of which include singers and Hebrew or Aramaic texts. Bernstein's music is clearly tonal, enlivened by syncopations and irregular meters, and infused with jazz and dance rhythms. Like Stravinsky and Copland, both of whom influenced him, Bernstein wrote very successful ballets, including *Fancy Free* (1944) and *Facsimile* (1946). Dance numbers play an important and dramatic role in his musicals *On the Town* (1944), *Wonderful Town,* (1953) and *West Side Story* (1957). Bernstein accomplished the difficult feat of bridging the worlds of "serious" and popular music. He died in 1990, mourned by people all over the world.

(Eileen Darby)

Tony and Maria meet on the fire escape in a scene from *West Side Story*.

WEST SIDE STORY (1957)

On January 6, 1949, the choreographer Jerome Robbins first suggested to Leonard Bernstein that they collaborate on a modern version of Shakespeare's *Romeo and Juliet* set in the slums of New York. Bernstein was very enthusiastic about the "idea of making a musical that tells a tragic story in musical-comedy terms, using only musical-comedy techniques, never falling into the 'operatic' trap. Can it succeed? . . . I'm excited. If it can work—it's the first." *West Side Story*—with music by Bernstein, book by Arthur Laurents, and lyrics by Stephen Sondheim—was created seven years later.

West Side Story deals with the conflict between gang rivalry and youthful love. The feud between the lovers' families in Shakespeare's *Romeo and Juliet* is transformed into warfare between two teenage street gangs: the Jets, native-born Americans led by Riff; and the Sharks, Puerto Ricans led by Bernardo. The plot revolves around a fight ("rumble") between the gangs and the doomed love of Tony (Romeo), a former member of the Jets; and Maria (Juliet), Bernardo's sister. Tony kills Bernardo after a vain attempt to break up the fight. Later he is shot by one of the Sharks and dies in Maria's arms.

Though it included rough street language and ended unhappily, *West Side Story* was a tremendous popular success and became an Oscar-winning musical film (1961). It was an unprecedented fusion of song and drama with electrifyingly violent choreography (by Jerome Robbins and Peter Gennaro). Compared with the average Broadway show, *West Side Story* contained more music, more complex and unconventional music, and a wider range of styles, from vaudeville (*Gee, Officer Krupke*) and Latin rhythms (*America*) to bebop fugue (*Cool*) and quasi-operatic ensemble (*Tonight*).

Tonight Ensemble

In the *Tonight* ensemble, Bernstein projects several different emotions at the same time: Riff, Bernardo, and their gangs excitedly planning for the upcoming fight; Anita—Bernardo's girlfriend—looking forward to the "kicks" she's "gonna get"; and Tony and Maria anticipating the joy of being together. Riff, Bernardo, and Anita sing quick, staccato tones in a narrow range, whereas Tony and Maria sing the legato, soaringly lyrical *Tonight* melody, heard in an earlier "balcony scene" on Maria's fire escape. As Verdi did in the Quartet from *Rigoletto*, Bernstein lets us hear the voices separately before combining them in an ensemble. Such dramatic ensembles were uncommon in musicals, which tended to feature solo songs with "hit" potential.

Side 16, band 5
CD 8 [22]

Listening Outline To be read while music is heard

TONIGHT ENSEMBLE FROM *WEST SIDE STORY* (1957), BY LEONARD BERNSTEIN

Riff, Bernardo, Anita, Tony, Maria, gang members, orchestra

Fast and rhythmic.

(Duration, 3:40)

22 0:00   1. *a.* Orchestra, menacing staccato melody with syncopations introduces
   0:07   *b.* Riff, Bernardo, and their gangs alternate and then sing together quick, staccato phrases with syncopations.

RIFF *mp* Marcato

The Jets are gon-na have their day _____ To - night. _____

   1:07   *c.* Anita repeats previous phrases.
23 1:25   *d.* Tony, lyrical *Tonight* melody.

TONY (warmly) *mf*

To - night, to - night Won't be just an - y night, To - night there will be no morn - ing star. _____

   2:18   2. *a.* Orchestra, *ff.*
   2:23   *b.* Riff, quick staccato phrases.
   2:40   *c.* Maria, lyrical *Tonight* melody, with Riff's staccato phrases, and brief interjections *(All right, Tonight)* by Tony and Anita. Tony joins Maria on *Tonight* melody.
   3:29   *d.* Voices join on sustained high tones *(Tonight), ff;* orchestral conclusion.

BASIC TERM

594   musical (musical comedy) (page 586)

X

ROCK

X

Tina Turner and Mick Jagger.

$\left[\!\left[\,1\,\right]\!\right]$ ROCK STYLES

The mid-1950s saw the growth of a new kind of popular music that was first called *rock and roll* and then simply *rock*. Though it includes diverse styles, **rock** tends to be vocal music with a hard, driving beat, often featuring electric guitar accompaniment and heavily amplified sound. Early rock grew mainly out of *rhythm and blues,* a dance music of African Americans that fused blues, jazz, and gospel styles. Rock also drew upon *country and western,* a folklike, guitar-based style associated with rural white Americans. In little more than a decade, rock evolved from a simple, dance-oriented style to music that was highly varied in its tone colors, lyrics, and electronic technology.

DEVELOPMENT OF ROCK

In the late 1940s, rhythm and blues became the dominant style among American blacks. The rhythm and blues of the 1950s differed from earlier blues in its more powerful beat and its use of the saxophone and electric guitar. Among the leading performers were Little Richard, Chuck Berry, Bo Diddley, and Fats Domino. Gospel-tinged vocal groups, such as the Drifters, and the soaring falsetto lead sounds of the Platters were also an important part of rhythm-and-blues style.

The earliest of the important rock and roll groups was Bill Haley and His Comets, whose *Rock Around the Clock* was the first big hit of the new style. Significantly, it was a film about youthful rebellion, *Blackboard Jungle* (1955), that popularized *Rock Around the Clock.* To many people at the time, the new music itself seemed rebellious in its loudness, pounding beat, and sexual directness. The image of a youthful rebel was also projected by Elvis Presley, who reigned as "king" of rock and roll.

During the 1960s, much music by black performers was called *soul,* a term that emphasized the style's emotionality, its gospel roots, and its relationship to the black community. Soul musicians included James Brown, Ray Charles, and Aretha Franklin. A type of soul music that blended rhythm and blues with popular music was known as *Motown,* after the name of a record company based in Detroit. Motown has been described aptly as a combination of "gospel rhythms, modern harmonies, soft melodies, and bright lyrics." Among the Motown stars were Diana Ross and the Supremes, and Stevie Wonder, whose first big hit came in 1963, when he was only thirteen.

A new era in rock history began in 1964 with the American tour of the Beatles, an English group. Along with the Rolling Stones (also English),

(New York Public Library, Music Collection)

During the 1950s, Chuck Berry was a leading performer of rhythm and blues.

(UPI/Bettmann Newsphotos)

Elvis Presley, who died in 1977 at the age of forty-two, was the "king" of rock and roll.

(Larry Hulst/Retna Ltd.)

Bob Dylan's songs of the 1960s often dealt with such contemporary issues as war and racial injustice.

the Beatles came to dominate the popular music scene in the United States. Under their influence, rock musicians of the middle and late 1960s explored a wider range of sources for sounds and musical ideas. They experimented with electronic effects, with "classical" and nonwestern instruments, and with unconventional scales, chord progressions, and rhythms.

Rock in the 1960s also absorbed elements of folk music and often had lyrics dealing with such contemporary issues as war and racial injustice. This development was spurred by the success of the songwriter and singer Bob Dylan, whose *Blowin' in the Wind*—a song against racial bigotry—articulated the feelings of many young people.

During the late 1960s, the popular music scene was enormously varied. The diversity of rock styles is reflected in the many terms that arose: *folk rock, jazz rock, classical rock, raga rock, psychedelic rock, acid rock*. This period saw the first rock musical, *Hair*, by Galt MacDermot; and the first rock opera, *Tommy*, written by Peter Townshend and featuring The Who, an English group.

In 1970 and 1971, rock music suffered major losses: the Beatles announced their dissolution, and, tragically, three leading performers died—

Jimi Hendrix and Janis Joplin, of drugs; and the Doors' Jim Morrison, of a heart attack. Yet during the 1970s rock was as popular as ever. This decade saw the continuation of many 1960s styles, the revival of early rock and roll, and the rise of a dance music called *disco*. Veteran performers of the 1960s—such as Bob Dylan, Stevie Wonder, and the Rolling Stones—continued to be active; but new stars also emerged, including Linda Ronstadt, Billy Joel, Bruce Springsteen, and the "disco queen" Donna Summer. For a while in the early 1970s, there was a nostalgic fascination with 1950s rock and roll and its pioneer performers, such as Chuck Berry. Record companies released many albums of repackaged old hits, and two films about early rock-and-roll personalities appeared *(The Buddy Holly Story* and *American Hot Wax)*. A blend of country music and rock called *country rock* became popular in the early 1970s. Country music itself moved into the musical mainstream as its stars (Johnny Cash, Dolly Parton, Willie Nelson, and others) won national popularity. Other musical styles of the 1970s included *reggae*, a music that sprang from political and social concerns in the West Indies; *funk*, which featured electrification and jazzlike rhythms; and *punk*, or *new wave*, a primitive form of rock and roll. Some groups, including Emerson, Lake, and Palmer, performed *classical rock*, consisting of rock arrangements of such compositions as *Pictures at an Exhibition*, by the nineteenth-century Russian composer Modest Mussorgsky. And during the 1970s and 1980s, jazz rock (or *fusion*) reached a wider audience than ever before through groups like Chicago, the Crusaders, and Weather Report.

In the early 1980s, new wave bands from Britain such as Police, Culture Club, and Eurhythmics were popular with American rock audiences. This "second British invasion" was comparable to the one that had been led by the Beatles during the early 1960s. Though their styles varied, most of these British bands made extensive use of electronic technology—synthesizers and computers—and often featured outlandish-looking performers. The 1980s saw a renewed interest among teenagers in *heavy metal*, a type of basic rock characterized by pounding drums, a heavily amplified bass, and unrestrained guitars played at peak volume. Heavy metal's lyrics, with their increasingly overt references to sex and violence, gave rise to concern about their possible effect on young people. Popular heavy metal bands include Metallica, Quiet Riot, Iron Maiden, Motley Crue, and Guns 'n' Roses.

Among young urban blacks, *rap music* developed. It began as a kind of rhythmic talking accompanied by a disk jockey who manipulated recordings on two turntables to create a collage of rhythmic effects. First popularized in black neighborhoods of east coast American cities, rap often depicts the anger and frustration of urban black youth. During the later 1970s and 1980s, groups such as the Talking Heads and Police also drew increasing inspiration from "exotic" sources, including African music and Jamaican reggae.

Guns 'n' Roses.

Heavy metal and rap continued to grow in popularity throughout the 1980s and into the 1990s. The audience for heavy metal has been, since its beginnings, mainly white working-class adolescents. Rap, on the other hand—although its major audience is still black young people—had by 1990 adopted stylistic features from other forms of popular music and had begun to attract new audiences. There was a highly successful rap show on cable television; rap artists included Vanilla Ice (the first white rap superstar) and M.C. Hammer.

Another significant trend of the 1980s was African popular music. Youssou N'Dour of Senegal, whose music mixed traditional styles with contemporary European-American pop accompaniments, became an international star—especially when he toured for Amnesty International with such rock icons as Bruce Springsteen and Sting. Paul Simon's album *Graceland*, recorded in 1986 with South African musicians, also helped increase worldwide interest in African popular music.

There was also an interest in other styles that combined older forms with the sounds of contemporary American and European popular music. *Zouk*, for example—a hybrid of Parisian and French Caribbean dance music—had widespread international appeal.

Having briefly examined the development of rock, we'll now consider its musical elements.

ELEMENTS OF ROCK

Tone Color

The electric-guitar sound of rock is very different from the brass-reed sound of the ''big band'' heard in earlier popular music. Rock music is amplified powerfully, and the guitar is often manipulated electronically to produce a wide range of tone colors. Along with singers (who also play instruments), a rock group typically includes two electric guitars (lead and rhythm), electric bass, percussion, and keyboard instruments such as piano, electric piano, and synthesizer. Some groups also include one or more trumpets, trombones, or saxophones.

Since the 1960s, a wide range of instruments not normally associated with popular music—from the harpsichord to the Indian sitar—were occasionally added to the basic rock group, particularly for recording sessions. Rock recordings began using such diverse sounds as electronic blips, crowd noises, and a symphony orchestra. During the 1970s and 1980s, rock musicians exploited the ever-expanding capacities of synthesizers and computers. Sophisticated electronic technology made it possible for a few performers to sound like a large ensemble.

The singing style of rock is drawn largely from black, folk, and country-and-western music. Although singing styles vary, they all are different from the crooning sound cultivated by earlier popular vocalists. Rock singers shout, cry, wail, growl, and use guttural sounds, as well as *falsetto*, a method of singing used by males to reach notes higher than their normal range. Nonsense syllables and repeated chants (such as *Yeah! Yeah! Yeah!*) are also featured.

Rhythm

Rock is based on a very powerful beat in quadruple ($\frac{4}{4}$) meter with strong accents on the second and fourth beats of the bar. The rhythmic excitement is heightened because each beat is subdivided into 2 equal notes. This produces 8 faster pulses, which are superimposed on the 4 basic beats. To get the effect, count out the following: 1-and-**2**-and-3-and-**4**-and. Rock of the 1960s and 1970s often combined complicated rhythms with this basic pattern; for example, the bass player might emphasize the offbeats—the *ands*. During the late 1970s and 1980s, some rock music became more rhythmically complex, as performers drew inspiration from the poly-rhythms of African music.

Form, Melody, and Harmony

Rock music is usually in 12-bar blues form (see Section 3 of Part VIII, Jazz); in 32-bar A A B A form (see Section 5 of Part VIII); or in variants of these forms. Earlier popular songs usually consisted of 4- or 8-bar phrases, but rock melodies sometimes contain phrases that are irregular in length. Rock songs tend to have short melodic patterns that are repeated several times. They are occasionally built on modes, rather than on traditional major or minor scales.

The harmonic progressions of rock are usually quite simple, often consisting of just three or four basic chords. Sometimes, the harmony can be restricted deliberately to only two chords, as in *Eleanor Rigby,* by John Lennon and Paul McCartney. Rock often uses chord progressions that are rare in earlier popular music.

BASIC TERM

rock (page 598)

[2]ᴿᴼᶜᴷ ROCK MUSIC IN AMERICAN SOCIETY

"Hey! That's our music; that was written for us!" shouted the fourteen-year-old Bob Dylan when he first heard Bill Haley's *Rock Around the Clock* in 1955. Like Dylan, millions of young people felt that rock music belonged to them and that it expressed their search for identity and independence. Many leading rock performers and songwriters were themselves in their teens or early twenties. In contrast to rock, popular music before the 1950s had appealed about equally to people of all ages.

As a result of the "baby boom" after World War II, there were more American young people in the 1950s and 1960s than ever before, and they had more money to spend, because of a generally rising economy. American industry quickly responded to this vast youth market, and rock music became a big business. Sales of electric guitars, phonographs, records, and transistor radios increased dramatically. Rock superstars struck it rich through record royalties, movie contracts, and astronomical concert fees. Rock performances took place everywhere: in auditoriums, gymnasiums, sports arenas, and baseball stadiums. A single concert by a leading group could gross hundreds of thousands of dollars and be seen by an audience of up to 75,000 people. There even were rock festivals, like the three-day Woodstock Music and Art Fair in August 1969. At that event, over 300,000 people listened in the open fields to the music of Joan Baez, Janis Joplin,

Jimi Hendrix, and the Jefferson Airplane, among others. *Woodstock*, one of the most important of many rock films, documented this gathering.

Often, rock performances were as much theatrical as musical events. From the earliest days of rock and roll, costumes and staging were essential to the show. For example, Elvis Presley's appeal was heightened by tight-fitting sequined pants, a leather jacket, and gyrations that led to the nickname "Elvis the pelvis." In the late 1960s, Jimi Hendrix smashed and burned his guitar on stage. The image of "psychedelic rock" was heightened by flashing strobe lights that simulated the sensations of a drug experience. Rock performances of the 1970s became even more theatrical. Alice Cooper—a man—appeared on stage with a boa constrictor and performed acts of simulated violence. The members of a group called Kiss wore macho glitter costumes and makeup influenced by the kabuki theater of Japan. Their act involved flames, smoke, and explosions. David Bowie, who wore women's clothing and dyed his hair bright orange, often said that his records were only "half there," because the visual aspect was missing. Some British new wave stars of the 1980s continued the tradition of David Bowie and were as famous for their outrageous appearance as for their music. Among the best known was Boy George of the group Culture Club, whose transvestite clothing, braided hair, rouge, and mascara were meant to shock. The theatrics and music of rock performers often generated hysterical excitement: fans screamed, moaned, and rushed the stage.

Rock songs often reflected trends in American life, such as increased openness about sexuality. Lyrics tended to be more sexually explicit than those of the sentimental ("moon-June-spoon") love songs of the 1930s and 1940s. (In fact, the term *rock and roll* originally had sexual connotations.) During the 1960s, rock performers often sang about the Vietnamese war, experiences associated with drugs, and the struggle for civil rights. And performers often wrote their own songs. For many young people of the time, rock music was part of a lifestyle that seemed less inhibited and less materialistic than that of their parents. They quickly adopted the longer hairstyles and casual dress popularized by rock stars. Within a short time, many older people also cultivated a casual appearance.

During the 1970s, rock became integrated into the mainstream of American popular music. Although rock concerts still appealed primarily to the young, a wide variety of rock records were purchased by people of all ages. And rock songs of the 1970s were less likely to deal with social and political issues.

Popular music of the 1980s, however, rediscovered an idealism recalling that of the 1960s. In 1985, for example, many leading rock stars recorded a song and video, *We Are the World,* that would eventually raise about $45 million for victims of famine. Many rock concerts benefited various social causes; perhaps the most spectacular was the 16-hour Live Aid concert (also in 1985) for African famine relief, which was telecast on an interna-

(Touchstone Pictures/Peter Sorel/Photofest)

Madonna as Breathless Mahoney in *Dick Tracy*.

tional satellite network and reached an audience of about 1½ billion people. (Among the performers in the Live Aid concert were Bob Dylan, Joan Baez, David Bowie, Paul McCartney, Sting, Madonna, Tina Turner, the regrouped Who, and Keith Richards and Ron Wood of the Rolling Stones.)

During the 1980s, women performers had a powerful impact on rock music. "Many of the new women rockers do a lot more than sing," observed one critic. "They play their own instruments, write their own songs, control their own careers." Their wide range of musical styles extended from pop and soul to funk, new wave, and heavy metal. Leading performers included Madonna, Cyndi Lauper, Donna Summer, Pat Benatar, Linda Ronstadt, Sheila E., Joan Jett, and the veteran Tina Turner.

ROCK MUSIC AND RECORDINGS

Unlike earlier popular music, rock spread more through radio and recordings than through live performances or sheet music. There were a growing number of radio stations, and many of them broadcast only rock music. Disk jockeys like Alan Freed—who popularized the term *rock and roll*—

became important personalities who strongly influenced musical tastes. Most early rock and roll records were produced by small, specialized companies. But the tremendous financial success of rock soon led major companies to enter the field as well. By the 1960s and 1970s, major companies were producing most rock recordings.

During the 1960s, the sound of rock recordings became quite different from what was heard at a live performance. Increasingly, rock groups took advantage of multitrack recording. "With a small group," wrote one record producer, "every instrument can be recorded on a different track. Each track has a separate volume control and a tone control to adjust to the desired treble or bass. Several kinds of echoes can be added to each instrument." Recording sessions were often a "layer cake" operation: each sound layer was produced separately and the different layers were combined later. The Beatles, for example, would first record the instrumental accompaniment to a song, a process that might take a whole day. Another day would be devoted to recording the voice parts. Then, various instrumental and electronic sounds might be added before the recording was complete. With such a complex process, it's no wonder that a record like their *Sgt. Pepper's Lonely Hearts Club Band* took as long as four months to be produced.

ROCK MUSIC AND TELEVISION (MTV)

The 1980s saw the development of MTV, a cable television network broadcasting rock videos. MTV gave a needed boost to the record industry and contributed to the popularity of many performers. An innovator in the use of rock video was Michael Jackson, whose documentary on the production of *Thriller* became one of the most widely sold prerecorded videocassettes ever made. Rock video adds a new dimension to the rock experience through a wide variety of visual effects that are often fantastic and provocative.

ROCK MUSIC AND DANCING

Since its beginning, rock music has accompanied a dizzying succession of dances, such as the twist, the frug, the monkey, the shake, and the mashed potato. In most rock dances of the 1960s, partners did not hold each other, as in earlier dances, but moved individually to the music's powerful beat. Most rock dances were improvisational and did not require dancers to learn a series of complicated steps. Among the best-known rock dances was the twist, associated with a New York nightclub, the Peppermint Lounge, and popularized in 1961 through a television performance by the singer Chubby Checker. By the 1960s, many adults became influenced by the youth culture and danced to rock music at nightclubs called *disco-theques*.

During the 1970s, thousands of discotheques—mostly featuring recorded music—mushroomed around the country. *Disco* became the dominant dance music. Many dances of the 1960s had been formless and improvisational, but dances of the 1970s—such as the hustle and its variants—often required intricate steps and turns. Moreover, these dances frequently required partners once again to touch each other. Also popular again were line dances, in which many dancers performed the same movements. The late 1970s and 1980s saw the development of *breakdancing*, a combination of dancing and gymnastics, often to rap music. In the early 1980s, the movie *Flashdance* conveyed the excitement of breakdancing to millions of people.

[ROCK **3**] THE BEATLES

The Beatles—the singer-guitarists Paul McCartney, John Lennon, and George Harrison, and the drummer Ringo Starr—have been the most influential performing group in the history of rock. Their music, hairstyle, dress, and lifestyle were imitated all over the world, resulting in a phenomenon known as *Beatlemania*.

All four Beatles were born during the early 1940s in Liverpool, England, and dropped out of school in their teens to devote themselves to rock. Lennon and McCartney, the main songwriters of the group, began working together in 1956 and were joined by Harrison about two years later. In 1962 Ringo Starr became their new drummer. The group gained experience by performing in Hamburg, Germany, and in Liverpool, a port to which sailors brought the latest American rock, rhythm-and-blues, and country-and-western records. In 1961 the Beatles made their first record, and by 1963 they were England's top rock group. In 1964, they triumphed in the United States, breaking attendance records everywhere and dominating the record market. Audiences often became hysterical, and the police had to protect the Beatles from their fans. Beatle dolls, wigs, sweatshirts, and jackets flooded the market. Along with a steady flow of successful records, the Beatles made several hit movies: *A Hard Day's Night*, *Help!* and *Yellow Submarine*.

The Beatles stopped touring in 1966, possibly because some of their most imaginative effects were achieved in the recording studio and could not be duplicated in live performance. For several years they devoted themselves to recording, producing such long-playing albums as *Sgt. Pepper's Lonely Hearts Club Band* (1967), *Magical Mystery Tour* (1967), *The Beatles* (1968; a double record set nicknamed the "white album"), and *Abbey Road* (1969).

The Beatles have so far been the most influential performing group in the history of rock.

In 1970 the Beatles disbanded to pursue individual careers. The fatal shooting of John Lennon in 1980 seemed to symbolize the end of an era.

The Beatles' highly original style derived from a variety of sources, including traditional blues, the rhythm and blues of Chuck Berry, the rock and roll of Elvis Presley, English folk songs, and the lyrics of Bob Dylan. The impact of Indian religions led Harrison to use the sitar. And the Beatles' brief period of experimentation with hallucinogenic drugs was reflected in some of their songs of 1967. In their early days, the Beatles strove for originality so strongly that they consciously eliminated clichés of melody and harmony from their songs. Their style evolved continuously, growing in sophistication with each new album.

The Beatles' vocal delivery sounded carefree and spontaneous, and Lennon's and McCartney's lyrics were unusually inventive. Their songs were often based on modes—rather than major or minor scales—and their harmonic vocabulary was richer than that of most rock music. Sometimes, their songs contained changes of meter and phrases of irregular length. Most striking was the Beatles' use of many electronic and instrumental sounds not previously associated with rock. Many of these novel features can be heard on the long-playing record *Sgt. Pepper's Lonely Hearts Club Band*.

SGT. PEPPER'S LONELY HEARTS CLUB BAND (1967)

Sgt. Pepper's Lonely Hearts Club Band, produced as a long-playing record, is among the Beatles' finest achievements and a landmark in the history of rock music. It was one of the first rock recordings to be presented as a unified song cycle with lyrics important enough to be printed on the record jacket. The cycle's thirteen songs are unified by the device of a music hall show in which the audience is entertained by a dazzling variety of acts. The opening two songs are addressed to the audience, and we hear the sounds of crowd noises, instruments being tried out, applause, and the brasses of Sgt. Pepper's band. The closing song of the first record side *(Being for the Benefit of Mr. Kite)* tells the audience about an evening performance. After *Within You Without You*, which opens side 2, we hear the laughter of the audience. Contributing to the record's musical continuity is the reprise of the opening *Sgt. Pepper's Lonely Hearts Club Band* as the next-to-last song, as well as the fact that there are no pauses between the first two songs and between the final three songs.

The impact of this record comes largely from its tremendous range of sounds and electronic effects. Audience noises, barnyard sounds, and weird orchestral tone clusters are heard, along with such instruments as the harpsichord, harp, and sitar. The record also has a wide range of musical styles. Along with traditional rock and roll, it includes a parody of a 1920s music-hall tune *(When I'm Sixty-Four)*, an old-fashioned melodramatic ballad using harpsichord and strings but no guitars or percussion

(She's Leaving Home), and a song featuring the exotic sounds of Indian music *(Within You Without You)*. We'll now focus on two of the record's most original songs, *Lucy in the Sky with Diamonds* and *A Day in the Life*.

Lucy in the Sky with Diamonds

Lucy in the Sky with Diamonds, the third song of the cycle, evokes a world of daydream and fantasy. But the dreamlike mood is shattered by a brusque refrain. Apart from its introduction, the song is made up of three sections that are repeated: A, B, and C. Sections A and B are relatively soft, gently pulsating, and in triple meter. In contrast, section C (the refrain *Lucy in the sky)* is loud, heavily accented, and in quadruple meter.

Listening Outline   To be read while music is heard

LUCY IN THE SKY WITH DIAMONDS,
FROM *SGT. PEPPER'S LONELY HEARTS CLUB BAND* (1967), BY THE BEATLES

A B C A B C A CC form

(Duration, 3:30)

Introduction
A

    1. *a.* Unaccompanied melody, synthesized sound suggests "electric harpsichord."
      b. Soft, triple meter, stepwise vocal melody repeats 3-note idea in narrow range, "electric harpsichord," electric bass; lightly stroked cymbals join.

B
*(Cellophane
flowers)*

    2. Moderately soft, triple meter, repeated-note melody, voice doubled by guitar and electronically manipulated to sound slightly "unreal," fuller accompaniment, electric bass more active, marks beat.

C (refrain)

    3. Loud, quadruple meter, single phrase sung three times (during some repetitions, phrase doubled at higher pitch), higher range than in sections A and B, driving rhythm, drummer accents second and fourth beats of each bar.

A

    4. Soft, triple meter, stepwise vocal melody.

B *(Newspaper
taxis)*

    5. Moderately soft, triple meter, repeated-note melody.

C (refrain)

    6. Loud, quadruple meter.

A

    7. Soft, triple meter, stepwise vocal melody.

CC (refrain)

    8. Loud, quadruple meter; fade-out at end.

A Day in the Life

A Day in the Life, the concluding song of the cycle, uses electronic effects with an inventiveness that was unprecedented in rock. Here, fantasy blends with harsh and humdrum reality. The song is outlined as follows: introduction–A A' A''–first interlude–B–second interlude–A''–postlude. In sections A, A', and A'', John Lennon sounds ''unreal'' as he sings of violence and war in a curiously detached way. Section A' begins with *He blew his mind out* and ends with a high note on *House of Lords.* Section A'' opens with *I saw a film today* and concludes with a fade-out on a trill-like setting of *turn you on.* These words generate the hallucinatory first interlude, in which a gigantic block of electronic and orchestral sound–superimposed over a percussive beat–gradually becomes louder and higher.

Suddenly, the massive sound is cut off, giving way to insistent pulsations and the soft ringing of an alarm clock. As though awakened from a bad dream, Paul McCartney describes ordinary events in his everyday life (section B). Section B contrasts with the opening sections because of its more powerful beat, livelier rhythms, and more natural vocal sound. *I went into a dream* ushers in the second interlude, in which far-off voices sing *ah* and the orchestral sound gradually becomes melodically prominent.

After the return of A'' *(I read the news)* and the final words *(turn you on)* comes a postlude similar to the first interlude but with an even more powerful buildup of electronic and orchestral sound. The postlude ends with a low E major chord that takes more than ½ minute to fade away. It is as though the slow fade-out attempted to resolve the tremendous tensions of the song cycle.

XI

NON-WESTERN MUSIC

XI

All over the world, music is an indispensable accompaniment to daily activities, magic rites, and ceremonies marking important phases of life. In this funeral ceremony of the Onitsha Ibo people of Nigeria, the chief blows an elephant tusk trumpet, an instrument symbolizing royalty.

[1] MUSIC IN NONWESTERN CULTURES

Nonwestern music reflects the diversity of the world's languages, religions, geographical conditions, and social and economic systems.* The varied peoples of the world have music that seems to express their distinctive values, beliefs, and ways of life.

The many different musical cultures each exhibit characteristic instruments, performance practices, tonal systems, and melodic and rhythmic patterns. Nonwestern societies differ in their range of musical styles as well. Some of these societies, for example, have only folk music, or music that is commonly performed by almost anyone in a village. Other cultures also have popular music, or music that is learned largely through recordings, films, and broadcasts. In addition to folk and popular music, some cultures also have classical music of a complexity that requires highly trained performers.

Nonwestern music offers a wide range of fresh listening experiences and can provide insights into cultures which are very different from our own. The enormous musical resources of nonwestern traditions have been an important source of inspiration for twentieth-century western music. The influence of Asian and African music has been felt by musicians as diverse as the French composer Claude Debussy, the British rock star George Harrison, and the African American jazz artist John Coltrane.

CHARACTERISTICS OF NONWESTERN MUSIC

Music of the nonwestern world is too varied to allow easy generalizations. Yet some features are common to most musical traditions. All over the world, music is closely linked with religion, dance, and drama. Music can serve as both a form of entertainment and an indispensable accompaniment to everyday activities, magic rites, and ceremonies marking important phases of life. In addition, music is often employed to communicate messages and to relate the traditions of a people.

---

*Discographies of nonwestern music may be found in several of the books that are listed in Appendix 5.

Oral Tradition

Nonwestern music is most often transmitted orally from parent to child or from teacher to student. Compositions and performance techniques are learned by rote and imitation. Music notation is far less important in nonwestern than in western culture. Many musical cultures—such as those of central Asia and sub-Saharan Africa—do not have notation. Even when notation exists, as in China and India, written music traditionally serves only as a record and is rarely used in teaching or performance.

Improvisation

Improvisation is basic to many nonwestern musical cultures. Performers usually base their improvisations on traditional melodic phrases and rhythmic patterns. In some parts of the world, including India and the middle east, improvisation is a highly disciplined art that requires years of training. Indian and Islamic musicians create music within a framework of melody types, each associated with a specific mood, a specific set of tones, and characteristic phrases. There are many melody types, and within each the improviser can create a practically limitless variety of music.

Most musical cultures have a repertory of traditional songs or instrumental pieces. In some cultures, these are relatively fixed and are performed similarly from generation to generation—as in Japan, where improvisation in classical music is practically nonexistent. But in other traditions, pieces are treated with great flexibility. In Iran (Persia) and sub-Saharan Africa, for example, performers freely vary melodies and add sections.

Voices

Singing is the most important way of making music in the vast majority of nonwestern cultures. Preferred vocal timbres vary widely from one musical tradition to another. In the middle east and north Africa, for example, singers cultivate a nasal, intense, strained tone. A more relaxed and open-throated sound is generally preferred by singers in sub-Saharan Africa. The vast range of vocal techniques includes shouting, crying, whispering, sighing, humming, yodeling, and singing through the teeth. A most amazing vocal technique is employed among the Tuvins, a Siberian people located northwest of Mongolia. A male Tuvin singer can produce two sounds at the same time: a low, sustained tone together with a high, eerie melody.

Instruments

Nonwestern instruments produce a wealth of sounds and come in a wide variety of sizes, shapes, and materials. Scholars usually group these instruments into four categories, based on what generates the sound.

(Metropolitan Museum of Art; gift of Alice E. Getty, 1946)

A chordophone: the mayuri, a peacock-shaped bowed string instrument from India.

1. *Chordophones* are instruments—such as harps and lutes—whose sound generator is a stretched string.
2. *Aerophones* are instruments—such as flutes and trumpets—whose sound generator is a column of air.
3. *Membranophones* are instruments—basically, drums—whose sound generator is a stretched skin or other membrane.
4. *Idiophones* are instruments—such as bells, gongs, scrapers, rattles, and xylophones—whose own material is the sound generator (no tension is applied).

The musical style of a culture is among the important factors influencing its choice of instruments. For example, chordophones (strings) are prominent in Islamic and Indian classical music, whose highly ornamented melodies require instruments with great flexibility of pitch. Idiophones and membranophones (such as bells, rattles, and drums) are features in sub-Saharan Africa, where rhythm is strongly emphasized and music is closely linked with dancing.

A culture's use of instruments is also influenced by its geography and raw materials. Bronze idiophones are prominent in southeast Asia, where metallurgy developed around 5,000 years ago. Indonesian orchestras (gamelans) contain up to eighty instruments, including bronze gongs, chimes, and xylophones. Instruments made of animal skins and horns are common in parts of sub-Saharan Africa, where these materials are easily found. Among the Aniocha Ibos of Nigeria, for example, drums are made of animal skins, and aerophones (winds) made from elephant tusks are used by the royal family and some chiefs. Where raw materials are scarce, as in the deserts of Australia, instruments may be few in number.

Along with musical style and geography, religious beliefs may influence the choice of materials. In Tibet, for example, trumpets and drums are made from the bones and skulls of criminals in order to appease demons. Instruments often have symbolic associations and are linked with specific gods and goddesses. They may be shaped like birds, animals, or fish.

Melody, Texture, and Rhythm

Most music of Asia, the near east, and north Africa emphasizes melody and rhythm, rather than harmony or polyphony. In the music of these cultures, the texture is often monophonic, consisting of an unaccompanied melody or a melody supported by percussion. In India and the near east, the melodic line is frequently supported by a drone, one or more tones sustained throughout the performance. In many parts of the world—such as north Africa, the middle east, southeast Asia, and the far east—music often has a texture in which all parts perform the same basic melody, but in versions that differ in ornamentation or rhythm. (This texture, called *heterophony*, is considered in Section 4.) Homophonic and polyphonic textures tend to be somewhat more common in sub-Saharan Africa than in most parts of Asia.

A wide variety of scales are employed in nonwestern music. Most often, they contain five, six, or seven tones. Nonwestern melodies commonly employ intervals smaller or larger than those standard in the west. Microtones—intervals smaller than the western half step—are frequent in the music of India and the near east.

Also, much nonwestern music employs very complex rhythms. For example, because of the complexity of the rhythms used, drummers in India and sub-Saharan Africa spend many years learning their highly sophisticated art.

INTERACTION BETWEEN NONWESTERN AND WESTERN MUSIC

During the twentieth century, nonwestern music has felt the impact of American and European music. This influence has been spurred by increased urbanization, adoption of western technology, and access to radios, films, recordings, and western instruments. Western elements are often found in the popular music heard in the large cities of Africa, Asia, and the near east. One example of such popular music is the *high life* of west Africa, which combines European instruments with the steady rhythm characteristic of Africa. Some composers in the nonwestern world combine traditional elements with western forms and styles. (Ravi Shankar's Concerto for Sitar and Orchestra is an example.) And in many areas, western and traditional music exist side by side. Yet there are vast areas of the world where traditional music is dominant. Many governments subsidize traditional performing groups to preserve their rich national heritage.

In the sections that follow, the traditional music of three areas—sub-Saharan Africa, India, and Japan—will be studied as a tiny sample of the vast wealth of nonwestern music.

<table>
<tr><td>

NONWESTERN

2

</td><td>

MUSIC IN SUB-SAHARAN AFRICA

</td></tr>
</table>

The African continent, which is more than three times the size of the United States, can be subdivided into two large geographical areas: north Africa, which includes such countries as Morocco, Algeria, Tunisia, and Egypt; and sub-Saharan Africa (south of the Sahara Desert), which includes Ghana, Nigeria, Mozambique, and Angola, among many other countries. The population of north Africa is predominantly Moslem and Arabic-speaking, and its music is closely related to that of the middle east. This section focuses on the music of sub-Saharan Africa, sometimes called "black Africa," and generally, throughout the section, the word *Africa* pertains to sub-Saharan Africa.

Sub-Saharan Africa, which is environmentally and culturally diverse, includes several thousand peoples with different religions, social customs, and ways of life. They speak over 700 different languages (more than are found on any other continent). Though urban growth and industrialization are transforming sub-Saharan Africa today, many Africans still hold to traditional ways of life. Most peoples have polytheistic religions, live in villages, and devote themselves to such traditional occupations as agriculture and cattle raising.

The music of sub-Saharan Africa is as diverse as its people. Even so, most of its music features complex rhythms and polyrhythms, percussive sounds, and a wide variety of instrumental ensembles. Vocal music is often performed by a soloist and a responding chorus. Of course, the different cultures of Africa have influenced each other. For example, in parts of sub-Saharan Africa, such as Ghana and northern Nigeria, musical styles have been influenced by Arabic culture.

MUSIC IN SOCIETY

Music permeates virtually every aspect of African life. It is used to entertain; to accompany dances, plays, religious ceremonies, and magic rites;

620

and to mark such events as birth, puberty, marriage, and death. Healers use specific songs and dances to treat the ill. There are work songs to accompany digging, grinding, chopping, and harvesting. Litigation songs are sung when people are in court arguing about property ownership. There are songs praising leaders, criticizing authority, and recounting history. Singing and playing instruments are so interwoven into the fabric of life that the abstract word *music*—as it is understood in the west—is not used by most African peoples. (However, there are words for *song, dance,* and *poetry.*)

An extraordinarily large number of songs are meant for particular occasions. For example, among the Fon—a people in Dahomey (in west Africa)—children sing a special song when they lose their first tooth. The Akan of Ghana have a ritual song to cure bed-wetters. The Tutsi of Rwanda—a small country in east central Africa that depends on cattle raising—have many different songs to praise cows and to accompany their care and feeding.

Music is essential to many African ceremonies. Among the Basongye of Zaïre, the funeral of an important person requires the services of a professional musician who announces the death and praises the deceased. The musician clowns to cheer up the people at the funeral, allowing them to vent emotion.

African music is closely associated with dancing; both arts are basic to many ceremonies, rituals, and celebrations. While moving, a dancer often sings or plays rattles or other idiophones that are held or tied to the body.

African music is also intimately linked with language. Many languages are "tone languages," in which the meaning of a word is determined by the relative pitch at which it is spoken. The same word can have four different meanings, depending on its pitch. Tone languages permit the use of music for communication. Drummers, trumpeters, and other musicians convey messages and tell stories by imitating the rhythms and pitch fluctuations of words. "Talking drums"—capable of two or more different pitches—are often used to send musical messages. A musician can even describe an event with the aid of a talking drum.

In Africa, music making is a social activity in which almost everyone participates. As a result, music is usually performed outdoors—in streets, courtyards, or village squares. There is spontaneous music making as well as performances by social and music groups at ceremonies and feasts. As in other cultures, the level of musical skill and training varies from one individual to another. Some highly trained musicians are employed at royal courts to entertain the monarch. Others are hired to sing songs of praise. Musicians may receive money or goods in return for their services. Musical tradition is orally transmitted, as are folklore and history. There is no musical notation, since the cultures of sub-Saharan Africa do not emphasize literacy.

African music is closely associated with dancing. While moving, a dancer often sings or plays an instrument.

ELEMENTS OF AFRICAN MUSIC

Rhythm and Percussion

Rhythm and percussive sounds are highly emphasized in African music. This emphasis reflects the close link between music and dance in African culture. African music tends to feature complex polyrhythms. Usually, several different rhythmic patterns are played simultaneously and repeated over and over. Each instrument goes its own rhythmic way, producing accents that appear to be out of phase with those of the other parts. Dancers may choose any of several rhythmic patterns to dance to. For example, while one dancer follows a pattern played with a bell, another may dance to the rattle, while yet another follows the drum.

Percussion ensembles consisting mainly of drums, xylophones, or rattles are widely employed. The instruments of percussion ensembles are carefully chosen to provide contrasts of tone color and pitch. The human body itself is often used as a percussion instrument. Hand claps, foot stamps, and thigh or chest slaps are common sounds in African music.

Vocal Music

African singers use a wide variety of vocal sounds. Even within a single performance a singer may shift from an open, relaxed tone to one that is more tight and constricted. Singers sometimes whisper, hum, grunt, shout, and imitate animal noises. Yodeling—the quick movement from a chest voice to a falsetto—is practiced by the Pygmies, among others.

Much African vocal music is characterized by a performance style known as *call and response,* in which the phrases of a soloist are repeatedly answered by those of a chorus. An exciting overlap of sound often results when the leader resumes singing before the chorus has completed its response. Singers are often accompanied by ostinatos (repeated rhythmic patterns) played by percussion. Typically, African vocal music has short phrases that are repeated over and over to different words.

Texture

Unlike many other nonwestern cultures, African societies often have music that is homophonic or polyphonic in texture. Several voice parts may sing the same melody at different pitch levels, occasionally producing a series of parallel chords. Some African peoples also perform polyphonic music in which the different melodic lines are quite independent.

AFRICAN INSTRUMENTS

A great variety of instruments and instrumental ensembles are found in Africa. Ensembles include from two to twenty or more players. Performing groups range from ensembles of instruments of indefinite pitch (bells, rattles, log drums) to those containing instruments of definite pitch (flutes, trumpets, xylophones, plucked lutes). There are also groups that combine instruments of both definite and indefinite pitch (flutes, drums, bells).

(Jacques Jangoux/Peter Arnold)

Two musicians play a slit drum while three others play membranophones.

Idiophones

The most common instruments in Africa are idiophones, such as bells, rattles, scrapers, xylophones, and log drums. Most of these instruments are struck or shaken, but others are scraped, rubbed, plucked, or stamped against the ground. Many—like rattles, bells, and stone clappers—are instruments of indefinite pitch. A few—like the xylophone and *mbira,* or *thumb piano*—are tuned instruments.

Xylophones are particularly important in Africa; they are played solo, in small groups, and in orchestras of from ten to more than thirty members. The Chopi, a people of southeast Africa, are noted for large xylophone ensembles including instruments of different sizes ranging from soprano to double bass. In some parts of Africa, a single large xylophone is played by several performers simultaneously. Xylophones have from about ten to over twenty slats, sometimes with gourd resonators attached. Spider webs are often placed over small holes in the resonators to create the buzzing sound favored by African musicians.

The *mbira (sansa, kalimba,* or *thumb piano),* which is native to Africa, is a melodic idiophone capable of producing elaborate melodies. From eight to over thirty tongues made of metal or bamboo are attached to a sounding board or box. The tongues are plucked with the thumbs and forefingers. The mbira's tone is often enriched by the jingle of shells or metal pieces attached to the resonator. Vocalists often use the mbira to accompany themselves.

Another important idiophone is the slit drum, a hollowed-out log with a long slit on top. Some slit drums are small enough to be held in the hand, while others are tree trunks over 20 feet long. Variations in the width of the slit allow two and sometimes four different tones to be produced when the slit is struck. The slit drum is used both as a "talking drum" for signaling and as a musical instrument, often together with membranophone drums.

Membranophones

Drums with stretched skins or other membranes are also important in African culture. They are essential to many religious and political ceremonies, and they are used for dancing and regulating the pace of work. "Talking drums" are employed to send messages over long distances. Drums are often considered sacred or magical; some Africans believe that drums contain the spirits of ancestral drummers. The manufacture of drums is usually accompanied by special rites, and drums are sometimes housed in special shrines and given food and offered sacrifices. Drums are often regarded as the property of the group, rather than that of an individual. And they frequently symbolize power and royalty. Some African chiefs are accompanied by official drummers when they move from place to place.

Drums are usually played in groups of two to four. However, in parts of east Africa—Burundi, Uganda, Rwanda—ensembles of up to fifteen drums are played by four to six performers. The drums are often tuned to different pitches and are used to perform melodic music similar to that of xylophone ensembles.

African drummers are among the most sophisticated in the world. They can produce not only complicated rhythms but a wide range of tone colors and pitches as well. Within an ensemble, drummers have specific roles. It is usually the chief drummer who has the freedom to improvise within the traditional framework. Other drummers repeat certain rhythmic patterns over and over.

Drums come in a wide variety of sizes, shapes, and forms. There are drums shaped like cones, cylinders, kettles, barrels, goblets, and hourglasses. They are made from logs, gourds, and clay. They may have one or two drum heads made from skins of such animals as snakes, lizards, goats, and monkeys. Some drums produce just a single sound; others—like the hourglass-shaped *pressure drum*—can produce a variety of pitches. The two heads of the pressure drum are connected by thongs; by varying the arm pressure on the thongs, a player can control the tension of the heads and so change the pitch. The pitches of the pressure drum often imitate the "tone language" spoken by the people. Sometimes, special devices are used to get certain sounds: for example, seeds or beads inside a closed drum or pieces of metal or small bells attached to a drum's rim.

Aerophones and Chordophones

The most common aerophones (winds) are flutes, whistles, horns, and trumpets. Reed instruments are less widespread. Flutes are usually made of bamboo, cane, or wood; horns and trumpets are made from animal horns, elephant tusks, wood, bamboo, and gourds.

Chordophones (strings) are used throughout Africa and come in many types and sizes. Most are plucked or struck, perhaps reflecting the African musician's preference for percussive sounds. One of the most widely used chordophones is the musical bow, which looks like a hunting bow. The string is plucked or struck with a stick. Some musical bows have a gourd resonator; with others, the player's mouth is used as the resonator.

We'll now study three examples of music from sub-Saharan Africa.

SONG FROM ANGOLA

Side 16, band 6
CD 8 [24]

A call-and-response pattern dominates this song from Angola. The performance involves (a) brief solos for male voice, (b) even shorter choral responses, and (c) longer phrases for chorus alone or for chorus together with the soloist. The song consists of four statements of the pattern ababc:

[24] 0:00
1. Solo (a)–chorus (b)–solo (a)–chorus (b)–longer choral phrases (c)

0:21
2. Solo (a)–chorus (b)–solo (a)–chorus (b)–longer choral phrases with single note interjected by soloist (c)

0:41
3. Solo (a)–chorus (b)–solo (a)–chorus (b)–longer choral phrases together with soloist (c)

1:03
4. Solo (a)–soloist with chorus (b)–solo (a)–soloist with chorus (b)–longer choral phrases together with soloist (c)

Notice how the soloist's voice—somewhat tense and nasal in quality—becomes increasingly intertwined with the chorus. In the background, several drummers perform different rhythms simultaneously.

MITAMBA YALAGALA KUMCHUZI

Side 16, band 7
CD 8 [25]

Percussive sounds and complex polyrhythms are featured in *Mitamba Yalagala Kumchuzi,* a dance song of the Zaramo people in Tanzania. First we hear percussion instruments—five tuned goblet drums, four tuned cylindrical drums, and tin rattles—producing a variety of rhythms, pitches, and tone colors. After about a ½ minute, the percussion instruments are joined by a group of voices singing a dance melody.

HINGANYENGISA MASINGITA

A xylophone orchestra of the Chopi people of Mozambique plays *Hinganyengisa Masingita,* one movement from a dance. A complete orchestral dance may contain as many as fifteen movements, most having their own lyrics sung by the dancers.

Side 16, band 8
CD 8 26

In this movement, the xylophone orchestra first is heard alone and then is joined by voices. Several times, a solo male voice is followed by a male chorus singing in unison. Excited high-pitched yodeling can also be heard. The singing dancers are inspired by the xylophone orchestra, which creates enormous drive through its ostinatos.

CLASSICAL MUSIC OF INDIA [NONWESTERN 3]

The musical traditions of India, which include folk and popular music, date back over 3,000 years and are thus among the oldest in the world. Between the twelfth and sixteenth centuries, Indian classical music developed two distinct traditions: *Karnatak music,* of south India, and *Hindustani music,* of north India (an area that now includes Pakistan). The centers of north Indian music were the princely courts, whereas south Indian music was performed in temples. The music of north India absorbed many Persian elements because many of its rulers came from Persia and were Moslems. The music of south India developed more along its own lines.

When India came under British rule during the nineteenth century, north Indian classical music was still performed mainly for small, elite audiences at princely courts. But aristocratic patronage declined during the twentieth century as India made the transition from British rule to independence. Many musicians lost their jobs around 1947—the date of India's independence—when almost 600 princely states of India were abolished as political units and merged with neighboring territories. Indian performers turned to the general public for support, just as European musicians did during the eighteenth and nineteenth centuries.

Today, Indian musicians broadcast on radio and television, make recordings, and compose music for films. Some teach in colleges or give concerts for large audiences. Many Indian artists now travel and give concerts throughout the world.

PERFORMERS

Indian performers consider their music to be spiritual in character. "We view music as a kind of spiritual discipline that raises one's inner being to divine peacefulness and bliss," writes Ravi Shankar (b. 1920), one of the most important Indian musicians. "The highest aim of our music is to reveal the essence of the universe it reflects; . . . through music, one can reach God." This spiritual emphasis is reflected in the texts of south Indian songs, which have religious associations. Indian musicians venerate their guru (master-teacher) as representative of the divine. A special initiation ceremony usually occurs when the guru accepts a disciple. The student is then expected to surrender his or her personality to the guru.

Musical traditions are transmitted orally from master to disciple, who learns by imitation, not by studying textbooks or written music. For example, Indian music students imitate their teacher phrase by phrase at lessons and sing or play along at concerts. Although India has various systems of musical notation, they give only the basic melodic and rhythmic elements. The development of these elements—the essential ornaments and musical elaborations—cannot be notated and must be learned from a teacher.

IMPROVISATION

Improvisation plays an important role in Indian music. In few other cultures is improvisation as highly developed and sophisticated. The improviser is guided by complex melodic and rhythmic systems that govern the choice of tones, ornaments, and rhythms. Before being allowed to improvise, young musicians must study for years and practice many hours a day mastering the basic rules and techniques. Improvisations are generally performed by a soloist and a drummer. They last anywhere from a few minutes to several hours, depending on the occasion and the mood of the performers and audience. Both vocalists and instrumentalists improvise.

ELEMENTS OF INDIAN CLASSICAL MUSIC

Indian music is based on the human voice—so much so that the pitch range of all Indian music is restricted to less than 4 octaves. Instrumentalists often imitate a vocal style of performance. Composed pieces are songs performed by the singer or instrumentalist, with the instrumentalist imitating vocal styles. And songs are used as a springboard for improvisation.

There have been many composers in south India, producing thousands of songs. The greatest composers were Tyagaraja (1767–1847), Muthuswamy Dikshitar (1775–1835), and Shyama Sastri (1762–1827). These three musicians were born in the same village and were contemporaries of Haydn, Mozart, and Beethoven; they are called the "musical trinity."

Highly embellished melody—both vocal and instrumental—is characteristic of Indian music. Melodies often move by microtones (intervals smaller than a half step). Melodic lines are subtly embellished by microtonal ornaments, tiny pitch fluctuations around notes. Slides of pitch provide graceful transitions from one note to another.

Indian melodies are almost always accompanied by a drone instrument that plays the tonic and dominant (or subdominant) notes throughout the performance. The basic texture of Indian music, therefore, consists of a single melody performed over an unchanging background. Rather than the harmonic progression and polyphonic texture of western music, there is melodic and rhythmic tension and relaxation. The main drone instrument is the *tambura,* a long-necked lute with four metal strings that are plucked in succession continually. The constant sound of the drone vitally contributes to the atmosphere of the music. Besides the soloist and the tambura players, there is a drummer who maintains the rhythmic structure and may also perform rhythmic improvisations.

Melodic Structure: Raga

In Indian classical music, melody is created within a melodic framework called *raga.* A *raga* is a pattern of notes. A particular raga is defined partly by the number of its tones and the pattern of its intervals. Each raga has an ascending and descending form with characteristic melodic phrases and tonal emphases. Particular ornaments and slides from one note to another give each raga its individuality. Two ragas are shown here:

Raga Malkauns

Raga Yaman Kalyan

The term *raga* comes from a word meaning *color* or *atmosphere,* and an ancient saying describes raga as "that which colors the mind." Ragas have many extramusical associations. Each raga is linked with a particular mood, such as tranquillity, love, or heroism. Ragas are also associated with specific gods, seasons, festivals, and times of day or night. They involve so many dimensions that Indian musicians spend a long period of time learning each one. Some distinguished musicians restrict themselves to performing only about a dozen ragas. Within the framework of a raga, great artists can create and improvise a limitless variety of music.

Rhythmic Structure: Tala

Rhythm is organized into cycles called *tala*. A **tala** consists of a repeated cycle of beats. Although beat cycles range from 3 to more than 100 beats in length, the most common cycles include from 6 to 16 beats. A cycle is divided into groups of beats. For example, the 10-beat tala called *jhaptal* is divided as 2–3–2–3, while the 10-beat tala called *shultal* is divided as 4–2–4:

Jhaptal

|1   2 |3   4   5 |6   7 |8   9   10|

Shultal

|1   2   3   4 |5   6 |7   8   9   10|

Each beat may be divided into smaller time values, just as a quarter note in western music may be divided into eighth or sixteenth notes. The most important beat is the first beat of the tala cycle. The soloist usually plays an important note of the raga on the first beat. Apart from the main beat, other beats receive secondary accents at the beginning of each group division. Singers and members of the audience often keep time with hand and finger movements on accented beats and hand waving on less important ones. Talas are performed in a variety of tempos ranging from slow to very fast.

The rhythm of Indian music is remarkably complex and sophisticated. Young drummers spend years with a master drummer memorizing hundreds of talas and their variations. Drummers and instrumental soloists sometimes have exciting dialogues in which rhythmically intricate phrases are rapidly tossed back and forth.

INSTRUMENTS

Although the most important performing medium in India is the voice, there are a dazzling variety of instruments of all kinds. In north Indian classical music, instruments have become about as popular as the voice. Many instruments are associated with specific gods and goddesses. For example, the flute is associated with the Hindu god Krishna, and the *vina*— a plucked string instrument—is linked with Sarasvati, the Hindu goddess of wisdom. We will describe only a few of the best-known instruments.

The **sitar** is the most popular chordophone of north India. It is a long-necked lute with nineteen to twenty-three movable frets. There are seven strings, which are plucked: five are used for melodies, and two supply drone and rhythmic effects. The sitar also has nine to thirteen sympathetically vibrating strings that give the instrument its characteristic sound.

These strings lie under the frets, almost parallel to the plucked strings. The most famous sitarist today is Ravi Shankar.

The *vina* is the most ancient plucked string instrument of south India. It has four strings for playing melodies, and three strings at the side of the fingerboard can be used for drone and rhythmic effects.

The *sarod* is a north Indian string instrument plucked with a plectrum of ivory or coconut shell. It has six main strings: four for melodies and two for drones and rhythm. Eleven to sixteen other strings vibrate sympathetically.

The *mridangam* is a two-headed barrel drum popular in south India. It is played with the open hands and fingers. The right drum head is tuned to the tonic, and the left head functions as a bass.

The north Indian counterpart of the mridangam is the **tabla,** a pair of single-headed drums played by one performer. The right-hand drum is generally tuned to the tonic note, and the left-hand drum functions as a bass drum. These drums, which are played with the hands and fingers, can produce a wide variety of pitches and tone colors. The tabla is vital to north Indian concerts and is used for solos as well as accompaniments.

MARU-BIHAG, **BY RAVI SHANKAR**

The performance here is an improvisation by the sitarist Ravi Shankar on the evening raga *Maru-Bihag*. As usual, the sitar is accompanied by a pair of drums (tabla) with the *tambura* (a drone instrument) in the background. In his spoken introduction to the recorded performance, Ravi Shankar illustrates the raga pattern and the tala (beat cycle) used as a basis for this performance. The ascending and descending melodic forms of the raga *Maru-Bihag* are:

Side 16, band 9
CD 8 27

Raga Maru-Bihag

The tala, played by the tabla, consists of 10 beats divided to give 2–3–2–3. In the illustration as well as the performance, it is not easy to perceive the beats. Each one is often subdivided into shorter drum strokes, and accents often come off the beat.

The performance opens with the *alap*, a rhapsodic introductory section in which the sitar is accompanied only by the tambura playing the tonic and dominant notes of the raga pattern. The sitarist plays in free rhythm,

(Loomis Dean, Life Magazine; © 1958 Time Inc.)

The sitarist Ravi Shankar is accompanied here by a tabla (a pair of single-headed drums) and a tambura (a drone instrument).

without regular beat or meter. Ravi Shankar conveys the basic mood and character of the raga by gradually unfolding its melodic pattern, character-istic phrases, and important tones. There are many long notes, microtonal ornaments, and slides from tone to tone. After opening with a downward glissando (glide) across the sympathetic strings, Ravi Shankar first explores the lowest notes of the melody and then plays slightly higher ones. In this performance the introductory section (alap) is 2 minutes in length. (In other performances, however, the alap can last as long as an hour.)

The entrance of the tabla playing the tala (beat cycle) marks the second phase of the performance. Ravi Shankar presents the *gat*, a short com-posed phrase that recurs many times. Between these recurrences, there are longer sections of improvisation. As the improvisation progresses, Ravi Shankar generates excitement by using increasingly rapid notes and by moving through the low and high registers of the sitar. This performance is a spectacular display of virtuosity and musical imagination.

BASIC TERMS

tambura (page 629)
raga (629)
tala (630)
sitar (630)
tabla (631)

KOTO MUSIC OF JAPAN

The rich musical culture of Japan embraces both folk music and a tradition of classical music that goes back over 1,000 years. Traditional Japanese classical music includes sacred and secular works, theater music, vocal and instrumental music, and works for orchestra, chamber ensemble, and soloists. A wide variety of styles, forms, instruments, and musical techniques are employed. We shall explore some characteristic features of this music by focusing on the koto, a plucked string instrument whose importance in Japanese music is comparable to the importance of the piano in western music.

THE KOTO

The **koto** has thirteen strings—of silk or nylon—that are stretched over a hollow sound board about 6 feet long. Each string has a movable bridge. The player tunes the thirteen strings by adjusting the placement of their individual bridges. The two most common koto tunings—called *hira-joshi* and *kumoi-joshi*—both employ only five different pitches:

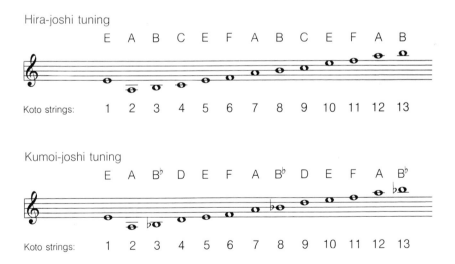

The strings of the koto are plucked with ivory plectra worn on the thumb, index finger, and middle finger of the right hand. The strings may also be struck and scraped with the plectra to produce a variety of tone

633

(Asian Art Museum of San Francisco)

The importance of the koto in traditional Japanese music is comparable to that of the piano in western music.

colors and musical effects. Two common right-hand playing techniques are a slide across the strings (resembling the glissando on western string instruments) and a rapid shaking of a single string (like a tremolo).

The koto is not limited to the pitches produced by plucking an open string. The player may raise the pitch of a string—usually by a half step or a whole step—by using the left hand to press down the string on the left side of the movable bridge. Left-hand pressure is also used to obtain ornamental pitch slides and "bent" tones.

HISTORICAL BACKGROUND

Like Buddhism, woodblock printing, and much else in Japanese culture, the koto originally came to Japan from China. It was imported sometime between 650 and 750, along with Chinese and Korean musicians who came to play in the Japanese court orchestra. The koto was used in Japanese court music (*gagaku*), which is among the world's oldest surviving orchestral music. By the tenth century, the koto was also used as a solo instrument by the court aristocracy. The earliest surviving solo koto music dates from the sixteenth century. This music, which is ceremonial in character and is therefore heard mostly in temples, was performed only by Buddhist priests, Confucian scholars, and aristocrats.

Most masterpieces of traditional koto music were composed during the Edo period (1615–1868), when the capital of Japan was moved to Edo (now Tokyo). During this period, Japan isolated itself from contacts with foreign cultures. However, an increasingly wealthy merchant class stimulated new developments in the arts such as color woodblock prints and the kabuki theater, a form of drama that combines acting with brilliant music and dance.

(Fusako Yoshida)

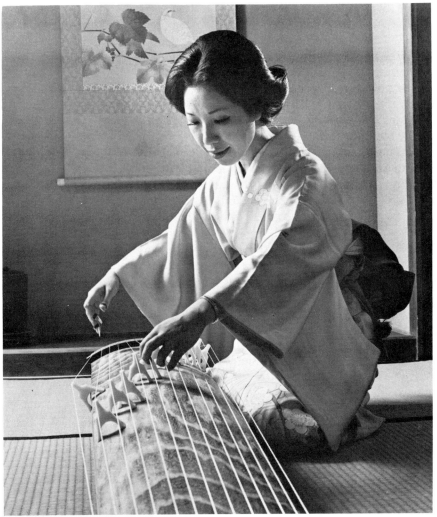

Fusako Yoshida, a "master of koto."

The early Edo period saw the rise of koto music intended for entertainment, rather than for religious rites. It was composed by blind professional musicians, not by scholars or priests. These blind musicians belonged to a special guild that protected their professional and economic interests. The guild also bestowed ranks, of which the highest was *kengyō*, or master of koto. Koto masters earned their living by teaching young women from well-to-do families. The blind musician Yatsuhashi Kengyō (1614–1685) is known as the founder of modern koto music.

KOTO MUSIC

The koto is used for solos and duets, for vocal accompaniments, and in combination with one or more other instruments (with or without voice). An important chamber ensemble consists of koto and voice together with the *shakuhachi* (an end-blown bamboo flute with five holes) and the *shamisen* (an instrument with three strings that are plucked, also spelled *samisen*).

The most important type of music for solo koto is a theme-and-variations form known as *danmono.* The theme is presented in the first section *(dan)* and then is varied in subsequent sections, which have increasingly faster tempos. New melodic material is also placed between phrases of the original theme. Each section consists of 104 beats in duple meter (except the first section, which has 108). Danmono pieces were composed during the seventeenth and eighteenth centuries. The most famous piece of this type is *Rokudan (Six Sections),* attributed to Yatsuhashi Kengyō. Since the nineteenth century, these solo pieces have often been arranged for two koto or for other instruments such as shamisen and shakuhachi.

Another basic form of koto music is *tegotomono,* a song cycle with extended instrumental interludes. The simplest type of song cycle consists of three parts: song–instrumental interlude–song. Tegotomono developed during the eighteenth century. Today song cycles are performed by an ensemble consisting of voice, koto, shamisen, and shakuhachi.

The Japanese koto repertory is made up of traditional pieces that are passed down from teacher to student and learned by rote. Rote learning was a necessity, since many koto masters were blind. Though a system of musical notation had long existed, musical scores were not used in teaching or performance until after World War II.

Most koto music is based on pentatonic (five-tone) scales that correspond to A–B–C–E–F or E–F–A–B–C on the piano. In this music, the precise quality of each individual tone is of great importance. The performer strives to give each tone the proper dynamic level, tone color, pitch inflection, and ornamentation. When the koto is used as part of a chamber ensemble, no instrument (or voice) is allowed to outshine the others. The instruments and voices blend together without losing their individual qualities.

Music for koto and other instruments or for koto and voice is usually heterophonic in texture. *Heterophonic texture* occurs when all parts perform the same basic melody, but in versions that differ in ornamentation or rhythm. However, the parts sometimes become so independent that the texture becomes polyphonic.

GODAN-GINUTA (NINETEENTH CENTURY), BY MITSUZAKI KENGYŌ

Godan-Ginuta, by Mitsuzaki Kengyō (?–1853), is one of the earliest and most brilliant pieces conceived as a duet for two koto. As its title indicates, *Godan-Ginuta* is composed of five sections (*godan* means *five sections*) and evokes the sound of cloth beating against a wooden block called a *kinuta* (*ginuta*). Japanese women once used the kinuta to clean and soften cloth in autumn, and so the music of *Godan-Ginuta* is associated with that season.

Side 16, band 10
CD 8 [28]

In this duet, the koto are tuned to different scales, and one instrument is pitched 5 steps higher than the other. The two koto are of about equal importance and often engage in a lively dialogue with rapid give-and-take. Variety is created through changes between monophonic, heterophonic, and polyphonic textures. Typical of koto music are the many tones which are "bent" upwards or downwards. Also characteristic are the duple meter and the flexible tempo, which is often held back or pressed forward. The rhythm of *Godan-Ginuta* is particularly exciting and features much syncopation. We'll now focus on the opening section of the piece, which is included in the record set.

Godan-Ginuta opens with the two koto playing long notes in unison. These tones represent the sound of the kinuta (wooden block for beating cloth). As the section unfolds, the tempo quickens and the rhythm becomes increasingly animated. Toward the middle of the piece we hear two characteristic koto sounds: a downward glissando, and rapid scrapes of the plectrum along the top of the string. This section of *Godan-Ginuta* ends with a point of repose when a long note is played in unison by the two koto.

[29] 0:00

1:20

BASIC TERMS

koto (page 633)
heterophonic texture (636)

APPENDIXES

[1] GLOSSARY AND EXAMPLE LOCATOR

Note: Musical examples are given for most of the terms in the glossary. Examples indicate (as appropriate) composer; title; movement (mvt), page (p) where discussed or page where listening outline (LO) appears; item on listening outline; words in text; side, band, CD, and track numbers (track numbers are in small boxes); and timings (in minutes and seconds, 0:00). Additional abbreviations are: supplementary sets of four cassettes, LPs, and CDs = supp sets; first, second, third, fourth, etc., = 1st, 2d, 3d, 4th, etc.

A B form See *two-part form.*

A B A form See *three-part form.*

Absolute music Instrumental music having *no* intended association with a story, poem, idea, or scene; nonprogram music.

A capella Choral music without instrumental accompaniment.
    Example Josquin Desprez, *Ave Maria;* p 110; side 2, band 3; CD 1 [44]

Accent Emphasis of a note, which may result from its being louder (dynamic accent), longer, or higher in pitch than the notes near it.

Accelerando Becoming faster
    Examples Bartók, Concerto for Orchestra, 1st mvt; p 503; LO slow introduction 2d; side 14, band 5; CD 7 [28]; 2:36
    Liszt, *Transcendental Étude* No. 10 in F Minor; p 335; LO 4b; side 9, band 6; CD 5 [20]; 1:49

Accompanied recitative Speechlike melody that is sung by a solo voice accompanied by the orchestra.
    Examples Handel, *Messiah, Comfort Ye,* starting at *The voice of him;* p 191; side 4, band 5; CD 2 [26]; 2:39
    Bach, Cantata No. 140, 5th mvt; p 183; supp sets, side 2, band 9; CD 1 [42]

Accordion Instrument consisting of a bellows between two keyboards (pianolike keys played by the right hand, and buttons played by the left hand) whose sound is produced by air pressure which causes free steel reeds to vibrate.

Adagio Slow
    Example Beethoven, Piano Sonata in C Minor, Op. 13 *(Pathétique),* mvt 2; p 273; side 8, band 3; CD 4 [37]

Aerophone Any instrument—such as a flute or trumpet—whose sound is generated by a vibrating column of air.

Aleatory music See *chance music.*

Allegretto Moderately fast
    Example Mozart, *Eine kleine Nachtmusik,* 3d mvt; p 218; side 5, band 2; CD 3 [7]

Allegro   Fast.
> Example   Vivaldi, *La Primavera (Spring)*, Concerto for Violin and String Orchestra, mvt 1; p 162; side 2, band 9; CD 1 59

Alto (contralto)   Female voice of low range.
> Example   Verdi, *Rigoletto*, Quartet, voice of Maddalena, p 393; side 11, band 4; CD 6 15

Andante   Moderately slow, a walking pace.
> Example   Haydn, Symphony No. 94, 2d mvt; p 215; side 5, band 1; CD 3 1

Answer   Second presentation of the subject in a fugue, usually in the dominant scale.
> Example   Bach, Organ Fugue in G Minor, p 142; LO 1*b*; side 2, band 10; CD 1 64 0:18

Aria   Song for solo voice with orchestral accompaniment, usually expressing an emotional state through its outpouring of melody; found in operas, oratorios, and cantatas.
> Examples   Mozart, *Don Giovanni*, Leporello's "catalog" aria; p 245; side 5, band 5; CD 3 21
> Puccini, *La Bohème, Mi chiamano Mimi;* p 406; side 12, band 1; CD 6 18 8:19

Arioso   A vocal solo more lyrical than a recitative and less elaborate than an aria.
> Example   Handel, *Messiah, Comfort Ye;* p 191; side 4, band 5; CD 2 25

Arpeggio   See *broken chord.*

Art song   Setting of a poem for solo voice and piano, translating the poem's mood and imagery into music, common in the romantic period.
> Example   Schubert, *Erlkönig (The Erlking)*, p 309; side 8, band 5; CD 4 45

Atonality   Absence of tonality, or key, characteristic of much twentieth-century music.
> Example   Schoenberg, Five Pieces for Orchestra, 1st mvt; p 486; side 14, band 1; CD 7 16

Augmentation   Variation of a fugue subject in which the original time values of the subject are lengthened.

Ballade   In medieval music, a French poetic and musical form with the structure A A' B, introduced by the troubadours.
> Example   Machaut, *Je suis aussi;* p 98; supp sets, side 1, band 2; CD 1 26

Ballett (fa-la)   Dancelike song for several voices, mostly homophonic in texture, with the melody in the highest voice and the syllables *fa-la* occurring as a refrain after each stanza; common in English Renaissance music.
> Example   Morley, *Now Is the Month of Maying;* p 117; supp sets, side 1, band 4; CD 1 32

Bar   Another term for *measure,* often used in jazz.

Baritone   A male voice lower than a tenor and higher than a bass.
> Example   Mozart, *Don Giovanni*, duet *Là ci darem la mano*, voice of Don Giovanni; p 247; side 5, band 6; CD 3 23

Baritone horn   Brass instrument similar in shape to the tuba, with a higher range, commonly used in bands.

Bass   (1) Male voice of low range. (2) See *double bass*.
Example   Mozart, *Don Giovanni*, Leporello's "catalog" aria; p 245; side 5, band 5; CD 3 ⟨21⟩

Bass clarinet   Member of the clarinet family, having a low range. Its shape is curved at the end before flaring into a bell.

Bass clef   Symbol on the staff indicating relatively low pitch ranges, such as those played by a pianist's left hand.

Bass drum   Percussion instrument of indefinite pitch, the largest of the orchestral drums.
Example   Britten, *The Young Person's Guide to the Orchestra*; p 35; variation 13; supp sets, side 1, band 1; CD 1 ⟨19⟩; 11:56

Bass fiddle   See *double bass*.

Basso continuo (figured bass)   Baroque accompaniment made up of a bass part together with numbers (figures) indicating the chords to be played above it. Usually the basso continuo is played by two instruments, a keyboard plus a low melodic instrument.
Examples   Monteverdi, *Orfeo, Tu se' morta*; p 154; side 2, band 7; CD 1 ⟨56⟩
Bach, Suite No. 3, gigue; p 174; side 4, band 3; CD 2 ⟨21⟩

Basso ostinato   See *ground bass*.

Bassoon   Double-reed woodwind instrument, made of wood, having a low range.
Examples   Ravel, *Bolero*, p 459; 1*d*; side 13, band 4; CD 7 ⟨13⟩; 1:47
Britten, *The Young Person's Guide to the Orchestra*; p 34; variation 4; supp sets, side 1, band 1; CD 1 ⟨10⟩; 4:08

Baton   Thin stick, used by many conductors, to beat time and indicate pulse and tempo.

Beam   Horizontal line connecting the flags of several eighth notes or sixteenth notes in succession, to facilitate reading these notes.

Beat   Regular, recurrent pulsation that divides music into equal units of time.

Bebop (bop)   Complex jazz style, usually for small groups, developed in the 1940s and meant for attentive listening rather than dancing.
Example   Parker, *KoKo*; p 579; side 16, band 4; CD 8 ⟨21⟩

Bitonality   Approach to pitch organization using two keys at one time, often found in twentieth-century music.

Blues   Term referring both to a style of performance and to a form; an early source of jazz, characterized by flatted, or "blue," notes in the scale; vocal blues consist of 3-line stanzas in the form a a' b.
Examples   Smith, *Lost Your Head Blues*; p 564; side 15, band 8; CD 8 ⟨17⟩
King Oliver's Creole Jazz Band, *Dippermouth Blues*; p 569; side 16, band 1; CD 8 ⟨18⟩

Bop   See *bebop*.

Bow   Slightly curved stick strung tightly with horsehair, used to play string instruments.

Brass instrument   Instrument, made of brass or silver, whose sound is produced by the vibrations of the player's lips as he or she blows into a cup- or funnel-shaped mouthpiece. The vibrations are amplified and colored in a tube that is flared at the end.

Bridge (transition)   In the exposition of the sonata form, a section which leads from the first theme in the tonic, or home, key to the second theme, which is in a new key.
> **Examples**   Mozart, Symphony No. 40 in G Minor, 4th mvt; p 212; LO exposition 2; side 6, band 5; CD 3 ⃞44; 0:28
> Beethoven, Symphony No. 5 in C Minor, 1st mvt; p 276; LO exposition 2; side 7, band 1; CD 4 ⃞2; 0:21

Broken chord (arpeggio)   Sounding of the individual tones of a chord in sequence rather than simultaneously.
> **Examples**   Mozart, Symphony No. 40 in G Minor, 4th mvt; p 212; LO exposition 1 (opening six notes); side 6, band 5; CD 3 ⃞43
> Beethoven, Symphony No. 5 in C Minor, 3d mvt (opening six notes); p 276; side 7, band 3; CD 4 ⃞15

Cadence   (1) Resting place at the end of a phrase in a melody. (2) Progression giving a sense of conclusion, often from the dominant chord to the tonic chord.
> **Example**   Chopin, Prelude in E Minor (last three chords); p 58; side 1, band 9; CD 1 ⃞25

Cadenza   Unaccompanied section of virtuoso display for the soloist in a concerto, usually appearing near the end of the first movement, and sometimes in the last movement.
> **Examples**   Mozart, Piano Concerto in A Major, K. 488, 1st mvt; p 257; LO recapitulation 5c; side 5, band 3; CD 3 ⃞16; 9:03
> Mendelssohn, Violin Concerto in E Minor, 1st mvt; p 340; LO development 3; side 9, band 7; CD 5 ⃞27; 6:40

Call and response   (1) In jazz, a pattern wherein one voice or instrument is answered by another voice, instrument, or group of instruments. (2) Performance style in which the phrases of a soloist are repeatedly answered by those of a chorus, often found in African and other nonwestern music.
> **Examples**   Smith, *Lost Your Head Blues*; p 564; side 15, band 8; CD 8 ⃞18
> Song from Angola (Gangele Song); p 626; side 16, band 6; CD 8 ⃞24

Camerata   In Italian, *fellowship* or *society*; a group of nobles, poets, and composers who began to meet regularly in Florence around 1575 and whose musical discussions prepared the way for the beginning of opera.

Cantata   Composition in several movements, usually written for chorus, one or more vocal soloists, and orchestra. The church cantata for the Lutheran service in Germany during the baroque period often includes chorales.

Cantus firmus   Melody—often a Gregorian chant—used as the basis of a polyphonic composition.
> **Example**   Perotin, *Alleluia: Nativitas*; p 96; side 2, band 1; CD 1 ⃞40

Castrato   Male singer castrated before puberty to retain a high voice range; the most important category of vocal soloists in opera during the baroque period.

Celesta   Percussion instrument of definite pitch, with metal bars that are struck by hammers controlled by a keyboard.

Cello (violoncello)   String instrument with a range lower than that of the viola and higher than that of the double bass.
> **Example**   Schubert, *Trout* Quintet, 4th mvt; p 314; LO variation 5; side 8, band 7; CD 4 [58]; 5:10
> Britten, *The Young Person's Guide to the Orchestra;* p 34; variation 7; supp sets, side 1, band 1; CD 1 [13]; 6:36

Chamber music   Music employing a small group of musicians, with one player to a part.

Chance (aleatory) music   Music composed by the random selection of pitches, tone colors, and rhythms; developed in the 1950s by John Cage and others.

Chimes   Percussion instrument of definite pitch, with suspended metal tubes that are struck with a hammer.

Chorale   Hymn tune sung to a German religious text.
> **Example**   Bach, Cantata No. 140, mvt 7; p 184; side 3, band 6; CD 2 [16]

Chorale prelude   Short composition for organ, based on a hymn tune and often used to remind the congregation of the melody before the hymn is sung.

Chord   Combination of three or more tones sounded at once.
> **Example**   Chopin, Prelude in C Minor for Piano, Op. 28, No. 20; p 8; side 1, band 2; CD 1 [5]

Chordophone   Instrument—such as a harp or lute—whose sound is generated by a stretched string.

Chorus   In jazz, a statement of the basic harmonic pattern or melody.

Chromatic harmony   Use of chords containing tones not found in the prevailing major or minor scale but included in the chromatic scale (which has twelve tones); often found in romantic music.

Chromatic scale   Scale including all twelve tones of the octave; each tone is a half step away from the next one.
> **Examples**   Purcell, *Dido and Aeneas, Dido's Lament,* repeated descending chromatic scale in bass; p 156; side 2, band 8; CD 1 [57]
> Bach, Mass in B Minor, *Crucifixus,* repeated descending chromatic scale in bass; p 170; supp sets, side 2, band 7; CD 1 [40]

Church modes   Scales containing seven tones with an eighth tone duplicating the first an octave higher, but with different patterns of whole and half steps from major and minor scales; used in medieval, Renaissance, and twentieth-century music and in folk music.
> **Example**   *Alleluia: Vidimus stellam;* p 90; side 1, band 13; CD 1 [36]

Clarinet   Single-reed woodwind instrument with a beak-shaped mouthpiece, cylindrical in shape with a slightly flared bell.
> **Examples**   Mozart, Symphony No. 40 in G Minor, 4th mvt; p 212; LO exposition 3*b;* side 6, band 5; CD 3 [45]; 1:20
> Ravel, *Bolero;* p 459; LO 1*c;* CD 7 [12]; 0:59
> Britten, *The Young Person's Guide to the Orchestra;* p 34; variation 3; supp sets, side 1, band 1; CD 1 [9]; 3:32

Clavichord Baroque keyboard instrument in which sound is produced by means of brass blades striking strings, capable of making gradual dynamic changes, but within a narrow volume range.

Clef Symbol placed at the beginning of the staff to show the exact pitch of each line and space.

Climax Highest tone or emotional focal point in a melody or a larger musical composition.
  Example Arlen, *Over the Rainbow;* p 53; melody B on *find;* side 1, band 8; CD 1 ⌷23⌷; 0:45

Coda In a sonata-form movement, a concluding section following the recapitulation and rounding off the movement by repeating themes or developing them further.
  Examples Mozart, Symphony No. 40 in G Minor, 1st mvt; p 252; LO coda; side 6, band 2; CD 3 ⌷36⌷; 7:54
  Beethoven, Symphony No. 5 in C Minor, 1st mvt; p 276; LO coda; side 7, band 1; CD 4 ⌷8⌷; 5:54

Complete cadence Definite resting place, giving a sense of finality, at the end of a phrase in a melody.
  Example Chopin, Prelude in E Minor (last three chords); p 58; side 1, band 9; CD 1 ⌷25⌷

Computer A tool used to synthesize music, to help composers write scores, to store samples of audio signals, and to control synthesizing mechanisms.

Concert overture Independent composition for orchestra in one movement, usually in sonata form, often found in the romantic period.
  Example Tchaikovsky, *Romeo and Juliet,* p 365; side 10, band 3; CD 5 ⌷38⌷

Concertmaster Assistant to the conductor; usually the principal first violinist in a symphony orchestra.

Concerto Extended composition for instrumental soloist and orchestra, usually in three movements: (1) fast, (2) slow, (3) fast.

Concerto grosso Composition for several instrumental soloists and small orchestra; common in late baroque music.
  Example Bach, *Brandenburg* Concerto No. 5 in D Major, pp 138 and 168; side 3, bands 1–3; CD 2 ⌷1⌷, ⌷6⌷, and ⌷7⌷

Conductor Leader of a performing group of musicians.

Consonance Tone combination that is stable and restful.

Contrabassoon Double-reed woodwind instrument with a register one octave lower than the bassoon's.

Contralto See *alto.*

Contrast Striking differences of pitch, dynamics, rhythm, and tempo that provide variety and change of mood.

Cool jazz Jazz style related to bebop, but more relaxed in character and relying more heavily on arrangements; developed around 1950.

Cornet Brass instrument similar in shape to the trumpet, with a mellower tone.

Countermelody   Melodic idea that accompanies a main theme.
Example   Haydn, Symphony No. 94, 2d mvt; p 215; LO variation 3; side 5, band 1;
CD 3 ⟨4⟩ ; 3:20

Counterpoint   Technique of combining two or more melodic lines into a meaningful whole.

Countersubject   In a fugue, a melodic idea that accompanies the subject fairly constantly.
Example   Bach, Organ Fugue in G Minor; p 144; LO 1*b;* side 2, band 10; CD 1 ⟨64⟩ ;
0:18

Crescendo (cresc.)   Gradually louder.
Example   Stravinsky, *Firebird Suite,* Finale; p 8; LO 1; side 1, band 3; CD 1 ⟨8⟩

Cymbals   Percussion instrument of indefinite pitch, consisting of a pair of metal plates, played by striking the plates against each other.
Example   Wagner, *Lohingrin,* Prelude to Act III; p 7; LO 1*a;* side 1, band 1;
CD 1 ⟨1⟩

Da capo   From the beginning; an indication usually meaning that the opening section of a piece is to be repeated after the middle section.
Examples   Bach, Cantata No. 140, 6th mvt, duet for bass and soprano; p 184; supp
sets, side 2, band 10; CD 1 ⟨43⟩
Mozart, *Eine kleine Nachtmusik,* 3d mvt; p 218

Da capo aria   Aria in A B A form; after the B section, the term *da capo* is written; this means *from the beginning* and indicates a repetition of the opening A section.

Decrescendo   Gradually softer.
Examples   Wagner, *Lohengrin,* Prelude to Act III; p 7; LO 3*c;* side 1, band 1;
CD 1 ⟨4⟩ ; 2:47
Tchaikovsky, *Romeo and Juliet;* p 365; LO recapitulation, first theme 1; side 10, band 3;
CD 5 ⟨44⟩ ; 11:58

Development   Second section of a sonata-form movement, in which themes from the exposition are developed and the music moves through several different keys.
Example   Mozart, Symphony No. 40 in G Minor, 4th mvt; p 212; LO development;
side 6, band 5; CD 3 ⟨47⟩ ; 1:57
Beethoven, Symphony No. 5 in C Minor, 1st mvt; p 276; LO development; side 7, band 1;
CD 4 ⟨6⟩ ; 2:57

Diminuendo   See *decrescendo.*

Diminution   Variation of a fugue subject in which the original time values of the subject are shortened.

Dissonance   Tone combination that is unstable and tense.

Dixieland   See *New Orleans jazz.*

Dominant chord   Triad built on the fifth note of the scale, which sets up tension that is resolved by the tonic chord.
Example   Chopin, Prelude in E Minor, next-to-last chord; p 58; side 1, band 9; CD 1 ⟨25⟩

Dotted note   Note with a dot to the right of it. This dot increases the note's undotted duration by half.

Dotted rhythm Long-short rhythmic pattern in which a dotted note is followed by a note that is much shorter.
Examples Chopin, Prelude in C Minor, rhythmic pattern long-long-long-short-long; p 8; side 1, band 2; CD 1 5
Bach, Cantata No. 140, 1st mvt; p 179; side 3, band 4; CD 2 10
Handel, *Messiah, For unto Us a Child Is Born*, on the words *and the government shall be upon*; p 193; side 4, band 7; CD 2 29 ; 0:58

Double bass ("bass fiddle"; bass) Largest string instrument, having the lowest range of the string family.
Example Britten, *The Young Person's Guide to the Orchestra*, variation 18; p 34; supp sets, side 1, band 1; CD 1 14 ; 7:53

Double stop See *stop*.

Double-reed woodwinds Instruments whose sound is produced by two narrow pieces of cane held between the player's lips; these pieces vibrate when the player blows between them.

Downbeat First, or stressed, beat of a measure.
Example Chopin, Prelude in C Minor, opening chord; p 8; side 1, band 2; CD 1 5

Dubbing In recorded music, the insertion of sounds, which may themselves be live or prerecorded, which then become part of the resulting piece of music.

Duple meter Pattern of 2 beats to the measure.
Example Tchaikovsky, *Nutcracker* Suite, *Dance of the Reed Pipes*; p 73; side 1, band 11; CD 1 31

Dynamic accent Emphasis that a note receives when a performer plays it more loudly than the notes around it.

Dynamics Degrees of loudness or softness in music.

Electronic instrument Instrument whose sound is produced, modified, or amplified by electronic means.

Embellishments Ornamental tones that are either improvised by the performer or indicated in the music by signs or notes in small print.

English horn Double-reed woodwind instrument, slightly larger than the oboe and with a lower range, straight in shape with an egg-shaped bell.
Example Tchaikovsky, *Nutcracker* Suite, *Dance of the Reed Pipes*; p 73; LO 1c; side 1, band 11; CD 1 31

Ensemble In opera, a piece sung by three or more solo singers.
Example Verdi, *Rigoletto*, Quartet; p 393; side 11, band 4; CD 6 15 ; 4:33

Episode Transitional section in a fugue between presentations of the subject, which offers either new material or fragments of the subject or countersubject.
Example Bach, Organ Fugue in G Minor; p 144; LO 1e; side 2, band 10; CD 1 65 ; 1:14

Étude In French, *study*; a piece designed to help a performer master specific technical difficulties.
Examples Liszt, *Transcendental Étude* No. 10 in F Minor; p 335; side 9, band 6; CD 5 17
Chopin, *Revolutionary* Étude in C Minor; p 329; supp sets, side 4, band 2; CD 2 31

Euphonium   Brass instrument similar in shape to the tuba and the baritone horn, with a higher range than the tuba's, commonly used in bands.

Exoticism   Use of melodies, rhythms, or instruments that suggest foreign lands; common in romantic music.

Exposition   First section of a sonata-form movement, which sets up a strong conflict between the tonic key and the new key; and between the first theme (or group of themes) and the second theme (or group of themes).
   Example   Mozart, Symphony No. 40 in G Minor, 4th mvt; p 212; LO exposition; side 6, band 5; CD 3 ⌷43⌷

✓ *Expressionism*   Musical style stressing intense, subjective emotion and harsh dissonance, typical of German and Austrian music of the early twentieth century.
   Example   Schoenberg, Five Pieces for Orchestra, 1st mvt; p 486; side 14, band 1; CD 7 ⌷16⌷

Fa-la   See *ballett*.

Figured bass   See *basso continuo*.

Flag   Wavy line attached to the stem on a note, indicating how long that note is to be held relative to the notes around it.

Flat sign   Symbol which notates a pitch one half step lower than the pitch that would otherwise be indicated—for example, the next lower key on the piano.

Flute   Woodwind instrument, usually made of metal, with a high range, whose tone is produced by blowing across the edge of a mouth hole.
   Examples   Bach, *Badinerie* from Suite No. 2 in B Minor; p 75; side 1, band 12; CD 1 ⌷34⌷
   Tchaikovsky, *Nutcracker* Suite, *Dance of the Reed Pipes*; p 73; LO 1*b*; side 1, band 11; CD 1 ⌷31⌷

Form   Organization of musical ideas in time.

Forte (f)   Loud.
   Examples   Mozart, *Eine kleine Nachtmusik*, 3d mvt; p 218; LO 1; side 5, band 2; CD 3 ⌷7⌷
   Vivaldi, *La Primavera (Spring)*, Concerto for Violin and String Orchestra, mvt 1; p 162; LO 1*a*; side 2, band 9; CD 1 ⌷59⌷

Fortepiano   Eighteenth-century or early-nineteenth-century piano, which differs from the modern piano in sound and construction.
   Example   Mozart, Piano Concerto in A Major, K. 488, 1st mvt; p 256; side 5, band 3; CD 3 ⌷10⌷

Fortissimo (ff)   Very loud.
   Example   Wagner, *Lohengrin*, Prelude to Act III; p 7; LO 1*a*; side 1, band 1; CD 1 ⌷1⌷

Fourth chord   Chord in which the tones are a fourth apart, instead of a third; used in twentieth-century music.

Free jazz   Jazz style which departs from traditional jazz by not being based on regular forms and established chord patterns; developed during the 1960s.

French horn Brass instrument of medium range, whose tube is coiled into a roughly circular shape and fitted with valves; commonly used in symphony orchestras and in bands. (Sometimes called simply a *horn*.)
   Examples Stravinsky, *Firebird* Suite, Finale; p 8; LO 1*a*; side 1, band 3; CD 1 8
   Britten, *The Young Person's Guide to the Orchestra*, variation 10; p 34; supp sets, side 1, band 1; CD 1 16 ; 9:40

French overture Common opening piece in baroque suites, oratorios, and operas; usually in two parts: the first slow, with characteristic dotted rhythms, full of dignity and grandeur; the second quick and lighter in mood, often starting like a fugue.
   Example Handel, *Messiah*, Overture; p 191; side 4, band 4; CD 2 23

Front line In Dixieland or New Orleans jazz, the group of melodic instruments which improvise on a melody, supported by the rhythm section.

Fugue Polyphonic composition based on one main theme, or subject.
   Example Bach, Organ Fugue in G Minor; p 144; side 2, band 10; CD 1 64

Fusion See *jazz rock.*

Glissando Rapid slide up or down a scale.
   Example Gershwin, *Rhapsody in Blue*, p 516; LO 1*a*; supp sets, side 7, band 3; CD 4 15

Glockenspiel Percussion instrument of definite pitch, made up of flat metal bars set in a frame and played by striking with small metal hammers.
   Example Stravinsky, *Petrushka*, opening scene; p 468; LO 4*c*; supp sets, side 7, band 1; CD 4 5 ; 2:37

Gong (tam-tam) Percussion instrument of indefinite pitch, made up of a large flat metal plate that is suspended and struck with a mallet.
   Example Britten, *The Young Person's Guide to the Orchestra*, variation 13; p 34; supp sets, side 1, band 1; CD 1 22 ; 12:54

Grand staff Combination of the treble and bass staves, used in keyboard music to encompass the wide range of pitches produced by both hands.

Grave Very slow, broad.
   Example Beethoven, Piano Sonata in C Minor, Op. 13 *(Pathétique)*, slow introduction; p 271; side 8, band 2; CD 4 30

Gregorian chant Melodies set to sacred Latin texts, sung without accompaniment; the official music of the Roman Catholic church.
   Example *Alleluia: Vidiumus stellam;* p 90; side 1, band 13; CD 1 36

Ground bass (basso ostinato) Variation form in which a musical idea in the bass is repeated over and over while the melodies above it constantly change; common in baroque music.
   Examples Purcell, *Dido and Aeneas, Dido's Lament;* p 156; side 2, band 8; CD 1 57
   Brahms, Symphony No. 4 in E Minor, 4th mvt; p 384; LO variations 4–8; side 11, band 2; CD 6 9 ; 1:03
   Bach, Mass in B Minor, *Crucifixus;* p 170; supp sets, side 2, band 7; CD 1 40

Guitar Plucked string instrument with six strings stretched along a fretted fingerboard.
   Example Lillian Hardin Armstrong: *Hotter Than That;* p 9; LO 4–5; side 1, band 4; CD 1 12 and 13 ; 1:19

Half step   Smallest interval traditionally used in western music; for example, the interval between *ti* and *do*.

Harmonics   Very high-pitched tones, like a whistle's, produced in bowed string instruments by lightly touching the string at certain points while bowing.

Harmony   How chords are constructed and how they follow each other.

Harp   Plucked string instrument, consisting of strings stretched within a triangular frame and tuned to a major scale.
   Examples   Tchaikovsky, *Romeo and Juliet;* p 365; LO introduction 1c and 2c; side 10, band 3; CD 5 $\boxed{38}$; 1:05
   Britten, *The Young Person's Guide to the Orchestra;* p 34; variation 9; supp sets, side 1, band 1; CD 1 $\boxed{15}$; 8:52

Harpsichord   Keyboard instrument, widely used from about 1500 to 1775, whose sound is produced by plectra which pluck its wire strings. The harpsichord has been revived during the twentieth century.
   Example   Bach, *Brandenburg* Concerto No. 5 in D Major, 1st mvt; p 138; LO 8c; side 3, band 1; CD 2 $\boxed{5}$

Heterophonic texture   Simultaneous performance of the same basic melody by two or more voices or instruments, but in versions that differ in ornamentation or rhythm; common in nonwestern music.

Home key   See *tonic key.*

Homophonic texture   Term describing music in which one main melody is accompanied by chords.
   Examples   Chopin, Prelude in C Minor; p 8; side 1, band 2; CD 1 $\boxed{5}$
   Arlen, *Over the Rainbow;* p 53; side 1, band 8; CD 1 $\boxed{22}$

Horn   See *French horn.*

Idée fixe   Single melody used throughout a long work to represent one idea.
   Example   Berlioz, *Fantastic Symphony;* p 349; supp sets, side 4, band 3; CD 2 $\boxed{32}$

Idiophone   Instrument—such as bells, a gong, a scraper, a rattle, or a xylophone—whose sound is generated by the instrument's own material with no applied tension.

Imitation   Presentation of a melodic idea by one voice or instrument that is immediately followed by its restatement by another voice or instrument, as in a round.
   Examples   Josquin Desprez, *Ave Maria,* opening words *Ave Maria;* p 110; side 2, band 3; CD 1 $\boxed{44}$
   Bach, Organ Fugue in G Minor; p 144; LO 1; side 2, band 10; CD 1 $\boxed{64}$

Impressionism   Musical style which stresses tone color, atmosphere, and fluidity, typical of Debussy (flourished 1890–1920).
   Example   Debussy, *Prelude to the Afternoon of a Faun;* p 452; side 13, band 3; CD 7 $\boxed{5}$

Improvisation   Creation of music at the same time as it is performed.
   Examples   Parker, *KoKo;* p 579; side 16, band 4; CD 8 $\boxed{21}$
   Shankar, *Maru-Bihag;* p 631; side 16, band 9; CD 8 $\boxed{27}$

Incidental music   Music intended to be performed before and during a play, setting the mood for the drama.

Incomplete cadence   Inconclusive resting point at the end of a phrase which sets up expectations for phrases to follow.
> **Example**   Arlen, *Over the Rainbow*, end of first phrase on the word *high*; p 53; side 1, band 6; CD 1 22

Interval   "Distance" in pitch between any two tones.

Inversion   Variation of a fugue subject in which each interval of the subject is reversed in direction.

Jazz   Music rooted in improvisation and characterized by syncopated rhythm, a steady beat, and distinctive tone colors and performance techniques. Jazz was developed in the United States predominantly by black musicians and gained popularity in the early twentieth century.

Jazz rock (fusion)   Style which combines the jazz musician's improvisatory approach with rock rhythms and tone colors; developed in the 1960s.

Kettledrums   See *timpani*.

Key (tonality)   Central note, scale, and chord within a piece, in relationship to which all other tones in the composition are heard.

Key signature   Sharp or flat signs immediately following the clef sign at the beginning of a piece of music, indicating the key in which the music is to be played.

Keyboard instrument   Instrument—such as the piano, organ, or harpsichord—played by pressing a series of keys with the fingers.

Keynote (tonic)   Central tone of a melody or larger piece of music. When a piece is in the key of C major, for example, C is the keynote.

Klangfarbenmelodie   See *tone-color melody*.

Koto   Instrument with thirteen silk or nylon strings stretched over a hollow sound board about 6 feet long; each string is tuned by adjusting the placement of a movable bridge. The koto is an important instrument in Japanese music.
> **Example**   Mitsuzaki Kengyō, *Godan Ginuta*; p 637; side 16, band 10; CD 8 28

Largo   Very slow, broad.
> **Example**   Chopin, Prelude for Piano in C Minor; p 8; side 1, band 2; CD 1 5

Leap   Interval larger than that between two adjacent tones in the scale.

Ledger lines   Short, horizontal lines above or below the staff, used to indicate a pitch that falls above or below the range indicated by the staff.

Legato   Smooth, connected manner of performing a melody.
> **Examples**   Arlen, *Over the Rainbow*, melody A; p 53; side 1, band 8; CD 1 22
> Bach, Organ Fugue in G Minor; p 144; LO 1a; side 2, band 10; CD 1 64

Leitmotif   Short musical idea associated with a person, object, or thought, characteristic of the operas of Wagner.
> **Example**   Wagner, *Die Walküre*, Act 1, Love Scene, *Sword*; p 419; side 12, band 2; CD 6 25 ; 5:42

Librettist   Dramatist who writes the *libretto,* or text, of an opera.

Libretto   Text of an opera.

Madrigal   Composition for several voices set to a short secular poem, usually about love, combining homophonic and polyphonic textures and often using word painting; common in Renaissance music.
   Example   Weelkes, *As Vesta Was Descending;* p 116; side 2, band 4; CD 1 ⃞47⃞

Major key   Music based on a major scale.
   Examples   Arlen, *Over the Rainbow;* p 53; side 1, band 8; CD 1 ⃞22⃞
   Contrast between major and minor keys is illustrated in Tchaikovsky, *Nutcracker* Suite,
   Dance of the Reed Pipes; p 73; LO 1, 2; side 1, band 11; CD 1 ⃞31⃞ and ⃞32⃞
   Haydn, *Surprise* Symphony, 2d mvt; p 215; LO theme, variation 2; side 5, band 1;
   CD 3 ⃞1⃞ and ⃞3⃞

Major scale   Series of seven different tones within an octave, with an eighth tone repeating the first tone an octave higher, consisting of a specific pattern of whole and half steps; the whole step between the second and third tones is characteristic.
   Example   Handel, *Messiah, Ev'ry Valley Shall Be Exalted*, downward major scale on first
   appearance of *-ley shall be exalted;* p 192; side 4, band 6; CD 2 ⃞27⃞

Marimba   Percussion instrument with tuned wooden bars, similar to the xylophone, but larger and having cylindrical acoustic resonators.

Mass   Sacred choral composition made up of five sections: Kyrie, Gloria, Credo, Agnus Dei; Sanctus, and Agnus Dei.
   Example   Machaut, *Notre Dame* Mass, Agnus Dei; p 100; side 2, band 2; CD 1 ⃞41⃞

Mass ordinary   Roman Catholic church texts which remain the same from day to day throughout most of the year: Kyrie, Gloria, Credo, Sanctus, and Agnus Dei.

Measure   Rhythmic group set off by bar lines, containing a fixed number of beats.

Melody   Series of single tones that add up to a recognizable whole.

Membranophone   Instrument—basically, a drum—whose sound is generated by a stretched skin or other membrane.

Meter   Organization of beats into regular groups.

Meter signature   See *time signature.*

Metronome   Apparatus which produces ticking sounds or flashes of light at any desired constant speed.

Mezzo piano (mp)   Moderately soft.
   Example   Ravel, *Bolero;* p 459; LO 1d; side 13, band 4; CD 7 ⃞13⃞; 1:47

Mezzo forte (mf)   Moderately loud.
   Example   Ravel, *Bolero;* p 459; LO 2d; side 13, band 4; CD 7 ⃞15⃞; 5:48

Microtone   Interval smaller than a half step.

Middle C   The note C nearest to the center of the piano keyboard, notated as the pitch on the ledger line below the treble clef and above the bass clef.

Minimalist music   Music characterized by steady pulse, clear tonality, and insistent repetition of short melodic patterns; its dynamic level, texture, and harmony tend to stay constant for fairly long stretches of time, creating a trancelike or hypnotic effect; developed in the 1960s.

Minimalist music (Continued.)
Example   Adams, *Nixon in China,* Act I, scene 2; p 548; side 15, band 6; CD 8 ⬚12⬚

Minor key   Music based on a minor scale.
Examples   Chopin, Prelude in C Minor for Piano; p 8; side 1, band 2; CD 1 ⬚5⬚
Contrast between minor and major keys is illustrated in Bizet, *L'Arlésienne* Suite No. 2;
p 69; LO 1, 2; side 1, band 10; CD 1 ⬚26⬚ and ⬚28⬚
Clara Schumann, Romance in G Minor for Violin and Piano; p 324; LO 1, 2; side 9,
band 3; CD 5 ⬚2⬚ and ⬚7⬚
Smetana, *The Moldau;* p 369; LO 2, 8; side 11, band 1; CD 6 ⬚2⬚ and ⬚7⬚

Minor scale   Series of seven tones within an octave, with an eighth tone repeating
the first tone an octave higher, composed of a specific pattern of whole and half
steps; the half step between the second and third tones is characteristic.
Example   Berlioz, *Fantastic Symphony,* 4th mvt, *March to the Scaffold,* downward minor
scale at opening of first theme; p 352; side 10, band 1; CD 5 ⬚29⬚ ; 0:27

Minuet   See *minuet and trio.*

Minuet and trio (minuet)   Compositional form—derived from a dance—in three
parts: minuet (A) trio (B) minuet (A). Often employed as the third movement of
classical symphonies, string quartets, and other works, it is in triple meter, ($\frac{3}{4}$ time),
and usually in a moderate tempo.
Examples   Mozart, *Eine kleine Nachtmusik,* 3d mvt; p 218; side 5, band 2; CD 3 ⬚7⬚
Mozart, Symphony No. 40 in G minor, 3d mvt; p 255; side 6, band 4; CD 3 ⬚40⬚

Moderato   Moderate tempo.
Example   Tchaikovsky, *Nutcracker* Suite, *Dance of the Reed Pipes;* p 73; side 1,
band 11; CD 1 ⬚31⬚

Modified strophic form   Form in which two or more stanzas of poetry are set to the
same music while other stanzas have new music; found in art songs of the Romantic period.
Example   Schubert, *Die Forelle;* p 312; side 8, band 6; CD 4 ⬚51⬚

Modulation   Shift from one key to another within the same piece.
Example   Mozart, Symphony No. 40 in G Minor, 4th mvt; modulation from G minor to
B flat major; p 212; LO exposition 2, 3; side 6, band 5; CD 3 ⬚44⬚ and ⬚45⬚

Monophonic texture   Single melodic line without accompaniment.
Example   *Alleluia: Vidiumus stellam,* p 90; side 1, band 13; CD 1 ⬚36⬚

Motet   Polyphonic choral work set to a sacred Latin text other than that of the
mass; one of the two main forms of sacred Renaissance music.
Example   Josquin Desprez, *Ave Maria;* p 110; side 2, band 3; CD 1 ⬚44⬚

Motive   Fragment of a theme, or short musical idea which is developed within a
composition.
Example   Beethoven, Symphony No. 5 in C Minor, 1st mvt, first four notes; p 276;
LO exposition 1*a;* side 7, band 1; CD 4 ⬚1⬚

Movement   Piece that sounds fairly complete and independent but is part of a
larger composition.

Musical texture   Number of layers of sound that are heard at once, what kinds of
layers they are, and how they are related to each other.

Musical (musical comedy) Type of American theater created to entertain through fusion of a dramatic script, acting, and spoken dialogue with music, singing, and dancing—and scenery, costumes, and spectacle.

> **Example** Bernstein, *West Side Story*, *Tonight* ensemble; p 594; side 16, band 6; CD 8 ⌷23⌷

Mute Device used to veil or muffle the tone of an instrument. In string instruments, the mute is a clamp which fits onto the bridge; in brass instruments, it is a funnel-shaped piece of wood, metal, or plastic which fits into the bell.

Nationalism Inclusion of folk songs, dances, legends, and other national material in a composition to associate it with the composer's homeland; characteristic of romantic music.

Natural sign Symbol used in notation of pitch to cancel a previous sharp or flat sign.

✓ *Neoclassicism* Musical style marked by emotional restraint, balance, and clarity, inspired by the forms and stylistic features of eighteenth-century music, found in many works from 1920 to 1950.

> **Example** Stravinsky, *Symphony of Psalms*, 1st mvt; p 475; side 13, band 2; CD 7 ⌷4⌷

New Orleans (Dixieland) jazz Jazz style in which the front line, or melodic instruments, improvise several contrasting melodic lines at once, supported by a rhythm section that clearly marks the beat and provides a background of chords; usually based on a march or church melody, a ragtime piece, a popular song, or the 12-bar blues.

> **Example** King Oliver's Creole Jazz Band, *Dippermouth Blues*; p 569; side 16, band 1; CD 8 ⌷18⌷

Nocturne In French, *night piece;* a composition, usually slow, lyrical, and intimate in character, often for piano solo.

> **Example** Chopin, Nocturne in E Flat Major, Op. 9, No. 2; p 328; side 9, band 5; CD 5 ⌷14⌷

Notation System of writing down music so that specific pitches and rhythms can be communicated.

Note In notation, a black or white oval to which a stem and flags can be added.

Oboe Double-reed woodwind instrument with a relatively high range, conical in shape with a small flared bell

> **Examples** Wagner, *Lohengrin*, Prelude to Act III; p 7; LO 2; side 1, band 1; CD 1 ⌷3⌷; 1:16
> Bartók, Concerto for Orchestra, 1st mvt; p 503; LO exposition 2a; side 14, band 5; CD 7 ⌷31⌷; 4:04
> Britten, *The Young Person's Guide to the Orchestra*; p 34; variation 2; supp sets, side 1, band 1; CD 1 ⌷8⌷; 2:28

Octave Interval between two tones in which the higher tone has twice the frequency of the lower tone.

> **Example** Arlen, *Over the Rainbow*, on opening word *Somewhere*; p 53; side 1, band 8; CD 1 ⌷22⌷

✓ *Opera* Drama that is sung to orchestral accompaniment, usually a large-scale composition employing vocal soloists, chorus, orchestra, costumes, and scenery.

Oratorio Large-scale composition for chorus, vocal soloists, and orchestra, usually set to a narrative text, but without acting, scenery, or costumes; often based on biblical stories.

Organ (pipe organ) Keyboard instrument with many sets of pipes controlled from two or more keyboards, including a pedal keyboard played by the organist's feet. The keys control valves from which air is blown across or through openings in the pipes. (The *electric organ* is an electronic instrument that is sometimes designed to imitate the sound of a pipe organ.)
  Example Bach, Organ Fugue in G Minor; p 144; side 2, band 10; CD 1 64

Organ point See *pedal point*.

Organum Medieval polyphony that consists of Gregorian chant and one or more additional melodic lines.
  Example Perotin, *Alleluia: Nativitas*; p 96; side 2, band 1; CD 1 40

Ostinato Motive or phrase that is repeated persistently at the same pitch, used in twentieth-century music to stabilize a group of pitches.
  Examples Ravel, *Bolero*; p 459; side 13, band 4; CD 7 12
  Stravinsky, *Symphony of Psalms*, 1st mvt, accompanying the opening words, *Exaudi orationem meum, Domine*; p 475; side 13, band 2; CD 7 4

Overture (prelude) Short musical composition, purely orchestral, which opens an opera and sets the overall dramatic mood. Orchestral introductions to later acts of an opera are called *preludes*.

Passacaglia See *ground bass*.

Pedal point (organ point) Single tone, usually in the bass, which is held while the other voices produce a series of changing harmonies against it; often found in fugues.

Pentatonic scale Scale made up of five different tones, used in folk music and music of the far east.
  Example Debussy, *Voiles*; p 455; LO 2; supp sets, side 8, band 1; CD 4 24; 2:15

Percussion instrument Instrument of definite or indefinite pitch whose sound is produced by striking by hand, or with a stick or hammer, or by shaking or rubbing.

Performer Person who plays or sings music.

Phrase Part of a melody.
  Example Arlen, *Over the Rainbow*, from the opening to the word *high*; p 53; side 1, band 8; CD 1 22

Pianissimo (pp) As softly as possible.
  Examples Haydn, Symphony No. 94 *(Surprise)*, mvt 2; p 215; LO theme, section a repeated; side 4, band 9; CD 3 1
  Chopin, Prelude in C Minor for Piano; p 8; LO 3; side 1, band 2; CD 1 7; 0:54

Piano Widely used keyboard instrument of great range and versatility, whose sound is produced by felt-covered hammers striking against steel strings.
  Examples Beethoven, Piano Sonata in C Minor, Op. 13 *(Pathétique)*; p 271; side 8, band 2; CD 4 30
  Chopin, Nocturne in E♭ Major; p 328; side 9, band 5; CD 5 14

Piano (p)   Soft.
   Examples   Wagner, *Lohengrin*, Prelude to Act III; p 7; LO 2; side 1, band 1; CD 1 ⟨3⟩; 1:16
   Stravinsky, *Firebird Suite*, Finale; p 8; LO 1a; side 1, band 3; CD 1 ⟨8⟩

Piccolo   Smallest woodwind instrument, having the highest range; a smaller version of the flute.
   Example   Sousa, *Stars and Stripes Forever*; p 36; LO 5; side 1, band 5; CD 1 ⟨19⟩; 1:55

Pipe organ   See *organ.*

Pitch   Relative highness or lowness of a sound.

Pitch range   Distance between the highest and lowest tones that a given voice or instrument can produce.

Pizzicato   Means of playing a string instrument by which the strings are plucked, usually with a finger of the right hand.
   Example   Tchaikovsky, *Nutcracker* Suite, *Dance of the Reed Pipes*, p 73; LO 1a–b; side 1, band 11; CD 1 ⟨31⟩

Polonaise   Composition in triple meter with a stately character, often for piano solo; originally a Polish court dance.
   Example   Chopin, Polonaise in A flat Major Op. 53; p 330; side 9, band 4; CD 5 ⟨10⟩

Polychoral motet   Motet for two or more choirs, often including groups of instruments.
   Example   Giovanni Gabrieli, *Plaudite;* p 123; supp sets, side 1, band 5; CD 1 ⟨33⟩

Polychord   Combination of two chords sounded at the same time, used in twentieth-century music.

Polyphonic texture   Performance of two or more melodic lines of relatively equal interest at the same time.
   Examples   Bach, Organ Fugue in G Minor, illustrates polyphonic texture based on imitation; p 144; side 2, band 10; CD 1 ⟨64⟩
   Bach, Cantata No. 140, 4th mvt, starting with entry of tenors, illustrates polyphonic texture based on the simultaneous presentation of different melodies; p 181; side 3, band 4; CD 2 ⟨13⟩

Polyrhythm   Use of two or more contrasting and independent rhythms at the same time, often found in twentieth-century music.
   Example   Stravinsky, *Petrushka*, opening scene; p 468; LO 1d; supp sets, side 7, band 1; CD 4 ⟨2⟩; 0:29

Polytonality   Approach to pitch organization using two or more keys at one time, often found in twentieth-century music.

Postlude   Concluding section; the section at the end of an art song which sums up its mood, played by the piano alone.
   Example   Robert Schumann, *Im wunderschönen Monat Mai;* p 319; side 9, band 1; CD 5 ⟨1⟩

Prelude   (1) Short piece usually serving to introduce a fugue or other composition; a short piece for piano. (2) See *overture.*
   Example   Chopin, Prelude in E Minor for Piano; p 58; side 1, band 9; CD 1 ⟨25⟩

Prestissimo   As fast a tempo as possible.
Example   Beethoven, String Quartet in C Minor, Op. 18, No. 4, 4th mvt; p 220; LO 7; side 8, band 1; CD 4 $\boxed{29}$; 3:31

Presto   Very fast tempo.

Primitivism   Evocation of primitive power through insistent rhythms and percussive sounds.
Example   Stravinsky, *The Rite of Spring, Sacrificial Dance;* p 474; side 13, band 1; CD 7 $\boxed{1}$

Program   Explanatory comments specifying the story, scene, or idea associated with program music.

Program music   Instrumental music associated with a story, poem, idea, or scene, often found in romantic music.

Program symphony   Symphony (a composition for orchestra in several movements) related to a story, idea, or scene, in which each movement usually has a descriptive title; often found in romantic music.
Example   Berlioz, *Fantastic Symphony;* p 349; side 10, bands 1 and 2; CD 5 $\boxed{28}$, $\boxed{32}$.

Progression   Series of chords.

Prompter   Person who gives cues and reminds singers of their words or pitches during an opera performance. The prompter is located in a box just over the edge of center stage, which conceals him or her from the audience.

Quadruple meter   Pattern of 4 beats to the measure.
Examples   Chopin, Prelude in C Minor for Piano; p 8; side 1, band 2; CD 1 $\boxed{5}$
Vivaldi, *La Primavera (Spring),* Concerto for Violin and String Orchestra, 1st mvt; p 162; side 2, band 9; CD 1 $\boxed{59}$

Quadruple stop   See *stop.*

Quintuple meter   Pattern of 5 beats to the measure.

Quotation music   Works which make extensive use of quotations from earlier music; common since the mid-1960s.
Example   Zwilich, *Concerto Grosso 1985,* 1st mvt; p 545; side 15, band 5; CD 8 $\boxed{10}$

Raga   Pattern of notes comprising a melodic framework used in the creation of an improvisation, characteristic of Indian classical music.
Example   Shankar, *Maru-Bihag;* p 631; side 16, band 9; CD 8 $\boxed{27}$

Ragtime   Style of composed piano music, generally in duple meter with a moderate march tempo, in which the pianist's right hand plays a highly syncopated melody while the left hand maintains the beat with an "oom-pah" accompaniment. Ragtime was developed primarily by African American pianists and flourished from the 1890s to about 1915.
Example   Joplin, *Maple Leaf Rag;* p 561; side 15, band 7; CD 8 $\boxed{13}$

Range   See *pitch range.*

Recapitulation   Third section of a sonata-form movement, in which the first theme, bridge, second theme, and concluding section are presented more or less as they were in the exposition, with one crucial difference: all the principal material is now in the tonic key.

Recapitulation (Continued.)
Example Mozart, Symphony No. 40 in G Minor, mvt 4; p 212; LO recapitulation; side 6, band 5; CD 3 [48] ; 3:14

Recitative Vocal line in an opera, oratorio, or cantata that imitates the rhythms and pitch fluctuations of speech, often serving to lead into an aria.
Example Mozart, *Don Giovanni*, introduction; p 245; side 5, band 4; CD 3 [20] ; 5:19

Recorder Family of woodwind instruments whose sound is produced by blowing into a "whistle" mouthpiece, usually made of wood or plastic.
Example Andrea Gabrieli, Ricercar in the Twelfth Mode; p 120; side 2, band 5; CD 1 [48]

Reed Very thin piece of cane, used in woodwind instruments to produce sound as it is set into vibration by a stream of air.

Register Part of the total range of an instrument or voice. The tone color of the instrument or voice may vary with the register in which it is played or sung.

Repetition Reiteration of a phrase, section, or entire movement, often used to create a sense of unity.

Requiem Mass for the dead.
Example Mozart, Requiem, *Dies irae;* p 262; side 5, band 2; CD 3 [27]

Resolution Progression from a dissonance to a consonance.

Rest In notation of rhythm, a symbol to indicate the duration of silence in the music.

Retrograde Variation of a fugue subject in which the subject is presented by beginning with its last note and proceeding backward to the first.

Rhythm Ordered flow of music through time; the pattern of durations of notes and silences in music.

Rhythm section Instruments in a jazz ensemble which maintain the beat, add rhythmic interest, and provide supporting harmonies. The rhythm section is usually made up of piano, plucked double bass, percussion, and sometimes banjo or guitar.
Example Parker, *KoKo;* p 579; side 16, band 4; CD 8 [21]

Ricercar Polyphonic instrumental composition which makes extensive use of imitation, often found in Renaissance music.
Example Andrea Gabrieli, Ricercar in the Twelfth Mode; p 120; side 2, band 5; CD 1 [48]

Riff In jazz, a short repeated phrase that may be an accompaniment or a melody.
Example Berlin, *Blue Skies;* p 573; side 16, band 2; CD 8 [19]

Ritardando Becoming slower.
Examples Liszt, *Transcendental Étude* No. 10 in F Minor; p 335; LO 5; side 9, band 6; CD 5 [21] ; 2:04
Tchaikovsky, *Romeo and Juliet;* p 365; side 10, band 3; CD 5 [40] ; 6:19

Ritornello In Italian, *refrain;* a repeated section of music usually played by the full orchestra, or tutti, in baroque compositions.

Ritornello (Continued.)

Examples Bach, *Brandenburg* Concerto No. 5 in D Major, mvt 1; p 138; LO 1*a*; side 3, band 1; CD 2 [1]

Vivaldi, *La Primavera (Spring)*, Concerto for Violin and String Orchestra, mvt 1; p 162; LO 1*a*; side 2, band 9; CD 1 [59]

Bach, Cantata No. 140, mvt 1; p 179; side 3, band 4, CD 2 [10]

Ritornello form Compositional form usually employed in the baroque concerto grosso, in which the tutti plays a ritornello, or refrain, alternating with one or more soloists playing new material.

Examples Bach, *Brandenburg* Concerto No. 5 in D Major, mvt 1; p 138; side 3, band 1; CD 2 [1]

Vivaldi, *La Primavera (Spring)*, Concerto for Violin and String Orchestra, mvt 1; p 162; side 2, band 9; CD 1 [59]

Rock First called *rock and roll*, a style of popular vocal music which developed in the 1950s, characterized by a hard, driving beat and featuring electric guitar accompaniment and heavily amplified sound.

Romance In nineteenth-century music, a short lyrical piece for piano or solo instrument with piano accompaniment.

Example Clara Schumann, Romance in G Minor for Violin and Piano; p 324; side 9, band 3; CD 5 [5]

Rondo Compositional form featuring a main theme (A) which returns several times in alternation with other themes, such as A B A C A and A B A C A B A. Rondo is often the form of the last movement in classical symphonies, string quartets, and sonatas.

Examples Beethoven, String Quartet in C Minor, Op. 18, No. 4, mvt 4; p 220; side 8, band 1; CD 4 [26]

Beethoven, Piano Sonata in C Minor, Op. 13 *(Pathétique)*, mvt 3; p 274; side 8, band 4; CD 4 [41]

Rubato Slight holding back or pressing forward of tempo to intensify the expression of the music, often used in romantic music.

Example Chopin, Nocturne in E Flat Major, Op. 9, No. 2; p 328; side 9, band 5; CD 5 [16]; 0:51

Saxophone Family of single-reed woodwind instruments.

Examples Parker, *KoKo*, p 579; LO 2; side 16, band 4; CD 8 [21]

Ravel, *Bolero*; p 459; LO 2*c*; side 13, band 4; CD 7 [15]

Scale Series of pitches arranged in order from low to high or high to low.

Scherzo Compositional form in three parts (A B A), sometimes used as the third movement in classical and romantic symphonies, string quartets, and other works. A scherzo is usually in triple meter, with a faster tempo than a minuet.

Examples Beethoven, Symphony No. 5 in C Minor, mvt 3; p 281; side 7, band 3; CD 4 [15]

Dvořák, Symphony No. 9 *(From the New World)*, mvt 3; p 376; supp sets, side 5, band 3; CD 3 [13]

Score Notation showing all the parts of a musical ensemble, with a separate staff for each part, and with simultaneously sounded notes aligned vertically; used by the conductor.

Secco recitative   Speechlike melody that is sung by a solo voice accompanied only by a basso continuo.
  Example   Mozart, *Don Giovanni*, introduction; p 241; side 5, band 4; CD 3 [20]; 5:19

Septuple meter   Pattern of 7 beats to the measure.
  Example   Brubeck, *Unsquare Dance*; p 43; side 1, band 7; CD 1 [21]

Sequence   In a melody, the immediate repetition of a melodic pattern on a higher or lower pitch.
  Examples   Arlen, *Over the Rainbow*, starting with *land that I heard of*; p 53; side 1, band 8; CD 1 [22]
  Mozart, Symphony No. 40 in G Minor, mvt 1; p 252; LO 1*a*; side 6, band 2; CD 3 [28]
  Beethoven, Symphony No. 5 in C Minor, mvt 1; p 276; LO 1*a*; side 7, band 1; CD 4 [1]

Serenade   Instrumental composition, light in mood, usually meant for evening entertainment.
  Example   Mozart, *Eine kleine Nachtmusik*, 3d mvt; p 218; side 5, band 2; CD 3 [7]

Serialism   Method of composing which uses an ordered group of musical elements to organize rhythm, dynamics, and tone color, as well as pitch; developed in the mid-twentieth century.
  Example   Babbitt, Composition for Synthesizer; p 540; side 15, band 3; CD 8 [8]

Series   See *tone row*.

Set   See *tone row*.

Sextuple meter   Pattern of 6 beats to the measure.
  Examples   Mozart, Symphony No. 40 in G Minor, 2d mvt; p 254; side 6, band 3; CD 3 [37]
  Bach, Suite No. 3, gigue; p 174; side 4, band 3; CD 2 [21]

Sharp sign   Symbol which notates a pitch one half step higher than the pitch that would otherwise be indicated—for example, the next higher black key on the piano.

Side drum   See *snare drum*.

Single-reed woodwinds   Instruments whose sound is produced by a single piece of cane, or reed, fastened over a hole in the mouthpiece, which vibrates when the player blows into it.

Sitar   Most popular chordophone of north India. It is a long-necked lute with nineteen to twenty-three movable frets. Seven strings are plucked and nine to thirteen strings vibrate sympathetically.
  Example   Shankar, *Maru-Bihag*; p 631; side 16, band 9; CD 8 [27]

Snare drum (side drum)   Percussion instrument of indefinite pitch, in the shape of a cylinder with a stretched skin at either end. A "snare" of gut or metal is stretched below the lower skin and produces a rattling sound when the drum is struck.
  Example   Ravel, *Bolero*; p 459; LO 1; side 13, band 4; CD 7 [12]

Sonata   In baroque music, an instrumental composition in several movements for one to eight players. In music after the baroque period, an instrumental composition usually in several movements for one or two players.
  Example   Corelli, Trio Sonata in E Minor; p 159; supp sets, side 2 bands 1–4; CD 1 [34] to [37]

√ ***Sonata*** (Continued.)

   Example   Beethoven, Sonata in C Minor, Op. 13 *(Pathétique); p 271; side 8, bands 2–4;* CD 4 30 , 37 , 41

√ ***Sonata form***   Form of a single movement, consisting of three main sections: the exposition, where the themes are presented; the development, where themes are treated in new ways; and the recapitulation, where the themes return. A concluding section, the coda, often follows the recapitulation.

   Examples   Mozart, Symphony No. 40 in G Minor, 4th mvt; p 212; side 6, band 5; CD 4 43
   Beethoven, Symphony No. 5 in C Minor, 1st mvt; p 276; side 7, band 1; CD 4 1

Sonata-rondo   Compositional form that combines the repeating theme of rondo form with a development section similar to that in sonata form, outlined A B A–development–A B A.

   Examples   Haydn, Trumpet Concerto, 3d mvt; p 234; side 4, band 9; CD 2 37
   Haydn, Symphony No. 94 in G Major *(Surprise)*, 4th mvt; p 233; supp sets, side 3, band 3; CD 2 12

Song cycle   Group of art songs unified by a story line that runs through their poems, or by musical ideas linking the songs; often found in romantic music.

Soprano   Female voice of high range.

   Example   Gershwin, *I Got Rhythm; p 42; side 1, band 6; CD 1* 20
   Purcell, *Dido and Aeneas, Dido's Lament; p 156; side 2, band 8; CD 1* 57

Sound   Vibrations which are transmitted, usually through air, to the eardrum, which sends impulses to the brain.

Sprechstimme   In German, *speech-voice;* a style of vocal performance halfway between speaking and singing, typical of Schoenberg and his followers.

   Example   Berg, *Wozzeck,* Act 3, scene 4; p 491; side 14, band 3; CD 7 20

Staccato   Short, detached manner of performing a melody.

   Examples   Tchaikovsky, *Nutcracker* Suite, *Dance of the Reed Pipes; p 73; LO 1b;* side 1, band 11; CD 1 31
   Haydn, Symphony No. 94 in G Major *(Surprise)*, 2d mvt; p 215; LO theme, section a; side 5, band 1; CD 3 1

Staff   In notation, a set of five horizontal lines between or on which notes are positioned.

Stem   Vertical line on a note indicating how long that note is to be held relative to the notes around it.

Step   Interval between two adjacent tones in the scale.

Stop (double, triple, quadruple)   Means of playing a string instrument by which the bow is drawn across two, three, or four strings at the same, or almost the same, time.

Stretto   Compositional procedure used in fugues, in which a subject is imitated before it is completed; one voice tries to catch the other.

String instrument   Instrument whose sound is produced by the vibration of strings.

String quartet Composition employing two violins, a viola, and a cello; usually consisting of four movements. (*Also,* the four instrumentalists.)

Examples Beethoven, String Quartet in C Minor, Op. 18, No. 4, 4th mvt; p 220; side 8, band 1; CD 4 26
Beethoven, String Quartet in F Major, Op. 18, No. 1, mvt 1; p 286; supp sets, side 4, band 1; CD 2 23

Strophic form Vocal form in which the same music is repeated for each stanza of a poem.

Example Robert Schumann, *Im wunderschönen Monat Mai*; p 319; side 9, band 1; CD 5 1

Style Characteristic way of using melody, rhythm, tone, color, dynamics, harmony, texture, and form in music.

Subdominant Fourth note (*fa*) of the scale, or the triad (chord) based on this note.

Example Smith, *Lost Your Head Blues*, repetition of the words *I was with you baby*; p 564; side 15, band 8; CD 8 17

Subject Theme of a fugue.

Example Bach, Organ Fugue in G Minor; p 144; LO 1a; side 2, band 10; CD 1 64

Suite In baroque music, a set of dance-inspired movements that are all written in the same key but differ in tempo, meter, and character.

Example Bach, Suite No. 3 in D Major; p 173; side 4, bands 1–3; CD 2 17, 19, 21

Swing band Typically, a large band made up of fourteen or fifteen musicians grouped in three sections: saxophones, brasses, and rhythm. They play swing, a jazz style which was developed in the 1920s and flourished between 1935 and 1945.

Example Ellington, *Concerto for Cootie*; p 575; side 16, band 3; CD 8 20

√ **Symphonic poem (tone poem)** Programmatic composition for orchestra in one movement, which may have a traditional form (such as sonata or rondo) or an original, irregular form.

Symphony Orchestral composition, usually in four movements, typically lasting between 20 and 45 minutes, exploiting the expanded range of tone color and dynamics of the orchestra.

Syncopation Accenting of a note at an unexpected time, as between two beats or on a weak beat. Syncopation is a major characteristic of jazz.

Examples Gershwin, *I Got Rhythm*; p 42; side 1, band 6; CD 1 20
Brubeck, *Unsquare Dance*; p 43; side 1, band 7; CD 1 21
Mozart, Symphony No. 40, 3d mvt, third note of melody; p 255; side 6, band 4; CD 3 40
Joplin, *Maple Leaf Rag*; p 561; side 15, band 7; CD 8 13

Synthesizer System of electronic components which can generate, modify, and control sound; used to compose music and to perform it.

Example Babbitt, Composition for Synthesizer; p 540; side 15, band 3; CD 8 8

Tabla Pair of single-headed drums in which the right-hand drum is generally tuned to the tonic note and the left-hand drum functions as a bass drum; the most important percussion instrument in north Indian music.

Example Shankar, *Maru-Bihag*; p 631; side 16, band 9; CD 8 27

Tala Repeated cycle of beats organizing the rhythm in Indian classical music.

Example Shankar, *Maru-Bihag*; p 631; side 16, band 9; CD 8 27

Tambourine Percussion instrument of indefinite pitch, consisting of a skin stretched across a shallow cylinder, with small circular plates set into the cylinder which jingle when the skin is struck or the cylinder is shaken.
 Example Bizet, *L'Arlésienne* Suite No. 2, *Farandole;* p 69; LO 2a, introducing dance theme in woodwinds; side 1, band 10; CD 1 ⟨28⟩; 0:33

Tambura Long-necked lute with four metal strings that are plucked in succession continually; the main drone instrument in Indian music.

Tam-tam See *gong.*

Tape studio Studio with tape recorders and other equipment used to create electronic music by modifying and combining recorded sounds.
 Example Varèse, *Poème électronique;* p 538; side 15, band 2; CD 8 ⟨7⟩

Tempo Basic pace of the music.

Tempo indication Words, usually at the beginning of a piece of music, often in Italian, which specify the pace at which the music should be played.

Tenor Male voice of high range.
 Examples Handel, *Messiah, Ev'ry Valley;* p 192; side 4, band 6; CD 2 ⟨27⟩
 Puccini, *La Bohème, Che gelida manina;* p 405; side 12, band 1; CD 6 ⟨17⟩; 4:14

Terraced dynamics Abrupt alternation between loud and soft dynamic levels; characteristic of baroque music.
 Example Vivaldi, *La Primavera (Spring)*, Concerto for Violin and String Orchestra, mvt 1; p 162; LO 1a; side 2, band 9; CD 1 ⟨59⟩

Thematic transformation Alteration of the character of a theme by means of changes in dynamics, orchestration, or rhythm, when it returns in a later movement or section; often found in romantic music.
 Examples Tchaikovsky, *Romeo and Juliet;* p 365; compare appearances of the love theme at LO exposition 3a and recapitulation 3a; side 10, band 3; CD 5 ⟨41⟩ and ⟨46⟩; 6:58 and 12:58
 Berlioz, *Fantastic Symphony;* compare *idée fixe* in 1st mvt; p 350; supp sets, side 4, band 3; CD 2 ⟨32⟩; in 4th mvt; p 352; basic set, side 10, band 1; CD 5 ⟨31⟩; 6:19; and in 5th mvt; p 353, basic set, side 10, band 2; CD 5 ⟨33⟩; 1:47
 Liszt, *Transcendental Étude* in F Minor; p 335; compare lyrical theme at LO 2a and processional theme at LO 3; side 9, band 6; CD 5 ⟨18⟩ and ⟨19⟩; 0:42 and 1:14

Theme Melody which serves as the starting point for an extended piece of music.
 Example Mozart, Symphony No. 40, mvt 1; p 212; LO 1a; side 6, band 2; CD 3 ⟨28⟩

Theme and variations Form in which a basic musical idea (the theme) is repeated over and over and is changed each time in melody, rhythm, harmony, dynamics, or tone color. Used either as an independent piece or as one movement of a larger work.
 Example Haydn, Symphony No. 94 in G Major *(Surprise)*, 2d mvt; p 215; side 5, band 1; CD 3 ⟨1⟩
 Schubert, Piano Quintet *(Trout)*, 4th mvt; p 314; side 8, band 7; CD 4 ⟨53⟩
 Copland, *Appalachian String*, section 7, theme and variations on *Simple Gifts;* p 523; side 15, band 1; CD 8 ⟨1⟩

Three-part form (A B A) Form that can be represented as statement (A); contrast (B); return of statement (A).
 Example Wagner, *Lohengrin*, Prelude to Act III; p 7; LO 1(A)–2(B)–3(A'); side 1, band 1; CD 1 ⟨1⟩

Three-part form   (Continued.)

Examples   Tchaikovsky, *Nutcracker* Suite, *Dance of the Reed Pipes;* p 73; side 1, band 11; CD 1 ⸢31⸣
Mozart, Symphony No. 40, mvt 3; p 255; side 6, band 4; CD 3 ⸢40⸣
Clara Schumann, Romance in G Minor for Violin and Piano; p 324; side 9, band 3; CD 5 ⸢2⸣

Through-composed form   Vocal form in which there is new music for each stanza of a poem.

Example   Schubert, *Erlkönig (The Erlking);* p 309; side 8, band 5; CD 4 ⸢45⸣

Tie   In notation of rhythm, an arc between two notes of the same pitch indicating that the second note should not be played but should be added to the duration of the first.

Timbre   See *tone color.*

Time signature (meter signature)   Two numbers, one above the other, appearing at the beginning of a staff or the start of a piece, indicating the meter of the piece.

Timpani (kettledrums)   Percussion instruments of definite pitch, shaped like large kettles with calfskin or plastic stretched across the tops, played with soft padded mallets.

Examples   Stravinsky, *Firebird* Suite, Finale; p 8; LO 2a; side 1, band 3; CD 1 ⸢9⸣; 1:27
Tchaikovsky, *Romeo and Juliet;* p 365; LO coda 1; side 10, band 3; CD 5 ⸢47⸣; 15:53
Britten, *The Young Person's Guide to the Orchestra;* p 34; LO variation 13a; supp sets, side 1, band 1; CD 1 ⸢19⸣; 11:56

Tonality   See *key.*

Tone   Sound that has a definite pitch, or frequency.

Tone cluster   Chord made up of tones only a half step or a whole step apart, used in twentieth-century music.

Example   Penderecki, *Threnody for the Victims of Hiroshima;* p 537; LO 1a; supp sets, side 8, band 3; CD 4 ⸢28⸣

Tone color (timbre)   Quality of sound that distinguishes one instrument or voice from another.

Tone-color melody   Succession of varying tone colors serving as a musical idea in a composition, used by Schoenberg and his followers.

Example   Webern, *Five Pieces for Orchestra,* 3d piece; p 497; side 14, band 4; CD 7 ⸢25⸣

Tone poem   See *symphonic poem.*

Tone row (set, series)   Particular ordering of the twelve chromatic tones, from which all pitches in a twelve-tone composition are derived.

Example   Schoenberg, *A Survivor trom Warsaw,* to the Hebrew words of *Shema Yisroel;* p 487; side 14, band 2; CD 7 ⸢19⸣

Tonic   See *keynote.*

Tonic chord   Triad built on the first, or tonic, note of the scale, serving as the main chord of a piece and usually beginning and ending it.

Tonic chord (Continued.)
   Example Chopin, Prelude in C Minor, opening and concluding chords; p 8; side 1, band 2; CD 1 ⑤

Tonic key (home key) Central key of a piece of music, usually both beginning and ending the piece, regardless of how many other keys are included.

Transition See *bridge*.

Treble clef Notation of a staff to indicate relatively high pitch ranges, such as those played by a pianist's right hand.

Tremolo Rapid repetition of a tone, produced in string instruments by quick up-and-down strokes of the bow.
   Examples Stravinsky, *Firebird* Suite, Finale; p 8; LO 1*a* (tremolo in string accompaniment); side 1, band 3; CD 1 ⑧
   Bartók, Concerto for Orchestra, 1st mvt; p 503; LO slow introduction 1*a–b*,; side 14, band 5; CD 7 ①

Triad Most basic of chords, consisting of three alternate tones of the scale, such as *do, mi, sol.*

Triangle Percussion instrument of indefinite pitch, consisting of a triangular length of metal suspended from a hook or cord, played by striking with a metal rod.
   Example Smetana, *The Moldau;* p 369; LO 4*a*; side 11, band 1; CD 6 ④

Trill Musical ornament consisting of the rapid alternation of two tones that are a whole or half step apart.
   Example Vivaldi, *La Primavera (Spring)*, Concerto for Violin and String Orchestra, mvt 1; p 162; LO 1*b*; side 2, band 9; CD 1 ⑥⓪; 0:30

Triple meter Pattern of 3 beats to the measure.
   Examples Purcell, *Dido and Aeneas, Dido's Lament;* p 156; side 2, band 8; CD 1 �57㊉
   Mozart, *Eine kleine Nachtmusik*, 3d mvt; p 218; side 5, band 2; CD 3 ⑦
   Verdi, *Rigoletto, La Donna è mobile;* p 393; side 11, band 4; CD 6 ⑬

Triple stop See *stop*.

Triplet In notation of rhythm, three notes of equal duration grouped within a curved line with the numeral 3, lasting only as long as two notes of this same length normally would last.

Trio sonata Baroque composition which has three melodic lines: two high ones, each played by one instrument; and a basso continuo, played by two instruments.
   Example Corelli, Trio Sonata in E Minor; p 159; supp sets, side 2, bands 1–4; CD 1 ㉞, ㉟, ㊱, ㊲

Trombone Brass instrument of moderately low range, whose tube is an elongated loop with a movable slide, commonly used in symphony orchestras, bands, and jazz ensembles.
   Examples Lillian Hardin Armstrong, *Hotter Than That;* p 9; LO 6*a*; side 1, band 4; CD 1 ⑭; 2:17
   Bartók, Concerto for Orchestra, 1st mvt; p 503; LO exposition, 1*b*; side 14, band 5; CD 7 ㉚; 3:48
   Britten, *The Young Person's Guide to the Orchestra*, variation 12; p 34; supp sets, side 1, band 1; CD 1 ⑱; 10:58

Trumpet Brass instrument with the highest range, commonly used in symphony orchestras, bands, and jazz and rock groups.
Examples Lillian Hardin Armstrong, *Hotter Than That;* p 9; LO 2; side 1, band 4; CD 1 [10]
Haydn; Trumpet Concerto, 3d mvt; p 234; side 4, band 9; CD 2 [37]

Tuba Largest brass instrument, having the lowest range, commonly used in symphony orchestras and bands.
Example Britten, *The Young Person's Guide to the Orchestra*, variation 12; p 34; supp sets, side 1, band 1; CD 1 [18] ; 10:58

Tutti In Italian, *all;* the full orchestra, or a large group of musicians contrasted with a smaller group; often heard in baroque music.
Example Bach, *Brandenburg* Concerto No. 5 in D Major, 1st mvt; p 138; LO 1a; side 3, band 1; CD 2 [1]

12-bar blues In vocal blues and jazz, a harmonic framework that is 12 bars in length, usually involving only three basic chords: tonic (I), subdominant (IV), and dominant (V).
Examples Smith, *Lost Your Head Blues;* p 564; side 15, band 8; CD 8 [17]
Oliver, *Dippermouth Blues;* p 569; side 16, band 1; CD 8 [18]

Twelve-tone system Method of composing in which all pitches of a composition are derived from a special ordering of the twelve chromatic tones (tone row or set); developed by Schoenberg in the early 1920s.
Example Schoenberg, *A Survivor from Warsaw;* p 487; side 14, band 2; CD 7 [18]

Two-part form (A B) Form that can be represented as statement (A) and counterstatement (B).
Examples Bach, Suite No. 2 in B Minor, *Badinerie;* p 75; side 1, band 12; CD 1 [34]
Bach, Suite No. 3, air, bourée, gigue; p 173; side 4, bands 1, 2, 3; CD 2 [17] , [19] , [21]
Haydn, Symphony No. 94 in G Major *(Surprise),* 2d mvt, theme; p 215; LO theme; side 5, band 1; CD 3 [1]

Unison Performance of a single melodic line by more than one instrument or voice at the same pitch or in different octaves.
Examples Handel, *Messiah, Hallelujah* Chorus, to the words *For the Lord God;* p 194; side 4, band 8; CD 2 [32]
Beethoven, Symphony No. 5 in C Minor, 1st mvt; p 276; LO 1a; side 7, band 1; CD 4 [1]

Upbeat Unaccented pulse preceding the downbeat.
Examples Vivaldi, *La Primavera (Spring)*, Concerto for Violin and String Orchestra, 1st mvt, opening note; p 162; LO 1a; side 2, band 9; CD 1 [59]
Chopin, Nocturne in E Flat Major, Op. 9, No. 2, opening note; p 328; side 9, band 5; CD 5 [14]

Variation Changing some features of a musical idea while retaining others.

Vibraphone Percussion instrument of definite pitch with metal bars, similar to the marimba, with tubular metal resonators driven by electronic impulses.

Vibrato Small fluctuations of pitch which make the tone warmer, produced in string instruments by rocking the left hand while it presses the string down.
Example Mendelssohn, Violin Concerto, 1st mvt 1; p 340; side 9, band 7; CD 5 [23]

Viola String instrument with a lower range than the violin and a higher range than the cello.
  Examples Schubert, Piano Quintet *(Trout)*, 4th mvt; p 314; LO variation 2; side 8, band 7; CD 4 55 ; 2:08
  Britten, *The Young Person's Guide to the Orchestra*, variation 6; p 34; supp sets, side 1, band 1; CD 1 12 ; 5:37

Violin String instrument with the highest range of the string family.
  Examples Clara Schumann, Romance in G Minor for Violin and Piano; p 324; side 9, band 3; CD 5 5
  Mendelssohn, Violin Concerto, 1st mvt 1; p 340; side 9, band 7; CD 5 23

Violoncello See *cello*.

Virtuoso Performing artist of extraordinary technical mastery.

Vivace Lively tempo.
  Example Wagner, *Lohengrin*, Prelude to Act III; p 7; side 1, band 1; CD 1 1

Voice categories of opera Voice ranges which include coloratura soprano, lyric soprano, dramatic soprano, lyric tenor, dramatic tenor, basso buffo, and basso profundo, among others.

Whole step Interval twice as large as the half step; for example, the interval between *do* and *re*.

Whole-tone scale Scale made up of six different tones, each a whole step away from the next, which conveys no definite sense of tonality; often found in the music of Debussy and his followers.
  Example Debussy, *Voiles*; p 455; LO 1a; supp sets, side 8, band 1; CD 4 21

Woodwind instrument Instrument whose sound is produced by vibrations of air in a tube; holes along the length of tube are opened and closed by the fingers, or by pads, to control the pitch.

Word painting Musical representation of specific poetic images—for example, a falling melodic line to accompany the word *descending*—often found in Renaissance and baroque music.
  Example Weelkes, *As Vesta Was Descending*; p 116; side 2, band 4; CD 1 47

Xylophone Percussion instrument of definite pitch, consisting of flat wooden bars set in a frame and played by striking with hard plastic or wooden hammers.
  Example Britten, *The Young Person's Guide to the Orchestra*, variation 13; p 34; supp sets, side 1, band 1; CD 1 21 ; 12:44

TONE COLOR AND
THE HARMONIC SERIES

What we perceive as a single musical tone is actually a mixture of a number of different tones heard at the same time. The pitches making up a single musical tone are called *harmonics* (or *partials*). To understand what harmonics are, recall that a musical tone is produced by a vibrating body, such as a string or a column of air.

A string vibrates not only in its entirety but also in segments such as halves, thirds, fourths, fifths, and so on. These vibrating segments produce faint tones that are higher in pitch than the *fundamental tone* (or first harmonic) produced by the string vibrating as a whole. The halves produce a tone twice the frequency of the fundamental tone, the thirds produce a tone three times the frequency of the fundamental tone, and so forth. The entire group of component pitches is called the *harmonic series*. Here are the first sixteen harmonics of the tone C.

(The seventh, eleventh, thirteenth, and fourteenth harmonics—indicated by black notes—are markedly out of tune with the scales used in western music.)

The color or timbre of a tone is determined by the number and relative intensity of its harmonics. For example, an oboe tone has almost all the harmonics, but a clarinet tone lacks the even-numbered harmonics.

String players can produce audible harmonics—high, whistlelike tones—by lightly touching the string at certain points. A light touch halfway along the length of a string produces the second harmonic, which is an octave higher than the fundamental tone.

KEY SIGNATURES

CHRONOLOGY

MIDDLE AGES (450–1450)		
Musicians	**Artists and Writers**	**Historical and Cultural Events**
		Sack of Rome by Vandals (455)
		Reign of Pope Gregory I (590–604)
		First Crusade (1096–1099)
Perotin (late twelfth century)		Beginning of Notre Dame Cathedral in Paris (1163)
		King John signs Magna Carta (1215)
	Dante (1265–1321)	
	Giotto (1266–1337)	
Guillaume de Machaut (c. 1300–1377)		
	Boccaccio (1313–1375)	
	Chaucer (c. 1343–1400)	Hundred Years' War (1337–1453)
		Black death (1348–1350)

RENAISSANCE (1450–1600)		
Musicians	**Artists and Writers**	**Historical and Cultural Events**
Guillaume Dufay (c. 1400–1474)		Fall of Constantinople (1453)
Josquin Desprez (c. 1440–1521)	Leonardo da Vinci (1452–1519)	Gutenberg Bible (1456)
		Columbus discovers America (1492)
	Michelangelo (1475–1564)	
	Raphael (1483–1520)	Martin Luther's ninety-five theses (1517)
	Titian (c. 1477–1576)	
	François Rabelais (c. 1494–c. 1553)	
Andrea Gabrieli (c. 1520–1586)		

670

Musicians	Artists and Writers	Historical and Cultural Events
Giovanni Pierluigi da Palestrina (c. 1525–1594)		Council of Trent (1545–1563)
Roland de Lassus (1532–1594)	Michel de Montaigne (1533–1592)	
William Byrd (1543–1623)		
Giovanni Gabrieli (c. 1555–1612)		
Thomas Morley (1557–1603)	Cervantes (1547–1616)	Elizabeth I, queen of England (1558–1603)
	William Shakespeare (1564–1616)	
		Spanish Armada defeated (1588)
Thomas Weelkes (1575–1623)		

BAROQUE (1600–1750)

Musicians	Artists and Writers	Historical and Cultural Events
		Jamestown founded (1607)
Claudio Monteverdi (1567–1643)		
	Peter Paul Rubens (1577–1640)	
Heinrich Schütz (1585–1672)		Thirty Years' War (1618–1648)
	Gian Lorenzo Bernini (1598–1680)	
	Rembrandt (1606–1669)	
	John Milton (1608–1674)	
Jean-Baptiste Lully (1632–1687)	Molière (1622–1673)	Louis XIV reigns in France (1643–1715)
	Baruch Spinoza (1632–1677)	
Arcangelo Corelli (1653–1713)		
Henry Purcell (c. 1659–1695)	Jonathan Swift (1667–1745)	Newton, *Principia Mathematica* (1687)
François Couperin (1668–1733)		
Antonio Vivaldi (1678–1741)		Louis XV reigns in France (1715–1774)
Johann Sebastian Bach (1685–1750)	Jean Antoine Watteau (1684–1721)	
George Frideric Handel (1685–1759)		

671

CLASSICAL (1750–1820)

Musicians	Artists and Writers	Historical and Cultural Events
	Voltaire (1694–1778)	Maria Theresa reigns in Austria (1740–1780)
		Frederick the Great reigns in Prussia (1740–1786)
	Benjamin Franklin (1706–1790)	Publication of the French *Encyclopedia* begins (1751)
Christoph Gluck (1714–1787)	Jean Jacques Rousseau (1712–1778)	
		Seven Years' War (1756–1763)
Carl Philipp Emanuel Bach (1714–1788)		Winckelmann's *History of the Art of Antiquity* (1764)
	Immanuel Kant (1724–1804)	
Joseph Haydn (1732–1809)		
	Goya (1746–1828)	
	Jacques Louis David (1748–1825)	
	Johann Wolfgang von Goethe (1749–1832)	Louis XVI reigns in France (1774–1792)
Wolfgang Amadeus Mozart (1756–1791)		American Declaration of Independence (1776)
Ludwig van Beethoven (1770–1827)		French Revolution begins (1789)
		Eli Whitney invents cotton gin (1792)
		Napoleon becomes first consul of France (1799)
		Battle of Waterloo (1815)

ROMANTIC (1820–1900)

Musicians	Artists and Writers	Historical and Cultural Events
	William Wordsworth (1770–1850)	
	J. M. W. Turner (1775–1851)	
Carl Maria von Weber (1786–1826)		
Gioacchino Rossini (1792–1868)		

Musicians	Artists and Writers	Historical and Cultural Events
Franz Schubert (1797–1828)	Heinrich Heine (1797–1856)	
	Eugène Delacroix (1798–1863)	
	Honoré de Balzac (1799–1850)	Revolutions in France, Belgium, Poland (1830)
Hector Berlioz (1803–1869)	Victor Hugo (1802–1885)	
	George Sand (1804–1876)	First Reform Bill in Britain (1832)
Felix Mendelssohn (1809–1847)	Edgar Allan Poe (1809–1849)	
Frédéric Chopin (1810–1849)		Revolutions of 1848; Marx and Engels, *The Communist Manifesto* (1848)
Robert Schumann (1810–1856)		
		Darwin's *Origin of Species* (1859)
Franz Liszt (1811–1886)		American Civil War (1861–1865)
	Charles Dickens (1812–1870)	
Richard Wagner (1813–1883)		Franco-Prussian War (1870)
Giuseppe Verdi (1813–1901)		
Clara Wieck Schumann (1819–1896)		
César Franck (1822–1890)	Fëdor Dostoevsky (1821–1881)	
Anton Bruckner (1824–1896)		
Bedřich Smetana (1824–1884)	Leo Tolstoy (1828–1910)	
	Emily Dickinson (1830–1886)	
Johannes Brahms (1833–1897)	Edouard Manet (1832–1883)	
Georges Bizet (1838–1875)	Paul Cézanne (1839–1906)	
Modest Mussorgsky (1839–1881)		
Peter Ilyich Tchaikovsky (1840–1893)	Claude Monet (1840–1926)	First group exhibition of impressionists in Paris (1874)
Antonin Dvořák (1841–1904)	Stéphane Mallarmé (1842–1898)	
John Philip Sousa (1854–1932)		
Giacomo Puccini (1858–1924)	Friedrich Nietzsche (1844–1900)	Bell invents telephone (1876)
Gustav Mahler (1860–1911)		
	Vincent Van Gogh (1853–1890)	
Richard Strauss (1864–1949)		Spanish-American War (1898)

TWENTIETH CENTURY

Musicians	Artists and Writers	Historical and Cultural Events
		Freud, *The Psychopathology of Everyday Life* (1904)
Claude Debussy (1862–1918)	Wassily Kandinsky (1866–1944)	Einstein, special theory of relativity (1905)
Scott Joplin (1868–1917)		
	Henri Matisse (1869–1954)	
	Marcel Proust (1871–1922)	
Arnold Schoenberg (1874–1951)	Gertrude Stein (1874–1946)	
		World War I (1914–1918)
Charles Ives (1874–1954)		Russian Revolution begins (1917)
Maurice Ravel (1875–1937)		
Béla Bartók (1881–1945)	Pablo Picasso (1881–1973)	
	James Joyce (1882–1941)	Beginning of Great Depression (1929)
	Virginia Woolf (1882–1945)	
Igor Stravinsky (1882–1971)		
	Franz Kafka (1883–1924)	Franklin D. Roosevelt inaugurated (1933)
Anton Webern (1883–1945)		Hitler Chancellor of Germany (1933)
Edgard Varèse (1883–1965)		
Alban Berg (1885–1935)		
	T. S. Eliot (1888–1965)	World War II (1939–1945)
Sergei Prokofiev (1891–1953)		
Bessie Smith (1894–1937)		
Paul Hindemith (1895–1963)		
Roger Sessions (1896–1985)		
George Gershwin (1898–1937)	William Faulkner (1897–1962)	
E. K. ("Duke") Ellington (1899–1974)	Henry Moore (b. 1898)	
	Ernest Hemingway (1899–1961)	
Louis Armstrong (1900–1971)	Louise Nevelson (b. 1900)	
Aaron Copland (1900–1990)	Isaac Bashevis Singer (b. 1904)	
Ruth Crawford-Seeger (1901–1953)		
Miriam Gideon (b. 1906)	Willem de Kooning (b. 1904)	
Dmitri Shostakovich (1906–1975)	Jean Paul Sartre (1905–1980)	

674

Musicians	Artists and Writers	Historical and Cultural Events
Elliott Carter (b. 1908)	David Smith (1906–1965)	
Olivier Messiaen (b. 1908)		Atomic bomb destroys Hiroshima (1945)
John Cage (b. 1912)		Korean war begins (1950)
Benjamin Britten (1913–1976)	Jackson Pollock (1912–1956)	
Billie Holiday (1915–1959)	Albert Camus (1913–1960)	
	Saul Bellow (b. 1915)	
	Robert Motherwell (b. 1915)	
Milton Babbitt (b. 1916)	Andrew Wyeth (b. 1917)	
Leonard Bernstein (1918–1990)		
Charlie Parker (1920–1955)	Alexander Solzhenitsyn (b. 1918)	American involvement in Vietnam increases dramatically (1965)
	Roy Lichtenstein (b. 1923)	
	Norman Mailer (b. 1923)	
Pierre Boulez (b. 1925)	James Baldwin (1924–1987)	
John Coltrane (1926–1967)	Allen Ginsberg (b. 1926)	American astronauts land on moon (1969)
Miles Davis (1926–1991)	John Hollander (b. 1928)	
Karlheinz Stockhausen (b. 1928)	Helen Frankenthaler (b. 1928)	Resignation of President Nixon (1974)
George Crumb (b. 1929)	Andy Warhol (1931–1987)	End of American involvement in Vietnam (1975)
Joe Zawinul (b. 1932)		United States and China establish diplomatic relations (1979)
Krzysztof Penderecki (b. 1933)		
Mario Davidovsky (b. 1934)		Revolution in Iran (1979)
Steve Reich (b. 1936)		Ronald Reagan inaugurated (1981)
Philip Glass (b. 1937)		Wars in Lebanon and the Falkland Islands (1982)
Charles Wuorinen (b. 1938)		Ronald Reagan inaugurated for second term (1985)
Ellen Taaffe Zwilich (b. 1939)		Nuclear accident at Chernobyl, Soviet Union (1986)
John Lennon (1940–1980)		George Bush inaugurated (1989)
John Adams (b. 1947)		Reunification of Germany (1990)
		Persian Gulf war (1991)
		Dissolution of Soviet Union; formation of Commonwealth (1991)

APPENDIX 5

BIBLIOGRAPHY AND SELECTED READINGS

GENERAL

Baker's Biographical Dictionary of Musicians, 7th ed. (Nicolas Slonimsky, ed.), Schirmer, New York, 1984.

Bowers, Jane, and Judith Tick (eds.): *Women Making Music: The Western Art Tradition,* University of Illinois, Urbana, 1986.

Downes, Edward: *The New York Philharmonic Guide to the Symphony,* Walker, New York, 1976.

Grout, Donald Jay, and Claude V. Palisca: *A History of Western Music,* 4th ed., Norton, New York, 1988.

Kamien, Roger (ed.): *The Norton Scores: An Anthology for Listening,* 5th ed., 2 vols., Norton, New York, 1990.

Lang, Paul Henry: *Music in Western Civilization,* Norton, New York, 1940.

Neuls-Bates, Carol (ed.): *Women in Music: An Anthology of Source Readings from the Middle Ages to the Present,* Harper and Row, New York, 1982.

The New Grove Dictionary of Music and Musicians (Stanley Sadie, ed.), 20 vols., Grove's Dictionaries of Music, Washington, D.C., 1980. The *New Grove* composer biographies are expanded and updated versions of articles from this dictionary and contain bibliographies as well as comprehensive lists of compositions.

Randel, Don (ed.): *The New Harvard Dictionary of Music,* Harvard, Cambridge, Mass., 1986.

Weiss, Piero, and Richard Taruskin (eds.): *Music in the Western World: A History in Documents,* Schirmer, New York, 1984.

I. ELEMENTS

Aldwell, Edward, and Carl Schachter: *Harmony and Voice Leading,* 2d ed., Harcourt, Brace, Jovanovich, New York, 1989.

Backus, John: *Acoustical Foundations of Music,* 2d ed., Norton, New York, 1977.

Carse, Adam: *The History of Orchestration,* Dover, New York, 1964.

Donington, Robert: *The Interpretation of Early Music,* St. Martin's, New York, 1963.

Harrison, Frank, and Joan Rimmer: *European Musical Instruments,* Norton, New York, 1964.

Kivy, Peter: *Music Alone: Philosophical Reflections on the Purely Musical Experience,* Cornell University Press, Ithaca, N.Y., and London, 1990.

Manning, Peter: *Electronic and Computer Music,* Clarendon Press, Oxford, 1985.

Manoff, Tom: *The Music Kit,* 2d ed., Norton, New York, 1984.

Marcuse, Sybil: *Musical Instruments: A Comprehensive Dictionary,* Norton, New York, 1975.

Meyer, Leonard B.: *Emotion and Meaning in Music,* University of Chicago Press, Chicago, 1961.

Sachs, Curt: *History of Musical Instruments,* Norton, New York, 1940.

Shapiro, Meyer: "Style," in Morris Philipson and Paul J. Gudel (eds.), *Aesthetics Today,* Meridian, New York, 1961.

II. THE MIDDLE AGES

Hoppin, Richard H.: *Medieval Music,* Norton, New York, 1978.

McKinnon, James (ed.): *Antiquity and the Middle Ages: From Ancient Greece to the Fifteenth Century,* Macmillan, London, 1990. (Part of the series *Man and Music.*)

Munrow, David: *Instruments of the Middle Ages and Renaissance,* Oxford, London, 1976.

Reese, Gustave: *Music in the Middle Ages,* Norton, New York, 1940.

Seay, Albert: *Music in the Medieval World,* 2d ed., Prentice-Hall, Englewood Cliffs, N.J., 1975.

Strunk, Oliver (ed.): *Source Readings in Music History: Antiquity and the Middle Ages,* Norton, New York, 1965.

III. THE RENAISSANCE

Brown, Howard Mayer: *Music in the Renaissance,* Prentice-Hall, Englewood Cliffs, N.J., 1976.

Lowinsky, Edward E.: "Music in the Culture of the Renaissance," in Paul Oskar Kristeller and Philip P. Wiener (eds.), *Renaissance Essays,* Harper and Row, New York, 1968.

Reese, Gustave: *Music in the Renaissance,* rev. ed., Norton, New York, 1959.

Strunk, Oliver (ed.): *Source Readings in Music History: The Renaissance,* Norton, New York, 1965.

IV. THE BAROQUE PERIOD

General

Bukofzer, Manfred F.: *Music in the Baroque Era,* Norton, New York, 1947.

Palisca, Claude V.: *Baroque Music,* 2d ed., Prentice-Hall, Englewood Cliffs, N.J., 1980.

Strunk, Oliver (ed.): *Source Readings in Music History: The Baroque Era,* Norton, New York, 1965.

Specific Topics

Grout, Donald Jay: *A Short History of Opera,* 2d ed., Columbia, New York, 1965.

Kerman, Joseph: *Opera as Drama,* new rev. ed., University of California Press, Berkeley, 1988.

Kobbés Complete Opera Book, rev. ed. (Earl of Harewood, ed.), Putnam, New York, 1972.

Newman, Ernest: *Great Operas: The Definitive Treatment of Their History, Stories, and Music,* 2 vols., Vintage, New York, 1958.

Newman, William S.: *The Sonata in the Baroque Era,* 4th ed., Norton, New York, 1983.

Smither, Howard E.: *Oratorio in the Baroque Era,* vols. I and II, University of North Carolina Press, Chapel Hill, 1977.

Weisstein, Ulrich (ed.): *The Essence of Opera,* Norton, New York, 1969.

Individual Composers

Bach

David, Hans T., and Arthur Mendel (eds.): *The Bach Reader*, rev. ed., Norton, New York, 1966.

Geiringer, Karl, with Irene Geiringer: *Johann Sebastian Bach: The Culmination of an Era*, Oxford, New York, 1966.

Corelli

Pincherle, Marc: *Corelli: His Life and His Music*, Norton, New York, 1956.

Handel

Hogwood, Christopher: *Handel*, Thames and Hudson, London, 1984.

Lang, Paul Henry: *George Frideric Handel*, Norton, New York, 1966.

Larsen, Jens Peter: *Handel's Messiah: Origins, Composition, Sources*, 2d ed., Norton, New York, 1972.

Monteverdi

Schrade, Leo: *Monteverdi, Creator of Modern Music*, Norton, New York, 1969.

Purcell

Westrup, Jack A.: *Purcell*, Octagon, New York, 1975.

Vivaldi

Pincherle, Marc: *Vivaldi: Genius of the Baroque*, Norton, New York, 1962.

V. THE CLASSICAL PERIOD

General

Blume, Friedrich: *Classic and Romantic Music*, Norton, New York, 1970.

Pauly, Reinhard: *Music in the Classic Period*, 2d ed., Prentice-Hall, Englewood Cliffs, N.J., 1973.

Pestelli, Giorgio: *The Age of Mozart and Beethoven*, Cambridge University Press, Cambridge, 1984.

Ratner, Leonard G.: *Classic Music: Expression, Form, and Style*, Schirmer, New York, 1980.

Rosen, Charles: *The Classical Style: Haydn, Mozart, Beethoven*, Norton, New York, 1972.

Rosen, Charles: *Sonata Forms*, 2d ed., Norton, New York, 1988.

Wellesz, Egon, and Frederick Sternfeld (eds.): *The Age of Enlightenment: 1745–1790* (vol. 7 of the *New Oxford History of Music*), Oxford, London, 1973.

Zaslow, Neal (ed.): *The Classical Era: From the 1740s to the End of the Eighteenth Century*, Macmillan, London, 1989. (Part of the series *Man and Music*.)

Specific Topics

Newman, William S.: *The Sonata in the Classic Era*, 3d ed., Norton, New York, 1983.
Ulrich, Homer: *Chamber Music*, 2d ed., Columbia, New York, 1966.

Individual Composers

Beethoven

Anderson, Emily (ed. and trans.): *The Letters of Beethoven*, rev. ed., St. Martin's, New York, 1964.
Arnold, Denis, and Nigel Fortune (eds.): *The Beethoven Reader*, Norton, New York, 1971.
Hopkins, Antony: *The Nine Symphonies of Beethoven*, University of Washington Press, Seattle, 1981.
Kerman, Joseph: *The Beethoven Quartets*, Knopf, New York, 1967.
Solomon, Maynard: *Beethoven*, Schirmer, New York, 1977.
Thayer, Alexander W.: *Life of Beethoven*, rev. ed. (Elliot Forbes, ed.), Princeton University Press, Princeton, N.J., 1973.
Tovey, Donald F.: *Beethoven*, Oxford, London, 1963.

Haydn

Geiringer, Karl, and Irene Geiringer: *Haydn: A Creative Life in Music*, 3d ed. (rev. and expanded), University of California Press, Berkeley, 1982.
Landon, H. C. Robbins: *The Symphonies of Joseph Haydn*, Rockcliff, London, and Universal Edition, 1955; supplement, 1961.
Landon, H. C. Robbins: *Haydn: Chronicle and Works*, 5 vols., Indiana University Press, Bloomington, 1976–1980.

Mozart

Anderson, Emily (ed.): *Letters of Mozart and His Family*, 2 vols., 2d ed. (A. Hyatt King and Monica Carolan, eds.), St. Martin's, New York, 1966.
Einstein, Alfred: *Mozart: His Character, His Work*, Oxford, New York, 1945.
Hildesheimer, Wolfgang: *Mozart*, Vintage, New York, 1983.
Mann, William: *The Operas of Mozart*, Cassell, London, 1977.

VI. THE ROMANTIC PERIOD

General

Abraham, Gerald: *A Hundred Years of Music*, 3d ed., Aldine, Chicago, Ill., 1964.
Dalhaus, Carl: *Nineteenth-Century Music* (trans. J. Bradford Robinson), University of California Press, Berkeley, 1989.
Einstein, Alfred: *Music in the Romantic Era*, Norton, New York, 1947.
Longyear, Rey M.: *Nineteenth-Century Romanticism in Music*, 2d ed., Prentice-Hall, Englewood Cliffs, N.J., 1973.
Plantinga, Leon: *Romantic Music*, Norton, New York, 1985.
Ringer, Alexander: *The Early Romantic Era: Between Revolutions, 1789 and 1848*, Macmillan, London, 1990. (Part of the series *Man and Music*.)
Strunk, Oliver (ed.): *Source Readings in Music History: The Romantic Era*, Norton, New York, 1965.

Specific Topics

Loesser, Arthur: *Men, Women, and Pianos: A Social History*, Simon and Schuster, New York, 1964.
Newman, William S.: *The Sonata since Beethoven*, Norton, New York, 1972.
Stevens, Denis (ed.): *A History of Song*, Norton, New York, 1961.

Individual Composers
Berlioz

Barzun, Jacques: *Berlioz and the Romantic Century*, 2 vols., 3d ed., Columbia, New York, 1969.
Berlioz, Hector: *Memoirs of Hector Berlioz* (Ernest Newman, ed.), Dover, New York, 1966.
Holomon, D. Kern: *Berlioz*, Harvard University Press, Cambridge, Mass., 1989.

Brahms

Gal, Hans: *Johannes Brahms: His Work and Personality*, Weidenfeld and Nicolson, London, 1963.
Geiringer, Karl: *Brahms: His Life and Works*, 3d ed. (enlarged), Da Capo, New York, 1982.
MacDonald, Malcolm: *Brahms*, Schirmer, New York, 1990.

Chopin

Hedley, Arthur: *Chopin*, rev. ed., Dent, London, 1974.

Dvořák

Clapham, John: *Antonin Dvořák: Musician and Craftsman*, St. Martin's, New York, 1966.

Liszt

Walker, Alan: *Franz Liszt: The Virtuoso Years, 1811–1847*, Knopf, New York, 1983.
Walker, Alan: *Franz Liszt: The Weimar Years, 1848–1861*, Knopf, New York, 1989.
Watson, Derek: *Liszt*, Schirmer, New York, 1989.

Mahler

Cardus, Neville: *Gustav Mahler: His Mind and His Music*, St. Martin's, New York, 1965.
de La Grange, Henry-Louis: *Mahler*, vol. 1., Doubleday, Garden City, N.Y., 1973.
Kennedy, Michael: *Mahler*, Schirmer, New York, 1990.

Mendelssohn

Werner, Eric: *Mendelssohn: A New Image of the Composer and His Age*, Free Press, New York, 1963.

Mussorgsky

Calvocoressi, Michael D.: *Modest Mussorgsky: His Life and Works*, Essential Books, Fair Lawn, N.J., 1956.

Puccini

Hughes, Spike: *Famous Puccini Operas*, 2d rev. ed., Dover, New York, 1972.

Schubert

Brown, Maurice J. E.: *Schubert: A Critical Biography*, St. Martin's, New York, 1958.
Brown, Maurice J. E.: *Schubert Songs*, University of Washington Press, Seattle, 1969.
Deutsch, Otto Erich (ed.): *Schubert: A Documentary Biography*, Dent, London, 1946.
Deutsch, Otto Erich (ed.): *Schubert: Memoirs by His Friends*, Black, London, 1958.

Clara Wieck Schumann

Reich, Nancy B.: *Clara Schumann: The Artist and the Woman*, Oxford University Press, New York, 1989.

Robert Schumann

Brion, Marcel: *Schumann and the Romantic Age*, Macmillan, New York, 1956.
Ostwald, Peter: *Schumann: The Inner Voices of a Musical Genius*, Northwestern University Press, Boston, Mass., 1985.
Schumann, Robert: *On Music and Musicians* (Konrad Wolff, ed.), University of California Press, Berkeley, 1983.

Smetana

Large, Brian: *Smetana*, Da Capo, New York, 1985.

Tchaikovsky

Abraham, Gerald: *The Music of Tchaikovsky*, Norton, New York, 1974.
Brown, David: *Tchaikovsky: The Early Years (1840–1874)*, Gollancz, London, 1979.
Brown, David: *Tchaikovsky: The Crisis Years, 1874–1878*, Norton, New York, 1983.
Brown, David: *Tchaikovsky: The Years of Wandering, 1878–1885*, Norton, New York, 1986.
Weinstock, Herbert: *Tchaikovsky*, Knopf, New York, 1973.

Verdi

Budden, Julian: *The Operas of Verdi*, 3 vols., Oxford, New York, 1978–1981.
Toye, Francis: *Guiseppe Verdi: His Life and Works*, Vienna House, New York, 1972.

Wagner

Goldman, Albert, and Evert Sprinchorn (eds.): *Wagner on Music and Drama: A Compendium of Richard Wagner's Prose Works,* Dutton, New York, 1964.

Millington, Barry: *Wagner,* Vintage, New York, 1987.

Newman, Ernest: *The Life of Richard Wagner,* 4 vols., Knopf, New York, 1933–1946.

Newman, Ernest: *The Wagner Operas,* Knopf, New York, 1949.

White, Chappell: *An Introduction to the Life and Works of Richard Wagner,* Prentice-Hall, Englewood Cliffs, N.J., 1967.

VII. THE TWENTIETH CENTURY

General

Austin, William: *Music in the Twentieth Century,* Norton, New York, 1966.

Machlis, Joseph: *Introduction to Contemporary Music,* 2d ed., Norton, New York, 1979.

Morgan, Robert: *Twentieth Century Music,* Norton, New York, 1991.

Salzman, Eric: *Twentieth-Century Music: An Introduction,* 3d ed., Prentice-Hall, Englewood Cliffs, N.J., 1988.

Slonimsky, Nicolas: *Music Since 1900,* 4th ed., Scribner, New York, 1971. Supplement, 1986.

Stuckenschmidt, H. H.: *Twentieth Century Music,* McGraw-Hill, New York, 1969.

Vinton, John (ed.): *Dictionary of Contemporary Music,* Dutton, New York, 1974.

Watkins, Glen: *Soundings: Music in the Twentieth Century,* Schirmer, New York, 1988.

Specific Topics

Ammer, Christine: *Unsung: A History of Women in American Music,* Greenwood Press, Westport, Conn., 1980.

Chase, Gilbert: *American Music,* 3d ed., University of Illinois Press, Urbana, 1984.

Hamm, Charles: *Music in the New World,* Norton, New York, 1983.

Hitchcock, H. Wiley: *Music in the United States: A Historical Introduction,* 2d ed., Prentice-Hall, Englewood Cliffs, N.J., 1974.

Kingman, Daniel: *American Music: A Panorama,* 2d ed., Schirmer, New York, 1990.

The New Grove Dictionary of American Music, 4 vols. (H. Wiley Hitchcock and Stanley Sadie, eds.), Grove's Dictionary of Music, New York, 1986.

Rockwell, John: *All American Music: Composition in the Late Twentieth Century,* Vintage, New York, 1984.

Schwarz, Boris: *Music and Musical Life in Soviet Russia, 1917–1981,* enlarged ed., Indiana University Press, Bloomington, 1983.

Southern, Eileen: *Music of Black Americans,* 2d. ed., Norton, New York, 1983.

Southern, Eileen: *Readings in Black American Music,* rev. ed., Norton, New York, 1983.

Individual Composers

Bartók

Stevens, Halsey: *The Life and Music of Béla Bartók,* rev. ed., Oxford, New York, 1967.

Berg

Carner, Mosco: *Alban Berg: The Man and the Work*, Holmes and Meier, New York, 1977.

Cage

Cage, John: *Silence*, Wesleyan University Press, Middletown, Conn., 1961.

Carter

Edwards, Allen: *Flawed Words and Stubborn Sounds: A Conversation with Elliott Carter*, Norton, New York, 1972.
Stone, Else, and Kurt Stone (eds.): *The Writings of Elliott Carter: An American Composer Looks at Modern Music*, Indiana University Press, Bloomington, 1977.

Copland

Berger, Arthur: *Aaron Copland*, Oxford, New York, 1953.
Copland, Aaron: *Our New Music*, McGraw-Hill, New York, 1941.
Copland, Aaron: *Copland on Music*, Norton, New York, 1963.
Copland, Aaron: *The New Music: 1900–1960*, rev. ed., Norton, New York, 1968.
Copland, Aaron, and Vivian Perlis: *Copland: 1900–1942*, St. Martin's/Marek, New York, 1984.

Debussy

Lockspeiser, Edward: *Debussy: His Life and Mind*, 2 vols., Cassel, London, 1962.

Gershwin

Jablonski, Edward: *Gershwin*, Northeastern University Press, Boston, Mass., 1990.
Jablonski, Edward, and Lawrence Stewart: *The Gershwin Years*, Doubleday, New York, 1973.
Schwartz, Charles: *Gershwin: His Life and Music*, Da Capo, New York, 1979.

Ives

Cowell, Henry, and Sidney Cowell: *Charles Ives and His Music*, Oxford, New York, 1969.
Hitchcock, H. Wiley: *Ives*, Oxford, New York, 1977.
Ives, Charles: *Essays before a Sonata and Other Writings* (Howard Boatwright, ed.), Norton, New York, 1962.
Kirkpatrick, John (ed.): *Charles E. Ives: Memos*, Norton, New York, 1972.

Ravel

Orenstein, Arbie: *Ravel: Man and Musician*, Columbia, New York, 1975.

Schoenberg

Rosen, Charles: *Arnold Schoenberg*, Viking, New York, 1975.
Schoenberg, Arnold: *Letters* (E. Stein, ed.), St. Martin's, New York, 1965.
Schoenberg, Arnold: *Style and Idea* (Leonard Stein, ed.), University of California Press, Berkeley, 1975.
Stuckenschmidt, H. H.: *Arnold Schoenberg: His Life, World, and Work,* Calder, London, 1977.

Stravinsky

Craft, Robert: *Stravinsky: Chronicle of a Friendship: 1948–1971,* Vintage, New York, 1973.
Stravinsky, Igor: *Poetics of Music,* Vintage, New York, 1956.
Stravinsky, Igor: *An Autobiography,* Norton, New York, 1962.
Stravinsky, Igor, and Robert Craft: *Conversations with Igor Stravinsky,* Doubleday, New York, 1959.
Stravinsky, Igor, and Robert Craft: *Memories and Commentaries,* Doubleday, New York, 1960.
Stravinsky, Igor, and Robert Craft: *Expositions and Developments,* Doubleday, New York, 1962.
Stravinsky, Igor, and Robert Craft: *Retrospectives and Conclusions,* Knopf, New York, 1969.
Stravinsky, Igor, and Robert Craft: *Themes and Conclusions,* Faber and Faber, London, 1972.
White, Eric Walter: *Stravinsky: The Composer and His Works,* 2d ed., University of California Press, Berkeley, 1980.

Varèse

Ouellete, Fernard: *Edgard Varèse,* Calder and Boyars, London, 1973.

Webern

Kolneder, Walter: *Anton Webern: An Introduction to His Works,* University of California Press, Berkeley, 1968.

VIII. JAZZ

General

Feather, Leonard: *The Encyclopedia of Jazz,* rev. ed., Horizon, New York, 1960.
Gridley, Mark C.: *Jazz Styles,* 2d ed., Prentice-Hall, Englewood Cliffs, N.J., 1985.
McCalla, James: *Jazz: A Listener's Guide,* Prentice-Hall, Englewood Cliffs, N.J., 1982.
Schuller, Gunther: *Early Jazz: Its Roots and Musical Development,* Oxford, New York, 1968.

Schuller, Gunther: *The Swing Era: The Development of Jazz 1930–1945,* Oxford University Press, New York, 1989.

Shapiro, Nat, and Nat Hentoff (eds.): *Hear Me Talkin' to Ya,* Rinehart, New York, 1955.

Tirro, Frank: *Jazz: A History,* Norton, New York, 1977.

Williams, Martin: *Where's the Melody? A Listener's Introduction to Jazz,* rev. ed., Pantheon, New York, 1968.

Williams, Martin: *The Jazz Tradition,* rev. ed., Oxford, New York, 1983.

Specific Topics

Blesh, Rudi, and Harriet Janis: *They All Played Ragtime,* 4th ed., Oak Publications, New York, 1971.

Charters, Samuel B.: *The Country Blues,* Rinehart, New York, 1959.

Keil, Charles: *Urban Blues,* University of Chicago Press, Chicago, 1966.

Williams, Martin: *Jazz Masters in Transition, 1957–1969,* Macmillan, New York, 1970.

Individual Composers

Ellington

Ellington, Edward Kennedy: *Music Is My Mistress,* Doubleday, New York, 1973.

IX. MUSICAL THEATER

Bernstein, Leonard: *The Joy of Music,* Simon and Schuster, New York, 1959.

Green, Stanley: *The World of Musical Comedy,* Ziff-Davis, New York, 1960.

Peyser, Joan: *Bernstein: A Biography,* Morrow, New York, 1987.

Stempel, Larry: "Broadway's Mozartean Moment, or An Amadeus in Amber," in Stephen Ledbetter (ed.), *Sennets and Tuckets: A Bernstein Celebration,* Boston Symphony Orchestra/David R. Godine, Boston, Mass., 1988.

Swain, Joseph: *The Broadway Musical: A Critical and Musical Survey,* Oxford University Press, New York, 1990.

Wilson, Edwin: *The Theater Experience,* 5th ed., McGraw-Hill, New York, 1991.

Wilson, Edwin, and Alvin Goldfarb: *Theater: The Lively Art,* McGraw-Hill, New York, 1991.

X. ROCK

Bergman, Billy: *Good Time Kings: Emerging African Pop,* Quill, New York, 1985.

Davies, Hunter: *The Beatles,* rev. ed., McGraw-Hill, New York, 1978.

Gillett, Charles: *The Sound of the City,* 2d ed., Dell, New York, 1972.

Marre, Jeremy, and Hannah Charlton: *Beats of the Heart: Popular Music of the World,* Pantheon, New York, 1985.

Miller, Jim (ed.): *The Rolling Stone Illustrated History of Rock & Roll*, Random House, New York, 1976.

Pareles, Jon, and Patty Romanowsky (eds.): *The Rolling Stone Encyclopedia of Rock and Roll*, Summit Books, New York, 1983.

Stapleton, Chris, and Chris May: *African Rock: The Pop Music of a Continent*, Dutton, New York, 1990.

XI. NONWESTERN MUSIC

General

Malm, William P.: *Music Cultures of the Pacific, the Near East, and Asia*, 2d ed., Prentice-Hall, Englewood Cliffs, N.J., 1977.

May, Elizabeth (ed.): *Music of Many Cultures: An Introduction*, University of California Press, Berkeley and Los Angeles, 1980. (Includes music examples on three 7-inch 33⅓ monaural soundsheets.)

Merriam, Alan P.: *Anthropology of Music*, Northwestern University Press, Evanston, Ill., 1964.

Nettl, Bruno: *Folk and Traditional Music of the Western Continents*, 2d ed., Prentice-Hall, Englewood Cliffs, N.J., 1973.

Reck, David: *Music of the Whole Earth*, Scribner, New York, 1977.

Titon, Jeff Todd (general ed.), James T. Koetting, David McAllester, David Reck, and Mark Slobin: *Worlds of Music: An Introduction to the Music of the World's Peoples*, Schirmer, New York, 1984. (There is a set of two accompanying cassettes.)

Specific Topics

Adriaansz, Willem: *The Kumiuta and Danmono Traditions of Japanese Koto Music*, University of California Press, Berkeley, 1973.

Chernoff, John Miller: *African Rhythm and African Sensibility: Aesthetics and Social Action in African Musical Idioms*, University of Chicago Press, Chicago and London, 1979. (There is an accompanying 90-minute cassette.)

Jones, A. M.: *Studies in African Music*, Oxford, London, 1959.

Malm, William P.: *Japanese Music and Musical Instruments*, Tuttle, Rutland, Vt., 1959.

Merriam, Alan P.: *African Music on LP: An Annotated Discography*, Northwestern University Press, Evanston, Ill., 1970.

Merriam, Alan P.: *African Music in Perspective*, Garland, New York, 1982.

Nketia, J. H. Kwabena: *The Music of Africa*, Norton, New York, 1974.

Shankar, Ravi: *My Music, My Life*, Simon and Schuster, New York, 1968.

Tracey, Hugh: *Chopi Musicians: Their Music, Poetry, and Instruments*, rev. ed., Oxford University Press, London, 1970.

Wade, Bonnie: *Tegotomono: Music for the Japanese Koto*, Greenwood, Westport, Conn., 1976.

RECORDINGS

BASIC SET

ELEMENTS

Records and Cassettes	Compact Disks	Selections
Side 1	CD 1	
band 1	1 – 4	Wagner: *Lohengrin*, Prelude to Act III
band 2	5 – 7	Chopin: Prelude in C Minor for Piano, Op. 28, No. 20
band 3	8 – 9	Stravinsky: *Firebird* Suite, Finale
band 4	10 – 15	Lillian Hardin Armstrong: *Hotter Than That*, Louis Armstrong and His Hot Five
band 5	16 – 19	Sousa: *The Stars and Stripes Forever*
band 6	20	Gershwin: *I Got Rhythm*
band 7	21	Brubeck: *Unsquare Dance*
band 8	22 – 24	Arlen: *Over the Rainbow*
band 9	25	Chopin: Prelude in E Minor, Op. 28, No. 4
band 10	26 – 30	Bizet: *Farandole* from *L'Arlésienne* Suite No. 2
band 11	31 – 33	Tchaikovsky: *Dance of the Reed Pipes* from *Nutcracker* Suite, Op. 71a
band 12	34 – 35	Bach: *Badinerie* from Suite No. 2 in B Minor

MIDDLE AGES

Records and Cassettes	Compact Disks	Selections
Side 1	CD 1	
band 13	36 – 38	*Alleluia: Vidimus stellam*
band 14	39	Estampie
Side 2	CD 1	
band 1	40	Perotin: *Alleluia: Nativitas*
band 2	41 – 43	Machaut: Agnus Dei from *Notre Dame* Mass

RENAISSANCE

Records and Cassettes	Compact Disks	Selections
Side 2	CD 1	
band 3	44 – 46	Josquin Desprez: *Ave Maria . . . virgo serena*
band 4	47	Weelkes: *As Vesta Was Descending*
band 5	48 – 51	Andrea Gabrieli: *Ricercar in the Twelfth Mode*
band 6	52 – 55	Praetorius: *La Bourée*

BAROQUE

Records and Cassettes	Compact Disks	Selections
Side 2	CD 1	
band 7	56	Monteverdi: *Tu se' morta* from *Orfeo*, Act II
band 8	57 – 58	Purcell: *Dido's Lament* from *Dido and Aeneas*
band 9	59 – 63	Vivaldi: *La Primavera (Spring)*, Concerto for Violin and String Orchestra, Op. 8, No. 1, from *The Four Seasons*; first movement (allegro)
band 10	64	Bach: Organ Fugue in G Minor *(Little Fugue)*
Side 3	CD 2	
band 1	1 – 5	Bach: *Brandenburg* Concerto No. 5 in D Major; first movement (allegro)
band 2	6	Bach: *Brandenburg* Concerto No. 5 in D Major; second movement (affetuoso)
band 3	7 – 9	Bach: *Brandenburg* Concerto No. 5 in D Major; third movement (allegro)
band 4	10 – 12	Bach: Cantata No. 140, *Wachet auf, ruft uns die Stimme*; first movement
band 5	13 – 15	Bach: Cantata No. 140, *Wachet auf, ruft uns die Stimme*; fourth movement
band 6	16	Bach: Cantata No. 140, *Wachet auf, ruft uns die Stimme*; seventh movement
Side 4	CD 2	
band 1	17 – 18	Bach: Air from Suite No. 3 in D Major, S. 1068
band 2	19 – 20	Bach: Bourée from Suite No. 3 in D Major, S. 1068
band 3	21 – 22	Bach: Gigue from Suite No. 3 in D Major, S. 1068
band 4	22 – 24	Handel: Sinfonia for Orchestra (French Overture) from *Messiah*
band 5	25 – 26	Handel: *Comfort Ye, My people*, from *Messiah*
band 6	27	Handel: *Ev'ry Valley Shall Be Exalted*, from *Messiah*
band 7	28 – 30	Handel: *For unto Us a Child Is Born*, from *Messiah*
band 8	31 – 36	Handel: *Hallelujah* Chorus, from *Messiah*

CLASSICAL

Records and Cassettes	Compact Disks	Selections
Side 4	CD 2	
band 9	37	Haydn: Trumpet Concerto in E Flat Major; third movement (allegro)
Side 5	CD 3	
band 1	1 – 6	Haydn: Symphony No. 94 in G Major *(Surprise)*; second movement (andante)
band 2	7 – 9	Mozart: *Eine kleine Nachtmusik*, K. 525; third movement (minuet)
band 3	10 – 16	Mozart: Piano Concerto in A Major, K. 488; first movement (allegro)
band 4	17 – 20	Mozart: *Don Giovanni*, K. 527; Act I, Introduction (opening scene)
band 5	21 – 22	Mozart: *Don Giovanni*, K. 527; Act I, "Catalog" aria *(Madamina)*
band 6	23 – 26	Mozart: *Don Giovanni*, K. 527; Act I, *Là ci darem la mano*
Side 6	CD 3	
band 1	27	Mozart: *Dies irae*, from Requiem, K. 626
band 2	28 – 36	Mozart: Symphony No. 40 in G Minor, K. 550; first movement (molto allegro)
band 3	37 – 39	Mozart: Symphony No. 40 in G Minor, K. 550; second movement (andante)

Records and Cassettes	Compact Disks	Selections
Side 6	**CD 3**	
band 4	40 – 42	Mozart: Symphony No. 40 in G Minor, K. 550; third movement (menuetto)
band 5	43	Mozart: Symphony No. 40 in G Minor, K. 550; fourth movement (allegro assai)
Side 7	**CD 4**	
band 1	1 – 8	Beethoven: Symphony No. 5 in C Minor, Op. 67; first movement (allegro con brio)
band 2	9 – 14	Beethoven: Symphony No. 5 in C Minor, Op. 67; second movement (andante con moto)
band 3	15 – 18	Beethoven: Symphony No. 5 in C Minor, Op. 67; third movement (allegro)
band 3	19 – 25	Beethoven: Symphony No. 5 in C Minor, Op. 67; fourth movement (allegro)
Side 8	**CD 4**	
band 1	26 – 29	Beethoven: String Quartet in C Minor, Op. 18, No. 4; fourth movement (rondo)
band 2	30 – 36	Beethoven: Piano Sonata in C Minor, Op. 13 *(Pathétique)*; first movement (grave; allegro molto e con brio)
band 3	37 – 40	Beethoven: Piano Sonata in C Minor, Op. 13 *(Pathétique)*; second movement (adagio cantabile)
band 4	41 – 44	Beethoven: Piano Sonata in C Minor, Op. 13 *(Pathétique)*; third movement (rondo: allegro)

ROMANTIC

Records and Cassettes	Compact Disks	Selections
Side 8	**CD 4**	
band 5	45 – 50	Schubert: *Erlkönig*
band 6	51 – 52	Schubert: *Die Forelle*
band 7	53	Schubert: Piano Quintet in A Major, D. 667 *(Trout)*; fourth movement (andantino)
Side 9	**CD 5**	
band 1	1	Robert Schumann: *Im wunderschönen Monat Mai* from *Dichterliebe*, Op. 48
band 2	2 – 4	Robert Schumann: *Aufschwung* from *Fantasiestücke*, Op. 12
band 3	5 – 9	Clara Wieck Schumann: Romance in G Minor for Violin and Piano, Op. 22, No. 2
band 4	10 – 13	Chopin: Polonaise in A Flat Major, Op. 53
band 5	14 – 16	Chopin: Nocturne in E Flat Major, Op. 9, No. 2
band 6	17 – 22	Liszt: *Transcendental Étude* No. 10 in F Minor
band 7	23 – 27	Mendelssohn: Concerto for Violin and Orchestra in E Minor, Op. 64; first movement
Side 10	**CD 5**	
band 1	28 – 31	Berlioz: *Symphonie fantastique*; fourth movement *(March to the Scaffold)*
band 2	32 – 37	Berlioz: *Symphonie fantastique*; fifth movement *(Dream of a Witches Sabbath)*
band 3	38	Tchaikovsky: *Romeo and Juliet*, Overture-Fantasy

Records and Cassettes	Compact Disks	Selections
Side 11	**CD 6**	
band 1	⊡1–⊡7	Smetana: *The Moldau*
band 2	⊡8–⊡11	Brahms: Symphony No. 4 in E Minor, Op. 98; fourth movement (allegro energetico e passionato)
band 3	⊡12	Brahms: *A German Requiem;* fourth movement (*How Lovely Is Thy Dwelling Place*)
band 4	⊡13–⊡15	Verdi: *La donna è mobile* and Quartet from *Rigoletto*, Act III
Side 12	**CD 6**	
band 1	⊡16–⊡19	Puccini: *La Bohème*, Act I; excerpt (Mimi's entrance through conclusion of act)
band 2	⊡20–⊡27	Wagner: *Die Walküre;* Act I, scene 3 (conclusion of love duet)

TWENTIETH CENTURY

Records and Cassettes	Compact Disks	Selections
Side 12	**CD 6**	
band 3	⊡28	Stravinsky: *Introduction, Omens of Spring—Dances of the Youths and Maidens, Ritual of Abduction,* from *Le Sacre du Printemps,* Part I
Side 13	**CD 7**	
band 1	⊡1–⊡3	Stravinsky: *Sacrificial Dance* from *Le Sacre du Printemps,* Part II
band 2	⊡4	Stravinsky: *Symphony of Psalms;* first movement
band 3	⊡5–⊡11	Debussy: *Prélude à "L'Après-midi d'un Faune"* (Prelude to "The Afternoon of a Faun")
band 4	⊡12–⊡15	Ravel: *Bolero*
Side 14	**CD 7**	
band 1	⊡16–⊡17	Schoenberg: Five Pieces for Orchestra, Op. 16, No. 1, *Vorgefühle*
band 2	⊡18–⊡19	Schoenberg: *A Survivor from Warsaw,* Op. 46
band 3	⊡20–⊡24	Berg: *Wozzeck;* Act III, scenes 4 and 5
band 4	⊡25	Webern: Five Pieces for Orchestra, Op. 10, No. 3 (very slow and extremely calm)
band 5	⊡26–⊡34	Bartók: Concerto for Orchestra; first movement
band 6	⊡35	Ives: *Putnam's Camp, Redding, Connecticut,* from *Three Places in New England*
Side 15	**CD 8**	
band 1	⊡1–⊡6	Copland: *Appalachian Spring;* Section 7 (Theme and Variations on *Simple Gifts*)
band 2	⊡7	Varèse: *Poème électronique*
band 3	⊡8	Babbitt: *Composition for Synthesizer* (excerpt)
band 4	⊡9	Crumb: *From Where Do You Come, My Love, My Child?* from *Ancient Voices of Children*
band 5	⊡10–⊡11	Zwilich: *Concerto Grosso 1985;* first movement (maestoso)
band 6	⊡12	Adams: *Nixon in China;* Act I, scene 2, opening

JAZZ

Records and Cassettes	Compact Disks	Selections
Side 15	**CD 8**	
band 7	13 – 16	Joplin: *Maple Leaf Rag*
band 8	17	Smith: *Lost Your Head Blues*
Side 16	**CD 8**	
band 1	18	Oliver: *Dippermouth Blues*
band 2	19	Berlin: *Blue Skies*
band 3	20	Ellington: *Concerto for Cootie*
band 4	21	Parker: *KoKo*

THE AMERICAN MUSICAL

Records and Cassettes	Compact Disks	Selections
Side 16	**CD 8**	
band 5	22 – 23	Bernstein: *Tonight* ensemble from *West Side Story*

NONWESTERN MUSIC

Records and Cassettes	Compact Disks	Selections
Side 16	**CD 8**	
band 6	24	Song from Angola (Gangele song)
band 7	25	*Mitamba Yalagala Kumchuzi*
band 8	26	*Hinganyengisa Masingita*
band 9	27	*Maru-Bihag*, excerpt
band 10	28	Mitsuzaki Kengyō: *Godan Ginuta*

SUPPLEMENTARY SET

Records and Cassettes	Compact Disks	Selections
		ELEMENTS
Side 1 band 1	CD 1 [1]–[25]	Britten: *The Young Person's Guide to the Orchestra* (Variations and Fugue on a Theme by Purcell)
		MIDDLE AGES
band 2	[26]–[28]	Machaut: *Je suis aussi*
		RENAISSANCE
band 3	[29]–[31]	Palestrina: Kyrie from *Pope Marcellus* Mass
band 4	[32]	Morley: *Now Is the Month of Maying*
band 5	[33]	G. Gabrieli: *Plaudite,* Motet in Twelve Parts for Three Choirs
		BAROQUE
Side 2 band 1	CD 1 [34]	Corelli: Trio Sonata in E Minor, Op. 3, No. 7; first movement (grave)
band 2	[35]	Corelli: Trio Sonata in E Minor, Op. 3, No. 7; second movement (allegro)
band 3	[36]	Corelli: Trio Sonata in E Minor, Op. 3, No. 7; third movement (adagio)
band 4	[37]	Corelli: Trio Sonata in E Minor, Op. 3, No. 7; fourth movement (allegro)
band 5	[38]	Vivaldi: *La Primavera (Spring),* Concerto for Violin and String Orchestra, Op. 8, No. 1, from *The Four Seasons;* second movement (largo e pianissimo sempre)
band 6	[39]	Vivaldi: *La Primavera (Spring),* third movement *(Danza pastorale)*
band 7	[40]	Bach: Mass in B Minor, *Crucifixus*
band 8	[41]	Bach: Mass in B Minor, *Et Resurrexit*
band 9	[42]	Bach: Cantata No. 140; fifth movement (recitative for bass)
band 10	[43]	Bach: Cantata No. 140; sixth movement (duet for bass and soprano)
		CLASSICAL
Side 3 band 1	CD 2 [1]–[8]	Haydn, Symphony No. 94 in G Major *(Surprise);* first movement (adagio; vivace assai)
band 2	[9]–[11]	Haydn, Symphony No. 94 in G Major *(Surprise);* third movement (minuet)
band 3	[12]–[14]	Haydn, Symphony No. 94 in G Major *(Surprise);* fourth movement (finale)
band 4	[15]–[17]	Mozart, Piano Concerto in A Major, K. 488; second movement (adagio)
band 5	[18]–[22]	Mozart, Piano Concerto in A Major, K. 488; third movement (allegro assai)
Side 4 band 1	CD 2 [23]–[30]	Beethoven: String Quartet in F Major, Op. 18, No. 1; first movement (allegro con brio)

Records and Cassettes	Compact Disks	Selections

ROMANTIC

Records and Cassettes	Compact Disks	Selections
Side 4	CD 2	
band 2	31	Chopin, Étude in C Minor, Op. 10, No. 12 (Revolutionary)
band 3	32	Berlioz, Symphonie fantastique; first movement (excerpt, idée fixe)
band 4	33 – 35	Mussorgsky, Boris Godunov; Coronation Scene
band 5	36	Mahler: Symphony No. 1; third movement (Funeral March)
Side 5	CD 3	
band 1	1 – 7	Dvořák: Symphony No. 9 in E Minor (From the New World); first movement (adagio; allegro molto)
band 2	8 – 12	Dvořák: Symphony No. 9 in E Minor (From the New World); second movement (largo)
band 3	13 – 18	Dvořák: Symphony No. 9 in E Minor (From the New World); third movement (scherzo: molto vivace)
Side 6	CD 3	
band 1	19 – 22	Dvořák: Symphony No. 9 in E Minor (From the New World); fourth movement (allegro con fuoco)
band 2	23 – 25	Mendelssohn: Concerto for Violin and Orchestra in E Minor, Op. 64; second movement (andante)
band 3	26	Mendelssohn: Concerto for Violin and Orchestra in E Minor, Op. 64; third movement (allegretto non troppo; allegro molto vivace)

TWENTIETH CENTURY

Records and Cassettes	Compact Disks	Selections
Side 7	CD 4	
band 1	1 – 7	Stravinsky: Petrushka; Act I, scene 1
band 2	8 – 14	Bartók: Concerto for Orchestra; second movement
band 3	15 – 20	Gershwin: Rhapsody in Blue
Side 8	CD 4	
band 1	21 – 25	Debussy: Voiles from Preludes for Piano, Book I
band 2	26 – 27	Carter: Sonata for Flute, Oboe, Cello, and Harpsichord; first movement (risoluto)
band 3	28	Penderecki: Threnody: For the Victims of Hiroshima

ACKNOWLEDGMENTS

PART-OPENING PHOTOGRAPHS

- I. Innervisions.
- II. Glasgow University Library.
- III. Schloss Rohrau, Vienna.
- IV. A. C. Cooper, by gracious permission of the Queen.
- V. Carnavalet Museum, Paris; Giraudon/Art Resource.
- VI. Lauros-Giraudon/Art Resource.
- VII. Art Institute of Chicago. Gift of Mrs. Gilbert W. Chapman.
- VIII. Photo Files.
- IX. Martha Swope.
- X. Anthony Suau/Black Star.
- XI. Peter Buckley/Photo Researchers.

MUSIC EXCERPTS AND MUSICAL TEXTS

Adams, John, and Alice Goodman. *Nixon in China*. Music copyright © 1987 Red Dawn Music BMI. Libretto © Alice Goodman 1990. Reprinted by permission.

Arlen, Harold, and E. Y. Harburg. *Over the Rainbow* from *The Wizard of Oz*. Copyright © 1938, 1939 (renewed 1966, 1967) Metro-Goldwyn-Mayer Inc. Assigned to Leo Feist, Inc. All rights of Leo Feist, Inc. assigned to EMI Catalogue Partnership. All rights controlled and administered by EMI Feist Catalog, Inc. International copyright secured. Made in USA. All rights reserved.

Bach, Johann Sebastian. Cantata No. 140. Translation by Gerhard Herz. In Roger Kamien (ed.), *The Norton Scores* (New York: W. W. Norton, 1970). Copyright 1970 W. W. Norton & Company, Inc.

Bartók, Béla. *Concerto for Orchestra*. Copyright © 1946 by Hawkes & Son (London) Ltd.; copyright renewed. Reprinted by permission of Boosey & Hawkes, Inc.

Bartók, Béla. *Six Dances in Bulgarian Rhythm* from *Mikrokosmos*, vol. 6, nos. 148–153. © copyright 1940 by Hawkes & Son (London) Ltd.; copyright renewed. Reprinted by permission of Boosey & Hawkes, Inc.

Berg, Alban. *Wozzeck,* Act III, scenes 4 and 5. Translation by Eric Blackall and Vida Harford. © 1923, 1931 by Universal Edition, A. G., Wien. English translation © 1952 by Alfred A. Kalmus, London. Copyright renewed. All rights reserved. Used by permission of European American Distributors Corporation, sole U.S. agent for Universal Edition.

Bernstein, Leonard, and Stephen Sondheim. *Tonight* from *West Side Story*. Copyright © 1957 (renewed) Leonard Bernstein & Stephen Sondheim, Jalni Publications, Inc., U.S. & Canadian publisher; G. Schirmer, Inc., worldwide print rights and publisher for the rest of the world. International copyright secured. All rights reserved. Used by permission.

Carter, Elliott. Sonata for Flute, Oboe, Cello, and Harpsichord. Copyright © 1962 by Associated Music Publishers. Reprinted by permission of Associated Music Publishers.

Copland, Aaron. *Appalachian Spring*. Copyright © 1946 by Aaron Copland; copyright renewed. Reprinted by permission of Aaron Copland, copyright owner; and Boosey & Hawkes, Inc., sole licensees.

Crumb, George. *Dance of the Sacred Life Cycle* from *Ancient Voices of Children*. Copyright © 1970 by C. F. Peters Corporation. Reprinted by permission of C. F. Peters Corporation. Texts by Federico García Lorca from *Gacela of the Dead Child* in *Selected Poems*, translated by Edwin Honig, copyright 1947, 1955 by New Directions Publishing Corporation; and *Yerma* in *Three Tragedies*, translated by J. L. Gili, copyright © 1960 by J. L. Gili. Reprinted by permission of New Directions Publishing Corporation, the heirs of Federico García Lorca, and J. L. Gili.

Ellington, Duke. *Concerto for Cootie*. © 1940, renewed 1967, by Robbins Music Corporation, New York.

Gershwin, George. *Rhapsody in Blue*. © 1924 (renewed) W B Music Corp. All rights reserved. Used by permission of W B Music Corp.

Gershwin, George, and Ira Gershwin. *I Got Rhythm*. © 1930 W B Music Corp. (renewed). All rights reserved. Used by permission.

Haydn, Franz Josef. Symphony No. 94 in G Major *(Surprise)*. Critical edition by H. C. Robbins Landon, vol. XI. © 1956 by Haydn-Mozart Presse, Salzburg. All rights reserved. Used by permission of European American Music Distributors Corporation, sole U.S. agent for Haydn-Mozart Presse.

Ives, Charles. *Three Places in New England*. © 1935, 1976 Mercury Music Corporation. Used by permission. Sole representative U.S.A. and Canada, Theodore Presser Company.

Lennon, John, and Paul McCartney. *A Day in the Life*. © Copyright 1967 Norther Songs. All rights controlled and administered by MCA Music Publishing, a division of MCA Inc., 1755 Broadway, New York, under license from Northern Songs. International copyright secured. All rights reserved MCA Music Publishing.

Mozart, Wolfgang Amadeus. *Don Giovanni*. Translation by William Murray. Copyright © 1961 Capitol Records. Reprinted by kind permission of Angel Records.

Mussorgsky, Modest. *Boris Godunov*. Translation by Louis Biancolli. Reprinted by permission of Louis Biancolli.

Porter, Cole. *You're the Top*. © 1934 (renewed) W B Music Corp. All rights reserved. Used by permission of W B Music Corp.

Puccini, Giacomo. *La Bohème*. Translation by William Weaver. Copyright © 1952 Capitol Records, Inc. Reprinted in *Seven Puccini Librettos in New English Translations* by William Weaver, © 1981, 1986 by W. W. Norton & Company, Inc.

Ravel, Maurice. *Bolero*. © 1929 Durand S. A.; Editions A.R.I.M.A. and Durand S. A. joint publication. Used by permission. Sole representative U.S.A. and Canada, Theodore Presser Company.

Schoenberg, Arnold. *Vorgefühle* from *Five Pieces for Orchestra*. Copyright © 1952 by Henmar Press, Inc., New York. Reprinted by permission of the publisher.

Schoenberg, Arnold. Suite, Op. 25, 1920–1923. Copyright by Universal Edition. Copyright renewed 1952 by Gertrude Schoenberg. Reprinted by permission of Belmont Music Publishers, Pacific Palisades, California.

Schoenberg, Arnold. *A Survivor from Warsaw*. Copyright © 1949 by Boelke-Bomart, Inc. Reprinted by permission.

Schubert, Franz. *Der Erlkönig* and *Die Forelle*. Translations from Philip L. Miller (ed.), *The Ring of Words*. Copyright © 1966 by Doubleday, a division of Bantam Doubleday Dell Publishing Group, Inc. Reprinted by permission.

Schumann, Robert. *Im wunderschönen Monat Mai*. Translation from Philip L. Miller (ed.), *The Ring of Words*. Copyright © 1966 by Doubleday, a division of Bantam Doubleday Dell Publishing Group, Inc. Reprinted by permission.

Smith, Bessie. *Lost Your Head Blues*. © 1925 Frank Music Corp.; renewed 1953 Frank Music Corp. International Copyright secured. All rights reserved. Reprinted by permission.

Stravkinsky, Igor. *Petrushka*, 1911. Copyright © by Edition Russe de Musique. Copyright assigned to Boosey & Hawkes, Inc. Revised edition copyright © 1947, 1948 by Boosey & Hawkes; copyright renewed. Reprinted by permission of Boosey & Hawkes, Inc.

Stravinsky, Igor. *The Rite of Spring*, 1913. Copyright © 1921 by Edition Russe de Musique (Russischer Musikverlag); copyright renewed. Copyright assigned 1947 to Boosey & Hawkes, Inc. Reprinted by permission of Boosey & Hawkes, Inc.

Stravinsky, Igor. *Symphony of Psalms*, © copyright 1931 by Edition Russe de Musique; renewed 1958. Copyright and renewal assigned to Boosey & Hawkes, Inc. Renewed 1975. Reprinted by permission of Boosey & Hawkes, Inc.

Verdi, Giuseppe. *Rigoletto*. Translation by William Weaver. © 1963 by William Weaver. Reprinted by permission of Doubleday, a division of Bantam Doubleday Dell Publishing Group, Inc.

Wagner, Richard. *Die Walküre*. Translation by William Mann. Reprinted by permission of William Mann.

Zwilich, Ellen Taaffe. *Concerto Grosso 1985*. © copyright 1985 by Mobart Music Publications, Inc. Reprinted by permission.

QUOTATIONS

Anderson, Emily (ed.). *Letters of Beethoven*, rev. ed., 1964. Reprinted by permission of Macmillan Publishing Ltd., London.

Anderson, Emily (ed.). *Letters of Mozart and His Family*, 2d ed. (A. Hyatt King and Monica Carolan, eds.), 1966. Reprinted by permission of Macmillan Publishing Ltd., London.

Barzun, Jacques. *Berlioz and the Romantic Century*. Copyright 1950. Reprinted by permission of Little, Brown & Company.

Copland, Aaron. *Our New Music*. Copyright 1941. Reprinted by permission of McGraw-Hill Book Company.

Cowell, Henry, and Sidney Cowell. *Charles Ives and His Music*. Copyright © 1955 by Oxford University Press Inc., renewed 1983 by Sidney Cowell. Reprinted by permission of the publisher.

Geiringer, Karl. *Haydn: A Creative Life in Music*, 3d rev. and enl. ed. Copyright 1983. Reprinted by permission of the University of California Press.

Large, Brian. *Smetana*. New York and London: Praeger and Duckworth, 1970.

Lockspeiser, Edward. *Debussy: His Life and Mind*. Copyright Edward Lockspeiser 1962. Reprinted by permission of Curtis Brown Ltd., London.

Newman, Ernest (ed.). *Memoirs of Hector Berlioz, 1803–1865*. New York: Alfred A. Knopf, 1932. Reprinted by permission.

Reich, Steve. Comments in interview with D. Sterritt, *Tradition Reseen*, in *The Christian Science Monitor*, Oct. 23, 1980. Reprinted by permission of Steve Reich.

Schoenberg, Arnold. *Style and Idea*, ed. Leonard Stein. Berkeley and London: The University of California Press and Faber & Faber, 1975. Reprinted by permission of the publishers.

Schwartz, Charles. *Gershwin, His Life and Music*. New York: Da Capo Press, 1979. Copyright 1973 by Charles Schwartz. Reprinted by permission of Charles Schwartz.

Stevens, Halsey. *The Life and Music of Béla Bartók,* rev. ed., 1967. Copyright © 1953, 1964 by Oxford University Press, Inc.; renewed 1981 by Halsey Stevens. Reprinted by permission of the publisher.

Stravinsky, Igor. *Chronicle of My Life.* London: Gollancz, 1936.

Stravinsky, Igor, and Robert Craft. *Expositions and Developments.* London and New York: Faber & Faber and Doubleday. © 1959, 1960, 1961, 1962 by Igor Stravinsky.

Thayer, Alexander. *Life of Beethoven,* rev. ed. (ed. Elliott Forbes). Princeton: Princeton University Press, 1973. Reprinted by permission.

Wilson, Edwin. *The Theater Experience,* 5th edition. New York: McGraw-Hill Book Company, 1991. The author gratefully acknowledges this source for information and ideas upon which the musical theater portion of this book is based.

Wilson, Edwin, and Alvin Goldfarb. *Theater: The Lively Art,* New York: McGraw-Hill Book Company, 1991. The author gratefully acknowledges this source for information and ideas upon which the musical theater portion of this book is based.

Zwilich, Ellen Taaffe. Comments on *Concerto Grosso 1985.* Reprinted by permission of Ellen Taaffe Zwilich.

INDEX

702

706

708

714